A SOCIOLOGY OF CONSTITUTIONS

Using a methodology that both analyses particular constitutional texts and theories and reconstructs their historical evolution, Chris Thornhill examines the social role and legitimating status of constitutions from the first quasi-constitutional documents of medieval Europe, through the classical period of revolutionary constitutionalism, to recent processes of constitutional transition. *A Sociology of Constitutions* explores the reasons why modern societies require constitutions and constitutional norms, and presents a distinctive socio-normative analysis of the constitutional preconditions of political legitimacy.

CHRIS THORNHILL is Professor of European Political Thought and Head of Politics at the University of Glasgow, where his research focuses both on the relations between legal and political theory and legal and political sociology and on processes of state formation and constitution writing in different European societies.

CAMBRIDGE STUDIES IN LAW AND SOCIETY

Cambridge Studies in Law and Society aims to publish the best scholarly work on legal discourse and practice in its social and institutional contexts, combining theoretical insights and empirical research.

The fields that it covers are: studies of law in action; the sociology of law; the anthropology of law; cultural studies of law, including the role of legal discourses in social formations; law and economics; law and politics; and studies of governance. The books consider all forms of legal discourse across societies, rather than being limited to lawyers' discourses alone.

The series editors come from a range of disciplines: academic law, socio-legal studies, sociology, and anthropology. All have been actively involved in teaching and writing about law in context.

Series editors

Chris Arup *Monash University, Victoria*
Martin Chanock *La Trobe University, Melbourne*
Pat O'Malley *University of Sydney*
Sally Engle Merry *New York University*
Susan Silbey *Massachusetts Institute of Technology*

Books in the series

Diseases of the Will
Mariana Valverde

The Politics of Truth and Reconciliation in South Africa: Legitimizing the Post-apartheid State
Richard A. Wilson

Modernism and the Grounds of Law
Peter Fitzpatrick

Unemployment and Government: Genealogies of the Social
William Walters

Autonomy and Ethnicity: Negotiating Competing Claims in Multi-ethnic States
Yash Ghai

Constituting Democracy: Law, Globalism and South Africa's Political Reconstruction
Heinz Klug

The Ritual of Rights in Japan: Law, Society, and Health Policy
Eric A. Feldman

The Invention of the Passport: Surveillance, Citizenship and the State
John Torpey

Governing Morals: A Social History of Moral Regulation
Alan Hunt

Justice and Reconciliation in Post-Apartheid South Africa
Edited by François du Bois and Antje du Bois-Pedain

Militarization and Violence against Women in Conflict Zones in the Middle East: A Palestinian Case Study
Nadera Shalhoub-Kevorkian

Child Pornography and Sexual Grooming: Legal and Societal Responses
Suzanne Ost

Darfur and the Crime of Genocide
John Hagan and Wenona Rymond-Richmond

Planted Flags: Trees, Land, and Law in Israel/Palestine
Irus Braverman

Fictions of Justice: The International Criminal Court and the Challenge of Legal Pluralism in Sub-Saharan Africa
Kamari Maxine Clarke

Conducting Law and Society Research: Reflections on Methods and Practices
Simon Halliday and Patrick Schmidt

Culture under Cross-Examination: International Justice and the Special Court for Sierra Leone
Tim Kelsall

The Gacaca Courts and Post-genocide Justice and Reconciliation in Rwanda: Justice without Lawyers
Phil Clark

Water on Tap: Rights and Regulation in the Transnational Governance of Urban Water Services
Bronwen Morgan

A Sociology of Constitutions: Constitutions and State Legitimacy in Historical-Sociological Perspective
Chris Thornhill

A SOCIOLOGY OF CONSTITUTIONS

Constitutions and State Legitimacy in
Historical-Sociological Perspective

CHRIS THORNHILL

CAMBRIDGE
UNIVERSITY PRESS

CAMBRIDGE UNIVERSITY PRESS
Cambridge, New York, Melbourne, Madrid, Cape Town,
Singapore, São Paulo, Delhi, Mexico City

Cambridge University Press
The Edinburgh Building, Cambridge CB2 8RU, UK

Published in the United States of America by Cambridge University Press, New York

www.cambridge.org
Information on this title: www.cambridge.org/9781107610569

First published 2011
First paperback edition 2013

A catalogue record for this publication is available from the British Library

Library of Congress Cataloging in Publication data
Thornhill, C. J. (Christopher J.), 1966–
A Sociology of Constitutions : Constitutions and State Legitimacy in Historical-Sociological
Perspective / Chris Thornhill.
p. cm. – (Cambridge Studies in Law and Society)
Includes bibliographical references and index.
ISBN 978-0-521-11621-3 (hardback)
1. Constitutional history. 2. Constitutional law – Social aspects. I. Title. II. Series.
K3161.T486 2011
342.02′9–dc22
2010051564

ISBN 978-0-521-11621-3 Hardback
ISBN 978-1-107-61056-9 Paperback

For Grace and John

CONTENTS

ACKNOWLEDGEMENTS

While writing this book I found myself in the company of a number of brilliant scholars, academics and intellectuals who either shaped my thinking in a general manner or offered advice or stimulation on particular points of fact and interpretation. In particular, I would like to mention Samantha Ashenden, Hauke Brunkhorst, Jean Clam, Emilios Christodoulidis, Daniel Chernilo, Photini Danou, Robert Fine, Poul Kjaer, Mikael Rask Madsen, William Outhwaite, Inger-Johanne Sand, Darrow Schecter, Irene Stolzi, Gunther Teubner, Adam Tomkins, Johan van der Walt and Stephen White. Most especially, however, I would like to thank Chris Berry and Gianfranco Poggi, who exceeded all normal bounds of collegiality in reading long sections of the book in its earlier stages and offering very helpful comments and suggestions. Of course, I do not expect that any of these people will agree with what I have written here, but (for better or for worse) I would not have written it without my intellectual exchanges with them. I would also like very warmly to thank Finola O'Sullivan at Cambridge University Press for encouraging me throughout this project.

Vital to the writing of this book were two research trips to the Max-Planck-Institut für Europäische Rechtsgeschichte in Frankfurt am Main. I found the Institute a magnificent place to work, and I am grateful to all its employees, albeit most especially to Frau Ursula Pohl, for their assistance in finding books and manuscripts for me during my sojourns there. I owe a similar debt of gratitude to the staff in the Rare Books Room at the British Library and in the Special Collections Library at the University of Glasgow.

In addition, I would like to express my gratitude to my students in politics at Glasgow University, in particular to those who have taken my courses on the history of political thought, fascism, and political legitimacy, for the fact that they have so consistently and intelligently challenged my preconceptions and forced me to consider and reflect on my ideas in new ways. I have found it a great privilege over the last five years to teach the young men and women studying in Glasgow, and much of my work has been thought out – either immediately or through more indirect engagement – in the company of students at Glasgow.

A NOTE ON TEXTS AND TRANSLATIONS

This book examines texts written originally in a number of languages, spanning many centuries, some of which have been translated into English and some of which have not. To guarantee some degree of uniformity in referencing, I have decided to refer to all works in original editions, and all translations of these editions are my own. I accept all responsibility for whatever shortcomings these translations might have.

~

Introduction

Why a sociology of constitutions?

During the emergence of sociology as an academic discipline the questions about the origins, status and functions of constitutions were widely posed. Indeed, for both thematic and methodological reasons, the analysis of constitutions was a central aspect of early sociology. Sociology developed, however ambiguously, as a critical intellectual response to the theories and achievements of the Enlightenment in the eighteenth century, the political dimension of which was centrally focused on the theory and practice of constitutional rule. In its very origins, in fact, sociology might be seen as a counter-movement to the political ideals of the Enlightenment, which rejected the (alleged) normative deductivism of Enlightenment theorists. In this respect, in particular, early sociology was deeply concerned with theories of political legitimacy in the Enlightenment, and it translated the revolutionary analysis of legitimacy in the Enlightenment, focused on the normative claim that singular rights and rationally generalized principles of legal validity were the constitutional basis for legitimate statehood, into an account of legitimacy which observed political orders as obtaining legitimacy through internalistically complex, historically contingent and multi-levelled processes of legal formation and societal motivation and cohesion.[1] This is not to suggest that there existed a strict and unbridgeable dichotomy between the Enlightenment, construed as a body of normative philosophy, and proto-sociological inquiry, defined as a body of descriptive interpretation. Clearly, some theories commonly associated with the Enlightenment pursued an evolutionary line of social reconstruction, and they rejected the idea that political legitimacy could be produced by singular acts of theoretical intelligence. Some theorists associated with the Enlightenment also specifically analysed constitutions in a proto-sociological perspective, and

---

[1] This culminated in Weber's famous account of legitimacy (1921: 122–30).

1

they accentuated the relativistic contingency of normative political forms.[2] However, if the political centre of the Enlightenment lay in the belief that political institutions obtain legitimacy if they enshrine constitutional laws translating abstract notions of justice and personal dignity into legal and normative constraints for the use of public and private power, sociology was first formed as a diffuse and politically pluralistic body of literature that opposed this belief. Sociology first evolved as a discipline that sought to promote reflection on the legitimacy of socio-political orders by elucidating the ways in which societies produce inner reserves of cohesion, obligation and legitimacy, without accepting the simplified view that these reserves were generated, and could be reliably authorized, by spontaneous external acts of reason. Formative for early sociology was thus a socially internalistic critique of the revolutionary constitutions and their catalogues of rights that, resulting from the Enlightenment, were established in the 1770s, 1780s and 1790s. Moreover, inquiry into constitutions might be seen as the defining element of early political sociology: it was in analysing constitutions and their functions that sociology raised its most profound questions regarding both the methodological/analytical methods and the political conclusions that supported the normative doctrines of the Enlightenment.

The rejection of normative constitutionalism was exemplified across the spectrum of pre- or proto-sociological analysis. At the very inception of modern social theory, for example, the works of Burke, De Maistre, Savigny, Bentham and Hegel can be loosely grouped together as – in themselves greatly divergent – endeavours to propose an anti-formalist theory of constitutional law.[3] At the centre of each of these theories was a negation of the principle that states acquire legitimacy from constitutional laws because these laws articulate simple promptings of universal reason to which states, in order to exercise their power in legitimate fashion, automatically owe compliance. Later, the early writings of Marx

---

[2] The Scottish Enlightenment appears as a forerunner of political sociology. David Hume, for example, argued that the principles around which pacified human societies tend to be organized – that is, the stability of possession, the transference of property by consent and the performance of promises – are not derived from immutable laws or invariably rational ideas of justice, but are in fact elements of social artifice or convention. In particular, Hume derided theorists who sought to calibrate all experiences of legitimate power in simplified or rationalized terms, and he especially denounced the 'fashionable system of politics' (1978 [1739–40]: 542). Adam Smith also prefigured later elements of political sociology by claiming that institutions of government, including separated powers, evolved, not through normative stimulus, but through the 'naturall disposition' of society (1978 [1762–6]: 347).

[3] This point has often been made. See my recent account in Thornhill (2010a).

also drew impetus from the conviction that the Enlightenment had proposed a misconstructed ideal of constitutional legitimacy. Marx (1958 [1844]) argued that the rationalist assumption that constitutions generate legitimacy for states could only be supported through a sociologically closed – or indeed *ideological* – construction of societal reality. In the first period of classical sociology, subsequently, the attempt to examine constitutions and their legitimizing functions as expressions of wider societal dynamics played a yet more central role. This was reflected in the works of Ferdinand Tönnies, Émile Durkheim and Max Weber, all of which proposed distinctive accounts of constitutional functions, and all of which aimed to observe the origins of constitutional norms, not in deductive prescriptions but in inner-societal and historically elaborated normative structures. At this juncture, sociological analysis of constitutions also began to cross the boundary between sociology and law, and in the period of classical sociology it must have appeared that constitutional sociology would soon establish itself as a distinctive line of jurisprudence. In France, first Léon Duguit and then Maurice Hauriou both accounted for constitutions and their functions in creating legitimacy as pronounced elements of an overarching social order (Duguit 1889: 502; Hauriou 1929 [1923]: 72–3). In Germany, Carl Schmitt later defined his constitutional theory as reflecting a strongly sociological approach to law, which ridiculed purely legalistic reconstructions of constitutional law and its legitimating force (1928: 121). One potent lineage in constitutional theory in the Weimar Republic in fact insisted on the use of sociological analysis of integration through constitutional law and constitutional rights to refute the legal positivist orthodoxy established in the late nineteenth century (Smend 1968 [1928]: 263). By the third decade of the twentieth century, in short, the anti-normative patterns of legal/constitutional analysis in the first wave of post-Enlightenment social theory were widely cemented in social and legal analysis, and the contours of a sociology of constitutions were clearly identifiable.

After 1945, however, the impetus of constitutional sociology decelerated, and in the longer wake of the Second World War more formally normative theories assumed central status in both constitutional theory and constitutional practice. In the practical domain, formal-normative constitutional methods and ideals assumed great importance during the push for constitutional order in the later 1940s and 1950s, at which time constitutions were widely deployed as instruments for consolidating Western-style democracy and obviating renewed collapse into political authoritarianism: relativistic and societally contingent attitudes to constitutional law were perceived as obstructing this objective. In the successive waves of post-authoritarian constitutional-democratic transition, in the 1940s, 1970s and 1990s, the model of the constitution as an institution guaranteeing basic rights and a separation of powers, and usually subjecting both executive and legislature procedures to statutory compliance with prior non-derogable norms, was widely adopted as a necessary construct whose normative validity and general functional utility were beyond question. To be sure, constitutional sociology did not entirely disappear after 1945. In Germany, elements of a functionalist sociology of constitutions were present first in the works of Helmut Schelsky (1965 [1949]) and then in the writings of Niklas Luhmann (1965; 1973; 1991). Jürgen Habermas's early analysis of constitutional legitimacy also contains a tentative and often revised sociological approach to the functions of constitutional law (1990 [1962]: 326–42). Constitutional formation assumes vital status in Richard Münch's sociology of modern political culture (1984: 311). In the United States, moreover, Talcott Parsons gave an important, although marginal, role to the constitution and the rights contained in it, which he saw as sources of far-reaching inclusion and structural stabilization (1969: 339).[4] Generally, however, the attempt to construct the rule of law and the public-legal regulation of governmental power as expressions of societal, rather than deductive/prescriptive, norms lost intellectual momentum in the later twentieth century. Indeed, for all their practical/political advantages and utility in stabilizing democratic regimes, the preponderance of normative principles in post-1945 constitutional discourse and practice weakened sociological understanding of the motives which lead societies to produce, and habitually to articulate, their grammar of legitimacy in constitutional laws. The fact that constitutional order has been promoted as a general ideal of legitimacy in post-1945 politics has tended to obstruct sociological inquiry into the deep-lying normative structure of society, and the increasing reliance of modern societies on relatively uniform patterns of constitutional organization has not been reflected in a consonant growth of society's self-comprehension in respect of its normative political foundations. In fact, it is arguable that in the later twentieth century the original and formative post-Enlightenment dichotomy between normative and sociological inquiries into constitutions and constitutional legitimacy reproduced and reconsolidated itself. In this process, the assumption that constitutional principles, especially those

---

[4] See my longer discussion of contemporary aspects of constitutional sociology in (2010a).

condensed into formal rights, could be definitively illuminated as normative objects became almost unshakably predominant.[5]

This situation, it needs to be noted, has begun to change in very recent years, and it is now possible to identify a number of theorists and researchers, working across the disciplinary distinctions between politics, law and sociology, who employ sociological or socio-theoretical methods to illuminate constitutions. This can be seen in the neo-functionalist legal sociology of David Sciulli (1992). It is evident in the quasi-ethnographic approach to constitutional formation in the writings of Kim Lane Scheppele. It is apparent more recently in the post-Luhmannian school of legal analysis, centred around Gunther Teubner, which, although largely focused on the changing sources of private law, has provided an outstandingly complex account of the pluralistic constitutional structures of modern society.[6] This is also manifest in the post-Habermasian constitutional analyses set out by Andrew Arato and, in particular, by Hauke Brunkhorst, who has developed a far-reaching model of constitutional formation that seeks to account for both the societal/evolutionary and the normative dimensions of constitutions and their legitimating intentions (2000: 55; 2002: 136). On this basis it is plausible to suggest that the sociology of constitutions, in different expressions, is gradually resuming its former importance in social theory. Indeed, it can be observed that, despite the prevalence of formal-normative orthodoxy in constitutional analysis in modern societies, the transformations in the constitutional design of Western societies in the last fifty or so years are slowly becoming objects of adequately sociological interpretation.

Despite this, however, it is also fair to say that, to date, the recent attempts at sociological constitutionalism, although often comprising research of the highest theoretical importance, have not succeeded in re-establishing constitutional sociology as a sub-discipline of law, politics or sociology. This is the case for two reasons. On one hand, recent sociological interpretations of constitutions have tended to focus on one particular aspect of constitutional formation – that is, habitually, either on the rights dimension of constitutions, or on the changing functions of constitutions in increasingly internationalized societies or societies with post-traditional political structures.[7] The constitution as a legal

---

[5] The most extreme case of this might be the theory of Dworkin, who argues that it is imperative to isolate 'the problem of rights against the state', and so pushes the case for a 'fusion of constitutional law and moral theory' (1977: 149).

[6] See the argument in Fischer-Lescano and Teubner (2006).

[7] Habermas and Brunkhorst might exemplify the first tendency and Teubner might be a case of the second.

apparatus emerging in, and functionally defined by, its structural integrity with a historically formed state has only rarely been placed at the centre of recent sociological inquiry, and the normative functions of classical state constitutions still assume a withdrawn role in sociology. There is, as yet, no encompassing sociological attempt to explain why states have tended to evolve around constitutions as classical documents of public law, and what exact sociological functions constitutions fulfil for states. Moreover, recent theories addressing the political functions of state constitutions have often tended to step outside the realm of strictly sociological methodology in accounting for the normative status of constitutions and constitutional rights. Specifically, they have often fallen back on the more deductive foundations of Enlightenment theory in their attempts to illuminate the reliance of modern societies on constitutional norms, especially in respect of rights.[8] Exactly which internal forces cause societies to produce constitutions and constitutional rights has not been explained without reliance on residually foundationalist theories of universal human nature or universal human reason. In consequence, we might consider that the founding sociological attempt to enable modern societies internally to comprehend their articulated normative structure has not been concluded. Indeed, modern societies still lack a conclusively sociological vocabulary for explaining their convergence around normatively restricted political systems and for elucidating their relatively uniform dependence on stable patterns of public-legal legitimacy, secured in constitutions.

This book, therefore, contains an attempt to draw together the existing, yet inchoate, threads of the sociology of constitutions, which date back to the very genesis of sociological interpretation. In the first instance, this book attempts further to consolidate the development of constitutional sociology in contemporary debate, and it wishes to contribute, in some measure, to the growing recognition of constitutional sociology as a free-standing field of intellectual inquiry. Naturally, this book is not intended to reflect any presumption that all practitioners of constitutional-sociological analysis will sympathize with the methodological approach adopted here. The book carries the consciously

---

[8] I have considered this problem elsewhere (Thornhill 2010b). In brief, though, this tendency is illustrated by the fact that Brunkhorst's sociology of constitutions relies on the assertion that the demand for solidarity is a constitutive disposition of human life (2002: 203). See also the neo-foundational approach to rights in Alexander (2006: 34, 69).

deliberated title *A Sociology of Constitutions* (that is to say, it is not called *The Sociology of Constitutions*). This reflects the anticipation that a number of other constitutional sociologies might either oppose or sit alongside this book without undue mutual inconvenience. Yet aspirations of the book are that it might add substance to the current literature addressing constitutions from a sociological standpoint, and that it might establish co-ordinates for the future direction of inquiry in this field.

In seeking to cement sociological analysis of constitutions, however, this book is also shaped by an attempt to re-articulate and reinforce the original ambitions of constitutional sociology. Like its remote precursors, it aims critically to reappraise and reconfigure the classical questions of post-Enlightenment normative political inquiry – that is, questions regarding the normative foundations of political legitimacy and legal validity, the essential content of constitutional laws and constitutional norms, and the reasons for the reliance of political institutions on normatively abstracted legal principles. In so doing, it wishes to account for the structure of political legitimacy without reliance on hypostatic or purely deductive methods, and it seeks to illuminate the fabric of legitimacy using socially internalistic paradigms. At one level, in this respect, unlike much early sociology, this book is not hostile to normative constitutional claims. In fact, this book shares the conventional position unifying most normative political theories arising from the Enlightenment, and it accepts as valid the common normative assumption *that particular political institutions (usually states) acquire legitimacy by means of constitutional documents, and that constitutionally enshrined subjective rights, protecting those subject to political power from non-mandated coercion and recognizing these persons as bearers of immutable claims to dignity, equality and like redress, are probable preconditions for the legitimate exercise of power.* This book, therefore, proposes a definition of political legitimacy which would be acceptable to most normative theories: it defines legitimate political power as *power exercised in accordance with public laws, applied evenly and intelligibly to all members of society (including those factually using power), which are likely to give maximum scope to the pursuit of freedoms that are capable of being generally and equally appreciated by all social actors.*[9] Against the

---

[9] The classical expression of this view occurs in the writings of Kant. Kant argues that a state with a legitimate 'republican constitution' reflects the formal 'laws of freedom' which human beings deduce as conditions of their autonomy (1976 [1797]: 437). These views now resurface in more contemporary debate in the works of Rawls and Habermas.

methods resulting from the Enlightenment, nonetheless, this book is shaped by the conviction that the constitutional structure of society and the legitimacy of political institutions can be illuminated only weakly by normative analysis. In fact, normative analysis is incapable of illuminating that object which it has made its most common analytical focus: rights-based constitutional legitimacy. In consequence, this book suggests that an encompassing sociological perspective is required to address these questions and to account for the motives underlying the constitutional construction of legitimacy, and it tries to cast light on the legitimating status of constitutions by examining the societal functions and the objective societal exigencies that are reflected in constitutional norms. Primarily, therefore, the book seeks to examine and explain, sociologically, why modern societies have tended, independently and with some consistency across socio-cultural variations, to elaborate constitutions, why societies tend to concentrate their political functions in constitutional form and why constitutions, and the normative reserves that they contain, prove vital to the stability of modern societies and the legitimacy of their political institutions. In this respect, although the book does not engage in great detail with the preconditions of distinct lines of normative analysis, it contains the implicit argument that the original sociological attack on the normative analyses of the Enlightenment needs to be re-initiated. In order for a valid explanation of the normative structure of modern society to be obtained, the constitution needs once more to be constructed as an eminently sociological object – that is, as an object formed by inner-societal forces and explicable through analysis of broad patterns of social formation.

What is a constitution?

One question necessarily and invariably faced by sociological inquiry into constitutional law is the question, *what is a constitution?* Indeed, this question has recurrently punctuated and stimulated the development of inquiries into public law that employ a sociological perspective. This question obtained central importance in the first aftermath of the French Revolution and its processes of constitutional formation in 1789/91: at this time, the definition of a constitution of itself separated theorists pursuing a normative orientation from theorists adopting a more sociologically oriented interpretive disposition. The Enlightenment in general was marked by a specific conception of political modernity, and it widely pressed the claim that the possession of a formally prescribed and written political constitution was a hallmark of progressively realized or *enlightened* modern societies. The first self-designated theorists of modern constitutionalism in fact tended flatly to deny that societies without single written constitutions possessed constitutions at all, and they saw societies without such documents as archaically structured and residually despotic.[10] This view, then, has been diversely reflected in conceptual-historical literature on constitutionalism, which often implicitly replicates the strict distinction between societies that possess and societies that do not possess constitutions – or at least between societies marked by modern and societies marked by pre-modern constitutionalism.[11] The earliest proto-sociological theories of the constitution, in contrast, were driven by a critical response to such clear distinctions, and they promoted a more nuanced, and historically variable, sense of a society's constitutionality and of the historical sources of its normative structure. Many theorists whose work anticipated the first emergence of legal sociology reacted to the constitutionalism of the French revolutionaries by denouncing as reductive the insistence that a constitution could only take the form of a single written document or a single catalogue of rights,[12] and they argued that all societies incorporate a particular, organically evolved legal order and a factual constitution.[13] More elaborated sociological analyses of the constitution subsequently also tended to dismiss the claim that there existed a clear distinction between societies with a written constitution and societies without a written constitution, and they viewed elements of constitutional order – rights, separated powers and so on – as evolving elements of society's inherent ethical structure.[14] More recent sociological interpreters have also usually accepted latitude in the definition of the constitution (Luhmann 1991: 179).

The concept of the constitution proposed in this book builds on earlier sociological taxonomies. It suggests that, long before the advent of

---

[10] Art. 16 of the French Declaration of Rights (1789) stated simply, 'A society in which the observance of the law is not assured, nor the separation of powers defined, has no constitution at all.'

[11] See McIlwain (1947: 81). It is claimed in further important literature that the concept of the constitution was an innovation specific to early modernity (Stourzh 1977: 304).

[12] This was exemplified by Bentham (2002) and Burke (1910 [1790]).

[13] See Savigny's claim that the 'production of law' reflects a process of natural-historical self-interpretation, in which the 'natural whole' or the integral spirit of the people externalizes its defining characteristics and its specific rationality in the form of law (1840: 21–2).

[14] This is implicit in Durkheim (1950: 92–3).

formally written constitutions, it was customary for societies to comprehend themselves as possessing a distinctively normative constitutional
shape, which could not be exclusively reduced to a single body of written
precepts. The strictly constrained account of the constitution is thus seen
here as a projection of normative analysis, which revolves around a
highly controlled construction of its object and its legitimating functions. A sociological approach to the constitution, in contrast, needs to
resist the suggestion that there occurred a radical caesura between early
modern and modern constitutions.[15] Indeed, it is fundamental to sociological examination of constitutions that, in perceiving constitutions as
documents reacting to conditions within a broad inner-societal environment, it opposes purely textual definitions of constitutionality, and it is
prepared to recognize societies as possessing a multiple and diffuse
constitutional apparatus. For normative analysis, it is clear that a constitution comprises a body of norms that (either adequately or inad-
equately) prescribes legal conditions for the public use of power and
forms a focus for normative debate about the self-conception of society
as a whole. For sociological inquiry, however, it is always possible that a
society might have a normative constitution that evades simple forms of
prescription and cannot easily serve as a singular focus for society's
self-reflection or normative self-construction. Indeed, a sociological
approach might observe constitutions as evolving through multi-levelled
historical/functional processes, and it might identify the suggestion that
categorical disjunctures occur in the formation of constitutions as
revolving around a simplification of society's functional structure.

In consequence, this book proceeds from a definition of constitutions
that denies that (for example) 1689, 1787–9 or 1789/1791 formed points
of categorical discontinuity in the legal-normative history of modern
society. For this reason, the book observes pre-modern and early modern
societies as possessing documents or legal arrangements that can clearly
be classified as constitutions and that pre-empt, and respond to the same
functional and general societal pressures as, post-Enlightenment constitutions. On the account offered here, in sum, a constitution has the
following features. It is a legal order impacting on the exercise of political
power that (a) contains an effectively established presumption of public
rule in accordance with principles or conventions, expressed as law, that

---

[15] It has recently been argued that in pre-1789 France the view was common that, although
France lacked a written constitution, the 'basic structure of society' could be viewed as
possessing an informal constitutional force (Vergne 2006: 127).

cannot easily (i.e. without societally unsettling controversy) be suspended; (b) is designed to constrain or restrict egregiously mandatory
use of power in both public and private functions; (c) allocates powers
within the state itself, and comprises some form of popular/political
representation in respect of questions perceived as possessing importance for all politically relevant sectors of society; and (d) expresses a
legal distinction between the form of the state and those persons assuming authority to borrow and enforce the power stored within the state. To
this degree, this book uses the more expansive definition of the constitution common in much classical sociological literature, and it defines
the constitution in terms that can be applied to many societies in different historical periods. In parallel to this, however, this book also limits its
view of the constitution by claiming that a constitution, although often a
socially embedded legal order, is characterized by the fact that it refers
primarily to *the functions of states*, and it establishes a legal form relating
to the use of power by states, or at least by actors bearing and utilizing
public authority. Some contemporary legal sociology has persuasively
argued that private laws obtain quasi-constitutional force (Teubner
2006): indeed, this view was central to the earliest works of constitutional
sociology.[16] However, the constitution is defined here as a distinctively
political structure, originally and enduringly typified by its function in
producing, restricting and refining power utilized by states. The constitution is thus observed as a restrictive order of public law that
possesses a distinct normative valence for those who use and those
who are subject to political power: it is an institution that allows societies
to construct and articulate power as the power of states. As such, the
constitution may assume a high level of variability across different
societies, and it may (quite obviously) exist at different levels of articulation and evolutionary prominence. Naturally, in medieval societies,
which possessed only a highly uncertain distinction between private law
and public law, the form of the constitution differed markedly from the
state-centric model prevalent in modern differentiated societies.
Moreover, many constitutional documents or aggregates of such documents in medieval societies possessed an incomplete normative structure, and they left many gaps in the legal apparatus of the state and were
scarcely applied across all regions included in a particular society.

---

[16] The use of private-law concepts to articulate a theory of constitutions was central to the
first historicist reflections on the public law of the Enlightenment. For an example, see
Hugo (1823 [1792]: 77).

Nonetheless, the definition of the constitution as a (however incomplete) order of *public law* (that is, a legal order describing conditions for the use of political power) allows us, ideal-typically, to examine the emergence and function of constitutions across a large number of societal settings, and it clearly specifies the distinctively political structure of societies that have constitutions. The constitution, in short, is observed in this book as a gradually evolving and highly variable social phenomenon, extant to different degrees in different societies. Yet it is determined by the fact that, both internally and externally, it creates legal conditions for the use of political power, and it possesses a certain primacy above other elements of the law and the political system.

In setting out this definition of a constitution, it is naturally impossible for this work to consider every single important constitution, either pre-modern or modern, and a high degree of selectivity has been exercised in deciding which constitutions should form objects of analysis. The guiding concern in this respect has been to identify processes of constitutional formation which condense and illuminate deep-lying and widespread transformations in society in different historical periods, and to analyse most extensively those constitutions that reflect substantial shifts or developmental patterns that are common to, or prefigure tendencies in, many societies. In particular, in attempting to elucidate how constitutions were first formed as objects that were internally interwoven with the construction and legitimation of political institutions, the book focuses on processes of historical evolution in societies that produced the proto-types for modern constitutions and modern states. It thus concentrates on decisive and characteristic periods of constitutional formation in European societies, and its primary objective is to clarify the social causes and functions of constitutions in the major European states.

A note on method and central concepts

This book deviates from most research on constitutions in that it proposes an approach to constitutional analysis that is at one and the same time historical and functional. In this respect, it places itself in a distinctive relation both to historical-political sociology and to more conventional functionalist sociology, and it combines elements of both methodologies to propose a method of constitutional inquiry that might be classified as *historical functionalism*. That is to say, central to the book is an endeavour to understand constitutions both as highly varied outcomes of inner-societal processes of historical/political formation, yet also to appreciate constitutions as institutions through which emergent European societies, in relatively generalized fashion, regulated and adapted to their underlying functional dimensions and exigencies. This methodological aspect of the book uses an account of the functional structure of modern societies, elements of which, in very broad terms, are shaped by the theory of European modernity outlined by Niklas Luhmann. In particular, the book employs select aspects of Luhmann's theory to show how constitutions have evolved through a process of historical *functional differentiation*, which, at a certain level of generality, decisively determined the overarching form of modern European society. Further, it adapts from Luhmann the view that, as separate realms of social exchange are differentiated, they elaborate meaningful concepts to unify and give *positive* (that is, internally abstracted) consistency to their communications. On this basis, it claims that constitutions have assumed legitimating prominence in modern society through their efficacy in enabling societies at once objectively and positively to reflect and control the differentiation of their diverse spheres of social exchange, and to simplify and consistently to distinguish the complexly interwoven functions resulting from their differentiated and pluralized evolutionary form. In this respect, the book suggests that the formation of constitutions has been caused by relatively generalizable evolutionary conjunctures, which, with inevitable differences, tend to characterize societies marked by a *pluralistic functional structure*. Naturally, this theory of socio-functional differentiation as the source of constitutional formation is not posited as a singular or universally identical causal source for the construction of constitutions, and throughout the book close attention is paid to salient variations of cultural and developmental structure in different societies. Nonetheless, the book observes that the pluralistic functional reality of modern societies has effectively necessitated the evolution of constitutions as instruments for the sustainable organization of political power.

In proposing a historical-functionalist method, however, this book moves away from much more conventional functionalist analysis and much historical/political sociology (including that of Luhmann) in that it places primary emphasis on the normative dimensions of modern society, and it is underpinned by a sociological analysis of *legal norms* as structurally central dimensions of modern social formation. In particular, the book is based in the argument that highly differentiated societies tend to require complexly articulated and prominent legal norms in order to stabilize and conduct their differentiated functions, especially in the political sphere, and that constitutions act as institutions that provide such normative political articulation for societies. In this respect, the book stands outside the main conflict-theoretical canon of historical-political sociology. It rejects the originally Weberian notion of politics as a socially dominating struggle for power (Weber 1921: 852), and it rejects the widespread historical-sociological view of political institutions as social forms whose origins reside solely (or largely) in conflict between social actors over the monopoly of power, usually consolidated through domination of the fiscal-military resources in society.[17] However, the book also rejects the main lineage of functionalist method, which is also characterized by extreme normative relativism.[18] As mentioned, one methodological purpose of the book is to examine and explain the prevalent normative configuration of modern societies, to comprehend the reasons why societies produce normative institutions, and so to illuminate constitutions as essential components of normative societal organization. To this end, the book seeks to outline a theory of norms to unsettle the conceptual dominance of analytical theory in normative inquiry: it attempts to apply a sociological method to show how modern societies tend, for functional motives, to promote the emergence of relatively generalized societal and legal-political norms, and how this can be identified (and even advocated) without reliance on hypostatically rationalist patterns of deduction and prescription. In

---

[17] See as primary examples Tilly (1975); Tilly (1985). For a more normatively inflected account of this, see Michael Mann's theory of *infrastructural power* (1984: 189), which views the growth in the state's power to 'penetrate civil society' as marked by a decline in its purely coercive status. For a more cultural perspective, see Corrigan and Sayer (1985). Yet, across methodological divides, the state-building process is still viewed as essentially one bringing about a conflictual convergence of society around a dominant bloc. I have assessed the literature in the classical canon of the historical sociology of states elsewhere (Thornhill: 2008), and I do not wish to repeat these points. Suffice it to say, though, that, in general, the historical-sociological account of the state revolves around the assumption, first promoted by Weber, Hintze and Schumpeter, that European states were formed as groups of actors who arrogated to themselves a monopoly of violence in society, and that the assumption of this monopoly is firmly tied to the need of states to gain fiscal supremacy in order to fund wars. In short, the *fiscal–military* paradigm in analysis of state building remains dominant. Recently, see Hopcroft (1999: 90); Kiser and Linton (2001).

[18] Naturally, the works of both Durkheim and Parsons contain an implicitly normative theory of social construction. But the latest position in this lineage, that of Luhmann, is resolutely anti-normative. Simply, Luhmann stated that political power has no necessary precondition *ab extra* (1981: 69). He added later that the legitimation of power is always a communicative act of 'self-legitimation' that occurs within the political system, and it 'excludes legitimation through an external system' (2000: 358–9).

general, therefore, the book uses a historical-functionalist method in order at once both to question the common normative indifference both of historical-political and functionalist sociology and to promote a theory of historically constructed norms that identifies the elaboration of a solid legal normative apparatus as a highly probable structural feature of modern societies. In its entirety, the book can be interpreted, not only as a historical-functional sociology of constitutions, but also as a historical-functional sociology of legal/political norms, which intends to analyse norms as objective institutions that are generated by inner-societal dynamics and functionally formative evolutionary processes.

It is in its approach to the normative fabric of modern society that the most controversial methodological aspect of this book becomes visible. Underlying the conception of the book, namely, is a theory of political power that positions itself in strict opposition to more widely established constructions of power and its social status. At one level, this book attracts controversy because it makes a sharp distinction between political power and the patterns of social influence, coercion and obedience, which are often characterized as power in other lines of sociology. The book thus places itself against the definitional basis of Marxist or Foucauldian micro-social analysis of power. It argues that the exercise of political power and the exercise of social power or coercion need to be quite sharply distinguished, that the use of political power needs to be viewed as the functional operation of a distinct set of institutions and exchanges in modern society, and that, in modern societies, the production and consumption of power are only required for a relatively circumscribed number of social objectives.[19] Of course, there is no intention in this book either to deny that exchanges in other spheres of society – for example, in the economy, in religion or in education – are to some degree supported by power, or to suggest that conflicts in these spheres do not refer to and presuppose strategies of coercion. However, the book claims that political power is not equally or even universally implicated in all spheres of social action. Additionally, it claims that modern societies have in fact characteristically evolved through a process in which the selective distillation of political power around a relatively discrete

---

[19] In this respect, the book borrows aspects of Luhmann's theory of power. Particularly useful in Luhmann's theory is the fact that he viewed power, in strict terms, as the medium of communication for the political system and for the political system alone. He saw the political system as communicating power precisely by the fact that it holds itself at a level of inner consistency against the patterns of exchange in other parts of society (Luhmann 1969; 1988: 1991).

number of functions has acted as a precondition of social stability and has approached an advanced stage of development. It is taken here as an insignia of modern society that societies learn to curtail their transfusion with political power, that persons and exchanges relevant for power are quite clearly demarcated from those not relevant for power, and that, together with economic, legal, religious and scientific exchanges, political power is necessarily held at a level of relative differentiation, abstraction and institutional exclusivity in relation to other spheres of social practice. Power, in consequence, is defined here, not as a static conflictual force, but as an evolutionary and adaptive social facility or a medium of social exchange that is used by societies for making decisions that possess highly generalized collective relevance, but is only marginally (or exceptionally) expended in legal, economic, scientific or other activities. Indeed, on this account, it is a determinant of modern societies that they are required to generate power in a characteristically and distinctively differentiated political form – that is, modern societies are structurally marked by the fact that they segregate power from singular persons, they require reserves of power that do not need to be policed and applied through local and highly controlled acts of coercion, and they possess a dominant tendency to augment and maximize the volume of selectively politicized power over which they dispose. Modern societies, thus, are defined by an incremental requirement for differentiated quantities of political power, by the need to evolve mechanisms to produce, manage and intensify their stores of power, and so also by an increased abstraction, differentiation and *multiplication* of their power. Although it intersects with aesthetic, religious, economic and (especially) legal authority, political power is not identical with these: these other realms of exchange are in fact normally defined by the fact that they only rarely borrow or support themselves with political power. Indeed, the distinction of political power in relation to other spheres of social exchange is one vital dimension in a modern society's intensification of the volume of usable power that it contains, and the relative abstraction of power against other social activities is a constitutive structural feature of modern society.

For this reason, this book also argues that modern societies are characterized by the fact that they rely on their ability to abstract and utilize political power as a largely *autonomous* facility, which, in most situations, is clearly distinguished from other patterns of social exchange. Inquiry into the relative autonomy of political institutions is, to be sure, a well-rehearsed debate: from Max Weber to Antonio

Gramsci, to Nicos Poulantzas, to Theda Skocpol, to Michael Mann, it has been argued that states are institutional actors in possession of a degree of (albeit curtailed) societal autonomy. The argument in this book builds in certain respects on such analyses, and it shares the widespread historical-sociological view that societies, especially in periods of rapid transition, converge around structurally autonomous political institutions, and that these institutions cannot be reduced to simple aggregates of economic influence. However, the emphasis of the argument proposed here is rather distinct from that evident in other examples of historical sociology. Central to this book, first, is the claim that modern societies are defined – in the first instance – by the fact that they require and produce, not autonomous political institutions, but rather autonomous reserves of political power: that is, the evolution of modern societies has depended on the capacities of these societies for generating quantities of political power that could be applied across complexly differentiated social terrains in reasonably positive, independent and easily *inclusive and reproducible* fashion, and whose utilization was not subject to endless local coercion or personalized controversy. The growing autonomy of political power, and the existence of capacities in society for the use of power in positive and replicable fashion, thus formed irreducible hallmarks of emergent modern societies. It was only through the abstraction of political power as a positive autonomous object that societies assumed features of spatial and temporal extensibility, positive inclusion and collective integration typical of modern social orders. Modern political institutions, then, first evolved, variably, as repositories of such abstracted and autonomous political power, and the progressive abstraction of political power gave rise to the formation of political institutions: political institutions were not initially identical with political power, and their development reflected the emergence of political power as a relatively autonomous and structurally independent social phenomenon. The defining characteristic of modern societies, thus, is that they are able to construct power at an increasingly refined level of positive force: institutions were first formed as part of a subsidiary process, in which power, as a positive phenomenon, was organized and distributed through society. Also central to this book, second, is the claim, accordingly, that, if political institutions possess some degree of autonomy, this is to be measured, not by their presumptive levels of societal penetration, mobilization or control, but rather by the degree to which they are able to use power in positive and self-authorizing fashion and to which they possess and unify institutional instruments (usually of a fiscal and judicial nature) that enable them to transmit power through society as an abstracted and internally reproducible resource.[20] The autonomy of the state, in short, depends on the autonomy of political power in society: political institutions obtain autonomy if they can produce and consume power as a relatively consistent and abstracted object, and societies unable to mobilize power in a relatively autonomous form are likely to be characterized by weak political institutions.

It is in this respect, then, that this book courts controversy most flagrantly. In suggesting that power is required and produced in modern societies as an autonomous and positive facility, it also suggests that political power has an intrinsic relation to law. Indeed, it argues that in the course of power's construction as a differentiated and positive medium of societal exchange, the intersection between law and power has necessarily increased: the intersection of power and law in fact serves the increasing need for autonomous reserves of positive power which characterizes modern societies. In this respect, this book again positions itself against micro-analytical and exceptionalist accounts of power and against analyses of power (i.e. Marxist or conflict-theoretical approaches) that observe law as a mere coercive instrument of political control. Against these positions, as discussed, the book revolves around the claim that in differentiated societies political power tends, over longer periods of time, to be constructed and applied in increasingly conventionalized fashion, and the wider abstracted specialization of power on a select number of exchanges means that power evolves as a facility that is only rarely applied as pure coercion.[21] As a result of this, political power also normally assumes correlation with a pronounced body of legal norms. Legal norms in fact facilitate the positive specialized and internally reproducible construction of political power, and power normally suffers from internal deficiencies if its legal-normative fabric (and the legal fabric of society more widely) is diminished or corrupted. In both these respects, the book adopts a controversial stance. While opposing analytical/deductive philosophy, as mentioned, it makes a strong case for the probable existence of a normative political structure in modern society, and it claims that through its formation as an autonomous resource power necessarily adopts a legal/normative form.

---

[20] Note my critique of Davidheiser (1992).

[21] Here I follow both Parsons and Luhmann in associating an increase in the differentiated reserves of power with a growth in options contained in society and a correlated diminution of physical violence (Parsons 1963: 243, 237; Luhmann 1988: 78–9).

While pursuing a historical-sociological line of inquiry, further, it rejects the conflict-theoretical model that prevails in much sociological analysis, and it suggests that the construction of power is most deeply marked, not by irreducible political conflict, but by patterns of normatively inflected self-reproduction, multiplication and *inclusion*. In fact, the book pursues its analysis of constitutions from a perspective that observes modern societies as containing an internal political disposition towards normative self-construction in order to augment the mass of power accessible within a society, and it suggests that this disposition is especially concentrated around constitutions (see Luhmann 1991: 201).

Finally, it needs to be noted that this book is conceived as the first in a series of books on the sociology of constitutions, and it is anticipated that it will be followed by a volume on the transformation of constitutional order in the increasingly internationalized societies of the contemporary world and by a volume on post-colonial constitutionalism. This fact reveals much about the rationale shaping this first volume. In the first instance, this volume is designed to illuminate the societal processes that originally constructed and gave rise to states in their specific form as constitutional states. In consequence, it focuses to a large degree on the formation of modern European states, from the medieval era into the era of high modernity. To illuminate this process, naturally, it is not possible to ignore the constitutional developments in revolutionary America and beyond, and Chapter III, addressing the first formal constitutions, discusses aspects of early American constitutionalism. However, although it is assumed that the analytical paradigm employed here can be applied (in part, at least) to post-colonial settings and the settings which borrowed European constitutional design at a late historical juncture, such constitution writing is a topic in its own right, it requires a subtly modified interpretive structure, and it is reserved for a further volume. Similarly, although it is also assumed that much of the analysis here can also be transferred to the formation of post-national constitutional systems, certain revisions and qualifications are again required to make this transfer sustainable, and this, too, must be held over for a subsequent work. This book, in short, is a book that seeks to illuminate the formation of centralized states as relatively autonomous repositories of political power, the role that constitutions play in this process, and the underlying normative apparatus of state power. The largely European focus of this book is explained by this ambition.

Medieval constitutions

The social origins of modern constitutions

The earliest modern constitutional arrangements can be identified in different European societies in the high medieval period: that is, in the later part of the twelfth century and throughout the thirteenth century. In this period, most European societies were beginning gradually to move away from the highly diffuse social order of early feudalism, which had itself supplanted the more vertical political structures of the Carolingian period, and the more advanced societies of this time witnessed a substantially increasing centralization of their political institutions and a growth in the inner consistency of their legal apparatus.[1] This does not imply that the highly localized jurisdictional structures based in lordship, lateral association and private force that characterized earlier feudalism had dissolved by the twelfth century. In fact, a recent outstanding monograph has persuasively demonstrated the contrary (Bisson 2009). However, by the later twelfth century many European societies were beginning to develop more regularly constructed legal and political systems, and they were in the process of devising at least the bare practical and conceptual instruments to make this possible. The transition from early to high feudalism was thus marked by a deep societal impetus towards more formal legal administration: this ultimately shaped the constitutional design of emergent centres of political power.[2]

---

[1] For samples of the vast literature on this theme, see Fournier (1917); Berman (1977: 894); Reynolds (1981: 223); and Brundage (2008: 3–4). For the classical treatment of this wider theme in English, see Berman (1983: 113).

[2] It needs to be acknowledged here that I use the concept of feudalism despite controversy over its validity. The use of this term was widely assailed in the 1960s, most vehemently by Richardson and Sayles (1963: 117), who described feudalism as 'a modern concept, an abstraction ... owing much to the desire of scholars for symmetry'. This term is now commonly viewed as a 'discredited formulation' (Bisson 2009: 31). In persisting in the use of this concept, I do not wish to make grand claims for feudalism as a term to define an

In earlier feudal societies, political power had normally been constructed through a pattern of societal organization in which kings, princes or other regents granted land and noble or seigneurial rights of private lordship to feoff holders, and, in return, feoff holders accepted certain, usually military, obligations towards feudal lords. Through this system, seemingly public resources of political and judicial power were obtained through private transaction and held as private goods in the hands of barons or territorial lords, who then assumed personal legal and judicial rights over those subordinated to them by feoff. Through this system, moreover, rulers widely conceded legal exemptions, immunities or other powers of jurisdictional autonomy to inhabitants of their territories, so that private islands of judicial independence proliferated outside vertical power relations.[3] It is widely documented that earlier feudal societies contained a distinctive inner legal order, and, as an overarching societal system, feudalism stabilized judicial structures in otherwise highly disordered social settings: the exchange of feoffs meant that the use of power by those in superior positions in the feudal chain was countervailed by the rights attached to feoffdom, and violations of feudal rights could be pursued at different levels in private feudal courts. Societies under early feudalism contained a diffuse, yet prominent, lateral legal apparatus, in which customary and personal rights and rights of status groups were articulated at various points in society, and judicial rights were strongly attached to private embedded relationships.[4] However, feudal societies, or at least societies at a relatively early stage of feudalization, were pervasively shaped by very irregular and personalistic patterns of lordship and legal settlement, and, as

overarching social system, with uniform characteristics and a clear beginning and a clear end. I simply use it to describe a particular mode of socio-political organization, accepted as a reality (albeit not in England) even by Richardson and Sayles (1963: 118), in which 'sovereignty was divided between the king and his feudatories'. A primary characteristic of feudal society, following this residual definition, was that *jurisdictional power was held in part in private hands*, society as a whole witnessed a 'collapse of public justice' (Bisson 1994: 71) and power was not 'experienced publicly and institutionally' (Bisson 2009: 14). See also Bloch (1949: 135). For this reason, feudalism is construed here as a societal regime in which power was applied, often by violent means, through lateral private bonds, and thus did not clearly exist as *political power*.

[3] There is a substantial body of literature on immunities. Immunity is defined here as an institution that at once placed royal power as a private good in the hands of bearers of an immunity, and allowed them to 'isolate themselves from the state' (Boutruche 1968: 132–3). It involved 'exemption from certain fiscal burdens' and delegation to the lord of 'certain judicial powers' (Bloch 1949: 122). This captures the sense of the immunity as a legal principle that at once supported and gradually fragmented centrally applied power.

[4] For analytical examples, see Milsom (1976: 58).

mentioned, feudal lords often purchased support for their power by allocating private rights or offering indemnities in respect of judicial force, taxation and service. For this reason, earlier feudal societies tended to be highly particularized and endemically violent, they embedded reserves of power in deeply privatized local and familial milieux, and they had limited recourse to a reliably centralized or regular legal apparatus. In the high medieval period, however, the decentred legal structure of early feudalism began to be supplanted through a gradual shift towards a societal order in which power was more directly mediated through central political actors, and social relations increasingly became subject to stable administrative control. Indeed, the high medieval era generally witnessed the beginnings of a deep transformation of political authority, such that centralized administrative institutions, which were increasingly funded, no longer solely by land tenures based in a particular lordship but also by taxation, began to act as the mainstay of political order: as a result of this, holders of political power very gradually began to construct their authority, not by granting seigneurial rights over land, but by raising revenues on the lands, offices and exemptions that they conferred on others (Wickham 1984: 27). This, in turn, brought an expansion in the size of government, it increased the mass of social exchange that was administered through governmental power, and it increased the need for regular consistent legal order to delineate the obligations underlying government.

The period of legal and political transition in question here was emphatically not a period of widespread *de-feudalization*: that is, it did not detach power from private land holding, or integrate rights and lands granted either as feoffs or under feudal immunity into a vertical state apparatus. Despite this, however, the later twelfth century and the thirteenth century gradually gave rise to an internal transformation of the deep-lying political structures of feudalism itself. Through this transformation, the balance between central power and feoff holding was tilted towards centralized agency. Both the diffuse holding of feudal rights, exemptions and unbridled (often violent) lordship were increasingly controlled by dominant figures in society, who were beginning (very tentatively) to acquire a monopoly of the instruments of political coercion. Through this process, albeit with substantial regional differences, the powers attached to lordship, to local privileges and to seigneurial rights were weakened. Indeed, throughout the entire transformation of feudalism, the feudal nobility, originally exercising power at a high degree of independence, experienced a slow change in political status: the private authority and independence of the nobility were slowly reduced, and in more advanced states the nobility was commonly brought into a more controlled and subordinate relation to central dynastic authority. Indeed, instead of locating power in private hands, feoffs, immunities and noble privileges came to act as legal devices for intensifying regalian powers, for strengthening the central authority of proto-state institutions, and for weakening actors (i.e. the nobility) defined by possession of privilege.[5]

If the transition from early to high feudalism was marked by an incipient centralization of the political system in European societies, it was also coloured by a further, more encompassing, transformation of society as a whole. In particular, this progressive change from political order based on lordship and private land tenure to political order based in administrative institutions can be seen as a broad reaction to the very early emergence of a differentiated and independent economic system in many European societies. The institution of a formal administrative system for securing political control responded to an aggregate of processes in which, throughout Europe, trade routes and more consistently monetarized patterns of commerce began to spread over increasingly large geographical areas (Lousse 1943: 123). The early emergence of a widening monetary economy meant that economic transactions were increasingly conducted through relations of contract, which presupposed replicable legal principles of personal autonomy that precluded feudal control,[6] and independent ownership of property and monetary reserves liberated some social groups from feudal affiliations. The progressive differentiation of society's economic interactions meant that most European societies of the high feudal period began to require administrative institutions whose functions could be performed at a growing level of social and personal abstraction and consistency, and societies increasingly developed instruments for using power to regulate highly diverse and regionally remote exchanges in generalized, predictable and replicable fashion. In some instances, most notably the northern Italian cities, in fact, the *public* power of emergent administrative organs began to evolve because of the expansion of distinctively *private*

---

[5] For important views on this structural change within feudalism, paving the way for the eventual supplanting of feudal order, see Mayer (1939: 457–87); Lousse (1943: 120, 294); and Wickham (2003: 6).

[6] On the relation between monetarization and the rise of contractual legal principles see Lopez (1998: 73).

modes of ownership in the economy (Goetz 1944: 93; Calasso 1949: 156). That is to say, the gradual extension of monetary transactions and individual property ownership and the disintegration of property-holding groups from feudal tenures created an early urban economic elite, and this class intensified its authority through techniques of governance and legal integration that were not tied to socially embedded customs and feudal arrangements (Bertelli 1978: 29; Dilcher 1967: 7; Faini 2004).

In the later twelfth and thirteenth centuries, in sum, it is possible to discern a broad set of transformative processes, which, in conjunction, at once disaggregated different spheres of social activity and diminished the local or personal embeddedness and the violent contestability of political power. As a result, European societies began to develop institutions that were able to utilize political power as a facility that was increasingly indifferent to the local, personal and patrimonial distinctions underlying feudal social structure, and which possessed a certain distinction or even tentative autonomy against other modes of social exchange. In consequence, these societies also began to require institutions that could organize their functions in a relatively firm and consistent legal apparatus. Indeed, the general restructuring of feudalism throughout the high medieval period was reflected most distinctively in the law, and, in promoting gradually generalized and differentiated patterns of social exchange, this transformative process clearly stimulated a growing need in most European societies for precise and increasingly constant legal forms. At a general level, this period witnessed a wide employment of more consistent legal formulae across very different spheres of society, and the widespread rise in the distinction between separate social practices meant that each set of social activities required constructs to support its exchanges at a growing level of internal abstraction: in particular, the first emergence of a relatively independent economy presupposed the use of legal forms that could be predictably applied to monetary transactions in very different locations. At a specifically political level, this period was marked by a need for legal instruments able to store political power in relatively stable, centralized form, to reinforce political institutions above the highly personal rights and customs of immunity and vassalage characteristic of early medieval societies, and to formalize relations between political actors and those granted feudal rights in increasingly settled legal arrangements. In addition, in view of their wider incremental differentiation, European societies of the high feudal era also experienced an increased need for political institutions that could transplant power inclusively across broad social divisions, and they evolved a requirement for institutions that could, over large geographical areas, refer to relatively stable and consistent constructions of themselves and their functions. In these different respects, therefore, European societies increasingly came to require new formations within the law, and the law became a crucial device both in the growing distinction of different spheres of functional exchange and in the widening circulation of political power which marked societies in the early process of feudal transformation. The high medieval period, in other words, induced a change in social structure in Europe in which power, separated from private lordship and particular privilege, was 'objectively defined' and increasingly transmitted across growing social distances (Bisson 2009: 415). The increasing regularization of the law was fundamental to this process.

Legal order in the church

The first and most important example of this process of legal formalization at the origins of high medieval society can be found in a sequence of institutional changes, beginning in the eleventh century, that occurred in the Roman Catholic church. Generally, in the early stages of the high medieval period the church assumed an increasingly distinctive role in emerging European societies, and it began, through a long process of reform, both to establish itself as the central institution in society and to acquire systematically ordered powers of jurisdiction and legal regulation that distinguished it from the local, personalized structures of feudal order. To be sure, this process did not take place in a political vacuum, and the distinction between processes of formalization in ecclesiastical law and similar processes in civil law cannot always be clearly drawn. For example, the tendency towards legal uniformity in the church was driven in part by the growing construction of the Holy Roman Empire as a concerted and increasingly autonomous body of political institutions: the increasing legal consistency of the church evolved almost in parallel to similar changes in the Empire, whose rulers progressively asserted their right to act in independence of the church, to assume independent territorial power and even to form a universal Empire. The reforms in the church thus (at least in intention) set the foundations for a period of *papal monarchy*, in which the papacy sought to suppress the claims of the Holy Roman emperors and to assert both worldly and spiritual authority throughout Christendom. Further, the conceptual foundations of legal reform in the church were in large part derived from Roman law. The increase in legal consistency in the church coincided roughly with the promotion of the science of Roman civil law in the medieval law schools in Italy, especially Bologna, and the ecclesiastical reforms were deeply influenced by ideas emanating from these schools (Helmholz 1996: 17–18). Despite this, however, as early as the late eleventh century the church had clearly assumed a uniquely ordered and centralized internal legal structure, and, to a greater extent than societal actors using the civil law, it instituted a uniform model of legal order, which began pervasively to transform European societies in their entirety. In particular, the church began to respond both to the endemic privatism and disorder of early feudalism and to the gradual differentiation and expansion of European societies by constructing for itself a legal apparatus that enabled it to make decisions and enforce its authority at an increasingly high level of inner autonomy and outer uniformity – that is, to circulate its power in increasingly regular and inclusive procedures across the local and jurisdictional fissures that underlay European societies in the condition of early feudalism. At the caesura between early and high feudalism, therefore, the church assumed distinctive status as an institution that, in reforming its legal apparatus, was able autonomously to confer consistency and unity on its particular functions, and so reproducibly to apply its power across the intra-societal boundaries of pre-modern social order.

To illustrate this analysis, during the high medieval period the Roman Catholic church began to extricate itself both from the tradition of territorial or private-dynastic control of the church (*Eigenkirchentum*) and from the integration of the church in the feoffs of the Holy Roman Empire, which had characterized the legal status of the church since the Carolingian period (Weise 1912: 19, 36; Tellenbach 1988: 57–8). At the centre of this transformation was the increasingly powerful declaration, expressed in the reforms of Gregory VII in the late eleventh century, that the pope possessed *plenitudo potestatis* in all matters of the church. This meant that no pope was bound by secular laws of custom, that each pope could assume authority to act, abstracted from all specific or embedded legal arrangement, as a *lex animata* for the church as a whole, and that papal legates could enforce church power across extensive geographical areas as commissioned representatives of the pope. The crucial point of law in this development was that, owing to the Gregorian reforms, popes followed Roman-law maxims in claiming the *ius condendi legem* (the power to legislate – that is, to introduce *new laws*), through which the papacy assumed for itself rights analogous to those of the emperors of classical Rome.[7] As the popes assumed supreme and general power in this manner, then, the church began to internalize an account of itself as containing a higher natural law, which was categorically distinct from local laws and could be generally invoked to authorize the actions and decisions of the church.[8] In the first instance, this idea of higher law allowed the church, externally, to assume a representative dignity and integrity through which it could separate itself from, and assert its autonomy against, the corpus of personal agreements that had previously supported the early-feudal interconnection between territorial lords and ecclesiastical potentates. In addition, however, this idea of higher law also allowed the church, internally, to define itself as a relatively unitary personality, and it created a legal structure in which ecclesiastical delegates could borrow (and thus, also, *represent*) the pope's power and appeal to a corporate personality in the church in order to make decisions or settle disputes across substantial regional and temporal divides. Through the ascription of supreme legislative authority to the pope, thus, the church obtained the ability to use its power at a dramatically heightened level of administrative generality, and this allowed the power of the church to overarch different regions and in principle to include all members of European society in a consolidated *ecumene*. Paradoxically, moreover, the assumption that the pope incarnated higher law permitted the church more fluidly to positivize its basic legal principles: it enabled the church to produce legal decisions from within an inner justificatory apparatus, to abstract a formal judicial order for its procedures and to store a set of clear principles to accompany and unify very diverse applications of its power. In all these respects, in and after the period of Gregorian reform in the late eleventh century the church progressively defined itself as a distinct fulcrum of power within society, and it invoked principles of higher law in order both to integrate and regularly to sustain the procedures in which it used its power and to augment the volume of power that it contained.

This progressive attribution of unitary legal power to the highest offices of the church was reflected at all levels of the church's internal

---

[7] This was stated in the famous Dictatus Papae of Gregory VII, in which the pope was accorded the power: 'pro temporis necessitate novas leges condere'. This document is printed in Caspar (1967: 203–8).

[8] Note the argument – 'Sed canones pro varietate gentium non variantur' – to support the universality of canon law (Weigand 1967: 169). I found excellent commentary on this in Leisching (2001: 214, 233).

organization. Throughout the reformist period, in fact, the entire operative structure of the church was placed on a firm legal basis. For instance, this period witnessed the formation of the monastic regime in the church, and it witnessed the institution of a formal concept of sacraments. It also witnessed the imposition of firm standards of behaviour and worship across churches in all countries under the papal see; and it witnessed the establishment of a stricter episcopal regime in which bishops were closely tied to Rome and were commissioned to impose the pope's will throughout the church in its entirety. In addition, during the Gregorian reforms and their aftermath the church even began to develop institutional features now considered characteristic of secular states: that is, it evolved new resources for raising fiscal revenue, it acquired devolved legal-administrative powers for codifying law and for issuing and promulgating new laws, and it reinforced its jurisdictional powers for enforcing positive law through specialized judicial procedures (Morris 1989: 388, 402, 575). Through these reforms, training in law became a qualification for ecclesiastical office, the papal curia was expected to process a dramatically increasing mass of litigation, and episcopal courts, with expansive administrative staffs, were appointed to conduct, delegate and uniformly control church legal affairs. Distinctive for this period was also the fact that the legal bureaucracy of the church increased markedly, and a specially qualified class of canon lawyers was required to preside over cases for legal adjudication. The legal order imposed by the reformist papacy, thus, led to a legal unification of the church as a whole, and throughout the church written law was used to transmit ecclesiastical power in a specifically consistent and general fashion.

Fundamental to this legal revolution in the church was a far-reaching revival and refinement of the canon law, through which distinct branches and procedures of ecclesiastical order were gradually underpinned by uniformly ordered legal principles, and both the church and the papal monarchy assumed independent and positive legal foundations. The revival of canon law was shaped, in the first instance, by a substantial expansion of legal learning, both in the ecclesiastical and in the secular realms, in the eleventh century. However, the refinement of canon law was also decisively stimulated by the rediscovery of older canonical collections, and it was pursued through a systematic reconstruction of existing canonical texts using principles of Roman law. This process resulted in the revision, redrafting and widespread promulgation of new collections of canon law. Most importantly, it culminated in the codification of Gratian's *Decretum*, which appeared towards the middle of the twelfth century, and, finally, in the Fourth Lateran Council of 1215, where a more uniform set of laws and judicial procedures was established for the church as a whole. In this respect, as above, it needs to be noted that this codification of ecclesiastical law was not fully separate from secular law, and it did not constitute an unrestricted endorsement of papal monarchy. In fact, some sections of Gratian's *Decretum* served as conceptual 'cornerstones for the doctrine of the universal Empire', to which the reformist papacy was opposed (Kienast 1975: 297). In fact, the *Decretum* claimed that imperial law was justified under divine law and that civil order depended on imperial law.[9] Vitally, though, Gratian's *Decretum* was designed systematically to differentiate church law from secular law, and it established a consistent and positive legal order to which judicial practices in the church could refer to explain their authority.

It was the systematic rewriting of ecclesiastical law, above all, that enabled the church to give a reproducible internal account of its functions and regularly to transmit principles of order across society. In particular, the codification of canon law had this result because it allowed the church to form itself as an institution whose power obtained a certain corporate legal integrity against distinct persons, including, tentatively, those factual persons that it incorporated and that used and dispensed its power. If the pope's claim to act as a *lex animata* was at the heart of the growth in ecclesiastical authority, therefore, this was augmented further by the systematic organization of canon law, which greatly extended the ability of the church to explain its authority and its validity as residing in a legal source distinct from any immediate subject or bearer of power. This assumption of a stable legal apparatus in the church meant that the church was able to apply power as an increasingly abstracted and autonomous phenomenon, and that it could presuppose flexible principles to underwrite diverse applications of its power. Naturally, this is not to suggest that at such an early stage the Roman Catholic church had begun to assume a corporate-constitutional or genuinely conciliar character. This eventually became the case in the fourteenth century, when theorists of ecclesiastical law began to accept the principle that the church possessed a legal personality (a *persona ficta*) that was distilled solely from law and that was at once internally consistent and constitutionally distinct from its particular representatives or executors. Both

---

[9] *Decretum Gratiani* (1676 [*c.* 1140]: 22).

canonists and political theorists of the later Middle Ages in fact ultimately claimed that the representative and doctrinal powers of the
church reposed, not in the person of the pope alone, but in the church
as a community of the faithful (*congregatio fidelium*), which had its
supreme constitutional organ in the church council (Tierney 1955: 4, 13).
John of Paris, for example, concluded that the power of the church had a
constitutional source that was not to be conflated with the pope and the
inner administrative hierarchy around the pope (1614 [*c.* 1302]: 45).
Similarly, William of Ockham insisted that the pope did not possess a
categorical 'fullness of power' in either spiritual or temporal matters.
Ockham in fact added to this the telling claim that Christian law should
be viewed as a 'law of liberty' – that is, as a law that was founded in the
institution, not of the pope, but of Christ, and which inspirited all members
of the church in equal manner (1940 [*c.* 1339]: 233). Marsilius of Padua also
endorsed conciliar ideas, and he argued that not the pope alone, but only a
'general council composed of all Christians', could represent the 'whole
body of the faithful' (1956 [1324]: 280). These conciliar theories thus
expanded the transpersonal or organic implications of earlier doctrines
of canon law, and, especially during the Great Schism (1378–1417), they
came to define the church as an order with an administrative and
doctrinal personality separate from all its functionaries, even the pope.
Even in earlier canonical discourses, however, the implication inevitably
became clear that, as an agent using and founded in generalized legal
principles, the church possessed a distinctly unified, positive legal personality, which it could invoke to support a substantial number of
devolved and personally indifferent administrative or judicial acts and
decisions. As a result, the church was able to claim singular authority for
the multiple decisions of its representatives, and it could refer to a set of
general internal norms that authorized its representatives to create, and
explain the necessity of, *new laws*. Indeed, in promoting the acceptance of
a canon law as a formal *lex scripta*, the church obtained the specific
benefit that it was able to override and remove old laws, to question the
authority of simple customs and embedded judicial practices and to
devise principles to support new legislation and appellate rulings.
Paradoxically, therefore, the schematization of canon law in the church,
which expressly derived the authority of ecclesiastical law from
the church's ability to incarnate divine law, substantially augmented
the reserves of legal autonomy, positive generality and reproducibility
contained in the church: the belief that law could be uniformly justified
by higher, even transcendent, principles deeply enhanced law's ability to

overrule local feudal agreements, to supplant private authority and to confer a perennial and flexible consistency on the church's legal order. Owing to this, the church was able dramatically to expand the volume of power that it contained and, gradually, it began to use its power, through law, as a personally autonomous, iterable and inclusive facility. Through the legal transformation of the church, in short, for the first time since late antiquity European societies acquired an institution that could autonomously explicate its use of power by referring to resources that it stored within itself, and could apply its power as relatively independent of external determinants and relatively insensitive to immediate consent, local resistance or accepted custom.

Throughout the course of its formation, to conclude, the legal order of the medieval church at once refracted and intensified a number of defining dynamics, transformations and problems in feudal society. In the first instance, it reflected a wide process of societal expansion, and it distilled the power of the church into a generalizable form that could be equally and iterably applied to all members of the Christian community. Vital for this was the fact that the canon law began to project a construction of the church as an overarching organic personality – that is, as a personality that retained an inner consistency against the particular bearers of its power, and could autonomously authorize, devolve and reproduce power in varied settings by referring to highly generalized and inclusive legal concepts. This brought the crucial benefit to members of the church that they were able to distribute power in a relatively stable and consistent fashion (that is, in written codes, formal judicial procedures and static juridical instruments) across geographically and temporally widening societies.[10] At the same time, however, the legal reforms in the church reflected a process in which society as a whole experienced an incremental differentiation into discrete functional spheres, and in which the densely interwoven mass of personal and seigneurial functions and immunities characterizing early feudalism was beginning to disintegrate. The formalization of canon law was also at the centre of this second process: canon law provided a body of terms in which, for the first time, one free-standing institution was able to delineate its functions as internally consistent and relatively indifferent to patterns of exchange and obligation in other social spheres, and to transmit its authority in a functionally unified and specialized manner.

---

[10] On the wider importance of written law in the creation of a positively abstracted legal culture, see Clanchy (1979: 46, 50); Keller (1991: 183); and Dreier (2002: 3).

The increasing reception of Roman law in the church, in particular, was the crucial element in each aspect of this process. Roman law stored the legal order of the church in clear written procedures, and this facilitated the emergence of a legal apparatus that could articulate its power, not in local or socially embedded agreements or customs, but in temporally and locally indifferent juridical categories (Radding 1988: 299).

Church law, the state and feudal transformation

This legal organization of the church as a source of inclusively transmissible power had resonances across medieval societies that extended far beyond questions of ecclesiastical jurisdiction, and it deeply shaped the secular political form of nascent European societies in their entirety. Indeed, just as the church had borrowed elements of Roman law and other ideas of legal personality from the secular arena, worldly political actors also began to replicate the church's legal and procedural innovations, and secular institutions increasingly employed techniques of legal-political abstraction that they appropriated from the church. The growing legal order of the church thus provided a general model of legal organization for early Western societies, and, by the later twelfth century, this had become formative for the initial construction of secular political power in its characteristically modern institutional form. In fact, in a number of ways the legal abstraction of the Roman Catholic church in the longer Gregorian period directly stimulated the growth and shaped the structure of early European states.

In the first instance, both before and during the period of ecclesiastical reform the church was in the forefront of the promotion of temporal legal order throughout European society, and secular authorities increasingly relied on the church and its legal apparatus to pacify society and to suppress the endemic violence and feuding that were characteristics of earlier feudalism.[11] Notably, the ecclesiastical ideal of the Peace of God (*Gottesfriede, Treuga Dei, Paix de Dieu*) – that is, the prohibition of feuding and private violence enforced by the church under threat of excommunication – acted at times, especially in the eleventh century, as a vital mechanism for establishing order in societies fragmented by the pursuit of justice through feuds, local lordship and private violence. In many cases, moreover, the Peace of God provided a direct stimulus for

---

[11] On the relation between the church reforms and the Peace of God, see Barthélemy (1999: 212). Generally, see Hoffmann (1964).

the imposition of peace in the realm by worldly actors, and secular leaders, both of territories and cities, used legal forms and oaths derived from the Peace of God in order to bring legal and judicial order to their territories and to solidify their own jurisdictional powers.[12] In this respect, the increasing consolidation of law in the Roman Catholic church clearly marked a crucial step towards the more general enforcement of law and political jurisdiction in the temporal sphere.

In addition to this, however, the legal reorganization of the church had its most significant external or secular consequences, not in any direct appropriation of ecclesiastical legal structure in the political arena, but rather in the protracted conflicts between the church and emergent states, which defined the political contours of high medieval society and are generally known as the investiture contests. These contests, beginning in the later eleventh century, were conflicts over jurisdiction, which were conducted both between the reformist papacy and the Holy Roman Empire, and – to a lesser degree – between the papacy and emergent smaller national dynasties. The central manifest issue in these conflicts was a controversy over the degree to which temporal rulers were authorized to anoint their own bishops and whether the dispensing of church offices fell under temporal authority. More generally, however, these contests centred around the legal question of whether representatives of the church were beholden to regents in whose territories they operated, and they raised the question, which had vital status in a period of rising functional specialization, whether ecclesiastical laws could prevail over local legislation and transcend the jurisdiction of particular regents.

It is often claimed that the investiture contests marked the beginning of an era of papal monarchy, in which the papacy rebutted the claims to universal Empire made by the Holy Roman emperors, and that through the resolution of these contests the papacy assumed extensive powers in relation to and even *over* worldly rulers, so that the church asserted its authority as the dominant political agent in European society (Calasso 1954: 171). In most instances, however, the investiture contests actually ended in a bilateral clarification of the legal relation between church and state, in which ecclesiastical power in spiritual matters was established as an exclusive principle and in which the exclusive authority of temporal

---

[12] This was vital in some of the earliest Italian *comuni*, where the urban constitutions were often legitimized by the exchange of oaths to keep the peace: the *treuga dei* was at the foundation of the *comuni* (Keller 1982: 67).

lords in matters of worldly significance was also clearly underlined. In England, the controversies in their strictest sense came to an end in the Concordat of London of 1107, which formulated a compromise between Henry I and Anselm of Canterbury. However, related conflicts continued and found their apotheosis in the murder of Thomas Becket in 1170. In the Holy Roman Empire, these controversies, which culminated in the excommunication of Heinrich IV, were resolved in the Concordat of Worms (1122). This concordat gave express legal form to an arrangement in which church power was sanctioned as unlimited *in spiritualibus* and imperial power was accepted as inviolable *in temporalibus*. Although it symbolically accepted papal supremacy in church offices, the Concordat of Worms also integrated the temporal elements of the church into the feudal system of the Empire, it placed the worldly possessions of the church under imperial law so that the emperor retained the right to confer ecclesiastical property in the form of regal rights (*regalia*), and it played a significant role in extending the feudal power of the Empire over all areas of worldly legislation.[13] Naturally, these agreements did not bring an end to the contests between church and state, and the papacy continued to claim that the pope possessed two swords, the spiritual and the temporal. A most notable example of this was the decretal, Per Venerabilem (1202), of Innocent III, which, while (reluctantly) accepting the claim of kings to supreme temporal jurisdiction, asserted that the pope had the power to decide whether candidates for imperial office were worthy of assuming this dignity. It was under Innocent, moreover, that the canon lawyers fully elaborated their theory of papal monarchy, and they defined papal powers in the church as specifically derived from Christ's original mandate (Pennington 1984: 38). Nonetheless, the diverse accords marking the end of the investiture contests put in place the foundations for a division of jurisdictional powers between church and state, and in principle they accepted a legal distinction of competence between these powers.

These legal controversies over investiture had the most far-reaching consequences for the secular-political structure of European societies. Indeed, one main result of these controversies was that political institutions began to design themselves around the same principles of positive legal order that had been consolidated in the church, and, in different

---

[13] For this interpretation see Classen (1973); Minninger (1978: 208); and Paradisi (1987: 387).

ways, conflicts over investiture stimulated a concerted migration of legal concepts from the church to the institutions of worldly power.

Most immediately, for example, the Gregorian era and its controversies over jurisdiction necessarily forced political actors in European societies clearly to explain and legally to justify their activities in those areas of social regulation that they contested with the church. This meant that nascent states assimilated elements of legal order applied in the church, and they began to approach law, as did the church, as a positive and internally consistent science, and to transform the law of the church for their own functional and explanatory purposes. In particular, on account of their contests with the church, political actors widely emulated the church in employing concepts of Roman law. Over a longer period of time, actors in secular institutions utilized Roman law to describe themselves, like the church, as actors with relatively independent legal personalities, and they were able to extract a constant construction of their functions to imply stable internal authorizations for their use of power and to define their power and their procedures for using their power in internally consistent and socially abstracted categories. In fact, in the wake of the investiture controversies emerging states also began to establish professionalized or at least laicized judiciaries, and to prescribe professional qualifications for bearers of judicial power.[14] The use of Roman law as the foundation for legal finding meant that law was increasingly administered by a privileged class of lawyers, who, like jurists in the church, were distinguished by specific qualifications and possessed a growing monopoly of legal authority. As indicated, moreover, the longer period of Gregorian reform coincided with the foundation of the Bolognese law school, which was established as the main forum for legal study in Europe by the middle of the twelfth century. The activities of this school centred, although not exclusively, on the study of civil law, and Bolognese law promoted the circulation and refinement of positive ideas of secular legitimacy. In particular, the elements of *lex regia* in Roman law began to form the basis for a strict doctrine of abstracted princely authority: at this time the first full systematic rendering of Roman law in Bologna, presumed to be the work of Irnerius, accorded to the prince a position above all other magistrates,[15] thus

---

[14] To exemplify, see Musson (2001: 47); and Reynolds (2003: 361–2).

[15] See the observation that the 'Romanum princeps' is 'caput omnium magistratum' (Irnerius? 1894: 21). In other earlier medieval glosses the prince was even described as the 'caput aliorum iudicum' (Fitting 1876: 148).

imputing to the prince an ultimate monopoly of worldly power. These ideas became progressively prevalent through Europe, and, spreading outwards from Bologna, Roman law was broadly employed throughout high medieval European society as a device for asserting the growing territorial supremacy of temporal rulers, and for constructing the state as a consistent and uniform legal personality, able, in some matters, to subordinate the church. The very origins of the modern concept of state sovereignty might in fact be discerned in the strategic appropriation by worldly states of the Roman-law principles of *plenitudo potestatis, plena potestas* and *lex animata*, which were increasingly used by reformist popes as formulae for constructing their own abstract legislative status.[16] In the Holy Roman Empire, for example, where the conflict over the balance of authority between church and state was at its most intense, Roman law was the legal medium in which this conflict was distilled and conducted, and emperors widely employed aspects of Roman law to claim a fullness of secular/territorial power. Early glossators of Roman law, notably Accursius, specifically borrowed the ecclesiastical idea of the *lex animata* to describe the status and powers of the Emperor in the Empire (see Krynen 2009: 173).[17] As discussed below, Roman law was commonly utilized to consolidate the civil foundations of imperial power in terms that directly mirrored and rivalled the descriptions of papal power offered by the canon law. In smaller proto-national societies, moreover, a similar process of legal translation can be observed, and national regents also began to use abstract notions of legal power to sustain their authority and to eliminate external legal influence from their territories.[18] The period of church reform, in short, was also a period of secular reform in which emergent states, however tentatively, began juridically to harden their legal form, and certain early states emulated the church by using the law – and specifically Roman law – to explain themselves as regularized bearers of socially abstracted administrative power.

At the deepest societal level, however, the process of legal abstraction in the church and the transfer of legal concepts between church and state were reflections of a more fundamental and encompassing process of societal transformation. Indeed, if the question of rights of jurisdiction

---

[16] This is discussed in Haller (1966: 40); Pennington (1984: 38); Paradisi (1987: 302); and Erwin (2009: 55, 72).

[17] Yet on the dialectical implications of the work of Accursius see Tierney (1963).

[18] See pages 50–5 below.

and ordinance was the primary object of legal dispute in the investiture contests, these controversies also revealed, and were shaped by, a less evident, deeper-lying structural problem in high medieval society, and the refined elaboration of legal power in both church and state caused by the controversies distilled a problem of still more profoundly constitutive importance for medieval politics. This, namely, was a question that touched on the central nerve of feudalism itself. It was the question, first, of whether any institution or group of institutions could separate itself from, or place itself above, the highly personal and locally embedded accords forming the underlying legal apparatus of feudal society. Second, it was the question of whether any institution or group of institutions could release itself from personal incorporation in feudal bonds and legislate in growing inner autonomy and consistency and as relatively specialized on a distinct, overarching and personally indifferent set of social functions. In this respect, the investiture controversies, although raising a particular question about the church's political status and authority, were actually expressions of a wider contest over the substance and future of feudalism *in toto*. These controversies influenced the political order of European societies by describing and enacting a broad change in the functional structure of early European societies, and they stimulated a migration of legal forms from church to state because they created an environment in which both church and state began to act simultaneously as distinctly constructed institutions.

The jurisdictional conflict between the church and the state was at root a legal controversy in which the church initially began to generate principles of social organization that negated the privatistic, functionally interdependent and personal attribution of power in early feudalism. In this respect, the investiture contests reflected a submerged dynamic of feudal transformation and even of incipient *de-feudalization* throughout European society as a whole, and they created a social conjuncture in which both ecclesiastical and political institutions began to separate their functions from the local and structural relations of feudal society in order to consolidate themselves as relatively abstract, specialized and internally consistent societal actors. It was for this reason that the investiture contests gave rise to a growth in legal order in both the church and the state. In the wake of the investiture contests, both the church and its rivals in early states experienced an increasing requirement for law, and they relied on a consistent legal apparatus as an instrument at once for organizing the integrity of their power in relation both to their own specific functions and to other spheres of practice, and for unifying their power so that it could be transmitted, in relative abstraction, across the widening social spaces that their functions now incorporated. Law, thus, became the instrument by means of which church and state began to organize their differentiated autonomy.

If the investiture controversies began to crystallize the abstracted form of church and the state as legally distinct and semi-autonomous entities, therefore, this is because the controversies brought a decisive fissure into the social order of feudalism, and after this time both state and church began to develop as institutions that were equally foreign to feudalism. Both church and state evolved into their modern form through a process of functional and institutional division and specialization, which, although born of feudalism, could not ultimately coexist with the diffuse principles of feudal order. Where the church and the state began to operate as distinct institutions – that is, as relatively autonomous institutional entities that used power in general and internally consistent categories, that increasingly negated locality and consuetudinal privilege and that relied on written and formally memorized principles to support their legitimacy and integrity – the legal arrangements of feudalism could not, in pure form, enduringly prevail.[19] The legal separation of church and state in the investiture contests was in fact only secondarily a separation of two rival institutional bodies: in its essence it was a conjoined separation of two general, differentiated and increasingly *public* structures of political agency from the densely interwoven and deeply personalized legal background of feudal society, and, as such, it both reflected and intensified a wider underlying process of feudal transformation in European society. In this respect, most vitally, the conflict of church and state, and the resultant migration of legal forms between ecclesiastical and political institutions, not only gave rise to the basic legal apparatus of the state: it actually formed a preparation for the far longer conflicts that would ultimately determine the political structure of modern European states. Both the growing functional distinction and the growing legal autonomy of church and state were the emergent preconditions for the separation of the state, not only from the church, but also from other sources of external private privilege and personal power, and the tentative formation of public legal forms in this period

---

[19] Tellingly, it has been observed that both church and states are entities that were naturally 'outside' the legal realm of feudalism (Olivier-Martin 1984: 202).

ultimately allowed emergent states to propose themselves as centres of coercion above those social groups holding power (through immunity and seigneurial indemnity) as a private attribute. The process of legal and judicial abstraction in the church thus laid the foundations for the gradual formation of European states as primary autonomous centres of public order, and it set the terrain for the consolidation of political power against particular actors and localities and for the ultimate termination of feudal patterns of socio-political organization more generally.

In these respects, the investiture contests can be seen as playing a formative role in the first construction of distinctively *political* forms of power in European society. The legal organization of the church reflected a process in which European societies began to require condensed reserves of political power to resolve matters of generalized significance, to evolve specifically political functions, and – accordingly – to abstract their political power as a functionally distilled and autonomous phenomenon – that is, as a resource that could be used positively, distinctively and consistently to address politically resonant questions and which was only marginally reliant on other spheres of practice for its authority. The emulation of ecclesiastical principles by worldly actors in the wake of the investiture contests was in fact, at the deepest level, caused by the fact that both church and state required a rudimentary public personality in order to apply power as a general abstract resource. The conflicts between church and state created a social condition in which worldly political actors were compelled to produce legal instruments and to extract clear principles for capturing their growing autonomy and for managing their power as a positive abstracted and increasingly public phenomenon, and they provided legal constructs in which new institutions could account for and apply their newly abstracted resources of public power. Indeed, more arguably, the investiture contests also began to reflect and consolidate a legal structure in European societies, in which different institutions were required independently *to produce* abstracted resources of power, and to find devices to expand and reproduce the quantities of power that they incorporated. Through the investiture contests, both church and state began to emerge as institutions required internally to generate their own power, and to exercise this power against the privatistic fabric of early feudal society. The emergent principles of public law at once described the separation of state from church and created a legal structure in which states could account for their power in positive form and increase the volume of power which they possessed.

Patterns of early statehood

The incipient formation of states through the disaggregation of the local and privatistic social order of feudalism assumed different form in diverse national/cultural settings, and a number of patterns of political formation through feudal transformation can be discerned. In each case, however, the law was the crucial agent in the transformation of feudalism. The law, initially abstracted and rationalized in the church, enabled states to stabilize themselves in the political vacuum that emerged as the personalistic fabric of feudalism incrementally lost structural importance.

Law and feudal transformation I: the Holy Roman Empire

Perhaps the classic case of state formation as incipient de-feudalization was the Holy Roman Empire itself. As mentioned, after the altercations over investiture and jurisdiction between church and Empire, the imperial executive began to deploy the hierarchical principles, and in particular the *lex regia*, of Roman law, as utensils for consolidating imperial authority both against the papacy directly and against the cities and territories which the Empire incorporated. Indeed, it is widely documented that the school of Roman law in Bologna had very close ties to the Empire, and the glossators in Bologna concentrated their work on providing commentaries on the *Digest* of Justinian in order to support imperial authority. As mentioned, the imperial party sought to define the medieval Empire as a revival of classical Rome, and emperors widely employed the *lex regia* of the *Digest*, and above all the principle that the prince's will has force of law (*quod principi placuit legis habet vigorem*), to insist on their authority to create law and to express the universal primacy of their temporal power.[20] In employing these concepts, the Empire was able at once to distinguish its power from that of the church and to define relations of supremacy and obedience between the emperor and those persons and regions holding power from the Empire in the form of feoffs. In this last respect, the consolidation of Roman law deeply altered the legal structure of feudalism in the Empire,

---

[20] The close links between Emperor Friedrich I (Barbarossa) and the legists in Bologna are of particular significance and widely documented. Notably, the Bolognese jurists described Friedrich I as embodying the *lex animata* (see Colorni 1967: 149).

and it progressively formed the imperial regime as a centre of distinctive public sovereign authority.

The legal process of feudal transformation in the Holy Roman Empire attached in particular to the question of immunities and regalian rights. As discussed, immunities, indemnities and *regalia* were a crucial element of legal control in many feudal societies: immunities and *regalia* formed a pluralistic legal reality through which a feudal lord, in return for payment or obligation, ceded jurisdiction over a particular territory to another person or corporate body.[21] Owing to the link between indemnities, *regalia* and judicial power, feudal societies were built around parcellated and cross-cutting jurisdictions, many localities were exempted from central jurisdiction by virtue of the fact that they were covered by immunity or indemnity, local or seigneurial justice was ordinarily conducted without central control, and many areas were subject to a number of jurisdictions at the same time. Rule by immunity or indemnity was thus a legal regime in which immunity or indemnity was applied in lieu of general law, and in which legal order was sustained through a multiplicity of agreements and overlapping powers (Buschmann 1999: 22). Moreover, in the earlier feudal order of the Holy Roman Empire both regalian grants of land and office and the immunities and indemnities attached to these grants had often been converted into hereditary holdings, so that the bearers of exemptions had over generations assumed a high degree of jurisdictional autonomy in different territories within the Empire. The legal transformation of feudalism in the Empire, however, which began in earnest under the intermittent regime of the Hohenstaufen (1138–1254), brought a deep change to this system of independent tenure, local jurisdiction and legal immunity, and it replaced the localizing and centrifugal use of privileges, immunities and bonds with a more formal system of legalized feudal hierarchy (*Lehnrecht*). This new style of legal order had the primary feature that the granting of *regalia* placed the recipient or recipients of a feoff under close imperial control, and it sought to prevent the permanent transfer or alienation of feoffs yielded as *regalia* without imperial consent. In 1180, most notably, the feudal bond (*Lehenband*) was strictly reformulated as a direct legal relation between the emperor and his subjects

---

[21] Immunities, as distinct from *regalia* more generally, were initially granted to ecclesiastical bodies. Eventually, though, their use often ran together with *regalia*. On the origins of immunities see Anton (1975: 1). On immunities as originally weakening central legal authority see Kroell (1910: 20). For a recent slight revision of this view, which nonetheless still examines immunities as elements of 'private jurisdiction', see Rosenwein (1999: 6, 15).

or vassals: this led to a stricter organization of the high nobility in the Empire. At this point, feudal law was transformed into a more clearly integrative apparatus for conducting government, and the law, based on a vertical obligation between lord and vassal, began to engender a more hierarchical political apparatus, in which subjects obtained their status and legal rights as corollaries of regal office and were consequently drawn into a more immediate relation to the Empire (Stengel 1948: 297). One crucial constitutional consequence of the investiture contests was that from this time onwards the imperial executive utilized *regalia*, not as legal grants for conceding immunities or indemnities and so for sustaining a diffuse or centrifugal legal order throughout the Empire, but as instruments of direct coercion and integration, binding actors in society into an increasingly uniform subjection to the Empire's administrative authority.

As a result of these legal changes, the governmental elite of the Holy Roman Empire was transformed from a loose ruling stratum into a more strictly regimented and centralized bloc, and subjection to this elite was increasingly consolidated through accountable office holding.[22] The main legal edicts promulgated by the Hohenstaufen dynasty can clearly be interpreted in the light of these tendencies. As discussed below, the centralistic policies of the Staufer were perhaps most evident in the degree to which they transformed the political landscape of northern Italy. The most exemplary process of feudal transformation effected by the Staufer, however, was evident in their regime in the Kingdom of Sicily (1194–1266), which, although not integral to the Empire, was in many ways a testing ground for the construction of post-feudal statehood. The Hohenstaufen regents of Sicily employed Roman law to create a proto-modern administrative state, combining a relatively centralized governmental and judicial system, a formal legal code, and a state bureaucracy imposing regal authority through special appointees. The statutes of the Hohenstaufen regime in Sicily, usually referred to as the Liber Augustalis (1231), expressly affirmed the *lex regia* as the basis of government and jurisdiction, and they were designed clearly to consolidate the territorial authority of the ruling family. These statutes – or royal writs – concentrated power in a form that was specifically opposed to feudal tenure: that is, they stipulated that the regime of the Hohenstaufen should appoint its own agents in place of local consuls or administrators, and that no local or customary use of political or legal

---

[22] See the argument in Haverkamp (1971: 160).

authority would be tolerated.[23] Any towns appointing their own administrators were subject to violent suppression (Conrad, Lieck-Buyken and Wagner 1973: 44, 77).

In analogy to this, many of the German territories in the Empire also experienced a process of attempted legal concentration at this time. The twelfth century and the early thirteenth century, in particular, were marked (albeit rather inconclusively) by a number of both local and general endeavours to impose conditions of legal regularity across the German territories of the Empire. This resulted in the implementation of a series of laws intended to establish uniform conditions of territorial peace, to consolidate imperial authority as the dominant source of law and, as a result of this, to transform informal customary procedures for law finding into a clear body of criminal law. This process was expressed in the promulgation of an early uniform penal code, the *Mainzer Landfriede* (1235), and in related proclamations stressing the royal origin of all supreme jurisdiction (Fischer 2007: 32). This process also coincided with the establishment of a regular (although still ambulatory) imperial court and the appointment of increasingly fixed judicial staff, which was designed to promote more uniform legal procedures throughout the Empire and in particular to suppress the use of feuds and private violence as sources of law (Franklin 1867: 66–72; Diestelkamp 1983: 50–1). In general, thus, this era witnessed a pronounced growth in the strictness of legal regulation, and it saw the introduction of the main law books of medieval Germany, most especially the *Sachsenspiegel* (and variants on this text) around 1230. Tellingly, in fact, contemporaries knew this text as the Law of the Emperor (*keyserrecht*) (Erkens 2002: 82).

The concentrated legal order of the Holy Roman Empire can be seen as a feature of an early state that resulted from the investiture contests and the attendant transformation of the legal relations of feudal society. The imperial state used formalized legal resources, borrowed originally – in part – from Roman law, in order to restructure the personal legal arrangements of earlier feudalism, and to translate the plural private jurisdictions and immunities of feudalism into a body of vertically (although still very incompletely) controlled *regalia*. In this context, the transformation of regalian law through Roman-legal principles constructed a basic form of autonomous public law (*ius publicum*), and this enabled the state to extract principles to support its power that at once

---

[23] My account is influenced by Friedl (2005: 21–9); Calasso (1971; 118); and Pepe (1951: 42).

reflected and rivalled the claims for juridical autonomy and internal consistency that underpinned the Gregorian church.[24] Through this process, a political system began to emerge that condensed political power into a distinct proto-modern administrative edifice. In particular, this regime succeeded, in a rudimentary manner, in projecting an independent legal order for itself, and in using law uniformly to enforce vertical territorial control. In addition, this regime succeeded in establishing office holding as founded in a direct relation to the state, and in so doing it created a legal/political apparatus which, unlike the privatistic apparatus of feudal power, functioned (albeit rudimentarily) as a generalized and in principle impersonal and extensible system of social domination.

Law and feudal transformation II: Italian city-states between church and Empire

A distinct process of state building resulting from the investiture contests and the incipient transformation of feudalism can be observed in the governance of the cities of northern Italy, the *comuni*, which were mainly under the rule of the Holy Roman Empire. In this context, the investiture controversies also provided an immediate impetus for the construction of political power in independent positive form, and in this setting, too, the controversies over secular and ecclesiastical jurisdiction acted to differentiate and consolidate political agency as a socially independent function, reacting strongly against the privatistically interwoven legal structures of earlier feudalism. The form of independent political power resulting from the transformation of feudalism in northern Italy, however, assumed a distinctively broad-based and socially integrative quality.

The first impulse behind the construction of relatively independent political institutions in the Italian city-states arose from the fact that the investiture contests led to a marked decline of episcopal power in many cities, and for this reason they created a setting in which new patterns of authority began to evolve. In many city-states, civic and political authority had originally been vested together in holders of episcopal office, and the bishops governing these cities had obtained the right to exercise civic rule through feudal immunities or *regalia* granted by the Empire.

---

[24] In agreement, see Dilcher (2003: 285–6); Kannowski (2007: 176).

Bishops often enjoyed a high degree of independence from the papacy, and they regularly presided over quasi-feudal regimes, sustained legally by imperial immunities:[25] One historian has argued that an 'alliance of monarchy and Episcopate' was the basis for governance in the cities before the eleventh century (Keller 1979: 332–3). However, as the cities became caught in the conflict between Empire and church, urban episcopal power was often substantially weakened. This was mainly due to the fact that the reformist papacy, in pursuit of monastic discipline and legatine centralization, sought to undermine the independent authority of bishops, to dissolve the feudal obligations, patterns of office holding and the imperial *regalia* supporting episcopal power, and to ensure that bishops were more strictly attentive to papal command. Most notably, for instance, Gregory VII excommunicated bishops who allied themselves with the imperial party in the investiture contests. This diminution of ecclesiastic power placed the Italian cities in a new and unusual legal situation. On one hand, the reduction of episcopal power freed civic authority in the cities from immediate supervision by the church, and it enabled the cities to obtain and enlarge autonomous communal structures. More importantly, in weakening the feudal ties between bishops and Empire this process also liberated the cities from the direct, or at least mediated, control of the imperial dynasty. In conjunction with this, however, it is also widely documented that cities first reinforced their administrative autonomy as they rejected the authority of the feudal lords in their surrounding rural territories and separated the administration of the urban communes from the regional legal order (Wickham 2003: 17).[26] The Italian cities, in other words, began to obtain institutional independence in a highly distinctive legal/political setting, from which, simultaneously, feudal-imperial, feudal-territorial and feudal-episcopal power was receding.[27] At this primary level, the dissolution of the close feudal ties between church and Empire in northern Italy gave rise to a political condition, often described as an 'anti-feudal revolution', in which, to speak metaphorically, a legal opening appeared, in which free-standing and impersonal political institutions had to be created and

---

[25] Dilcher argues that the urban bishop became the 'feudal lord' of the city (Dilcher 1967: 64). See also Keller (1982: 58).

[26] In Pisa it is documented that the conflict with the rural powers in the *contado* was the preamble to a subsequent conflict with the bishops (Volpe 1902: 195–9).

[27] This is a common argument. See Hegel (1847: 137); Dilcher (1967: 66); Bertelli (1978: 17); and Occhipinti (2000: 20).

new sources of political authority, centred in a new, less personalized legal apparatus, had to be instituted (Calasso 1949: 156).

Most of the northern Italian cities responded to this unprecedented legal situation by taking steps to avoid renewed reintegration under the direct dominion of the Empire. In particular, most cities sought strategically to consolidate the indemnities through which they had initially established their semi-autonomous legal status, and they endeavoured to expand the rights obtained through *regalia* to establish a foundation for a more fully independent order of civic government. In this process, in the first instance, powers of government and jurisdiction, originally attached in many cities to urban bishops, were placed in the hands of freely appointed urban consuls (*consoli*): these consuls were usually drawn from outside the ranks of the most powerful feudal groups, and they were intent on elaborating the political apparatus outside inherited structures of personal status and affiliation (Dilcher 1967: 172, 177; Faini 2004). In many cases, this first stage of political formation had occurred as early as the beginning of the twelfth century. Notably, however, the quest for autonomy on the part of the cities culminated in the formation of the Lombard League in 1167, in which cities banded together to resist imperial ambitions to reimpose regalian overlordship. At this point, the northern Italian cities witnessed a rapid increase in the power of their civic authorities, and they began more consistently to act as semi-independent communes, possessing increasingly firm legislative and – most vitally – judicial responsibility for their populations. From this time on, the constitutional system of consular government was progressively supplanted by a model of public governance concentrated around more formally ordered and often professional offices. The later twelfth century saw a general 'reinforcement of oligarchical powers' in the cities (Bertelli 1978: 55), as judicial authority was separated from other urban responsibilities and condensed in the *podestà*: that is, in magistrates and judicial office holders, sometimes originally appointed by the Empire, and often called from outside the city in question, who assumed supreme judicial power and ruled by standard legal procedures in the cities.[28] After this time, the autonomy of the cities was repeatedly threatened, but it continued to expand. By 1275, the Empire had effectively renounced control of the Italian cities, and the urban *podestà* operated as independent centres of political power.

---

[28] For a comprehensive account of the supplanting of consuls by *podestà*, see Zorzi (2000).

The battle for the autonomy of the Italian city-states was inevitably fought, in part, as one dimension of the larger legal battles between the papacy and the Empire, and, accordingly, the changing status of the cities was widely reflected in constructions extracted from Roman law. On one hand, for example, the coterie of Roman civil lawyers employed by the Empire rejected the legality of claims to independence expressed by the cities, and they sought to entrench regalian authority and reclaim the cities as direct dominions of the Empire. At the Diet of Roncaglia (1158), when the Empire clearly had the upper hand in the struggle with the cities, the emperor called on the doctors of Roman law in Bologna to support him. These lawyers duly asserted that the imperial will should act as the foundation for government, and they sought to demonstrate that all laws, liberties, judicial offices and *regalia* in the Empire were derived solely from the emperor's express and voluntary approval.[29] Backed by the civil lawyers of Bologna, in fact, the imperial party eventually attempted to conduct a thorough reorganization of the Empire as a personal-bureaucratic state, and to impose on northern Italy a strict regime similar to that later pioneered in the Kingdom of Sicily.[30] Indeed, the emperor used the opportunities afforded by his military victories over the cities to reacquire all the *regalia* that had been given to the Italian communes, and effectively to subject the cities to immediate imperial jurisdiction.

An interim end of the conflicts between the Empire and the Lombard League was sealed in the Peace of Constance (1183), however, and after this time concepts of Roman law were widely employed, against the Empire, to reinforce the power of the cities. At a most general level, the essential legal principle of communal autonomy – namely, the principle that the *comuni* possessed an autonomous legal personality outside the feudal relations that bound the Empire, the episcopate and the imperial aristocracy together – marked (arguably) a triumph of Roman law over the personalistic elements of Germanic law (Mayer 1909: 443; Volpe 1976: 67, 101). More specifically, the Peace of Constance recognized the cities as possessing independent *regalia*, and it played a crucial role in the legitimization of the cities as legal entities obtaining a degree of sanctioned constitutional and legislative autonomy within the Empire.

---

[29] See the documentation of the Curia Roncaglia (Pertz 1837: 110–14). See the near-contemporary account of the consultation between Friedrich I and the 'four masters' of Bologna (Schmale 1986: 88–9).

[30] This point is made in Sütterlin (1929: 8); Vergottini (1952: 207); and Zorzi (1994: 87).

Moreover, it accepted the validity of the customary statutes and documented *consuetudines*, which many cities already possessed, and in so doing it sanctioned the free exercise of judicial power by the *comuni* of the cities.[31] Additionally, the Peace of Constance also defined the administrative organs of the cities as bodies that were authorized independently to introduce their statutes, and it acknowledged urban political elites as entitled to transform customary laws into acts of written public order and so, in effect at least, freely to create *new laws*. In each of these respects, the end of the first Lombard conflicts gave rise to a deep (although still tentative and piecemeal) reconstruction of the legal order of the cities. It created an environment in which principles of secular law, loosely influenced by Roman-law concepts, could be used to establish new patterns of post-feudal public governance, and a written legal order instituted a positive and generalized political apparatus for urban centres.

In addition to this constructive use of civil law, the cities of northern Italy also borrowed elements of canon law to support their cause, and they found in the Roman-law arguments of the canonists, themselves often hostile to the Empire, an effective support for their independence. Many canon lawyers, like the papacy itself, were keen to affirm the customary legislative powers of the semi-independent Italian cities, which they saw as a vital bastion against the intensification of imperial power, and they often provided legal assistance for urban rulers and *comuni* who aimed to explain and strengthen their legal foundation. Indeed, many earlier commentaries on canon law entailed a *de iure* recognition of the claims to statutory autonomy and even semi-sovereign power asserted by the rulers of individual administrative organs within the Empire:[32] the view was quite common among earlier canonists that the independence of particular states in the Empire had sound claim to legal validity and that the Empire had no entitlement to assume universal territorial power. Seminally, for instance, the canonist Alanus Anglicus argued that each ruler had the same authority in his kingdom as the emperor in his.[33] Later commentators on civil law, such as Bartolus and Baldus, then applied these ideas to the Italian cities, and

---

[31] The Pax Constantiae conceded 'jurisdiction in criminal and pecuniary cases' and 'in other matters relating to the well-being of citizens' to the cities (Pertz 1837: 175–80).

[32] This argument is strongly asserted in Onory (1951: 226) and Calasso (1957: 122). It is contested in Catalano (1959: 29).

[33] This text is printed in Schulte (1870: 90). See a similar claim in the *summa* of Étienne de Tournai (Schulte 1891: 12).

they argued that office holders in the Italian city-states were, in proportion to the dignity of their office, entitled to presuppose relative autonomy under law (Bartolus 1555: fol. 11; Baldus 1616: fol. 13). Indeed, Bartolus and Baldus recognized the city-states as possessing quite manifestly a legitimate *ius statuendi*, and they used principles of natural law, derived from the *ius gentium* of Roman law, to accord to the Italian city-states the right to pass laws without full authorization by the Empire. This interpretation of civil law underwrote a legal structure, in which the urban *comuni* could assume the right to unify the customary laws that had traditionally been applied in informal fashion in the cities. Moreover, this made it possible for an elite and increasingly professionalized class of learned judges to reform the hitherto rather haphazardly applied fusion of custom, regalian liberties and ecclesiastical edicts that had formed the legal structure of cities, so that urban legal codes could be compiled to form a reasonably systematic and, above all, positively alterable statutory system.

Gradually, in sum, the use of Roman law and elements of canon law in the northern Italian cities created a legal culture in which statutes became the primary positive foundation of authority, and from the later twelfth century onwards most cities began to design statutes in which they defined and codified their underlying legal principles. As a corollary of this, most cities began to set these principles apart from common life, and they introduced strict procedures to ensure that their laws were formally and equitably applied: in many cases, the urban statutes stipulated that, to ensure impartiality of judgment, foreign judges should be appointed to administer the laws. Early examples of this formal organization of law were the quasi-constitutional consular documents instituted in Pisa and other cities in the twelfth century. These included the Constitum Consulum Comunis in Pistoia (1117), the Pisan Constitutum Legis and the Constitutum Usus (*c.* 1160), and, most importantly, the Breve Consulum Civitatis of Pisa (1162). Indeed, the *constituti* of Pisa and Pistoia contained procedural rules regarding the obligations and elections of consuls (Bonaini 1854: 6–9; Rauty and Savino 1977: 47). By the mid thirteenth century, as analysed below, most cities of northern Italy had produced statutory accounts of their basic political functions and responsibilities, and they used techniques of legal codification to create a positive and autonomous overarching legal apparatus for the urban polity.[34]

---

[34] On the connection between writing, legal positivization and the formation of public law see Keller (1991: 183).

In the Italian cities, to conclude, the legal disputes between church and state, the transformation of feudalism and the early construction of positive abstracted forms of statehood were three aspects of the same inextricably conjoined process. In this second case, the conflict between church and Empire gave further impetus to the tentative emergence of early states, and states began to develop as positively founded and increasingly *public* political actors that filled an open legal space created as the complex feudal nexus between church and Empire was dissolved. Of crucial importance in this was that the Italian cities began to concentrate their power around statutes and they attached great constitutional importance to securing the *ius statuendi*: statutes became the constitutional form in which nascent states expressed and administered their increasing powers of positive political autonomy.

Law and feudal transformation III: the consolidation of central monarchy

A series of related developments was also evident in England. In this regard, first, some cautionary observations need to be made. High medieval England cannot be compared directly with other European states and societies. For example, it is debatable whether English society ever, or at least for very long, possessed fully characteristic features of feudal organization.[35] Even before 1066, English society had been marked by a high level of statehood and an 'exceptionally powerful and unified' order of royal lordship (Bartlett 2000: 201), and it gave only limited recognition to feudal justice. By the twelfth century, then, England was already in a process of de-feudalization, and it was beginning to evolve rudimentary administrative, jurisdictional and fiscal features typical of modern central states. Despite this, however, the conflicts between church and early state in England had implications that reflected the same underlying processes as in other regional settings. Indeed, these conflicts were again flanked by, and they in turn intensified, a dynamic of legal and political transformation, in which the diffuse corpus of feudal law was subject to systematic statutory organization, and in which a monarchical executive began to emerge that possessed substantially enhanced reserves of positive legislative power.

Two processes acquired particular prominence in this context. In the first instance, the aftermath of the investiture controversies in England

---

[35] As the salient view in this polemic, see Richardson and Sayles (1963: 91).

was generally characterized by a formal consolidation of the legal system that reinforced and intensified monarchical power. In England, although there was only limited reception of Roman law, the high medieval period, and especially the reign of Henry II, saw a thorough systematization of the legal apparatus of state. This process involved a rapid increase in the formality of judicial procedure, the establishment of reliable precedents for ruling cases, the integration of local courts into one overarching legal system subordinate to a central court, the more extensive use of general eyres (in fact established, debatably, by Henry I) to supervise the provision of justice in local courts, and, in total, a thorough laicization and regular central organization of judicial process.[36] By 1200, the primary foundations of the English common law, destined to last for centuries, were already established. Notably, then, the principles of English judicial order were further formalized in Magna Carta (1215), which at once clarified feudal law and enshrined a set of normative principles that could be invoked to resolve controversy over judicial procedure. Although most obviously an attempt to curb the use of royal power against a baronial oligarchy, Magna Carta arose from a context in which plaintiffs found substantial benefits in a stable judicial order, and it reflected a positive evaluation of regular centralized royal justice (Holt 1992: 121–3). Indeed, Article 18 of Magna Carta evidently reinforced royal justice: the document as a whole 'demanded more justice' (Stacey 1987: 9), and it led to the holding of county courts with increased regularity (Palmer 1982: 25). In addition to this, in England the later feudal era was also marked by the fact that, as in other settings, leading political actors detached the law from its more customary and embedded forms, they slowly integrated the originally private functions of baronial and seigneurial courts into a judicial hierarchy, and, in so doing, they progressively transformed the law into a more positively malleable medium of social exchange (Adams 1926: 185; Denholm-Young 1939: 89). This began with the institution of assizes under Henry II, which, as the 'headspring of English legislation', allowed regents and royal commissioners to form and alter legal edicts by regulating and settling inequalities in customary law (Jolliffe 1961: 239). By the later medieval period, baronial courts were mainly restricted to initiating cases for settlement in royal courts, and, correlatively, the use of general statutes as instruments for introducing new laws had increased exponentially: this culminated in

---

[36] See Stenton (1965: 26); Keeton (1966: 204); Turner (1985: 74); Hudson (1996: 150); and Musson and Ormrod (1998: 2).

the large swathes of statutory legislation introduced during the reign of Edward I.[37] The earlier organization of the common law through royal writ under Henry II thus ultimately created a framework in which common law itself could be flexibly altered and augmented by positive legal statutes.

These two legal processes – first, the formal structuring of common law and, second, the expansion of the state's positive statutory powers – were fundamental to the building of central political institutions in England, and together they formed a transformative process that pierced the legal arrangements typical of feudalism.[38] Indeed, the assumption of statutory powers by the government during the high feudal period is widely viewed as reflecting the historical process in which England was transformed 'from a feudal to a national state' (Prestwich 1972: 224), and it created the foundations for a governmental order able to apply political power across the entire national territory, in growing indifference to particularities of territory, privilege or status. The first English statute is usually seen as the Statute of Merton of 1236 (Wilkinson 1948–58: 242). However, the Statutes of Westminster introduced by Edward I in 1275 and 1285 were perhaps the decisive moment in the formation of the English monarchy as a political system that could legislate independently of feudal custom and whose power was condensed in positively authorized institutions. Notably, these statutes coincided with the Quo Warranto legislation of Edward I, which aimed to sever the law from private jurisdiction, to restrict judicial privileges granted under feudal order, and to ensure that laws were subject to central statutory monarchical control (Ault 1923: 5; Sutherland 1963: 1).

In France the controversies over the limits of papal and royal power reached their highest levels of intensity rather later than in other European countries, and the subsequent process of feudal transformation also approached conclusion at a somewhat retarded juncture. However, processes similar to those in other countries were also identifiable in France. In the first instance, for example, the period of early Capetian rule saw a re-establishment of monarchical power as a source of public authority: it was marked by a sustained attempt on the part of

---

[37] For this analysis see Plucknett (1922: 30; 1949: 10).

[38] Maitland famously saw the reforms of Henry II as giving England a more centralized legal-political order than any other state in Europe (Pollock and Maitland 1895: 146). This thesis has been repeatedly disputed, most notably in Milsom (1976: 186). But for a moderating pronouncement see Biancalana (1988: 535).

the monarchy to transform and consolidate feudal obligations, to suppress independently exercised seigneurial privileges, and to use regalian powers to bind the lords of the realm into a direct juridical relation to the crown. This naturally coincided with an intensification of the law, through which the monarchy attempted to salvage its jurisdictional powers from the feudal privatization to which they had fallen prey in the eleventh century and to transform by statutory means the customary constitutional order of French society.[39] During the reign of Philip Augustus (1180–1223), the machinery of justice underwent a significant transformation, and royal writ was expanded as a medium for settling disputes. By the end of the reign of Philip Augustus full assizes were held in many towns. The period 1190–1200 is commonly regarded as marking a crucial turning point in the regularization of the French judicial apparatus (Baldwin 1986: 137). Similarly, the teaching of Roman law at French universities expanded substantially under the Capetians, and Roman law became a vital tool for reinforcing secular political order. In 1219, in fact, the pope even issued a bull to suppress instruction in Roman law at the University of Paris. These processes then continued under the later Capetians. In 1278, for example, Philippe III issued procedures to ensure that supreme jurisdictional powers were to reside solely in the *parlement* (the sovereign court of the monarchy, performing the highest judicial and certain limited legislative functions). By this time, royal justice prevailed over local and ecclesiastical jurisdiction, and the *parlement* began to perform many functions previously performed by feudal courts.[40]

This formalization of the state's legal order culminated in the later decades of the thirteenth century in a series of protracted and envenomed altercations over temporal jurisdiction between the late Capetian kings and the papacy. This led both to a substantial transfer of judicial power from the papal church to the French monarchy and to a concerted attempt by the monarchy to centralize and regularize legal procedures. During the famous jurisdictional conflict between Philippe le Bel and Pope Boniface VIII, most notably, the monarch conducted a systematic reorganization of the *parlement* in Paris, and he called on specialists in Roman law, notably the *légistes* Pierre Dubois, Pierre Flotte and Guillaume Nogaret, to articulate juridical concepts to strengthen his jurisdictional powers. Accordingly, the

---

[39] See the classic analysis in Lemarignier (1965: 163, 169).
[40] On these points see Boutaric (1861: 208); and Rigaudière (1988: 233).

légistes offered a legal justification of monarchy that defended royal powers against a series of inflammatory bulls circulated by Boniface VIII.[41] In particular, the *légistes* argued that the claim to temporal powers by a pope was tantamount to heresy, and that the king of France had no 'sovereign on earth save God' (Rivière 1926: 104, 118).[42] Philippe himself opposed the church by offering the classical definition of royal power as a quasi-sovereign attribute, stating that it was inconceivable that '*in temporalibus nos alicui subesse*' (Dupuy 1963 [1655]: 44). Through the analyses of the *légistes*, therefore, a clear concept of monarchical sovereignty, founded in Roman law, began to emerge, and the French monarchy arrogated to itself supreme responsibility for maintaining peace and order in the realm. Notably, this doctrine was intended to support the French monarchy, not only in relation to the pope, but also in relation to the universalist claims of the Holy Roman Empire: it stated that the monarch assumed powers of sovereignty in France that were in no way inferior to the powers of the emperor in the Holy Roman Empire. This argument finally assumed emblematic form in the anonymous tract, *Le songe du vergier*, of the 1370s, which stated that the French king held 'his realm from God alone' and was fully entitled to make, alter and interpret laws (1982 [*c.* 1378]: 55, 28). In according these semi-sovereign attributes to kingship, the *légistes* also set out relatively systematic principles to determine the competence of different courts, to augment royal authority in the courts, and to oversee courts and prevent judicial irregularity. The period around 1300 saw the introduction of stricter protocols in the royal courts and the institution of fixed judicial personnel. During this time the *parlement* began to grow in authority and to specialize more exclusively in judicial matters, and it was becoming a fixed institution in Paris. Its regularity and professionalism grew substantially under the influence of legist doctrine. Under Philippe le Bel, Roman law was also utilized as an ideal tool for promoting systematic understanding of French law, and it was even claimed that Roman law was an integral part of French customary law.[43]

---

[41] A most inflammatory declaration of papal power was the Unam Sanctam bull of 1302. The most extreme statement of this position was the (apparent) bull Deum Time, which stated: 'We want you to know that you are subject to us in both spiritual and temporal matters.' However, this was a forged bull, fabricated in order to legitimize monarchical reaction.

[42] On the formation of the doctrine of monarchical sovereignty in France see David (1954: 76).

[43] On these matters, see Chénon (1926: 508–10); Bloch (1964: 43); Bisson (1969: 366); Aubert (1977: 7–11); Strayer (1980: 218); Shennan (1998: 22–3).

As in other countries, therefore, the formation of the French state evolved through a profound transformation of feudalism. This process was integrally linked to the rationalization of the instruments of justice, which was itself intensified by the longer process of formal differentiation between state and church. In both England and France, in fact, the high medieval period was at once structurally dominated by the concerted endeavour of actors around the state to claim jurisdictional rights from the church, by the – closely related – suppression of feudal laws and indemnities, and by the concentration of increasing jurisdictional power in the emergent state, through which these actors were able to negate the privatistic and centrifugal legal forces in society. In particular, like the Italian cities, these societies also began to produce principles close to modern ideas of state sovereignty, and proto-state institutions began to be identified as dominant repositories of political power, exercising a monopoly of force both against the church and against the local reserves of feudal authority.

Constitutions and the formation of early states

This account of patterns of early state formation is not intended to be exhaustive, and it addresses only the main lineages of political construction in Europe in the wake of the investiture contests. Many variant patterns of this process can be identified. Indeed, even the basic principle that states resulted from sustained legal discord between ecclesiastical and worldly powers, which in itself reflected a deep-lying, although intermittent, process of feudal transformation, can only be applied to those medieval societies that, in a more or less obvious manner, possessed a feudal structure and were originally marked by a close interaction between bearers of political power and the papal church. A very important partial exception to these patterns, for example, was Spain. In Spain, it is often (although not universally) argued that feudalism existed only in a weak and rather under-evolved form: indeed, it is seen as characteristic of medieval Spain both that political offices remained recuperable by the monarchy,[44] and that, owing to high levels of social

---

[44] For the classic expression of this view see Sánchez-Albornoz (1942: 265). For commentary see Lourie (1966: 61, 63); O'Callaghan (1975: 165–7, 263); and Linehan (1993: 192–5). This view is often (in my opinion, very persuasively) disputed. For salient revisions of this view see Barbero and Vigil (1978: 15); Estepa Díez (1989); and García de Cortázar (2000: 561).

militarization, peasants could extricate themselves from feudal servitude with relative ease. Moreover, it might also be observed that in Spain the concentration of monarchical power was widely flanked by a recurrent growth in seigneurial autonomy, and the pluralistic interdependence between central jurisdiction and the privileges of the *señorios* remained higher and more embedded in Spain than in other societies.[45] Importantly, furthermore, in Spain there was no investiture contest or directly analogous event, and the emergent state of Castile-León gradually evolved into a Catholic monarchy, in which worldly rulers claimed to act as defenders of Roman Catholicism. However, in key respects the case of Spain was deeply analogous to the evolutionary patterns underlying other states. In Spain, the lines of authority between state and church were also clearly drawn by the later Middle Ages. Moreover, Spain, too, saw a strengthening of royal authority in the later twelfth century, and the consolidation of the monarchy was flanked by the prevalent use of Roman law to concentrate jurisdictional power in the state.

Despite these partial qualifications, however, it can be argued that the formalization of the law in the Western church and the translation of legal constructs from church to state in and after the investiture contests produced a crucial impetus for the formation of the proto-typical institutions of modern European states. This was intimately tied to the capacity of formal law for responding to changes in social structure in feudal society and for constructing political power as a relatively abstracted phenomenon, focused on a series of distinct and increasingly public functions. The emergence of consistent and abstracted legal principles in the church intersected with the wider dynamics of social transformation, and these principles enabled both the church and the state to separate themselves from the interwoven socio-legal structure of feudalism and to consolidate their power as relatively autonomous entities. Above all, the generalization of law in the church enabled the state to borrow from the church a projection of itself as the unique and consistent source of law, and states gradually adopted this principle of legal generality in order at once to secure their institutional consistency,

---

[45] It is arguable that in medieval Spain monarchy and *señorios* enjoyed something close to a symbiotic relationship, and the high medieval period witnessed a growth and proliferation of seigneurial power: Estepa Díez (1989: 219, 240); de Moxó (2000: 71). It has been widely argued that, despite monarchical claims to highest jurisdictional power in Spain, the parcellation of judicial force was endemic (Rodríguez-Picavea 1994: 366–7).

to explain, justify and transplant their political power throughout society, and to capture, manage, and apply in the form of statutes, relatively autonomous reserves of power. In England, for example, the idea of the monarch as the fount of justice became widespread through the first expansion of royal government: the Angevin monarchy, for all its recurrent despotic proclivities, was specifically defined and obtained legitimacy as a *law state*, in which the instruments of justice were condensed around the monarchy and the king acted as the 'highest source of justice' or even as a *judicial king* (Jolliffe 1955: 32; Bartlett 2000: 178).[46] In the Holy Roman Empire, the emperor was expressly conceived as the source and custodian of all law, and the preservation of legal order was viewed as the highest duty of the emperor. The *Sachsenspiegel*, the main secular legal code of the territories of medieval Germany, clearly defined the emperor as 'the common judge of all' (III, 26). In France, the need to provide justice was almost an article of faith for the Capetian kings: throughout the early formation of the French state the monarchy explained its legitimate right to legislate as deriving from its custodianship of justice.[47] In Spain, too, a codified law book, *Las Siete Partidas*, was introduced and promulgated throughout Castile-León in a period of far-reaching legal innovation undertaken by Alfonso X in the mid thirteenth century. Spanish society remained marked by a very high level of legal particularism, and the aspiration to legal uniformity remained unfulfilled. However, this law book also defined the monarchy as the primary centre of justice, and it aimed to concentrate the most important elements of jurisdiction around the crown (II,1,1).[48] The close interdependence of state and law was thus the most vital conceptual construct in the slow emergence of post-feudal states possessing, or aspiring to possess, a monopoly of political power, and the formation of distinctively political institutions was closely correlated with the abstraction of a general legal apparatus. In fact, decisively, in each case considered above it was the interdependence of law and state that allowed the state to project itself as a public body or actor, and this construction of the state played the most vital role in enabling states to organize and apply their power as a distinct, positive and autonomous facility.

In many instances, the processes of generalized legal formalization that defined high medieval European society involved little more than

---

[46] On this in general see Marongiu (1953: 702).

[47] This is a common argument. But in this case see Petit-Renaud (2001: 180–1).

[48] I refer to the 1807 edition of the *Siete Partidas*.

the establishment of formally drafted summaries of existing common laws or customs. In most cases, it was not until a much later point in history that judicial power was fully centralized and a consolidated body of public law was established. In most European countries supreme judicial functions were still attached to unstructured royal courts, which were convened as the monarch moved around the land. Nonetheless, it remains the case that most European societies in the period of nascent state formation were marked by the principle that general and consistent laws were required to supplant private justice and private violence as the source of judicial settlement, and the law was expected to restrict the degree to which personal agreements, settlements or individual decisions were used to satisfy society's need for jurisdiction.[49] Furthermore, most societies of this time also began to utilize law, not as a body of norms embedded in diverse customs or local practices, but as a more positive medium, which could be produced from legal reserves that society stored in consistently written and reliable form, and whose application was subject to principles of professional regularity and formal qualification. The increasingly dominant motive in legal finding from this time onwards, in short, was that law was expected generally and iterably to traverse diverse social fields, and a body of law was required that could authorize and reproduce singular principles from within itself. In order to fulfil the growing requirement for legal iterability, the law began to reduce the influence of external considerations on judicial procedure and law-finding more generally, it distilled itself into internally refined, consistent and professionally differentiated and documented forms, and, in this form, it became possible for law to cross many social spheres and to apply political power at a high level of generality, inner consistency and reproducibility. At the very formative origins of the political institutions of European society, in consequence, it is possible to identify what might be defined as a normative relation of *differentiated interdependence* between political power and positive law. High medieval societies, in particular, were characterized by the progressive formation of differentiated political institutions, which could structurally isolate themselves from other areas of human practice and autonomously circulate, as statutes, resources of political power across society as a whole: by 1200, most societies had begun to construct power, in distinction from laterally configured lordship and feoffdom, as distinctively *politicized power* (Bisson 2009: 484). This consolidation of

---

[49] For general literature on this, see Kaeuper (1988: 145); Harding (2002: 33).

politics and political power, however, presupposed a close relation between politics and positive law, through which the developing political system increasingly presupposed juridically formalized categories of law in order meaningfully and reliably to use, and, in fact, to produce and augment, its power. The formation of states as differentiated autonomous institutions applying increasingly positive reserves of power only occurred because of the interpenetration of political institutions with the law. Formal law was the primary precondition of statehood: formal law was at once a normative construct that allowed early states to define and project a foundation for their growing autonomy, and a functional instrument that enabled them to reduce their own residual privatism and to transplant power positively across widening and increasingly de-feudalized (less and less privatistic) societies.

In this relation, however, it can also be observed that the existence of a general legal apparatus was not the sole prerequisite for the first abstraction of political power and the first construction of states in the process of feudal transformation. In addition to this, the articulation of political power as an increasingly autonomous and positively generalizable social medium also meant that power was forced to support its diffusion through society by constructing an increasingly uniform account of its addressees: that is, by imagining its addressees as distinct and abstracted from their natural or regional particularities, and by projecting an idea of those subject to law that could be consistently and reproducibly presupposed as the terrain to which law was applied. One further precondition for the growing autonomy and the widening circulation of political power, therefore, was that power began to utilize procedures and principles of legal *inclusion*, which it could use to support and accompany the particular acts of its application. This in itself was partly accomplished through the establishment of a general written legal order: written laws allowed nascent states to perceive their subjects as uniform legal constructs, and so to apply power to their subjects in simplified, internalized and routinized fashion. Additionally, however, the detachment of power from particular persons and locations in the wider transformation of feudal order also, of necessity, meant that states began to co-opt and integrate a growing number of social actors into the political apparatus in order to authorize their statutory power, and states invented procedures in which the recipients of power were drawn into a direct, controlled and replicable relation to political power. The first general diffusion of power through emergent modern societies, in consequence, was internally linked to an increase in power's internal inclusivity: *abstracted generality* and *positive inclusion* might in fact be seen as the vital, reciprocally formative characteristics of political power as it first emerged as a differentiated and autonomous societal facility. For this reason, it is notable that many of the legal codes that were introduced in later medieval Europe clearly provided, not only for consistent judicial order and legal regularity, but also for an expansion of the state to include, and give representative powers to, (selected) relevant political actors. The English Magna Carta, for instance, was a document that possessed (albeit limited) constitutional implications, and it made clear provision, not only for legal rule and legal respect for acknowledged freedoms, but also, in Article 12, for the convocation of representative assemblies to approve exceptional levies. Shortly after Magna Carta, Bracton's commentary on English law also enunciated the principle that royal power was subject to both legal and political limits, and that the intensification of power in the monarchy necessarily presupposed certain norms of popular inclusion and elected representation. There is, Bracton stated, 'no *rex* where will rules rather than *lex*' (1963 [*c.* 1235]: 33). In Castile, similarly, the *Siete Partidas* expressed the constitutional presumption that royal power could only be exercised across society if it was derived from a 'balanced relationship' between sovereign and subjects (O'Callaghan 1975: 372). Although using selected principles of Roman law to authorize the king's statutory powers, the *Partidas* instilled a moral/inclusionary dimension in the law, and they even stipulated (1.1.18) that the king could not revoke laws without 'the great counsel of all the good men of the realm' (O'Callaghan 1989: 127). A further example of this was the Swedish Land Law, introduced by Magnus Eriksson in the fourteenth century. This law expressly provided for governance by council-constitutionalism, and it obligated the king both to respect 'the ancient Swedish laws' and to consult members of a permanent royal council on matters of general importance (Upton 1998: 1).

The earliest positive construction of modern European states, therefore, did not only presuppose a necessary relation between the general growth of state power and the general positive abstraction of the law. This process also presupposed recognition of the fact that the state's power could only be legally generalized across society if it was underscored both by constant legal formulae and by inclusionary arrangements by means of which it could at once integrate its addressees and harden preconditions for its support. The first construction of political power had a twofold normative character: it presupposed legal norms for its transmission and legal norms for its procedures of inclusion. Indeed, if the introduction of general law codes was part of a wider process in which states transformed their legal foundations from custom to statutes and so assumed capacities for positively generalized legislation, those states that established strong inclusionary devices to sustain their legal systems normally experienced greatest success in introducing statutes, pursuing positive processes of legal enactment and fulfilling the basic functions of statehood. On these grounds, if the first stage in the transition from early feudalism and privatistic lordship to the rudimentary establishment of modern statehood was integrally bound to the process of power's positive legal organization, this path also widely presupposed an increasing interdependence of power, law and a rudimentary system of inclusive constitutional representation. The generalized use of law and power normally required an inclusionary apparatus that acted evenly to integrate social actors within the sphere of political power, to solidify uniform societal conditions for the application of law and to create a climate of general responsiveness to law.[50] In fact, the earliest – very tentative – formation of the European state as an agent consolidating its autonomy under public law widely depended on the capacity of the state for quasi-constitutional inclusion.

Early states and constitutions

The correlation between the early formation of European statehood, the generalization and positivization of law, and the construction of a constitutional order to sustain early states was visible in different ways in a number of national settings. In each of these settings, as above, the specific conjuncture between these processes corresponded to the distinctive pattern of feudal transformation or gradual de-feudalization that marked particular societies.

Italian city-states

The case of the Italian cities has been briefly considered above. As discussed, the initial emergence of the Italian cities occurred, simultaneously, in the context of a conflict over jurisdiction between the papacy and the Holy Roman Empire and in the context of a conflict over regalian rights between the Empire and powerful urban administrations. In these conflicts, the cities assumed autonomy by gradually asserting positive

---

[50] This point is corroborated in Bisson (2009: 529–72).

statutory control of legal and judicial functions. These processes, and their political outcomes, naturally followed a different course in different cities, and many local variables affected the formation of different communes. To speak very generally, however, Italian city-states, whose jurisdictions were originally based in privileges granted by the Empire, began to act as distinct administrative and judicial entities – *comuni* – around the middle of the eleventh century. By 1100, many northern Italian cities are documented as possessing a communal authority. In 1117, for example, Milan (belatedly, given its status) obtained the status of an independent municipality. By 1154, Florence possessed its own independent judicial apparatus. Subsequently, after the Peace of Constance (1183), the *comuni* progressively acquired, despite ongoing disputes with the Empire, the (still very rudimentary) features of modern statehood: that is, they were authorized to administer justice, to summon armies, to impose duties and raise taxes, and even – in some cases – to elect magistrates.

In addition to this, it is notable that, as these city-states consolidated their functions outside inherited personal and legal forms, they were also obliged to produce increasingly inclusionary arrangements to underpin their statutory authority, and they instituted general procedures to ensure support for their power throughout their societies. For this reason, the early Italian city-states experienced a proliferation of formulated legal documents that prescribed norms for the regulation of public matters (that is, for fiscal and judicial processes), that laid down principles for the election and selection of temporal magistrates, and that contained elaborate mechanisms for avoiding the arbitrary use of power. In other words, it was crucial to the process of their autonomous political/judicial expansion that, in parallel to their intense activities of legal construction and statutory revision, the Italian *comuni* elaborated extensive, although also clearly highly limited, provisions for popular representation and veto and approval in political decision making. The growing statutory autonomy of the cities was thus structurally reliant on an underlying inclusionary constitutional order.

In the earliest stages of their political formation, the highest political authority in the cities, as discussed, was allocated to informally appointed consuls. The consular period was characterized by only the most rudimentary constitutional apparatus, which was normally restricted to prescribing procedures for electing consuls and to imposing oaths of integrity and probity on bearers of office (Rauty and Savino 1977: 47). By the later thirteenth century, however, some cities, notably Florence, had developed much more complex documents to dictate principles for the assumption of public office, and in many cases these documents subjected the exercise of public power to clear principles of accountability. By the 1280s, in fact, Florence had acquired a constitutional order, entailing provisions for citizen participation, which contained express rules for the maintenance of uniform justice for all members of society and – above all – for the suppression of private violence (Rondoni 1882: 45–58), and which sought to guarantee an impersonal legal order as a matter of express public interest: it evidently provided a legal/judicial framework for establishing the *comune* as an early *res publica*. Subsequent constitutional documents in Florence also regulated election to public office, and they enunciated the categorical principle that the use of power within the city must refer to and be determined by existing written statutes (Caggese 1921: 4). Most importantly, the Florentine Ordinances of Justice of 1293 stipulated that the consent of substantial sections of the population was the precondition of legitimacy in the exercise of communal power, and the Ordinances provided legal support for intermittent periods of rule by the *popolo*: that is, by governments founded in the approval of powerful members of the middle-class, confederated in guilds. These Ordinances also directly invoked the principle that matters of common interest had to be approved by all (*quod omnes tangit debet ab omnibus approbari*) as the foundation for communal rule (Najemy 1979: 59): that is, theoretically, they reflected the principle that sustainable power was power that included all politically relevant sectors of society, and they made public authority directly contingent on laws receiving common consent. In Bologna and Padua, similarly, documents of the 1280s set procedures for elections, and they stipulated that government had to be conducted in conformity with existing statutes.[51] Indeed, the Sacred Ordinances introduced in Bologna in 1282 provided foundations for guild-based quasi-republican government, and these, too, were focused on suppressing private violence between powerful groups of magnates. These principles were then widely reproduced in the statutes of other cities.

Naturally, these descriptions are not intended to suggest that, by the thirteenth century, the Italian cities possessed the characteristics of fully evolved and constitutionally determined states. The converse was in fact the case for a number of reasons. First, it is not clear that the *comuni* existed as fully public bodies. Their legislative processes were generally

---

[51] For Padua, it was stated that election to office of *podestà* was not to be made *contra formam statuti* of the Padovan *comune* (Gloria 1873: 6). For similar principles in Bologna see Fasoli and Sella (1937: 5).

founded in a balancing of horizontally structured private interests, and sovereign power was often inseparable from the immediate prerogatives of potent social groups, which meant that political authority remained rooted in specific milieux and professions. Government often vacillated between the magnates and the guilds, and much legislation was devoted both to enacting particular interests and to suppressing oppositional groups, who pursued motives of private justice in order to unsettle the *comune*. Second, it has also been widely observed that, if the *comuni* were formed as organs that cut through the feudal ties binding the cities to the Holy Roman Empire and the imperial aristocracy, they always existed alongside other channels of obligation, and they were not constituted as finally sovereign or independent institutions. Neither the feudal apparatus of the Empire nor the private associations of interests within the cities were ever fully brought under the force of the judicial authorities of the cities – the *podestà*. Moreover, the level of private violence in the cities remained very high, and it is difficult to claim that the *comuni* possessed an administrative apparatus enabling full public or sovereign control of the city or, in fact, even an approximate monopoly of force. Third, over a longer period of time the communal origins of the constitutions of the city-states were partly eroded. Most, although not all, cities progressively abandoned the broad-based model of government. Most opted instead, first, for a pattern of government in which power was removed from the *comune* and placed in a *signoria*, which in most (but not all) settings tended to assume a relatively closed oligarchical form.[52] Later, then, most cities ultimately settled for government by an aristocratic *principato*, which centralized more power in one single dynastic elite. One commentator has observed that as early as 1300 much of northern and central Italy was under 'despotic rule' and that the 'period of effective autonomy' in the communes was very brief (Jones 1965: 71–2). In some cases, the transition from commune to *signoria* led to the consolidation of the city-states as quasi-territorial states, in which urban regions secured their power against the Empire by adopting hierarchical patterns of sovereign jurisdiction. In other cases, in seeming paradox, the transition from *comune* to *signoria* re-accentuated the private/familial control of political power, and it even involved a partial reintegration of the cities into the neo-feudal legal order that still prevailed in the Empire. In general, however, the advent of the signorial

---

[52] Florence was the crucial exception, where, initially, the *signoria* extended political representation across class boundaries (Becker 1960: 423).

regimes led to a more monistic system of government above the plural
sources of power in the commune, and it prefigured the later, more
highly integrated, models of monarchical statehood. For all these qualifications, nonetheless, it remains the case that the Italian city-states of
the high to later medieval era approached a type of statehood that
separated public from private power to a greater degree than in most
European societies in the earlier stages of feudal transformation, and that
these cities also possessed institutions through which governors could
exercise power across society from a relatively constant base. The most
politically refined of these states were defined both by the consolidation
of judicial and statutory powers in a fixed executive and by the solidification of intermittently free-standing legislative institutions. Indeed,
in some cases, most notably that of Florence, the Italian city-states
eventually succeeded in devising a complex apparatus for raising public
finance and consolidating public debt, thereby further reinforcing their
independent political structures.[53]

Whatever their level of public construction, it was clearly fundamental
to the emergence of statehood in the Italian cities that they elaborated a
quasi-constitutional legal apparatus, and they tied the use of political
power both to legally pronounced rules and preconditions and to
acceded procedures of limited representation. Indeed, the emergence
of rudimentary urban constitutions was a crucial element in the process
through which the cities were able to extract their power from private or
feudal milieux, and to regularize their power in predictable procedures: it
was only by means of a series of entrenched legal and constitutional
statutes that the cities were able to stabilize the form of political power
and to apply their power in generally accepted procedures. The emergence of a political system as a functionally consolidated set of institutions, which possessed at least some degree of positive consistency
against private power, relied crucially on the fact that its resources of
power were supported by a constitutionally integrative or *inclusive*
apparatus. The autonomous political order of the Italian cities, in other
words, was founded both in the fact that these cities produced generalizable reserves of positive and statutory law and in the fact that they
availed themselves of inclusionary functions offered by early constitutions. By fusing these elements, the Italian cities were able to extract a

---

[53] This occurred in Florence in 1345. For detailed analysis of this and its constitutional
implications see Becker (1966: 17; 1968: 157–8).

public structure for themselves which enabled them to utilize political power at a distinctive level of autonomy and general inclusion.

The Holy Roman Empire

The connection between state building and constitutional formation obtained its most striking expression in the Italian city-states. However, related phenomena were also evident in other societies. Indeed, in other social settings the aftermath of the investiture controversies also led to the development of states organized around a quasi-constitutional apparatus, and other states also began to distinguish and generalize their power by assuming a form in which they could account for themselves as inclusive centres of social integration.

This tendency could be observed in the Holy Roman Empire itself. After the stricter assertion of the *lex regia* in the years following the investiture controversies, the Holy Roman Empire began to form itself around a distinct constitutional order, and the idea that the imperial prerogative was the sole basis of legislation was sharply undermined in the later Middle Ages. This idea was quite widespread in the works of later commentators on Roman law, notably the post-glossators writing after the classical period of Bolognese commentary, who rejected the universalistic claims of the Empire and argued that imperial power was only sustainable within constitutional constraints. Yet this view also had earlier origins. For example, Azo clearly stated that the emperor had the authority to make laws (*ius condendi legem*). But he also stated that new laws and statutes had to be made in consultative fashion and presupposed consent 'per principem and per populos' for their validity (1506: 9). However, perhaps the defining step in this respect occurred in the thirteenth century, when an increasingly strict constitutional framework was established both to determine appointment to imperial office and to bind emperors to Electors after their assumption of office. The role of Electors was mentioned in the *Sachsenspiegel*, and it was acknowledged by Friedrich II in the 1230s. In 1276, then, King Rudolph committed himself by oath as required to obtain the consent of the Electors in major acts of legislation, especially those concerning the alienation of imperial lands (Krammer 1913: 169). This process culminated in the promulgation of the Golden Bull of 1356, in which the imperial Electors assumed formally enshrined rights of participation in government in the Empire. Chapter 2 of the Golden Bull stipulated that whoever should be prospective emperor should recognize and reinforce all rights, privileges and customs of the Electors, who were defined as 'the most immediate organs of the Holy Empire' (Weinrich 1983: 337). This section of the Golden Bull in principle defined the Empire as a polity with an organic constitution, through which the state obtained a legal identity that was clearly distinct from those holding office – even highest office – within it. Chapter 12 of the Bull stated that the Electors should convene each year to deliberate on matters of importance for the Empire (Weinrich 1983: 357). Through this provision the Electors effectively assumed the status of constituted organs within an imperial state.

In parallel to this constitutional organization of the imperial executive, moreover, the high to later medieval period was also marked by the increasing introduction of provisions for a delegatory system of government at regional or territorial level throughout the Holy Roman Empire: that is, by an increase in regional representation, established through a constitution of territorial estates (*Landstände*), especially in questions pertaining to taxation and fiscal supply. As a result of this, in 1231 legislation was introduced in the Empire that stated that in particular territories princes were not at liberty to pass new laws without the express consent of regional estates. The recognition of regional estates as constitutionally authorized participants in legislation was further cemented in subsequent acts of constitutional legislation, and by the 1290s the rights and privileges of the *Landstände* were expressed and sanctioned in increasingly contractual form. In 1311, the Ottonische Handfeste, the so-called Magna Carta of the German estates, was promulgated. This document enshrined the rights of estates, it protected noble jurisdictional privileges, and it placed a prohibition on arbitrary taxation by territorial princes. Throughout the fourteenth century, subsequently, further regional charters were introduced. In many cases, these arrangements either endorsed or presupposed a condominium between princes and estates as the form of government, and they created the basis for a constitution (*Ständeverfassung*), in which the estates played a key role in territorial government. This arrangement of constitutional balancing gradually replaced the more diffuse and personalized holding of power that characterized feudalism in its earlier form, and it bound powerful and wealthy members of society, often holding land and office under privilege and immunity, into a more unified and stable political order.[54] Indeed, the emergence of formal constitutional structures in the

---

[54] On the integrative dimensions of the process of estate formation see, classically, Below (1885: 48); Brunner (1968: 189–90).

German lands acted at once to integrate powerful social actors into nascent states and to establish early territorial governments as political orders with relatively secure and inclusive procedures of regional domination and a relatively firm monopoly of territorial power. In both these respects, the quasi-delegatory arrangements of estate-based governance brought great solidity to early territorial states in Germany, and they played a vital role in assimilating addressees of power into expansive (even proto-national) societies, in unifying territorial domains, and in solidifying the power of political institutions over increasingly cohesive and extended territories.

In the longer wake of its consolidation as a body of institutions distinct from the papacy, therefore, the Holy Roman Empire clearly began to assume the form of a multi-levelled state with a subtly balanced and articulated constitution. At the end of the Middle Ages, this constitutional apparatus of the Empire came under intense strain because of the increasing territorial power (derived from feudal *regalia* and immunities) of the princes, which eventually eroded the substance of the Empire. However, these arrangements persisted well into the early modern era, and even for a long time after the Reformation the use of political power in the Empire was dominated by an equilibrium between three political groups: the regional estates, the imperial estates and actors around the emperor himself. In this instance again, in consequence, it can be observed that, in order to stabilize itself as a political order capable of applying political power in generalized fashion across diffuse social terrains, the Empire was obliged to evolve a wider organic personality and to incorporate impersonal methods for integrating and unifying its territory. Indeed, the emergence of the Empire as a public order, overarching a number of private domains and capable of dislocating power from private actors, structurally presupposed, not only that it contained a formal legal order, but that it could selectively integrate private actors in its corporate structure. In so doing, it obtained a transpersonal legal system for itself and it created conditions of factual legal regularity and probable inclusionary compliance throughout society.

The central monarchies

In England, similarly, the formation of the state as an increasingly positive apparatus for using power depended on the construction of a proto-constitutional order. In the first instance, for example, it can be observed that under the conventionalized expectations of early feudalism members of the English monarchy exercised power from a residually private domain in society. Although having a general land tax at their disposal, English monarchs were expected to live and finance their operations either through intermittent feudal aids or *from their own resources* (i.e. from revenues raised on their own lands). The progressive growth and centralization of the monarchy as a central and increasingly dominant source of justice and order, however, meant that the English monarchy rapidly required more money, and that the feudal apparatus for levying funds was insufficient. Consequently, in order to obtain funds to support the exercise of centralized power, the monarchy was obliged, in a gradual process, at once to sever itself from the personal structure of feudalism and to introduce new patterns of direct and indirect taxation. To facilitate this, it integrated prominent sectors of society into the perimeters of the emergent governmental order, and it promoted the use of consultative parliaments to obtain revenue (Hoyt 1950; Wolffe 1970: 25): indeed, earliest parliaments, like the general eyres in the judicial sphere, were part of a royal strategy for reducing local influence in administration and for pursuing effective centralization of government.[55] The need for tax thus intensified a dynamic of de-feudalization in the English state, and, driven by its monetary needs, the monarchy began to construct itself as a complex of institutions that possessed extensive consultative mechanisms and inclusionary procedures for underwriting its extractive powers. To be sure, the emergence of the early English state as a public constitutional order, in which monarchs performed distinctively public duties and recruited support from public office holders, was not completed in the medieval period. Yet it was already clear in Magna Carta that any effective conduct of government presupposed inclusionary, representative foundations. Indeed, even the assizes of Henry II required common assent for the passing of legislative acts and legal rulings (Butt 1989: 81; Maddicott 2010: 75, 90). Throughout the thirteenth century, subsequently, a fully parliamentary order began to emerge, and parliamentary assemblies, evolving out of the king's court, gradually assumed well-defined, semi-constitutional powers. By the middle part of the thirteenth century, the concept of parliamentary authority was clearly established in England (the earliest use of the term is dated to 1236) (Butt 1989: 79; Maddicott 2010: 226). This period was also marked by a series of baronial plans and petitions for constitutional reform, designed to reinforce the representative

---

[55] This theory seems self-evident. But to support it see Plucknett (1956: 153).

powers of parliament. The Paper Constitution (attributed to 1244) and the Provisions of Oxford (1258) were salient among these documents. Indeed, the Provisions of Oxford created a full, although short-lived, constitutional system, in which governmental power was placed under direct baronial control by means of an appointed council. By 1300, then, the assemblies gathered to grant taxes had acquired a form close to that of constituted national assemblies, and at this point it was assumed that the king could only raise tax in *pleno parliamento* (Willard 1934: 13; Clarke 1936: 8; Butt 1989: 150).

In the English case again, therefore, as the state began to utilize power in increasingly autonomous fashion and as it transposed its legal operations into a positive statutory form, it relied on an elaborate constitutional apparatus to unify its addressees and to produce support and legitimacy for its decisions. Although the monarchical state extended its power at the expense of the baronial class, early parliaments allowed the crown partly to integrate this class and they provided the monarchy with consensual instruments for passing and applying laws through society. It is documented, for example, that the period of baronial revolt against the monarchy in the thirteenth century, far from dissipating the Angevin policies of administrative centralization, reinforced the central judicial order of the state. The Provisions of Westminster (obtained by the barons in 1259 and reissued 1263), notably, limited powers of franchise courts and other private jurisdiction and reinforced appellate powers of the king, and the rise of parliament brought the courts under direct monarchical jurisdiction (Treharne 1932: 171; Palmer 1982: 292). The growth of parliamentary procedures thus strengthened a framework in which the monarchy could construct its power as power inclusively generated and applied throughout society, and it instituted an acceded set of conventions through which state power could be legitimized and experienced as public power, and the private goods of subjects (taxes) could be more regularly and peacefully transacted through the state. In this respect parliaments greatly simplified the statutory operations of government. Indeed, the rise of parliament coincided exactly with the rise of statutory legislation in England, and the state's increasing need to authorize new laws across all society interlocked with a rapid inclusionary expansion of parliament. The highly generalized statutory production under Edward I, notably, was marked by a widening of parliamentary power and an increasing use of parliament as the 'main instrument of public governance' (Maddicott 2010: 283). The formation of governmental power as legislatively independent and positively abstracted, in consequence, had its defining precondition in a defined constitutional order. This early constitution acted to unify the widening territorial domains in which power was applied, to detach political power from pure private interests or prerogatives and selectively to integrate social groups who were politically weakened by the rise of statehood. In both respects, the medieval constitution made possible the early use of power as a generalized social facility.

A similar process can also be identified in the kingdoms of León and Castile in medieval Spain, which possessed a particularly strong constitutional tradition. During the eleventh and early twelfth centuries, the rudimentary beginnings of a representative tradition were already clearly in evidence in these societies.[56] In 1188, the Cortes of León, and later of Castile-León, was founded as a representative assembly, comprising, as well as prelates and nobles, elected representatives of towns with a municipal organization. This assembly possessed pronounced legislative functions, especially in fiscal matters, and it was accepted as a point of constitutional principle that no new laws or taxes could be introduced or vital political decisions taken except in a council comprising bishops, nobles and good men (Procter 1980: 51). The convocation of councils and assemblies was often, as in England, bound to the king's commitment to observe customary laws of the realm, especially in respect of the equal provision of justice and consensual levying of fiscal reserves. Both the supply of taxation to the monarchy and the exercise of both statutory and jurisdictional force depended on the monarch's respect for established constitutional agreements, and representative assemblies acted at once both to limit the private authority of royal prerogative and to support a general, more inclusionary and more immediately flexible, use of royal power across society.[57]

France followed a slightly different path in this respect. It has often been noted as a distinctive feature of medieval French history that representative parliaments were slow to be formed as organs of state that were substantially different from judicial chambers. Owing to this fact, it is often claimed, French parliaments lacked the ability to assume constitutionally formative legislative power (Pollard 1920: 43; Maddicott 2010: 450–1), and medieval France was only able to develop a relatively weak system of representation. Whether this is true or not, it remains the

<hr />

[56] For background see Colmeiro (1883: 8, 115, 118–20); O'Callaghan (1989: 9–19).
[57] For the argument that the monarchy of Castile-León depended for its territorial 'consistency' on a balance between estates, see González (2006: 157).

case that the consolidation of the French monarchical state as a substantially independent and geographically extensive centre of power occurred in a period characterized by a pronounced dynamic of constitutional formation. During the reign of Philippe le Bel, most strikingly, the French monarchy asserted its independence from the papacy by claiming that the monarch embodied not merely private royal power, but the power of the national community of France as a whole: that is, the power of the 'communautez des villes'.[58] Moreover, owing to his conflicts with Boniface VIII, Philippe le Bel was the first monarch (in 1302) who summoned the Estates-General, comprising the orders of clergy, nobility and third estate, to deliberate affairs of the realm. Further, in part because he began to institute a regular taxation system distinct from the feudal *taille*, he oversaw a substantial increase both in the consultative functions of the estates and in the frequency of their convocation (Boutaric 1861: 19; Bisson 1972: 548; Krynen 1993: 270). Both Philippe le Bel and subsequent Capetian kings utilized the estates both to secure the 'independence of the crown' from the papacy and to stabilize the fixed apparatus and revenue supplies of the monarchy (Bardoux 1877: 29). Even the *légistes*, for all their extensive justifications for the diminution of papal power, were decidedly not apologists for royal absolutism. The *légistes* were in fact keen to frame the legitimacy of royal power within a broadly constructed constitutional apparatus, and they identified integral constitutional support as a precondition of the sovereign autonomy of the state (Pegues 1962: 225). In France, therefore, the process of feudal transformation did not only lead to the early formation of the state as a distinct and functionally specialized centre of sovereignty: it also of necessity produced a need for a legitimating national constitution to facilitate the state's increasing statutory and judicial functions.[59]

It has been argued in highly influential literature on medieval constitutionalism that medieval societies possessed a constitutional structure that was clearly distinct from that of modern societies. On this account, medieval societies contained customary constitutions, in which counterweights to royal power were derived from consuetudinal laws, interpreted by actors in the judiciary: it was only in early modern societies that elite actors began to use legal principles to weaken royal power and to force a constitutional

---

[58] See the 'Lettre des Nobles du Royaume de France' (1910 [1302]: 13).

[59] The correlation in France between the growth of sovereignty and the constitutional 'dialogue between the sovereign and his realm' has been brilliantly observed in Petit-Renaud (2001: 363).

order on the legislative functions of government (McIlwain 1947: 87). The argument proposed here, however, suggests that this analysis, although correct to identify a constitutional apparatus in medieval societies, requires revision. The account offered here implies that the basic dimensions of constitutional rule were established in many European societies by the high medieval period, and that such constitutions, prefiguring their later functions, were a necessary prerequisite for the political differentiation and functional specialization of these societies and so also for the formation of strong governmental systems. Of course, this is not to claim that medieval societies possessed constitutions in the modern sense of a formally acceded set of basic norms for the state. However, if the two primary elements of constitutional rule are, first, the existence of a prescribed legal order, usually containing strong ideas of right and entitlement, to determine conditions for the exercise of power, and, second, the existence of representative and consultative mechanisms in matters of common societal importance, it is difficult to argue that constitutional rule was not a prominent feature of governance in many medieval societies. Constitutions in fact developed in medieval European societies as necessary responses to wider exigencies, caused by deep-lying processes of social transformation, which continued to stimulate the formation of constitutions into the modern era.

At a practical level, the first elements of a constitutional apparatus in proto-modern states evolved – quite simply – because the density of governance increased. That is to say, as states required more and more resources to perform their growing judicial functions they also needed adequate public mechanisms for expressing and securing support. In particular, the institutions of representative government in early constitutional states developed specifically because the more personal and informal structures of feudal governance proved incapable of managing the volume of administration and of levying the volume of revenue that were required for the conduct of governmental affairs. In England, France and Spain, for instance, both the assemblies of estates and the regular courts of law are normally seen to have grown out of the more informal *curia regis*, in which royal government had originally been consolidated,[60] and the establishment of these more inclusionary institutions permitted a heightened flexibility and specialization in the administrative resources of the state. The practical function of

---

[60] Baldwin (1913: 308); Pollard (1920: 112); Aubert (1977: 1, 259); Estepa Díez (1988: 57); O'Callaghan (1989: 19); Sicard (1990: 68); Maddicott (2010: 153).

constitutions thus resulted, in the first instance, from an extension of the state's administrative procedures, and it enabled the state to acquire much more refined, internally cohesive and socially sensitive instruments of administrative co-ordination.

Additionally, however, modern states assumed their first quintessential features as they began to utilize political power as a distinctly abstracted and general medium of exchange and, in particular, as they initially assumed *statutory powers* of legislation: that is, as, often using techniques borrowed from the church, they began to transform customs into positive laws, autonomously to pass legal acts, and to use power in general positive form across increasingly diverse and differentiated societies. The fact that laws were increasingly *written* in textual form might be seen – across different regional contexts – as a technique for minimizing power's sensitivity to locality, privilege and status in society, and for holding both power and law in a condition of differentiated abstraction and generality.[61] This defining feature of modern states also relied on the existence of representative and consultative functions in the state: that is, on a rudimentary constitution. The emergent states of the medieval era that possessed the greatest and most easily enforceable statutory power were ordinarily those that possessed elaborate and inclusive mechanisms (that is, representative constitutions) for producing and demonstrating wide societal inclusion. Indeed, the existence of a constitutional structure was normally a precondition for the formation of a state able effectively to integrate its population, raise revenue in addition to feudal levies and both incorporate, and utilize its power consistently across, wide territories. For this reason, representative constitutions, and the patterns of unified inclusion and compliance that they helped to articulate, were crucial instruments in the transposition of legal order from the informal arrangements of feudalism on to the positive-legal or statutory foundations of early modern statehood. In fact, in many societies statutes and constitutions were often contained within the same document, and together they provided preconditions for the state's use of power that were at once socially acceded, determined by positive decisions and separated from singular or personal actors (McIlwain 1947: 24; Holt 1972: 505). In this respect, then, it can be concluded that states developed constitutions because it was by using constitutions that they were able to disarticulate their power from

---

[61] The necessary hostility of the aristocracy to written law seems sociologically self-evident. But this point is expressly made in Kejř (1992: 204).

exclusively private prerogatives, and progressively to reconstruct this power as an autonomous, positively generalizable – gradually *public* – societal resource. Constitutional inclusion, in fact, was the mechanism that enabled societies to stabilize and manage their increasingly autonomous reserves of power and to make effective use of power as it was abstracted from more immediate patterns of consent and coercion. The end of feudalism and the attendant formation of political power as an abstract and positive resource, in other words, were necessarily parts of a constitutional process.[62]

In contributing in this manner to the positive construction of political power, early constitutions also performed wider and more fundamental functions for early European states. In particular, representative constitutions, as inclusionary foundations for the rule of law, emerged as institutions that both reflected and accelerated the transformation of society as a whole, and they changed society from a loosely decentred aggregate of private persons into a stratified and decisively *included* political community, capable of reacting in a uniform, general and inclusive manner to matters of potentially generalized political resonance. The first emergence of European societies as geographically extensive sources of integration and motivation was in fact closely linked to the growth of general constitutional laws and general patterns of political and territorial inclusion. As discussed, the modern European state began to emerge as a body of institutions that suppressed the private/seigneurial rights guaranteed under feudalism and so deeply altered the status of noble elites. In establishing constitutions, however, states were also able incrementally to convert these private rights into rights that were held, or at least negotiated, within and through the state, and this allowed the state both to transform private (feudal) rights into constitutive elements of public order and more easily to include bearers of such rights in the jurisdictional purview of the state. Emerging modern European states, in other words, relied on a representative constitution because they required a form in which political power could be applied evenly across society and in which, correlatively, society could be unified and brought into a uniform relation to power. As rudimentary constructions of public law, therefore, constitutions began (gradually) to form political power as abstracted *inclusionary power*: but they also

---

[62] The relation between early constitutional formation and the end of feudalism has often been observed in different settings (Spangenberg 1912: 130; Bosl 1972: 321; Ganzo 2008: 421).

began to form societies as *inclusionary societies*, in which power could be utilized as a more evenly circulated resource, and in which all social domains became more evenly responsive to the growing, differentiated power of the state. The formulation of the key normative principle of medieval constitutionalism – *quod omnes tangit debet ab omnibus approbari* – can be seen in this context.[63] This principle allowed states to reflect on and consolidate the relatively abstracted autonomy and the increasing generality of their power by expanding their administrative resources, by integrating more members of society (however selectively) in functions of the state and by ensuring that relevant sectors of society received power in internally pre-formed fashion. The first typical constitutional structure of European states was thus a *dualistic constitution*. The first modern constitutional order was a political condition of society in which certain powers were centralized in the state, yet in which representatives of prominent feudal groups politically subordinated by the state (the nobility and the baronial class) were selectively co-opted in the periphery of the expanding administration and their legal titles and privileges were constitutionally recognized as sources of entitlement within the state. In the still highly fragmented political landscape of medieval Europe, this dualistic constitutional relation between regents and prominent social elites made the autonomous construction and inclusionary application of political power possible.

The initial abstraction of political power in the formation of European societies, to conclude, was shaped by a twofold normative impulse. Political power required the law for its transmission and reproduction through society, and it required the law for the inclusion of its addressees. As power first became political power, it inevitably assumed the internal normative shape of *constitutional law*.

---

[63] On the application of this concept in England see Maddicott (2010: 227–8).

2

Constitutions and early modernity

Constitutions and the rule of law at the end of the Middle Ages

The fact barely needs emphasis that in late medieval societies European states did not increase their jurisdictional power or reinforce their ability to separate statutory acts from local custom and agreement in a linear or conclusive fashion. Many later medieval societies were endemically afflicted by lawlessness, and many societies, especially in the fifteenth century, witnessed a forfeiture of state authority through civil war and internecine strife.[1] Nonetheless, in most European societies with relatively established political structures the centralistic constitutions of the high medieval period did not disintegrate in the later Middle Ages, and the last decades of the medieval era witnessed both a renewed growth in the positive statutory power of the law and an increase in the uniformity and concentration of legal order. Indeed, in much of Europe the latter period of the Middle Ages experienced the formation of more strictly organized monarchies, which renewed and reinvigorated the centralizing tendencies discussed in Chapter 1.

In England, for instance, after the dynastic conflicts of the fifteenth century the early Tudor administration began centrally to strengthen both the fiscal and the judicial apparatus of the state and to extend royal law more consistently across society. This period of English history is usually viewed as an era in which, after the Wars of the Roses, the machinery of royal justice resumed sufficient strength to suppress particularistic, compacted and even clientelistic patterns of law finding in the counties, and royal courts again became effective instruments of government.[2] In France, in partial distinction, by the fifteenth century

---

[1] This was particularly, but not uniquely, acute in England, and the resultant condition is often described as 'bastard feudalism' (Stone 1968: 96–134; Bellamy 1989). This was also endemic in Spain, where the ceding of royal jurisdiction was widespread through the fourteenth century (Nader 1990: 77).

[2] This is accepted even by historians sceptical about the use of the term 'bastard feudalism' (Carpenter 1983: 235).

the extension of central power during the era of high feudalism had, due to protracted military depredation, yielded, in part, to a process of institutional decentralization. Because of this, monarchs appointed regional governors to regulate financial and judicial matters in areas originally subject to feudal authority. This meant that, owing partly to the physical dimensions of the country, the importance of municipalities and villages grew significantly in France, and these obtained semi-independent legal and jurisdictional status. Despite this, however, the aspiration towards unitary statehood and legal order remained strong and it was progressively reasserted towards the end of the Middle Ages. By the 1430s, during the last part of the Hundred Years War, France again had a central *parlement* in Paris. Shortly afterwards, royal *parlements* were established in the provinces. In 1454, the Ordonnance of Montils-les-Tours was passed. This statute prescribed the uniform editing of customary laws in the provinces: this process was not completed for over a century, but it was designed in part to dictate the primacy of royal statute over seigneurial laws and centrally to regulate the apparatus of justice (Grinberg 1997: 1021). The late medieval period thus saw a substantial tightening and refinement of the judicial divisions of government, and this continued through the sixteenth century.[3]

In the Holy Roman Empire, similarly, the last decades of the Middle Ages witnessed a steady growth in the density of statehood, as a result of which both the jurisdictional and the fiscal powers of the Empire were augmented. The Middle Ages effectively came to an end in the Holy Roman Empire in 1495: this year saw the final establishment of a permanent central court (*Reichskammergericht*) for the German parts of the Empire. This court, mainly applying Roman law, was created primarily to suppress feuding and private lawgiving, and it imposed a common legal code (*Ewiger Landfriede*) throughout the German territories. During the first decades of its institution, this court was also at the centre of a comprehensive reform of the judicial administration. Among other innovations, this period saw the introduction in the Empire of more systematic procedures for trial, and it eventually witnessed the implementation of a comprehensive catalogue of criminal law (the Carolina of 1532) (Angermeier 1984: 216–17). In this context, it is notable that, although it was founded by the emperor, the central legal apparatus was established largely because the imperial princes demanded the institution of a high court, and the court ultimately

---

[3] Generally on these points see Doucet (1948: 167); Major (1960: 5–7); Glasson (1974: 8–9).

reflected a compromise between the constitutional designs of the Electoral princes and the centralizing ambitions of the Habsburg rulers.[4] In the high medieval period, as discussed, the push for a central court and a general legal order had usually been the prerogative of the imperial executive, and the promotion of a stable legal system was intended, in part, to reduce the territorial power of princes and the nobility; indeed, this objective survived in part into the fifteenth century, and in the first half of this century the impetus for legal centralization was still commonly associated with the imperial party.[5] By the late fifteenth century, in contrast, the power to impose territorial peace had been ceded by the imperial party to the territorial princes: the princes now pursued their own policies of concerted legal pacification, and it was, to some degree, their interests that were reflected through the central court. At one level, the creation of the new court weakened the Electors, as the laws that founded the court called into question the privileges that they had obtained under the Golden Bull, and the court again subjected their territories, albeit with certain immunities, to the jurisdiction of the Empire,[6] and it was (albeit to no avail) intended as a device to facilitate regular fiscal supply.[7] Yet the court also reinforced the constitutional position of the princes. In particular, the formation of a central court ensured that the princes could influence imperial jurisdiction, it removed supreme judicial power from the hands of the emperor, and it meant that the emperor could be subject to legal decisions and his power determined in legal categories. Through the establishment of the court, in any case, both the imperial control of the law and the protracted search for territorial peace came to an effective end, and the mechanisms for enforcing peace in the Empire reflected a constitutional balance between Empire and princes.

In most European societies, in sum, the final decades of the Middle Ages were marked by a substantial concentration of the apparatus of legal and political control. In particular, the institutions attached to monarchical government were beginning, after the widespread disorder

---

[4] For this point see Angermeier (1966: 489, 539, 253; 1984: 253); Durchhardt (1996: 4).

[5] The Reformatio Sigismundi, which was the main imperial reform document of the earlier fifteenth century, was clear in demanding the universal introduction of a law book based in Roman law, to be applied through imperial courts (1497 [c. 1438]: 14).

[6] On this crucial point see Angermeier (1966: 550); Weitzel (1976: 87); Diestelkamp (1983: 49–63).

[7] The reforms also tentatively foresaw the implementation of a common tax (Schmid 1989: 223–4).

of the later Middle Ages, to reconsolidate a monopoly of legal authority in society, and the ability of central political organs both to pass laws and to rule over legal cases in predictable fashion increased significantly. As in the high medieval era, however, at this stage in European history the imposition of the rule of law did not simply reflect a simple extension of royal prerogative, and the process of political centralization was not solely effected through social coercion or extraction. On the contrary, the intensification of legal and political order at the end of the fifteenth century usually arose from a set of political arrangements in which consensual supports for the process of centralization were reinforced: the consolidation of central legal and political institutions relied on a growing body of representative structures. In fact, in the last decades of the medieval period most European societies continued to witness an increase in the inclusionary and even representative dimensions of government, and this period generally consolidated the dualistic constitutions which had first accompanied and facilitated the formation of the earliest European states.

The extension of the inclusionary aspects of statehood at the threshold of early modernity in Europe was, to be sure, not a universal fact. In many Italian settings, as mentioned, the pluralistic constitution of the medieval *comuni*, often destabilized by the military engagements between different cities, rapidly gave way to more oligarchical regimes, in which popular institutions fell, in part, under the sway of leading families.[8] Some cities, such as Florence and Venice, retained their republican structure for longer than others. However, just as governmental power over Milan was assumed by the Viscontis and then the Sforzas, Florence also eventually fell into the embrace of the Medici family. By the early sixteenth century, after the short popular revival under Savonarola, the Florentine republican regime was effectively dissolved.[9] After this time, the republic was increasingly defined, not as an inclusive corporate order, but as an artificial coercive edifice, largely dissolved from prior legal constraints and representative obligations.[10] In the Italian cities governed by dynastic oligarchies, a pattern of statehood began to emerge, in which the personal and sectoral privileges of different social groups were restricted, and political

---

[8] The point has been well made, though, that republican statutes did not simply disappear and the transition from one regime to the other was not seamless (Chittolini 1991: 34, 37).

[9] Stephens dates the erosion of the Republic to the period 1471–80 (1983: 23). In agreement, see Rubinstein (1997: 151).

[10] Note Botero's argument that the 'principal foundation of every state is the obedience of subjects to the superior' (1590 [1589]: 17).

power was progressively condensed in a centralized bureaucracy. Indeed, it has been widely noted that these oligarchies pre-empted the model of the 'absolutist' state, which later became prevalent in much of Europe.[11] That is to say, the regimes in these cities tended to integrate new families in government at the expense of those holding established privileges, and they diminished the political status of particular societal privileges or indemnities by transforming bearers of privileges into actors within the expanding state administration. Moreover, in reaching for support beyond late-feudal elites, these oligarchies solidified bases of political approval through different strata of society, and they used their powers of legislation and jurisdiction in uniformly inclusionary fashion and in relative indifference to private status (Kent 1978: 5; Najemy 2006: 471). Above all, in centralizing the means of coercion and extending laws in relative uniformity across all members of society these later Italian city-states brought about a close fusion between *state* and *territory*, and they began to consolidate their institutional order as evenly concentrated within fixed spatial boundaries. In Castile, processes analogous to those in the Italian cities were also evident. To be sure, in Castile many elements of the medieval constitutional tradition survived to the beginnings of the early modern period. Through the fourteenth century, successive monarchs had repeatedly confirmed that no new taxes could be levied without consultation in the Cortes. In 1387, Juan I pledged that no acceded laws could be abrogated without the agreement of the Cortes, thus placing a factual limit on the authority of the crown. However, the statutory powers of the monarchs expanded significantly in the late medieval era, and by the fifteenth century the consultative institutions of the earlier period were (arguably) in decline and the nobility was (temporarily) in retreat (de Dios 1982: 119; Carretero Zamora 1988: 66; Nieto Soria 2002: 247). After the establishment of the Catholic monarchy, which united Castile and Aragon, the crown was able to introduce laws in the form of ordinances, which assumed statutory force without prior approval through the Cortes (Edwards 2000: 51).[12]

Despite this, however, most late medieval European monarchies and principalities were characterized by an extension of their delegatory and representative procedures. In Poland, for instance, the middle of the fifteenth century saw a concerted reinforcement of the representative

---

[11] There is a huge body of literature on this. For some examples see Rodolico (1898: 75); Baron (1966: xxvi); Martines (1968: 424).

[12] On the weakening of the Cortes under the Catholic monarchy see Carretero Zamora (1988: 46–51); Suárez Fernández (2003: 124).

dimensions of the constitution, and the Polish king accepted that major decisions of state required prior approval by small regional parliaments (*sejmiki*). A central bicameral parliament (*sejm*) was established after 1492, and regional assemblies began to send deputies to represent noble interests in a newly constituted chamber. In 1505, a long period of charter granting culminated in a formal law, the *nihil novi* statute, which placed political power in the hands of the aristocracy and bound the king to obtain the support of the assembled nobility whenever he introduced new legislative acts. This effectively assured legislative equality for the Polish nobility, and it created a parliamentary system, dominated by the aristocracy, whose force was unrivalled in Europe. Ultimately, the union of Lithuania and Poland in 1569 was also ratified by parliaments of both states, and it is habitually claimed that the union was designed to preserve those noble interests (freedom from taxation, right of habeas corpus, right to elect deputies, rights to participate in election of kings) that were traditionally represented in local and national assemblies (Dembkowski 1982: 3, 210).

In France, as mentioned, the central governmental order constructed by the Capetian monarchs had fragmented under the pressures of war in the fourteenth century, and by the end of this century the importance of the Estates-General had also declined. Indeed, much historiography has argued that after 1439, when Charles VII obtained consent to collect annual national taxes, the significance of constitutional consensus in France was dramatically reduced, and the monarchical state began to assume early 'absolutistic' characteristics (Marchadier 1904: 131; Lewis 1962; Wolfe 1972: 33, 51). Despite this, however, it has equally been noted that even in the fourteenth century local representative institutions still played a vital role in the French polity (Lewis 1968: 351–3). More importantly, the progressive reassertion of monarchical power in the later fifteenth century was accompanied by an active revival of estates (both general and provincial) and other representative bodies, and these served both as legal checks on royal power and as integrated components of the growing administrative system of government (Major 1960: 16). The creation of a more compact and ordered princely state during the Renaissance in fact specifically presupposed a consultative constitution in which estate assemblies, albeit primarily at a provincial level, served both to support and administratively to extend state power across society (Doucet 1948: 339; Major 1960: 61). Subsequently, in the sixteenth century, French provincial assemblies become more powerful, and they began to assume distinct institutional form, comprising stricter rules of procedure, duties and membership. The principle of the constitutionally balanced polity was also pervasive in the theoretical literature of late fifteenth-century France, and it was expressed in exemplary fashion by Claude de Seyssel. Seyssel defined the French state as a monarchy in which the exercise of regal power was subject to three sources of normative constraint: religion, justice and policy (1961 [1519]: 119). This contained the implication that the royal will was accountable to *parlements*, and that it could not contravene the statutory ordinances, 'made by kings themselves and subsequently confirmed and approved from time to time' which acted as a de facto constitution for the realm as a whole.

A further example of this tendency towards semi-organized condominium as the basis for later medieval governance was the English polity. It has been widely observed that during the Wars of the Roses the Lancastrian party sought to cement its legitimacy by promoting an integrative model of government, giving relatively large sectors of society a role in the political process (Pickthorn 1934: 134–5). Throughout the fifteenth century, the principle that royal prerogative was limited was sharpened, and it was accepted that kingship was an office to which prescribed duties and obligations were attached. Further, the convention of invoking the authority of parliament to demonstrate the legitimacy of legislation was reinforced, and the presumption that new laws and new taxes could only be introduced through statutes approved by parliament was strong (Chrimes 1936: 61, 75; Ladner 1980: 62). The constitutional doctrines that supported Lancastrian government, exemplified by John Fortescue, also expressed strong hostility to monarchical absolutism. Fortescue argued for a mixed royal and political constitution, balancing royal prerogative and parliamentary power (1942 [c. 1470]: 79). He defined royal power as subject to counsel and obligated by customary principles of common law and natural law, and he insisted that parliamentary mandate and royal will needed to be constitutionally conjoined in the making of statutes. In England, Fortescue stated plainly, statutes were not imposed by a king 'able to change the laws of his kingdom at pleasure' or to preside over his people 'with a power entirely regal' (1942 [c. 1470]: 25).

The processes of state formation and constitutional construction that occurred in the Holy Roman Empire at the end of the Middle Ages were particularly indicative of this broad societal connection between centralistic legal-political consolidation and representative inclusion. As discussed, the formation of a central judicial system at the end of the Middle

Ages was reflected in an implicit constitutional balance between the imperial party and the territorial princes. Additionally, however, the creation of the central court was also flanked by a wider step-wise constitutional settlement, in which fixed imperial Diets (*Reichstage*) were established to deliberate and resolve matters of importance for the Empire. In these Diets, which at once replaced the movable courts and personal assemblies of the medieval era and established procedures for the representation of princely interests, it was expected that major questions should be settled on a consensual basis. Further, after 1519 it became habitual for emperors, on assumption of office, to commit themselves to quasi-contractual electoral pledges (*Wahlkapitulationen*) as prerequisites of legitimate imperial governance. These contracts rapidly obtained implicit constitutional status, and they were widely invoked to bind and judge the exercise of imperial power.[13]

As in the earlier medieval period, further, this constitutional balance between the imperial party and the princes in the Holy Roman Empire acted as one aspect of a multilayered process of state formation in the Empire, and the Empire continued to develop as a diffuse polity in which power was consensually structured at multiple institutional junctures. In fact, in the last century of the Middle Ages many of the duchies and principalities within the Empire began to assume a much stricter inner constitutional order, as the regional estates also demanded greater rights of political consultation and participation in important decisions, especially those regarding taxation. In many parts of Germany, thus, the century prior to the Reformation witnessed the formation of semi-autonomous territorial states with a constitutionally sustained political constitution: this pattern of statehood is traditionally called the *Ständestaat*. At least in its ideal-typical construction, this was a political order in which the constitutional balances of the earlier territorial regimes were tightened, and different estates (in some areas, including clergy, an early mercantile class and the peasants) were accommodated as collaborative and politically represented actors in an increasingly cohesive administrative structure. Central to the formation of the *Ständestaat* was a process in which regents began to transform different social estates, who were in many cases originally dynastic vassals and holders of feudal rights, into ranks and orders within the institutional hierarchy of a distinct territory. As such, then, the estates provided

---

[13] For these details, see Kleinmeyer (1968: 20, 101–6); Oestreich (1977: 61); Moraw (1980); Neuhaus (1982: 26).

regulatory support for regents through their territories, and, in return, their rights and freedoms, which they originally held as private/personal rights under feudal laws, were progressively translated into rights of co-optation and representation within a central political order. The *Ständestaat* marked a momentarily balanced or hybrid model of statehood, in which the plural and embedded rights of feudal society were gradually articulated as rights obtained within and through a formal state apparatus. However defined, the *Ständestaat* reflected a pattern of state building in which the representative or delegatory dimension of governance performed a key and increasing role. In Saxony, for example, estates began to negotiate on an organized basis with territorial lords in the 1430s, and a representative order in fiscal questions was consolidated by the 1450s. In Brandenburg, it was agreed in 1472 that regents would not sell land without formal approval of the estates. In Prussia, the estates became an integral part of government in the course of the fifteenth century. In Württemberg, where a particularly robust set of constitutional arrangements ultimately emerged, Diets were also regularly convoked by the fifteenth century, and the Tübingen treaty (1514) formally enshrined principles of representation and fiscal control for the estates.[14]

For each of these reasons, the type of early sovereign statehood particular to the German regions of the Holy Roman Empire – that is, the pattern of territorial supremacy (*Landesherrschaft*), entailing the partial transfer of jurisdictional rights in a particular region from the Empire to one prince, duke or count[15] – was only sustainable because territorial regents engaged in firm constitutional arrangements with their subjects. Underlying the formation of territorial rule was an evolutionary shift in which the personal rights and obligations of feudal law (*Lehnrecht*) were supplanted by regionally concentrated

---

[14] On these points see Küntzel (1908: 100); Näf (1951a: 68); Helbig (1955: 418, 451); Carsten (1959: 6–12).

[15] This is the crucial concept for understanding state building in late medieval Germany. *Landesherrschaft* describes a principle of territorial domination exercised by princes who originally obtained land and jurisdictional rights under *regalia* granted under feudal law and eventually transformed their holdings into hereditary goods, over which they consolidated their dominion. This transformation can be seen to have presupposed a wider transformation of feudal tenure and feudal relations, in which inhabitants of land originally bound to their lords by feudal obligations had to be mobilized as consenting subjects. On the rise of *Landesherrschaft* see Krieger (1979: 341); Willoweit (1983). On the process of de-feudalization implied in the construction of territorial power see Stengel (1904: 300); Klebel (1960).

rights and authorities (*Landrecht*), and in which power was tied to fixed geographical spaces and specific rights of localized authority: this transition from diffuse personal law to vertical territorial law depended on consensual instruments for consolidating and administering the regions to which power, in increasing uniformity, was now applied.[16] The inclusion of estates in government gave structural solidity to emerging territorial states, it allowed political actors to detach power from the fluid personal arrangements of feudalism, and it integrated the people of one territory in a relatively uniform and regimented manner within the political system. In fact, in the German regions, the transformation of the variable power of feudal society into a regime of regionally centralized dominion presupposed that states could construct relations of compliance in which all relevant members of society recognized themselves as subject to the same power in similar fashion, and this, in turn, presupposed that power was utilized on an integrative, consultative foundation.[17]

The emergence of an estate-based polity at the end of the Middle Ages was not peculiar to the German territories. Throughout the fifteenth century, the states of the Netherlands also developed a powerful consensual apparatus, in which individual provinces established representative assemblies to deliberate matters of military and fiscal significance. These assemblies then sent delegates to the States-General, which, in rudimentary form, were first convened in 1464, and were obliged to consult with local bodies before arriving at major decisions (Parker 1977: 30–3; Koenigsberger 2001: 32; Tracy 2008: 45). Indeed, in some parts of the Netherlands the tradition of governmental consultation through regional estates went back as far as the early thirteenth century: a charter of rights for the estates in Brabant was in place as early as 1312.

In each of these examples, the processes of later feudal societal formation and territorial intensification that shaped the transition from the Middle Ages to early modernity in Europe normally created states with a pronounced constitutional order: in fact, outside smaller cities, where oligarchical power was more easily sustainable, some element of constitutional formation was a widespread prerequisite for the rejuvenated

---

[16] On the increasing 'dualism between land law and feudal law' towards the end of the Middle Ages see Droege (1969: 410).

[17] In the Brandenburg constitution of 1472, the terms 'lordship' or 'dominion' (*Herrschaft*) and 'subjects' (*Unterthanen*) are tellingly introduced together, and they act as structurally correlated concepts (Näf 1951b: 67).

growth of statehood at this time. Notably, the consolidation of statehood still tended, in most polities, to depend on the preservation of a *dualistic constitution*, whose origins clearly lay in the multiply privatized legal order of feudalism. That is to say, at the caesura between medieval and early modern Europe most states still employed constitutional arrangements to maintain a balance between actors within the political system and actors (usually members of the nobility endowed with seigneurial or patrimonial authority) outside the state, and constitutional conventions were in most cases employed to guarantee a body of external social rights, privileges and exemptions, the bargained preservation of which enabled actors within states to purchase social acceptance for the rising power of central polities.[18] The margins of the political system still remained blurred and fluid: these late medieval constitutions expressed an equilibrium between originally private privileges or charters and the claims of public order, and they mobilized compliance for the state by specifically recognizing that some localities, freedoms and functions could not be subsumed under state power. At the same time, however, these constitutions also acted incrementally to expand the periphery of the state: that is, they established a loose inclusionary order on which the state relied for the execution of basic uniform functions – such as legal enforcement and the maintenance of fiscal supply – in specified territories. To follow the argument of J. Russell Major, therefore, in many cases late medieval society was marked simultaneously by the 'revival of royal authority' and by the promotion of a constitutional balance between regents and provincial estates (1960: 16). In fact, each of these two dynamics at once presupposed and intensified the other, and the widening of representative constitutional structures allowed increasingly powerful states to engender support for their policies (especially in fiscal matters), to avail themselves of an administrative apparatus that could consolidate their power, and to concentrate their power around firm territorial boundaries. Similarly, Werner Näf has plausibly concluded that the original dualistic relation between monarchs and parliaments or estates that characterized the late medieval era was in fact a constitutional and territorial *partnership*, in which both parties relied on each other and both, in collaboration, gave rise to the basic legal, administrative and fiscal structure of the modern state (Näf 1951a: 242). Each of these arguments implies, as Peter Blickle has also observed, that in the late Middle Ages the concentration of monarchical power, the increasing

---

[18] For ideal-typical reconstruction of the dualistic constitution see Bosl (1974: 55).

princely control of land, tax and courts, and the wider 'territorialization and intensification of government' were necessarily sustained by the emergence of multi-levelled representative and inclusionary structures (1973: 435).[19] As in the earlier medieval period, therefore, the social abstraction of political power was closely correlated with the promotion of inclusionary mechanisms to support power's reproduction and distribution through society. These mechanisms in fact enabled the state to produce and sustain a sufficient mass of power to conduct its growing body of functions and to increase the volume of positively generalized power available in society.

The Reformation and the differentiation of state power

This vital correlation between late medieval state building and constitutional formation obtained its most intense expression in those states which, in the course of the sixteenth century, either fully renounced their political attachment to the Roman Catholic church or underwent substantial political disruption owing to religious reform.

In each society that experienced an (either complete or partial) Reformation, the period of religious transformation at once responded to and intensified the two processes which had formed the vital political dimensions of European societies under high feudalism. The Reformation revolved, at a most manifest level, around a continued differentiation of the state from the church, and, in consequence of this, it led, evidently, at once to an increase in the functional autonomy of political power and to a general centralization and consolidation of the institutions of state power (gradually recognizable as modern states). Still more fundamentally, however, the Reformation was an event that at once reflected and was induced by a multi-causal increase in the positivization and formalization of legal relations in society, which resulted from earlier processes of legal secularization and feudal decline in European society. In the Reformation, therefore, the two dominant political tendencies of the Middle Ages – the abstraction and intensified autonomy of political power and the positive abstraction of power's legal foundations – coincided to stimulate a period of extreme structural upheaval in European society as a whole. The Reformation, most essentially, was an occurrence in which the status of power as a relatively autonomous phenomenon was greatly accentuated and in which the

---

[19] For similar views see Hintze (1962a [1930]: 133); Bosl (1974: 44, 107).

legal construction of political power underwent a process of dramatically accelerated positivization.

The over-layering of centralistic political abstraction and legal positivization in the Reformation was apparent, first, in the fact that all states converting to Lutheranism vehemently attacked the use of canon law in their territories, and the success of particular princes and regents in conducting a Reformation and reinforcing their political institutions depended on the ability of these regents to suppress the system of legatine authority imposed by the papal courts. The first legal precondition of the Reformation, thus, was that regents were powerful enough to eradicate external or sacral elements from their legal orders. One of the most powerful political origins of the German Reformation lay in the fact that princely rulers of nascent states objected to the imposition of ecclesiastical jurisdiction (and the attendant ecclesiastical taxes and indulgences, which deprived them of revenue) in their lands. In consequence, they utilized Luther's theological attack on the canon law, driven by his early antinomianism, to campaign for an exclusion of papal jurisdiction from worldly power, to reduce the legal power of the church in secular territorial government, and so to strengthen their legal, jurisdictional and fiscal authority in their territories.[20] In the course of the Reformation, German Evangelical states began to integrate the canon-law courts, they began to consolidate more complete territorial control of judicial procedures, and they transformed canon law and objects of ecclesiastical-legal procedure into inner elements of state jurisdiction.[21] In so doing, these states suspended large swathes of legislation embedded in the judicial fabric of their societies, and they greatly augmented the jurisdictional and statutory authority of single princes. In England, a similar process occurred, and the first concrete impulse for the Reformation, the divorce of Henry VIII, entailed an assertion of royal exemption from, and then supremacy over, the courts of church law, which was formalized in the Act in Restraint of Appeals (1533). This

---

[20] As early as 1515 Luther argued that obedience to law cannot bring salvation. Law, he argued, 'inflates people' and 'makes them boastful' (1960 [1515–16]: 245). Justification, he claimed, can only occur as a passive experience of grace which is indifferent to law. The most famous case of royal opposition to papal courts was the divorce of Henry VIII. But this was widespread throughout Germany, and by 1555 all Evangelical territories had substantially augmented their jurisdictional power in both church and state. In the Netherlands, the contest over ecclesiastical regulation was a primary cause of the first revolt against Catholic Spain.

[21] See Heckel (1956); Mauer (1965: 253); and the contributions in Helmholz (1992).

then led to the submission of the judicial powers of the clergy and the integration of the canon-law courts into the sphere of royal jurisdiction: Thomas Cromwell prohibited the university study of classical canon law, and the need for a new body of canons was stated as early as the mid 1530s. The courts of common law in fact assumed a large amount of the business formerly treated in the church courts, and they did much to extend royal authority over all matters of the realm. Reflecting this transformation in the law, moreover, the Reformation saw, in all Evangelical societies, the emergence of new patterns of legal analysis, often drawing on Roman law, which employed decisively positive templates for examining conditions of state power, legitimacy and legal justice. During the Reformation in the German states, for example, legal theorists such as Johann Oldendorp began to use specifically secular concepts of natural law for deducing reproducible normative foundations for judicial acts (1549: 90). In England, an analogous tendency became manifest in the works of Christopher St German. St German proposed a model of legal and political authority which denounced the powers accorded to ecclesiastical courts and ascribed all legitimate secular power to the state. Above all, he argued that the parliamentary monarchy, as a consensually legitimized executive, should assume 'absolute power' in all legislative and judicial matters (1532: 24), and that the common law should form the basis for all legal finding.[22]

The connection between these two processes of political consolidation and legal positivization was evident, further, in the fact that those states that converted to one or other variant on the Evangelical faith assumed regulatory authority over the church as a whole, and they transformed the church from a source of external legal-normative obligation into an institution governed under a territorial constitution. Naturally, this process was marked by striking variations: no fully general pattern of church government developed in the Reformation. However, all states that underwent a Reformation assimilated the sacral laws of the church into their administrative apparatus. This began in the later 1520s in some German territories, as secular rulers reacted to the alarming spread of iconoclasm, lay preaching and disorder in the church by imposing orders of visitation to supervise teaching and worship in the church and to establish

---

[22] Even before the Reformation was fully in process, St German included both 'particular customes' and 'statutes made in parliament' among the sources of the laws of England (1613 [1523]: 17). Like Oldendorp, St German also took the principle of 'equitie' as the basis for positive law (1613 [1523]: 55).

conformity in articles of faith. In the German territories, the first formal church constitutions of the later 1530s, pioneered by Philipp Melanchthon,[23] defined care of the church as a primary duty of territorial authority and they provided for the appointment of religious superintendents and the formation of an Evangelical consistory to regulate the church, both of which were accountable to princely power.[24] Territorial supremacy over the church in the German states was in fact constitutionally established in the two primary documents of the German Reformation: that is, in the Confessio Augustana of 1530 and the Religious Peace of Augsburg (1555). The first document, comprising the founding articles of faith of Lutheranism, declared that the church should be seen solely as a spiritual institution, holding only the power of the keys, and it implied that princely authorities should defend and protect the church in the worldly arena (Art. 28). The Peace of Augsburg enunciated the juridical principle that came to underpin the Evangelical state church: *cuius regio eius religio*. This was gradually interpreted by Evangelical lawyers to the effect that papal jurisdiction in sacral matters was suspended, and territorial princes assumed the (as yet not constitutionally sanctioned) right to reform the church (*ius reformandi*) and to impose confessional uniformity in their territory (Stephani 1612 [1599]: 16, 51–2). From 1555 onward, it was loosely accepted in most states of the Holy Roman Empire that Evangelical princes were authorized to dictate ecclesiastical policy, and the church was directly subject to territorial rule.

Outside the German heartlands of the Reformation, Sweden was perhaps the most complete example of the incorporation of the reformed church within the state: indeed, Gustav Vasa organized the Swedish church as a simple 'department of state' (Roberts 1968a: 116). In England, through the sixteenth century the form of the ecclesiastical polity varied greatly from monarch to monarch. Vitally, however, Henry VIII appointed Thomas Cromwell to act as vice-regent in spiritual matters as early as 1535, and in this role he was given full responsibility for regulating ecclesiastical affairs. The Elizabethan settlement of 1559, in turn, authorized parliament, under royal supervision, to legislate over matters in the church.

---

[23] Philipp Melanchthon concluded seminally that the territorial prince should act as the *Patronus* of the church (1836 [1541]: 684).

[24] The classic case of this is the *Wittenberger Gutachten* of 1538, partly penned by Melanchthon, which provided for government of the church through immediate command of the territorial prince (1851 [1538]).

In different ways, in short, the Reformation brought towards a conclusion the conjoined process of political abstraction and legal positivization which had underpinned many European societies in the Middle Ages, and it created an environment in which worldly states experienced an expedited growth in the abstraction and the social centrality of their power and in which the legal foundations of their general authority and single statutory acts were defined in increasingly positive terms. Despite these common political features unifying different patterns of the Reformation, however, great care needs to be exercised in order to maintain historical accuracy in assessing the Reformation as an epochal event in the history of European state building. It is too easy to see the Reformation as a moment in which European states, in a relatively uniform manner, simply assumed full contours of statehood. It is surely not the case, as even the most learned historians have asserted, that the Reformation created a legal/political condition in which sovereign states immediately exercised complete positive jurisdictional authority.[25] In fact, in different parts of Europe the process of legal/political positivization underlying the Reformation stimulated very diverse patterns of state building, none of which immediately engendered fully evolved sovereign princely states.

In England, notably, the Tudor regime, reinforced by the Reformation, began to acquire the hallmarks of modern sovereign statehood. The formal concept of the state as an actor able to exercise a monopoly of legislative power was not widespread at this time. However, in the early 1530s Thomas Cromwell was able to describe the polity of England as an institution possessing qualities close to undivided sovereignty, and, to legitimize the break with Rome, he asserted that the state was able to pass statutes and provide justice in all matters and without any superior.[26] Through the Tudor period, the power of royal courts was substantially reinforced, and monarchical control over both the fiscal system and the means of jurisdiction was consolidated.[27] Moreover, the amount of business transacted through the state administration also expanded substantially, leading to a further concomitant growth in state authority. Of particular importance, moreover, was the fact that

---

[25] Speaking of the German states, Harold Berman argued (in my view, rather absurdly) that the Reformation marked the 'ascendancy of the prince and his high magistracy' and constituted a 'final stage in the transition … from the *Ständestaat*, rule by estates, to the *Fürstenstaat*, rule by princes' (2003: 65).

[26] On this see Lehmberg (1970: 164). Yet on the limits of sovereignty see Loades (1997: 1–4).

[27] For discussion see Hoyle (1994: 1177).

the edifice of state emerging under the Tudors was beginning clearly to assume characteristics of a public apparatus: that is, it departed from the model of semi-private governance characteristic of the Middle Ages, it organized its administrative (and especially its fiscal) mechanisms as devices to sustain its general rule across a national kingdom, and it clearly relied on reserves of general social recognition and support that were deeply rooted across different echelons of society.[28] In the Netherlands, similarly, the Reformation also brought about an accelerated consolidation of state power. This process deviated markedly from the state-building dynamics of the English Reformation. The underlying structure of the modern state in the Netherlands was not created until the Pragmatic Sanction of 1549, which transformed the seventeen provinces of the Netherlands into one administrative entity, and, even after gaining independence from Habsburg Spain, the Dutch provinces did not form an integrated central unitary order: they were, in fact, opposed to conventional notions of sovereignty. However, the Reformation and the resultant religiously motivated revolt against Spain clearly brought unprecedented autonomy to the States-General, which governed the Dutch Republic. Between 1576 and 1581, the States-General began to operate as an independent government. The Reformation thus led to the transformation of the States-General into an effective centre of sovereign republican statehood, able to exercise powers of jurisdiction formerly held by Habsburg rulers (Tracy 2008: 291).

In the German territories, as mentioned, the Reformation also significantly reinforced the territorial dominance (*Landesherrschaft*) of princely regents. In the course of the Reformation, in particular, the claim to ecclesiastical supremacy made by Evangelical princes placed intense strain on the constitution of the Holy Roman Empire, and, owing to the support of the emperor for the papal church, it finally became clear that the Habsburgs could not rule the Holy Roman Empire as a centralized dynastic state under one set of supreme institutions. By 1555, the assumption of ecclesiastical supremacy by princely estates greatly strengthened their claims to jurisdictional independence within the Empire, and the princes became the clearly ascendant force in the constitutional conflict between estates and Empire (Angermeier 1984: 317). Notably, in the German regions the Reformation reinforced the power

---

[28] See primarily Elton (1966: 4, 150). Yet it should be noted that at a fiscal level this sometimes involved reinforcing elements of feudalism. For this view see Buck (1990: 209).

of secular regents because the assumption of ecclesiastical autonomy by territorial regents consolidated the conversion of land held through feudal immunity into land held under independent jurisdiction, which meant that princes were able to declare that they governed their lands under rights of territorial sovereignty. Despite this, nonetheless, in the princely territories of the Holy Roman Empire the Reformation did not create an aggregate of political institutions even remotely approaching modern notions of statehood. Even after 1555 many political functions were not ceded by the Empire to the territories. In fact, the structural determinants of statehood often eluded territorial regents in German areas for well over a century: in many territories a complex body of interwoven feudal, territorial and imperial jurisdictions persisted long after the Reformation, and the controversy over jurisdiction and the limits of territorial power remained 'by far the most important theme' in constitutional debate in sixteenth-century German states (Willoweit 1975: 34). It was only around 1600, as exemplified by the seminal work of Andreas Knichen, that jurists began even tentatively to define German princes as possessing 'universal and superior' powers in a territory (1603 [1600]: 17). Territorial supremacy was not consolidated as a practical reality until considerably later.

The Reformation, in consequence, was not a singular state-building occurrence: its causes, immediate consequences and longer-term political results in respect of state formation were highly varied and contingent. In fact, in the German context it cannot unreservedly be argued that the Reformation led in any immediate way to a reinforcement of statehood. The Holy Roman Empire was already, albeit to a limited degree, constructed as a state before the Reformation began in 1517: this state was then dismantled in the wake of the Reformation, and it was only after 1648 that it was slowly replaced by similarly well-integrated particularistic state institutions. In one respect, however, it is possible to discern a certain overarching uniformity in the Reformation and its results. The longer-term state-building significance of the Reformation resided, namely, not in any universal increment of state integrity and density, but in the fact that it dramatically intensified the processes of *political abstraction* and *legal positivization*, which had from the outset supported the construction of statehood in Europe. In the European polities that experienced a conversion to the Evangelical faith, in consequence, the period of Reformation had one common characteristic: it led to the creation of judicial and political institutions, in which the counterbalancing of different legal sources was reduced, the influence of (sacral or customary) external law on territorial jurisdiction was diminished, and legal and political order was consolidated around positive statutes, enforced by a relatively monistic executive. The results of the Reformation, in short, might be most accurately observed, not in uniform state construction, but in the intensification of the autonomy of political power. In bringing towards conclusion the positive abstraction of political power, however, the Reformation created preconditions, varying substantially from region to region, for the formation of integral, ultimately even *sovereign*, states.

If the processes of legal and political transformation in the Reformation fell short of creating generalized models of statehood, they had the consequence that worldly political actors in those societies that experienced a Reformation were confronted with broadly analogous societal objectives, and they were faced with similar requirements in relation to the production and legitimation of political power. The Reformation had the outcome, first, that actors utilizing power were required, often in highly precarious and unprecedented settings, to formulate singular and autonomous accounts of their authority and new explanations for their inclusionary functions. In addition, the Reformation also meant that, as they eradicated external and conventional sources of law, states became largely exclusive centres of political power and jurisdiction, and they were obliged, often against extremely unstable backgrounds, independently *to produce* the power that they needed to fulfil their basic functions: that is, they witnessed an increased societal need for statutory legislation, and they were compelled to transform their institutional order to adapt to these requirements. The shared characteristic of societies shaped by the Reformation, therefore, was that – to a large degree – states began to act as positive and increasingly undivided centres of jurisdictional power, they experienced and used power as a highly contingent and normatively unsettled phenomenon, and they were obliged to generate and maintain more power (without external assistance) to respond to their increasing functions of statutory legislation and social inclusion, for which they were also compelled to provide positive and independent legal justifications. This meant that, as customary and religious sources of law were in part extirpated from the political system, states (or institutional orders close to states) needed to generate *more power* for their societies, and, in face of deep societal polarization and loss of traditional legitimacy, they were expected to explain and apply this power as a highly abstracted and autonomous resource. If the political construction of later medieval European societies had reflected an increasing abstraction and autonomy of political power, therefore, it was in the Reformation that this process gained its conclusive expression. Subsequently, it was as a response to the need for the positive production of political power that European societies after the Reformation developed (with substantial temporal variations) their distinctive patterns of sovereignty and statehood.

Positive law and the idea of the constitution

It is of the greatest importance in this process of legal positivization and consolidated political abstraction during the period of the Reformation that the reliance of emergent states on an internal constitutional fabric also increased. Naturally, it was not the case that all post-Reformation states evolved according to an identical constitutional pattern. In the longer wake of the Reformation, different states responded to the problems arising from their growing administrative density in different ways. However, the simultaneous positivization and abstractive expansion of statehood at this time meant that states began to require more ramified inner structural and inclusionary dimensions. In fact, as an event that transposed the legal basis of states onto positive premises, the Reformation generated a multi-levelled set of requirements for legitimacy and inclusion in nascent European states, and at each level it tended to promote the formation of a constitutional political order within Evangelical societies. Constitutional formation, in other words, was a mechanism that allowed states in post-Reformation societies both to adapt to and to organize the increased mass of abstracted and precarious power that they contained, and to adjust to the problems of self-explanation and inclusion arising from the rapid positivization of their power's foundations. In most Evangelical states, consequently, the Reformation had the immediate result that it reinforced the constitutional power of parliaments and estates, and in most Evangelical societies parliaments and estates were utilized to recruit support for the Reformation and to legitimize decisions of regents in questions concerning rapid religious reform and intense political upheaval. In fact, parliaments, reflecting broad constitutional presuppositions, often filled a justificatory void in states undergoing dramatic religious transformation, and they enabled states to assume legitimacy while conducting highly disruptive and legally unprecedented executive processes.

In Sweden, for example, although Gustav Vasa invoked the plenitude of royal power to vindicate the Lutheran conversion of the state, representative estates, present in the *riksdag*, played an important role in paving the way for the Reformation and for ensuring its approval (Roberts 1968a: 58, 139, 219). After this time, Sweden developed a powerful constitutional system, in which throughout the sixteenth century parliament acted as a vital instrument in cementing monarchical authority. Similarly, in Denmark in 1536 Christian III called a meeting of the Rigsdag to endorse the Reformation. In Poland, the early move towards Reformation gained extensive support among the noble estates, the *szlachta*, and the Execution Movement, often sympathetic to the Reformation, urged the creation of a state based in a reformed church, comprising a reinforcement of the bicameral system and stronger laws to protect the interests of the gentry. In the lands to the east of the Holy Roman Empire, generally, the noble estates were often at the forefront of the Reformation and the religious conflict gave further vitality to the constitutional cause of the estates (Schramm 1965: 5–6, 233; Bosl 1974: 141; Eberhard 1981: 28).

In the English Reformation, although the Henrician regime saw an expanded use of royal prerogative, a similar pattern was observable. Through the Reformation, the principle of rule by king-in-parliament became a key legitimating device of royal government. The ability of the king to refer to parliament as a source of support and approval in legislation helped to elevate the king above more consuetudinal legal obligations, and it instilled a heightened flexibility in the legislative system. In particular, this formula enabled the king to suspend constitutions made by the clergy, and to incorporate the clergy and the canons under the jurisdiction of secular statutes. At the beginning of the English Reformation, the Reformation parliament, convened in 1529, was held for almost seven years, and it served as a vital instrument in the reforms. Subsequently, Henry VIII obtained parliamentary support to enforce statutes removing papal jurisdiction in England: the 1533 Act in Restraint of Appeals, the 1534 Dispensations Act, the 1534 Act of Submission of the Clergy and the 1539 Act of Proclamations were among the most important examples of this use of statutes. Throughout the entire period of the Reformation, in fact, English monarchs were able to employ parliamentary mechanisms to ratify acts and statutes that greatly augmented their judicial power and consolidated their authority in both state and church.[29] Notably, both the Henrician and the Elizabethan Acts of Supremacy were authorized as acts of

---

[29] The Treason Act of 1534 is a good example of this (Elton 1972: 284).

parliament. The constitutional juncture between king and parliament thus played a pivotal role in forming the early modern English state during the Reformation, and the legitimating constitutional presumptions attached to parliamentary consultation underpinned the emergence of the state as a sovereign centre of political power, capable of separating its acts from both external religious laws and customary norms. Indeed, the ability of the state to legislate in positive statutory fashion during this period of positive legal proliferation depended on its recognition of a parliamentary constitution as the *form of government*.[30] By the 1560s, anticipating the conceptual framework of the mid-Stuart period, Thomas Smith declared that parliament, including the monarch, was the 'most high and absolute power' in England, and that no 'Bill of Law' was valid without prior approval in parliament (1621 [1583]: 34, 37). Smith developed this theory to define the state as a unitary inclusionary body, and he even claimed that parliament was a place where every Englishman 'of what preheminence, state, dignitie or qualitie' was present 'either in person, or by procuration and Atturney'. Similarly, John Hooker defined parliament as 'the heist, cheefest, and greatest Court', which, by virtue of the fact that it 'consisteth of the whole Realme', 'may jointly and with one consent and agreement: establish and enact any Laws, orders, & Statutes for the common welth' (1572: 31). Underlying this strengthening of the English parliament, notably, was a deep and far-reaching constitutional shift. The formation of a monarchical/parliamentary order in the sixteenth century gradually created a new and highly inclusive internal constitution for the state: the idea of the state centred, under public law, on parliamentary representation replaced the medieval convention of government by a mixture of higher laws and customary privileges, and it substantially augmented both the central position of parliament in the state and the mass of positive power which the state could dispense through society.

The Reformation in the German states necessarily gave rise to a twofold process of constitutional construction. The first result of the Reformation in the German parts of the Holy Roman Empire was that it consolidated both the overarching constitutional relation between the Empire and the growing territorial and princely states and the balanced internal relation between the princes and the regional estates

---

[30] For excellent analysis see Dunham (1964: 26). For an outstanding discussion of this and the constitutional controversies attached to it (i.e. the erroneous grounds for the denunciation of Tudor government as despotic), see Heinze (1976: 85).

(*Landstände*). Naturally, the acrimony between the Empire and the imperial princes and princely estates (many, although not all, of whom converted to Lutheranism or Calvinism) was greatly exacerbated by the Reformation. The already fraught constitutional link between princes and the imperial party was further burdened by religious controversy, and after 1530 negotiations between Empire and estates at imperial Diets often degenerated into military conflict, which made the relative constitutional position of Empire and estates uncertain. By about 1600, however, the position of the imperial estates had been structurally reinforced: by the first decades of the seventeenth century it was widely acknowledged that the Empire was internally formed as a constitutional order, and that the exercise of imperial power was constrained by legal norms reflecting princely interests. During this time, princes claimed the right to act as participatory members in the legal form of the Empire, and this gave rise to an influential body of imperial constitutional law (*Reichsstaatsrecht*). The crucial constitutional argument in this body of law was that a constitutional distinction had to be made between the sovereignty of the Empire and the sovereignty of the emperor: that is, the majesty of the Empire was a *real* majesty whereas that of the emperor was a *personal* majesty, and the personal majesty of the emperor was merely derived from, and secondary to, the *real* majesty of the Empire. The most important principle arising in this context was the claim that the Empire should be seen, not as the patrimony of an imperial dynasty, but as an organic political entity, of which Electors, other imperial estates, and the emperor himself were constitutive elements.[31] These ideas articulated a definite constitutional structure for the Empire, and they centred on the idea that the Empire possessed an organic personality that transcended, and could be normatively isolated from, all its factual composite parts. At an express level, of course, the formation of a body of public law in the Empire was a result of positional and confessional conflicts between different constitutional actors in the Empire. At a more functional level, however, it resulted directly from the facts that the legal foundations of the Empire had become precarious through the Reformation, the Empire had lost its support in customary legal bonds, and it was obliged

---

[31] Reinhard König gave seminal expression to this doctrine (1614: 646). He asserted that it was only as a representative of the real (or constitutional) majesty of the Empire that the emperor was entitled personally to make laws, so that the emperor, as a person, was always subject to the constitutional laws of the Empire: the emperor, in fact, was merely an organ of state.

to extract for itself a wider abstract account of its source and functions in order to produce and support the volume of power that it now required. The increasingly articulated or distinctively *public-legal* constitution of the Empire thus immediately reflected the rise in its abstraction and autonomy.

In addition to this constitutional conception of the Empire, however, in most German territories that converted to Evangelical doctrine regional assemblies also played a substantial role in sustaining territorial power during and after the Reformation. As in other societies, German princes or territorial regents habitually called on their local estates to support the introduction of reformist policies, and, to secure their adherence, they were compelled to widen their procedures for consultation and inclusion. The basic institutions of constitutional rule were solidified in many German territories during the Reformation, and in certain cases the estates showed signs of assuming permanent and integrated status within the formal order of territorial states. For example, in Hesse, although the estates were not consulted prior to the Reformation, regional estates obtained prominent political functions through the Reformation period: this was due in part to the fact that the spiritual estate was excluded from political negotiations after 1527. From the 1530s, then, the noble territorial estate effectively acted as an internal component of government. In Saxony, the estates participated extensively in the process of reform, and important acts of ecclesiastical policy were introduced at the instigation of the estates. In Brandenburg, the estates obtained a particularly powerful position through the sixteenth century, and by the middle of this century they possessed almost exclusive control of the fiscal apparatus of the emerging territorial state.[32] The construction of the German territorial state as a positive integrated polity was thus reliant on the fact that, in different settings, territorial rulers were able to draw on multiple forms of structural sustenance throughout society. In the initial wake of the Reformation, the constitutional balance between imperial Diets, territorial Diets and local Diets was often deeply reinforced, and the century following the Reformation saw estates assume a general position of unprecedented power (Oestreich 1969: 282; Neuhaus 1982: 33–4).

The increase in the power of constitutional institutions during the sixteenth century was most notable and most dramatic in the

---

[32] On these separate points see Siebeck (1914: 27); Reden (1974: 163); Fürbringer (1985: 44–9).

Netherlands, and the Dutch Reformation created an exceptionally strong constitutional system. Indeed, whereas in other societies the estates merely assisted regents in the Reformation, in the Netherlands the religious changes culminated in the Dutch revolt, in which, as discussed, the estates deposed the ruling dynasty and initiated a lengthy experiment in republican governance. In the last decades of Habsburg rule in the Netherlands, the regional estates had already become very powerful institutions: one reason why Habsburg rule came to an end was that before the revolt the estates refused to obey Habsburg directives regarding taxation, and they were able independently to raise taxes and to dictate terms of supply for the Habsburg government. Through the Reformation, subsequently, the religious and political interests of the estates in the Netherlands began to converge, and religious dissidence coincided with the independent use of political power by the estates. The lower nobility widely converted to Calvinism, and its members used their strong hold over fiscal institutions to resist the reimposition of Roman Catholicism, to revolt against the Habsburgs and progressively to establish a new governing body. Through the revolt, the estates were able, relatively simply, to use their power to create a separate fiscal system, which enabled them successfully to oppose the Empire militarily (Tracy 1990: 183, 211; Koenigsberger 1994: 149; Fritschy 2003: 63). The broad-based estate-led constitution that was established in the Netherlands during the Reformation era ultimately proved to be a highly effective administrative instrument, and it played a vital role in maintaining support for the Dutch state through the course of its separation from Habsburg rule (Hart 1993: 173).

Across these very diverse settings, to conclude, the Reformation at once stimulated and concentrated a number of transformative processes in European states, each of which tended, normally, to force states both to assume a tightened unitary form and to intensify their constitutional structure. During this time, as discussed, states typically renounced highly external sources of legal validity and legitimacy, they became more conclusively reliant on positive statutory powers of legislation, and, habitually in extremely contingent environments, they were required to supply internally autonomous accounts of their power to support acts of legislation. During this time, in consequence, societies were marked by a rapidly growing abstraction of statehood and state power: many societies came to converge around actors able positively to use power to regulate societal conflicts, they experienced a growing need for institutions able to create and consume power in autonomous statutory fashion, and all volatile societal conflicts were progressively directed immediately to the state. As a result of these processes, many societies evolved a heightened need for deep-rooted mechanisms to support and elucidate their use of power, and their use of power as a positive resource depended on their production of *inclusionary power*: they required instruments of societal integration and constitutional co-option in order both positively to generate and reinforce and effectively to apply their power. In fact, the thickening of the constitutional structure of European states in the wake of the Reformation allowed states both to respond to the growing societal need for positive legislation and cohesively to consolidate their power in unpredictable and highly contingent societal contexts. In the first instance, the recurrent gathering of parliaments in different post-Reformation European states had the practical purpose that, both factually and symbolically, it gave a broad foundation to the state, and it permitted the state to articulate new forms of legitimacy and inclusivity in face of new uncertain requirements for statutory legislation. In addition, however, the state's growing constitutional integrity had the outcome of giving a corporate or organic density to the emergent structure of the state, and it infused the state with a personality that allowed it, even in absence of conventional justification, positively to underwrite its power and more coherently to support its acts across the diverse functions and the geographical and temporal distances that it now incorporated. The increasing role of parliaments and estates at this time thus acted to resolve a positive/definitional problem for the state, and the expansion of a representative constitution, or a body of public law inside the state, allowed states effectively to organize the abstraction of their power by reflecting their power as consensually founded, and, to an increasing degree, to use their power as a constant, positive and evenly inclusionary resource. Both practically and conceptually, in sum, the rise of constitutional principles after the Reformation was a response to the increase in the positive contingency and the uncertainty of the political power which states had at their disposal, and constitutional mechanisms provided an inner apparatus in which states could control and gather support for their newly abstracted reserves of power. The constitution made it possible for states to absorb their growing positivity, and to mobilize reserves of power in settings in which power had become simultaneously condensed and uncertainly authorized. After the Reformation, in consequence, a constitutional model began to emerge in which the state assumed all political power in society for itself, in which external – either religious or local – power structures were increasingly assimilated into the positive form of the state, and in which states utilized consensual techniques of public law to produce and to account for growing reserves of positive political power that they contained.

Constitutions and fundamental law

These constitutional developments in sixteenth-century Europe were also flanked by the emergence of a doctrinal corpus of ideas which began to explain the positive unity and autonomy of states in consistent fashion and proposed fixed categories to account for the power of states. In the first instance, the aftermath of the Reformation in many societies saw the formulation of a strong doctrine of *fundamental laws* (*leges fundamentales*), which, often sustained by ideas of natural law, was used to express the form and content of state power. This theory, based in the claim that states were defined and constrained by a distinct and stable body of inviolable legal norms, clearly had its origins in the judicial ideals of the Middle Ages, and it reflected the medieval belief that regal power was curtailed by customary rights and privileges. However, in many ways this doctrine differed notably from the legal maxims of the later Middle Ages, and it mirrored the rise of the state in its distinctive modern positive form: as such, it marked the formation of a distinct and specialized corpus of *public law*. In particular, this doctrine tended to renounce the principle that fundamental laws were derived from societal norms or conventions existing outside the state and placing external limits on state power. Instead, albeit tentatively and without clear or linear conceptual certainty, it began to propose a definition of statehood that accepted the growing abstraction and relative monistic autonomy of the state, and that insisted on the state's fundamental-legal or constitutional form in order, specifically, to preserve the state's internal abstraction and to prevent the re-submergence of statehood into its personal or societal origins. The longer aftermath of the Reformation, thus, witnessed the development of a normative constitutional doctrine that clearly reflected the growth and centrality of the state and began to fashion a model of legitimacy to cement the power of states constructed as autonomous orders. Indeed, just as the most rudimentary elements of public law had emerged after the investiture contests as concepts that intensified the abstraction of political power, post-Reformation doctrines of fundamental law began to offer concepts of legitimacy that enabled states to retain inner consistency and autonomy and more reliably to produce and utilize power as a positive societal facility.

The rise of the doctrine of fundamental laws was evident in most societies that experienced a Reformation. As discussed, in the Holy Roman Empire the idea that the imperial state was at once formed and constrained by acceded legal principles was prevalent by the first half of the sixteenth century, and electoral compacts possessed a semi-contractual status as early as 1519. However, the later sixteenth century witnessed a deep reinforcement of the doctrine of fundamental laws: as mentioned, in the years after 1600 the imperial state was commonly defined by a body of organic laws that clearly differentiated it from any factual persons that temporarily utilized its power. In this respect, notably, between 1519 and approximately 1600 the principle of fundamental laws was transformed from a doctrine of practical external compacts into a theory of the state's internal organic personality. By the early seventeenth century, this doctrine found accentuated expression in the works of Althusius, who argued that any legitimate polity must be structured by pre-existing invariable laws, and it must legislate in accordance with absolute principles of natural right. Althusius argued that 'universal law' was 'the form and substantial essence of sovereignty [*majestatis*]', and he described all members of the polity, including the prince, as bound by such universal law (1614 [1603]: 174, 177). This doctrine, although clearly insisting that laws placed strict checks on state power, changed the substance of earlier constitutional theory as it observed fundamental laws as *internal* components of the state and began to imagine the state as a legitimately autonomous actor, capable of utilizing an abstracted account of its own legal structure to produce and reflect internal justifications for its power. The emergent doctrine of quasi-natural fundamental laws thus described a transformation in the inner structure of the state, and it allowed the state to construct a highly contingent and generalized analysis of its power, which, in relative indifference to external agents, it could propose to accompany all acts in which it expended its power. This subtle change in the construct of fundamental laws in the sixteenth century projected a positively consistent and self-contained model of statehood, and it acted, not legally to circumscribe, but in fact to produce a conceptual design to maximize the amount of power contained within the state and dramatically to facilitate societal expenditure of political power.

In England, the idea that the state was bound by a set of fundamental laws and inviolable institutional arrangements was also well established by the later sixteenth century. In its original implications in the English setting, this theory pulled in two distinct, yet also residually overlapping, directions. On one hand, this doctrine accentuated the external common-law basis of the English constitution. In the last years of the sixteenth century, for example, Richard Hooker defined the best state as a state 'tied unto the soundest perfectest and most indifferent rule; which is the rule of law' (1989 [1593–1662]: 146). The view that the state was bound to 'fundamentall lawes' was then formulated in *The Elements of the Common Lawes of England* by (the eminent monarchist) Francis Bacon.[33] Underpinning these declarations was the principle that the state obtained legitimacy by accepting the external norm of the rule of law, and – by extension – that the law courts were privileged custodians of the constitution. The first years of the Stuart era, subsequently, gave cause for an accentuation of this debate. By 1610, although stating his respect for the common law, James I began simultaneously to resist informal-customary legal constraints on his power and to increase expectations of monetary supply from parliament. James I in fact ultimately insisted on the *royal prerogative* as an untouchable element of the constitution, and he defined the office of judges as to 'interprete the law of the King, whereto themselves are also subject' (1994 [1616]: 206). This led to a period of prolonged controversy in which parliament and courts assumed growing constitutional prominence, and the common-law principles of non-derogable rights and judicial constraint were invoked with greater vehemence to restrict royal legislation and jurisdiction. For example, in *Dr Bonham's Case* (1610), Edward Coke, dismissed by James I in 1616, famously concluded that courts of common law were authorized both to contradict royal prerogative and even, under some circumstances, to 'control acts of parliament' (Plucknett 1926: 34). In this regard, Coke's ideas looked back to earlier conventionalist theories of statehood, insisting on external customary legal limits on all acts of socially abstracted power. On the other hand, however, a doctrine of fundamental laws also emerged, in which lawyers (at times reticently) construed parliament itself, and legislation endorsed by parliament, as expressions of a fundamental law.[34] In parliamentary debates over supply in 1610, for instance, it was strenuously argued that 'parte of the law of England is that the king cannot impose without assent of parliament' (Gardiner 1862: 58–9), and the principle was asserted that parliamentary

---

[33] See the Epistle Dedicatory in Bacon (1639 [1597]).

[34] On the shaky foundations of the 'liaison between the Bench and parliament', see Waite (1959: 147).

debate and approval of taxes were integrally aspects of an 'ancient, general and fundamental right' under the English constitution (Tanner 1952: 246). Indeed, Coke himself repeatedly cited acts of parliament in petitioning against royal rulings, and he recurrently defined parliament as the primary institution and guarantor of the common law (Gough 1955: 64). At one point, notably, Coke argued that the 'weighty matters' of the realm 'ought to be determined, adjudged, and discussed by the course of parliament': they ought not to be judged by judges in courts of civil law or common law. He concluded that 'judges ought not to give any opinion of a matter in parliament, because it is not to be decided by the common law' (1797 [1628–44]: 14). For these reasons, the doctrine of fundamental laws in England contained rather conflicting dimensions, and it served simultaneously to constrain and to reinforce the positive power of the state. At one level, this doctrine insisted that statutory legislation was externally bound by the courts of law. Yet, at a different level, it accounted for parliamentary statutes themselves as internally legitimized by fundamental laws. In view of the nuanced equilibrium between consuetudinal constraint and statutory autonomy which it promoted, however, the doctrine of fundamental law in the English setting gradually expressed a model of statehood in which the statutory authority of parliament was tied a priori to an overarching public-legal order, and the exercise of statutory power internally presupposed the recognition of constitutional limits on the use of its legislative force. In this case again, therefore, the expansion of constitutional doctrine also described and underscored the growing autonomy of the state, and it traced a public construction of political power to facilitate the production and use of power in increasingly autonomous form.

It was during the religious wars in France, however, that theories of unshakable fundamental laws received their sharpest expression (Höpfl 1986; Schilling 2005: 375). Sixteenth-century French politics was generally marked by a substantial body of constitutional thought, and at this time it was accepted as a non-derogable principle that France was governed in accordance with customary laws, and that conventions of public representation needed to be preserved.[35] For example, Jean du Tillet argued that, although monarchs stood above legal conventions and were entitled to introduce statutes and change laws, they were obliged to seek wise council and respect the customs of the people (1579: 96). Innocent Gentillet argued that the kingdom of France was founded in

---

[35] For a typology of these arguments see Jouanna (1989: 167, 325–6).

'good laws', governed by kings advised by royal councils and benefiting from the 'good and virtuous advice' of the Estates-General and provincial assemblies (1609 [1576]: 82, 88). Pierre Rebuffi, although accepting the need for strong royal power, also argued that princes wishing to pass laws required both the approval of God and the consent of the people (1581 [1550]: 18). Bernard de Girard du Haillan developed the most institutionally refined version of these claims, and he asserted that all princes were bound to principles of justice enunciated in courts of law, and that legitimacy in the exercise of power presupposes communication between the monarchy and the people through estates (1572 [1570]: 5, 27–8). Indeed, Henri II was instructed in 1549 that the 'true and solid glory of the King' was evident in his willingness 'to submit his highness and majesty to justice, to rightness, and to the observation of his ordinances' (Zeller 1948: 80). These ideas clearly fostered a limited constitution in sixteenth-century France: through the era of religious transformation it was progressively accepted that the monarchy was constituted around six fundamental laws, acknowledged as 'unchangeable and inviolable' (Doucet 1948: 66), which included laws regarding royal succession, regency, the inviolability of Catholicism as the state religion, and the inalienability of the royal domain. These principles acted to tie the monarchy to a minimal constitutional order, and to abstract a minimally independent public personality for the state (Mousnier 1974: I, 505).

It was among the most adversarial parties in the French wars of religion, however, that the strictest and most compelling principles of fundamental law were formulated.[36] Among the Calvinist theorists of this time, Théodore de Bèze argued that the foundations of a polity must reflect divine law: no people, he claimed, was allowed to form a state in contravention of God's law, and the power of each state had to be constitutionally limited, so that lower magistrates could remove sovereigns from office if they tended towards tyranny (1970 [1574]: 44–5). In this, de Bèze employed principles of neo-natural law in order to construct a fully constitutional model of state legitimacy, which made the power of the state at once absolutely contingent on law and absolutely distinct from those persons who utilized its power. The radical constitutional ideal of the state typical of French Calvinism culminated in the notorious anonymous pamphlet, *Vindiciae contra Tyrannos* (1579). This pamphlet in fact gave earliest expression to the modern concept of

---

[36] In agreement, see Schilling (2005: 375).

legitimacy, and it defined the legitimate state as a state acting in compliance with legal norms external to the monarch. It concluded that 'legitimate princes' are those who 'receive laws from the people' and are bound by a double legal obligation, both to the people and to God (Celta 1580 [1579]: 105, 136). Such abstracted views were not the exclusive domain of the Huguenots. On the contrary, the theorists of the Catholic League also expounded a doctrine of fundamental laws to define state legitimacy. The *ligueurs* argued that the monarchy was accountable to absolute and quasi-theocratic principles of natural right, that, in consequence, the monarchical state was subject to inviolable laws, and that monarchs were to be appointed by the people and were commissioned by the people to preserve the true faith.[37] Both extreme camps in the era of religious war, thus, endorsed a universal model of state legitimacy, in which religious and consensual rights of subjects articulated a clear distinction between the legal order of the state and persons momentarily using its power, and it fully authorized the reclaiming of state power from rulers in breach of the constitution.

Both at a practical and at a conceptual level, consequently, the formation of European states as increasingly unitary and increasingly positive actors after the Reformation produced a deep need for a conceptually articulated constitutional apparatus in the state. This was reflected in the first consolidation of modern public law. European societies, divided by bitter religious controversy and subject to a dramatic positivization of their political foundations, sought uniformly to produce patterns of legal consistency and popular inclusion in order to express and preserve their political power. In particular, the idea of the state as constitutionally formed by abstract fundamental laws began to emerge as a conceptual structure through which states could observe the sources of their power as distinct from local persons or agreements and as *internal* to their own structure. In distinction from their pre-Reformation prototypes, this enabled states, however precariously, to acquire legitimacy for their political order in a highly volatile social and intellectual landscape, to produce and utilize their power in increasing autonomy, and to adapt their political power to new degrees of positivity and inclusion. At face value, self-evidently, debates about fundamental law often had little connection with the positivization of power or the acceptance of the contingency of state authority. On the contrary, in the

---

[37] For example, see Cromé (1977 [1593]: 54, 78). On the constitutional tendencies of the *ligue*, see Constant (1996: 169, 243).

setting of the French wars of religion much constitutional doctrine aimed at the establishment of a quasi-theocratic magistrature, and it was expressly shaped by a rejection of positive constructions of the law. For this reason, it has been widely observed that subsequent processes of state formation, particularly in France, reflected an endeavour to release the functional structure of the political system from religious controversy and to stabilize a de-theocratized political apparatus above the violent antagonisms prevalent throughout society.[38] This argument has clear factual validity, and it is not contested here. In fact, before and during the French wars of religion more positivist theories of state also began to gain momentum. Certain theoretical factions, looking forward to the simpler statism of the seventeenth century, began to promote an account of the state as indifferent to religion and determined solely by political laws (L'Hospital 1824 [1560]: 394–5). However, beneath the surface of the theocratically charged constitutional doctrines of the protagonists of the wars of religion, the idea of fundamental laws also served, in slow reflexive fashion, to outline the contours of a concept of statehood in which the law expressed a clear distinction between the state and the persons using its power, and in which – accordingly – the state, even where defined in theocratic categories, was able to propose a positive and internalistic source for its authority, which substantially augmented the power stored in the state. The translation of dispute over positive law into debate over divine law enabled states to detach their legal sources from specific persons, customs or privileges and to extract from their own functions a highly coherent definition of their power. This, in fact, formed a definition of their power, strictly, under *public law*: it was a definition which states could separate from external laws and from their own momentary operations, and which they could stabilize in their own apparatus as a static legal self-construction. States were then able to remove this self-construction from factually existing social conditions and internalize it as a clearly articulated and internally perennial justification for their functions. This, in turn, helped states to satisfy the requirements for inclusivity and legitimacy arising from their newly acquired positive fullness of power, and it enabled them to generate an autonomous description of themselves to differentiate, unify, simplify and authorize their power in their diverse operations.

---

[38] This point is a commonplace in historical literature. For some influential versions of this see Oestreich (1969: 190); Koselleck (1973 [1959]: 11); Saunders (1997: 89).

The extreme polarization of legal debate in the religious controversies after the Reformation might, in consequence, be viewed as a moment in which European societies subjected the positive form of the law to most intense dispute and contest, but in which, even counter-intentionally, they extracted a model of statehood capable of producing and using political power in heightened positive and autonomous fashion. The constitutional idea of the state as containing and constrained by a corpus of natural or fundamental laws, above all, began to allow states to generate power at a growing level of inclusivity and iterability and more easily to satisfy the requirement for political decisions (statutes) characteristic of early modern societies. The constitutional principles of fundamental law and natural law became devices through which states sought to imagine their own unity and inclusivity and in which they devised a unitary internal construction, distinct from the semi-private dualistic constitutions of medieval society, to support and connect the varied acts of power's application. Public law progressively emerged as a construction of the state which transformed the private constraints on state power of medieval constitutionalism into an internal autonomous description of the state, and as such it greatly augmented the volume of power that the state contained. As in earlier periods of state formation, in other words, in the Reformation and its aftermath, it was the evolving concepts of constitutionalism that made the positive production of power, and resultant forms of statehood, possible, and the growing abstraction of political power presupposed and relied on a constitutional apparatus for its effective usage and production. Each incremental step towards positive statehood was mirrored by an increase in the integrity and abstraction of constitutional order. The formation of the constitution as a body of public law, internal to the state, marked a decisive transition from the weak statehood of medieval society to the stronger statehood of early modernity.

Early modern constitutional conflicts

Despite the impetus towards political concentration and constitutional formation after the Reformation, in early modern Europe many states proved unable to condense their functions into a durable unitary constitutional structure. In many instances, states were deeply strained by the degree to which they became objects of general politicization, and they fragmented, both practically and conceptually, under the pressures caused by their need to produce power to incorporate a large volume of social exchanges, many of which they were forced to hold at a high level of internal intensity. In consequence, few early modern European states reached a conclusive constitutional settlement that served permanently to defuse their inner antagonisms, to unify their political functions or to offer a final set of public principles to accompany and positively to authorize their laws. In particular, most early modern states struggled unitarily to integrate the diverse social interests which they had previously reflected in a dualistic constitutional structure, they encountered difficulties in applying power as an even, unified and public resource throughout society, and they were often brought to crisis point by debilitating conflicts between centralistic and dualistic constitutional forces in society. These conflicts normally became evident in questions concerning legal status and monetary supply, and throughout the course of their development in the early modern era European states tended prominently to externalize their structural weaknesses and lack of public cohesion in relation to these questions.

The intensification of statehood during the Reformation era, in short, did not lead to a conclusive process of state building, and some unitary patterns of state construction were less effective than others. Dualistic contests between political actors and private centres of interest remained dominant political determinants throughout early modern European history, and most societies struggled to distil political power in a positively autonomous or reliably integrated apparatus. Indeed, the defining political problem in most European societies of the post-Reformation period centred enduringly (as before the Reformation) around the constitutional instruments which they employed for extracting power from private/personal privilege and for solidifying their foundations in relation to centrifugal social groups (especially the nobility). Post-Reformation states, therefore, can be broadly categorized in terms of the constitutional mechanisms which they deployed for maintaining political power at an adequate level of abstracted autonomy. A comparative analysis of different states indicates that some constitutional designs were more or less effective than others in preserving political power at a level of usably differentiated abstraction and in enabling states to utilize political power as a positively constructed object.

The constitution of absolutism

Some states in early modern Europe reacted to the increasing societal requirement for abstracted political order by seeking to suppress, in part by coercive means, the dualistic/consensual apparatus of government that had emerged in the Middle Ages. Initially, this was most pronounced in societies that did not experience a Reformation, and whose states were not required to expand their inclusionary processes to legitimize religious transformation. Indeed, some states developed strategies for the unitary concentration of power that, to some degree, enabled them to circumvent or weaken established constitutional procedures of delegatory consultation in respect of legal and fiscal disputes. It is for this reason that some states in early modern Europe are habitually seen as embodying a system of governmental 'absolutism'.

Spain

One early example of a state based in a selective suppression of medieval constitutional organs was Spain, where the establishment of the Catholic monarchy after 1469 and the subsequent assumption of power by the Habsburgs after 1516 created a state with features later typical of 'absolutism'. That is to say, a state began to emerge in Spain in which leading actors cemented their power by centralizing administrative structures, suppressing seigneurial privileges and attempting to secure increased direct monarchical control of the judicial and fiscal organs.[39] In particular, this state (albeit to a debatable extent) curtailed the representative capacities of the Cortes, and the monarchical executive was able, to some degree, to stabilize its power above local centres of noble deputation and authority in society. The foundations for this system were set as early as 1348, when the Ordenamiento de Alcalá confirmed the jurisdictional supremacy of the monarchy in Castile.[40] Subsequently, the position of the Cortes came under further attack, and by the sixteenth century the number of representatives was reduced and the legislative capacities of the Cortes were limited to rights of voting over taxation and presenting grievances. Throughout this period, it was commonly acknowledged (in principle, at least) that the monarchy possessed a fullness of power, and, both in Castile and later in Aragon, the constitutional power of the nobility was diminished. This was spelled out by Bernabé Moreno de Vargas, in whose *Discourses on Spanish Nobility* noble rights were seen as derived from the monarch and kings exercised powers as *monarcas*

---

[39] For succinct analysis see de Dios (1985).

[40] This should not be taken too literally, as it preceded the realm of Enrique II, who was profligate in ceding jurisdiction over land and cities (Nader 1990: 77).

absolutas (1622: fol. 7). After 1664, finally, the Cortes of Castile was reduced to an organ possessing mainly ceremonial status.

The weakening of the Cortes in Castile was not a linear or conclusive process, and well into the early modern era the Castilian Cortes continued to play a role in deliberating on decisions regarding key matters of state – that is, war, peace and tax. Indeed, it is well documented that the Cortes remained intermittently influential until the later seventeenth century, and that the strengthening of central monarchical power by no means incapacitated the Cortes.[41] It is now widely accepted that, owing to the parlous finances of the monarchy, the Castilian Cortes managed to claw back some power in the later sixteenth and earlier seventeenth century (Jago 1981: 310; Elliott 1986: 96; Thompson 1994: 190), and it has even been claimed that the Cortes retained a 'formidable position' in Castilian government (Thompson 1990: 81). Long parliamentary sessions were normally held precisely in periods of most sustained monarchical authority; the monarchy was discernibly reinforced in periods of heightened reliance on the Cortes. In Aragon, moreover, where noble powers were more solidly preserved, the Cortes retained greater influence than in Castile: the Aragonese Cortes, consisting of permanent deputations since the early fifteenth century, was integral to the legislative process and its competences were clearly formalized in an official protocol of the 1580s, and by the late sixteenth century a body of constitutional law existed defining the Cortes as an organ representing the entire nation.[42] In fact, in both Castile – and, to a substantially greater degree – in Aragon, at the inception of the early modern era, period constitutional arrangements settled around a pattern of government by compactual constitutional rule: *pactismo*. *Pactismo* described a constitutional regime in which the monarchy obtained licence to legislate by acknowledging in contractual fashion certain private legal and judicial privileges existing in society, in which the passing of particular laws was tied to clear preconditions and redress of particular grievances, and in which delegates of privately privileged groups granted taxes to the monarchy in return for singular acts of redress and for the preservation of particular customary rights (Torres 1989: 122).

---

[41] This view is especially associated with the work of Charles Jago (1981; 1985). Notably, though, it is also documented that during the reign of Philip IV the Cortes were in session for thirty of forty-four years (Stradling 1988: 134).

[42] See de Blancas (1641: 196).

Despite this, nonetheless, it remains arguable that early modern Spain was marked, however variably, by monarchical attempts to undermine the Cortes, and the Cortes was widely perceived as a bastion of noble privilege against the monarchy. This was manifest in the ultimate suspension of the Cortes. It was also manifest in the fact that successive monarchs sought to circumvent the Cortes, either by negotiating with other bodies for supply or by selling charters to corporate actors, usually to towns (Nader 1990: 158). Indeed, a tendency towards the weakening of representative power might also – more arguably – be identified in the system of *pactismo* itself, which appeared, superficially, to support the position of the Cortes. Owing to the model of *pactismo*, the representative functions of the Cortes was at times restricted to the brokering of particular compacts and specific agreements. The establishment of private pacts as the basis of monarchical rule meant that the convoking of assemblies and the recognition of general laws did not, even within a limited political society, involve a process of fully general inclusion or representation: assemblies acted primarily to provide particular legal – or even *civil-legal* – protection for private arrangements and legal privileges (Torres 1989: 126; González Antón 1989: 220). Indeed, it is arguable that *pactismo* privatized the monarchy as a whole, and thus eroded the public integrative structure of the state in its widest dimensions. Under such conditions, the fully representative qualities of the Cortes were diminished, and it acted primarily as a particularistic bargaining agent and source of judicial arbitration. To be sure, even when the meetings of the Cortes became sporadic and less formal, it retained a position within the constitutional order of the state. However, *pactismo* might be seen as a constitutional order that limited the general representative functions of parliamentary organs, and in fact implicitly re-privatized and weakened their abstracted and inclusionary force.[43]

At one level, in consequence, the model of government in early modern Spain acted as a response to the growing requirement in society for condensed statehood, and during the rise of the Spanish Empire it manifestly established a political apparatus capable of high levels of military mobilization. Indeed, this political system can easily be seen as a distinctive type of constitutional rule, which stabilized the monarchy in its institutional form and used selective means of societal

---

[43] Notably, *pactismo* was despised by the 'popular mass' (Maravall 1972: 290). On the particularism implicit in *pactismo* see further González Antón (1989: 220).

interpenetration to generate relatively reliable sources of income for the monarchy. However, the constitutional arrangements supporting the Spanish state had a number of consequences that also weakened unitary state construction, and in many respects they augmented the power of seigneurial actors that had traditionally used their judicial privileges to oppose the elaboration of a strongly abstracted central state. Indeed, although often characterized as following an 'absolutistic' pattern of state building, Spain (albeit with marked distinctions between Castile and Aragon) was the only major European state, which, having transformed itself from a late-feudal aggregate of privatistic interests into an early modern public order, began intermittently, in the sixteenth century, to relapse into the diffusely external and privatistic constitutional structure of the feudal era. It is widely observed that in Spain the ancient immunities granting seigneurial rights were pervasively reasserted in the early modern era. Indeed, by the seventeenth century the monarchical state had been restructured so that it acted in essence as a stratum of directive power above the private and patrimonial competences of the nobility and the separate administrative jurisdictions of the cities, and this period saw a widespread fragmentation of royal power. Through the later seventeenth century, thus, Spanish society was marked by extremely low levels of social integration and legal order (Thompson 1990: 89), and extremely high levels of particular local autonomy.

This internal weakening of statehood in early modern Spain was primarily caused by fiscal pressures resulting from military overstretch and intensified war financing, and the crisis of the Spanish state was by no means solely the result of constitutional defects. Nonetheless, both the privatistic configuration of the Cortes and the acceptance of *pactismo* as a diffusely dualistic model of governance based in recognition of privileges outside the state were distinctive features of early modern governance in Spain, and both these characteristics compounded the crisis of the Spanish monarchy, which became increasingly febrile through the seventeenth century. Indeed, the partial collapse of state power in Spain was at once caused by and symptomatically reflected in the fact that it was a monarchy that never fully integrated its consultative organs and permitted its inclusionary apparatus to persist in partially external structure. This ultimately led, not to a structural reinforcement of a semi-autonomous monarchical or even 'absolute' state, but in fact to a re-particularization of authority both within the state and throughout society more widely. As a result of this, the Spanish monarchs were increasingly bound, not by acceded general or *public* laws, but by the countervailing force of seigneurial rights and liberties,[44] and by the external power of private agents who had managed to purchase and maintain reserves of state power and judicial authority.[45] By the seventeenth century, therefore, although the powers of the Cortes were limited, royal authority was still checked by powerful counterweights. Yet these were located, not in any inner constitutional apparatus within the state, but in centres of seigneurial authority: in the *señorios*. One historian has argued persuasively that *pactismo* was a cover for the 'absolute power of the *señorios*' and that it directly impeded the formation of a strong central state and a strong uniform judicial order (Latorre 2003: 92). The decline, or particularistic fragmentation, of the power of the Cortes, in short, coincided with a decline in the power of the state. The crisis of the Spanish constitution focused on the Cortes marked a partial return to the medieval constitutional pattern, which led to an extreme lack of state integrity. This tendency was partly redressed towards the end of the seventeenth century, when the monarchy again attempted to decompose seigneurial power. In this instance, too, however, the monarchy did not succeed in elevating itself above its late-feudal structure of residual particularism, and a high level of governmental privatism remained a feature of Spanish government until the twentieth century.

It would be inaccurate to suggest that the so-called absolutistic style of government employed in Spain meant that the early modern Spanish state did not possess a constitution. As discussed, in early modern Spain the monarchical state was powerfully balanced by an amalgam of *pactos*, exemptions and local indemnities that restricted the force of general laws. However, this externalistic constitutional apparatus proved deleterious for the Spanish monarchy, and the 'absolutistic' experiment proved unable to create a powerfully autonomous state with reliable control of judicial or fiscal processes (see Dios 1985: 36; Mackay 1999: 59). It created a state that, despite the precocious rise of statehood in Spain, persisted in a residual dualist form, in which central authority was precariously supported and limited by private and regional powers outside the state, and in which political authority, within and outside the state, was exposed to a process of seigneurial re-privatization

---

[44] See analysis in Kamen (1980: 228); González Antón (1989: 220); Castellano (1990: 131); Mackay (1999: 2, 4, 11).

[45] Thompson set out this argument and claimed that the 'chronic degeneration of effective state power' in Spain saw the creation between 1625 and 1668 of 'at least 169 new lordships or baronies, each with primary and secondary jurisdiction' (1994: 217–22).

(Thompson 1990: 91). One notable historian has argued simply that by the late sixteenth century legal order in Castile had been so fundamentally fragmented by the selling of royal charters and indemnities that there no longer existed a 'law code common to all Castilian municipalities' (Nader 1990: 157). The fact that the constitution of state relied on the sanctioning of diffuse fiscal pacts and legal guarantees through society meant that the inclusionary integrity of the state was undermined, the state was not required or able to bind powerful particular actors into its structure, and it did not elaborate consistent institutional preconditions for unitary integration. On this basis, the 'absolutist' system of government in early modern Spain caused a traumatic degeneration of governmental authority, it obligated the use of state power to private compacts, it failed to produce an adequately articulated pattern of public order – or of *public law* – for the state, and it prevented the state from overcoming the pluralistic structure of social embeddedness that it had assumed in the Middle Ages. The pattern of 'absolutist' political evolution in Spain, in other words, marked one distinctive constitutional process of unitary state formation. However, this process produced a state that possessed limited control over its societal boundaries, that was not able to mobilize power at a level of high public abstraction or generality, and that at times risked forfeiting its quality as an integrally constructed state.

France

In France, similarly, the later period of early modernity was defined by the formation of a state that attempted to sustain its unitary structure by suppressing sources of dispute over political functions, and by eliminating articulated constitutional checks on royal prerogative.

At the beginning of the seventeenth century, French society as a whole was still perceived as regimented around a plurality of hierarchically organized orders or corporations and estates, each of which had its internal privileges, legal distinctions and administrative functions. This meant that societal structure was determined by multiple forms of power and status, and that the judicial and fiscal power of the central state could only be applied as proportioned to a highly pluralistic sectoral landscape of liberties, privileges and immunities. Charles Loyseau's argument that orders formed a quasi-natural social hierarchy, in which the 'state' (*estat*) of each person was determined by affiliation to an order and by the particular marks, signs and ornaments pertaining to this order, precisely captured the decentred and particularistic fabric of French social structure at this time (1665 [1610]: 4). Most notably, the society of orders in France militated against the formation of a strongly abstracted political system. That is, the fact that in this society power was tied to local and professional distinctions and legal and fiscal exemptions impeded the formation of a unitary fiscal and judicial apparatus in the state, and, in allocating governmental authority to corporate actors and estates, it ensured that basic functions of the state remained under private control. Throughout the early decades of the seventeenth century, however, the French monarchy began progressively to consolidate itself above the society of orders: it did this by combating the local and sectoral division of society, by strategically weakening hereditary orders and sources of immunity, by bringing the disparate orders of society under more immediate and evenly inclusive state jurisdiction, and by reducing the authority of estates.

In the aftermath of the Reformation era and the religious wars, in consequence, the instruments of corporate representation were employed with increasing rarity in France, and the constitutional structures of the later Middle Ages were allowed to fall into disuse. Most notably, the Estates-General were not called after 1614 until 1789, and as early as the first decade of the seventeenth century, Henri IV began consciously to curtail the power of organic institutions and, above all, to limit the corporate bodies that conventionally served the political interests of the nobility. In pursuing these policies, the French monarchy, in particular after the accession of Louis XIII, attempted (with only partial success) to rectify the fiscal problems that it suffered through protracted involvement in warfare by imposing larger and more uniform taxes throughout society, by ensuring that taxes were collected by a distinct class of royal officials (i.e. not by the estates themselves), and in some cases by simply ignoring the fiscal powers and privileges of regional assemblies and securing taxation by regularly mandated means.[46] At the core of this process was a progressive suppression of social orders and seigneurial distinctions, and royal policies reflected an endeavour, especially in fiscal matters, to restrict singular exemptions under law, and to apply fiscal edicts uniformly across society. In particular, this meant that the monarchy was obliged to construct an internal administrative apparatus that allowed it (to some degree) to detach taxation from

---

[46] The origins of this strategy have been plausibly traced to the religious wars (Hickey 1986: 30, 31, 45).

traditional or structurally enmeshed groups of rights and exemptions and instruments of approval, to separate contribution to tax revenue from social standing, and to establish centrally the levels of revenue required from particular regions and persons (Moote 1972: 99; Ranum 1993: 28–9). The transformation of the state's fiscal system led to a growing depersonalization of the state's administrative order, and it articulated an increasingly general line of exchange between the state and the economy, in which economic functions and obligations were constructed as relatively independent of hereditary or personal status. In this respect, the 'absolutistic' structure of the French monarchy clearly served to reinforce the state's unitary form and the positive abstraction of its power, it suppressed diffuse or dualistic elements in the state, and it helped, vitally, to clarify the lines of intersection between the state and the economy and, gradually, to detach forms of legal address and inclusion from private spheres of activity. The 'absolutistic' design of the state clearly heightened the positive force of the state's power, and it enabled the state to legislate more autonomously across society and simply to construct the categories in which it integrated its addressees.

In conjunction with this, the earlier seventeenth century also saw a transformation of the internal constitutional features of the French state. Instead of seeking to obtain monetary supply by negotiating with the assemblies or corporate estates, the monarch began to utilize the *parlements* (that is, the sovereign courts, designed to register laws and initially endowed only – or primarily – with judicial functions) as organs for transacting and documenting fiscal arrangements. One main motive for this, at least until the middle of the seventeenth century, was that the monarch was able to treat the *parlements* in much more peremptory style than the corporate estates, and he was able to use *parlements* to conduct fiscal business with limited resistance.[47] This policy of elevating the constitutional status of the *parlements* was not an ultimate success, and the role of the *parlements* in the construction of the compact, post-feudal state in France remained deeply ambiguous. In the early seventeenth century, the *parlements* gradually assumed limited representative competence and, as the estates became weaker, they began to act as the primary focus of political/constitutional controversy and opposition to the monarch. Owing especially to the fact that, as sovereign courts, they were authorized to submit remonstrances regarding new acts of law and

---

[47] Members of the *parlements* initially viewed themselves as 'king's men' (Jouanna 1989: 33).

fiscal measures introduced by the monarchy, they increasingly used their power to block the wider concentration of the governmental apparatus. This was especially the case because the members of the *parlements* were normally office holders, whose position could be held as a private venal privilege in a family for a long period: in consequence, the *parlements* became a forum for private, vested or even neo-seigneurial resistance to the construction of a centralized state. Nonetheless, the relocation of constitutional exchange from the estates to the *parlements* marked an attempt on the part of the monarchical executive to internalize sources of conflict within the state, to stabilize the executive apparatus in a relatively impermeable form, and to administer the vital interests of the state in a more internally controlled institution. Indeed, the French monarchy repeatedly attempted to bring the *parlements* under its direct influence, to limit the independence of judicial actors in the state, and to restrict the powers of budgetary remonstrance exercised by the *parlements*. In this respect, too, the formation of the state as an 'absolutist' monarchy reflected both the heightened differentiation and the unitary construction of the state apparatus, and it reflected the wider stratificatory transformation of the corporate structure of society as a whole.

In addition to this, the formation of a more 'absolutistic' state in seventeenth-century France was reflected in the expansion of the state administration, in the gradual formation of a semi-professionalized civil service, and in the progressive expulsion of centrifugal private interests from the state's administrative structure. For example, through the course of the seventeenth century the French monarchy gradually eroded the political functions and status of locally privileged or corporate actors by creating a specialized administrative body, first, of judicial and financial office holders (*officiers*) and, second, of personally appointed *commissaires*. Both the *officiers* and the *commissaires* were agents who executed royal business through the realm, especially in matters concerning taxation, jurisdiction, and religious observance, and they gradually set the foundations for the emergence of a class of professional functionaries. The corps of office holders, who usually obtained offices by venal transaction from the monarch, was first established as part of an attempt both to expand royal revenue and to preserve delegated public functions (especially responsibility for raising revenue) under direct royal control and to escape the privatization or renewed enfeoffment of public authority characteristic of feudal political order (Mousnier 1945: 2–4). Indeed, although by 1789 office holders were habitually derided as agents of feudal reaction, the allocation (often for money) of state offices in justice or finance was initially a strategy devised by the monarchy expressly to promote the *de-feudalization* of public power – that is, at once to obtain revenue for the public purse, and to remove state authority from the ancient nobility possessing judicial powers strongly rooted in land and seigneurial entitlement (Jouanna 1989: 98; Bien and Godneff 1988: 401; Bossenga 2006: 63). As a result, the formation of a class of *officiers* reflected the ambition, of defining prominence for the constitution of later medieval France, to separate administrative power from feudal jurisdiction, and this class formed the administrative core of the state during its first period of consolidated abstraction. By the middle of the seventeenth century, however, the number of offices had escalated and the rights and tenures over public duties attached to different offices had become more solidified, so that the office holders began to hold private stakes in state administration and to threaten the cohesion of the state. In consequence, they were in part supplanted by a new class of functionaries: the *commissaires*. The *commissaires* obtained strictly specific and temporary royal commissions, issued immediately under the king's great seal, their functions were classified direct enactments of royal will, and their institution was designed, once again, to minimize private alienation of royal power.[48] Notably, Jean Bodin made a clear distinction under public law between state servants holding *offices* and state servants holding *commissions*, and he underlined the risks accruing to the state through the granting of permanent venal offices, especially in the judiciary (1986 [1576]: 45, 61).

Salient among the ranks of the *commissaires* were the *intendants*. Originating under Henri II and obtaining formal commissions in the later sixteenth century, during the reign of Louis XIII the *intendants* were formed as an independent elite body of mainly non-venal functionaries, who, although often of noble provenance, played a key role in the attempted eradication of private power from the administration of the French state. Receiving orders directly from the general controller of finance, the *intendants* were commissioned to impose royal demands in respect of taxes and justice in the provinces,[49] and they were utilized to

---

[48] The grand *ordonnance* passed by Louis XIII in 1629, and sometimes known as the Code Michau, clearly explained both the levels of obedience due to bearers of *lettres de committimus* and the temporal and functional specificity of the commissions (Ordonnance 1630: 57–8). This document played an important role in weakening the consultative dimensions of French government.

[49] For samples of the vast literature on the *intendants* see Laferrière (1896: 153, 161); Dupont-Ferrier (1930: 190); Gruder (1968: 70); Kiser and Linton (2001: 422).

transmit royal power immediately from the monarchical centre to the social periphery: notably, their rise coincided with the concentration of fiscal and judicial authority in the *conseil du roi* and other personal councils around the king. The legal status of the *intendants* changed over time. By the middle of the seventeenth century, the *intendants* with responsibility for financial administration had begun to assume more personal powers, analogous in some ways to ministerial appointments, and this was eventually formalized by statute (Antoine 2003: 194–5, 461, 568). However, as royal agents with formal duties, the *intendants* acted throughout the seventeenth century to relieve the estates of their responsibility for gathering taxes, and they gradually became primary pillars of royal authority throughout France.[50] In general, in fact, through the seventeenth century the *commissaires* began to approach a functional condition of administrative specialization (i.e. they were allocated very particular royal duties to conduct), and they brought many social functions previously covered by provincial corporations under the sway of the monarchy (or the state) (Mousnier 1974: II, 495, 566). In this regard, the construction of the early modern French state revolved around a recognition that the functions of political administration traditionally conducted at a local level or effected through arrangements based on local privilege and private entitlement had to be regulated in a specifically and independently political manner. The initial development of a specialized and semi-professionalized civil service formed part of a process in which the political system assimilated those functions in a society that possessed a distinctively political content, and the nascent state administration both segregated itself from private sources of power and status and eliminated the need for local or personal agreement in the particular acts of its exercise of political power. Through this development, the resources of power within society were clearly delineated against private functions or marks of personal status, and groups bearing distinct and particular social rights (usually the nobility) were gradually either suppressed or transformed into commissioned organs of state power.

In all these respects, in sum, the basic structure of the French monarchy in the earlier seventeenth century was integrally shaped by the processes of political abstraction, legal generalization and unitary institutional formation that more generally accompanied the formation of early modern states and early modern societies. The French monarchy consolidated itself as a state that suppressed both estate-based legal/

---

[50] For samples see Kettering (1978: 84–8); Smedley-Weill (1995: 121); Major (1997: 283).

monetary privilege and late-feudal opposition by seeking to assimilate the noble class into the state bureaucracy, by endeavouring to purchase the support of this class by offering distinctions and privileges that had immediate remunerative benefit to the state, and – most importantly – by conferring venal office on people outside this class, in order to undermine noble dominance (Giesey 1983; Beik 1985: 337). These processes of administrative transformation were also reflected in the increasing generalization of the law in France in the second half of the seventeenth century. The ordinances imposed by the Code Louis of 1667–70, most particularly, still preserved special distinctions of status for the nobility and recognized certain noble jurisdictional privileges. However, this code laid down a general order of hearings and legal procedures, it formed a legal apparatus that was relatively indifferent to status, and it expanded the functions of royal councils as courts of last resort, able to override the judicial rulings of the *parlements* (1670: 19). At its core, thus, the emergence of French 'absolutism' was a process that suppressed the diverse and pluralistic constitutional dimensions of later feudal society in order to generate distinctively abstracted and internally consistent stores of power for society, and in which specifically commissioned political actors were designated to circulate political power through society in even and generalized fashion. As a result of this, the state evolved a form in which, to an increasing degree, it could apply power to different social strata in relatively uniform and generalized manner, and the preconditions of state power (especially fiscal revenues) could be secured without incessant personalistic controversy.

It would, in consequence, be absurd to deny that the emergence of 'absolutism' contributed dramatically to the modernization of French society: self-evidently, the balance between administrative centralization and office-holding patrimonialism at the centre of the monarchy brought a rapid intensification of state power, and it clearly consolidated the French monarchy in the international arena. Like Spain at the same time, however, the formation of 'absolutism' in France also revolved around two distinct paradoxes, which ultimately, over a long period, depleted its power. First, the rise of the absolutist governmental style and weakening of inherited instruments of representation did not involve a thorough suppression of the state's constitutional structure. In fact, second, in its attempt at centralization the French monarchy not only failed to eliminate constitutional counterweights to its power; it was also forced to assume a constitution that ultimately obstructed its emergence as a fully developed and autonomous political actor.

First, most manifestly, the French monarchy retained a residual constitutional order because it was widely presupposed that, for all its growing power, the monarchy was bound by a number of basic laws and norms, which continuously defined the structure of the state. These laws were rather diminished variants on the fundamental laws acknowledged in the sixteenth century. However, the expectation of royal adherence to laws of succession, laws of religious obligation, laws of majority and laws regarding the inalienability of the French territory remained strong. Moreover, it was also assumed that certain positive laws constrained monarchical power, and that the monarch could not arbitrarily contravene time-honoured institutional conventions (see Lemaire 1907: 271; Saguez-Lovisi 1984: 25). Even those theorists who supported monarchical 'absolutism' clearly insisted that France possessed a constitution that ensured that the state was juridically distinct from the person of its monarch and placed limits on the exercise of power. Close to the origins of the absolutist state, Jean Bodin and, later, Cardin Le Bret, both of whom are seen as staunch advocates of absolutism, were emphatic that monarchical legislation remained subject to customary constraints (Bodin 1986 [1576]: 193; Le Bret 1635 [1632]: 14–15).

Second, limits were placed on the power of the absolutist state by virtue of the fact that the reinforcement of the state bureaucracy, itself reflecting the anti-privatistic policies of the French monarchy, also contained constitutional implications. The bureaucratic intensification of the state structure was marked, in fact, not only by an incipient deprivatization of the civil service, but also by a reduction of the private status of the monarchy itself. During the early period of 'absolutism', a clear distinction was made between the administrative order of the state and the natural/physical will of the monarch, and the French monarchy created an administrative system that, although enacting a royal chain of command, possessed a distinct and abstracted permanence against the monarch. Above all, the administrative reforms that formed the basis for governmental 'absolutism' saw the final transformation of the monarch from a personal bearer of high seigneurial privileges located within a mass of private societal agreements into a pivotal focus of public authority, and they redefined royal power as a constant political resource that was insensitive to, and able to prevail over, privileges and personal entitlements. The main architect of early French absolutism, Richelieu, was notably committed to the formation, not of a political order using power as a personal/monarchical property, but of an abstract rational state, in which the concentration of power around the king was intended to simplify and confer symbolic cohesion on the bureaucratic apparatus in which power was factually distributed (Pagès 1946: 111; Church 1972: 16). In this respect, 'absolutism' drew its force from the precondition that the state was a positive actor, whose extensive reserves of power were of necessity constitutionally distinct from immediate factual bearers of office. The bureaucratic personality of the state, in fact, was the primary precondition of its emergent unitary and positive structure, and the unitary consistency of the state clearly presupposed that it contained a rudimentary organic constitution.

In addition to this, the French monarchy in the seventeenth century was also marked by a constitutional structure because, like the Spanish monarchy, it was incapable of suppressing private legal sources of obstruction, and a number of institutions formed potent correctives to the centralizing power of the monarchy. Primarily, as mentioned, under Louis XIII the *parlements* increasingly acted as irritants within the monarchical state, and the king repeatedly took measures to curtail their powers.[51] Indeed, the French monarchy was recurrently unsettled by unresolved conflicts over jurisdiction, noble privileges, prerogative power and preconditions of fiscal stability, and these were commonly articulated through the *parlements*. As a corps of high-ranking *officiers*, the members of the *parlements* were often motivated by the desire to push back the powers of the monarchy, to preserve their own (venal) judicial privileges against the uniform order of the central state, and to resist the centralistic authority of the various monarchical *commissaires*, especially the *intendants*, whose administrative commissions included judicial functions that diminished the powers of the sovereign courts and excluded members of the *parlements* from government (Bonney 1978: 135). These conflicts between the centralizing force of royal administration and the private claims of the judiciary found initial expression in the king's Édit de Saint Germain (1641). This statute made it illegal for *parlements* to intervene in business conducted by the *intendants*, and it sought to invest more judicial power in the state administration: it gave early expression to the notion of the *administrateur-juge*, which later became fundamental to French judicial structures (Burdeau 1994: 43). These conflicts then culminated in the Fronde, beginning in 1648–9; this was a deeply destabilizing elite revolt that led to a short civil war, caused by the fact that judges of the Parisian

---

[51] In the Code Michau of 1629 Louis XIII tried to reduce the period of time in which *parlements* could submit remonstrances (Ordonnance 1630: 38).

parlement demanded the suppression of the *intendants*, refused to register new tax laws and used their positions as *parlementaires* to defend both their own privileges and the privileges of those subject to new fiscal extraction. For a short time after the suppression of the Fronde, the courts became less politically vocal and more compliant instruments of the royal will, and, regardless of noble opposition, laws were often passed in prerogative style: through *lits de justice*. Louis XIV in fact withdrew the power of remonstrance from the *parlements* in 1673. However, after the death of Louis XIV the *parlements* again began to play a politically destabilizing role. From this time on, the friction between crown and *parlements* continued, and it at times assumed politically crippling intensity. Throughout the Ancien Régime, in short, the *parlements* operated as semi-constitutional bodies, which refracted the fiscal and judicial conflicts at the centre of the French monarchy. It was in the *parlements*, often through the use of prerogative means, that the monarchy's attempts to stabilize its unitary structure had to be fought out, and it was in the *parlements* that the primary sources of constitutional opposition to the crown were channelled. The *parlements* were the nodal point in the ongoing conflict between the monarchical state administration on one side and the semi-patrimonial judiciary on the other, which defined French institutional history up to 1789.

Of the greatest importance in this conflict was the fact that the composition of the *parlements* was such that the French state retained an element of constitutional privatism at its legislative and fiscal core. The fact that the members of the *parlements* assumed office venally and often came to preserve office as a hereditary patrimonial privilege meant that the persons responsible for the key public functions of approving legislation and taxation obtained these duties as members of a private corps of office holders, possessing particular corporate distinctions and privileges, which they naturally wished to defend. In particular, this meant that the office-holders in the *parlements*, although hostile to royal absolutism, were often committed to preserving local powers and seigneurial privileges and exemptions. As such, in fact, they simultaneously opposed both royal prerogatives and the establishment of general or national representative organs and general or national judicial forms, and they commonly obstructed state actors who sought to legislate in generalized fashion and to override the private interests of corporate society. The element in the state's structure (i.e. its legislative, judicial and – in corollary – fiscal dimensions) in which it had the greatest need for positive authority and autonomous flexibility, in short, remained a dimension of its power in which it was forced to negotiate with highly particular vested interests, and in which its need for autonomy inevitably brought it into confrontation with a residual constitutional privatism. In giving judicial privileges to office-holders, the Bourbon state privileged exactly those social sectors which, especially in fiscal questions, had a strong interest in blocking general laws, and the result of this was that the state preserved within its vital organs certain private groups that had not been – and in fact could not be – fully integrated into the state and fully brought under the more general rule of law;[52] these groups, then, were the people with whom it was compelled to conduct its defining constitutional conflicts. The private rights and privileges of office holders thus retained determining power in the activities of the French monarchy, and the state struggled autonomously to fulfil its main objectives as a state – that is, to pass general laws and to raise general taxes – because of its judicial/legislative reliance on the *parlements* and their privately motivated members. Indeed, after the end of the suppression of the *parlements* enforced by Louis XIV, it has been widely (although not unanimously) claimed that the *parlementaires* assumed a position in the forefront of the 'feudal reaction' through the eighteenth century, by which the centralistic state-building functions of the absolutistic elites were partly undermined by the new feudal-bureaucratic class of the *noblesse de robe*, whose members owed their status to venally transacted offices (Ford 1953: 246; Gruder 1968: 205). As in Spain, in consequence, in France the 'absolutistic' state-building experiment did not succeed in eradicating private countervailing power through society, the actual degree to which the state possessed an abstracted monopoly of social power was always limited, and, for all its attempts at 'absolutistic' centralization, the state retained an informal constitution that was plagued by lateral semi-patrimonial counterweights.

The primary consequence of this aggregate of processes was that throughout the seventeenth century the French monarchy was unable to avoid constitutional restrictions, and it did not consolidate itself as an abstracted and quasi-autonomous bearer of political power in society. In fact, the French monarchy retained a quasi-privatistic constitution, in part determined by its obligations to external prerogatives. Above all, the fact that the French monarchy elected to transact its most vital business

---

[52] Egret notes that the *parlements* were perceived as opposing certain fiscal bills for reasons that were not fully 'disinterested', and they undermined the attempts of the monarchy to create a reliable fiscal order (1970: 107–9).

not through public institutions but through venal office holders, meant that the state was unable to extricate its power from private milieux or to consolidate itself as a distinctively public order. The proliferation of venal offices in the monarchical state meant that, like the Spanish monarchy, the state of French 'absolutism' existed in a societal constitution in which its exposure to internal privatistic resistance was high and the danger that its offices could be retranslated into private/patrimonial or *dualistically* constructed rights or benefices remained palpably destabilizing. In particular, this meant that the state was not able to generalize its power equally across society, it was forced to prioritize, preserve and placate seigneurial interests in its legislative processes, and – in the final analysis – it could only use power at a relatively low level of positive abstraction, uniformity and intensity. In this case, too, 'absolutism' comprised a constitutional structure in which the state could only evolve to a limited level of autonomy and unitary cohesion: the constitution of 'absolutism' ultimately impeded the formation of integral statehood and autonomously usable reserves of power in French society.

Prussia and smaller states

After 1648, less representative and inclusionary techniques of government were also emulated throughout northern Europe. In many major Lutheran or Calvinist states, royal executives also began (at least sporadically) to limit the constitutional power of estates and to govern at a higher degree of societal independence than had previously been possible. In Denmark, for example, a new *lex regia* was passed in 1665, which substantially expanded the scope of royal power. This document, which remained secret, conferred on the king the 'sole authority' to pass and enforce law (Lockhart 2007: 249). By the later seventeenth century, even in Sweden, which (as discussed below) had previously possessed one of the strongest constitutional designs in Europe,[53] Karl XI was able to impose severe restrictions on the constitutional authority of his council, to remove other constraints on his political status and to set the stage for a short 'absolutist' experiment that lasted until 1719.

In the German territories, the longer aftermath of the Reformation raised legal and constitutional problems very different from those in consolidated monarchies, and the formation of unitary state executives was hardly feasible in the earlier seventeenth century; the developing

[53] See below, pages 134–7.

states in the German territories were necessarily marked, for long periods of time, by high levels of inner and outer constitutional dualism. The defining constitutional problem for most of the larger German states resided in the fact that supreme powers of jurisdiction in single states remained precariously divided and contested between territorial courts and imperial courts, and for long after the Reformation the relation between territorial states and Empire was shaped by a series of legal/ constitutional arrangements that prevented the territorial states from assuming entirely sovereign or unitary political authority. Most distinctively, the legal powers of some territorial states were fragmented by the fact that their subjects possessed rights of appeal to the imperial courts, and only a small number of the territories possessed jurisdictional competences that could not, in some matters, be overruled in the appellate system of the Empire. In the longer wake of the Reformation, therefore, most German regents devoted much of their constitutional energy to securing (or, more normally, attempting to secure) the *privilegium de non appellando illimitatum* – that is, a legal immunity granted by the Empire, which authorized the effective (although still often incomplete) legal independence of the territories from imperial appellate courts.[54] In consequence, well after 1600 most German states were still partly obligated by originally feudal entitlements and immunities in the exercise of their jurisdictional authority, and their power was still balanced both by legal prerogatives of the Empire and legal prerogatives of their own subjects. As a result, the primary conflicts of German states in the seventeenth century remained determined, to a large degree, by an external constitutional relation between Empire and particular territories, and this outer dualism, more than any inner dualism, was the main focus of legal-constitutional weakness and controversy. Fully evolved foundations for statehood were not established in the German territories until well after 1648. In many cases, German territorial states did not become the sole centres of fiscal and jurisdictional power until the eighteenth century, or even as late as 1806.

After the end of the Thirty Years War in 1648, however, the tendency towards the expansion of princely authority and the curtailment of the traditional powers of the estates, which was already a feature of more integrally constructed monarchical states, began to shape the temporally retarded process of state formation in German territories, and in some

---

[54] For example, Bavaria did not finally receive this privilege until 1620. Prussia did not have the privilege for all its – admittedly highly composite – territories until 1746.

cases this generated a constitutional structure similar to that in other 'absolutistic' states. The emergence of an absolutist pattern of state organization was perhaps most obvious in Prussia: in fact, the birth of Brandenburg-Prussia as a major state is commonly traced to the fact that, in the aftermath of 1648, the ruling electoral house of the Hohenzollerns progressively diminished the political liberties and functions of regional noble estates. The first step in this process was the Recess of 1653, in which the political authority of the estates in Brandenburg was selectively restricted. This recess formed a semi-constitutional compact in which, on one hand, the estates granted money and approved standing taxes, substantially increased during the Thirty Years War, for the Great Elector, who later used this to support a permanent royal army. As a result, the estates lost the power to veto taxation and to convene full parliamentary assemblies, and they renounced a good part of their status as quasi-representative actors. However, in this compact, by way of recompense, the nobility also retained and strengthened important rights and indemnities: the noble estates received guarantees for their powers of patrimonial authority over their lands and peasants, the jurisdictional structure of serfdom was intensified in lands held by the nobility, and nobles were partly exempted from central taxation.[55] Subsequently, after the formal union of Brandenburg and Prussia, the Hohenzollerns began, between the 1660s and the 1680s, more consistently to suppress the power of the estates in East Prussia, which had previously been under feudal obligation to Poland and Sweden. In particular, the Elector suspended the right of the estates in East Prussia to approve taxation, and he integrated permanent revenue-raising mechanisms into the state. Other German states, similarly, took steps to weaken the role of the estates at this time. Indeed, in some states, in particular Bavaria, the influence of the estates had begun to decline as early as the later sixteenth century (Lanzinner 1980: 250).

In parallel to this, throughout the course of its emergence as a major political force the Prussian ruling dynasty strategically emulated administrative patterns established in Spain and France. This was apparent, first, in the fact that its agents sought to assimilate previously potent political actors – usually members of the noble estates, still possessing embedded feudal rights – into the state administration: that is, it offered to accommodate members of the nobility as high-ranking civil servants

---

[55] See the *Corpus Constitutionum Marchicarum* (1737–55: 438, 440).

or in senior military offices, and it transformed private noble privileges into tokens of state-controlled social distinction, status and qualification (Baumgart 1969: 134; Wyluda 1969: 42–126; Vierhaus 1990: 214). It has been repeatedly observed that the elite administrative actors in Prussia, as in France, were designed to curtail noble power: in Prussia administrative *Kommissarien*, modelled on French *commissaires* (Hintze 1962b [1910]: 245–9), were also appointed to absorb functions into the state that had previously been performed by bearers of local or seigneurial authority.[56] However, the strategy of the Prussian ruling family was not exclusively repressive: it was also keen to placate the nobility by preserving noble status and social privileges within the administrative departments of the state, so that many social positions, primarily in the army, were reserved for the nobility. The creation of permanent standing armies, which distinguished many monarchies at this time, played a particularly vital role in Prussia. The army served both to intensify the controlling power of the governmental regime and to provide professional compensation for members of the nobility whose ancient privileges had been hollowed out by the process of political centralization. The Prussian military system, in sum, at once absorbed and perpetuated the status of the Prussian nobility (Büsch 1962: 93); indeed, it preserved the status of the nobility in its original feudal function as a 'class of warriors' (Hofmann 1962: 116).

As in other 'absolutistic' states, in consequence, the Prussian state consolidated its unitary form through a process of half-coercive and half-compensatory political assimilation of privately privileged elites. Through this process, political power was at once centralized and applied more generally through society, variations of status under law were partly eradicated, and, in some respects, society began evenly to converge around the reserves of legal power cemented in the princely state.[57] Despite this, nonetheless, as in other societies with a seemingly 'absolutistic' socio-political structure, Prussia also retained a strong body of societal counterweights and lateral balances, which obviated the concentration of political power in the bureaucratic state. Indeed, Prussian absolutism also evolved on a constitutional pattern that permitted only a highly selective process of political centralization and ensured that state power remained exposed to pervasively privatistic centrifugal forces.

[56] For a view qualifying this classical argument see Sieg (2003: 97).
[57] For a brilliant account of this core process see Rachel (1905: 319).

In this respect, most notably, the Prussian ruling house was unable to dissolve either the corporate constitution or the locally pluralistic fabric of Prussian society, and it was forced to accept the continued potency of external private and seigneurial limits on its power. As discussed, for example, the Recess of 1653 guaranteed certain legally enshrined privileges for the estates in Brandenburg: the recess certified that princely power in fiscal matters was not to encroach on the jurisdictional authority of the aristocracy, and in their domains the nobility retained jurisdictional privileges as quasi-constitutional rights. The local powers of quasi-sovereign rule possessed by the nobility were endorsed and perpetuated as a precondition for their military co-operation, and the class status and privileges of the nobility were, in part, preserved from 1653 until the early nineteenth century. The state's assertion of political primacy over the estates, in consequence, was predicated on a complex set of compromises, in which the ruling house committed itself to uphold the traditional rights of the nobility in local affairs and to guarantee noble interests in the highest echelons of the state (Büsch 1962: 135; Wehler 1987: 246). Central to Prussian absolutism was an implicit bargain between nobility and monarch, which meant that the central control of state power was accepted in certain areas of social regulation (primarily in matters regarding military security), yet that powers of centralization had to be purchased through a reinforcement of local and seigneurial authority in other areas. The nobility emerged, in short, as a class whose formal political status was diminished through the system of territorial 'absolutism', but whose social and territorial privileges were, in some respects, enhanced. As in other 'absolutistic' societies, the abstracted public transmission of power depended on a residually privatistic constitution of the state and of society more widely, and the reserves of power condensed in the administrative executive could only be applied to a limited and clearly predetermined range of societal exchanges. Under Prussian 'absolutism', effectively, state power was only usable as a resource situated above a still diffusely and pluralistically structured political society, in which the state's monopoly of power in a select number of regulatory matters was secured by the formal recognition of its secondary status in many others.

There has been much criticism of the concept of absolutism as a term for categorizing patterns of early modern state construction. Most particularly, this term has been rejected both by historians who deny that early modern states were able to assume absolute power (Hartung and Mousnier 1955: 7; Willoweit 1975: 2; Collins 1995: 1) and by historians who suggest that states never desired to legitimize themselves as uncurtailed centres of coercion.[58] In relation to these debates, two distinct views are proposed in the analysis provided above, both of which suggest that extreme caution must be exercised when the concept of absolutism is employed. The account given above seeks to add to scepticism about the historical reality of absolutism by claiming, first, that 'absolutist' states always possessed a de facto constitutional order, and they were inevitably checked by a manifest set of external countervailing powers. Second, it gives further emphasis to this point by arguing that societies distinguished by 'absolutistic' techniques for constructing and using power tended, owing to their externalistic constitutional apparatus, to develop very weakly unified states, which were endemically threatened by disaggregation into their constituent patrimonial parts, and they normally produced political power at a low level of intensity and generality and in a form marked by high degrees of regional and patrimonial unevenness. The constitution of 'absolutism', in other words, was an organizational response to the increased need for positive techniques for generating and circulating political power that uniformly cast the societal form of early modern Europe. As such, the constitution of 'absolutism' promoted the evolution of the state as an increasingly unitary and emergent modern political apparatus; to this degree, 'absolutism' marked a construction of political power as adapted to the processes of differentiation, abstraction and legal-political positivization that shaped early modern European societies more widely. However, the constitution of absolutism was an organizationally incohesive reaction to these processes: under 'absolutism' the state remained deeply enmeshed with originally dualistic or centrifugal centres of interest, and it struggled to distil power as an internally abstracted object or to apply political power as a flexible positive facility. The political constitution of 'absolutism' tended to reflect a wider societal conjuncture in which state and economy were only loosely differentiated, and in which states were compelled to resort to personalized regulation of the economy and erratic brokering with embedded economic groups in order to raise taxation and pass laws. As a result, state institutions lacked efficient techniques for economic control, and – for all these reasons – the state remained reliant on private and quasi-patrimonial sources of support through society in order to mobilize its basic monetary, military and jurisdictional resources. For these reasons, 'absolutist' states were

[58] See Dreitzel (1992: 139–40). For a resumé see Henshall (1996).

usually, over longer periods of history, ineffective as unitary political orders, and their basic positive functions of autonomous or abstracted statehood were habitually undermined by their half-coercive, half-privatistic structure. Indeed, in many instances the weakness of these states was the result of the fact that they did not evolve more generally inclusionary constitutions, they failed to disconnect public functions from private prerogatives and milieux, and they did not elaborate a formal and internalistic public-legal order in order autonomously to construct their power and systematically to conduct legislative processes. This private diffuseness of the political constitution created a vicious circle for 'absolutist' states: the weak constitution created a weak, privatistic state, and a revolutionary transformation of both the entire state and the entire society in which the state was located was required to create a strong, inclusionary state apparatus.

Early classical constitutionalism

If some societies of early European modernity organized their expanding political functions by concentrating political power in the state administration and weakening consensual mechanisms for regulating legislation and public finance, some societies, at the same time, produced alternative institutional models to abstract their political power and to unify and order their political functions. Indeed, some early modern societies responded to the growing abstraction of power and to the societal demand for the unitary production of political power by widening their systems of political representation and by internally formalizing negotiated techniques for structuring their exchanges with societal agents subject to political power, especially in the economy. The emergence of early classical constitutionalism, thus, evolved as a line of state building forming a parallel to absolutism, and it marked a related yet distinct institutional reaction to the increased need for differentiated and positivized resources of political power that characterized European societies after the Reformation.

Sweden

Through the sixteenth century, the Swedish monarchy had tended towards the formation of a moderately autocratic political regime, albeit one supported by a strong parliament. However, by the late sixteenth century it was expounded in constitutional doctrine, notably in the seminal works of Erik Sparre, that royal authority depended on the 'authority of law' and presupposed delegated consultation (1924 [1585]: 85). By the early decades of the seventeenth century, the Swedish monarchy began to adopt a particularly refined and powerful body of constitutional laws and documents. First, for example, in the Charter of January 1612 the new king, Gustav Adolf, promised, as a precondition of his coronation, that no new laws were to be introduced and no old laws rescinded, and that no new taxes were to be raised or fiscal burdens increased, without the collaboration and consent of both the royal council and the estates. Through this Charter, the Swedish monarchy, in modernized form, was reconnected with its late medieval origins, and it was framed anew as a constitutional order, bound to preserve the rule of law and to co-opt parliamentary councillors to advise on legislation.[59] This Charter was followed by the Rikstag Ordinance of 1617, in which a parliamentary apparatus was organized, and in which the delegatory procedures of the parliament were regularized, so that both the number of estates, including a fourth estate of peasants, and the nature of their representative freedoms, were firmly prescribed. The effect of this ordinance was that parliamentary ratification became a prerequisite for endorsement of taxes. In 1626, the Riddarhusordning was added to this corpus of constitutional laws, and the council of the nobility was constitutionally recognized as a governing Council of State (Schieche 1964: 406): the high nobility thus acted as a vital adjunct to royal power. The crucial text in this sequence of constitutional documents, however, was the Form of Government of 1634. Article 5 of this document stated that members of the king's council had the duty to ensure that the king ruled in accordance with the law of the land and showed 'constant care for the rights, dignity, advantage and welfare of King and people'. Article 45 of this document stipulated that resolutions of national Diets should be 'held as binding' by all subjects of law (Roberts 1968b: 20, 26). This document also provided for the institution of distinct governmental departments, each formally organized around the same general principles. In addition to this, in the Judicature Ordinance of 1614 Sweden received a court of appeal, and procedures for the equitable conduct of trials were laid down.

The constitutional system established in Sweden, naturally, contained salient imperfections: it was vulnerable to circumvention, it did not entirely negate the possibility of taxation by prerogative (Roberts 1991: 78), and it

---

[59] The Swedish crown had held national assemblies from 1359 and a *riksdag* from the 1430s (Schück 1988: 24).

did not prevent Sweden's ultimate decline into a more absolutist mode of governance after 1680. Moreover, the Swedish constitution was distinct from that of other early modern constitutionally balanced states in that the period of constitutional concentration was accompanied by a weakening of some parliamentary powers in respect of fiscal rights, and by increasing noble exemption from taxes (Lindegren 1985: 321). Indeed, the period of Sweden's imperial expansion, and of its closely related constitutional evolution, saw an extensive increase in crown land given over to the nobility for immediate revenue (Lindegren 1985: 325). Members of the nobility were in many respects the main beneficiaries of these constitutional processes. Nonetheless, the body of constitutional texts in seventeenth-century Sweden created an equilibrium between the non-noble estates and the nobility, and it enabled the monarchical executive at once to maintain its traditional support among the burghers and the peasants while also enshrining the liberties of the aristocracy. In this respect, the Swedish constitutions established a working arrangement at the centre of the state, through which the state could both appease the nobility and construct a political bulwark against the dominance of noble interests (Roberts 1962: 43, 50). This was facilitated by the fact that Sweden was never a fully feudal society, and the peasants tended to utilize their distinctive constitutional powers to seek alliance with the monarch in order to defend themselves against the imposition of serfdom. In addition to this, these constitutional settlements allowed the Swedish state consistently to order its legal apparatus and to organize lines of monetary supply, and they created a framework in which the crown could negotiate with the peasantry over taxation. At the same time, furthermore, the adoption of these constitutional arrangements also allowed the Swedish state to evolve an independent administrative apparatus and a largely non-venal civil service,[60] which could perform functions of state at a relatively high degree of abstraction and as relatively detached from particular or structural distinctions in society. One key purpose of the constitutional documents was that they helped to preserve an impersonal order of service in the state during periods of warfare, in which those persons factually bearing the power of the state were in combat overseas – or dead.

In each of these respects, the presence of a rudimentary body of written constitutional law in Sweden acted to stabilize the emergent

---

[60] On the growth of state bureaucracy in Sweden see Lindegren (1985: 309); Lockhart (2004: 7).

state as an independent public order, to consolidate the state as an abstracted bearer of social functions, and to augment the unitary and public power of the state. Above all, if the crucial precondition of an effective and self-reliant early modern state resided in its ability to secure general conditions of monetary supply, to establish a clear intersection with the economy, and so, necessarily, to de-privatize its social foundations, the constitutional apparatus deployed in Sweden provided (for a short time) an expedient technique for the partial accomplishment of these preconditions. The Swedish system might be seen as the first elaborated example of a monarchical state using consensual regulations to pursue its own political differentiation and positive unitary consolidation. In this case, the parliamentary mechanisms for manifesting consensus allowed the monarchy at once to negotiate with bearers of economic resources as formally external to its own structure, to project itself as a publicly constructed order and to legislate over matters of state in relatively positive and autonomous fashion.

The Dutch Republic

A highly distinctive variant on the early modern constitutional state developed in the Dutch Republic, which came into existence through the treaty of the Union of Utrecht in 1579, which cemented the Dutch revolt. At one level, strikingly, the Dutch Republic was constitutionally shaped by a rejection of the modern unitary state: it evolved through a noble rebellion against the Habsburg dynasty to preserve the chartered corporate rights and privileges of provincial and urban estates against Habsburg rule. In the first instance, the protagonists of the revolt legitimized their actions under the terms of a Habsburg Charter, prior to the Pragmatic Sanction of 1549. This document itself referred to the principles of lordship formulated in the contract of the Joyous Entry of 1356, in which the exercise of lordship in Brabant (especially in fiscal matters) was tied to the consent of the provincial estates. Throughout its initial formation, therefore, the Dutch Republic was characterized by an impetus against the construction of the state as a centralized political system, and the members of the States-General were clearly commissioned to guard the privileges of cities and provinces against any hegemonic political centre. To be sure, the Union Treaty of 1579 necessarily entailed the transfer of some powers – that is, of foreign policy and, notionally, of taxation – from the cities to the States-General. Moreover, after 1618 the office of the *stadhouder*, held by the princes of Orange, acted alongside the States-General as a powerful source of leadership in

Holland and in the republic as a whole (Price 1994: 136). In certain respects, therefore, the Dutch Republic evolved on a constitutional pattern that consolidated power in a centrally elected government. Yet, in other respects, this constitutional order retained its origins in the compacts of later feudal society, and it preserved, at least outwardly, a distinctively anti-modern and highly provincial constitutional form. Indeed, no one town or province was able to monopolize the States-General, and the power of supreme governmental authority in the growing republic after 1579 remained attached to a regionally balanced and loosely co-ordinated system of government.

At the same time, however, the informally pooled constitution of the Dutch Republic devised a state order that was clearly abstracted against highly privatistic regional interests and could legitimize itself as an independent and public organic body. In particular, it was a distinctive feature of the Dutch constitution that, in resisting full centralization, it preserved a high degree of local accountability and, especially in fiscal questions, it reinforced the local patterns of revenue raising and fiscal scrutiny that were already in place before the revolt: despite the pledges of signatories to the Union of 1579 to centralize taxation, a fully centralized fiscal order was slow to develop. Precisely because its public finances were subject to local administration and state revenue was subject to open review, the republic proved very effective in generating public confidence and obtaining capital reserves, and it showed great success in stabilizing its monetary foundations. Although falling short of a fully centralized modern state, therefore, the early Dutch Republic was able to use a consensual/constitutional apparatus to motivate trust in key functions of state, and the system of local/constitutional control of state decisions, established within a relatively small national terrain, meant that it was able to presuppose acceded instruments for structuring its economic base and for conducting public operations (especially in monetary matters) at a high level of evident regularity. Indeed, the constitutional arrangements existing through society meant that the state was even able to stimulate the formation of independent credit institutions, which further increased its revenue supply and intensified its structural autonomy: the Dutch Republic, notably, was the first European state to develop a central bank (Bank of Amsterdam, 1609). In the case of the Dutch Republic, therefore, the existence of an inclusionary constitution was the most vital precondition for the reinforcement of state power, and the preservation of constitutional mechanisms for raising revenue and approving legislation overcame structural weaknesses that, in other settings, would have dragged prohibitively against the formation of a stable state.

England

In England, as discussed, the initial period of Reformation witnessed a rapid concentration of power in the monarchy, in the royal courts and in parliament. This relocation of power was supported by the temporary and informal constitutional settlements following the Act of Supremacy, in which both the power of the monarchy and the power of parliament increased. However, over a longer period of time this balanced governmental apparatus was undermined by a series of protracted legal conflicts. Central to this, as mentioned, was the fact that the courts of common law began to invoke embedded customary rights to resist both royal prerogatives and parliamentary statutes, and even to revive medieval notions of time-honoured authority to propose a less autonomously abstracted model of state power. By the earlier seventeenth century, consequently, the English polity was showing acute signs of fracturing under the weight of jurisdictional power that it had absorbed, and antagonism between royal courts and common-law courts began to form a deep constitutional fissure in the English state. In this conflict, courts of common law were habitually used both to challenge rulings handed down by the tribunals of the king and to call into question the sovereign powers of statutory legislation that the monarchy had arrogated to itself.[61] Gradually, in fact, the courts of common law began to imagine themselves as appointed guardians of an ancient constitution, acting as a potent rival to the powers of statute and fiscal levy secured by the parliamentary monarchy. The overlapping jurisdictional powers and the multiple contradictory notions of statutory and customary authority existing in the English political system thus proved deeply inimical to the successful operation of the state, and it meant that the state struggled to articulate a clear jurisdictional basis for its functions or to promote a clear unitary conception of its power and its legitimacy to support its legal acts.

In very broad terms, the constitutional controversies that unsettled the English polity in the earlier Stuart period can be attributed to two primary factors. In the first instance, as outlined, these controversies were caused by simple contests over jurisdiction: the courts of common law set their jurisdictional power against royal prerogative, and

---

[61] For discussion see Tanner (1966: 41); Hart (2003: 39).

principles of common law were invoked, factually, as constitutionally inviolable sources of law, able to limit and counteract laws introduced by royal ordinance or parliamentary statute. As discussed, these ideas underwent a rapid ideological inflation through the earlier part of the seventeenth century, and principles of judicial inviolability became fundamental to analysis of the legitimacy or illegitimacy of the Stuart regime.[62] For example, the great common lawyers of the early seventeenth century, most notably Edward Coke, recurrently defended courts of common law as bastions even of *natural law*,[63] and they saw inherited common-law rights of royal subjects as part of the natural substance of society. One salient reason for the loss of legitimacy by the Stuart monarchy in the 1620s, in fact, was that the king repeatedly connived with judges, and judges were often discredited as agents in the pay of the monarchy and embodying a royal strategy to corrupt the inviolable fabric of the common law (see Reeve 1989: 137).[64] A second factor giving rise to these controversies, however, was that parliament itself was often (although by no means invariably) characterized as a court of common law, which was sanctioned by, and in turn provided protection for, the rights accorded to subjects under common law: in consequence, the existence of a strong parliament was accorded crucial importance for the survival of particular or customary liberties. Ultimately, this view of parliament induced crisis in the English monarchy in the longer build-up to the Civil War, because Charles I, beset by opposition, sought to legislate in vital religious and fiscal matters without due parliamentary consultation. Owing to the rising cost of increasingly technologically intensive wars, the monarchy experienced a rapid increase in its need for revenue in the 1620s and 1630s, and it lacked fully consensual mechanisms to generate supply to match these needs. In response to the resultant fiscal crisis, powerful actors within the monarchical executive embarked on the fateful policy of raising revenue by coercive means – that is, primarily, by forced loans, introduced without parliamentary support or after the enforced proroguing of parliaments. This brought

---

[62] Much of the following is treated expertly in Zaller (2007: 267–354). Although I find this work impressive, I have not borrowed any analysis from this account.

[63] Hence the subversive significance attached to the courts of common law in England, which were viewed as repositories of customary law and natural law at the same time. In his report of Calvin's case, Coke argued that natural law was 'Part of the Law of England' (2003 [1608]: 195).

[64] One historian has observed that Charles I used the judiciary as a 'political weapon' (Black 1976: 64).

the monarchy into acute conflict with parliament, whose members saw their power overridden by prerogative fiscal devices, and, in this respect again, it created a perception that the monarchy was intent on demolishing the symbolic bastion of the common-law liberties of English subjects.

As a result of this, in the period before the Civil War actors attached to the parliamentary cause were able to insist on the common law as the basis for an internal constitution of state by which the king himself could be held to account and even judged, and they began to employ parliament as a constitutional court of law. As early as 1628, as Conrad Russell explained, members of parliament were forced to choose whether to show support for either the common law or the king, and most elected to endorse, not a monarchical, but a common-law construction of the constitution (1979: 368–9). It was in this context that the Petition of Right, drafted by leading parliamentarians as a summary of existing common-law liberties, was proposed and agreed, and the Petition of Right acted as a constitutional focus for the growing parliamentary attempt to restrict royal prerogative and legal abuse. By the early Civil War, then, some lawyers and legal theorists had begun to enunciate the principles of common law in a vocabulary close to that of modern constitutionalism, and the idea of a constitution as an express legal corpus within the state manifestly began to condition the exercise of royal power.[65] In 1641, the Grand Remonstrance accused the king of 'subverting the fundamental laws and principles of government' (Kenyon 1966: 231). In 1643, Henry Parker, the eloquent proponent of parliamentary authority, examined the common law as an effective constitution, marking a clear distinction between the legally legitimized polity and non-legitimate personal rule, and so separating the public order of the state from singular persons with temporary authority to use its power. Parker defined the legitimate state as one in which the king was 'regulated by the Law' (1643: 4). In consequence, he insisted that offices

---

[65] Thirty years earlier the term 'constitution' had not quite assumed this meaning, and it still retained elements of its Latinate implication as a statute or body of positive laws. Importantly, by this stage the modern sense of the word was clearly coming into view. In his famous speech of 1610 James Whitelocke stated that the proposed taxes of James I were 'against the natural frame and constitution of the policy of this kingdom, which is *jus publicum regni*, and so subverteth the fundamental law of the realm' (Prothero 1913: 351). However, in parliament in 1610 the 'power to make constitutions' was also defined as equivalent to the power to make by-laws or to introduce local acts of legislation (Foster 1966: 193).

of state needed to be seen as distinct from all power of particular persons, and that those seeking to re-particularize or to use power for private ends needed to be opposed. He stated, 'If the Monarchy or Regal Authority itself be regulated, then whatsoever is done by the king, undeniably without and beyond the limits of that Regulation, is not *Regal Authority*. And therefore to resist Notorious Transgressions of that Regulation is no Resisting of Royal Authority' (1643: 4). On this basis, Parker concluded that it was prescribed by the common law – that is, by '*Constitution of this Government*' – that in the matters of greatest 'Importance for publick benefit' the king was obliged to seek and give heed to parliamentary consultation. During the Civil War, subsequently, these principles of common law were taken as the grounds for the constitutional indictment of Charles I and his strategies for avoiding parliamentary approval of laws: the prosecutors of the king asserted that, in seeking to legislate without parliament, the monarch had broken the 'limited government' entrusted to him and failed to 'govern by the laws of the land, for the good of the people and the preservation of their rights' (Woolrych 2002: 432). Prior to his execution, in fact, Charles I expressly rejected the legal division of office and person implied in the common-law constitution, and he insisted on his regal status as implying a simultaneous embodiment of public office and personal power (Smith 1994: 218). The parliamentary case, naturally, rested on the claim that the public office of the king was defined under common law, and this office contained normative implications by which the natural/physical person of the king could be impeached and put to death.

For these reasons, the polity of earlier seventeenth-century England possessed an inner constitutional structure, in which practical (fiscal) and normative (legal/judicial) antagonisms could easily infect and cause one another to escalate, and friction between components of an imperfectly unified legal order could become channels for wider practical malfunctions in the political system. The English state of the earlier Stuart era, in effect, suffered a crisis of legitimacy in both its functional and its normative dimensions. That is to say, the monarchical state encountered a situation in which it could not fulfil its functional needs (i.e. raise tax) without contravening normative expectations and without stimulating normative resistance (i.e. without encroaching on perceived and theoretically enunciated liberties). However, it could not easily obtain normative legitimacy (i.e. justify itself before the law and before parliament) without accepting certain functional restrictions (i.e. accepting constraints on monetary supply). Both aspects of this legitimacy crisis, however, were induced by the fact that the state had not yet evolved an effective and fully unitary functional apparatus to regulate its exchanges with either the law or the economy: that is, it had not yet formalized a legal/constitutional system in which law could be used easily and impersonally to transmit power, and it had not successfully separated economic exchanges from personal interests or organized its procedures of economic negotiation in a stable, differentiated structure.[66] The legitimacy crisis of the early modern English state, in short, was a crisis caused by incomplete unitary construction and incomplete positive political abstraction. Above all, it was induced by the fact that, under acute fiscal pressures induced by international military commitments, the state was obliged to hold both its legal and its economic interactions at a very high level of personal and political resonance, and the politicization of these exchanges illuminated the precarious unity of the state as a whole.

Against this background, the constitutional order that was progressively elaborated throughout the period of Stuart rule and the revolutionary interregnum in the middle of the seventeenth century formed a sequence of vital adaptive responses to the inner unitary weakness of the English state. Indeed, the period of rapid revolutionary transformation in the English monarchy throughout the seventeenth century gradually established a political order that was capable of conducting its functions at a higher level of public generality and inclusion than had previously been the case, and it established legal mechanisms within the political system which prevented the normative breaches and functional controversies that had previously disrupted the operations of state. Moreover, this period saw the construction of a constitution, as a public-legal order, which allowed the state coherently to integrate sources of resistance and to elevate the positive abstraction of its power.

In the first instance, in the long step-wise process of constitutional equilibration that ran through the seventeenth century, the English state obtained a more consistently uniform normative and judicial order, and this enabled it both to avoid unsettling juridical conflict and to simplify its unitary structure. The documents forming the constitutional settlements of the seventeenth century, initially, had the characteristic that they recognized the general rule of law, they rejected political encroachment in judicial procedure, and, in principle, they recognized all people as entitled to equal and fair treatment under law (Kenyon 1966: 83).

---

[66] For background see Dietz (1964: 127); Cust (1987: 34).

This latter point was central to the Petition of Right of 1628. It was reiterated in the Grand Remonstrance, which placed specific emphasis on judicial integrity. Oliver Cromwell's law reforms then also introduced measures to ensure fair judicial procedure.[67] This principle was finally confirmed by the Declaration of Rights in 1689. Through these petitions and statutes, concepts derived from the common law were accepted as normatively universal, and the extent to which royal courts could deviate from these standards was (in theory) subject to constitutional regulation. Indeed, these statutes and petitions also meant that the state as a whole was increasingly defined through reference to general and fundamental legal norms – or, as stated in the Grand Remonstrance, to 'fundamental laws and principles of government' – which were notionally extracted from the common law. In this respect, these statutes and petitions cemented the expectation both that those bearing state power were required to acknowledge and respect the 'laws which concern the subject in his liberty', and that all use of power in society was conducted according to abstractly acceded norms (Kenyon 1966: 231, 240).

In each of these respects, the growing constitutional order of the state brought great advantages to the political system. In internalizing a fixed legal construction of its foundations in this fashion, first, the state was able at once to reduce the political volatility attached to the law, to control its own intersection with the law and progressively to consolidate its unitary differentiated structure by limiting private conflicts over law. The acceptance of the common law as a constitutional apparatus, further, meant that the state was able to propose a coherent normative definition of itself to support its power, and to acquire a unitary set of procedures which simplified its use of power. Moreover, the normative corpus of the common law, conceptually absorbed within the state itself, provided the state with an apparatus in which it could internalize the sources of its authority, extirpate private or dualistic elements from its inner structure and adopt a public-legal order that exponentially increased the volume of power which it had at its disposal. The idea of the common law as a normative constitutional order within the state thus substantially heightened the power of the state. After the 1640s parliament was able to invoke a common-law constitution in order to assume semi-sovereign independence and, in fact, constitutionally

---

[67] Cromwell opposed full judicial independence. However, his reforms, notably Arts. XIX and LXVII of the 'Ordinance for the better Regulating and Limiting the Jurisdiction of the High Court of Chancery' (1654), were important for their provisions against executive law finding. This document is published in Firth and Rait (1911: 949–67).

to place its monopoly of legislative power above all conventionally acceded fundamental laws (and so, also, above all other judicial power).[68]

In addition, the constitutional order created during the longer period of the English Revolution also constructed the state as a political order with a balanced representative constitution, in which ratification by parliament became a precondition for legitimate statutory legislation. Naturally, views on the constitutional status of parliament varied greatly. The dominant view of the parliamentarians of the 1640s was that parliament was the highest focus of sovereign power, standing even above the common law. William Prynne stated this most boldly, claiming simply that the 'High Court of Parliament' was the 'Highest Souveraigne power of all the others, and above the King himselfe' (1643: 33). The Nineteen Propositions of 1642 clearly claimed that 'statutes made by Parliament' had authority to override other sources of authority, and that the 'justice of parliament', not the justice of privately appointed judges, was the supreme judicial force in the nation (Kenyon 1966: 246). Even before the execution of Charles I, the Commons of England declared that 'the people' were 'the original of all just power' and that 'the commons of England, in parliament assembled, being chosen by, and representing, the people' were in possession of 'the supreme power in the nation' (Davies 1937: 160). In his reply to the Nineteen Propositions, Charles I himself conceded that the legislative authority of parliament was an element of a balanced organic order of state, of which the monarch was merely one part.[69] Although lamenting the fact that his 'Just, Ancient, Regall Power' was 'fetched down to the ground' by the present parliament, he specifically acknowledged the existence of a mixed constitution in England, stating that 'In this Kingdom the Laws are jointly made by a King, by a House of Peers, and by A House of Commons chosen by the People, all having free Votes and particular Privileges.'[70] Subsequently, Cromwell's Instrument of Government of 1653 confirmed that 'supreme legislative authority of the Commonwealth of England' resided in the Lord Protector and the people assembled in parliament.

---

[68] The principle behind this point was captured in an anonymous pamphlet which argued that fundamental laws formed the 'politique constitution' of the commonwealth and imposed laws of consultative procedure, nature and equity on the king. Under such laws, however, parliament could not be guilty of 'Arbitrary Government' or contravention of fundamental law because the 'law was not made between Parliament and people, but by the People in Parliament betweene the King and them' (*Touching the Fundamentall Lawes* 1643: 8). Parliament, in other words, *was* the fundamental law.

[69] See the analysis in Weston and Greenberg (1981: 39).

[70] Charles I, 'His Majesties Answer to the Nineteen Propositions of Both Houses of Parliament' (1999 [1642]: 160, 168).

Article VI of the Instrument of Government stipulated that laws were not to be 'altered, suspended, abrogated, or repealed, not any new law made, nor any tax, charge or imposition laid upon the people, but by common consent in Parliament' (Kenyon 1966: 342–3). Through the revolutionary period, in short, parliament came to be considered as an institution that could not be dissolved or prorogued at royal behest, and it was accorded increasingly fixed duties, legislative competences and procedures, and, owing to its authority to form cabinets, substantial executive power. The rights of parliament, although weakened after the Restoration, were specifically acknowledged in the Triennial Act (1664), forming one part of the Restoration settlements: the Restoration was indelibly shaped by acceptance of an ordered parliament as a necessary organ of government (Seaward 1989: 77). These principles were then fundamental to the constitutional settlements of the Glorious Revolution of 1688–9. In 1688, parliament assumed the power to select and appoint English monarchs, and it functioned as a constitutional organ able to prescribe implicit contractual terms to those monarchs that it deemed fit to exercise power. The Convention Parliament of 1688–9 in fact acted in many respects like a constitutional assembly (with all the animosities typical of such assemblies), and it bound the power of William III to clear constraints and used the monarchical interim to extend its own legislative power.[71] Most notably, the 1689 Declaration of Rights was prefaced by an extensive attempt to discredit James II, and, almost as an effective contract between king and realm, it prohibited the non-parliamentary use of regal power in passing and enforcing laws (Williams 1960: 28).

In this regard, too, the seventeenth-century constitution greatly expanded the practical power of the state. The constitution that gradually emerged through the Interregnum, the Restoration and the parliamentary revolution of 1688–9 had the specific distinction that, in sanctioning the legislative power of parliament, it established an attributive structure that clearly identified the law's source, strictly separated the power of the state from the standing of singular persons, and conclusively consolidated the positive legislative operations of the state. The growing (yet still incompletely realized) idea of parliamentary sovereignty acted as a principle that greatly simplified the operations of the state: it assuaged the dualistic or polycratic elements in the state that had previously obstructed the use of

---

[71] It is noted, however, that William III accepted the crown before approving the Declaration of Rights (Speck 1988: 114). For a recent brilliant revision of common perceptions of the activities of the Convention Parliament see Pincus (2009: 283–6).

its power, it established clear procedures of political inclusion and it enabled the state to utilize its power at a previously unforeseen level of abstracted autonomy. In particular, it is notable that, although the ideal of parliament's obligation to the common law did not disappear, the assumption that parliament could be obligated to the courts of law began to recede during and after the Interregnum: by 1700 the principle of the statutory primacy of parliament was clearly prevalent.[72] If the revolutionary processes of the middle of the seventeenth century had been shaped by the joint insistence on the inviolability of common-law rights and on the authority of parliament, therefore, after 1688 the second of these principles took pronounced precedence over the first. This conceptual adjustment meant that, even where it was nominally sustained by the common law, parliament began to extricate itself from externalistic conventions and to remove quasi-legislative powers from the judiciary, and it concentrated its own power within a tightly defined, internally consistent, institutional organ. The doctrine of parliamentary supremacy, in short, created a regular fissure between polity and judiciary, did much to disaggregate the distinct legislative and judicial powers vested in parliament, set the foundation for the subsequent emergence of a unitary state with singular monopoly of jurisdictional power, and protected the state from dualistic destabilization through half-internalized controversies between legislators and judges.[73] This diminution of external judicial power was welcomed, not only by monarchists who had been threatened by countervailing claims to judicial power implied in the common law, but also by parliamentarians, who had initially insisted on powers of judicial review enshrined under common law to support their claims, yet who also saw judges as inclined to royalism and viewed the independence of the law courts as eroding the authority of the parliamentary order.[74] The ascription of full statutory powers of legislative

---

[72] Cromwell's judicial legislation stipulated that 'No Decree shall be made in Chancery against an Act of Parliament' (Firth and Rait 1911: 959).

[73] This point is also made in Grey (1978: 846); Burrage (2006: 415).

[74] In England, parliament, like the monarchy, was desperate to reduce the influence of centres of judicial power outside parliament – i.e. courts of common law. See the exclamation in the Commons Debates of 1621: 'The Judges are Judges of the Law, not of the Parliament. God forbid the state of the Kingdom should come under the sentence of a Judge' (cit. Mosse 1950: 128). Thus, although parliament called on the common law for its own justification, it also saw the limiting of common-law authority as a precondition of its sovereignty. Later, note John Pym's defence of parliamentary supremacy against judges who 'presume to question the proceedings of the House' (cit. Jones 1971: 138). On attempts to expel lawyers from the Commons and on the hatred of the Levellers for lawyers see Veall (1970: 100, 107, 203).

control to parliament resolved disruptive problems of this kind: the progressive reinforcement of parliament through the later years of the seventeenth century meant that the conflict between royal courts and parliament was attenuated, and the extent to which the state could be split through the politicization of particular acts of legislation and particular processes of judicial finding was restricted. Indeed, this period also witnessed a more systematic ordering of the common law and statutes, through which boundaries of competence between judicial and legislative organs were still more clearly defined.[75]

The rise of the parliamentary constitution, in other words, expressed a potent inclusionary dynamic through which dualistic or centrifugal elements of the English polity could be more coherently welded together. The symbolic connection of parliament and the common law had deeply felicitous implications in the emergence of the English state, and it enabled a powerful unitary legislature to develop, which was able to account for itself, normatively, as a custodian of time-honoured liberties and freedoms, yet which could also legislate with unprecedented levels of abstraction and positive autonomy. If the constitutional idea of fundamental law emerged in England in the earlier seventeenth century as part of an attempt to articulate residually medieval ideas of convention against the power of the monarchical executive, therefore, this idea ultimately fused with parliament to create a constitution containing a potent independent legislature acting both as internally bound by, yet also as released from, socially embedded basic laws. In this condition, the English parliament was able to act as an organ that internalized the diffuse dualistic constitution and the normative expectations of later medieval society into the state, and that condensed the laws of this society, not as a normative legal body of fundamental laws standing outside the political apparatus, but as the *state's own constitution*: as an internal constitution of public law, serving to articulate and expand the state's own power and positively to transmit the state's own legal acts.

In combining ideas of parliamentary autonomy and uniform legal rule in this fashion, crucially, the English constitutional settlements of the seventeenth century also formed a political system, in which parliament obtained firm control of the levers of finance, which meant that taxation could not be introduced without the endorsement of the assembled parliament. This was stated in the Petition of Right, which defined 'common consent by Act of Parliament' as the basis for new taxes

---

[75] See the account of this in Shapiro (1974).

(Kenyon 1966: 84). This was then confirmed in the *Instrument of Government*, and it was finally refined in Article 4 of the Declaration of Rights. These agreements began formally to recognize the idea of personal rights (that is, rights against fiscal depredation) as constitutive and actionable constitutional principles, and they began to express the conviction that parliament protected rights of persons in all aspects of their social lives and that parliament was an objective guarantor for a primary group of collective personal entitlements. Most importantly, however, the constitutional reinforcement of parliamentary powers of fiscal control had the practical result that the fiscal opposition between monarch and parliament was terminated, or at least substantially palliated, and that the political system as a whole acquired monetary instruments to stabilize its unitary functions. Indeed, the period of revolutionary constitutionalism in England was also a time of substantial fiscal rationalization, in which the procedures for securing monetary supply for the state were dramatically improved. The fact that the English state of the later Stuart period was a state that endorsed parliamentary review of taxation meant that, like the Dutch Republic, the state was able to generate a high level of social trust in its activities, and this allowed it exponentially to raise its capacities for obtaining revenue. It is notable, above all, that, as the monarchy renounced more prerogative approaches to securing its fiscal base, the finances of the state improved substantially, and the period of greatest parliamentary control of revenue coincided with an increase in the state's monetary buoyancy.[76] As in the Dutch Republic, this relatively easy relation between crown and creditors meant that the state was able to borrow money on trust, to found a national debt and even to establish a central lending bank, which at once further enhanced its credit supply and stimulated the growth of capital in private markets (Dickson 1967: 45). On this count, therefore, the constitutional guarantee for parliamentary ratification of fiscal measures also softened the earlier destabilizing interpenetration between economic and political questions, and it created a series of mechanisms that allowed both state and economy to evolve both in relative autonomy and in a reciprocally beneficial relation. In this respect again, the revolutionary

---

[76] For examples of the mass of literature on this, see North and Weingast (1989: 805, 817, 819); Brewer (1989: 89); Carruthers (1996: 119); Braddick (2000: 221); Stasavage (2003: 173). Importantly, crucial elements of the taxation system of the Restoration period were introduced during the Interregnum. They were legitimized by popular (or at least parliamentary) approval and subsequently retained as expedient (Ashley 1962: 83; Tanner 1966: 125; Wheeler 1999: 148).

constitutional texts of seventeenth-century England greatly augmented the abstracted and unitary power of the state, and they greatly expanded the state's capacities for the general and positive distribution of political power.

Of further benefit for the construction of the English state was the fact that, as they established parliament as a permanent and legally protected body of state, the constitutional settlements of the Stuart era allowed the state, in albeit very tentative manner, palliatively to internalize sources of political conflict and aggressive resistance in society. Through these constitutional arrangements, the state was able reliably (although not conclusively) to divide its legislative, judicial and executive functions, and it developed a largely separate parliamentary organ, independently sanctioned by the constitution, into which it could channel social conflicts and to which issues of the highest social volatility could be referred for legislative regulation. This pattern of organization substantially expanded the administrative flexibility of the state, and it greatly diminished the political controversy attached to the boundaries between the political system and other parts of society. More importantly still, as discussed, the incorporation of parliament as a distinct legislative organ allowed the state to internalize previously potent bearers of private privilege and sources of political dissent, to convert externalistic or private conflicts into disputes that could (to some degree) be settled within the state, and so to weaken the power of private actors that had previously been protected by customary laws. In the earlier documents of the English constitution, thus, the *separation of powers* began tentatively to emerge as a principle that stabilized the state both above society and its own day-to-day operations, that helped further to transform the dualistic elements of earlier constitutional arrangements into inner components of the state, and that endowed the state with more complex facilities for engaging with and pacifying social conflict. This was highly relevant for the financial condition of the state: it meant that parliament could exercise its powers of fiscal control and the state could obtain revenue through relatively stabilized procedures of negotiation. Most importantly, however, the fixed institution of parliament meant that the state, in very rudimentary manner, began to evolve internal organs in which adversarial opinions could be articulated and dissenting positions expressed without the danger that these would immediately lead to the unsettling of the state itself. In the documents resulting from 1688, in particular, the state limited its tendency to prohibit rival outlooks, and it established a legal order in which it could both integrate, and also

gradually mollify, highly divergent political stances.[77] This very gradual institutionalization of opposition in parliament, although not concluded until well into the eighteenth century, meant that the English
state was able to entertain and express a number of views about its
particular governmental policies without exposing itself to unmanageable levels of insecurity.[78] The possibility that legitimate – or even
loyal – opposition could exist as an internal element of the state itself
meant that the state was able to separate its power from momentary
controversies and control obstructions to its power and that, very
slowly, it acquired capacities for placating serious sources of obstruction and even for transforming these into elements of public order.

In each of these points, the incremental formation of the English
constitution throughout the Stuart period amounted to a supreme act
of unitary and independent state building. In many ways, it marked a
highly successful process of abstractive and differentiated political formation, and it exponentially extended the reserves of power which the
state was in a position to produce and utilize. This was in fact directly
reflected in even the most divergent theoretical constructions and controversies of the era, many of which acted conceptually to intensify the
positive structure of state power. Throughout the revolutionary period,
much theoretical literature centred around the extraction of a prominent
constitutional formula to simplify and increase the autonomous power of
the state. That is, this literature created and enriched a vocabulary in
which government was constructed as a commonwealth, subject to rule,
not by physical persons, but by abstracted laws, and in which political
power was required to explain itself as an internally consistent and
positively abstracted phenomenon in society (Scott 2004: 133). This
was evident in the writings of republican protagonists in debate, such
as Marchamont Nedham, who argued that states with republican constitutions – based in the 'due and orderly succession of their supreme
assemblies' and separate from natural or particular actors – were able to
maintain large reserves of distinctively political authority, and to assume
a degree of positive sovereignty not accessible to states based in natural

---

[77] Note the unsettling prohibition of Nonconformist factions through the 1680s and its
resolution after 1688 (Lacey 1969: 153, 163).
[78] This is exactly what had been missing before the Civil War (Sharpe 1992: 715). It should
be clear that the relation between political factions was not immediately pacified after
1689. For evidence to the contrary see Rose (1999: 62–104). However, even this documentation shows that the state was acquiring the facility that it could incorporate rival
views as countervailing parts of its structure.

hierarchy (1767 [1651–2/6]: 14, 85). James Harrington also argued that government, defined, *de iure*, as a 'civil society of men' that was 'instituted and preserved upon the foundation of common right or interest', was far more effective in applying political power than government founded in 'private interest' (1887 [1656]: 16). At the monarchical end of the spectrum of controversy, even royalists such as David Jenkins, who asserted that 'the Regality of the Crown of England is immediatly subject to God and to none other', defined the state as formed by a corporate constitution, which placed the king beneath an internal law and bound the king to accept acts of parliament (1647: 7). Notably, the work of Thomas Hobbes also gave rise to a doctrine of collective obligation, which played the most vital conceptual role in augmenting the power of the state. Hobbes proposed a theory in which the state drew power and legitimacy from its internalization of a public will, which could never be factually identical with private interests or acts of volition (1914 [1651]: 66). In incorporating this will, the state emerged as a public contractual order or 'artificial personality', that was able, in its corporate artifice, to eliminate countervailing personal forces (i.e. the church, the independent courts and the aristocracy), to concentrate all power singularly within its own structure and to apply its power across all society as a generalized, equally inclusive and personally insensitive social resource.

The common idea of the state as a public body thus acted throughout revolutionary England to provide a conceptual device that mirrored the expansion in the state's growing capacities for producing and transmitting power, and it formed a store of terms inside the state from which political power could project motives for its acceptance at a high level of social autonomy and internal abstraction. In all their different dimensions, in fact, the English constitutional innovations of the seventeenth century created a highly internal apparatus of public law for the state, which it could use to concentrate and preserve the abstraction of its political power. This allowed the state at once to abstract itself from other spheres of society, to soften the volatility of its exchanges with interests located in other parts of society, to exclude actors with privatistic claims to power, and gradually to internalize those actors within society that possessed the most acute political relevance. In all their different dimensions, therefore, these documents and processes dramatically increased both the volume of power stored in the state and the positive facility with which this power could be employed. The constitutional order that evolved in revolutionary England, thus, might be viewed as a distinctively effective solution to the accelerated abstraction and positivization of political power which marked the threshold of early European modernity.

The constitution and the function of constitutional rights

The most important accomplishment of the seventeenth-century English state, however, was that it began to utilize *constitutional rights* as internal instruments of formal political abstraction and pervasive socio-political inclusion. At this historical juncture, civil and political rights began discernibly to play a vital role in stabilizing the differentiated position of the political system in society, and this again greatly reinforced the inclusionary circulation of political power throughout society as a whole.

In the course of all the processes described above, the English Revolution established the principle of parliamentary authority (if not supremacy) in legislation as one component of a balanced constitution. Through this constitutional revolution, the common laws, which had originally been designated by common-law judges either as institutes to sanction particular privileges or as eternal protectors of socially embedded natural rights, were positively integrated *within* the state: far from acting as external normative limits on power, rights became parts of the state's internal functional, public-legal apparatus. After 1688, parliament was placed above particular fundamental laws, and the 'consent of parliament' itself became the fundamental law of the constitution (Williams 1960: 28). Parliament, acting now as an integrally fixed organ of the polity, identified itself both as a legislator legitimized by the rights inhering in ancient common laws and (at the same time – however paradoxically) as factually and positively enforcing its own laws throughout society, whose normative content it defined as derived from rights. Indeed, although the principles of rule by law and governance by parliamentary statute are often perceived as antinomies, the success and distinction of the post-revolutionary English constitution lay precisely in the fact that it offered legitimacy to the legislature as an organ that both implicitly internalized general principles of law (rights) and was authorized to legislate as a fulcrum of autonomous statutory power. The conventional antagonism between law (the judiciary) and the state (the administration) was (at least symbolically) resolved in the earlier documents of the English constitution, and under the post-1688 constitution parliamentary legislators began to present themselves, even in their acts of positive statutory legislation, as the legitimate custodians of basic common-law rights, such as rights of equality before the law, of equal legal redress, of free disposition over private property, and of protection from arbitrary fiscal extraction. In particular, the parliamentary constitution after 1688 tied together procedural rights (i.e. rights of legal redress), proprietary rights and rights of representation, and, as described by John Locke, it established the parliamentary legislature as an organ that proclaimed and obtained *natural* legitimacy by passing positive laws that represented and protected all three sets of antecedent rights at the same time (1960 [1689]: 364). In justifying itself through reference to rights in this manner, the parliamentary state obtained several distinctive practical benefits, and its legitimating fusion of positive law and internal obligation to rights greatly expanded its legitimacy and facilitated its autonomous functional operations.

Most obviously, first, the establishment of a parliamentary system that drew its positive statutory legitimacy from its implicit preservation of rights under common law meant that the English state was in a position to incorporate an internal and normatively extensible account of its own foundations, which it could use to accompany and simplify its procedures, and which greatly raised the probability that its legal decisions would be met with compliance. In this respect, the fact that the English constitutional state could declare as a prior position that it was constrained to legislate in accordance with laws derived from rights, and that it recognized all members of society as bearers of rights, meant that the state could presuppose confidence through society, and it obtained an exponentially increased liberty in its normal positive legislative, judicial and fiscal operations. Additionally, second, as it sanctioned rights-based principles of judicial uniformity and founding legal order, the state evolved a technique to reduce the personalistic elements of its power, and to obtain a more secure and less unwieldy structure of *legal inclusion* for its addressees. This culminated in the 1701 Act of Settlement, which, reinforcing similar provisions in the Declaration of Rights, ruled that the tenure of judges rested, not on royal pleasure, but on their behaviour and competence (*quamdiu se bene gesserint*): in this statute, judges became, in the last instance, accountable to parliament, and the administration of law was separated from all prerogative and personal favour and defined primarily as the application of rights (Williams 1960: 59). This statute at once limited variations in the wider legal fabric of society, and it reduced the degree to which the state exposed its power to private conflicts or private access. Through its construction as a legal order based in rights, in consequence, the post-revolutionary English state also acquired a more stable legal periphery for the application of its power, and it began internally to simplify and pre-construct both the social terrains in which it utilized power and the procedures by means of which its power was distributed. Furthermore, third, the principle that parliament was the inviolable sovereign organ of the people also promoted the idea that all people, as members of the founding sovereign body, possessed highly generalized rights, which formed the implicit basis for all acts of statutory legislation, and this, too, reinforced the positive inclusionary functions of the state. Whereas earlier traditions of representation and free assembly had promoted representative assemblies as expressions of the freedom of singular persons or singular groups to assert particular entitlements, to insist on particular embedded privileges or to influence particular points of policy, the incremental constitutional revolution in Stuart England gave clearer expression to the idea that, as rights holders, all members of society were equally co-implied in the authorship of laws, and that, because of this, laws had to reflect, to be constrained by and to enact certain immutable and imprescriptible general rights. This aspect of the English constitutional settlement formed a body of public law which, in separating the state from manifest particularism, dramatically extended the integrative dimensions of the state. It created a legal order, both factual and symbolic, which greatly facilitated the integration of social actors into the state's legal and political reserves, which gradually eliminated particular and vested obstructions to the circulation of power through society as a whole, and which, in separating power from particular persons, intensified and simplified the power available to the state. Most importantly, however, in defining itself as a formal repository of general legitimate rights in society the parliamentary/constitutional state established after 1688 clearly asserted that it held both a monopoly of societal rights and a monopoly of societal power, and that other – particular or local – rights were valid only insofar as they were consonant with and confirmed by the state: the state, thus, was the supreme bearer and custodian of rights, and so also the supreme bearer of society's political power, and, as such, it was uniquely entitled to expect obedience.

The constitutional rights that were implemented as internal components of public law through the seventeenth century, in sum, acted both practically and normatively to minimize the potentials for a collapse of legitimacy in the English state, they enabled the state to articulate its functions in more consistently controlled procedures, and they greatly augmented the volume of usably abstracted power that the state possessed. Above all, the aggregate of constitutional rights instituted during and at the end of the struggles between parliament and monarchy in early modern England clearly expressed the belief that the state must be viewed as a public entity, that its public quality was defined and exercised under laws independent of the groups of persons factually utilizing its power, and that the public sources of the state's authority were distinct from any personally negotiated set of privileges and agreements. The fact that the state acknowledged those subject to its power (notionally) as uniform rights holders allowed the state to extract an account of itself as a universally public body, which assumed power by principles detached from any singular or private entitlement. This public-legal dimension of rights was the functional wellspring of the English constitution. At one level, these constitutional principles acted to remove personal influence from the state: the 'advice of private men' was formally effaced from government, and all 'matters as concern the public' were to be brought before the 'great and supreme council' of parliament and not 'debated, resolved and transacted' elsewhere (Kenyon 1966: 244). Additionally, however, these principles also reduced the dualistic elements in the state: as it gradually implemented a uniform body of norms to determine rights of access to state power, the emergent English constitution condensed all political power into the state, and it drew all members of society into a uniform relation to power. Through its constitutional reference to rights, therefore, the state obtained a device in which its sovereign abstraction could be at once asserted and legitimized, and in which other rights (in particular, rights attached to powerful actors outside the state) could be diminished and subject to state control. The constitutional rights-based state evolved as the most powerful device for strengthening political authority, for eliminating particular sources of political power in society or in the margins of the state, for integrating all political actors into the state, and for circulating power through society in simplified, differentiated and generalized form. The rights-based transformation, in England, of the dualist constitution of later feudal society into a more monistic or internal order of state was perhaps the decisive step in the construction of a distinctively modern state, and it was the decisive achievement of the constitution growing from the protracted period of English revolution.

On balance, to conclude, the longer period of early modern European history gave rise to states in a distinctive, although still undeveloped, modern form. Most societies of this period began to converge around unitary or *sovereign* political institutions that were clearly distinct from institutions relating to other social spheres, most members of society began to enter a relatively and even uniform relation to state power, and power began to be transfused through society in relatively positive, even and structurally neutral fashion. The construction of a constitution entailing mechanisms for parliamentary deputation and provisions for basic rights (both in the state and in the judiciary) proved a highly effective device for cementing the differentiated political form of emerging modern societies. Indeed, while medieval societies had possessed the normative tendency to produce rudimentary forms of *public law* to abstract their political resources, early modern societies subjected this normative evolution to far-reaching refinement: these societies began successfully to evolve rights structures as instruments both for consolidating and differentiating their political resources, for condensing their power in unitary institutions, and for transmitting their power, in internally reproducible form, throughout society. Constitutions and constitutional rights, in short, began to be identified as the most adequate normative mechanisms of transmission for political power, and constitutions and constitutional rights came to act as internal instruments for producing and authorizing political power as a positive, public or *sovereign* social facility. Those societies that did not evolve normative institutions of this kind, often those retaining 'absolutistic' structures, tended to circulate political power at a lower level of autonomy, generality and differentiation: they tended to possess, in factual terms, *less power.*

3

States, rights and the revolutionary form of power

The progressive formation of sovereign states in many European societies in the sixteenth and seventeenth centuries was part of a substantial
transformation in the basic structure and application of political power,
which saw an increase in the volume of power and the mass of political
decisions required by different societies. Indeed, the formation of states
reflected a process in which power became political power in the modern
sense of the word: it constructed power as a resource that was relatively
indifferent to singular persons, that was not fully reliant on direct
conflict or coercion for its usage, and that contained a positive internal
structure which allowed it to be applied inclusively and reproduced
across significant structural, regional and temporal variations in particular societies. The construction of states, beginning with the disruption
of feudalism in the high Middle Ages, is widely viewed in historical-
theoretical literature as a process of concerted expropriation, in which
regents, in order to heighten their extractive force, coercively eliminated
all intermediary authorities between themselves and those subject to
power.[1] However, the primary feature of this process was not, in fact,
that power was applied more coercively or became more *forceful*. On the
contrary, this process meant that power was refined as a differentiated
social object, that it was utilized in increasingly constant procedures, and
that it was defined and applied in legal formulae that could be used, in
internally replicable manner, to regulate very different questions across
wide social boundaries. This had the result, in turn, that power was
transmitted to all social agents in increasingly uniform and inclusive
fashion: through its internal transformation, power constructed its societal addressees at a growing level of inner consistency and legal
uniformity. This of course does not mean that European states were
fully formed by the seventeenth century. Similarly, this does not mean

---

[1] This view is most famously associated with Charles Tilly (1975: 24), but it is widely
replicated in historical literature; see, for example, Wehler (1987: 221).

that by this time distinctions of private status and locality were eradicated from the use of power. On the contrary, by the end of the later seventeenth century only the most centralized European societies had begun to develop fully structured states, and even these were scarcely in a position to distribute power evenly throughout all territories and across all social divisions. If the essential modern experience of political power is that all members of society receive power in immediately equivalent and relatively unobstructed fashion from a central public authority, this condition was not reached in most societies until the nineteenth century. In some European societies, in fact, it took longer still. Nonetheless, the most striking feature of early modern European societies was that they witnessed an intensified change in the form and the circulation of political power: they were marked by an incremental tendency to employ political power as a generalized, positively abstracted and uniformly applicable substance.

Through this process of growing political abstraction, European states also gradually began – with substantial variations – to consolidate themselves around a series of distinctive structural characteristics. First, states increasingly evolved institutional mechanisms for integrating powerful private groups into their administrative apparatus. Second, states gradually developed more regular boundaries, or patterns of articulation, in their relation to other social spheres, and they began to produce devices and acceded procedures for simplifying and formalizing their interactions with the economy, with religion and with potentially destabilizing exchanges in other parts of society. Third, states also began to control and to limit 4the number of issues that had to be filtered through the political system, and in employing power as a uniform commodity, organized in distinct procedures, they evolved instruments to ensure that each particular application of power did not have to be negotiated with consolidated bearers of local authority or structural status and that many social exchanges could be conducted without an immediate or palpable requirement for power. Central to the structure of modern political power, in sum, was the fact that states assumed the ability to act as relatively positive public actors, capable of extricating and presupposing constant and positive foundations for their use of power through society, and they established iterable and relatively uncontroversial principles and public procedures which allowed them to apply and reproduce power in abstracted inclusionary fashion and to withdraw the internal basis of political power from incessant contest.

As indicated above, this process of general political abstraction in society should not be viewed as exclusive to one kind of political order, and, across manifest distinctions, these tendencies typified all consolidated European states in the later early modern period. Nonetheless, the English state, established through the reforms of the later seventeenth century, was a salient example of early statehood that enabled political actors to legislate without uncontrolled integration of social themes into the decision-making apparatus, without requiring an endless and exhaustive redefinition of the principles on which state power was founded, and without reliance on obdurate private bargains through society. This should under no circumstances be seen to imply that by the later seventeenth century the English state had established itself as a fully abstracted public or sovereign order. Yet, by the first decades of the eighteenth century, the English state had obtained a certain limited public status, and it had acquired the ability to project itself as a perennially consistent public personality, which greatly facilitated its use of power. Notably, it had begun to stabilize itself as a body of administrative organs situated above the divergent interests of society, it possessed the beginnings of a ministerial order that was independent of the persons factually consuming power, and it had begun to elaborate a system of limited representation and sanctioned opposition that allowed it both to adjust and to harden its social foundations without constant risk of overthrow.[2] Most especially, the fact that the British state now contained the rudimentary elements of a party apparatus, in which state power was rotated between two political groupings, which, for all their real antagonism, tentatively accepted aspects of the basic form of the state and identified the state as distinct from individual actors or interest, meant that power was not entirely bound to personal chains of command or to allocated ranks or affiliations. Naturally, this development should not be simplified, and, owing to the weakness of parliamentary procedure and the persistent allocation of office through courtly patronage, the principle of legitimate political opposition was not commonly established in England until the 1730s.[3] Gradually, however, this principle endowed the state with heightened flexibility in its administrative reactions, it meant that the state could respond to complex social challenges without placing the foundations of its legitimacy in question, and it enabled the state to overcome the diffuse privatism of feudal politics by deploying

---

[2] See the famous accounts in Plumb (1968: 158); Roberts (1966).
[3] Classically, see Foord (1964: 18–33).

techniques of inclusion to ensure that conflicts over power were conducted, internally, within the state itself. The emergence of an early party
system, in other words, allowed the political system to stabilize itself
around a distinction between government and state, or government and
constitution, and this constitutional extraction of the state from the everyday mechanisms of government greatly consolidated the state as a societally abstracted repository of positive power. This process was condensed
in Henry Bolingbroke's argument that, if unified by recognition of certain
constitutional principles, political parties were crucial for national political
liberty and brought reserves of solidity to the state (1786 [1733–4]: 312).
Later in the eighteenth century, Edmund Burke reinforced this point by
claiming that political parties were essential organs of governance, and
that political opposition was, in some circumstances, a vital device for
holding 'the constitution to its true principles': the abstracted distinction
between state and government thus presupposed the presence of oppositional parties (1775 [1770]: 100). Indeed, the fact that the English political
class began to divide into two separate party-political factions, the progressive Whigs and the conservative Tories, brought the distinctive
advantage that the nobility could interpenetrate with social groups emerging from the independent economy, and the state could evolve an integrative ideology in order incrementally to include increasingly powerful
social groups without undergoing fundamental transformation.

If the societies of early modern Europe were generally oriented
towards the abstractive maximization of their reserves of power, therefore, the existence of a regular or public-legal internal constitution,
exemplified by that of the English state, was a key component in this
process. In addition to this, however, it was of vital importance in this
process that the most advanced states began to cement their adaptive
structure around the normative concept of personal subjective rights,
and the uniform laws shaped by such rights. In many instances, the
rights sanctioned by early modern constitutions were little more than
formalized compilations of existing particular rights and privileges.
However, most states of the later early modern period were marked by
a tendency to internalize an abstracted image of those subject to power as
bearers of general subjective rights, to construct rights as uniform attributes of persons under law, and to apply law primarily to persons as *rights
holders*. In each respect, rights, as abstracted and prominent components
of constitutions, played an extremely important role in the positive
expansion of political power. Indeed, rights evolved – to an ever increasing degree – as inner elements of power's abstracted autonomy.

This growing status of rights was reflected – first – in the evolving patterns of public law in early modern Europe, and many states at this time began to envisage their power as correlated with and authorized by uniform and publicly sanctioned rights. Indeed, the gradual emergence of unified bodies of public law, containing elementary provisions for rights, was a general characteristic of early modern states that had reached a high degree of centralization and inclusion, and which, as a result, had weakened their local administrative supports and eroded the privilege- or estate-based societal constitution surviving from the medieval period. Such states used uniform rights to replace the complex feudal structures of society (rights based in estates, towns and corporations) with a monistic order comprising integrally controlled patterns of integration, in which rights were allocated directly by actors in the state, and they used their rights to include social agents in an increasingly even and predetermined manner in political decisions. The formation of the state as a centre of territorial inclusion was thus flanked by an expansion of internal state-conferred rights, and a rights-centred order of public law became a necessary basis for the abstracted power of the state.

The growing functional reliance of European societies on articulated public laws and increasingly formal rights was in fact one of the main reasons for the wide diffusion of natural-law ideals in early modern Europe, which culminated in the political doctrines associated with the Enlightenment. Throughout Europe in later early modernity, doctrines of natural law began to promote the idea that political power was legitimate only if it was applied to subjects holding certain stable rights, and if it was constrained by general practical principles of natural law condensed into rights. These doctrines immediately accompanied and facilitated the construction of European states as societal actors possessing a highly abstracted volume of legally transmissible power, and they greatly contributed to the production of state power as an autonomous and adaptively differentiated phenomenon. Indeed, throughout the last century of early modern European history, the theoretical corpus of natural law played the most profound role in substantiating the power of states. In implying that law could be legitimized by reference to singular general principles, and that it was justified if it reflected social agents as bearers of inherent rights, natural law allowed states to impose increasingly uniform legal regimes across society, to overarch and eliminate the particular authorities of local or intermediary actors, and internally to store positively usable justifications for their legal structures. As discussed, this obtained its clearest expression in the works of

Locke, whose theory of rights helped to concentrate the state as the primary source of sovereign power and allowed the state to imagine itself as applying law to an equal and even group of addressees, situated outside its own structure. In other societies, however, philosophers of natural law engaged still more directly in the processes of public-legal codification which underscored the positive formation of statehood. Leibniz's doctrine of natural law, for instance, culminated in his compiling a general legal code for the German states of the Holy Roman Empire.[4] Moreover, by the mid eighteenth century natural-rights theories were clearly invoked as an impetus for positive legal centralization in growing territorial states. In Prussia, Samuel Cocceji's theory of natural rights acted as the template for the systematic construction of legal procedure, for judicial reform, and for the separation of courts from the state executive.[5] In France, likewise, natural-law principles had crucial status in the repeated attempts of the monarchy throughout the eighteenth century to unify the judicial apparatus. Advocates of legal reform, whether favouring or opposing the concentration of legal authority around the monarchy, used natural-law constructs to found positive principles of judicial uniformity and abstraction.[6] In each case, the conceptual attempt to deduce natural foundations for the law acted both to intensify the power condensed into states, to explain general terms for the monopoly of power held by states, and to establish formulae for the simplified positive circulation of power throughout society more widely.

However, the politically abstractive function of rights was primarily manifest, not in public law, but in the sphere of civil law or common law, especially as this related to economic and monetary activities. The case of England has already been briefly discussed. In England, the state began at an early stage to identify legal persons under common law as bearers of (rudimentary) subjective proprietary rights, which could not be violated by any natural or artificial person (Atiyah 1979: 86). A basic principle of private subjective rights was in fact already implicit in the conflicts between Edward Coke and James I. However, the revolutionary era witnessed a growth in the potency of private rights in England, and

---

[4] Leibniz argued that natural law, as it guides society towards perfection, must serve practical human interests (1693: 10).

[5] Cocceji used principles of natural law to insist on the need for a formally independent judiciary, separate from the executive body of the state, which could ensure that the functions of law were systematically defined and implemented (1791–9 [1713–18]: 159).

[6] See note 25 below.

this also brought benefits to the state. In particular, the rise in the significance of rights under private law gradually acted to trace the boundaries and limits of state inclusion, and it delineated spheres of activity covered by rights as normally irrelevant for political power and removed from the public arena. In this respect, private rights greatly facilitated the formation of the state, not only as an abstracted construct, but also as a functionally specialized bearer of power. Indeed, the state's ability to abstract itself as a public order was closely correlated with its ability to define some social functions as covered by private rights and so as not eminently political. Like public laws, private rights enabled the state to solidify itself against private actors, to preserve private activities outside the state, and to avoid an excessive or blurred politicization of spheres of society not internal to the political system.

The increase in the status of private rights gathered pace through the eighteenth century, and in most cases it was immediately connected with a consolidation of state power. In England, this assumed characteristic expression in the works of William Blackstone. Blackstone, notably, insisted on simple principles of natural law in order to justify rights of personal autonomy in private society. However, he also used natural law to cement the power of the state by endorsing the principle of parliamentary sovereignty, and he offered a definition of parliament as an institution legitimized by subjective rights.[7] Similar processes were also, albeit to a lesser degree, accomplished in other national settings. The Savoyard state in Piedmont, for example, saw repeated acts of legal codification in the early decades of the eighteenth century. These reforms were designed at once to support state power, to establish royal tribunals above local and seigneurial courts, and to specify and preserve private rights and singular claims to ownership (Viora 1928: 186).[8] The main private-law compilation of eighteenth-century Austria, the Codex Theresianus (never enforced), was also centred around a definition of property ownership as an unrestricted right exercised by single persons over objects,[9] and it aimed to secure the direct and uniform legal rule of the monarchy throughout the Habsburg crown lands. Similar processes

---

[7] Blackstone argued that society is formed in order to 'protect individuals in the enjoyment' of 'absolute rights', and he observed that the state, insofar as it protects rights of singular persons, obtains a 'natural, inherent right' to pass laws and to demand uniform compliance (1979 [1765–9]: 47).

[8] As elsewhere, the reforms in Savoy had a pronounced 'anti-noble' impetus (Quazza 1957: 169).

[9] See Codex Theresianus (1883 [1766]: 42).

also took place in Prussia, notably in the preliminary drafting of a civil code under Friedrich II.[10] More tentatively, eighteenth-century France experienced parallel innovations, and the concept of ownership as a singular right of personal disposition and entitlement began to assume prominence in the course of the eighteenth century. The early and middle decades of the eighteenth century, in particular, gave rise to a wave of legal doctrine, especially the works of Boutaric, Bourjon and Pothier, which sought to synthesize French common law by applying principles of legal rationalism to the existing legal corpus. The treatises of these jurists did not finally distil a concept of purely private rights, they did not advocate the elimination of all privileges, and they did not efface from law all local or seigneurial power: in fact, the contrary was the case.[11] However, Pothier began to construct legal rights and entitlements as distinct from social rank, and to determine principles of ownership to separate economic activities from political functions (1830b: 145). Similarly, Bourjon sought to restrict patrimonial office holding, to concentrate judicial power in the monarchy, and to offer a systematic account of freedom of contract.[12]

In none of these European societies, notably, were all private rights strictly liberated from political control. However, theories of rights began to provide unitary regulation for questions of private economic activity, and they progressively brought private resources into a structured external relation to the state. As in the sphere of public law, then, these innovations were functionally vital to the rise of statehood, and, in stipulating certain rights as generally valid across society, they enabled the political system at once to distinguish its own functions from the economy, to produce clear categories to preserve its functional abstraction, and so to simplify its inclusionary application of power. In fact, legal documents constructing private rights gave rise to the characteristic feature of modern societies that political power was condensed in the state, but that many spheres of exchange, containing activities distinguished by personal rights, were detached from constant state jurisdiction: singular proprietary rights traced the progressive separation of state and society, and they enabled states to position themselves as societal

---

[10] See pages 171–2 below.

[11] Boutaric argued that in France powers of jurisdiction were patrimonial and that those subject to jurisdiction could not opt for their cases to be heard under other jurisdiction (1751 [1745]: 45).

[12] On these distinct points, see Bourjon (1767 [1747]: 211, 306, 409–413).

actors located within an increasingly pluralistic and functionally specialized societal landscape, in which other spheres of exchange also possessed a high degree of abstraction and autonomy. In addition to this, in
fact, by the eighteenth century other private rights, apart from economic
rights, were also widely acknowledged, especially in respect of religion, and
partial rights of confessional freedom and tolerance were promoted in most
early modern European societies. To be sure, few states offered equal rights
to bi-confessional populations: in most states, in fact, political stability
became most imperilled where religious plurality was reflected at state
level, and the restriction of the political resonance of dissent against a
state religion was a common precondition of the positive stability of early
modern statehood. However, most European states applied selective rights
of religious freedom and even tentatively adopted latitudinarian principles
to prevent – where possible – religious controversies from migrating across
society into the political system.[13]

In these different respects the, at least rudimentary, recognition of
basic political and certain private and civil rights by early modern
European states served to stabilize state power in a reasonably abstracted
form, to ensure that not all conflicts or questions in society converged
around the state, and to underscore the emergent pluralistic differentiation of society in its entirety. Additionally, however, it is worth noting
again that, if one of the primary challenges for early states was the need
to overcome their residual dualism or inner-structural pluralism and to
consolidate their power over the private interests that originally possessed a stake in the state, rights, both public and private, contributed
vitally to this process. Indeed, many early modern states continued to
exist in a precariously unified condition of statehood, and they were
intermittently exposed to the danger of privatistic *re-particularization*:
in particular, states were susceptible to destabilization owing to the
threat that their ability to unify and balance the private interests that
they incorporated could be eroded, that public offices might be privately

---

[13] A salient example is the English Act of Toleration of 1689. Less well documented are the
religious implications of the Treaty of Westphalia (1648) for the German states. The
treaty gave express sanction to the equality of different confessions, including
Calvinism. A degree of religious tolerance was fundamental to the rise of Prussia: an
Edict of Toleration was passed in 1685 to allow Huguenots to obtain residence in
Prussian territory. Apologists of enlightened absolutism in Prussia were also keen to
prompt religious tolerance. For example, Nicolaus Gundling defined religious tolerance
as a particularly effective way of guaranteeing public security (1743: 787). Samuel
Pufendorf also suggested that restraint in addressing religious dissidence was beneficial
for the state (1687: 168).

reclaimed or enfeoffed by potent privileged actors (especially in the nobility) outside the state, and that they might once again dissolve into loose aggregates of persons protected by private rights and privileges (Mousnier 1945: 2). However, as they acquired the capacity internally to construct different social groups as bearers of general rights and to delineate different spheres of activity as covered by rights, states acquired highly effective devices for preserving themselves against loss of internally unified autonomy. In particular, rights made it possible for states to dictate the activities in which private groups could appear relevant for the state, to impose highly selective restrictions on the processes in which actors outside the state needed to be politically internalized, and generally to consolidate their boundaries against prominent bearers of private or local status. Rights thus allowed states to reconstruct the diffuse dualistic structure that they had carried over from the later feudal period as an integrated internal constitution, and they enabled states to include social groups under law while ensuring that this inclusion was partial and pre-structured and that most addressees of power were held outside the state. This gave to the state heightened reserves of flexibility, as it allowed the state to legitimize itself as socially inclusive and accountable yet also to limit its structural porosity as a public organ. If early modern states, in short, had originally been founded in a dualistic political regime, in which the sources of constitutional order and agreement were external to the state, modern states separated themselves from their private interwovenness with society and transformed their constitutional order into an internal apparatus: the allocation of uniform rights to persons under law played a vital role in this.

Rights and constitutions, in sum, began to emerge in later early modern Europe as the most adequately articulated form of political power, and these normative institutes played a deeply formative role in the creation of the state as a positive political agent. The separation of public law and private law, which underpinned the emergence of early modern states, was a process in which two distinct sets of rights (public and private) served, in distinct yet overlapping fashion, to abstract and maximize the power preserved within states. Rights and constitutions in fact gradually began to express a *revolutionary* form of modern power: they allowed power to apply itself through society at a high level of generalization, autonomy and pluralistic legitimacy, they allowed members of society to be included in power in uniform fashion, and they dramatically raised the level of inclusivity at which power could be utilized.

Constitutional crisis and failed state formation

Across different European societies, the evolution of the characteristic instruments and legitimating procedures of modern statehood remained a complex and tortuous process. Throughout the later early modern period, as previously mentioned, many states encountered obstructions to the formation of their power as an abstractly centralized and uniform societal phenomenon, and they often struggled to distribute their power through even, uniform laws. Indeed, many states failed to consolidate a constitutional order to facilitate their reliable use of power, and their ability to perform functions of statehood remained uncertain. In each case of this kind, the weakness of the state was closely tied to the fabric of rights existing in society, and the structural problems of European states were normally caused, in part at least, by the fact that states encountered difficulty in generating a fully internal system of rights, and their normative capacity for uniform legislation was blocked by potent rights inside and outside the political system, which preserved and reinforced selective social privileges. Increasingly, in fact, the solidity of emergent European states was defined by the extent to which they were able to produce laws founded in generally constructed rights to replace the diffuse constitutional order that had been formed in the early stages of feudal transformation. At the threshold of political modernity, the constitutional integrity of different states widely depended on their success in combating and assimilating structurally embedded rights, and states sustaining an uneven rights apparatus tended to experience malfunctions in their legislative operations and were often susceptible to destabilization.

Poland and Sweden

One pattern of eighteenth-century constitutionalism, accordingly, was found in states that substantially retained the weakly integrated constitution that had accompanied their formation in the late medieval period. Key examples of this were Poland and Sweden. It is notable, in this respect, that for much of the early modern era Poland and Sweden were, with England and the Dutch Republic, the European states that possessed the most elaborated constitutional structure. However, in contrast to England, in both Poland and Sweden the constitutional order of the state retained pronounced dualistic features, including particularistic guarantees over rights, which by the eighteenth century proved fatally damaging for the state.

In the case of eighteenth-century Poland, the fact that the constitution guaranteed rights of statutory veto and regional control to the noble estates led to a far-reaching fragmentation of state power around personalities and localities, and it clearly impeded the consolidation of state power in a densely integrated political apparatus (see Hoensch 1982: 328). Indeed, as the noble estates used their rights routinely to oppose new taxes, the estate-based constitution ultimately made Poland vulnerable to external military intervention: it was ultimately responsible (in part) for the partition of Poland, which began in the 1770s. It is notable, in fact, that the response of the Polish political elites to the onset of partition was to draft a progressive national constitution (finalized in 1791), which was arguably the first modern constitution in Europe. This constitution was designed internally to strengthen the state and to preserve it against internal erosion, and it provided for rights-based judicial regularity, separated powers and some degree of national representation.[14] The provisions of this constitution, however, were deeply contested by the nobility, and, although it instituted a primary legislature accountable to the popular will, it reserved distinct recognition for noble privileges and elements of feudal law in respect of the peasantry, and it only 'gingerly' admitted persons outside the *szlachta* to the national franchise (Duzinkiewicz 1993: 69). Moreover, the 1791 Constitution was never fully enforced, and it was swept away by the partitioning powers. Poland thus remained an extreme example of a state that did not fully integrate medieval estates into a centralized unitary state apparatus, and its integrity was undermined by the unregulated power of the estates and by the haphazard exercise of particular rights by the nobility.

The eighteenth-century Swedish constitution contained certain similarities with the Polish case. In Sweden, as mentioned above, the powerful constitutional arrangements of the seventeenth century were abrogated in a series of royal decisions initiated in 1680, in which Charles XI restricted the power of the nobility and the Council of State and drastically diminished the powers of legislative ratification, veto and policymaking held by the legislative Diet. At this time the Swedish monarchy summarily curtailed the force of aristocratic constitutionalism, and the king opted instead for a model of concentrated bureaucratic legal rule, supported strongly by the commoners (Barudio 1976: 102; Upton 1998: 46). However, the absolutist regime established in the 1680s

---

[14] For discussion see Lukowski (1991: 94–5).

was ultimately rejected, and after 1718, which marked the beginning of the Age of Freedom, it was supplanted by a more representative system, centred in a formally written constitution (introduced in 1719 and revised in 1720). This constitution, expressly designed to strengthen the state, gave very substantial co-legislative powers to the assembly of estates (s. 4), it insisted that the ministerial executive was accountable to the estates (s. 14), and it initiated a brand of parliamentary rule that was distinct from the gentry constitutionalism of the previous century (Roberts 1986: 9, 82).[15] The parliamentary system of this era mirrored the British polity in that it, too, gave rise to two rival political parties, the Caps (conservative) and the Hats (progressive), through which different branches of the nobility vied for power. Despite this, however, the eighteenth-century Swedish polity clearly succeeded only moderately in placing the state above private interests, and it remained dominated and debilitated by noble factionalism. Indeed, it has been noted by both near-contemporary and more recent commentators that the Swedish state in the Age of Freedom was close in form to an oligarchical system, in which the nobility arrogated both legislative and executive powers, and it was marked at once by a deep disregard for popular rights and liberties and by extensive privatization of public office (Sheridan 1778: 154–5; Roberts 1973: 34–6). The parliamentary constitution was ultimately overthrown in 1772, and Sweden reverted to a more authoritarian monarchical system. In particular, the overthrow of the 1720 Constitution resulted from the fact that the nobility had grown anxious at the fact that the lower estates were beginning to act as concerted force in the Riksdag, capable of overruling the nobility and threatening to transform parliament into an organ of more fully democratic inclusion. The constitution was repealed through a coalition of retrenchment between the monarch and the nobility in order to preserve noble privileges (Metcalf 1982: 258–9; Roberts 2003: 194–201), and the return to semi-absolutism at this point was intended to reconsolidate privilege and private power within the state. Sweden too, thus, was a prominent example of a state in which noble privileges in the political system led originally to a strong representative governmental order and yet, ultimately, countervailed the construction of an inclusively unified state.

In both Poland and Sweden, for very diverse reasons, the function of parliament as a guarantor of noble privileges preserved a dimension of

---

[15] Rutger von Seth kindly helped me with translations of the *Regeringsformen* of 1719. This and other relevant texts are printed in Brusewitz (1916).

constitutional dualism in the state. This placed limits on the state's capacities for unitary modernization and for full rights-based inclusion. In effect, it prevented the complete construction of the state as an autonomous public order, and it left the state highly vulnerable to private power.

Prussia and smaller German states

An alternative example of a state weakened constitutionally by a conflict between general constitutional rights and structural privileges was Prussia. In the course of the eighteenth century in Prussia, semi-constitutional rights were in fact introduced, with the specific aim of intensifying state power and eradicating the dualism of earlier constitutional arrangements. By the middle of the eighteenth century, for instance, the Prussian monarchy had embarked on a campaign to efface the constitutional residues of feudal privatism through a far-reaching reform of the legal and judicial apparatus. Like other 'absolutist' dynasties of the eighteenth century, the regime of the Hohenzollerns promoted a strengthening of state power through extensive legal rationalization and anti-seigneurial codification. Indeed, although the Recess of 1653 had preserved jurisdictional rights of the nobility, this agreement was clearly not accorded final validity in Prussia throughout the eighteenth century. The legal reforms of the eighteenth century were in part intended to curtail noble autonomy in judicial matters and centrally to impose a uniform legal order and uniform rights of legal redress across all actors in society.

This process of political concentration through uniform allocation of legal status, shaped by concepts of natural right, was discernible in the first general law code of eighteenth-century Prussia: the Codex Fridericianus, introduced between 1747 and 1749. This code prescribed uniform legal procedures for the courts of law, thus guaranteeing basic rights of legal access and hearing, and it sought to subordinate questions of fiscal importance to an independent central judiciary. Indeed, in parallel to similar proposals for legal reform in the Habsburg territories, the establishment of a common judicial order in Prussia was clearly intended to detach legal control from the noble estates and to relocate judicial authority from local actors into the civil service.[16] Additionally,

---

[16] See Kocher (1979: 14, 18, 28). Koselleck states simply: 'The law of state pierced through the order of estates' (1977: 37).

however, this process of legal/political schematization also assumed a quasi-constitutional dimension. The centralization of judicial authority inevitably presupposed that the state, in itself, evolved a neutral legal consistency, and that the general status of the law, increasingly formulated through reference to natural rights, acted to reduce the private power, not only of potent seigneurial actors outside the state, but also of regents themselves: the growing uniformity of the law also prohibited egregious infraction by persons (even monarchs) momentarily using the power stored in the state. By the middle of the eighteenth century, therefore, the Prussian monarchy began openly to legitimize itself, at least rhetorically, through reference to its independent legal and administrative functions, and the exclusion of private/patrimonial influence from the law began to produce an idea of the state as an impersonally transcendent and powerfully overarching legal order, based in equal legal obligation.[17] This process of early-constitutional law reform ultimately gave rise to a comprehensive legal code for Prussia, the Allgemeines Landrecht of 1794, which was drafted, among others, by Carl Gottlieb Svarez. The Landrecht, conceived in antipathy to the nobility as a political force (Schwennicke 1998), was intended to generalize the foundations of the law, to integrate members of society as evenly as possible under state authority, and to include all persons as bearers of rights and entitlements under law. Svarez in fact favoured a highly abstracted concept of the state. He insisted that national law had to be founded in principles of natural right and personal autonomy, and he applied principles of natural law as institutions for enforcing political centralization and for bringing private actors under the 'highest territorial jurisdiction' (2000 [1791–2]: 69). In these respects, Prussia was a striking example of a state that began strategically to create a uniform rights-based legal order for itself in order to heighten its ability to apply political power evenly through society and to divest itself of its earlier dualistic dimensions. The abstraction of the state and the reinforcement of the state's constitutional order and rights structure were thus closely integrally conjoined.

At the same time, however, the state of eighteenth-century Prussia was only able to obtain a very incomplete degree of political unity and abstraction, and it retained certain underlying dualistic features. To be sure, if compared with the Habsburg crownlands, the strength of the Prussian executive over the noble estates was firmly established, and, by

---

[17] Friedrich II famously styled himself *the first servant of the state* (1913–14 [1777]: 235).

the middle of the eighteenth century, the law was concentrated in relative uniformity across Prussian territories. Austria retained a more pluralistic constitution throughout the eighteenth century: in fact, Austria was prevented by the imperial authority of the emperor, whose power and legitimacy depended on the preservation of a constitutional balance between regional estates and territorial princes, from establishing a fully evolved system of territorial rule (Strakosch 1976: 8, 17). Nonetheless, a dimension of socio-constitutional polycracy also persisted in the Prussian state throughout the early modern period, and even the Landrecht did not cement the state as a fully positive or public agent. The Landrecht in fact comprised a delicate compromise between the centralistic impulses of the monarchy and the local/centrifugal forces of the estates and nobility, and it clearly reconfigured the original bargain through which the noble estates had accepted confirmation of their social privileges as a condition for their transformation into a functional corpus within the state.[18] For example, the Landrecht promulgated a single law code for all inhabitants of Prussia. Yet it also, with qualifications, recognized the independence of 'provincial decrees and the statutes of singular communities' (Introduction, § 2). In fact, Svarez expressly accepted the legitimacy of patrimonial courts as representing a 'competence of the noble landowner', and he acknowledged that not all power could be concentrated in the state (2000 [1791–2]: 69). Similarly, the Landrecht proclaimed that 'general rights of the human being' were founded in 'natural freedom'. Yet it also accepted that some rights were to be judged as acquired through birth or status (Introduction, §§ 82–3). Most importantly, the Landrecht defined 'the right to tax' as a 'sovereign right' of the state. Yet it acknowledged that some persons were exempted from fiscal contribution by 'contracts or express privileges' (Part 14, §§ 2–4). Throughout the later eighteenth century, in short, Prussia remained an internally dualistic or even polymorphous state. This was reflected in the fabric of rights that underpinned Prussian society, and the socio-structural and regional variability of rights remained a powerful obstruction to the full unitary formation of the state.

In other German territories in the Holy Roman Empire, the estates also retained an ambiguous constitutional status throughout the eighteenth century, and other states were defined by a high degree of structural dualism or even pluralism. On one hand, in most territories

---

[18] See Koselleck (1977: 24). Excellent on this is Birtsch (1995: 145).

regional estates, led by the local nobility, acted de facto as integrated and subordinate elements of political systems ruled by princely regents: a basic degree of territorial sovereignty (*Landeshoheit*) was established in most particular societies. Yet, on the other hand, the powers of princely regents in their own particular territories remained defined and restricted by customary laws and by the constitution of the Empire as a whole. In most regions, in fact, the internal power of the territorial state was subject to clear formal and informal limits, and it was checked by regional estates, which were recognized under imperial law as independent bodies with customary rights which, under the imperial appellate order, could be appealed and reclaimed against territorial rulers. In certain cases, the regional estates were very effective in resisting the concentration of power around the unitary territorial state. As late as 1770, for example, the duke of Württemberg was forced, in the course of a series of fiscal negotiations, to recognize the estates as 'corpus repraesentativum' of the territory (Vierhaus 1990: 108). In the great compilations of imperial public law written during the eighteenth century, regional estates (*Landstände*) were routinely defined as constitutionally entitled representative organs, which acted as effectively distinct from, and authorized constitutionally to oppose, the imperial estates (*Reichsstände*): that is, the highest princely regents. For example, the great early positivist constitutional theorist, Johann Jakob Moser, interpreted the public law of the eighteenth-century Empire as a balanced constitution, founded in a multilateral 'contract' unifying, on one side, the emperor and the imperial estates and, on the other side, the territorial sovereigns and the regional estates or parliaments (*Landstände*) in the territories (1766–82a: 540). Moser reserved particular venom for the 'servants of sovereignty' – that is, the princes and their administrators who pledged themselves to limitless territorial power (1766–82b: 1146). Slightly later, Johann Stephan Pütter also defined the Empire as a constitutional order, based in a three-level internal equilibrium (1777: 42, 57).

Owing to the intersecting jurisdictions of territories and empires, in sum, most German territorial states retained a twofold constitutional composition: they integrated regional estates as components of their inner constitution, yet their regents, and their estates, possessed a specified position within the overarching constitution of the Empire as a whole. Consequently, these states retained a deeply uneven inner legal order, they consumed power and authority in a fashion reflecting a plurality of local and intersecting jurisdictional and appellate rights, and they struggled to elaborate a unified constitutional order to control their functions.

France

Analogous weaknesses and related constitutional problems were evident in the Bourbon monarchy in eighteenth-century France. As discussed, the earlier consolidation of 'absolutism' in France had revolved around an assault by the monarchy on seigneurial rights and privileges, and this period led to increasing uniformity in the legal foundations of the state. Despite these innovations, however, well into the eighteenth century the French state continued to operate at a high level of interpenetration with privatistic elements in society, and state functions were impeded by the persistence of regional, seigneurial and corporate claims to legal status, rights and entitlement.

The pluralistic fabric of the French state was particularly manifest in the fact that seigneurial rights of property ownership and seigneurial rights of legal jurisdiction remained interwoven. In France, as in other 'absolutistic' societies, private ownership of land remained a source of distinction under law: owners of landed property obtained seigneurial exemptions from particular laws, especially in respect of taxation, and even (albeit rarely) certain rights of legal precedence and powers of private jurisdiction.[19] This uncertain boundary between economic and legal/political status, reflecting a residually feudal blurring of public and private spheres, meant that the monarchical state could not legislate evenly over all matters of political importance, it could not apply laws equally through society, and its laws concerning judicial and fiscal questions were necessarily marked by high levels of regional or structural sensitivity. In addition, this pluralism was also evident in the fact that residues of feudal rights dictated that land was often an object of multiple ownership, and clear single rights of proprietary disposition over goods were not fully established (Chénon 1923: 91). This had the result, primarily, that monetary exchanges relating to agrarian production remained partly controlled by a legally privileged aristocratic elite. However, this also meant that monetary transactions could not easily be subject to uniform laws and that the monarchical state could not construct rights of property in fully abstract or generalized categories. Moreover, the internal intersection between the political system and private social groups was also visible in the highly corporate structures of economic management and association that prevailed in France. This had the consequence, first, that, despite all the attempts of the monarchy to suppress them,

---

[19] For contemporary commentary see Pothier (1830a: 4–5).

guilds, orders and corporations held far-reaching powers of autonomous professional self-regulation and jurisdiction, they reserved statutory control over many professional and economic activities,[20] and they conferred privileges on their members which determined procedures of legal access and inclusion in certain social functions. Professional functions were thus not assimilated to the simple statutory operations of the state: actors in the state routinely secured compliance by confirming the myriad privileges that determined the corporate form of French society, and a legal medium for addressing all persons in society as singular equivalent agents did not exist.[21] Further, this also meant that positions of economic advantage were often transacted through political channels and corporate membership brought privileged access both to economic benefits and to legal status (Taylor 1964: 488–9).

Throughout the eighteenth century, in consequence, political and economic structures in France overlapped almost insolubly, and the formation of the monarchical state as a positive centre of power was greatly obstructed by this. This characteristic of the French state had the most damaging consequences in the fiscal apparatus of the state. It meant that in fiscal matters the monarchy was unable to extricate itself from the mass of private legal agreements in society, and it could neither legislate uniformly over budgetary supply nor effectively maximize its revenue: by the 1780s, owing to its fiscal predicaments and its embroilment in unaffordable wars, the Bourbon monarchy was bankrupt. As a result, this period witnessed numerous reformist attempts to enforce a clear distinction between economic exchange and political structures, and to construct a uniform legal and fiscal regime, relatively indifferent to privilege and indemnity, consonant with this separation. Plans of this kind were pioneered by the physiocrats, who advocated a partial liberation of private, and especially agrarian, property both from state control and from multiple ownership.[22] In the mid 1770s, Turgot sought, in his famous Six Edicts, to implement physiocratic measures, and he launched a reformist attempt to increase state revenue by restricting the privileges attached to corporations and reducing the power of private actors in

[20] For analysis both of the functions of the corporations and of royal legislation against them, see Gallinato (1992: 183–4).

[21] One historian has gone as far as to claim that, as 'French society was organized corporatively', the 'individual had essentially no standing' (Fitzsimmons 1987: 270).

[22] Under physiocratic influence, for example, Turgot defined land as the 'unique source of all wealth' and favoured the integration of agriculture into a free market, based in the 'circulation of capital' (1844a [1766]: 34, 45).

regulating trade and controlling labour supply, and by generally consolidating the legal independence of economic practice (Sewell 1980: 72;
Sonenscher 1989: 283). Subsequently, shortly before the revolution of
1789, an Assembly of Notables was convened in Paris to discuss the fiscal
crisis of the monarchy: this Assembly was presented with a series of
projects to liberalize the economy, to reduce the extent to which privilege
caused intersection between private status and public judicial functions,
and, once more, to facilitate the raising of royal credit.[23] These projects
were generally supported by a doctrine of singular personal rights, and
they aimed to impose a uniform legal and monetary order to establish
single persons as bearers of proprietary entitlements and to ensure that
the economic activities of legal addressees were located and uniformly
constructed outside the state.[24] However, these attempted reforms were
unsuccessful. It has been well noted in recent research that fiscal privilege
was already 'circumscribed' by 1787, and that by and large the Notables
showed willingness to renounce some privileges (Gruder 2007: 37).
Nonetheless, the proposals for reform submitted to the Notables triggered endemic internal resistance, and the French monarchy was unable
autonomously to alter its fiscal laws: this was caused, not least, by the fact
that many powerful actors called on to deliberate the functions of state
were private or neo-seigneurial beneficiaries of fiscal rights and privilege,
and they rejected the strict segregation of political functions from private
privilege because this imperilled their own corporate standing and
benefits. The internal and external privatism of the eighteenth-century
French monarchy, therefore, remained a vicious paradox that prevented
the stabilization of the state, and throughout this period the state was
marked by acute structural problems caused by its inadequate abstraction and differentiation.

The greatest problem of the French monarchy in the decades before
1789, however, resulted from the fact that, as in earlier controversies, its
procedures for introducing new legislation were adversely affected by the
prerogatives of venal and hereditary office holders in the *parlements*.
Indeed, the monarchy invariably struggled to legislate on issues that

---

[23] On this, see Egret (1962: 33–5, 130); Stone (1986: 5–9). It is of vital importance that the
economic reforms were accompanied by a Decree Concerning the Administration of
Justice (1788), which reduced powers of seigneurial justice.

[24] Turgot's edict against corporations of 1776 claimed (in semi-Lockean vocabulary) that it
was vital to allow all French subjects the 'full and entire enjoyment of their rights',
especially in respect of the ownership of the products of human labour – the 'inalienable
right of humanity' (Turgot 1844b [1776]: 304–6).

touched the privileges of the members of the *parlements* – especially taxation – and it could not subordinate the judicial order of the *parlements* to one unitary legal system. As a result of this, throughout the eighteenth century the constitutional conflicts that had earlier culminated in the Fronde began to reappear: the Bourbon monarchy was, once again, repeatedly forced into bitter conflict with the *parlements*, and it sometimes suspended them altogether in order to pass new laws and fiscal packages. Prerogative suspension of the *parlements* occurred in the early 1750s and, more dramatically, in the early 1770s. In the latter case, Louis XV and his chancellor, Maupeou, sought to circumvent noble resistance by exiling members of the Parisian *parlement* and conspiring to replace the courts with a more compliant (and less venal) judicial order: the assault on the *parlements* was closely tied to an attack on venality of office (Egret 1970: 132; Doyle 1996: 117). The tension between the monarchy and the *parlements* then came to a head in the May Edicts of 1788, in which the king ordained before the Assembly of Notables that the *parlements* should be replaced with a single plenary court to register all laws, and that the privileges of the courts should be suspended and a uniform judicial structure imposed throughout France (Egret 1962: 270–5; Bell 1994: 181). This provoked great antagonism among the noble class, and it meant that the nobility represented in the *parlements* began to assume an intensified oppositional role as a focus for wider national constitutional resistance to the state (Gruder 2007: 3–4).

At one level, therefore, in the latter decades of the Ancien Régime some members both of the *parlement* of Paris and of the lesser regional *parlements* began to perceive their functions as public/constitutional obligations patterned on the English parliament, and, although not elected, they defined their duties in increasingly constitutionalist terms. This view was even seconded by proto-republican political theorists before 1789. Gabriel Bonnot de Mably, for example, advocated a transformation of the *parlements* into fully representative assemblies (1972 [1758]: 168). In general, the members of the *parlements* insisted that effective registration of laws in the *parlements* was one of the 'fundamental laws' of the French state: this law, they claimed, ensured that the state retained a perennial and organic legal form, and it even enabled the nation as a whole to consent to and to take part in the 'formation of laws' (Bickart 1932: 43, 73). By 1788, the *parlement* of Rennes was able to declare itself and other *parlements* the 'depositories and the inflexible guardians of the laws' of the French polity (Bickart 1932: 96). Indeed, the *parlements* even went as far as to construe themselves as custodians of 'an original contract' between state and society, and on this basis they suggested that some acts of the monarchy might be formally classified as 'anti-constitutional' (Vergne 2006: 263, 434). At a different level, however, whereas the English parliament was an integrated institution of state containing elected and (albeit nominally) accountable delegates, the French *parlementaires* occupied a dual status both within and outside the state. Although assuming (normally purchased) office within the state, the members of the *parlements* defended powerful vested interests against the central state, they preserved a piecemeal judicial order giving extensive sanction to corporate rights, and they clearly fragmented the judicial unity and the legislative autonomy of the state (Vergne 2006: 90). Crucially, for example, the *parlements* opposed Turgot's assault on the corporations, and they sought to defend the privileged pattern of economic control (Horn 2006: 25). Through their dual status, the *parlements* in fact perpetuated confusion between 'public power and private property' in the French polity (Mousnier 1945: 622), they dragged against the formation of the state as a public entity, and they prevented the state from applying its power as a relatively abstracted and even social facility. Indeed, many prominent *lumières*, notably Voltaire and d'Holbach, combined their advocacy of a free rational state founded in common natural rights with a vehement contempt for the *parlements*, whose particularism they viewed as blocking rational legal and judicial reform.[25]

For these reasons, the French state of the later eighteenth century existed in a condition of barely suppressed monetary and legislative crisis, often veering towards bankruptcy and statutory deadlock and presiding only over a highly fragmented and semi-privatized judicial order. This was caused in no small part by the fact that the monarchy possessed a socio-constitutional system for deliberating over its fiscal and legislative processes that made it impossible for the state to free itself from private motives and obstructed the construction of private actors and private prerogatives as irreducibly external to the political system. As a result, the fiscal problems encountered by the state necessarily assumed the dimensions of major constitutional traumas, and the state's endeavours to pass general fiscal laws inevitably engaged it in conflict

---

[25] See the claim of d'Holbach that judicial power needs to be seen as an 'emanation of sovereign authority' and that judges should not exercise 'legislative power' (1773: 220–2). See, likewise, the argument of Voltaire denying the claims to constitutional powers made by the *parlements* (1771: 5–6). For a general account see Echeverria (1985: 156, 232).

with the private interests situated at its constitutional core. Each fiscal problem underlined and intensified the need for constitutional reform and for the formation of a public order that could allow legislation and financial levying without highly privatized internal negotiation and opposition. However, the French state possessed a constitution that made a reform and unitary construction of its functions impracticable: those actors that constitutionally controlled the form of the state's power had a vested interest in preventing its fundamental reform, their social position depended structurally on the persistence of inner dualism in the state, and they remained 'firmly attached to civil feudalism' (Garaud 1958: 156).[26] From the 1750s to the 1780s, in fact, members of the *parlements* were often among the most vocal advocates of a re-convention of the Estates-General, and they clearly perceived that the state could not legislate effectively without a more systematic de-privatization of its consultative apparatus. Protest in the *parlements* at their suspension in 1788, notably, was a key reason for the summoning of the Estates-General in 1789. Tellingly, however, the *parlementaires* and other members of the nobility were widely recalcitrant in acceding to the abolition of representational privilege (i.e. representation by orders) in the Estates-General (Fitzsimmons 1987: 284). The revolutionary laws passed after 1789 then soon abolished the *parlements*, and leading members of the revolutionary executives observed powerful judges as a deeply corrosive force in the state. Moreover, as office holders and bearers of originally feudal privilege, many members of the *parlements* were put to death during the revolution caused by the Estates-General of 1789, which they had helped to summon.

On these grounds, eighteenth-century France might be viewed as the most significant example of a state that endeavoured centrally to abstract its power and to construct the law as a uniform corpus of norms, but that possessed mechanisms of inclusion and exclusion that obviated this. The primary reason for the weakness of the French state of the Ancien Régime was that, through its abiding constitutional privatism, it did not possess uniform legal categories in which to extract a clear construction of its functions and limits, or to reflect, differentiate and externally to define its legal addressees, and it was prevented by its inner corporate dualism from codifying laws in an adequately stable and internally

---

[26] On this see also Stone (1981: 17, 77). Note, however, the recent analysis of Gruder, who emphasizes the role of the aristocracy in creating a revolutionary culture before 1789 (2007: 4).

uniform rights structure. Both in their production and application, laws of the French polity remained deeply interwoven with privatistic milieux and interests, the state was unable to establish a constitutional order to detach its legislative functions from private status, and its recognition of multiply overlayered public and private rights meant that it could not legislate over external (primarily monetary) functions without internal constitutional disruption.

Constitutional revolutions and the form of political power

In very general terms, therefore, by the eighteenth century some European states were approaching a relatively high level of effective differentiation and positive abstraction. These were normally states that were able to distinguish and control their own societal boundaries, and to determine, with reasonable consistency, what was internal and what was external to the state. These states were usually states that had acquired a written or an informal constitution. The most effective constitutions of this era were those, first, that used a growing public-legal body of *political rights* (usually explicated through natural-law doctrine) to provide for controlled social representation within the state, and to extract a definition of the state which ensured that its legislative functions remained protected from undue or repeated external private influences (including from actors using power within the state). Second, the most effective constitutions of this period were those that used *civil or private rights* to ensure that members of society were (more or less) equally reflected in the legal system as bearers of certain general substantial and procedural claims: that is, habitually, as endowed with rights of equality before the law, and as entitled to certain basic and uniform rights of free ownership, movement, confession and opinion. The most effective constitutions of this era, thus, were those that at once allocated and clearly distinguished between private rights and public rights, and that employed both sets of rights to avert the unsettling coalescence of private and public power.

The view is not expressed here that by the middle or later decades of the eighteenth century public and private rights, even under the most advanced states, were extensively or invariably applied. Clearly, the contrary was the case: even in more state-centred societies such as England, rights were limited and repeatedly subject to dispute and abrogation. Yet by this time the constitutional state, ensuring both public and private rights, was surely emerging as the form of polity that was most adequately adapted to the extensive, pluralistic and functionally specialized demands for power in modern society. This had largely to do with the growing status of subjective-personal rights (both public and private). States that struggled to structure their power in positively abstracted or effective inclusionary manner were usually states that maintained a varied or polystructural rights regime, that accepted high degrees of personal distinction under rights throughout society, and that preserved a blurred boundary between private rights and public rights. If the eighteenth century – the era of Enlightenment – was the age of rights, therefore, the reason for this was that by this point in European history, owing to the growing differentiation of societal structure as a whole, political power had evolved into a condition in which it could not be abstractly circulated or supported throughout society if it did not internalize a generalized rights-based construct of itself and its addressees.

Rights revolutions

The major rights revolutions of the later eighteenth century can both be examined against this background. Indeed, both the American and the French revolutions of 1776 and 1789 can be interpreted as political events in which states, both at an institutional and at a conceptual/ reflexive level, underwent an accelerated internal transformation, as a result of which they began to utilize highly refined constitutions and constitutional rights to legislate consistently across society, and to organize their power as a general, inclusionary and autonomously abstracted facility. In the early part of the revolutionary era (that is, in the first decades of the period 1776–1848), therefore, rights began to act as instruments through which states brought towards completion the processes of differentiation and positive inclusionary abstraction through which they had originally been formed as states, and rights played a decisive role in the formal consolidation of political power.

The American constitutions

The constitutions established in revolutionary America had their original source and reference in the English judicial context, and, for this reason, in early American constitutional debate rights initially expressed a distinctively defensive attitude. In particular, the normative background both to the particular state constitutions founded in America in the 1770s and 1780s and eventually to the Federal Constitution of

1787–9 was formed by ideas of rights derived from the English common-law tradition. These ideas were recognized in America through a long history of colonial charters, which in many cases guaranteed common rights of English subjects, extensive colonial liberties, and partial rights of local assembly and representation for inhabitants of the American colonies.[27] English rights began to assume heightened constitutionally formative status in America in the course of the 1760s, as residents of the colonies invoked rights under English law to oppose seemingly non-mandated taxation by the English parliament through the Stamp Act and the Townshend Act. The constitutional movement in America in fact first drew impetus from the insistence that rights guaranteed in England under the rule of English law should also apply in the colonies, and it reflected the belief that all British subjects had equal rights under common law. Most notably, early American constitutionalism was shaped by the Lockean view that no English subjects could legitimately be taxed without their express agreement and taxation could not be selectively levied. Transposed into the colonial setting, this meant – of necessity – that the first American constitutionalists rejected the Blackstonian doctrine of the positive statutory supremacy of parliament established in England in the longer wake of 1688. They invoked older, more defensive, conceptions of honoured rights and judicial protection to oppose the authority of singular parliamentary statutes (Reid 1976: 1120; Snowiss 1990: 16).

In general terms, therefore, the first constitutional debates of revolutionary America expressed the very cautious and self-protective idea that rights formed customary checks on state power. Through an incremental process, however, in the 1760s debate about rights under English law expanded into a broader account of the corporate rights of colonial societies, and the demand for private entitlements under English law began to give rise to the conviction that colonial assemblies were institutions mandated to represent and preserve common-law rights. This process gathered pace, notably, in the Stamp Act Congress that met in 1765 to deliberate opposition to British taxes. The Declaration of Rights proposed by the Stamp Act Congress stated (Art. 2): 'That His Majesty's liege subjects in these colonies are entitled to all the inherent rights and

---

[27] It is usually claimed that the Pennsylvania Charter of Privileges (1701) was the key precursor of later rights-based documents (Schwartz 1977: 50). This Charter provided that for 'the well governing of this Province and Territories, there shall be an Assembly yearly chosen, by the Freemen thereof'.

privileges of his natural born subjects within the kingdom of Great Britain.' These rights were attached in particular (Art. 3) to defence against fiscal expropriation, and, accordingly, the Declaration stated: 'That it is inseparably essential to the freedom of a people, and the undoubted rights of Englishmen, that no taxes should be imposed on them, but with their own consent, given personally, or by their representatives.' Negative rights concerning property and taxation, in short, became the axis around which the legitimacy, not only of the colonial fiscal system, but in fact of the entire legislative order of the English parliament in America, was observed and contested (Mullett 1966: 83; Kruman 1997: 10, 93). The first stage of independent institution building in America was founded in a self-protective legalism, and it was born from a highly defensive and juridified climate of debate,[28] which insisted on rights of institutional autonomy, not primarily as positive expressions of political activity, but as institutes for preserving historical liberties against the power of imperial government.

This essentially defensive concept of rights was also reflected in the earliest state constitutions of America. These constitutions were commonly drafted, under endorsement of the Continental Congress, as documents that accentuated earlier rights guaranteed under English law and emphasized the prohibitive dimension of rights to construct an alternative to colonial rule by the British crown. In particular, these constitutions typically proceeded from an idea of the legitimate state based in a Lockean defence of rights of equality, freedom and proprietary integrity. This was evident in the resolutions of the First Continental Congress (1774), which derived the rights of 'the inhabitants of the English colonies in North-America' both from 'the immutable laws of nature' and from 'the principles of the English constitution'. The first resolve of the Continental Congress justified the rights of the colonies by stating that the first settlers 'were at the time of their emigration from the mother country, entitled to all the rights, liberties, and immunities of free and natural-born subjects, within the realm of England'. The classical example of this was the 1776 Virginia Declaration of Rights, which became the basis for many subsequent catalogues of rights. Article 1 of this Declaration stated: 'That all men are by nature equally free and independent, and have certain inherent rights, of which, when they enter into a state of society, they cannot, by any compact, deprive or divest

---

[28] Speaking of America, Burke famously mused: 'In no country, perhaps, is law so general a study' (1981 [1775]: 123).

their posterity.' Notably, the more defensive quality of rights was visible in the fact that in many constitutions rights under English law were specifically invoked and preserved. This was the case in the first declaration of independent sovereignty, that is, the Mecklenburgh Resolutions of 1775. Article III of the resolutions stated that 'every one of our former laws' was still valid, but that 'the Crown of Great Britain' could not be seen as 'holding rights, privileges, or authorities therein'. This principle was, by way of example, repeated in the 1776 constitution of Delaware (Art. 25), which stated that the 'common law of England ... shall remain in force' unless it was 'repugnant to the rights and privileges' contained in the constitution and the principles that it protected. The four constitutions written prior to independence in 1776 in fact specifically provided for a reconciliation with the British crown (Tarr 1998: 67).

In these primary respects, early constitutionalists in revolutionary America identified in rights a broad function similar to that possessed by rights in the English context before the Civil War. That is to say, rights were used to restrict sovereign power (in this instance, the power, not solely of the British king, but also of the king's parliament in Westminster), and to insist on customary entitlements as immune to political encroachment. Indeed, this process began, in distinct form, to re-express some of Coke's injunctions against king and parliament in the first decades of the seventeenth century. At the same time, however, this restrictive concept of rights also gradually promoted a political ethic, which, in separating American rights from their English provenance, began – inevitably – to denounce the English creed of virtual representation in parliament, and claimants to defensive rights in America progressively expressed a more active demand that they should assume some of the sovereign statutory powers attributed to the Westminster parliament (Selsam 1936: 170; Wood 1969: 176). Although cautious in origin, therefore, doctrines of rights in America began to emphasize local sources of authority and legislative power, they imagined the state as formed by particular and individual experiences of participation and freedom, and they ultimately conceived the legitimate state as a repository of directly represented *national* or even *popular* sovereignty, which presupposed representative autonomy for the American colonies (Pole 1966: 537; Wood 1969: 383; Reid 1989: 33, 145; Kruman 1997: 159). Defensive political controversy over fiscal rights, in short, also generated principles of shared identity and political community in revolutionary America, it unified bearers of fiscal grievances and claimants to singular legal protection into one increasingly political group of actors, and the demand for rights under English law incrementally redefined groups of self-protective American property owners and taxpayers as a formative, and practically sovereign, political community. As an example of this, among the first wave of state constitutions, the rights contained in the 1776 constitution of Pennsylvania, the most fully republican of all the revolutionary documents, came close to expressing a comprehensive doctrine of constituent popular sovereignty, cemented in a supreme unicameral legislature (Selsam 1936: 191; Williams 1989: 551–5). This constitution stated (Art. III): 'That the people of this State have the sole, exclusive and inherent right of governing and regulating the internal police of the same.' It added (Art. IV): 'That all power being originally inherent in, and consequently derived from, the people; therefore all officers of government, whether legislative or executive, are their trustees and servants, and at all times accountable to them.' Other state constitutions in the first wave of constitution writing up to 1777, although normally replicating the split legislature of the British state, proceeded from the assumption that 'all political power is vested in and derived from the people only' and that the people of each state 'ought to have the sole and exclusive right of regulating the internal government and police thereof'.[29]

In revolutionary America, in sum, rights acted as elements of state construction and political consolidation in two quite divergent ways. Rights were configured both as negative, defensive and even customary checks on state power and, equally, as positive, formative expressions of national cohesion and popular engagement, and these distinct dimensions in rights joined to form a powerful constitutional impulse towards independent statehood. In fact, these two dimensions of rights ultimately performed distinct, yet closely interdependent, structural functions, which together served to cement and intensify the political power of the American states, and ultimately of the new republic itself. This was evident, initially, in the negative status of rights.

First, the negative reference to rights in the American revolutionary constitutions meant that emergent centres of political authority, both at state and later at federal level, could be separated out of the colonial legal system, and directly legitimized both through and in contrast to this system. The fact that the new states could construe themselves as defenders, against the British crown, of traditionally established and sanctioned rights meant that these states possessed from the outset a higher-norm

---

[29] Arts. 1 and 2 of 1776 constitution of North Carolina. See also Arts. 1 and 2 of the 1776 constitution of Maryland.

vocabulary through which they could organize themselves as institutional bodies 'distinct from and superior to' the imperial government against which they reacted (Wood 1969: 266). In this respect, rights, construed as the defensive starting position for the formation of the political system, allowed colonial states to develop rapidly as institutions focused on a distinct and apersonal set of responsibilities, and as capable of justifying these functions in emergent and unpredictable settings (Douglass 1989: 133). This, in turn, created a legitimating environment in which power could be transferred in relatively simple fashion from the English parliament to colonial assemblies and, later, to the federal state, and it meant that a set of established principles could be used to insulate the state-building transition against extreme disorder or loss of legitimacy. Indeed, the negative articulation of common-law rights played a vital role in the state-building process in America because it made available a pattern of *ex-nihilo* validity for the American states. This had the result that states could use rights to internalize explanations of their power that were at once constant, recognized, and yet also highly fluid, and through reference to these rights states were able rapidly to legislate at a high level of independence (Wood 1992: 252). The fact that American states could refer to a tradition of rights-based judicial opposition to the English crown within England thus greatly strengthened their impetus for independence, and it offered a legal structure in which states could pre-empt challenges to their legitimacy and generally consolidate their power.

Second, the defensive conceptions of rights integrated in early American state constitutions fulfilled the function that they checked unregulated use of authority by the new independent states, and they propitiously shaped the inner institutional architecture of the polities established at this time. In the first instance, the emergence of rights-based constitutions helped to construct particular states with consistent procedures for fulfilling their most essential functions. For example, most state constitutions provided for regular judicial procedures, entitlement to fair trial, equal security under law and personal protection from encroachment by state power. Equally importantly, most constitutions also provided uncontroversial instruments for raising revenue through parliamentary agreement.[30] To exemplify both these points, the 1776 constitution of North Carolina contained guarantees for judicial

---

[30] As one example, see the provision in the 1776 constitution of New Hampshire: 'That all bills, resolves, or votes for raising, levying and collecting money originate in the house of Representatives.' Further, see the 1776 constitution of New Jersey (Art. 14): 'That the

regularity and equality (Arts. 7–14), consensual taxation (Art. 16), and freedom of conscience (Art. 19), and it prohibited all legal privilege (Art. 22). Likewise, the 1776 constitution of Pennsylvania set laws for administrative accountability (s. 22), independent judicial procedure (s. 23), judicial equality and fairness (s. 25), and legally regulated fiscal levying (s. 41). In each of these respects, rights performed the vital function that they simplified the use of political power, and they clearly articulated and controlled the points of separation between the state and other parts of society. In addition to this, however, these constitutions also progressively provided for an inner rights-based differentiation of state functions.[31] Indeed, in the American context rights instituted a principled commitment to the *separation of powers*, and, although this separation was only haphazardly organized in the earliest state constitutions (see Corwin 1925: 514–15; Tarr 1998: 76–7), rights were gradually applied to mark out the limits of competence for judiciary, legislature and executive, and to prevent both legislature and executive from exceeding certain allotted functions. This was accomplished through rights to fair trial, which presupposed the closure of judicial process to political intervention, and rights to freedom of movement, expression, assembly and legislative participation, which placed legal limits on the powers of the executive in relation both to the legislature and the judiciary. In this respect, rights gradually brought the functional benefit that they enabled states to segregate their judicial procedures from the executive, and to protect processes of legal inclusion from volatile

townships, at their annual town meetings for electing other officers, shall choose constables for the districts respectively; and also three or more judicious freeholders of good character, to hear and finally determine all appeals, relative to unjust assessments, in cases of public taxation; which commissioners of appeal shall, for that purpose, sit at some suitable time or times, to be by them appointed, and made known to the people by advertisements.' See also the 1776 constitution of Pennsylvania (s. 41): 'No public tax, custom or contribution shall be imposed upon, or paid by the people of this state, except by a law for that purpose: And before any law be made for raising it, the purpose for which any tax is to be raised ought to appear clearly to the legislature to be of more service to the community than the money would be, if not collected; which being well observed, taxes can never be burthens.' Similar clauses are found in most early constitutions.

[31] For example, the Declaration of Rights in the 1776 constitution of North Carolina stated (Art. 4): 'That the legislative, executive, and supreme judicial powers of government, ought to be forever separate and distinct from each other.' This insistence on the separation of powers became stronger after 1776. Note the clause in the 1786 constitution of Vermont (Ch. II: VI): 'The legislative, executive and judiciary departments shall be separate and distinct, so that neither exercise the powers properly belonging to the other.'

political pressures. Moreover, this arrangement meant that rights allowed states to integrate the sovereign body of citizens in a discrete and controlled fashion in an institutional setting (the legislature), which was formative for the entire system yet whose direct consumption of power was limited. Furthermore, through the separation of powers, rights also enabled the state to ensure that final political authority was concentrated in a distinct functional location (the executive) which was withdrawn from day-to-day consultative and judicial exchanges. On each point, the separation of powers created an institutional order in which no one part of government was fully responsible for producing political legitimacy, and no part of government was fully and exclusively central to the political process.[32] The simultaneous triadic convolution and partition in the functions of the state established a highly effective system for managing political power. It cemented an administrative order in which the state as a whole could distinguish itself from the sum of its parts, and thus reproduce its power at a heightened level of internal legitimacy. Further, it enabled the state to guard against the possibility that one of its components or one group of persons using its power might be forced to provide all legitimacy for its acts or be burdened with an excess or unsustainable volume of power. In their implications for the inner structure of early American states, rights fulfilled their more typical functions in negatively securing state power, and they both clearly simplified the relations between state power and other social functions and distinctively articulated the internal boundaries in the mechanics of state power.

At the same time, however, in the revolutionary American setting the positive dimension of rights was also central to the process of state construction. In particular, the fact that the idea of rights was increasingly correlated with the idea of the sovereign nation, and that rights were perceived as entitlements to equal representation in the state and its legislative functions, instituted a formula for power that complemented the negative aspect of rights and contributed decisively to the structural consolidation of post-colonial polities in America. In particular, the foundation of rights in a representational doctrine of equal national

---

[32] This was not spelled out in all state constitutions. But, for example, I/V of the 1780 constitution of Massachusetts declared that 'All power residing originally in the people, and being derived from them, the several magistrates and officers of government vested with authority, whether legislative, executive, or judicial, are the substitutes and agents, and are at all times accountable to them.'

sovereignty also helped to make it possible for states to account for themselves as authorized by a highly abstracted and internal source of legitimacy, and this, together with the negative reference to rights, provided a secondary *ex-nihilo* justification and reinforcement for state power. This principle was already clear in the Mecklenburgh Resolutions, whose authors defined themselves as representing 'a free and independent people' who 'of right ought to be a sovereign and self-governing association, under the control of no power, other than that of our God and the General Government of the Congress'.

Most importantly, the concept of national sovereignty permitted states to internalize a source of authority which they could use to accompany all applications of their power and all acts of political inclusion, and it made it possible for states to apply their power at a high level of abstraction across society. In reflecting and describing themselves as national-sovereign actors, in fact, states began to envision themselves as qualified to legislate for persons which they already factually *included*, and so to circulate power through society as effectively produced and authenticated by those to whom it was applied. In this regard, the idea of rights-based national-popular sovereignty in early America became a crucial term both for constructing political power as an inclusive societal resource and for promoting its iterable transmission across society. The fact that power could explain itself as invariably formed by those persons to whom it was applied substantially enhanced the inclusionary dimension and perceived validity of power, and – in particular – it heightened the ease with which power could be formed and employed in uncertain transitional contexts. The concept of national or popular sovereignty, then, became foundational for the particular state constitutions, which, although reluctant to support universal male suffrage, widely professed to draw power from the sovereign people and to pass laws immediately authorized by, and so factually including, their subjects. Although up to 1784 only the constitution of Massachusetts (1780) was ratified by the people through any actual show of consent, popular sovereignty was recognized as a legitimating general principle for the new states. Again, this was most emphatic in the constitution of Pennsylvania. In its Declaration of Rights, this constitution stated (Art. V): 'That government is, or ought to be, instituted for the common benefit, protection and security of the people, nation or community.' It added to this the principle that 'the community hath an indubitable, unalienable and indefeasible right to reform, alter, or abolish government in such manner as shall be by that community judged most conducive to the public weal'. The direct sovereignty of particular states was also supported by the Articles of Confederation (ratified 1777–81), which, in Article 2, strongly protected the immediate exercise of sovereignty of single states.[33]

Both the negative and positive dimensions of rights in the American revolutionary context proved to be vital elements in the production and construction of political power for the transitional society of America after its revolutionary break with Britain. Most crucially, however, it needs to be noted that in early America neither negative nor positive principles became politically formative in undiluted fashion. On the contrary, the positive ideal of national sovereignty was always dialectically checked and filtered by negative rights, and it was in negative conjunction with rights that the positive principle of national self-legislation assumed effective foundational status for new American states. Indeed, the defensive functions of rights served constrictively to moderate the more volatile implications of the idea of national sovereignty, and the primary negative rights underlying the American polity contained institutes that selectively preserved the integrity of the emergent state apparatus and obstructed tendencies towards precarious over-inclusion stimulated by principles of wholly integrated sovereignty.

To be sure, the very earliest constitutions usually, in the spirit of Tom Paine's republicanism, expressed bold proclamations of popular sovereignty and anticipated only weak constraints on the popular legislature.[34] Moreover, not all early state constitutions contained bills of rights, or consistently separated judicial, legislative and executive functions, and many imputed a high degree of sovereign latitude to legislative institutions. It has been noted that the commitment to preserving inviolable property rights in the states was originally weak (Bruchey 1980: 1157; Treanor 1985: 699). Nonetheless, after 1776, the original cautious functions of rights became more and more pervasive in revolutionary state construction, and in most states rights were increasingly used to limit the legislative powers of government and to place mandatory constraints on the sovereign authority assumed by parliamentary bodies. The state constitutions written after the Pennsylvania constitution of 1776, in fact, tended specifically to use rights to stabilize the political apparatus and to measure and curtail the sovereign powers accorded to the legislature: constitutions drafted from 1777 on widely reflected a move away from the simple republicanism that infused

---

[33] On controversy over this and the ultimate shift from state to federal sovereignty, see Jensen (1940: 161, 176, 239; 1950: 43).

[34] For comment see Tarr (1998: 65, 86–7).

the first wave of state constitutions (Williams 1988: 416–20). For example, seminally, the 1777 constitution of New York contained provisions for a strong executive to balance the legislature (Arts. 17–19). The 1777 constitution of Georgia defined rights as institutes to restrict sovereign legislative authority.[35] Similarly, the 1777 constitution of Vermont (II, 8) stated that members of the legislature 'shall have no power to add to, alter, abolish, or infringe any part of this constitution'. The 1780 constitution of Massachusetts (Part 2, Chapter 1, Art. 4) only allowed the legislature to establish 'orders, laws, statutes, and ordinances, directions and instructions' as long as these were expressly 'not repugnant or contrary to this constitution'. Throughout the later period of constitution drafting, additionally, bills of rights were widely used in a more circumspect fashion, and they became 'longer, more detailed, and stronger in their prohibitions', thus paving the way for the more proportioned model of internally balanced governance advocated by the Federalists (Lutz 1980: 68). This was not a universal tendency, and even some post-1787 state constitutions, notably the 1790 constitution of Pennsylvania, still espoused a strong theory of popular sovereignty. Even in these cases, however, rights were usually employed with restrictive functions in mind. In the second wave of state constitution drafting, therefore, the principles of negative constrictive rights and positive popular sovereignty were balanced against each other, and rights were routinely employed to restrict access to legislative power and to limit the mass of exchanges over which legislators were allowed to pass laws. Indeed, earlier American state constitutions ultimately constructed national-legislative sovereignty around the representation of *pre-defined rights* (i.e. rights regarding property, taxation, judicial security, etc.), and they ensured that representative duties of legislation fell to those with an interest in preserving rights that had received prior sanction (i.e. that they were owners of property).[36] In this respect, the early American constitutions gradually formed an organizing matrix that enabled most states at once to obtain legitimacy through wide claims to popular sovereignty, yet also, at the same

[35] Art. 7 declared: 'The house of assembly shall have power to make such laws and regulations as may be conducive to the good order and wellbeing of the State; provided such laws and regulations be not repugnant to the true intent and meaning of any rule or regulation contained In this constitution.'

[36] Note the declaration in the 1776 constitution of Pennsylvania (s. 17) that 'representation in proportion to the number of taxable inhabitants is the only principle which can at all times secure liberty'. Note also the provision in the 1776 North Carolina constitution (XVI): 'That the people of this State ought not to be taxed, or made subject to the payment of any impost or duty, without the consent of themselves, or their Representatives in General Assembly, freely given.'

time, to limit the factual inclusion of their constituents: that is, they implemented rights in a form that allowed emergent states both to reflect themselves as possessing inclusive legitimacy and authority, yet also to prepare and manufacture both the origin of their power and the social terrains to which their power was applied. In asserting that their positive sovereignty depended on negative protection of rights, therefore, states again used rights as an internal apparatus which extracted a construction of the state as a stable order of public law, but which also ensured that many exchanges in society were not defined as relevant for the political system, that social actions either covered by or indifferent to rights-based legal sanction were ordinarily excluded from power, and that state power – both in its source and its application – was only applied as a highly specialized and abstracted resource.

Rights, in sum, performed a threefold function of abstraction, differentiation and inclusion for new states in the revolutionary American setting. First, in expressing entitlements under inherited law, rights traced out lines of negative justification and higher-norm legitimacy and abstraction in the state. Second, in organizing procedures for judicial integrity, fiscal scrutiny and institutional specialization in the state, rights acted to effect processes of political exclusion and procedurally to delineate the state's internal and external functional boundaries. Third, in promising powers of participation and national representation, rights allowed states, for the first time in modern history, to obtain legitimacy through the claim that they derived their positive power – their sovereignty – directly and exclusively from those persons subject to this power. Through this third inclusionary implication of rights, states began to explain themselves as using power generated by their subjects, and they obtained legitimacy by claiming that all addressees of power were integrated in and subject to power as *their own power*. In this principle, states obtained a dramatically heightened formula of abstractive inclusion for their power, and this enabled states to elaborate internal grounds for the ongoing reproduction and the evenly inclusive application of their power. It is noteworthy in this, however, that the divergent implications of rights were not elaborated as conflicting principles. In fact, these principles reinforced each other as related structural components of statehood. In particular, positive rights of national sovereignty, even in their first formulation, were not pursued in the direction of factually and comprehensively inclusive sovereign statehood. Instead, the inclusionary implications of national sovereignty were gradually qualified by the fact that sovereign powers of political formation were policed by other rights: it was the coalescence of rights of sovereignty with other particular (formal and negative) rights that made the enduring formation of state power in America possible. The American states were able gradually to construct themselves as independent political organs and to develop effective legislative competences because they sanctioned a precisely constrained interplay between the inclusive and the exclusive functions of rights, and, after the first ebb of revolutionary/democratic or republican fervour, they insisted that representation of the sovereign nation must be entrusted to agents whose delegated functions and legislative actions were prescribed and preformed through established rights. By founding their legitimacy in this dialectical fusion of sovereignty and rights, the American state constitutions developed a conclusive technique for managing the boundaries of the political system, and they evolved a device both for organizing and including the sources of their abstracted power and its legitimacy and for preselecting those exchanges that the state was required to incorporate.

Ultimately, these interwoven functions of rights culminated in the Federal Constitution itself. On one level, to be sure, the Federal Constitution assimilated the positive implications of rights. Although it was less able to mobilize pure-republican legitimacy than the individual state constitutions, the concept of popular sovereignty, in modified form, was placed at the centre of the Federal Constitution. The Federal Constitution contained an implied idea of national citizenship, national equality under law (Art. 4.2), and national representation, and, although it recognized some state rights as limits on federal power, it drew its originating legitimacy from the same positive principles as state constitutions. Despite this, however, the defensive construction of rights again played a substantial role in the construction of the federal state. As is well documented, the revolutionary period in America was marked by a deep conflict between parties urging the formation of a strong federal state and those parties favouring the concentration of sovereignty in particular states. In this setting, it was initially the opponents of the federal state, the Anti-Federalists, often repeating earlier arguments directed against the Westminster parliament, who adopted a defensive conception of rights and were keen to promote a Bill of Rights to place checks on federal authority. In exemplary fashion, for instance, Luther Martin argued that a Bill of Rights would 'serve as a barrier between the central government and the respective states and their citizens' (Mason 1964: 77). The Federalists themselves only gradually came to view a formal Bill of Rights as necessary, and a separate catalogue of rights was not added to the Federal Constitution until 1791. This delay was due in part to the initial belief of the Federalists that human rights could not be fully enumerated and that any attempt to systematize rights must leave some rights unmentioned and vulnerable to violation. This delay was also due to the view, expressed by Alexander Hamilton in *Federalist* 84, that the constitution in itself already de facto comprised a Bill of Rights (Madison, Hamilton and Jay 1987 [1787–8]: 477). Additionally, however, the late acceptance of a Bill of Rights resulted from the conviction, expressed by James Madison, that governments only exercise powers specifically allotted to them, and that any formal catalogue of rights reflected a vague, dangerously expanded view of the extent of state power. Governments, in Madison's view, only laid legitimate claim to limited functions, and they could never encroach on natural human rights: the precautionary circumscription of the federal state with catalogues of rights was, consequently, superfluous (Mason 1964: 80–1). Nonetheless, by 1791, the Federalist framers, and particularly Madison, reacted to amendments proposed by the state ratifying conventions, and they drafted a bill based on those already contained in many state constitutions.[37] In the early federal era, in consequence, the use of rights was tied, across the spectrum, to the belief that rights served, not positively to form or transfer power to states, but defensively to restrict and selectively to filter state power.

These negative rights in the Federal Constitution played a core role in constructing statehood in the early American republic. As in the state constitutions, the establishment of a Bill of Rights in the Federal Constitution had the primary outcome that it removed crucial social issues from the centre of political intensity, and it reduced potentially destabilizing controversy around the state. This was evident, for example, in provisions for rights of judicial equality, which separated the law from constant political exposure. This was also evident in the question of religion: the constitutional guarantee of rights of religious freedom (already highly refined in colonial charters) and the independence of the church acted to remove religious conflict from the sphere of political control. In addition, the fact that the federal constitution gave endorsement to singular rights of ownership by protecting persons from expropriation helped to ensure that the political system was relatively indifferent to economic conflicts, and, in defining questions of ownership as covered by primary rights, it was able internally to limit the social

---

[37] For a helpful account of Madison's change of mind see Dumbauld (1958).

activities that were internalized by the state and to pre-construct its responses to its constituents.[38] In fact, although property rights were in the main treated rather implicitly in the Federal Constitution, the constitution as a whole was designed to protect private rights of ownership, it entrenched rights of property under the Contract Clause (Art. 1, 10, 1) and the Fifth Amendment, and it determined property as an object of rights which was categorically withdrawn from the reach of legitimate state power. This was clear enough in preceding bills of rights, notably the Virginia Declaration of Rights, which defined 'the enjoyment of life and liberty, with the means of acquiring and possessing property, and pursuing and obtaining happiness and safety' as a primary right of human association. In cementing a full list of subjective rights, therefore, the Federal Constitution removed swathes of regulatory responsibility from the state, and it created a body of legal institutions and procedures that – in relatively apolitical manner – could both deflect social issues from the state and preserve a sphere of functional liberty around the state. Moreover, this stabilizing impact of rights was also manifest in the question of taxation. The Federal Constitution (Art. 1.7) provided that all 'bills for raising Revenue shall originate in the House of Representatives'. In securing rights of popular revenue control, the constitution produced a simplified apparatus for regulating public finance, which restricted dispute over that source of controversy. As in earlier proto-constitutional polities, in fact, it enabled the state to fund a national debt, and even to create a central bank. It is widely documented that the push for a central federal state was largely dictated by exigencies of public finance and the need to create a taxation system able to raise a public debt to cover costs incurred during the revolutionary wars.[39]

For these reasons, the Federal Constitution provided a particularly potent constitutional formula for supporting a strong central state in the era of early state construction. At one level, the reference to popular or national sovereignty enabled the new American state to accomplish what no earlier national state had achieved: that is, to extract a body of public law which separated the functions of state from private activities and provided a unifying and legitimating basis to sustain particular acts of state. National sovereignty was in fact the absent formula in state-building processes in European societies, and other states had suffered residual

---

[38] For sardonic commentary see Morgan (1988: 233).

[39] For various accounts see White (1948: 507); Jensen (1950: 302); Ferguson (1961: 289–305).

weakness or internal pluralism because they had not been able to abstract and construct their power by appealing to national sovereignty: national sovereignty was the key instrument for effective abstractive state building, and it was distinctively elaborated as a principle of public law in the setting of revolutionary America. In founding its public law in rights of national sovereignty and equality, the Federal Constitution created a legal arrangement that enabled the state to define and internalize the grounds for its monopoly of power in society, to accompany its use of power with abstracted, internal and reproducible justifications, and so to legislate, in relatively even, positive fashion, across the politically relevant exchanges of society. In addition, however, the Federal Constitution, to a greater extent even than the state constitutions, had the notable feature that it used negative rights, in dialectical fashion, both as elements of sovereign inclusion and as instruments to police its inner structure and integrity, and this reinforced the state-building functions of the concept of public sovereignty. This dialectic was manifest in provisions for the separation of powers and in injunctions on absolute legislative supremacy contained in the constitution (Art. 1.9). More vitally, however, in sanctioning a formal Bill of Rights and in validating other rights at an implicit level, the constitution used private rights to separate many social exchanges from the sphere of political power, it designated many social questions as not requiring political power, and it thus depoliticized much of society and many of its own functions. In each of these respects, by 1791 the Federal Constitution brought towards completion the implicit social functions of rights in the European context, and it created a political order centred around an abstracted or *public-legal* state structure that was able both to legislate in relative autonomy and, as both corollary and precondition of this, to limit social politicization and to cement its own boundaries in relation to the rest of society. The politically abstractive dimension of the constitution arose directly from its fusion of ideals of national sovereignty and defensive rights. The demand for sovereignty impelled the extraction of the constitution as a body of public law which could be stored in the state and used both to accompany its legislative acts and, inclusively, to reproduce its power. Yet the demand for rights also ensured that the structure of public law remained differentiated from other activities, and rights strictly governed the distinction of private and public functions. Whereas previous and contemporary political systems in Europe struggled to maintain legislative sovereignty because of their uneven rights fabric, the American constitution used national sovereignty to create the state as a public order and it utilized rights to delineate the extent and limits of state power. In so doing, it solved the problems of uncertain differentiation and endemic re-particularization typical of other constitutions. It thus became the template for the modern differentiated (sovereign) state, able to use its power as an abstracted and autonomous facility.

The Federal Constitution made perhaps its most enduring contribution to the stabilization of state power by virtue of the fact that, building on the judicial provisions of some earlier state constitutions, it established strong principles for judicial review of statutes and new legislation by the courts of law. A vital dimension of the constitution, thus, was that it instituted a Supreme Court to protect constitutional principles in legislation and to ensure compatibility of single statutes with constitutional norms. This provision (rather vague in the Federal Constitution itself) was reinforced almost immediately under the Judiciary Act (1789): this Act cemented the powers of the national courts, it assigned to the courts the power (increased after 1803) to review statutes in the light of constitutional norms, and it appointed marshals to enforce federal constitutional law in different states. This rights-based strengthening of judicial power, in fact, might be viewed as the most distinctive and characteristic innovation in the constitutional apparatus of the American republic. The idea of judicial review of legislation was fundamental to American constitutionalism. If the English Revolution had grown from a contest between judiciary and parliament and had ultimately utilized judicial rights to create a sovereign legislature, able to legislate in independence of the law courts, the American Revolution deviated substantially from this pattern of political abstraction. To be sure, the first state constitutions were hardly consistent in placing legislative power under judicial control (Tarr 1998: 72). However, even prior to independence, the principle of strong judicial power ran through the entire American Revolution like a deep pulse.[40] In some cases, county courts had gone as far as to overturn contested colonial legislation, including the Stamp Act. In America, the rise of legislative power was closely linked to the belief that the law itself was a reservoir of rights. Indeed, the belief that statutes had to be checked by courts produced a model of higher law that supplanted the principle of statutory supremacy in eighteenth-century English constitutionalism, and it played a primary role in first allowing early American politicians to

---

[40] On pre-1787 cases of judicial review see Corwin (1925: 521). On the anti-Blackstonian implications of this see Snowiss (1990: 16, 20, 90).

authorize the transfer of power to colonial assemblies (Grey 1978: 873). This emphasis on judicial power became programmatic in Hamilton's account of the judiciary in *Federalist* 78, which argued that the constitution must be regarded by all judges as 'a fundamental law', and in case of 'variance' between the norms of single statutes and the norms of the constitutional text 'the Constitution ought to be preferred to the statute' (Madison, Hamilton and Jay 1987 [1787–8]: 439).

The tendency towards reinforcement of judicial power in the institution of the Supreme Court gave rise to what has often been perceived as the central paradox in early American history: namely that the Federalists, who considered the central constitutional state a political ideal, wished to limit this power through the establishment of horizontal controls on legislation through the courts (Rodell 1955: 43). However, it is not necessary to see the commitment to a central state and to judicial power as a paradox. In fact, the creation of a supreme legal institution to act as protector of the constitution and to preserve the state's highest legislative legitimacy brought a number of significant structural and functional benefits for the new American state, and the transfer of a portion of state power to judges greatly expanded the effective power of the state.

First, at a practical level, the institution of a Supreme Court helped to consolidate the federal state at a practical level, and it was utilized by parties committed to building an authoritative central state. The foundation of the court was closely tied to the Supremacy Clause (Art. VI) of the Federal Constitution, and it reflected a strategy to transfer judicial power from particular states to the federal state: the assertion of the constitution as highest law in the courts entailed a process of national-political concentration. Indeed, early members of the Supreme Court were usually Federalists, and they were prepared to use the court to maximize the power located in the federal state. The outcome of this was that, through a number of precedents in the 1790s, both statutes and court rulings were progressively tested for consistency with the constitution, and laws seen as violating the constitution were deemed void by the federal judges.[41] In addition, moreover, the judiciary became responsible for resolving highly resonant questions regarding the division of competence between the federal state and the individual states. The courts were charged with responsibility both for stabilizing and asserting primacy of federal power through arbitration of federal–state disputes

---

[41] On this and early post-1789 practice of judicial review see Currie (1985: 55, 70).

and, at the same time, for checking and 'limiting the reach of national government' and preserving, through recognition of the rights of states, the particular liberties of individual agents within the states.[42] Through subsequent practice the courts obtained authority to use limited powers of judicial review to police the legislative procedures of national (sovereign) government and, under some circumstances, to declare co-ordinate branches of government as acting *ultra vires*.[43] Central to each of these processes was the (albeit ambiguous) conviction that the constitution enunciated the 'original right' of the people, that legislative acts contrary or 'repugnant' to this primary constitutional right could not have force of law and that courts were specifically appointed to determine that principles of national constitutional law were uniformly prevalent (Van Alstyne 1969: 16, 36, 37).

Second, the existence of a Supreme Court consolidated the federal state at a deeper functional and conceptual level by virtue of the fact that it conferred an inviolable status on the Federal Constitution itself. Under the protection of the court, the constitution came to represent a law above all other laws, and the body of norms contained in the constitution was distinguished from the more informal, positive or statutory constitutions existing in common-law states (Haines 1944: 17). The court formally enabled the new American state, drawing legitimacy from the constitution, to explain itself as singularly authorized by a corpus of higher norms, which it used the courts to sanction, preserve and extract from everyday contestation. In this respect, in fact, it was the creation of a Supreme Court that enabled the American republic fully to obtain benefits of the constitution. By placing the constitution under protection of the courts, the state was able simply to internalize its constitution, to support all its legislative acts through overarching reference to the constitution and positively to reproduce its power as legitimate power, yet also to ensure that the constitution (the state's original source of legitimacy) was extricated from daily processes of political controversy around the state. The Supreme Court thus at once condensed and displaced the power held in the state, and it transformed the constitution into a politically withdrawn document to authorize and control the use of state power.

Third, by designating the Supreme Court as a guardian of the normative sources of its legitimacy, the federal state obtained a mechanism that

---

[42] See Choper (1980: 247); Fried (2004:15). See also, classically, Wechsler (1954: 559–60); Schmidhauser (1958: 11–17).
[43] See analysis of *Marbury v. Madison* in Choper (1980: 62); Wolfe (1986: 81–3).

allowed it to govern its relation to the sovereign body from which it derived its power and legitimacy, and to translate national sovereign power into a form that could be effectively and generally utilized through society. The Supreme Court performed this function in various ways. At one level, the court acted as an instrument by means of which the most central questions of sovereign legislation could be referred to subsidiary institutions, and laws could be tested in accordance with politically withdrawn norms. This meant that as, gradually, judges acquired the power to declare acts of Congress unconstitutional, the concentration of political power around the legislature was dispersed, and the constitution of the state, supposedly expressing the primary force of national sovereignty, could be extracted from everyday political conflict, so that the constitution was only rarely required to be subject to contest or openly politicized. Judicial review strictly limited the full localization of political power at any one point of sovereignty in the state, and it enabled the state, in part, to reduce the volatility of many of its sovereign functions. Additionally, however, the creation of a Supreme Court asserting powers to protect the constitution had the outcome that the will of the people, which the state purported to represent and from which it obtained legitimacy, was not entitled to shape the actual structure of the state or to gain immediate influence on the constitution. In consequence, the state obtained a mechanism through which it could structure and anticipate the precise forms in which it included its constituents, and it precisely determined its inclusion of the popular will. This was perhaps the decisive distinction between the constitutionalist visions of Federalists and Anti-Federalists, many of whom wished to preserve easier powers of amendment and to guarantee closer identity between the state and its subjects (Kruman 1997: 58). The early American republic, thus, utilized judicial review both to legitimize and stabilize itself, distinctively, against the English crown and against the more volatile acts – the 'various and interfering interests' and the 'spirit of party and faction' examined by Madison in *Federalist* 10 – of its own sovereign constituents (Madison, Hamilton and Jay 1987 [1787–8]: 124). In each respect, the fusion of sovereignty and rights was foundational for an abstracted and effective political system.

Through the incipient judicialization of sovereign power, in short, the American state instituted a body of recursive and functionally expedient principles at its own core. In its deeper functional dimensions, the doctrine of judicial power enabled the American republic rapidly to construct its political order, predictably to unify and give consistency to its widening legislative processes, and internally to control and explain the use of its power. The construction of statutory power as checked and authorized by a judiciary acting to preserve constitutional norms created a reservoir of legitimacy through which the new American state insulated itself against its own precariousness, absorbed uncertainty about its authority and reproduced internal legitimacy to cover the rapidly growing need for statutory legislation.[44] The federal state claimed to derive legitimacy from a constitution embodying the national will of the people. Yet, in designating this will as expressed in a number of higher-order *fundamental laws* and as concentrated in a catalogue of formal rights, the state adopted an instrument to ensure that the legislative expressions of this will were in fact checked by lawyers and interpreted by the courts, who then became guardians of the will (that is, the rights) of the people.[45] The partial displacement of sovereign power from the legislature to the courts meant that the sovereign people remained both present and absent in the state's structure, and it instituted procedures that counteracted a full politicization of the state. The Supreme Court established a circular relation between the popular will, the constitution and the courts, which meant that each of these organs produced legitimacy for the state, but none became an exclusive focus of over-intense political controversy. The Supreme Court allowed the state at once to authorize itself through reference to the higher-law expressions of the popular will contained in the constitution. Yet, at the same time, it allowed the state to avoid direct articulation or interpretation of the popular will. Indeed, in referring the legislative acts of the popular will to the judiciary, the constitution served factually to prevent the state from directly confronting the source of its legitimacy, it imposed limits on the extent to which the actual will of the people ever required express declaration, and it enabled the state to legitimize itself, dialectically, through the simultaneous inclusion and exclusion of the popular will. At the heart of the system of judicial review established after 1787-9, therefore, was an act

---

[44] A point close to this is made in Rakove (1997: 1059-60).

[45] Hence Hamilton's repeated claim that 'no other way' to protect constitutional limits existed 'than through the medium of the courts of justice; whose duty it must be to declare all acts contrary to the manifest tenor of the constitution void' (Madison, Hamilton and Jay 1987 [1787-8]: 438). See also Madison's record from the Federal Convention, noting the need to place a 'check on the Legislature' by means of a Supreme Court (Farrand 1911: II, 79). Note, though, that Madison was also cautious about judicial review (Snowiss 1990: 97).

of *exclusionary self-depoliticization* within the state: in creating a court to supervise the legislative acts of the national will and to ensure their compliance with prescriptions and rights enshrined in the constitution, the state employed principles of rights to curtail the *immediate* manifestation of the national will. By these means, the state was able to use instituted constitutional rights both internally to structure its responses to matters requiring legislation and to remove the inclusive centre of its political sovereignty from direct or intense politicization. Indeed, its strong judicial dimension meant that the constitution itself was transformed into an extracted element within the state, which accompanied and controlled the use of state power and through which the state could guarantee legitimacy, but which only exceptionally became an integrated component of the cycles of political engagement attached to legislative functions. The constitution, flanked by the Supreme Court, thus acted to construct a sphere of relative apolicity around the highest functions of the state: the state internalized a document through which it could simultaneously explain itself as the political expression of the people, yet also hold the exact factual demands of this will at a level of implicit latency.

In each of these respects, the early constitutional construction of the American republic can be seen as an experiment in which rights – in both their negative and their positive dimensions – enacted a legitimating process of controlled political in- and exclusion in the state apparatus. Rights-based constitutional procedures formed a technique for constructing a central state that was authorized by the idea of national sovereignty, yet that both reduced the impact of the more democratic claims of the state constitutions and expelled the sporadic or pluralistic expressions of the will of the people from the final structure of the state. It barely requires emphasis that the leading Federalists were intent on building a national-sovereign state that made only scarce concessions to full democracy, and they insisted on the unsustainability of any pure identity between government and governed. This was illustrated by Edmund Randolph, speaking in the Federal Convention, who identified the 'chief danger' for the state as arising 'from the democratic parts of our constitutions'. Randolph complained that none of the state constitutions 'provided sufficient checks against the democracy' (Farrand 1911: I, 26–7). Similarly, Madison warned in the Convention against 'equality of suffrage' (Farrand 1911: I, 37). In *Federalist* 10, Madison described democracy as liable to suppress 'both the public good and the rights of other citizens'. He concluded that 'popular government' could only exist if governmental power was entrusted to popular representatives who were not the people (Madison, Hamilton and Jay 1987 [1787–8]: 125). Madison made a strict distinction between republicanism and democracy, and he stressed that a republic needed to be based in the 'delegation of the government . . . to a small number of citizens' (Madison, Hamilton and Jay 1987 [1787–8]: 126). The Federal Constitution, therefore, was ultimately constructed at once as a bearer of federal sovereignty against state sovereignty and as a bearer of *national* sovereignty against pure *popular* or *democratic* sovereignty. In both these respects the Supreme Court, and the equilibration of the negative and the positive aspects of constitutional rights, performed a vital function.

For all these reasons, the early American republic emerged more generally as a polity that, at different levels, employed rights both to articulate principles of legitimacy for political order and to organize its functions in a manageably abstracted fashion. The federal state used rights to assume and justify its monopoly of power in society: by referring to itself as a repository of rights it gave internal foundation to its exclusive authority. Yet it also used rights to check and internally to police its power, to reduce its power to particular specified functions, and to restrict the possibility of its own excessive politicization. Much literature on the American Revolution is coloured by a controversy over the question whether liberal rights or republican principles were the main determinants in the course of constitution formation, and whether the federal state eventually emerged as a state marked by power-limiting liberal rights or power-forming republican sovereignty (Appleby 1984: 18, 22; Adams 2001: 301–14). From the perspective outlined here, however, this dispute revolves around a false antinomy. It was in fact the convergence of liberal and republican elements that facilitated the construction of the American republic. Rights acted both as active sources of legitimacy and as negative checks on power, and through both these correlated dimensions they served to form the state as a positively abstracted and effective sovereign actor: the state's positive formation depended, dialectically, on its reflexive self-restriction. Rights, therefore, clearly served as instruments of simultaneous political in- and exclusion: they allowed both the individual states and the federal state to apply power positively and evenly across society, but they also controlled the boundaries of the state against extreme expansion or over-inclusion.

The wider societal corollary of these constitutional tendencies was that early post-revolutionary American society began to be formed simultaneously around a growth in the 'public power of the state' and a factual reinforcement and promotion of the 'private rights of individuals' (Wood 1992: 325). In other words, American constitutionalism instituted a framework in which public power gained in uniformity and consistency, and in which the state abstracted and expanded its power as a positive and publicly usable facility. Yet it sustained this public power by using rights to secure a realm of relatively apolitical freedom around and outside the state, which meant that most personal liberties were exercised and most social controversies were voiced in relative indifference to state power. The power of the state resulted from a substantial depoliticization of society, which the constitution, its provisions over rights and review, and its controlled mechanisms for in- and exclusion, at once promoted and underwrote. The general dialectic between inclusionary state construction and exclusionary political selection or even depoliticization implied throughout the history of constitutional foundation thus culminated, momentarily, in the state constitutions of revolutionary America, and ultimately in the Federal Constitution itself. Through this process it became clear that the abstractive and differentiated construction of political power, as gradually formed in the European political environment, was most adequately accomplished by states preserving patterns of rights-based or higher-norm positive/internal self-validation, techniques for the self-displacement of power and political self-restriction, and instruments for simultaneously including and excluding persons and societal exchanges in and from power. In revolutionary America, the experimental fusion of nationally authorized sovereign (republican) power and politically withdrawn constitutional (liberal) rights allowed states with these features to develop.

The French constitutions

The American experiment in constitutional formation grew rapidly from a tax revolt into a state-building laboratory, in which claims over constitutional rights detached the state apparatus from colonial and monarchical authority and legitimized a new state as a powerful public and autonomous construct. In America, the insistence on rights of sovereignty was initially turned defensively against a different state: Great Britain. For this reason, the American constitutions phrased principles of public sovereignty and equality in rights holding in terms that were not primarily focused on questions of inequality between Americans: the proclamation of national unity and sovereignty as the substructure of the state was articulated (to a large degree) without critical resonance for the fibre of American society. For the longer-term consequences of the American constitutions, however, it is vital to observe that, once transplanted back to a European setting, the balanced principle of rights and national sovereignty enunciated in America impacted dramatically on inner-societal structures under European states, and formed the basis for a state-building process that was directed, not against colonial authority, but against stratified privilege. In the European context, specifically, the American constitutions provided a model for the general construction of power that could be utilized both experimentally to refound political systems and to weaken private residues within the state. As documents that justified state power by articulating higher-norm principles of sovereignty and rights against imperial power, these constitutions fused in combustible manner with the anti-feudal evolutionary trajectory of most European societies, and they provided a new public-legal template for expressing the deep-lying process of legal positivization, political abstraction and structural centralization which shaped these societies.

The first replication of the state-building dimensions of the American Revolution occurred in revolutionary France, after 1789. As discussed, the French monarchical state survived into the late eighteenth century as a diffuse and obdurately interlocked amalgam of public and private authority. The power of the state was limited by bearers of privileged office, and society as a whole was unevenly included in political power and unevenly subject to legal authority. As also discussed, this had debilitating constitutional consequences for the state, especially in fiscal matters, and the Bourbon monarchy was critically hamstrung in its attempts to detach matters pertaining to public revenue from private interests, corporate liberties, and questions of status. This meant that the state was always forced to hold a large volume of social exchanges at a high and varied level of political contestation, it struggled to legislate positively and generally over its most pressing problems, and it invariably confronted a mass of privately motivated internal social obstructions to its power. Indeed, the French monarchy was compelled to attune its legislative acts to the highly personal and particular demands and rights of the people that it incorporated, and it lacked a general legal order for controlling its inclusion of those subject to its laws. Turgot, notably, informed Louis XVI in plain words about the cause of the fiscal malaise of his state. He observed: 'The cause of the evil, sire, results from the fact that your nation does not have a constitution. It is a society composed of different badly unified orders, of a people whose members are barely connected by social bonds. As a consequence almost nobody cares for anything but his own particular interest' (1787 [1775]: 9). Later, at the Assembly of Notables in 1787, Calonne expressed the view that the weakness of France was caused by the lack of *loi commune*, which could be imposed across society regardless of immunity, privilege and other legal variation (see Behrens 1963: 468).

On these grounds, the revolution that began with the convention of the French Estates-General in 1789, although clearly expressing the volitional reaction of certain social groups to conditions of governance under late absolutism, was in the first instance a functional reaction within the political system to the haphazardly unsustainable internal order and the unenforceable power of monarchical authority under the Ancien Régime. Indeed, the first acts of legislation during the revolutionary period figured as devices for simplifying and maximizing the power contained in the French state and for manufacturing a societal environment in which this power could be easily and more inclusively produced and applied. The first piece of legislation to perform these functions was the famous law of early August 1789, in which the newly established National Constituent Assembly decided to abolish the legal residues of feudalism and to declare illegitimate the seigneurial powers still preserved by the nobility, especially those rights concerning tax exemptions and patrimonial jurisdiction. It has been forcefully argued in the historical literature that feudalism was already obsolete in France by the time of its statutory abolition in 1789, and it has been persuasively shown that many privileges had long since either fallen into disuse or were no longer in the hands of the nobility (Chaussinand-Nogaret 1976: 63; Gruder 2007: 37). Moreover, it has been demonstrated that many seigneurial conventions remained in force after 1789: even the Rural Code of 1791, which reinforced some provisions of 1789, was based in a compromise over the implications of feudal entitlement and collective rights (Jones 1988: 82, 137; Woloch 1994: 171). Nonetheless, the anti-feudal laws of the early revolution had the distinction that they succeeded, where previous royal legislation had failed, in creating a unitary legal order for the state. In so doing, they initiated a process in which uniform principles of rights were applied through society to eradicate particularistic interests from the state's structure and to concentrate the state's monopoly over its reserves of political power.

The first thrust of the laws of 1789 was that they effaced the traces of private/feudal authority from the state by separating rights under law from local or personal standing, and they defined status and entitlement under law as derived, not from socio-structural position, but from general legal-subjective personality. In the first instance, this was reflected in the fact that rights of property were detached from feudal privilege, and feudal proprietary rights were transformed into rights held, not under personalistic convention or authority, but under generally consented contracts. These laws in fact gave formal expression to the principle of individual integrity in ownership and legal standing, and they abolished (in part) the system of shared ownership of crops and land, through which lords had possessed time-honoured rights to taxes on the products of their feoffs. In this regard, these laws, jointly with the secondary – more powerful – anti-feudal laws introduced in the 1790s, served to designate persons under law as individual and uniform agents, to simplify the imputation of legal rights and claims and, consequently, to harden the external lines of differentiation between public authority and privately held resources. Second, these laws acted to dissolve the remnants of the legally cemented fusion of land tenure and jurisdictional power, they separated questions of legal entitlement from questions of local or customary authority and they at once restricted the powers of patrimonial justice that still applied in some regions and ensured that all persons were formally equal before the law and (notionally) had equal access to judicial hearing (see Markoff 1996: 44). In this respect, notably, the anti-feudal laws were supplemented, in the constitution of 1791, by laws banning corporations, which also acted to diminish the legal impact of private status and privilege and finally brought a 'reduction of all citizens to an equal submission to the law' (Sewell 1980: 89).

In these different respects, the swathe of anti-feudal laws passed in the early stages of the revolutionary era in France created a setting in which the emergent republican state was able significantly to increase both its inclusionary unity and the level of abstract intensity at which it could circulate its power through society. In applying formal constructs of legal personality and singular subjective rights to split apart the overlapping entitlements imputed to social agents under seigneurial law, these laws meant that the state obtained an internal apparatus to include particular social agents both more generally and more selectively in the political exchanges of society: that is, the state was only required to include social agents as bearers of economic interests, as addressees of law or as contestants for a portion of state power, but not in all these capacities at the same time. In this respect, these laws ensured that it was more difficult for actors to invade or privately to monopolize state power, and the state was able to refer to and assimilate societal actors in political exchanges as constituents of an equal and evenly constructed *external* environment. In fact, as it replaced the multiple rights and privileges of seigneurial communities with the uniform juridical rights of contractually autonomous equal subjects, the state acquired a uniform legal corpus that at once markedly expanded its own general power and increasingly made other agreements in society – previously constructed in pluralistic fashion – dependent on the state and the rights that the state autonomously allocated and legally underwrote. This construction of the state as a primary allocator and guarantor of rights greatly intensified the power stored in the state. At a more practical level, moreover, the abolition of privileges and exemptions under law also meant that the state was able to integrate members of society in a more controlled manner into its vital functions, and, in particular, that it could apply general fiscal laws without risking unabated constitutional friction with actors within its inner structure. The end of seigneurial law – and of privileges and corporations more widely – thus brought the benefit to the state that, in eradicating status, privilege and affiliation as determinants of fiscal contribution, it was able to implement a rational and centralized fiscal system in parallel to its increasingly ordered judicial system, and so gradually augment its fiscal revenue. Notably, the fiscal system put in place through the revolutionary period, although often revised, formed the basis of French taxation until the early twentieth century.

At this primary level, the very first statutory acts of the early revolutionary regimes in France acted fundamentally to promote the simultaneous differentiation and consolidation of state power, and this acted legally to simplify the boundaries of the state, to tighten and regulate its processes of political in- and exclusion and to solidify society around power vested in the state. This dimension of the revolutionary legislation was then reinforced in the 1789 Declaration of the Rights of Man. Article 1 of the Declaration, for instance, renounced the principle of social distinction as a qualification for rights, and it constructed all members of society as equal addressees of the law. Articles 6 and 7 protected rights of judicial equality and procedural integrity. Article 17 guaranteed rights of individual property ownership under law. Article 14 enshrined the right of public consent to taxation. Articles 10 and 11 supported rights of free expression and belief. Article 15 began to prescribe clear duties to public officials, and to set the legal basis for a fully professional (and less venal) civil service. In these respects, this proto-constitutional document aimed to separate out the public functions of society from their previous interdependence with private authority, to construct a firm legal and institutional boundary between the state and those persons and social exchanges subject to its power, and distinctively to delineate the contexts in which inclusion in state power was required. The promulgation of natural rights in 1789 intersected closely with the anti-seigneurial laws to promote (in principle) a public and internally consistent model of statehood, which was able to legislate in relatively differentiated and autonomous fashion and to position its power against internally controlled and uniform social environments.

The implementation of these laws sanctioning uniform rights, constructed within the political system, was followed rapidly by the establishment of a uniform judicial order and by a revolutionary formalization of the instruments of justice. Indeed, one distinct impetus of the early revolutionary legislation in France was that it favoured a strict separation of powers within the state, in which all legislative functions were placed in the parliament, all administrative functions were placed in the *pouvoir constitué* of the executive, and judges were appointed to highly specific judicial commissions and strictly prohibited from exercising any political influence. If the American Revolution had possessed a strongly favourable attitude to judicial power, the converse was true for the French Revolution. The French Revolution, reflecting the long-standing political conflict in France between state administration and the judicial power of the *parlements*, tied its revolutionary transformation of the state to an intense hostility towards independent judicial activity. Indeed, the leading revolutionaries expressly associated judicial freedom with the corporatistic traces of feudalism, and they introduced measures almost immediately to consolidate the state administration against the courts of law.[46] In 1789, the *parlements* were suspended, never to be reconvened, and a committee for judicial reorganization was established. The report on judicial reform, presented by Thouret to the Constituent Assembly in 1790, condemned the corrosive effects of the corporate spirit of the pre-revolutionary judiciary (Carré 1912: 201), it denounced the patrimonial control of judicial rights and powers, and it reflected scathingly on the fact that in the Ancien Régime the judiciary had seen fit to emulate 'legislative power' and had 'disturbed the operations' of the administration (Thouret 1790: 2–3). In August 1790, in consequence, laws were passed to ensure that judicial functions remained separate from administrative procedures, and a

---

[46] For an account of the 'profound distrust of the judge' in the French Revolution, see Badinter (1989: 19). Generally, see Burdeau (1995: 47); Lafon (2001: 102).

strict principle of separated powers was applied to guarantee that neither administrative functions nor legislative operations were subject to review by the courts.[47] The independent judiciary of the Ancien Régime became an early strategic victim of the revolution, and regional *parlements* and the last vestiges of the seigneurial courts were quickly replaced by justices of the peace, initially elected, who were placed under direct state control.[48] These laws marked the beginning of both the tradition of legislative supremacy and the tradition of independent administrative law (*droit administratif*) that became typical of subsequent French constitutional politics.[49] In particular, these laws brought a strict curtailment of judicial powers of statutory and administrative review, and they expressed the principle that acts of state could be subject to review by organs within the administration itself: they in fact gave rise to the principle of the *juge gouvernemental* (Bigot 1999: 101; Le Yoncourt 2006: 33). The years 1790 and 1791 also saw both a wholesale restructuring of the French judicial system and the introduction of a universal code of penal law. Taken together, these provisions gave a pronounced articulation to the boundary between the state and society, they eliminated particular judicial access to the state, and they enabled the state to construct and apply power to its addressees in highly externalized categories, which could be easily generalized from within the state itself.

The state-building functions of the early acts of revolutionary legislation were substantially reinforced in the 1791 Constitution, which provided for the transformation of the Bourbon dynasty into a constitutional monarchy and designated the king himself as a representative of the nation and primary civil servant. This constitution reinforced earlier provisions in respect of rights and legal status. Its preamble stated that hereditary distinctions were not admissible as qualifications for special legal rights and that all seigneurial and patrimonial courts were abolished. Additionally, it finally proscribed the venal acquisition of office, and in so doing it erased one of the most structurally damaging feudal residues from the judicial apparatus of the state. Under the catalogue of rights, the constitution also repeated earlier provisions for equal rights of persons before the law, for personal rights of proprietary autonomy and

---

[47] For classic comment see Laferrière (1896: 477).

[48] For analysis, see Woloch (1994: 350); Jones (1988: 267); Godechot (1951: 117). For more detail see Bell (1994: 189).

[49] On the origins of *droit administratif* and its expansion after 1789, see the classic account in Dareste (1862: 166–9).

for personal rights of freedom of expression. Moreover, the 1791 Constitution generally intensified the veto on independent judicial power in earlier documents: it stated clearly that the courts were not allowed to 'interfere with the exercise of legislative power', and it made arrangements for a court of last resort (Tribunal de Cassation) to address appeals and preserve judicial integrity for the entire nation (Chapter V). It also provided for a limited system of national representation, in which electoral rights were based (following the promptings of Emmanuel Sieyès) in *active citizenship*: that is, in a formal property qualification. The powers of the elected legislature included control of the public purse.

In each of these respects, the 1791 Constitution, building on preceding pieces of legislation, responded directly to pronounced problems of political abstraction in French society. These documents acted to transpose the state onto more conclusively abstracted public foundations, and they marked a decisive attempt to liberate the state from its hazy integrity with private motives and interests. In separating legislative and judicial powers, first, the 1791 Constitution reacted against the blurred lines of public power crystallized in the *parlements* of the old regime, and it ensured that half-internal judicial counterweights to the state were removed. In enshrining rights of judicial equality, proprietary integrity and autonomy, freedom of expression, confessional freedom and so on, moreover, it gave to the state an apparatus in which it could distinguish its power from exchanges within these social spheres, and in which it could refer to precise formulae in order to regulate its exchanges at the boundary with each of these areas of practice. In separating the state from its vestigial attachment to feudal privileges in the economy and the law, therefore, the 1791 Constitution endowed the state with capacities for legislating positively and evenly over a number of diverse social contents, for filtering and organizing its responses to the issues addressed to it, and – above all – for pre-constructing and limiting the processes through which its power had to be applied. As in America, the principles of rights contained in the first French constitution acted as instruments of pre-ordered in- and exclusion within the state, and, as such, they contributed very greatly both to the distinction and intensification of state power in society and to the wider differentiation of society as a whole.

At the same time as using rights to shape the conditions of its inclusion and differentiation, however, the state founded in the French revolutionary period, following earlier American constitutions, also utilized the principle of the nation, national sovereignty and sometimes even popular sovereignty to construct and explain its power. In revolutionary France, as in America, the concept of the nation was used to define the sovereign community of equal citizens, who were unified in their rights and who, by virtue of rights, possessed a claim to be formatively represented in the state. Additionally, however, this concept was used to denounce the privilege-based social order of the Ancien Régime, and the concept of nationhood specifically demanded a form of governance based in equality under law and the eradication of private or singular distinction. In the first stirrings of the revolution, thus, it was argued that the nation was the community of persons that recognized no legal distinction and no hereditary entitlement, and that all legitimate legislation presupposed its authorization by a nation configured in this way. This concept of the nation was already implicit in the foundation of the Constituent Assembly in July 1789, in which (unprecedentedly) deputies were viewed as representatives, not of privileged localities, but of the nation as a whole (Burrage 2006: 79). The revolutionary implications of nationhood were elaborated by Sieyès, who, in 1789, construed the nation as the 'group of citizens belonging to the common order', bound by 'a common law, and a common representation' and thus admitting no legal privilege (1839 [1789]: 45). He also used this concept to justify the original formation of the Third Estate assembled by the king in 1789 as one sovereign legislative body, renouncing all distinctions of social gradation, whose collective sanction was the sole source of legitimate law. The idea of the nation as a legally homogeneous sovereign power then pervasively shaped the ideas, the composition and the self-legitimization of the National Assembly, and it underpinned both the Declaration of the Rights of Man and subsequent constitutional texts. Article 3 of the Rights of Man stated that: 'The principle of all sovereignty resides essentially in the nation. No body nor individual may exercise any authority which does not proceed directly from the nation.' Central to the 1791 Constitution, subsequently, was the proclamation that all power was derived from the nation of citizens. It stated: 'Sovereignty is one, indivisible, inalienable, and imprescriptible. It appertains to the nation; no section of the people nor any individual may assume the exercise thereof.'

In France, in consequence, the concept of the nation offered a legitimating principle through which the emergent French state could define itself as nationally integrative and extract an account of its power as a focus of public-legal, sovereign legislative agency. Above all, the concept of national sovereignty enabled the state to reduce its porosity to private power, and to elevate itself above the privatistic socio-political relations of late feudalism. As in revolutionary America, the principle of national sovereignty acted, next to formal rights, as the second wellspring in the construction of an integral autonomous state. In implying that the state's power was derived from those persons to whom it was applied, this principle created an abstracted foundation on which the state could manage its inclusionary processes, produce laws that could be evenly and positively applied across society and generally augment its store of power. As in America, thus, the concept of national sovereignty employed to justify the governments of revolutionary France effected a dramatic increase in the density, centrality and inclusivity of the French polity. The founders of the 1791 Constitution were in fact under no illusions about the nature of their labour in this respect. They clearly recognized that, in invoking uniform principles of national sovereignty, they perpetuated and intensified the ambitions for political abstraction and state integrity held dear by the regents of the Ancien Régime. However, owing to their invocation of rights and nationhood to simplify the structure of power's application through society, they were able to concentrate far more power in the emergent state executive than had been the case under the pre-1789 monarchy (Church 1981: 110; Brubaker 1992: 49).[50] In this, the constitutional fathers of 1789–91 fulfilled the earlier dreams of 'absolutist' French monarchs, which had been thwarted by the corporatistic privatism of society under the Ancien Régime, and they came close to constructing the strong and territorially unified state with a single judiciary and a single administrative order to which earlier monarchs had only been able fancifully to aspire (Woloch 1994: 37; Vergne 2006: 94). The definition of power as *national power*, in short, comprehensively increased both the volume of political power in society and the inclusionary facility with which it could be utilized.[51] If early modern French political history had been dominated by a conflict between the particularistic idea of the rule of law based in the (feudal/patrimonial) judiciary and the general idea of the rule of law based in (monarchical) administration, this conflict was finally settled in the

---

[50] The function of rights as instruments for eliminating social obstructions to state power had already been recognized under Turgot. Further, Turgot's chief clerk, Pierre-François Boncerf, published a tirade against feudal law in which he argued tellingly that 'the eminent domain of sovereignty is more effective than suzerainty, legislative authority more powerful than feudal authority, and the right of the citizen forms bonds more precious than those between vassal and seigneur' (1776: 59).

[51] On the medieval origins of this see Weidenfeld (2001: 85).

revolution. At this time the administrative rule of law prevailed: this victory of 'absolutistic' ideals, however, was a victory which could only be accomplished through the concerted triumph of the sovereign nation and the overthrow of the monarchy, whose attempts at administrative reform had been undone by its own residual privatism and lack of national inclusivity. As in America, it was only when it founded itself on the national will that the French state could finally abstract an autonomous public legal order.

In this respect, to be sure, it needs to be noted that in revolutionary France the balance between republican (national-sovereign) and liberal (rights-based) constitutional ideas was rather distinct from that in America. In France, rights did not immediately assume the same potent exclusionary and restrictive functions which they performed in America. Notably, in France, owing to the endemic hostility to judicial independence, legislative functions were not immediately subordinate to the rulings of a binding catalogue of rights, and the early part of the revolution was shaped by a strong presumption in favour of direct exercise of sovereignty by the national will. Throughout the revolutionary era in France, in fact, both the nature of representative government and the locus of popular sovereignty were hotly contested, and the demand for an immediate legislative identity between government and governed was more persistently asserted than in America.[52] During the Jacobin interlude of 1793-5, for example, Robespierre reserved a Rousseauian scepticism for political representation of anterior rights and interests, and he sought to preserve a high degree of integrity between legislative, judicial and executive bodies, through which each of these institutions remained equally accountable to the popular will. He even argued that 'constitutional government', securing the stability of the state through administrative finesse, would have to wait until the period of 'revolutionary government', founding the Republic as a more direct expression of the will of the people, was concluded (1910 [1793]: 274). In addition, Robespierre expressed caution about basic rights (especially rights of property) and – in particular – about judicial autonomy: the Jacobins attacked the autonomy of the courts with particular vehemence, they dismembered the judicial system that evolved from the Declaration of Rights, and they even rendered courts subordinate to particular rulings of the legislature (Halperin 1987: 121-4, 267). The Constitution of 1793 contained particularly strong anti-judicial measures in order to protect

[52] See analysis in Rosanvallon (2000: 20); Cowans (2001).

administrators from judicial intervention. As a result of this, in France the popular will was first admitted to the state as a highly volatile force, and the height of the revolution was shaped by intense controversy over the location of this will, the methods for its inclusion in government and the need to transfuse all organs of state with its dictates.

Despite this, in revolutionary France the creed of national-popular sovereignty also – albeit gradually – began to adapt to and configure itself around the restrictive and dialectical principles, shaped by rights, that had marked revolutionary America. Although the notion of popular sovereignty remained intermittently central to French republicanism, the idea that the executive should be bound by direct vertical account-ability to the legislature was not uniformly endorsed through the revolu-tionary era. With the exception of the short period of Jacobin rule, most of the revolutionary executives were based on the limited, anti-Jacobin principle of representative government first enunciated by Sieyès. In fact, Sieyès contributed in vitally enduring fashion to the revolutionary formation of the French state by arguing, first, that, although the nation was always the sovereign, the nation was only represented by those among its particular members who were active citizens (property own-ers). Moreover, he concluded, second, that the actual exercise of sover-eignty by actors in a legislature could not be premised in factual unity between the sovereign legislature and the sovereign people. There existed, he claimed, a necessary distinction between the principle of popular sovereignty and the factual exercise of sovereignty:[53] it was only through its proportioned representation that the sovereign will of the people could be translated into the factually effective exercise of sovereign power – that is, 'good social administration' (1839 [1789]: 137).

Even in periods of intense conflagration, in consequence, the models of representative sovereignty pioneered in revolutionary France largely sanctioned the principle that the will of the people could only become concretely formative of state power in highly controlled and pre-manufactured settings. Furthermore, although the rights enshrined in the revolutionary constitutional documents were not placed in the custody of separate courts, rights remained pervasive filters for the popular will. This was the case, most obviously, because after 1789 rights provided the basis for a regular legal order in which, despite dramatic disruptions, presumption in respect of rights acted as a regulative force for statutory legislation, and it dictated procedures for conventionalized

---

[53] On the centrality of this problem in French republicanism see Gauchet (1995: 47–8).

legal finding. Although the judiciary was not conceived as a counter-vailing force, in fact, the Tribunal de Cassation remained an important institution after its foundation in 1790, and rulings of this court were (albeit variably) influenced by rights. In addition to this, further, in the longer wake of 1789, especially in the post-Thermidorean era (1795–9), a growing body of administrative law began to emerge which, in absence of extensive judicial control, placed internal restrictions on the arbitrary use of executive authority. This allowed the state at once to vest power in a unified administration and legally to control and proportion its appli-cation. Most importantly, however, rights checked and filtered the pop-ular will because, implicitly, they ensured that most activities covered by rights were conducted outside the state. This meant that activities rele-vant to rights only exceptionally required express politicization, that objects for legislation were pre-selected, and that, in observing persons as rights holders, the state could define the conditions under which the demands and activities of these persons might assume formative rele-vance for the use of state power.

In France, as in America, therefore, the reference to the founding nation as the sovereign source of power created a legal apparatus in which political power was able to propose itself as authorized by those subject to it, in which its positive/inclusionary circulation through soci-ety was greatly enhanced by this implicit authorization, yet in which it could also police its differentiation from, and its measured inclusion of, those persons whom it constructed as its original volitional/legitimating sources. Above all, by referring to itself as a state founded in national sovereignty – that is, based in an abstract subject detached from partic-ular persons or locations – the revolutionary French state produced a conceptual structure of public law that ultimately enabled it both to exclude private actors and to integrate wide and diverse fields of society in its exchanges. It was thus able, progressively at least, to use this constitution to include members of society equally and evenly under law. At the same time, however, popular sovereignty fused with rights to create a reference through which the state was able to exclude the people in most of their factual activities, so that the sovereign body of the people was at once both inclusively present and exclusively absent in the operations of the state. In this respect, the conjunction of national sovereignty and rights made it possible for the state to project a relatively uniform and legally defined environment for its functions and for the general application of its power, and it allowed the state abstractly to construct its origins and pre-emptively to select and delineate the societal settings in which it used its power. Vitally, in short, a constitution combining national sovereignty and rights as sources of legitimacy allowed the state dramatically to intensify its reserves of usable abstracted power.

In all these respects the provisions for rights and national sovereignty in the French constitutional texts of the revolutionary era marked a culminating moment in the evolutionary logic inscribed in constitutional formation from the earliest constitutional documents of medieval Europe. The 1791 Constitution performed the abiding function that it allowed the French state autonomously to organize its exchanges with bearers of particular interests as external to itself, it hardened the state's boundaries against unnecessary internalization of private motivations, and it enabled the state positively and inclusively to control and reproduce its power within its own structure. It was only with the invention of a state deriving its legitimacy from a rights-based national-sovereign will that the process of political construction underlying European society from the twelfth century could be brought towards completion: it was only in the constitutional principle of *national inclusion* that political power could finally be distilled as an abstracted and positively inclusive social resource. In a wider context, moreover, the 1791 constitution of France and the rights that it imputed to social agents also brought towards completion the underlying process of societal reconfiguration attendant on constitutional formation. The principles of rights and sovereignty established in the first French constitution put an end to the particular or corporate rights of feudal society, and they conclusively transformed society from a diffusely structured array of particular status-defined groups, diversely and pluralistically related to the state, into an evenly ordered mass of – in principle – functionally autonomous individuals, selectively included in and excluded from political power. The relations between these individuals, then, were increasingly mediated through the state: that is, through rights guaranteed by the state as a centre of representative sovereignty. In this respect, this 1791 Constitution and its provisions for rights created preconditions both for the formation of a generally inclusive society and for the institution of a strong general state, to which all subjects had (in principle) an equal and uniform relation, and which was functionally authorized, by rights, to exercise a monopoly of political power in society.[54]

---

[54] In agreement, see Raumer (1967: 182).

Constitutional rights, in sum, although habitually perceived as limits on the state, first assumed formal prominence as institutes that were deeply formative both of independent state power and of the societal constellation in which state power could be exercised. By the end of the eighteenth century, the modern European state was formed as an institution consolidated around uniform rights: constitutional rights acted as the structural precondition of the modern state and of modern society more widely. If 'absolutism' had acted as a progressive technique for the unitary production of positive power in early modern Europe, thus, the political impetus of 'absolutism' failed because government not underpinned by principles of rights and national/sovereign representation remained lacking in inclusive cohesion, and it was unable to abstract its power against the inherited privatism of privileged society. The abstracted production and transmission of positive political power could only be accomplished by states founded in rights-based national sovereignty: indeed, the increase in rights in society brought a directly correlated increase in power. Absolutism thus found both its apogee and its nemesis in early constitutional democracy.

After the rights revolutions I: the Bonapartist temptation

In Europe, the years directly following the great constitutional revolutions stretching from the 1770s to the 1790s were marked by an increasingly reflected recognition that the selectively abstractive dimension of rights-based constitutionalism could be isolated from its sovereign democratic claims, and that constitutional rights possessed clear utility as instruments for the technically measured centring of society around state power. While the first modern constitutions constructed strong states because of their anti-privatistic and strongly inclusionary principles, therefore, the proto-democratic line of constitutionalism culminating in early revolutionary France soon ceded ground to a second wave of post-revolutionary constitution writing, which normally adopted a more programmatic and controlled approach to constitutional functions of state reinforcement. The period after 1795 saw a continued impetus towards the formation of constitutions imputing subjective rights under general law to those persons obligated to the state. Yet, albeit with variations across different settings, the constitutions of the initial post-revolutionary era also began more strategically to diminish the element of popular sovereignty in previous legal texts, and to renounce the commitment to state legitimacy through expansive societal inclusion. These constitutions generally marked the inception of a period of more distinctly instrumental constitutionalism, in which constitutions were employed, often under royal fiat, both for steering European societies towards a condition of restricted and supervised political inclusion and for controlling the initial absorptive expansion of state power caused by the concept of popular sovereignty.

As mentioned, the French Jacobin constitution of 1793 was clearly an exception to this tendency. This constitution contained provisions both for a deep-rooted unicameral democratic order and for substantial social/ material rights: it thus abandoned the clear separation of private rights and public laws that had characterized the 1791 Constitution. Aspects of this constitution were also emulated in a number of short-lived and, in some cases, brutally suppressed Italian republics of the later 1790s, which were strongly influenced and supported by the French Directory and later by the Napoleonic armies.[55] For instance, the Bolognese constitution of 1796 guaranteed a catalogue of basic rights, and it stressed the entitlement of all citizens to participate in making laws (Art. 20). The principles of unitary statehood and democratic sovereignty were also central to the Batavian constitution of 1798, established in Holland following the French-inspired revolution of 1795 (Schama 1977: 320). Indeed, more expansive ideals of popular sovereignty persisted still longer in constitutional peripheries. In the last throes of the Napoleonic wars, for example, Norway was constituted as a state (albeit still under Swedish dominion) for the first time in more than four hundred years. This was accomplished through the progressive, semi-democratic constitution of 1814, which abolished personal privileges (Art. 23), placed legislative power in the parliament (Storting) (Art. 49), and prescribed regular elections (Art. 54). Despite this, however, the more widespread pattern of post-revolutionary constitutionalism was set directly in France. In France, the Jacobin constitution of 1793 was never implemented, and its commitment to integral-democratic sovereignty was not factually tested. After 1795, France embarked on a course of much more selective constitutionalism, which, while still accepting the formal principle of popular sovereignty, deployed constitutional law to place checks on the volatile politicization of society triggered by the 1791 Constitution and, still more, by the unenforced 1793 Constitution.

This functional transition in constitutionalism after the Jacobin experiment was reflected, initially, in the French constitution of 1795 itself, which marked the culmination of the Thermidorean reaction. The

---

[55] See the excellent discussion of this in Davis (2006: 94–5).

1795 Constitution remained committed to republican concepts of sovereignty. In its list of rights it stated boldly (Art. 6) that 'the law is the general will, expressed either by the majority of the citizens or the majority of their representatives', and that 'sovereignty resides essentially in the universality of citizens' (Art. 17). It also retained the core rights of man, placing particular emphasis on rights of 'security' (Arts. 1, 4) and judicial equality (Art. 3). Following the judicial violence of the Terror, it emphasized principles of due process under law, and it took pains to eliminate judicial arbitrariness and retroactive laws (Arts. 7–14). In the main body of the text, it instituted a fully separate judiciary (Art. 202), including a high court with reinforced powers to assess accusations against members of the legislature (Art. 265).

Crucially, however, the Thermidorean constitution also reflected a deeply held intention to bring to an end the sovereign inclusivity of the revolutionary era. This was evident, first, in the fact that it sought to eliminate executive-led republicanism by binding popular sovereignty to the majority will of electors and repressing claims to sovereign authority by individuals or small groups. Moreover, it placed a list of duties next to its catalogue of rights, and it defined rights as entitlements obtained through legal observance and obedience (Arts. 5–7). Further, it abandoned some of the popular rights, such as those to education and subsistence, espoused in 1793, and, in the list of duties, it gave property rights singularly high status: it specified property ownership as the foundation of social order (Art. 8). Additionally, the 1795 Constitution favoured a Girondist concept of representation: it stipulated a high property qualification for those nominated to stand in the electoral assemblies that controlled access to the legislature and other public functions (Art. 35). One of those contributing to the constitution, Boissy D'Anglas, tellingly explained that sovereign powers needed to be reserved for the wealthiest and most educated members of society, whose possession of property he saw as anchored in the 'social order', and whose right to govern was founded in the 'state of nature' (1795: 22). Furthermore, the 1795 Constitution rejected the model of undivided sovereignty in the 1793 Constitution by opting for a bicameral legislative system (Art. 44), in which a Council of Elders was appointed to review legislation, and it established a small executive Directory, comprising five members. Most important, however, was the fact that the 1795 Constitution began more emphatically (albeit still inconclusively) to sanction the notion that the constitution needed to be viewed, not only as a practical guarantor of popular sovereignty, but also, as in America, as a supra-positive norm, standing above and regulating the factual exercise of sovereign power. In the deliberations on the 1795 Constitution, Sieyès suggested that the constitution was a 'corpus of obligatory laws', which had to be placed under judicial custodianship and preserved, as inviolate, from particular or sporadic expressions of sovereign force.[56] To this end, Sieyès acted against the dominant anti-judicial theme of the French Revolution by proposing that a constitutional jury should be established to limit the sovereignty of the state to the terms and rights enshrined by the constitution and, in acting as 'a court of appeal for the constitutional order', to offer neutral resolution in cases of perceived constitutional infraction. He interpreted the constitutional jury, tellingly, as a 'conserving depositary' of the original constitutional act (Troper 2006: 525, 537). These proposals were not accepted in 1795, but they became important elements of later constitutional debates.

Revolutionary constitution writing in France, in consequence, reached its interim conclusion in a constitutional design – that of 1795 – which derived the legitimacy of the state from the sovereign will of the people, but that projected strict mechanisms to ensure that the state was never factually identical with this will and remained distinct from the factual persons from which it obtained its inclusive legitimating force. This idea was first proposed by Sieyès. However, it was later elaborated in the early liberal doctrines of Benjamin Constant, who argued for a *pouvoir neutre* or 'pouvoir préservateur' to check the power of the legislature, and to conserve the anterior rights of human beings, declared in the constitution, as necessarily withdrawn from the state and its sovereignty (1991 [1810]: 401). Underlying these models of constitutional rule was the principle that the constitution represented the people most effectively if it relieved them of incessant factual responsibility for sovereign governance. Indeed, the principle began to surface in the 1795 Constitution that rights guaranteed freedoms most consistently if they made sure that members of society were not fully included in the exercise of power.[57] In this respect again, the 1795 Constitution acted, dialectically, as an instrument that more schematically both in- and excluded the sovereign force of the people. That is, it incorporated this force as at once an internal mainspring for power's positive autonomy and a device for simplifying

---

[56] Sieyès's views on the need for a legal 'guardian' for the constitution are reprinted in Appendix 4 in Troper (2006).

[57] The 1795 Constitution looked forward to Constant's later view that rights offered freedoms as *modern freedoms*: that is, as freedoms that were expressly not predicated on constantly politicized or immediately formative sovereign actions (1997 [1819]).

its societal transmission, yet it also acted as an instrument for differentiating the state from other parts of society: especially from those
people from whose inclusion it purported to derive legitimacy.

This increasingly technical/dialectical aspect of constitutionalism
found its most extreme expression under the early years of the
Napoleonic regime in France. The early Bonapartist system worked
within evident constitutional constraints. In many respects, although
often characterized as dictatorship, Napoleon's 1799 Constitution was
conceived in continuity with the provisions made in 1791 for constitutional monarchy, and it was intended selectively to conserve the achievements of the early period of revolution.[58] Even after the constitutional
reforms of 1802, when the authoritarian powers of the Napoleonic
executive were reinforced, it is doubtful whether Bonapartist rule fell
completely outside the pattern of constitutional governance. Indeed, his
elevation to imperial grandeur after 1804 did not mean that Napoleon
governed wholly without parliamentary checks, and his regime preserved (albeit highly limited) countervailing powers in the state.[59] At
Napoleon's first accession to power, however, the constitutional dimensions of his regime were clear and pronounced. Initially, for example,
Napoleon was appointed to act as one of three consuls, alongside Sieyès
and Roger Ducos, and his authority was counterbalanced by a powerful
Senate. Most notably, the 1799 Constitution, once again bearing the
imprimatur of Sieyès, was intended to complete the establishment of
separate powers, effective public representation and particular subjective
rights, which had been projected in earlier documents. The 1799
Constitution in fact included, not just the conventional three, but no
fewer than five distinct powers, each of which was designed to be
proportioned to a particular functional objective, and each of which
was expected to hold the others in equilibrium and ensure that particular
freedoms in society were not annexed by one part of the state (Godechot
1951: 478). These powers comprised, first, a legislative power that was
divided between two assemblies: that is, between a *tribunat*, which processed
and presented laws before the legislature, and a legislature, which finally
accepted or rejected these laws. These powers included, second, an executive
structure divided between an executive power and a governing power. The
governing body included Napoleon himself and two other consuls, both,

---

[58] For this view see Thiry (1947: 228); Thiry (1949: 122); Godechot (1970: 798).

[59] For strong criticism of the interpretation of Napoleon's regime as dictatorship, see Pietri
(1955: 8); Kirsch (1999: 212).

until the reforms of 1802, appointed for ten years: the First Consul was entitled to present draft laws to the legislative bodies and both to promulgate and to execute laws (Arts. 25, 41, 44), and the Second and Third Consuls had a 'consultative voice' (Art. 42) in this process. These powers also entailed, third, a separate judicial order, and a conserving power (*pouvoir conservateur*): the Senate. In respect of the latter, Sieyès thought that the Senate, of which he would be president, ought to act as the custodian of state authority: so that the Senate might, in some circumstances, overrule the *tribunat* or government on questions of legislation and act as an 'interpreter and guardian of the supreme law' that was enshrined in the constitution (Vandal 1903: 497, 515). Sieyès even envisaged the institution of a Great Elector to supervise the application of constitutional provisions, to ensure that at no point in the system of balances was power unduly concentrated or personalized, and, if necessary, to counteract the power of the First Consul. Ultimately, this institution was not accepted, owing to the opposition of Bonaparte.[60] Moreover, the powers of review ascribed to the Senate were reduced in the revised constitution of 1802 (Art. 54).

In addition, the 1799 Constitution originally foresaw that representative assemblies would play a significant role in the business of the state. It is calculated that the 1799 Constitution provided for a basic electoral franchise of over five million voters: that is, of primary voters, who elected communal lists, from whom departmental notables and members of the legislature were selected, under Napoleon's supervision, by the Senate (Campbell 1958: 54). To be sure, from the outset the Bonapartist regime diluted the representative principle embodied in earlier constitutions, and in the 1802 reforms this principle was weakened further. For example, under the 1799 Constitution elections were conducted at cantonal level, and in the revised constitution of 1802 the presidents of cantonal assemblies and electoral colleges for these assemblies were normally appointed by the First Consul (Arts. 5, 23). After 1802, moreover, the First Consul could nominate his own appointees for the Senate (Art. 63), and he transformed the Senate into a much more compliant organ of the executive. Nonetheless, the 1799 Constitution did not abandon the principle that the supreme powers of the state were legitimized by their immediate representative connection with the people, and that power must be exercised by those who enjoyed the confidence of the people. In 1799, therefore, power was surely not re-personalized in dictatorial

---

[60] For an account of this see Thiry (1947: 230); Lepointe (1953).

fashion: those assuming public office and functions were not released from representative obligations, and they were not authorized to exercise power as a private commodity. In some questions, parliaments continued to function throughout the regime. Indeed, for Napoleon parliamentary assemblies retained an important role in his techniques of raising revenue, and they performed consultative functions that assisted the consolidation of state finance characteristic of his regime (Collins 1979: 15).

In these respects, Napoleonic government remained within the category of constitutional rule. At the same time, however, the first Bonapartist constitution of 1799 had strategic features that distinguished it from the mainstream of early, proto-democratic constitution writing. First, although it incorporated separate clauses protecting rights of citizenship, personal inviolability and protection from wrongful arrest (Arts. 76–82), this constitution contained no specific bill of rights. Second, this constitution was not approved by a constituent assembly, and the legitimating claim that it arose spontaneously from the sovereign will of the nation was strongly qualified: it was in fact approved by plebiscite. In addition, the constitution provided for a substantially reduced franchise, in which, as mentioned, members of representative bodies and other public functionaries were elected from local and regional lists of delegates, and the election of delegates to public functions had to be endorsed by the Senate (Art. 20), whose membership was partly controlled by the First Consul. Third, this constitution was also specifically designed as a counter-revolutionary document. It was intended both to cement and to bring to a halt the demands for active rights and sovereign power that had been intermittently expressed during the revolutionary era, and it was designed selectively to preserve some and to reject other aspects of revolutionary legislation in accordance with their utility in strengthening the administrative order of the state. Fourth, this constitution also, initially, declared Napoleon First Consul for a period of ten years, and it restricted the potency of institutional counterweights to the personal executive. Indeed, contrary to the original plan for the constitution set out by Sieyès, the First Consul was accorded a monopoly of legislative power, competence for legislative initiative, and the right to nominate ministers and members of the Council of State.

In its ambiguous fusion of representative-democratic and anti-democratic principles, therefore, the first Bonapartist constitution was an attempt to create a governmental system which secured the functional advantages accruing to states from the principle of national sovereignty, from the establishment of general laws and from the recognition of limited societal rights, yet that also welded these principles together to construct a hardened and functionally consolidated administrative apparatus. This constitution played out the concept of constitutionalism against the concept of democracy, and it deliberately intensified the dialectical balance between national sovereignty and legally guaranteed personal rights contained in earlier constitutions. This constitution reflected the sense that the constitution itself was sufficient to ensure adequate representation of the people, and it indicated that the people, in their factual existing quality, required only minimal or 'theoretical' inclusion in the state (Bourdon 1942: 82). Indeed, it implicitly suggested that the purpose of the constitution, while guaranteeing certain civil liberties, was to relieve persons throughout society of the burdens of actively engaged political freedom. To this end, the Napoleonic regime specifically selected as legitimate those rights that it deemed politically neutral, and, although protecting private rights, it weakened those rights that had a pronounced political content: that is, rights of expression, agitation and immediate participation (Woloch 2001: 186). Under the arrangements of 1799, in fact, the final locus of popular sovereignty was transferred from the parliamentary legislature to the Senate, which was supposed to ratify all acts of state under observance of their compatibility with the norms in the constitution: maintenance of the constitution thus became the primary obligation and guarantee of sovereign power. For the first short period of Napoleonic rule, in consequence, the constitution began to operate as a nominal higher-law instrument, and it was intended to maintain minimal conditions of liberty outside the state, to curtail access of particular social actors to the actual organs of statehood itself, and to allow the state at once to internalize and politically to withdraw (that is: to *depoliticize*) the inclusionary sources of its legitimacy.

The early constitutional regime of the Napoleonic era was a system designed to piece together rudimentary and substantially depleted elements of constitutional liberalism in a form that supported an executive-led oligarchical regime. The residual reliance of the constitution on basic aspects of liberalism such as separate powers, (curtailed) parliamentary representation and private/personal rights enabled the state to obtain the functional benefits of liberalism: that is, to extract its structure from private milieux and to authorize its societal inclusivity, to pre-structure its societal environments and to generalize procedures for using political power. Yet the Napoleonic order specifically employed these institutions to curtail the openness of the state to actors throughout civil society, and to condense the exchanges between state and other areas of society into highly formulated intersections. Important in this respect was the fact that the political constitution of Bonapartism was supplemented by the introduction of the Napoleonic Civil Code (Code Napoléon) in 1804. This code implemented a rights-based legal apparatus for the organization of civil life, and it constructed a legal order providing for the attribution and preservation of singular proprietary rights (Arts. 544–546), and for ensuring the inviolability and integrity of freely entered contracts (Arts. 1101–7). The Civil Code was also intended to limit judicial independence, and it placed a clear veto on constructive law finding by judges. Flanked by the Civil Code, then, the Napoleonic constitution formed a political system that sustained a strong centralized state on one hand, able to maintain minimal requirements of consensus and support through society, and a rigorously privatized rights-based social order on the other, in which a corpus of civil rights ensured that many areas of private regulation were at once brought under clear judicial structures and excluded from recurrent state control. In this regard, the Napoleonic state, at least in its early years, consolidated the dialectical dislocation of state and society, which had first culminated in the extracted apparatus of public law in the revolutionary documents of 1789 and 1791, and it defined legal parameters for the simultaneous growth of centralized public authority and the structuring of a legally ordered private economy. In so doing, the early Napoleonic constitution replicated some constitutional-monarchical ideals of 1789, which first shaped the constitutional endeavour of Sieyès and others, and it provided the foundation for the evolution of limited monarchical liberalism, which became the constitutional norm throughout the nineteenth century. Above all, the constitution of Bonapartism was an extended reflection of the restrictive and exclusionary functions that were, from the outset, implicit in liberal constitutionalism. This system fleshed out a constant authoritarian potential within liberal constitutional practice, and it strategically utilized the potentials for the intensification of state power always inherent in liberal constitutions. Bonaparte himself was hardly a critic of constitutional ideas. He argued simply that a constitution 'must be made in such a manner that it does not irritate the actions of government and so force it to violate it' (Thiry 1949: 101). In principle, he identified the constitution as an integral, yet withdrawn, principle of order within the state, through which the state regulated its societal boundaries, eliminated external checks on its power and externalized legitimating constructions of its factual sovereignty.[61]

After the rights revolutions II: monarchy limited and intensified

Restoration France

Elements of this instrumental reorientation in constitutional design were again evident, in different fashion, in the restoration constitution that followed the collapse of the Napoleonic regime: the imposed Charte of 1814. The Charte established a constitutionally limited monarchical system, which, although intermittently swayed by ultra-royalist groups, was intended to preserve in a monarchical order those elements of revolutionary legislation that reinforced the stability of the state.[62] On one hand, the Charte made general (although deeply ambiguous) provisions for partial parliamentary control of the executive, it upheld the (selective) liberation of property effected in 1789, it sanctioned (in diminished form) the rights of judicial equality and personal liberty in the revolutionary documents, it reduced noble rights (Art. 71), and it retained clauses securing the inviolability of property enunciated under the Code Napoléon of 1804. The Code Napoléon in fact remained foundational for French civil law throughout the nineteenth century. Yet the Charte also accorded full judicial supremacy to the monarch (Art. 57), it placed legislative initiative in the person of the monarch (Art. 16), it made only equivocal provisions for legislative elections, and it enabled far-reaching monarchical control of the executive (Art. 13). The Charte thus again concentrated authority in a powerful personal executive, and it sharply curtailed the claims to popular sovereignty and political rights expressed in earlier constitutions. Tellingly, more liberal actors in the political establishment of the restoration, notably Constant, endorsed a system of government in which sovereignty, although residing in the 'universality of citizens', was not expressed through any identity between the factual body of the people and its governmental institutions, but in a form limited or 'circumscribed' by basic rights (1997 [1815]: 312, 319).

---

[61] This paradox in Bonapartism is well captured by Brown (2006: 236), who describes the Brumaire as revolving around a fusion of liberal principles and anti-democratic strategies.

[62] For discussion of such continuity see Bastid (1954: 361–83); Sellin (2001: 203).

Notable in the 1814 constitution was the fact that it aimed to avoid provoking extreme political controversy, and it was intended to prevent the unchecked migration of societal antagonisms into the state. To this end, it left many principles of political order undeclared, and it was able to accommodate a number of different regimes. In the first instance, powers of government were shared between the king, an upper chamber and a deeply reactionary chamber of representatives, the *chambre introuvable*. Progressively, however, the Charte was utilized to countervail renewed tendencies towards royal autocracy, and the stipulations of the Charte, especially its cautious rulings on the core question of ministerial responsibility, were cited to undermine the legitimacy of the increasingly authoritarian Bourbon monarchy in the later 1820s. Indeed, the Charte was ultimately invoked to authorize the July Revolution of 1830, which reacted against the dissolution of the Chamber of Deputies and the suppression of the free press imposed by Charles X. During the July Revolution and the resultant establishment of the Orléanist executive, the wording of the 1814 Constitution was altered. After 1830, for instance, the monarch was accorded his title, not by God, as in the Charte of 1814, but by the nation, and laws were introduced to prohibit censorship of the press, and to ensure that meetings of the upper chamber were public and open (Art. 27). Furthermore, the 1830 Constitution made important provisions to increase the legislative initiative of parliament (Art. 15). However, the change of regime did not necessitate an entirely new constitution, and the constitution was able to offer legitimacy for the bureaucratic progressivism of the Orléanists without a political redefinition of the state. Under the cautious guidance of François Guizot, the July monarchy in fact elaborated a pattern of limited representation that extended the constitutional reaction against full sovereignty commenced in 1795 and reinforced in 1814, and it continued to draw strength and legitimacy from a highly restrictive application of liberal ideals.[63] Speaking for the liberal royalist Doctrinaires, Guizot argued that a system founded in the 'equal right of individuals to exercise sovereignty' was 'radically false'. As an alternative, he advocated representative government, which he defined as government founded, not in popular sovereignty, but in 'reason' (1855 [1821–2]: 108, 112). The 1814 Constitution and its variant forms after 1830 thus consolidated a tradition of constitutionalism that was strategically aimed

---

[63] For brilliant analysis of Guizot's moralizing view of democratic legitimacy see Rosanvallon (1985: 190).

both at raising the intensity of state power and at mollifying the politicization of society. To this end, it provided (at most) for a very cautious
widening of the political content of the state apparatus, and it legitimized
itself through reference to rights and freedoms that structurally presupposed the exclusionary non-identity of the state and factually existing
members of society.

Spain

Following the Napoleonic invasion, Spanish society also obtained a
constitutional order designed to consolidate state power at a level of
selectively inclusive abstraction. This process began with the abdication
of Carlos IV and the passing of the Napoleonic Statute of Bayonne in
1808, which cleared the path for the ultimate formation of a constitutional monarchy in Spain. This continued in antiseigneurial legislation
of 1811, and it culminated in the 1812 Constitution of Cadiz, drafted
outside territory controlled by Napoleon. This constitution created a
limited constitutional or 'moderate' monarchy, in which monarchical
power was constrained by a formal rights regime, and partial legislative
powers were vested in the parliamentary Cortes. In Article 3, the Cadiz
Constitution defined sovereignty as pertaining to the nation (notably –
not to the people), and it expressed an organic concept of national
sovereignty by fusing the idea of the nation as primary legislator with
the idea of the nation as a repository of historically formed basic laws.
This constitution also had the peculiar distinction that it utilized constitutional conventions imported from France in order to strengthen
Spain against French hegemony, and the constituent Cortes in Cadiz
invoked rights of national resistance and traditional independence to
legitimize the new constitution (Moran Orti 1986: 68–9).

Most notably, the Constitution of Cadiz was shaped by an attempt
finally to erase the privatistic power of the *señorios* from Spanish society,
and it acted to separate, as earlier in France, legitimate from non-
legitimate seigneurial rights: that is, to abolish seigneurial rights entailing private ownership of public resources (that is, rights with political,
fiscal or jurisdictional force) and to convert seigneurial rights with
merely economic substance into private rights of persons (Arts. 2, 4).
In consequence, this constitution borrowed from France the idea that a
national/sovereign constitution could be used to cut through the traditional privileges of late-feudal society in order to reinforce and rationalize the power of the state, and fully to integrate within the state the

offices and powers susceptible to privatization under the vestigial structures of feudalism. In early nineteenth-century Spain, significantly, the
jurisdictional powers of the nobility and the resultant seigneurial legal
patchwork remained substantially more entrenched than had been the
case in pre-1789 France, and the 1812 Constitution was clearly charged
with the task of rectifying the traditional jurisdictional and legislative weakness of the Spanish monarchy. In this case, therefore, the concept of the
nation was emphasized in order to nationalize the residually patrimonial
power of the monarch (Sebastiá Domingo and Piqueras 1987: 52), and it was
promoted to assist the monarchical state (now defined as a state bearing the
dignity of national sovereignty) in eliminating the quasi-political competences of the nobility, and in consolidating the powers that it had relinquished through its earlier feudal 'debility' (Moxó 1965: 39). The 1812
Constitution was suspended by the king in 1814, and many of its anti-
seigneurial provisions were rescinded. However, many of these reappeared
in further legislation of 1823 and in the liberal constitution of 1837.[64] It was
in fact only in 1837 that Spain's path towards a limited constitutional order
was settled and a state was created that clearly (although still with qualifications) reflected the generalized anti-privatistic political structure of a functionally specialized and inclusive society. Nonetheless, as a document that
combined an anti-feudal construction of rights and a structurally condensed
recognition of national sovereignty, the Constitution of Cadiz enacted
principles analogous to those of the constitutions in France during the
later revolutionary era. In its cautious avoidance of ideas of popular sovereignty, moreover, it distinctively utilized the idea of law's national source to
extract power from potent private agents and to distil power in the state,
yet also firmly and selectively regulate the boundaries between the state and
its addressees.

German states

In most German states, in partial analogy, the revolutionary and
Napoleonic periods stimulated processes of cautious constitutional
reform, often shaped by a clear state-building design. For example, the
longer aftermath of the French Revolution saw the establishment of
constitutions in some of the German states, notably in Bavaria and
Württemberg in 1818 and 1819 respectively, which had obtained sovereign status through Napoleon's dissolution of the Holy Roman Empire

---

[64] For a longer account see Hernández Montalabán (1999).

in 1806, and these constitutions were evidently conceived as devices to consolidate state power in post-feudal societies.

The constitution of Württemberg was the only German constitution of this period that was not imposed by a ruling dynasty. It contained strikingly progressive provisions for equal rights before the law (§ 24), equal access to public office (§ 22) and freedom of conscience, opinion, contract and ownership (§ 27–30), and it established an effective legislative veto for the estates, ordered in a bicameral parliament (§ 88, 124). However, this constitution also pursued a policy of tactical modernization: that is, it selectively strengthened the democratic dimensions of the polity in order to eliminate noble privileges in fiscal and jurisdictional matters (§ 92), and it prescribed strong public control of judicial process, even providing for a limited constitutional court (§ 195) in order to harden state authority against private-judicial corrosion. In Bavaria, the reformist establishment under Maximilian Montgelas pursued a policy of constitutional foundation determined to guarantee national representation and a property-based franchise as early as 1808. The reforms conducted by Montgelas were shaped by the belief that the constitutional doctrine of popular sovereignty could be invoked as an instrument that at once inclusively simplified society and stabilized and intensified state power against the nobility (Hofmann 1962: 32). The 1808 constitution (never fully enforced) was thus conceived as part of a strategy for solidifying the state. At one level, it pursued this goal by prohibiting serfdom (I, § 3), by largely abolishing noble privileges under law (I, § 2, § 5), and by ensuring that the state exercised its newly obtained sovereign force in uniform judicial and fiscal policies: the constitution and subsequent laws also strongly restricted the powers of patrimonial courts. At a different level, it pursued this strategy by granting political rights in order to ensure that rights did not entail a private stake in the power claimed by the monarchy, to construct less particularistic procedures of political inclusion, and to make sure that all members of society showed equal obedience to the state (I, § 7). The 1808 constitution of Bavaria clearly reflected the conviction that only a state organized under a constitution granting general rights to subjects of the crown could detach political power from territorial or patrimonial tenures, and that a national constitution was required to construct a simple and uniform relation between state and society.[65] The anti-feudal policies essayed by Montgelas suffered

---

[65] On the Bavarian constitution as an instrument of sovereignty, see Hofmann (1962: 283–6); Doberl (1967).

a number of setbacks through late-feudal reaction. Indeed, the 1818 Constitution, which was more generally implemented, gave renewed recognition to noble privileges of patrimonial jurisdiction: these were not finally abolished until 1848.

Even in the German states in which no formal constitution was enacted, certain elements of revolutionary legislation were implemented to create a quasi-constitutional order, and the state-building techniques utilized under the revolutionary and the Napoleonic regimes also assumed influence in polities less strictly regulated by a formal order of public law. As discussed, for example, Prussia had obtained a uniform legal code in 1794, which imposed a general procedural order on the law courts. After the Napoleonic invasion, a process of legal and economic reform, shaped by the belief that the French Revolution had awakened the 'sleeping forces' of the French nation through its constitutional reforms, was initiated by the great Prussian reformers Stein and Hardenberg.[66] The reforms conducted by Stein and Hardenberg after 1806 were also, in part, marked by direct hostility to the seigneurial powers of the nobility. Indeed, the reformist administration came repeatedly into conflict with the regional nobility, which habitually blocked and weakened the reform policies and sought to restore governmental and patrimonial conditions close to those that existed before the Napoleonic period.[67] Nonetheless, this period saw both the abolition of the feudal rights on land (including serfdom) and the removal of legal barriers preventing intermarriage and other forms of mobility between social classes. This period also witnessed an intensification of debate about rights in the civil sphere, and the attempt gathered momentum to recast laws of property ownership in accordance with principles of Roman law and to eliminate legal principles of divided tenure, multiple collective privileges and shared possession.[68] This did not lead to the introduction of a general code of civil law in the German states, yet throughout the German states inherited legal relations, especially in

---

[66] See the *Rigaer Denkschrift* (1931 [1807]: 305).

[67] The reformers made no secret of their dislike for the old nobility. Stein and his close collaborator Johann August Sack concluded that a 'constitution and organisation of the estates' were imperative in the attempt to remove 'all traces of the feudal system' and to inhibit the power of the nobles: the nobles, Sack opined, were solely committed to their own 'crudest egotism' and were 'totally useless for anything except for preventing what is good' (Stein 1961: 352).

[68] The classic example of this was the attempt of Savigny to deduce rights of ownership from the singular will of the property owner (1837 [1803]: 25).

respect of property, were slowly converted into more organized form. As in France, in particular, Roman law was employed in the wake of the Napoleonic invasion to clarify rights of singular economic autonomy, and to cement the division between political and economic competence. Central to the Prussian reforms after 1806 was also an attempt to abolish the judicial powers of the Prussian gentry. As late as 1800, many judicial powers in Prussia were still in the hands of the nobility, and earlier attempts to subject these powers to regular state control remained inconclusive. Even by the middle of the nineteenth century patrimonial courts, although increasingly subordinate to local state administration, had not disappeared in the rural areas of Prussia (Wienfort 2001: 34, 79, 151, 251). In 1807, however, the reformers announced measures to integrate patrimonial courts into the state, and senior reformers sought to impose more rigorously generalized procedures for legal order and to eliminate constitutional weaknesses caused by private courts.[69] As in the previous century, therefore, a general rights structure was imposed in Prussia to reinforce state power and to exclude private/dualistic sources of authority from the state.

The reformist period in Prussia also witnessed an (unsuccessful) attempt, led by Hardenberg, to establish a constitution providing for formal national representation, and it saw the tentative emergence of an independent legislative body within the Prussian state. Like other reforms, the plan for a written state constitution in Prussia was conceived as a means for simplifying and solidifying state power. Hardenberg's design for a constitution was not shaped in the first instance by a desire for popular representation. On the contrary, as in Bavaria in 1808, the constitution was proposed as the centrepiece of a design for a strong sovereign Prussian polity, capable of acting in administrative autonomy against dualistically structured and actively Frondist social groups. In particular, Hardenberg's constitutional ideal deviated from classical theories of representation in that it opposed the strict separation of powers, and it envisaged that the civil service would play a key role in receiving delegations from social interest groups and conducting reforms (Koselleck 1977: 162; Wehler 1987: 446).[70] The constitutional project was driven by the view that only an integrative constitution and a national assembly could limit provincial power, pressurize the nobility,

---

[69] Altenstein's *Denkschrift* of 1807 announced that all private or patrimonial courts had to be integrated into the state (1931 [1807]: 510).

[70] Hardenberg suggested that parliamentary representation might lead to an 'amalgamation' of popular delegates and the reformist elements in the civil service (Huber 1957: 296).

create mechanisms for fiscal levying required by the state in its financially depleted circumstances after the wars with Napoleon, and so generally consolidate the administrative power of the state.[71] These plans for constitutional reform, however, were eventually brought to nothing by the old nobility and their speakers at the Prussian court, who rejected the attempt implicit in constitutional formation to impose general taxes, to create a political, legal and fiscal order that cut through patrimonial boundaries[72] and to construct bearers of power in formulae indifferent to inherited or local status. Eventually, in 1817, Hardenberg created a Council of State, which assumed some representative functions and concentrated the power of the state administration as the primary reserve of political authority. But this fell far short of a representative or constitutional system.

The opposition of the Prussian nobility to the reformist projects conducted by Stein and Hardenberg after 1806 contained an important constitutional paradox, which strikingly underlines the defining status of modern constitutions in relation to medieval constitutionalism. The Prussian estates acquired significantly increased constitutional importance during the French revolutionary era, and both the financial weaknesses of the state caused by the revolutionary and Napoleonic wars and the resurgence of proto-parliamentary ideas spread from Paris by the revolution meant that estate-based power, which had in any case been reinvigorated in the later eighteenth century, was further reinforced in the reformist period.[73] As early as 1798, a Diet was convoked in East Prussia, in which delegates demanded a catalogue of measures to liberalize the economy and to establish principles of equality through law. In 1808, then, a further Diet of estates was convened in East Prussia, and after 1809 the committee of estates assumed more central representative functions. Diets were also organized in Brandenburg in 1809–10. These processes reflected a substantial rise in influence on the part of the estates in Prussia, and the estates, led by the nobility, assumed a position in which they could use semi-elected authority to participate in modernizing and restructuring the state. Some members of the nobility even contemplated a voluntary renunciation of hereditary jurisdictional privileges to the state, and they began to envisage transforming

---

[71] For this view see Zeeden (1940: 112); Koselleck (1977: 209); Botzenhart (1983: 448); Neugebauer (1992: 233–4).

[72] See Simon (1955: 61); Klein (1965: 167, 192); Koselleck (1977: 313).

[73] For discussion see Botzenhart (1983: 431); Neugebauer (1992: 197–217); Gehrke (2005: 2).

themselves from orders of structural privilege into functional organs within the state (Neugebauer 1992: 239). Throughout the earlier nineteenth century, the concept of the estate (*Stand*) remained a deeply controversial constitutional principle in Prussia. Progressive sectors of political society urged a redefinition of the estate, which aimed to establish estates as 'representatives of the people',[74] acting to integrate diverse social interests within the administrative apparatus of the state. This remained one of the most pervasive arguments of German liberalism before 1848. Conservatives, in contrast, argued that the organic constitution of estates reflected a natural order of corporate society in which, not the 'entire mass of the people', but the particular rights of social groups obtained representation.[75] Such conservatives opposed the monistic integration of estates within the state and sought to preserve a social order based integrally on the dualistic assertion of embedded rights. In Prussia, therefore, the conflict between the dualistic-privatistic principle of late feudal constitutionalism and the monistic public-legal principle of modern constitutionalism received its paradigmatic expression. For the most part, the Prussian estates ultimately rejected their redesignation as politically integrated representative groups, and they offered strong resistance to the reforms in order to preserve their particular external prerogatives. Members of the nobility largely opposed the establishment of a national/constitutional system of representation, and the Prussian elite attempted instead to preserve the social constitution based in local power and diffuse privileges.[76]

The major German states, Prussia and Austria, in fact, did not obtain full written constitutions until 1848–9. Indeed, the concluding documents of the Congress of Vienna prohibited the establishment of representative constitutions in major German states. Article 1 of these documents defined sovereignty as a princely attribute, and Article 57 stated that princely sovereignty had no limits except in customary rights. Articles 54–56 stated that only estate-based dualist constitutional arrangements were legitimate in the German states, and that no internal system of representation was to be established. As a result of this, provincial estates were established in Prussia in 1823: they acted to reconsolidate the 'older

---

[74] The quote is from the pre-eminent popular liberal thinker of the Vormärz, Karl von Rotteck (1997 [1819]: 19).

[75] This was the view of Friedrich von Gentz, conservative commentator on the French Revolution and its aftermath in Germany (1979 [1819]: 218–19).

[76] See Vetter (1979: 146); Vogel (1981: 48); Botzenhart (1983: 444–6); Neugebauer (1992: 229).

German constitutions' of the pre-1789 period and to prevent the convergence of society around broad-based state executives (Rauer 1845: 1–2). This tendency set the foundations for a constitutional system in which privatistic elements were allowed to survive in the state, and legislative power remained largely in the hands of particular and local elites. To be sure, there were striking exceptions to this tendency. The 1831 constitution of Saxony, although accepting obligation to an estate-based model, contained a powerful legislative chamber, some of whose members were elected in provincial elections. The 1831 constitution of Hesse, analogously, remained nominally committed to estate-based delegation. Yet it also contained a powerful catalogue of rights and, crucially, it made provision for a semi-elected legislature with the power to initiate laws. Nonetheless, the longer period of post-Napoleonic reform and restoration created an especially fateful legacy for many German states. The reforms substantially reinforced the central power of the state bureaucracy: during the reforms, as Hegel enthusiastically observed, the civil service was formed as a liberal elite, it acted as the force behind modernization, and it even assumed quasi-constitutional functions in restricting the prerogatives of monarchy (1969 [1821]: 473). After 1820, however, the state administration was increasingly populated by more conservative figures, who reattached central state power to more particular interests. This meant that by the middle decades of the nineteenth century many larger German states were marked by a condition of statehood, in which private interests were concentrated in the administration of powerful central states. In fact, the subsequent development of the Prussian state, and later also of the German state, was deeply shaped by the fact that during the post-1806 reforms the central authority of the state was reinforced, yet this process was not flanked by an effective exclusion of private power (see Koselleck 1977: 409).

Britain

The intensification of state power through constitutional inclusion was also evident in other states that did not acquire a single written constitutional order. In the later eighteenth and early nineteenth centuries, for instance, Britain also experienced a change in constitutional structure that heightened its inclusionary power and abstracted authority. Although in the late eighteenth century British political debate was marked by wide hostility to the French Revolution, and theorists at diverse points along the spectrum reviled the formal declaration of revolutionary rights in 1789,[77] the British polity at once prefigured and emulated aspects of the wider rights-based constitutional transformations of this time. On one hand, through the eighteenth century the original constitutional conception of parliament as a balance against monarchical power was revised, and both the fiscal and statutory competences of parliament were substantially extended. Parliament, in fact, became the primary centre of governance, and it was increasingly conceived as an organ of full representative sovereignty (Cannon 1969: ix–xiii; Dickinson 1976). Blackstone stated this clearly in arguing that parliament, of which the king was one element, possessed 'supreme and absolute authority' (1979 [1765–9: 143]). In this respect, further, parliamentary power incrementally broke through the local structure of noble authority, and it established a more generalized public foundation for the use and legitimization of political power. Moreover, despite violent attempts at reactionary retrenchment after 1789, governmental and monarchical powers were finally divided in the eighteenth-century English state: the state assumed an increasingly impersonal constitutional order, and single politicians were able, if required, to act independently of the monarchy and to remove ministries endorsed by the king. As a result of this, both parliament and civil service evolved towards an increased level of independence, and the power of government was concentrated in distinct ministries, each containing a distinct administrative apparatus (Parris 1969: 49, 82). Through the later eighteenth century, therefore, the British state generally experienced a process of internal concentration typical of states under more formal constitutions.

This process culminated in, and was in return reinforced by, the Reform Act of 1832. This law increased the number of voters admitted to the electorate, it enfranchised new industrial centres,[78] and it eradicated constituencies (rotten boroughs) that provided support for local and noble authority. In so doing, the Reform Act distributed entitlement to political representation 'more evenly' across the country (Chester 1981: 106), it reduced the importance of local power through more general political inclusion, and – vitally – it began to allocate political/representational rights, not on a communal or local foundation, but as entitlements of singular persons. In each respect the Reform Act expanded and regimented the integrative basis of the state, and, although surely not in definitive fashion, it acted to sever political inclusion from

---

[77] See by way of examples Burke (1910 [1790]: 59); Bentham (2002: 30–1).

[78] An example of this was my own adopted city, Glasgow, which, despite its size, was represented before 1832 by one quarter of an MP.

informal structures of local deference and patronage: after 1832, the tendency towards party alignment became more rigid, and parties formed a stronger link between executive and society.[79] The Reform Act was intended at one level as part of a strategy of social palliation, and it was guided by the assumption that electoral reform was a device for avoiding revolutionary upheavals stimulated by the autocratic shift in British policy under Pitt and Wellington (Hill 1985: 230; Turner 2000: 218). Yet, in widening the foundations of the state, the Reform Act also performed the functionally intensifying objectives of other constitutions. The progressive integration of the population in the political system, further augmented by subsequent reform acts, acted as part of an inclusionary regimentation of state power, and it was closely linked to the growing statutory sovereignty of parliament and the rise and influence of parliamentary parties. One major outcome of the Reform Act, significantly, was a constitutional reinforcement of the office of prime minister and other ministerial departments, and a wider consolidation of the state as a public order. The expansion of electoral inclusion thus stimulated and provided legitimacy for a restriction of personal influence on the state executive, for a rationalized reinforcement of state power as distinct from personal authority, and for a marked growth in the effective power of the state.

Across the whole wave of post-revolutionary constitutional construction, constitutional reform – either wholesale or piecemeal – was used to institute a determinably public form for the state, and constitutions created inclusionary instruments in which state power could unify widening societies and transmit itself more easily and positively across these societies. At this time, most European societies responded to their longer-term processes of political abstraction, differentiation and generalized inclusion by adapting, in a manner reflecting their distinct structure, proto-democratic constitutional techniques for separating public from private functions, for extending the power of central states and for promoting inclusive patterns of support to utilize their power. Most states employed national constitutions and constitutional rights to suppress extreme dualism or polyarchy in their exercise of power and to establish preconditions under which they could consolidate their power as self-contained institutional actors. Moreover, most states began to rationalize the system of their civil laws and formally to juxtapose their

---

[79] For discussion, see Phillips and Wetherell (1995: 434). On the pre-history of this see O'Gorman (1982: 63).

inner public-legal structure to uniformly constructed rights-based legal relations located outside the state. As in earlier settings, the growth in the volume of rights underwritten by states was directly reflected in the effective power of states. Rights acted as a normative formula in which states constantly augmented their inclusive effective power.

Constitutions, in other words, performed the most vital functions of selective political inclusion for European states in the early decades of contemporary society, and these functions enabled states to operate as such. The expansion of statehood in increasingly modern European societies both coincided with and presupposed the formation of constitutions as documents of functionally proportioned inclusion. In most cases, nonetheless, the consolidation of political structure in society remained partial, post-Napoleonic societies were only loosely integrated around abstracted reserves of political power, and most European states employed elements of constitutional design developed in the French Revolution in order specifically to prevent a fully inclusionary increase in political power. Above all, rights remained very weakly enacted in society, and in most settings their power to shape social structure was limited: private inner-societal authority remained strong, and rights acted primarily to liberate a limited political superstructure, which often fused closely with private power. Only gradually did rights clear the terrain for subsequent, more extensive processes of inclusionary social formation and political abstraction.

Constitutions and social design: 1848

Of the three constitutional elements implicit in the French Revolution – private rights, political rights and national sovereignty – the first was the principle that exercised the strongest immediate influence. As discussed, through the decades that followed the revolution of 1789 this principle allowed states to simplify and attenuate their primary attachment to the second two principles, and subjective rights were widely employed by states to restrict the immediate exercise of popular sovereignty in governmental power without relinquishing the benefits of internal public-legal order and uniform political inclusion. Towards the middle decades of the nineteenth century, however, in many settings the increasingly uniform societal structure that had emerged from the revolutionary era began to generate social and political movements insisting on more universally expansive political freedoms and more centrally authoritative and socially integrative states. In particular, this period saw a widespread inflation of the concept of national sovereignty, in which, in conjunction with rights, the idea of national self-legislation began to act as the leading impulse of inclusionary political formation. This reached an apotheosis in the (largely unsuccessful) constitutional revolutions of 1848, when in many European societies the demand for constitutional formation and rights-based representation coincided with an impetus towards the construction of states founded in more fully and cohesively integrated national societies. The period prior to 1848, as a whole, might be viewed as one in which the inclusionary and politically abstractive implications of rights became more pervasively and fundamentally embedded in the structure of European societies. This had the result that societies assumed more homogeneous shape (often appearing as *nations*), and it meant, accordingly, that these societies experienced a more pronounced requirement for generalized and articulated reserves of political power. The construction of societies comprising uniform rights-holding social constituencies (nations) and requiring consonantly abstracted constitutional states, which was tentatively anticipated in the earlier revolutionary period, thus assumed heightened expression in 1848.

The growing constitutional significance of nationhood expressed itself in several, quite distinct patterns of political transformation and state formation in the period of revolutionary change around 1848. In cases such as France, first, the salience of national sovereignty was expressed in the formation of more radically inclusive, or even democratic, constitutions, which used the idea of national-sovereign self-legislation to terminate the bureaucratic gradualism of post-revolutionary institutional conditions and fully to realize the constitutional promise of equal inclusion in the political system expressed in 1789. The rise of national sovereignty was expressed, second, in national state building (sometimes with an irredentist dimension) within existing empires or supra-national states. In such cases, the idea of national sovereignty began to bring about a more even anti-privatistic distribution of power within territories, especially those under Habsburg and Ottoman rule, controlled by late-feudal imperial bureaucracies, and the vision of the sovereign self-legislating people facilitated the construction of societies opposing and traversing imperial boundaries. Third, the growing significance of national sovereignty was also expressed in the incremental formation of unified national states, such as Italy and Germany, which were formed through the fusion of loosely connected cultural blocs which had formerly been under diverse administrative control. In such cases the concept of national sovereignty began to authorize the construction of societies at a heightened degree of political inclusion, and the belief in the nation as constituent power began to extend societies and their political reserves more easily across local and feudal frontiers. In each case the rising prominence of national ideas of sovereignty remained correlated with the functions of social inclusion and general political construction expressed by constitutional rights, and the growth of national statehood formed an intensified manifestation of the impulse towards political abstraction and general inclusion originally contained in rights-based constitutionalism. Following different patterns in different settings, the emphatic expansion of nationhood in early nineteenth-century Europe marked a process in which societies were progressively formed, through personal rights, as cohesive and regionally extensive, in which the local privatistic design of society was dissolved, and in which, accordingly, societies required states as strongly abstracted centres of power, formally situated against relatively ordered and inclusive societies. In most cases, in fact, the rise of national sovereignty reflected a social order that was already deeply shaped and integrated by general subjective rights, and the impetus towards national statehood reflected a requirement for political power adequate to a society constructed and rendered uniform and stabilized by the construction of social agents as uniform rights holders.

France: popular democracy

In France, the revolutionary movement of 1848 culminated in the overthrow of the administrative liberalism of the Orléanist regime, and it led to the formation of the Second Republic. As France already possessed a moderately centralized state, the defining debates of 1848 revolved primarily, not around national integrity, but around the substantial content of rights and the inclusionary extent of sovereign power. The Second Republic was founded, first, in the proclamation of a democratic franchise reflecting the full sovereignty of the nation (Art. 1): it rejected the Orléanist aversion to comprehensive popular sovereignty, and it temporarily reinvigorated Jacobin ideals. Second, the constitution of the Second Republic was conceived, initially, as an attempt to fuse bourgeois-republican and socialist-democratic political concepts in order to thicken the content of the rights established in 1791. At least initially, the founders of the Second Republic promoted highly inclusive ideas of citizenship as the basis of political legitimacy. On one hand, the constitution of 1848 sanctioned classical liberal rights, and it provided for the usual rights in respect of property, belief, education and equal access to public office. Additionally, however, the founders engaged deeply in debates over rights as instruments of *material inclusion*, and early drafts for the constitution contained clauses acknowledging a strong presumption in favour of *material rights*: especially rights to employment and to decent living conditions. During the process of constitution writing, however, the different revolutionary factions turned on each other and the bourgeois factions rapidly suppressed the more radical revolutionary groups. Accordingly, the social ideals of the constituent assembly faltered, and the material rights promised in the Assembly were weakened in later drafts of the constitution. For instance, Article 7 of the provisional constitution of June 1848 already marked a move away from the original aspirations of the constituent body, and it described the right to work – in the vaguest terms – as a right that society must recognize by 'productive and general means'.[80] In the final constitution, this commitment was further diluted, and the right to gainful employment was treated, not as a formal entitlement, but as a protected liberty. Article 13 of the 1848 Constitution stated that 'the constitution guarantees to citizens the freedom to work', and it declared that society 'promotes and encourages the development of labour': it thus abandoned the full inclusionary scope of its first conception. Nonetheless, the 1848 Constitution still established a strong principle of popular sovereignty, and it provided for a unicameral legislature (Art. 20), based in universal male suffrage, and for a nationally elected president. In this case, above all, the principle of national sovereignty acted as a device for selectively reinforcing the state, and as Karl Marx (perhaps inadvertently) recognized, its function was to organize power in a strong state executive, and to establish the state as a powerful, yet abstracted actor capable of applying power independently across society (1958–63 [1852]: 197).

Greece, Belgium, Hungary and the early Risorgimento

The second pattern of national constitutional formation first (momentarily) became reality in Greece, in the initial stages of the unification process that gradually gave rise to the modern Greek state. In Greece, the early aftermath of the French Revolution and the first influx of revolutionary ideas had stimulated a body of constitutional thought, plotting the liberation of Greece from Ottoman rule. Ultimately, after the wars of

---

[80] For comment, see Bastid (1945: I, 277).

independence against Turkey, the first Greek constitution (only partially applied) was drafted in 1822, and it was followed by revised documents in 1823 and 1827. The 1822 Constitution, although influenced by the French Thermidorean constitution, did not fully separate executive and legislative functions, and members of the executive retained control of military units and the state administration. It is also notable that, at such an early stage in the process of nation building, this constitution, although notionally centralistic, performed only weak integrating functions for the state, and it secured only loose control of the governmental periphery (Dakin 1973: 105; Argyriadis 1987: 68). Moreover, the resultant republic was short-lived, and it was soon replaced by a more authoritarian system. Nonetheless, the 1822 Constitution of Greece created a rudimentary state apparatus, and it contained sufficient symbolic power to draw members of an emergent society into an increasingly immediate and unified relation to the state. In partial analogy to this pattern, the Belgian constitution of 1831, highly influential for later constitutions of multi-ethnic societies owing to its provisions for language rights, concluded the separation of the Belgian provinces from Holland by providing a structure for a cautiously progressive constitutional monarchy. This constitution, strongly informed by the assimilation of Napoleonic law in Belgian provinces under French rule up to 1815, reflected the unitary construction of society under rights-based law by breaking dramatically with estate-based constitutions (Juste 1850: 301). It created a governmental order with two elected chambers (Arts. 47, 53), it gave the elected legislature (albeit representing only a tiny franchise) final control of legislation (Art. 28) and – above all – it made strict provisions for ministerial accountability to the legislature and it removed ministerial power from dynastic authority (Art. 89).

The prominence of national constitutionalism in anti-imperial national state building gained most exemplary expression in Hungary. In Hungary, the constitutional movement clearly incorporated two distinct state-building impulses: it consolidated both the inner-societal anti-feudalism and the strong external claim to national/territorial sovereignty typical of early constitutional foundation. Up to 1848, elements of feudal social order remained strongly embedded in Hungary. To be sure, after the 1820s reformist principles had become increasingly pervasive. However, there was no constitution in Hungary except for an assembly of organic laws. Serfdom still existed in rural areas, the delegatory order of estates, led by the aristocracy, remained intact, and administrative power was based in regions or counties (*vármegye* or comitats) overseen by the aristocracy. The comitats retained powers to tax, to enforce laws and to preside over patrimonial courts, and, although not without reformist elements, government at comitat level provided a bastion for noble defence of ancient privileges (see Révész 1968: 123; Stipta 1998: 473–7). This came to an end in the anti-Austrian national uprisings of March 1848. As a result of this revolt, by April 1848 the parliament of estates, under the leadership of the gentry, introduced a sweeping body of liberal reformist legislation, which at once removed many remaining elements of feudal administration from Hungarian society and accorded greatly extended powers to a centralized and autonomous national government. This process did not entail the establishment of a full constitution, and in any case the reformist movement was eventually brutally suppressed by Austrian and Russian troops. However, this legislation, strongly indebted to the Belgian constitution, created a quasi-constitutional national order in Hungary, effectively forming Hungary as a distinct state within the Habsburg monarchy. At one level, the 'April laws' (subsequently subject to authoritarian revision) established popular representation and a democratic legislative process, and they abolished fiscal, judicial and executive privileges for the nobility. In this respect, the April laws eroded internal sociostructural boundaries, and they tentatively established a unitary political system within Hungary. These laws thus consolidated uniform constitutional rights to enact an inner-societal state-building process. At the same time, however, the April laws were also designed to regulate and strengthen the position of Hungary within the Habsburg empire. The construction of an elected parliament involved an attempt to formalize relations between Hungary and Vienna and to consolidate an autonomous national government in Pest (Révész 1978: 126). The April laws were thus also intended as a state-building exercise in external politics. Owing to the resultant conflict with the Habsburg authorities, this in fact led to Kossuth's (unrealized) declaration of Hungarian independence in April 1849. In both its internal and its external dimensions, therefore, the revolutionary experiment in Hungary reflected the dual potential of constitutional formation as a technique for simultaneous rights-based social inclusion and uniform social construction and (as corollary) intensified political abstraction and state building.

Similarly, 1848 saw the drafting of constitutions in many Italian cities: in fact, the European national-constitutional movement of 1848 began in Palermo. During the revolutionary fervour, some Italian states established constitutional systems in which monarchical power was combined with a representative order and guarantees over basic rights. For instance, Sicily established a highly progressive, although short-lived, monarchical constitution. This constitution gave exclusive legislative power to a parliamentary assembly, elected by full male franchise, and, while preserving a monarchical executive, it instituted a supreme bicameral parliament (Arts. 4–5), and it provided for minister-ial responsibility (Art. 68), judicial independence (Art. 72) and rights of political engagement. In Piedmont-Sardinia a constitutional monarchy was established, which was founded in classical liberal rights, the divi-sion of legislative power between monarch and two chambers (Art. 3) and ministerial responsibility (Art. 67). In the Papal States, too, a far-reaching democratic constitution was drafted in 1849 to support the Roman Republic founded in late 1848. This constitution, although the reforms preceding it were initiated by Pius IX himself, ended the tem-poral power of the pope, established ministerial responsibility (Arts. 43–44) and created a permanent representative system based in exten-sive manhood suffrage (Arts. 17, 23). Notably, most of these constitu-tions made scarce specific reference to national unity. However, the Roman Constitution defined itself as promoting Italian nationality, and the wider process of constitution drafting was shaped by a growing demand for Italian self-rule and for the expulsion of the Habsburgs from northern Italy. Moreover, this process was also shaped by the assump-tion that the constitutionally enforced rule of law would ultimately unify all Italian territories under the same power, and the ambition of creating a strong and constitutionally regulated political order overlapped with the ambition of establishing a unified nation.[81]

Germany

As in Italy, in 1848, the loosely associated states of the German Confederation also experienced a process of intense constitutional recon-struction, in which expectations of private rights and rights of political representation converged with a demand, far more potent than in Italy, for a unitary national state. In 1848, progressive constituencies in differ-ent German states, including Prussia and Austria, proclaimed, separately, the need for liberal constitutions. At the same time, a national

---

[81] To support this, although Italian nationalism remained relatively weak, we can observe the rise of national symbolism during 1848 and the choice of an Italian flag and a standard Italian language for the Roman Republic.

Constituent Assembly was convened in the *Paulskirche* in Frankfurt, comprising delegates from states of the German Confederation and other states within the Habsburg territories, to create a constitution for all Germany. The Constitutional Assembly in Frankfurt was faced with multiple state-building and nation-building tasks. On one hand, it attempted to construct the unified German *state* as an integrated national polity within defined territorial limits, to found the legislative power of the state in the designated rights of the German people (Section 4, Art. 3, § 93), and, at least in questions of public law, to assert national laws over the laws of particular German states. In addition, it sought to construct the German *nation* as a uniform body of citizens represented in an elected legislature, endowed with common rights of conscience, property, education, expression, intellectual inquiry, and political activity and association (Section 6, Arts. 4, 5, 6, 7, 8, 9). The all-German constitution of 1848–9 in fact represented the most literal attempt to utilize the state-building functions of constitutionalism, and its framers sought at one and the same time to employ a constitutional document to create the people as a source of power for the state, to ensure that state power was distributed evenly and inclusively through a particular society, and to construct the state itself, *ex nihilo*, as a central and fully monopolistic bearer of power. At the core of this endeavour was the deeply-lying conviction that a constitution guaranteeing national inclusion and uniform personal rights was required to elaborate a state able to act as the sole focus of identity and political unity within German society. Indeed, in enshrining the extracted principles of national/territorial sovereignty and personal rights under law, the German Constitution of 1848–9 was designed finally to wrest power from the nobility and the ministerial bureaucracy, and to build a fully public and conclusively sovereign state on that foundation. The constitution was centred in the principle that rights allocated through the state weakened power in the margins of the state, and that inclusion through national sovereign affiliation and through private and political rights was a precondition for a powerfully autonomous state. At the head of its catalogue of rights, in consequence, the constitution of 1848–9 emphatically proscribed distinctions of status before the law, and it abolished all use of titles not attached to an office: that is, external to the state (Section 6, Art. 2, § 137). Furthermore, it loudly prohibited private courts and the dispensing of justice on a patrimonial basis (Section 6, Art. 10, § 174). Leading members in the progressive and radical factions of the constituent assembly in Frankfurt expressed the view that the formation of a representative constitution was needed as a strategic concluding

step in a long process of political de-privatization, through which the dualistic estates of the German territories could finally be converted into
inner components of a fully evolved state: only a deep-rooted rights-
based national constitution, they argued, could rectify the persistent
privatism and weakness of German statehood.[82] At this point in
German history, therefore, the principle became reflexively clear that
strong states presupposed constitutions and constitutional rights, and
societies unified by rights converged uniformly around central national
executives.

Across diverse patterns of revolution and state construction, the widespread political nationalism typifying the middle decades of the nineteenth century mirrored and extended the wider inclusionary dynamics
of societal transformation after 1789. In all lines of national-sovereign
state formation culminating in 1848, the concept of the sovereign nation
as the source of power served both to remove political authority from
embedded elites and to enable power to cut across the sectoral and
patrimonial boundaries that still marked the inner structure of particular
societies. In all cases, the principle of national sovereignty promoted a
greater inclusivity in power, and, in increasing the extensibility of different societies, the idea of power as belonging to a nation raised the level of
abstraction at which power could be produced and utilized. Moreover, in
each line of national state formation characteristic of this time, the
expansion of national power was closely linked to the construct of rights,
and rights consolidated and fused with nationhood to shape and structure the underlying process of administrative consolidation and extensive societal inclusion. Demands for national statehood around 1848
were normally stimulated by the fact that the societies experiencing
national revolution had already gained a high degree of internal
uniformity through their transfusion with subjective legal rights. As a
result of this, they possessed a structural propensity for conceiving
themselves in uniform and unified legal categories (as nations), and so
also for receiving power from central states, simply and uniformly
counterposed to other functions in society. In emergent anti-imperial
states, for example, independent state formation was normally accelerated by the unsustainability of late-feudal empires in the face of widening
societies drawn together under post-Napoleonic civil law. This was

---

[82] For example, Friedrich Christoph Dahlmann, a leading liberal delegate in 1848, claimed
that the traditional estate-based system in Germany could be transformed by a constitution into a strong modern state (1924 [1835]: 124–32).

especially prominent in anti-Habsburg national revolts and movements, which occurred in societies, for example in northern Italy, Poland and Hungary, in which rights-based civil law, resulting from late absolutistic codifications and Napoleonic influence, had found wide resonance and had done much to dissolve society from its localized pre-revolutionary structure. In nascent unified national states, alternatively, the enforcement of rights-based legal orders had created an increasingly uniform societal environment before the edifice of national statehood was created, and in these settings, too, a process of de facto legal unification preceded and smoothed the path for the revolutionary proclamation of national statehood. Much of Italy, for instance, had implemented revolutionary civil laws after 1795, and most parts of Italy had (haltingly) adopted Napoleonic civil legislation, which at once created a 'concrete terrain' for a unified nation and anticipated the possibility of 'legislative unification' (Ghisalberti 1972: 35). Indeed, the step-wise reception of the Napoleonic codes in Italy had established principles of civil equality, equal entitlement to private rights and general uniformity under law that deeply pre-structured the emergent conditions of national statehood (Ghisalberti 2008: 258).[83] Much of Germany, likewise, had also been, either directly or indirectly, subject to legal principles derived from Napoleonic rule. Each line of national state formation at this time thus gained specific momentum in societies integrally suffused with rights-based civil law, and it responded to a requirement in such countries for commensurately abstracted and inclusionary patterns of statehood. These societies then consolidated nationhood as comprising a uniform claim to rights, as obliterating the inner-societal vestiges of late feudalism, and as leading to the convergence of society around an administrative order able to include all people equally (as members of a nation) in its power.

It is of the greatest importance, however, that the actual constitutional model stabilized in the major European states before, during or after 1848 was settled through a formal renunciation of the more expansive promises of national self-legislation in the revolutionary proclamations of 1848–9. In different ways after 1848, European states reverted to a model of constitutionalism that used limited catalogues of rights to separate the state from particular interests and factually to limit the democratic

---

[83] In Italy, some Napoleonic law was initially removed after 1815. But subsequent legal codes, culminating in the *codice civile* (1865) for all Italy, were strongly influenced by Napoleonic ideas. For discussion see Ghisalberti (1995: 19, 80, 91).

element of national sovereignty. As discussed, in France the constitution of 1848 only contained a reduced version of the rights originally anticipated as the outcome of the revolution. In late 1851, this constitution was removed by a Bonapartist *coup d'état*, and the Second Empire reaffirmed the basic disjuncture, characteristic of authoritarian-liberal states, between a formally independent and quasi-prerogative state apparatus and an economic system based in subjective rights of proprietary autonomy. Events in Italy formed a partial analogy to this. In Italy, the only constitution to survive post-revolutionary repression was the constitution of Sardinia-Piedmont: the Statuto Albertino. This contained provisions for basic rights, including individual liberty (Art. 26), freedom of the press (Art. 28), freedom of property (Art. 29) and freedom of assembly (Art. 32). However, it was flexible in its approach to political representation and integration, it reserved to the monarch the right to approve and promulgate law (Art. 7), and it placed only ambiguous constraints on executive power. In the German states, the planned constitution for a unified Germany was not enacted, the National Assembly in Frankfurt was eventually suppressed by Prussian troops, and the revolutionary era concluded with the imposition of a highly restrictive constitution in Prussia. Indeed, as in France, the Prussian constitutions of 1848–50 were imposed through an effective *coup d'état*, in which the Prussian monarchy, acting in conjunction with the ministerial bureaucracy and the army, used prerogative legislation to suppress the progressive parliamentary-constitutional faction, first, in Prussia and, subsequently, in the German states more generally (Grünthal 1982: 65). The Prussian Constitution in fact remained in some respects a Bonapartist constitution. The infamous Article 105 of the 1848 Constitution contained substantial provisions for rule by emergency decree. Similar provisions were preserved in Articles 45 and 51–52 of the 1850 Constitution.

In each of these instances, two points have particular salience. First, even in the middle of the nineteenth century the full potentials of the revolutionary constitutions of the late eighteenth century were not realized. Constitutions that remained enduringly in force contained mechanisms for restricting the expansionary implications of popular sovereignty. Second, by 1848 a heightened element of reflexivity had become apparent in the application of constitutional laws, and a weakened version of the Bonapartist principle that constitutions could be routinely employed as restrictive models of social design was now conventional. Constitutions were imposed in order selectively to simplify and generalize the functions of the state, yet also to ensure that states did not become fully inclusive and did not fully renounce their attachments to particular dynasties and personal elites. Notably, the only revolutionary constitutions that survived the outbursts of 1848, those of Piedmont-Sardinia and Prussia, were in fact counter-revolutionary constitutions (*constitutions octroyées*), and they were used to preserve a private/familial monopoly of power while ensuring that this monopoly could be applied in a system of public law adapted to the generally uniform structure of a modern society.

4

Constitutions from empire to fascism

Constitutions after 1848

As discussed, the revolutionary constitutions of the later eighteenth century did much to consolidate the power of central states, and in supplying the idea that the nation of rights holders was the origin of legitimate state power they greatly simplified the social abstraction and circulation of political power. The constitutions of 1848, then, consolidated the state as a broad-based body of institutions, and they at once heightened the power of states and distributed power in more even fashion through society by enunciating the principle that all members of a national society had a common and equal relation to political power. In both periods, the forming of constitutions continued a process of political distillation that had shaped most European states throughout the seventeenth and eighteenth centuries, and the patterns of liberal-national constitutional formation that culminated in the middle of the nineteenth century extended the centralistic and inclusionary impetus of earlier constitution writing. Indeed, as discussed, the liberal-national constitutional movement resulted directly from the primary state-building tendencies of the age of 'absolutism'. Naturally, this does not imply that the constitutional models that emerged in the age of revolution did not profoundly alter the inner organization of states, and that their emphasis on popular sovereignty and rights-based self-legislation did not produce a condition of more equal legal and political inclusivity in society in which a popular legislature played an increased role in governance. However, the revolutionary constitutions of the period 1789–1848 formed a structural continuum with the administrative innovations typical of 'absolutism'. It was in these constitutions that the attempt of 'absolutistic' states to abstract an inclusionary and generalizable form for political power was finally accomplished. National-liberal constitutionalism eventually consolidated itself as a dominant mode of governance in Europe precisely because its core principle of popular sovereignty, correlated with the concept of citizenship as rights holding, was successful in concentrating political power as a generally abstracted resource, and it was more effective than personal/monarchical rule in weakening society's local and patrimonial structures. The early form of constitutional democracy, thus, emerged as a political system that, more than any previous political model, adequately reflected the growing autonomy of political power and enabled societies to use power as a positive iterable phenomenon. As discussed, the tendency towards accelerated nation building in the constitutional movements of the middle part of the nineteenth century immediately reflected both the growing abstraction of political power and the increasing construction of societies around uniform processes of political inclusion, in which the separation of political power (state) and the rest of society (nation) was organized through generally articulated rights.

In the same way that absolutist states governed in spite of particularist opposition, however, states founded in national-liberal constitutionalism were also opposed by social groups who possessed entrenched regional and status-determined authority, and in the nineteenth century the national-constitutional ideal of autonomous statehood found its main adversaries in conservative elites. As discussed, privileged social groups had originally approached central states with deep scepticism. Nonetheless, by the eighteenth century an informal compromise had been established in many European societies, in which regents and dynastic families assumed a monopoly of political power in society and old elites obtained a constitutionally protected position within the state: this usually presupposed that the nobility sacrificed its political liberties in return for guarantees over social privileges and status. Throughout the nineteenth century, however, this familiar antagonism began to reproduce itself in a new form, and bearers of local and hereditary status necessarily perceived centralized constitutional states as perpetuating, now in far more threatening fashion, the more general statist attack on their particular liberties and noble indemnities. Even in the later nineteenth century, in consequence, many European societies contained sporadically influential conservative factions, such as the Carlists in Spain and the *légitimistes* in France, who continued to oppose the central state and dedicated themselves to the preservation of the local/corporatistic structure of society. Both at a political level and at a social level, in consequence, the centralistic design of constitutional states arising in the era of revolution did not provide a conclusive pattern of convergence for legally and politically unified societies, and it was only through subsequent adjustment that states obtained solid foundations in society.

The constitutional orders of European states after 1848 were normally marked by a double process of entrenchment, and they typically preserved a pragmatic balance between centralistic principles of government, reflected in a unitary state apparatus and a general legal system, and the embedded prerogatives of established elites. After 1848, most European states possessed rudimentary features of constitutional order. That is to say, they guaranteed some basic mechanisms of representation, and they normally provided for clear public procedures to determine the introduction, promulgation and enforcement of laws. Moreover, the societal basis of states was increasingly impervious to collective private privileges and, even in more traditional societies, Roman-law concepts of singular personal rights, separating private activities from institutionally defined state structures, became prevalent. However, most states also fell substantially short of uniform constitutional inclusion, and they retained legal instruments to ensure that constitutional provisions concerning the rule of law and the legal foundations of the state were selectively and unevenly applied. Indeed, after 1848, most states reverted to a pattern of constitutional construction that was designed to appease and even to co-opt traditional elites and to guarantee that those groups with vested regional and personal privileges were not fully alienated from the state.

To illuminate this, after 1848 few states entirely relinquished the essential integrative dimensions of constitutional statehood, and even those that opted for more authoritarian-governmental structures did not revert to a pre-constitutional political order. For example, even in France during the Second Empire an implicit constitutional structure remained intact. Following the neo-Bonapartist assumption of power in 1851, the authoritarian constitution of 1852 was imposed throughout France, and it abrogated many constitutional achievements of 1848 and before. However, even in this period of French constitutionalism, executive powers were subject to clear constraints: the daily conduct of government by semi-accountable elites was flanked by a restricted system of election and representation, administrative acts were subject to control by a senate, and a general legal order was preserved (Price 2001: 65). Moreover, throughout the Second Empire accountable political institutions and counterweights to the Caesaristic executive were increasingly strengthened. After 1860, in fact, the French polity was defined by a clear liberalization of constitutional design, and by an increase in political participation. Indeed, in its centralistic impetus Bonapartism paved the way for the re-establishment of inclusive political citizenship

as a principle of governance perhaps more effectively than less authoritarian political systems (Berton 1900: 362; Deslanges 1932: 593;
Hazareesingh 1998: 89, 245).

More generally, however, the typical constitutional design of the
period after 1848 was one that, while accepting the need for inclusive
legal principles and procedures adapted to a thinly nationalized societal
and political structure, continued to strengthen the position of private
elites in the state. Across different national settings, the standard constitutional form of this era was an intermediary model of statehood, in
which an apparatus of formal public law coexisted with a political order
facilitating private access to political power.

An extreme example of this was the post-1848 Prussian state, whose
constitution gave high-ranking members of the nobility privileged use of
executive power. The revised Prussian constitution of 1850, formed
through a series of progressively reactionary counter-revolutionary
octrois between late 1848 and 1850, instituted (Art. 65, 1) a split legislature, in which a dominant position was given to the First Chamber,
redefined after 1855 as a House of Lords (*Herrenhaus*), which, among
others, comprised members of the high aristocracy and royal appointees.
Additionally, in April–May 1849 the Prussian king used emergency
provisions in the 1848 Constitution (Art. 105) to introduce an estate-
based voting system for the elected Second Chamber, in which different
social groups were unevenly enfranchised on the basis of their income
status, and obtained bloc voting rights in proportion to their contribution to fiscal revenue. This system of representation, although not finally
renouncing the principle of general electoral rights, hinged on a neo-
feudal idea of the state as a stratified body of particular interest groups,
which defined government as elected to represent a natural/corporate
hierarchy of estates. Similarly, the polity of later nineteenth-century
Austria contained a striking example of a constitution designed to solidify
the power of the nobility. In 1848 and 1849, two separate constitutions were
introduced in Austria. The 1848 Constitution placed a bicameral legislature
alongside the executive authority of the Kaiser (§ 34). It also sanctioned
limited basic rights and the general rule of law, and, vitally, it gave
increased recognition to the Habsburg crownlands and endorsed free
choice of language for their inhabitants (§ 4). The 1849 Constitution
(never really enforced) promoted the abolition of remaining feudal legal
relations, patrimonial jurisdiction and noble monopoly of state office
(§ 26, 27, 28, 100), and it established a bicameral parliamentary system,
with an upper chamber comprising deputies elected on a regional basis

(§ 40). However, this constitution, which was an imposed constitution and never assumed full legal force, was suspended in 1851: 1852 saw the abandonment of the plan for a centrally elected chamber of deputies and a partial return to estate-based deputation. This assumed more constitutionally ordered shape in the Oktoberdiplom of 1860, which, although sanctioning earlier federal rights and giving limited recognition to regional assemblies (Art. 1), stated that laws had to be passed and ratified by the *Kaiser*. Subsequently, this system was revised in the Februarpatent introduced by Schmerling in 1861. This document, which in itself was intended to avert a full constitutional reform of the state, established a bicameral imperial council, containing imperial nominees and elected representatives of the crownlands. It was, however, only in 1867 that the representative constitutionalism initiated in 1848 firmly took root in Austria, and that concessions to the nobility were tempered. In 1873, parliamentary supremacy was consolidated and by 1907 reforms were conducted to ensure the authority of parliament and to introduce universal manhood suffrage. Even states that adopted relatively liberal or at least moderate conservative constitutions, such as Spain after 1845, retained a constitutional model preserving regional and local/territorial power. Notably, the Spanish constitution of 1845 instituted a split legislature, including an upper chamber, or senate, to which the nobility had privileged access (Art. 15), and this ultimately obstructed progressive reform and left power in the hands of personally appointed cabinets.

In each of these cases, a constitutional pattern developed after 1848 which ensured that political power rested with a monarchical executive, supported by groups endowed with hereditary privilege, and in which the role of parliamentary assemblies did not, in all respects, conclusively exceed the representative dimension of earlier dualistic constitutions. Although they reflected the growing centralization and nationalistic construction of society by recognizing social agents as obtaining formally equal status under law, the constitutions instituted at the end of the revolutionary period pursued a policy of very minimal political centralism and regular inclusion, and they permitted heterogeneous social, regional and ideological elements to coexist as formative components of the state. In consequence, the states that were formed in most European societies after 1848 were states that had only a partially integrated constitutional form, that were inconclusively constructed as unitary public orders, and that still attached power to potent vested interests and allowed power to be channelled through patronage, favour and standing. Moreover, because of their inherent personalism, these states habitually struggled to detach power from private tenures, to institutionalize political opposition, or even to rotate government: as a result, they lacked flexible options for the application of power. These states were, in other words, states that were incompletely formed as states, and their ability to apply power autonomously through society was restricted.

Constitutions in the imperial era

The combination of the limited rule of law, the partial preservation of private elite privileges, and the underlying minimalism of post-1848 constitutions ultimately provided a partial template for the constitutions of the imperial era, which were formed in the latter decades of the nineteenth century. This claim of itself requires two qualifications. First, it is self-evident that in the later nineteenth century not every European state or society possessed uniform imperial features. Indeed, the concept of empire itself contained very different implications in different societies at this time. For example, Britain and France ruled over rapidly growing colonial empires, whereas Russia and Austria controlled more established dynastic empires. After 1870, the newly formed German state invoked the notion of empire to legitimize a process of unified nation building and national-territorial consolidation. In contrast to this, Spain lost most of its empire in the course of the nineteenth century. Italy was excluded from the race for colonies until the late nineteenth century, and it did not acquire substantial dominions until after 1912. In consequence, it is questionable whether the concept of an imperial age can be applied across Europe as a whole. Nonetheless, it is proposed here that certain characteristics, with very strong variations, were common to European societies in the later nineteenth century, and that all, however diversely, were pervasively shaped by factors connected with imperialism. Notably, most European societies of this time, propelled by increasingly rapid industrial and technological transformation, were generally marked by territorial concentration and expansion, within one newly unified agglomerate of states or in colonies overseas. Moreover, most states were shaped by the reality or the growing expectation of extensive colonial annexation. As a result, most states used imperial slogans to produce symbolic legitimacy, and, vitally, by the 1890s the policies of major European states were increasingly defined by conflicts of interest and influence with other imperial blocs. In particular, these expansionary tendencies had the general result that most European states witnessed heightened requirements for social control and mobilization, and the imperial era in general witnessed a rapid rise in the intensity and penetration of statehood. To this extent, it is possible to discern certain common features of European societies in the imperial era, and to observe ways in which each state was affected by imperialism.

Second, in addition, it needs to be very clearly noted here that in respect of electoral enfranchisement, guarantees over procedural order in legislation and general legal rule, most constitutions of the imperial period reflected a *very substantial inclusionary advance* on the first post-1848 constitutions. Indeed, the beginning of the imperial period after 1870 normally saw a striking acceleration in the process of political inclusion and intensification in European societies. European states of this era usually pursued more committed policies of unitary institutional consolidation, and in most settings the basic executive and ministerial structure of the state gained rapidly heightened integrity against particular bearers of power. Moreover, most constitutions of imperial Europe, with significant variations, promoted the tentative beginnings of mass-political organization, and an increase in parliamentary competence and party-political organization and inclusivity usually accompanied this process. Throughout Europe, thus, the imperial period brought both an extension of national franchises and a correlated consolidation of domestic statehood.

Despite this, however, the constitutions of European states in the imperial period remained shaped by constitutional minimalism and by a residual acceptance of elite pluralism as a basic foundation of public order. Indeed, in many cases the constitutions of imperial states were technically designed to stabilize the state as a restricted apparatus, able both flexibly to balance different elite groups and personal interests in its structure and to preserve a thin executive structure above the antagonistic conflicts of civil society, which possessed increasing political relevance.

Like earlier constitutions, the primary characteristic of the constitutions of the early imperial era was that they produced a synthesis of the disparate political elements of emergent liberal societies, and they enshrined a set of legal arrangements in which privileged private interests could be integrated into a state apparatus that sanctioned the basic liberal principles of legal generality and uniformity. This fusion was made possible by the fact that states in the imperial era remained very loosely integrated states, which had renounced the categorical inclusionary pledges of republican constitutional doctrines, and their constitutions allowed great latitude in the definition of the state's direction. This was made possible by the fact, further, that conservative elites gradually secured clear and distinct benefits from the models of statehood that took shape in most of Europe in the wake of 1848, and the liberal proponents of centralized legal and constitutional order proved increasingly willing to co-operate with traditional elites and to accept a greatly attenuated version of their original ideals of state legitimacy. Most importantly, the early imperial period was the historical epoch in which the social forces (that is, the growing middle class) that had traditionally supported the central legal state began (although still not without tension and equivocation) consistently to accommodate the forces of political conservatism, which had traditionally opposed the central state and the general rule of law. As a result of this, first, the imperial era was a period in which models of constitutional statehood were promoted that fostered an alliance between traditionally statist and traditionally anti-statist groups within society. Second, notably, it was a period in which enthusiasm for the central state became gradually integral to common conservative outlooks, so that (at least intermittently) a conceptual union of the two forces that had previously vied for influence in the process of state formation was established. Third, it was a period in which traditional liberal policies of legal regularization and codification were pursued in an attitude of strategic placation towards conservative groups, and in which even the more systemic drafting of economic laws and singular rights retained a conciliatory dimension and did not sweep away the traces of seigneurial privileges. Owing to these tendencies, in fact, most states of the imperial era remained weakly unified states, and, following varying patterns, their appeasement of vested elites persistently obstructed their formation as structurally integral public actors, able to utilize their power at a high level of general intensity.

Italy

In Italy, for example, after the hasty and haphazard process of national unification in the early 1860s the formal constitution remained unchanged from 1848, and, supplemented by the national legal reforms of 1865, the Statuto Albertino of Piedmont-Sardinia was extended to form the internal legal foundation of the unified Italian state. As discussed, the Statuto was a skeletal, flexible constitution, and, apart from its provisions for constitutional monarchy and its limited guarantees for personal rights, its commitment to a determinate institutional order was limited. Under this document, a governmental system emerged that combined aspects of liberal constitutionalism and the basic elements of representative democracy: that is, it guaranteed the rule of law, a constrained monarchical executive, and rights of personal economic autonomy, and it endorsed a limited (although still significant) representative-democratic parliament, albeit based in a very small franchise, countervailed by an appointed senate. It has been noted that in Italy a powerful parliamentary legislature developed with surprising rapidity under the Statuto, and the Statuto clearly facilitated the beginnings of a semi-democratic representative state (Di Lalla 1976: 116; Romanelli 1979: 37; Kirsch 1999: 129). Nonetheless, in some of its features, notably its ambiguous stipulations for ministerial responsibility (Arts. 65, 67), the Statuto favoured weakly integrated statehood. The constitutional order of unified Italy was essentially one that stabilized the state apparatus above society as a body of functional institutions with only restricted inclusionary substance and in which power was habitually transacted in closed personalistic fashion. Indeed, in the later nineteenth century, the Italian polity was defined by the emergence of a system of deeply personalized parliamentary governance widely identified as *trasformismo*, which was in large part attributable to the Statuto itself and its attenuated commitment to a strong and electorally accountable executive. This governmental model was pioneered under the progressive leadership of Agostino Depretis in the 1870s and 1880s, and until the extensive suffrage reforms of 1912 it served, intermittently, as the working basis of government in Italy. Under *trasformismo*, governmental decisions were made by the personal brokering of agreements between factions and informal groups in the parliament, and inter-party associations and diffuse cross-milieu alliances were routinely constructed to create a mandate for particular acts of legislation. In the absence of an evolved party democracy, *trasformismo* served within parliament as a technique for administering consensus in government and for garnering ad hoc support for the executive, and outside parliament as a technique for consolidating leading liberal interests in society more widely and for gradually cementing the authority of a powerful progressive class, which used parliament to guarantee its influence (Perticone 1960: 92; Salomone 1960: 110; Agócs 1971: 647). As such, *trasformismo* was a pattern of rule that was expected gradually to broaden the foundations of the unified state through the cautious widening of the executive elites and the very tentative inclusion of different milieux, factions and regional groups in decision-making functions, and so to create a national political culture to support the precariously constructed edifice of the new Italian state. However, owing to its personalistic structure, *trasformismo* strongly encouraged bureaucratic clientelism, and it prevented the emergence of a conclusively representative political system (Ghisalberti 2000: 189, 203). It also meant that much legislation was introduced without full parliamentary approval and that extra-parliamentary personal support for legislation was often vital: it prevented parliament from becoming the centre of political authority (Rebuffa 2003: 92–4). This mode of governance culminated in the periods in which Giovanni Giolitti held the office of prime minister in the 1890s and after 1900. These periods were marked by the conduct of government through informal accords and by the widespread use of personal contacts within a parliamentary elite to obtain support for legislation from increasingly disparate social groups and their delegates.

It should be noted that the programme of *trasformismo*, refined in the political strategies of Giolitti, was not entirely flawed. Although based in a limited, technical constitution, the Italian polity soon established itself as a moderately integrative state, and it outstripped many other states in its positive legislative capacities. In particular, liberal Italy showed notable success in the sphere of labour legislation. The first decade of the twentieth century witnessed a significant opening to the left, punctuated by Giolitti's legislation establishing workers' insurance, mediation in labour disputes and favourable conditions for moderate unions. Despite this, however, until 1912 the policies of *trasformismo* meant that the social foundations of the state necessarily remained local, particular and personalized, and, as the power of national government was sustained through isolated compromises, the state struggled to detach its power from particular personalities and prerogatives. Italian politics was marked by a weak distinction between government and opposition, and the rotation of power was often dictated by personal concerns and clientelistic favours. Moreover, the power of the Italian state was also subject to acute regional variation, and, despite the use of local prefects to centralize the administration, in many southern areas regional authorities remained outside the absorptive pull of *trasformismo* and basic functions of the central state were scarcely accomplished (Elazar 2001: 34–5). Both at a formal and at a material level, therefore, the constitutional state of liberal Italy was characterized by a relatively low level of generality and a moderate level of inclusivity. Most crucially, Italy remained a weakly integrated state, which struggled reliably to impose direction on society as a whole, and its constitution was clearly adjusted to its level of inclusionary power.

Germany

Some related features can be identified in the constitutional order of imperial Germany (*Kaiserreich*), which was established after Bismarck's work of national unification had been concluded in 1871. The 1871 Constitution, substantially based on the constitution of the North

German Confederation that Bismarck wrote while on vacation in late 1866, was also very flexibly worded, and it contained aspects of very different conceptions of statehood. Like other documents of this era, its essential intention was to stabilize a thin political superstructure above society, and to establish for society a limited apparatus of general coercion and legal control that did little to dislodge entrenched social positions. At one level, the Bismarckian constitution fell into the broad terrain of liberal constitutionalism: it used positivist ideas to guarantee the rule of law, it insisted on publicly disclosed procedures for legislation, and it balanced the supreme executive powers of the *Kaiser* with competences accorded to a council of federal delegates (Bundesrath) and an elected parliament (Reichstag), both of which possessed a portion of legislative power (Art. 5). It also, notably, endorsed a very advanced system of manhood suffrage. Despite this, however, the Bismarckian constitution was largely silent on the question of basic rights, and it mainly addressed rights as institutions under civil law. Moreover, this constitution had the distinctive feature that it left extensive powers – notably in fiscal and judicial functions – in the hands of the federal states, so that the imperial state did not in all respects act as the supreme organ of political power. In particular, it preserved the regional power of the Prussian aristocracy within the newly unified Reich. It ensured that Prussian interests were disproportionately represented in the Federal Council (Art. 6), which was under the fixed presidency of the Kaiser (in fact, the king of Prussia) (Art. 11). Further, under this constitution the regional parliament of Prussia (Preußischer Landtag), which was still (until 1918) based in the weighted franchise of 1849, had a prominent position, so that Prussian interests could be easily within and asserted against the Reich. The unified state of imperial Germany, in consequence, was also a weakly integrated state, and many basic institutions of state power were not fully brought under central state authority. Notably, the revenue-raising capacities of the state were low, the state's control of the judiciary was limited and the ability of the state to enforce policy across all regions remained precarious. It was also not until 1900 that Germany obtained a fully uniform Civil Code, and even this document clearly acknowledged the inner pluralism of the state by preserving certain elements of seigneurial law (Blasius 1978: 222; John 1989: 96).

In addition to this, the 1871 constitution of Germany, although in principle sanctioning a parliament elected by universal suffrage, constructed the state on a quasi-Caesaristic foundation, and it stabilized the executive (originally around Bismarck himself) as a semi-prerogative ministerial body. Indeed, the constitution contained provisions to ensure that the impact of parliamentary debate on national policy was limited, it placed strict limits on the legislative powers of the Reichstag (Art. 23), and it expressly prohibited the assumption of ministerial office by members of parliament (Arts. 9 and 21). Ministerial office was almost without exception assumed by appointees, whose accountability to parliament remained minimal (Mommsen 1990: 64), and because of this the thread of responsibility between the ministerial body and the Reichstag was tenuous. Moreover, the elected members of the legislature were not authorized to form governmental cabinets, or unilaterally to initiate legislative acts. As a result of this, in turn, the policies of the parties in the Reichstag normally centred on arrangements to create informal coalitions to prevent the passing of legislation, and political parties tended to be structurally weak and defensive. The parties of imperial Germany remained highly milieu-specific, lacking broad integrative force, to some degree rooted still in private associations, and capable only of performing negative functions in the legislative process.[1] Above all, in consequence, in imperial Germany state power was residually diluted by, or in fact not conclusively distinguishable from, local, regional and private authority, mechanisms for the routine rotation of governmental power were under-evolved and personalized, and the constitution necessarily resulted in government by a limited and semi-independent executive, placed above, and selectively interacting with, disparate private groups in civil society.[2]

It is habitually asserted that the state of imperial Germany was a strong state, able extensively to mobilize society and, in particular, to dictate economic policy to an unusual degree.[3] Owing to its personalistic design, however, by most reliable indicators (especially fiscal competence and judicial control) the state created by Bismarck was a weak state. Throughout the imperial era, in fact, there existed certain crucial questions of social direction over which the state could not reliably legislate, and which were normally removed from the state's jurisdiction by the vested interests solidified at its core. The key example of this was

---

[1] This was Max Weber's view (1922 [1917]: 221).

[2] For one sample of the vast literature on the 'crippling' of political organs in imperial Germany resulting from the interpenetration of the political system with private associations, see Puhle (1970: 361).

[3] This is the myth propagated by the claim that imperial Germany was a Caesaristic political system based on a hegemonic agrarian/industrial coalition of 'rye and iron' which acted as a prerogative 'instrument for the co-ordination of organized interests and the control of the public sphere' (Stürmer 1974: 181).

fiscal legislation. One of the defining problems of imperial Germany was that the state struggled to reform its taxation system and, in particular, reliably to impose inheritance tax. Attempts uniformly to impose such taxes, most notably in the unified liberal-conservative parliamentary coalition of 1907–9, led to the dissolution of government. A further matter which resisted legislative control was the status of Prussia within the empire. Both the reform of Prussia's internal political apparatus and its hegemony in the Reich were questions that could not easily be addressed or altered under the existing constitution. In short, imperial Germany was a key example of an incompletely formed state in which local and private elites assumed powerful positions within the central state.[4] In these positions, these elites at once utilized the state for their own objectives and residually impeded the full consolidation of the state as a set of autonomous institutions possessing a positive monopoly of legislative power.

Spain

Such characterization can be applied still more strictly to Spain in the imperial era. After a series of constitutional experiments, including a short-lived republican interlude in 1873–4, Spain obtained a more enduring constitutional order in the restoration constitution of 1876. Like other constitutions in the imperial era, the 1876 Constitution was a limited constitution, and it was strongly marked by a 'coexistence of diverse political conceptions' and by a reluctance to endorse one model of government as categorically valid (Sanchez Agesta 1955: 344). In the first instance, this document gave limited recognition to liberal conventions: it enshrined basic positive principles of general legal rule, it guaranteed a catalogue of rights (albeit subject to repeated suspension), and it placed partial legislative power in the elected Cortes (Art. 18). However, the progressive aspects of the constitution were counterbalanced by the fact that the power to convoke and dissolve the Cortes was accorded to the monarch, and the Cortes was organized on a bicameral model in which the elected parliament was checked by the senate, comprising, among others, royal family and appointees, and senior military, administrative and ecclesiastical figures (Arts. 21–22). Most importantly, it was a salient working feature of the Canovite

---

[4] Not for nothing has one historian observed that in imperial Germany the 'boundaries between private and public interest almost entirely disappeared' (Winkler 1972: 12).

constitution that it organized political representation and inclusion through the pattern of governmental *caciquismo*: that is, through a political structure in which the nomination of deputies for the Cortes was widely monopolized by leading families and members of the nobility in particular local constituencies, and nominees, or *caciques*, secured their hold on their constituencies through clientelistic offering of benefits and personal patronage. Owing to this system, which, as in Italy, served to maintain central government in a highly localized society, elections were often uncontested or their outcomes dictated by informal pacts or effective transactions, and real legislative power was not wrested from private social milieux. As a result, political parties were weak, power was concentrated in the hands of a parliamentary oligarchy and state power was routinely traded as an object of patronage and even subject to clientelistic 'enfeoffment' (Varela Ortega 1977: 354). The Spanish state of the imperial era, in consequence, was also a state that constructed and applied its power at a relatively low level of inclusion and generality, it was based in a complex fusion of public and private functions, and it struggled to assume a monopoly of coercive power in society (Kern 1974: 75). Indeed, the Canovite constitutional apparatus was a striking example of a political order in which the residues of seigneurial power persisted in the institutions of a liberal state.[5] Through this coexistence, the state incorporated inner reactionary forces that decelerated its full formation as a state, and the constitution merely preserved a thin stratum of governance above society that substantially protected and relied on potent private interests.

The constitutional cases of Italy, Germany and Spain, in sum, demonstrate how, during the earlier part of the age of imperialism, many European states were structurally founded in a pattern of low legislative capacity, weak national/territorial control and highly uneven social inclusion. These states typically developed a minimalist positivist constitutional apparatus that ensured that many areas of government both within the state and outside the state remained unregulated, and certain societal privileges were not subject to generalized legal jurisdiction. This dimension of states in the imperial era was not an oversight. Nor, as is often remarked, was it a refusal, on the part of the architects of the imperial constitutions, to adopt a clear political direction (Mommsen 1990: 11–38). On the contrary, the preservation of inner and outer

---

[5] The term *caciquismo* in fact originates in relations of vassalage in Latin America. On this see Tusell (1976: 75); Ortega (1977: 353–4).

pluralism in the state was a distinct and pragmatically necessary strategy of state construction at this juncture in European history: it was a technique for forming states around a pragmatic working balance between the disparate liberal and conservative groups that the politically relevant constituencies of European societies contained, and it was precisely the low intensity of the states designed through this balance that enabled these states to perform even basic functions of general societal regulation. The most extreme cases of weak statehood in the imperial period, exemplified by the newly unified polities of Italy and Germany, were induced by the fact that states were forced rapidly both to elaborate constitutional devices to extend political power across new nations and to harden societal foundations for their functions of statehood at the same time. These states, in fact, were called on to perform extensive inclusionary functions of statehood before they had been consistently solidified as states, and they were required to accomplish this in societies to which the experience of unitary statehood was new. In such instances, states simply relied on local structures and existing elites to perform functions of governance, and they remained embedded in a social reality in which the use of central power only became possible through a coalescence of the state with local, private or clientelistic sources of order. A further, more uniform, cause of the weakness of states in the imperial era, though, was the fact that in many instances key actors in the earlier processes of state formation had not been able to subordinate the nobility and other collective sources of privilege to the central power of the state. In the earlier nineteenth century, as discussed, many states had only selectively introduced a system of general rights under law, they had only precariously enforced uniform legal principles through society and they had continued to sustain their functions by relying largely on the remnants of a dualistic constitution, in which private and public authority were informally but necessarily conjoined. This model of statehood then persisted, in some societies, into the imperial era. For this reason, the constitutions of many states in the later nineteenth century were of necessity *residually dualistic*: that is, they were polities in which powerful social groups were not fully incorporated within the state, and in which constitutions bought acquiescence for the central state by placating dominant social actors, whose power then wandered irregularly between the private and the public domain.[6]

---

[6] Again, an extreme example of this is Germany, where Bismarck frequently toyed with the idea of replacing the parliamentary system with a corporate body.

The minimalism of these constitutions was an institutional design that allowed a loose fusion of liberal and conservative interests in the fabric of the state, and, in so doing, it facilitated the basic circulation of uniform reserves of power through society. To ensure that this was possible, however, these states were forced to ensure that many questions of social privilege, status and hereditary entitlement were not directly politicized and many exchanges through society were not assimilated into the functions of the state.

Russia

The most extreme example of a nineteenth-century state founded in a fragile constitutional balance between central administrative organs and vested local powers was late imperial Russia, where the relation between high conservative social groups (i.e. the nobility) and the central monarchy assumed highly distinctive features. In the first instance, the middle decades of the nineteenth century were witness in Russia to a pervasive expansion of the state administration: this was widely driven by enlightened civil servants who aspired to create a social order based in regular legal and administrative procedures (Emmons 1968: 9; Lincoln 1982: 201). As in other European countries, the expansion of the central state administration brought the Russian ruling dynasty into direct conflict with the old nobility, whose authority was still founded in noble immunities, patrilineal privilege and extensive seigneurial jurisdictional rights, including rights of feudal tenure over serfs. It is against the background of this conflict, then, that the Great Reforms of 1861 were conducted: in emancipating the serfs, the reforms at once weakened the material basis for noble privilege and jurisdiction in Russian society and extended the power of the state administration into parts of society formerly under aristocratic jurisdiction.[7] In belated symmetry with other European societies, therefore, the central state in Russia consolidated its power through an assault on the local privileges and patrimonial rights of the nobility, especially in the courts of law. Indeed, the emancipation of 1861 was followed almost immediately, under the Judicial Reform statute of 1864, by a process of far-reaching legal transformation, in which provincial law courts were restructured, judicial arbitrariness was restricted, judicial rulings were made public, the judiciary became

---

[7] On the hostility of the nobility to the reforms and the ultimate triumph of the state bureaucracy, see Yaney (1973: 31); Field (1976: 292); Wcislo (1990: 43).

independent and (eventually) professionalized and the principle of
equality before law was reinforced (Yaney 1973: 389; Lincoln 1990: 62,
105). This statute, a key element in the body of reform legislation, played
the most crucial role both in limiting the autocratic power of the
monarchy and in reducing the local or private power of the nobility.

Significantly, the expansion of state power prior to and after the Great
Reforms left the Russian state with depleted fiscal and administrative
capacities. This was due, in part, to the fact that the central administration now assumed responsibility for functions previously conducted at a
local level by the nobility: it thus required increasing reserves of public
finance to fulfil these functions. However, the fiscal side of this problem
also had earlier causes: throughout the early 1860s the treasury had been
in high alarm over the level of public debt incurred during the Crimean
War (Starr 1972: 222). One outcome of both these processes, however,
was the introduction in 1864 of a reform that established self-governing
assemblies (*zemstvos*) in different localities, which were to be elected by
the local population in three distinct estate-like bodies. Primarily, the
zemstvos performed administrative functions in regions whose traditional hierarchical order had been destroyed: the *zemstvos* assumed
functions in respect of local administration and taxation previously
performed by the nobility. Additionally, however, the *zemstvos* also
gradually assumed quasi-constitutional features, and they began to act
as representational counterweights both to the state administration and
to the prerogative powers of the imperial dynasty.

It has been widely observed that the Great Reforms were not intended
to destroy the Russian nobility. The nobility's loss of seigneurial jurisdiction was softened by special tax exemptions and by guarantees for
noble privilege in local government, and in 1902 legislation was even
passed to assist the nobility in paying mortgage debts and to preserve
noble monopoly of land ownership.[8] However, the reforms clearly led to
a political marginalization of the nobility. Indeed, after the reforms many
nobles were forced to seek new modes of political representation, and
many began to engage in the politics of the *zemstvos*, often forming loose
alliances with the gentry and other social factions.[9] As a result of this, the
zemstvos became a key forum for the diffuse anti-autocratic political
tendencies that gained momentum in the last decades of imperial Russia,

[8] See Ascher (1988: 28) and, on the laws of 1902, Becker (1985: 85).
[9] See the account in Manning (1982a: 28, 43). It is calculated that nobles amounted to
above 40 per cent of *zemstvo* membership (Galai 1973: 7).

and many nobles and members of the gentry drifted through the *zemst-vos* into the Liberation Movement, an influential political grouping that urged moderate constitutional reform in the imperial state. The activities of the *zemstvos* in this movement culminated in the Zemstvo Congress of 1904. This Congress witnessed the formation of a pro-reform constitutionalist majority among different groups in the *zemstvos*, which demanded the establishment of limited representative government throughout Russia. The political intentions of the *zemstvo* activists have often been questioned, and their constitutional ambitions were clearly still, in part, intended to secure elite privileges outside the central state, and to fight incorporation of the nobility within the state bureaucracy: they are viewed as forming a constitutionalist group that at once rejected the central bureaucracy and yet also normally fell short of endorsing fully democratic constitutional reform (Manning 1979: 51). Ultimately, however, the *zemstvos* played a substantial role in the half-completed constitutional revolution of 1905, and in particular they helped to force the tsar to commit himself to the October Manifesto in that year. This Manifesto, extracted against a background of general strikes and rising political insurrection, promised fundamental civil freedoms for the Russian population, committed the tsar to an extension of suffrage and the convocation of a national parliament (Duma), to be ascribed fixed and irrevocable legislative powers. This period of national reform finally resulted in the Fundamental Laws of April 1906, which, while reserving substantial veto powers and rights of ministerial control for the tsar, created the first basic constitution and system of national representation for the modern Russian state.

The emerging constitutional order of late imperial Russia, thus, contained important parallels to other states in the imperial era, and it, too, hinged structurally on a precarious balance between centrist interests concentrated in a state bureaucracy and the diffuse privileges of powerful elites. In Russia, to be sure, the central bureaucracy was more markedly personalistic and prerogative than that of other states: notably, the imperial family utilized the civil service more strictly as a chain of autocratic command. In many respects, moreover, gentry constitutionalism was stimulated, through the *zemstvos*, in a fashion reminiscent of aristocratic resistance in other European states at an earlier historical juncture. Indeed, the term 'gentry fronde' to describe the constitutional activities of the *zemstvos* is especially apposite: this description captures both the anti-imperial and the anti-centralist motivations of the *zemstvos*, which remained a source of simultaneously progressive and reactionary opposition both in the authoritarian imperial state and in the reformed imperial state after 1905.[10] Nonetheless, the constitutional force of the *zemstvos* again illustrates how the structure of states in the imperial era remained broadly rooted in a constitutional dualism, in which the administrative power of the state was ambiguously both supported and fragmented by politically suspended members of the nobility and other corporate elites. In fact, Russia had the distinction among imperial states that its failure internally to accommodate landed elites caused an unusual, although temporary, fusion between some sectors of the nobility and the gentry and more progressive constitutional/democratic sectors of Russian society.

France

Partial alternatives to these patterns of diffuse or weakly consolidated statehood existed in France and Britain: in societies, that is, in which by the later nineteenth century states possessed a relatively high level of public density and political inclusivity. In this context, the briefly worded constitution of the Third Republic of France, introduced in 1875, occupied the middle ground in the spectrum of governmental integrity in different European societies. This constitution, naturally, stood outside the category of imperial constitutions as, after 1870, France was a republic, and, although it (initially) contained a powerfully symbolic presidency reflecting the interests of the majority monarchists in the National Assembly, it was founded as an alternative to the Caesaristic design of the Second Empire. Nonetheless, the founding document of the Third Republic shared some common features with other constitutions of the age of empire. For instance, first, this constitution contained no formal catalogue of rights, and it located questions of rights in the sphere of civil law and administrative law. Second, this constitution allowed great flexibility and tactical minimalism in the definition of governmental legitimacy. Although it committed itself by legal resolution to the core doctrines of general suffrage and republican rule, the representative system of the Third Republic was originally centred around a powerful second chamber, designed to restrict the force of popular democracy (Mayeur 1984: 57). Above all, the founders of the Third Republic symbolically refused to define the state as a localized centre of sovereignty. Indeed, prominent commentators on the constitution concluded that the Third Republic reflected a strictly limited, pragmatically realistic and decisively

---

[10] For this term, see Manning (1982a); Fallows (1985).

anti-Jacobin conception of popular sovereignty, in which sovereign power was commonly vested in diverse institutions of state and not derived from one primary formative act or one unitary expression of sovereignty (Durkheim 1950 [1900]: 85; Duguit 1921 [1911]: 495). Underlying the transition from the Second Empire to the Third Republic, in fact, was a widespread and deeply rooted conceptual process, in which earlier doctrines of national sovereignty and legislative power were transformed into a gradualist and highly positivistic theory of 'republican legalism', which perceived the formation of republican states as a process, not of spontaneous engagement, but of elite-led legal engineering and gradually inclusionary social 'pacification' (Nicolet 1982: 156–64).[11] The 1875 Constitution was thus marked by the initial sense that the stability of the state depended on the fact that it should – specifically – not be required to perform extensive functions of foundation or inclusion, and that the actual direction of government should not be prescribed in constitutionally exclusive principles.

In these respects, the 1875 constitution of France had a clear similarity with other constitutions of this era in that it was intended to institute a technical order of governance above the primary conflicts of society. At the same time, however, the constitution of the Third Republic clearly exceeded other constitutions of the imperial era in its exclusion of private groups from the state and in its ability to consolidate the state as a substantially public order. Vitally, in Article 6 the constitution made ministerial responsibility the cornerstone – or the 'essential element' – of the state, and it defined ministers, both particularly and collectively, as bearers of strictly public functions (Esmein 1928: 257). Moreover, although it rejected higher-norm provisions for control of statutes, it contained a limited entrenchment clause (Art. 8) to ensure that the public form of state could not easily be altered by simple legislative decisions. Indeed, the Third Republic, although sworn to the republican concept of popular sovereignty, also witnessed a tentative increase in support for external judicial control of sovereign power.[12] Owing to

---

[11] For examples of positivist republicanism, see Littré (1879: 444). Littré saw the *theoretical rule* of the people as coincident with the *factual rule* of bourgeois elites, guaranteeing the rule of law through society (Scott 1951: 99). On the Third Republic as an 'absolute republic', see Rudelle (1982: 289).

[12] After three decades of the Third Republic, leading constitutionalists acknowledged the 'political preponderance' of the legislature but argued that the lack of judicial control was *très regrettable* (Jèze 1925 [1904]: 385). Hauriou, although clear about the prescribed separation of judicial and legislative functions, also argued that 'control of the constitutionality of laws' was the 'logical consequence of the supremacy of the national constitution' (1929 [1923]: 267).

these principles, this constitution was also able to construct a state apparatus that was fully distinct from singular persons, to promote ideas of loyal opposition and to allow different political parties to rotate in the use of power. Above all, it created a ministerial executive that was designed to efface personal privilege from state power. Leading republicans of the 1870s, notably Jules Ferry, were able to observe the state of the Third Republic as an organ of 'general interest', which was fully separate from any personalistic or quasi-feudal obligations (Barral 1968: 278). Gradually, in fact, the 1875 Constitution provided effective positive foundations for the exercise of state power, it strengthened the distinction of the state from specifically embedded interests and it consolidated the state as a deeply inclusive public order. In consequence, the Third Republic gradually evolved capacities for applying laws at a higher level of generality and inclusivity than many other European states. Unlike the governments of Spain, Germany and Italy, it was able positively to extend the sphere of legal-political regulation, across regional and functional differences, to incorporate a large array of societal exchanges. In particular, this can be seen in the packages of labour law introduced by republican parties in France: most notably the laws of 1884, which authorized the free formation of trade unions and sanctioned rights of economic coalition, the industrial arbitration law of 1892, and the moderate syndicalist laws before and after 1900 that promoted municipal labour exchanges (*bourses du travail*) to co-ordinate union organization and worker education. By 1899, in fact, the Waldeck-Rousseau administration brought a socialist minister, Alexandre Millerand, into government. On these grounds, the Third Republic was an example of a state whose constitution, at least intermittently, led to a rise in both the integrity of its institutions and the inclusive force of its laws.[13] In this instance, the limited commitment to republican integration in the 1875 Constitution provided a foundation for a sustainable and increasingly deep-structured polity, in which the state's controlled and selective inclusion of society widened its capacities for the general circulation of power.

Britain

A further alternative pattern of constitutional formation and polity building in the imperial age was evident in the constitution of Britain.

---

[13] An important article on this point stresses that the republican governments of the Third Republic were able to legislate 'independently of elite interests' (Friedman 1990: 152).

Imperial Britain was a state that possessed a relatively high level of administrative solidity (Chester 1981: 362), and it was capable of utilizing statutory power, to a large degree, in autonomous and uniformly inclusive fashion. By the late 1880s the British state had, through a series of quasi-constitutional reforms, acquired a broad-based male franchise (although one still including only roughly half of all working-class men), and it at once drew support from and applied power to society in relatively generalized and recursive style. In addition, the British state was strengthened by the fact that it possessed the beginnings of a mass-democratic party system, in which political parties were directly involved in the formation of governments, and it was able to control social inclusion and parliamentary mobilization by means of two (usually) quite simply differentiated party-political factions. The fact that there were only two major parties until after 1900 meant that the British state could control its reactions to matters for legislation, that the distribution of power between government and opposition could be procedurally simplified, and that the ascription of power to individual politicians occurred at a low level of personalism and without disruptive resonances for the state as a whole. Through these processes, the state obtained an apersonal structure under public law, which greatly inflated the mass of effective power that it contained. Even theorists close in some questions to conservative principles, such as Dicey, were adamant that the 'sovereignty of Parliament and the supremacy of the law of the land' were 'the two principles which pervade the whole of the English constitution' (1915 [1885]: 406).

Of particular significance in the British constitution of the later nineteenth century was the fact that the strength of the parliamentary apparatus, which had been established at a very early stage, meant that liberal and conservative interests acted as coexistent elements of the state, and highly particularist interests of regional conservatism did not drag too heavily against the state's legislative operations. As a consequence, the British state possessed an advanced degree of autonomy in its legislative policies, and it was able consistently to draw most questions of social distinction and most objects of social contest under positive state jurisdiction. Crucially, for example, Britain had already begun to impose permanent income tax in the 1840s, and throughout the imperial era the British state was clearly able to implement statutes that weakened power attached to aristocratic land tenures. Furthermore, by the late nineteenth century the British state, like its counterpart in France, had also begun to assimilate aspects of the labour movement. Throughout the latter stages of the nineteenth century the more repressive legislation for control of labour markets was repealed, and trade union activity was decriminalized in the early 1870s. By the first decade of the twentieth century the labour movement had been integrated, via the Liberal Party, into the margins of the political mainstream.[14] The expansion of the state's statutory authority, however, culminated in the policies of Lloyd George in the years before the First World War. In particular, this was reflected in the reform of the House of Lords (1911), which cut the veto powers of the Lords, in the 1909 budget which aimed to increase inheritance tax and in the cautiously labour-friendly packages introduced in the National Insurance Act of 1911 and the Trade Union Act of 1913. None of this is meant to say that in the imperial period the British state was not an inherently conservative state. Indeed, it is patently clear that in Britain in the imperial era the aristocracy possessed privileged access to the executive. However, it was a conservative state in which conservatism had fused with liberal statism at an early formative stage, and it was able independently to legislate against entrenched interests of conservative elites. Indeed, the fact that as early as the eighteenth century a preliminary variant on liberalism, Whiggism, had been able to assert itself in Britain as a potent outlook meant that by the imperial era liberal concepts of statehood were able to traverse and include a number of social groups, and most factions in society were prepared (notionally, at least) to accede to a concept of the state as an inclusive public order under general laws. In legislating positively over labour, then, liberal politicians were also able gradually to lower the inclusionary threshold of the political system in society, and internally further to solidify and generalize the state's foundation and to harden it against particular elites. To a greater extent even than that of France, the nineteenth-century British constitution provided for a strongly integrated state which was able to use political power at a reasonably high (although surely not unconstrained) level of autonomy and generality.

On balance, through the imperial period the strongest states (that is, the states able to apply their power at the highest level of general autonomy and inclusion and statutory positivity) were those states that possessed the most elaborate and embedded constitutional structure, usually containing, to a limited degree, inclusionary elements of mass democracy. States that fell short of semi-democratic constitutionalism normally encountered

---

[14] On this gradual process, see Steinfeld (2001: 192); Curthoys (2004: 236). One historian has described the Liberal Party as 'the principal working-class party' in late nineteenth-century England (Tanner 1990: 19). On the importance of the partial integration of labour as a source of post-1918 democratic cohesion, see Luebbert (1987).

obstructions in their use of power, and they were only able to apply power in diffuse and selectively partial manner through society. Early democratization in the imperial era, in other words, was not a process that externally transformed already existing states: it was an internal dimension of the longer process of state building and political abstraction, and the construction of powerful and socially integrative states increasingly presupposed their inner formation around an early democratic model.

The First World War and the tragedy of the modern state

The transformation of statehood 1914–1918

If the revolutionary period 1789–1848 was the period of most intense state building and constitutional formation in modern Europe, the second period in which the foundations of modern statehood underwent expedited consolidation was the First World War. During the First World War, the integrative functions of modern statehood were dramatically extended, and states were forced to develop constitutional mechanisms to exercise their power at an exponentially heightened level of societal inclusivity and generalization. Indeed, it was in the course of the First World War, arguably, that the longer dynamic of state formation underlying the history of European societies approached completion, and states began to operate as evenly inclusive and politically monopolistic actors, forced to incorporate all members of society in broadly parallel procedures, and capable of mobilizing large volumes of power to sustain their functions.

Different European states experienced and were constitutionally affected by the First World War in a number of different ways. Manifestly, in the course of the war all European societies experienced a very steep increase both in the general density of statehood and in the volume of social exchanges regulated by and transacted through the state. This expansion of state authority was caused, first, by the fact that states were required to mobilize resources and manpower for the war. In consequence, the state's objectives of economic regulation and control grew to unprecedented levels between 1914 and 1918, and the level of state-sector employment and the number of governmental departments required to perform military and related functions of co-ordination rose in concomitant manner.[15] Moreover, this broad increase

---

[15] In the case of Britain, W. H. Greenleaf calculates that in 1914 there were twenty clerks for the purchase of munitions, and that in late 1918 the same office had a staff of over 65,000 (1983: 57).

in the political density of society also meant that states required more and more revenue, and monetary reserves were channelled through the state to a hitherto unimagined degree.[16] As a result, the war brought deep changes in the fiscal regimes of most European states, it raised the capital requirements of states to levels unknown in pre-1914 societies, and it necessarily burdened different states with extremely high rates of public debt, and so forced them constantly to alter and maximize their sources of revenue.[17] In addition to this twofold intensification of the public domain, however, European states were also transformed during the war by the fact that, in conjunction with their need to increase revenue, they were required selectively to direct capital (from both public and private sources) into sectors of the economy relevant for the war. In the latter stages of the conflict, in fact, they were called on directly to manage labour supply, to regulate industrial production and to negotiate with different parties in the production process. In this respect, states also began to act as integral partners of big business, and state officials assumed responsibility, for the sake of the war effort, for commissioning products and even for steering business policy and investment and directly shaping industrial design. This had the further result that state executives were required strategically to intervene in antagonisms arising from production, and they were expected in many instances to assume immediate powers of palliative arbitration in hostilities over production and military supply. The state, thus, became an effective party in industrial conflict.

The general outcome of this multidimensional expansion of state functions after 1914 was that European states – albeit with substantial national differences – dramatically elevated their levels of interpenetration with society, and the intersection of state power with previously private exchanges increased beyond recognition. Moreover, as they assumed directive and arbitrational responsibility for production and labour-market regulation, European states widened their periphery to allow a range of new social groups, using different channels of influence, to assume influential political positions close to centres of power, and immediately to impact on statutes and public policy. For this

[16] On Britain in this respect see Cronin (1991: 60–1). On Germany see Feldman (1997: 25–51). On Italy see Vivarelli (1991a: 429); Forsyth (1993: 101–24).

[17] For Britain it is calculated that the internal debt was as high as £6,142 million by 1919 (Tomlinson 1990: 51). Britain, however, was relatively effective in covering wartime outlay through tax. It covered 20 per cent of expenditures through taxation. Italy covered only 16 per cent, whereas France and Germany covered less than 2 per cent, and financed the war through loans (Forsyth 1993: 69).

reason, traditional distinctions of status became less important, and the state's growing mobilization of society meant that it relied on and included different social groups more evenly and equally. In itself, however, the growing structural coalescence between the state and other parts of society had a series of further, more specific consequences.

First, for example, one result of the First World War was that political parties quickly assumed vital importance for the stabilization of national regimes. As discussed, in many pre-1914 states political parties had played a limited role, and the political apparatus had normally been constructed above the parties in the legislature, which, in consequence, were ordinarily marked by low levels of integration and organization and high levels of clientelism. During the war, however, the wider convergence of state administration and private activity meant that the influence of parties grew rapidly, and even states with under-evolved party systems began to depend on societal support mediated through parties: most states in the First World War experienced a very rapid transition from limited-constitutional to party-democratic statehood. For example, after the first mass elections of 1913, Italy saw the consolidation of a mass franchise, an increase in the professional organization of political parties and dramatically rising levels of societal politicization during the war. A similar tendency towards increased party organization, from a more advanced starting point, was evident in Britain. In Germany, likewise, the unity and influence of the Reichstag increased substantially after 1914, and by the end of the war, despite the unwillingness of the Kaiser to sanction a democratic constitution, parliamentary parties had begun semi-independently to organize a cross-party pro-democratic majority (Bermbach 1967: 41; Grosser 1970: 150). Notably, moreover, those political parties representing organized labour assumed particularly heightened utility for states during the war. These parties provided vital integrative functions for belligerent states by acting as mechanisms of societal mobilization, penetration and co-optation between the state and the industrial workforce: the channels of communication between socialist parties and political executives were substantially widened in most countries after 1914. In Britain, for example, members of the Labour Party assumed cabinet office during the war. Indeed, in Germany, although the Social Democratic Party had been strategically excluded from governmental office before 1914, socialist politicians were able to acquire ministerial office before the end of the war, albeit only as defeat loomed in late 1918.

In addition to the rise of political integration through mass-political parties, second, the First World War also had more concrete daily implications for organizations representing the labour force, and it widened the intersection between state and society in other ways. As they were required to mobilize organized labour for the war effort, in particular, many states introduced legislation that offered trade unions legal and material rewards for their commitment to the military economy. In some cases, such legislation even began to accommodate unions in a tripartite decision-making apparatus, combining delegates of labour, business and government, and it gave unions a powerful voice in public deliberations over industrial policy. Naturally, much labour legislation in the war was simply coercive, and it was designed to reinforce prerogative planning and high-intensity industrial mobilization (see Rubin 1987: 13). Yet trade unions were able to use wartime pressures to negotiate a more advantageous legal position for their memberships, and some pieces of legislation effectively incorporated union delegates in state planning. The classic example of this was the German Auxiliary Service Law of 1916, which at once aimed at full civilian mobilization and compensated unions for their support of the war by enshrining a powerful body of material rights (i.e. rights of coalition and collective bargaining) for the union members. Indeed, in Germany it was openly suggested through the war that a new system of economic management was in the process of being established, in which state, unions and business were densely conjoined as co-directive economic organs: some analysts even billed this as a model of 'state socialism' (Zunkel 1974: 31).[18] However, the emergence of a diffuse system of socio-political co-optation was a characteristic, with variations, of all belligerent states. In France, for example, moderate unions were encouraged to found a system of shop-steward delegation to support the war effort, and instruments of conciliation and arbitration, based in a 'new relationship' between business and labour, were established to prevent strikes in sectors of production relevant for the war (Horne 1991: 15). In Britain, Lloyd George's Munitions Act of 1915 served simultaneously to apply coercive strategies to the labour market and to create more favourable preconditions for union bargaining.[19] Even in Italy, where the war

---

[18] Generally, see Feldman and Steinisch (1985: 19–20). On the political implications of the Auxiliary Service Law, see Kocka (1973: 115).

[19] On France and Britain see Horne (1991: 15, 208, 219). On the Munitions Act and its coercive content see Northcott (1917: 213).

saw the implementation of very repressive restrictions on labour mobility, the bargaining position of unions was progressively reinforced and unions played an important role in daily government (Tomassini 1991: 85; Vivarelli 1991b: 127). In addition to their reliance on support from traditionally included private elites, therefore, throughout the First World War many European states were also obliged to secure support from organizations of industrial production, both in management and in the labour force. In many cases, belligerent states were compelled to underpin their increased regulatory operations by entering unprecedented relationships with entrepreneurs, labour parties and trade unions, and they began, at both a political and an economic level, to generate a framework for incorporating both organized business and organized labour in the extended peripheries of state power. It has tellingly been observed, in consequence, that the war created a 'precorporatist experience' in many European societies (Adler 1995: 90), in which the formal apparatus of state administration intersected in haphazard fashion with a dense web of private associations and bargaining parties. Throughout the war, in short, European states at once expanded the range and density of their power. Yet they were also forced to found their widening functional structure on sporadic bargains between social groups originally external to the state, and they entered complex material exchanges in order to support and apply their power through society.[20]

Of further significance in this respect was the fact that the structure of European states changed during the First World War because the basic civil constituencies of states and political parties also experienced a dramatic alteration in the years of combat. Most obviously, as they were mobilized for the war (either in industry or at the front), the populations of European societies assumed a relationship of unprecedented *immediacy* to state power, and the war created societal settings in which members of different social strata and inhabitants of different regions encountered each other in relationships that were dictated by the state, that were relatively indifferent to societal status and private distinction and, vitally, that were unified by common hostility to military adversaries. The result of this was that, in many cases, the intensification and extension of state power in the war was accompanied by an incubated dynamic of socio-national homogenization or intensified *nation*

---

[20] The analysis proposed by Guido Mellis of the formation in Italy of a 'parallel' administration standing beside the 'state bureaucracy' is particularly illuminating in this instance (1988: 38).

building, in which the increase both in the evenness and the density of political inclusion was reflected in uniform patterns of emotional affiliation and societal convergence. This was especially prominent in more recently unified national societies, such as Italy and Germany, in which the war also drew people from previously unconnected regional locations into new experiences of proximity. The deep nationalization of European societies in the First World War, therefore, was closely correlated with the conclusive construction of the state as an evenly inclusive centre of political power, and the military intensification of political power after 1914 was formative for the final establishment of European nationhood.

In the First World War, thus, most European societies saw a dramatic leap in the density of statehood and in levels of social convergence around state structures. In most European societies it was only in the course of the war that the defining features of modern statehood – that is, the equal centring of society around state power and the even circulation of power through society by the state – finally became reality, and it was only through the wartime processes of mobilization and deepened inclusion that European states finally assumed the monopolistic capacity for transmitting power through societies in their entirety. The most pronounced overarching result of these overlayered processes, however, was that in European societies states finally approached a full monopoly of political power at a point in history at which this power was subject to dramatic transformation. The final formation of European statehood occurred at a moment when states were obliged exponentially to extend their functions, and principles of legal/political inclusion established in nineteenth-century polities no longer served to abstract political power and were no longer remotely sufficient to maintain and stabilize reserves of state legitimacy. Owing to the widening of the state periphery in the course of the First World War, specifically, post-1914 states were required to produce legitimacy by meeting expansive demands for the incorporation of citizens at once as material claimants, as participants in conflict over distribution processes in the economy and – significantly – as members of increasingly equal and intensely nationalized political communities. European states, therefore, finally assumed full legal and political centrality in different societies at a point where the inclusionary force of law alone was no longer adequate for the state's functions of political integration and generalization, and political inclusion presupposed ramified processes of material regulation and societal interpenetration. Indeed, it is of the highest importance to observe that the consolidation of statehood in the First World War was widely effected, not only through material bargaining, but also through the use of prerogative military legislation: in each belligerent society the incorporation of citizens – both politically and materially – in the periphery of the state was conducted through the use of mandatory emergency laws, legitimized by provisions for the suspension of normal judicial procedures and constitutional rights in conditions of military mobilization. In Britain, as discussed, the mobilization of the workforce was accomplished by means of strict labour-market control. In Italy, likewise, exceptionalist decrees were used to mobilize and integrate the labour force (Tomassini 1991: 59). In Germany and Austria, most importantly, the period of combat saw a dramatic expansion of the scope of emergency laws, especially in questions of economic control.[21] In the last years of the war, Germany was effectively governed by a quasi-dictatorial regime, in which executive power was substantially placed in the hands of the Supreme Military Command.

Throughout Europe, to conclude, the First World War generally created a societal conjuncture that had dramatically expansionist implications for the political system and ultimately fateful consequences for the longer and wider process of political abstraction underlying European state formation. First, the war meant that most European states assumed fully consolidated functions of statehood at a time when they were compelled to mobilize and integrate their constituencies in a number of different social dimensions. They were expected, not only inclusively to generalize their legal foundations, but also both to expand their allocation of material goods and, using corporate models, to co-opt and intersect with disparate private associations in order to pursue their allotted processes of inclusion. European statehood finally became a concrete historical condition at a historical juncture when its legal foundations were no longer equal to their functions, and the models of public law through which states had extracted their power from private activities had lost inclusionary purchase. In addition, moreover, the war meant that most European states first performed fully monopolistic functions of statehood by suspending the juridical patterns of self-restriction that had characterized the polities of the nineteenth century, and they were forced to secure their rapidly escalating functions of integrative control by abandoning the rights fabric which they had traditionally used for political inclusion and by pursuing a highly

---

[21] On Austria see pages 300–1 below. On Germany see Boldt (1980).

coercive – or exceptionalist – application of legal power. In short, the First World War saw the emergence of a legal-political order in which European states obtained vastly increased, highly generalized and deeply inclusive reserves of political power. Yet it also gave rise to a legal-political order in which they were required to legitimize and apply their power by at once expanding and dismantling the (already precarious) reserves of legal inclusivity and autonomy that they had constructed before 1914. The construction of European states as fully inclusive actors coincided with an erosion of the legal and political structure through which they had initially approached a condition of relative abstraction and autonomy. The final formation of states involved a negation of previous patterns of selective inclusion, and it widely coincided with a reduction in the abstracted autonomy of political power.

The transformation of statehood after 1918

The end of the First World War did not substantially diminish the material density of European states, and it did not induce a return to more legally restrictive patterns of political inclusion. On the contrary, the heightened co-ordinating and integrative functions accorded to wartime states were substantially carried over into the constitutional structure of the states formed after 1918. At a most obvious level, after 1918 all major belligerent states reacted to their rising levels of inclusivity by finally establishing a constitutional order according full legislative power to an elected parliament. After 1918, thus, all major belligerent states completed the representative inclusion of their male constituents, and they ascribed high prominence to political parties. In addition, however, most post-1918 European states were exposed to further events that created additional inclusionary pressures and expectations. Indeed, the aftermath of the war gave rise to a series of processes that placed additional integrative burdens on European states, and led to a further expansionary transformation of European statehood.

First, for example, the armistice of 1918 stimulated a large wave of unemployment in much of Europe, as, in economies that were already full of surplus labour caused by demobilized soldiers, companies that had either expanded too rapidly in the war or were bloated on public funds were suddenly forced to shed jobs, so that many people required material support. Second, the Bolshevik revolution of 1917 spread alarm through western European governments, and it fostered anxiety that failure effectively to sustain the system of material integration instituted during the war would have deeply destabilizing consequences, and might cause Bolshevik-style uprisings outside Russia. Many European states in fact experienced short-lived communist experiments after 1917. Examples of this were the short-lived Soviet Republic in Bavaria founded by Kurt Eisner in 1918, other communist insurrections in many German cities in late 1918 and the revolution led in 1919 by Béla Kun in Budapest. More generally, third, most European societies witnessed very high levels of industrial agitation after 1918, and even in under-developed capitalist economies the stability of capitalism as the primary mode of economic organization was intensely imperilled.[22] The combi-nation of these events had the outcome that the states emerging from the First World War were required to perpetuate their already highly charged functions of material inclusion, and they were forced to extend the quasi-corporate structures developed in the war in order to palliate economic hardship and to assuage apprehension about the revolutionary proclivities of their constituents.

In most European states, in consequence, the conditions after armi-stice led to a continuation of the techniques of social inclusion and control devised in the war. In some states, this occurred through rela-tively restricted (although still vitally significant) political reforms, which selectively retained some aspects of the wartime political appara-tus to bring towards completion a process of political enfranchisement that had already reached an advanced stage before 1914. Britain, where the division of the Liberal Party created an opening for a slow and more consistent inclusion (or at least appeasement) of the labour movement, was a key example of this pattern.[23] In Britain, rising demands for material inclusion caused by the war were softened in part by the already powerful absorptive function of political parties, and the British state was able to adapt to a substantially extended political franchise and a con-sonant rise in the power of labour without a fundamental transformation of its structural and legitimating foundations.[24] In other post-1918 societies, however, the dynamic of rapid political and material inclusion driven by the war gave rise to a process of constitutional transformation

---

[22] For example, after 1918 Spain had the fourth-highest level of industrial unrest in Europe (Martin 1990: 211).

[23] On the social reforms pioneered by Lloyd George to consolidate and extend the 'wartime consensus' after 1918, see Morgan (1979: 109).

[24] For example, the Lloyd George Liberals saw the extension of the franchise as a chance to expand their influence through a progressive but anti-socialist platform (Cowling 1971: 224).

that substantially redefined the established limits and substance of state-hood and necessitated rapidly revised sources of legitimacy.

In Italy, although the Statuto Albertino of 1848 remained in force after 1918 as the *formal* state constitution, the *material* constitution of the state was thoroughly altered during and after the war. This reform process had begun, as mentioned, with the franchise extension of 1912, and it continued with the institution of universal male suffrage in 1918. Through these rapid electoral reforms, the founding structure of the Italian state was deeply modified, and the inclusion of new social sectors in the political process, especially after 1918, brought an influx of new parties and politicians into parliament, which led to a full democratization of the political system and the abandoning of policies of *trasformismo*. Beginning with the 1919 elections, parties elected by national majorities assumed responsibility for forming the state executive, and the integrative role of parties, as organs for structuring and representing interests in civil society as a whole, expanded significantly. Owing to the parliamentary influence of the Italian Socialist Party (PSI), moreover, after 1918 the legal functions of the state were challenged by the fact that trade unions obtained access to state power, and they used this access to demand the continuation, under a democratic order, of elements of the wartime system of corporate political economy.

In this regard, it needs to be clearly stated that, unlike, diversely, Germany and Spain, post-1918 Italy did not experience a fully corporate revolution, and it did not obtain a constitutional system founded in corporate/material rights. Nonetheless, in the aftermath of the war it was vocally demanded, across divergent points on the political spectrum, that the liberal constitutional state in Italy should be expanded to include a material/corporate dimension, and the state should respond to its growth in political inclusivity by granting material and collective rights to economic actors, and even by extending its foundations to include full democratic control of the economy (Adler 1995: 123). On the political left this view was associated with the revolutionary syndicalist movement: theorists such as Sergio Panunzio, who later followed Mussolini into the Fascist movement, had in fact argued before the war that the modern state, promising political rights to an industrial workforce, could only preserve legitimacy if it evolved a corporate constitution – that is, a constitution able fully to incorporate the workforce in the state and to generate legitimacy by assuming and preserving an integral identity between state and society (Roberts 1979: 67). Subsequently, principles of reformist syndicalism assumed deep significance for the trade union movement during the *biennio rosso*: that is, the period of intense quasi-revolutionary activity after 1918. At this time, syndicates widely attempted to preserve for the labour movement the powers accorded to the unions in the war (Vivarelli 1991b: 129–30), and as early as 1917 both the Socialist Party and the trade unions urged the foundation of a democratic political system incorporating an element of economic parliamentarism. This varied left-oriented advocacy of a post-liberal corporate polity culminated between 1920 and 1922 in drafts for a national Council of Labour, supposed to act as an economic parliament sitting alongside the political legislature (Lanciotti 1993: 303–6). On the political right, similarly, as early as 1914, nationalist syndicalists such as Alfredo Rocco (later Mussolini's Minister of Justice) had also argued for a corporate reconstruction of the liberal legal order. Rocco asserted that in mass democracies liberal legal principles reflecting inviolable rights of private initiative had to be renounced, and he suggested that mass-democratic states could only acquire legitimacy by means of a legal order powerful enough to subordinate particular economic prerogatives to the national interest and to integrate and represent an identical national will overarching *all* productive dimensions of society.[25] Indeed, the short-lived national republic of Fiume in 1920 was also centred around a corporate constitution, drafted by Alceste De Ambris.

Through the post-1918 period, therefore, the Italian state underwent a twofold inclusionary transformation. At an institutional level, the executive, traditionally at once ultra-sensitive to parliamentary groups and detached from parliament owing to its obligation to the monarch, underwent far-reaching political reform in which it was expanded in order fully to incorporate mass-democratically elected parties. At a more societal level, organized economic groups acquired powerful and often destabilizing political positions, and the expectation grew, across varying political faultlines, that the formal constitutional functions of the liberal state had to be demolished in favour of a corporate constitutional system. This was shaped by the assumption, intensified through wartime experiences, that political integration of citizens was a multidimensional process, that substantial material laws and rights of material inclusion were required to produce sustainable legitimacy for the state, and that a truly legitimate constitution immediately reflected both the political and the material will of the people.

---

[25] This is the essence of the address given by Alfredo Rocco and Filippo Carli to the Congress of the Nationalist Association in 1914 (quoted in Spirito 1934: 75).

The key example of deeply transformative constitutional transition after 1918, however, was the case of Germany. After the end of the war and the collapse of the Hohenzollern monarchy in late 1918, the emergent democratic state in Germany experienced a number of profoundly incisive constitutional changes. All of these, in different ways, at once built on wartime corporate experiences and radically extended the inclusionary foundations of statehood.

First, as in Italy, the immediate aftermath of the war saw a fundamental change in the role of political parties in Germany. As discussed, in imperial Germany political parties played a role that was not absolutely central to the decision-making process: the link between the ministerial executive and the Reichstag was frail, and the legislative functions of the state did not fully rely on party-democratic initiative. Notably, in fact, the legal status of parties remained equivocal in Germany after 1918, and the 1919 constitution of the Weimar Republic did not classify political parties as public organs of the state (Art. 20). Moreover, certain counterweights to the power of democratically elected parties persisted under the 1919 Constitution: in particular, the executive was structured around a president elected by general plebiscite, who retained important powers of parliamentary veto. Nonetheless, after 1918, political parties became fully integrated elements of the German state: the Weimar Constitution bound the executive to strict principles of ministerial accountability before parliament (Arts. 54, 56, 59), and it enormously augmented the competences of the elected legislature (Art. 68).

Second, owing at once to its proximity to Russia, to the extent of its wartime quasi-corporate integration of the labour force, and to the pivotal role of the Social Democratic Party in the constituent assembly in early 1919, the emerging democratic state of post-1918 Germany was founded, almost by necessity, as a state with a pronounced *material constitution*. A number of different parties – primarily the Roman Catholic party (Zentrum), the Social Democrats and the left liberal party (Deutsche Demokratische Partei) – contributed to the constitutional drafting process, and the constitution finally reflected a compromise between the social groups speaking through these parties. However, the joint influence of the Social Democrats and the left liberals was particularly strong:[26] a fundamental aspect of the Weimar Constitution

---

[26] Represented primarily by Hugo Preuß, the left-liberal conception of the legitimate constitution had a strong corporate inflection. Preuß argued for 'organic social law' as the basis of the state (1889: vii), and he claimed that a legitimate state condensed its power and legitimacy, not solely in an abstracted legal personality, but in a corporate/material personality.

(ratified July 1919) was that it subjected previously private spheres of social exchange to far-reaching state jurisdiction, and, echoing the Russian constitution of 1918, it allocated rights as rights of productive groups and classes. In addition to the usual guarantees of property and free contract, which it enshrined in Articles 152–153, the Weimar Constitution gave expansive legal protection to the workforce (Arts. 157, 160–161), and it guaranteed rights of union activity, rights of co-determination at the place of work, and rights of shop-steward representation (Art. 165). In fact, it provided for the eventual nationalization of key industrial enterprises (Art. 153(2)), and it foresaw an overarching system of labour law, in which the state was expected to offer arbitration in industrial conflicts and to organize labour law around a progressively reconciled equilibrium between labour and management.[27] During the drafting of the constitution, it was even projected that trade unions would be accorded certain quasi-legislative functions in respect of economic management in the new democracy, and that unions would generate material legitimacy for economic statutes. These ideas of material constitutionalism had already assumed substance before the constitution was ratified: they were cemented through laws of late 1918, which instituted a system of collective bargaining and the creation of a Central Community of Labour (Zentralarbeitsgemeinschaft) in 1918, to act as a forum for inter-associational statutory negotiations over wages and production conditions. Indeed, the structure of the post-1918 German state had, to a large degree, been determined prior to the actual constitutional process, and representatives of business and labour had decided as early as late 1918 that the constitution was to accommodate corporate or even quasi-syndicalist arrangements (Albertin 1974: 660). However, these principles were formalized in the constitution in 1919. They were reinforced in 1920, with the passing of a co-determination law, and in particular in 1923, with the creation of a system of state arbitration in wage disputes, which in part integrated different actors in industrial negotiations into the state (Englberger 1995: 183).

In these respects the Weimar Constitution placed itself strikingly outside the theoretical perimeters of liberal constitutionalism and, reflecting diverse conceptions of political corporatism, it committed the Weimar Republic to a system of pervasively inclusionary welfare

---

[27] This never became reality. But on singular elements of this planned experiment, entailing objectively binding collective-bargaining agreements (1918), laws for a chamber of labour, and laws for labour tribunals (1926), see Bohle (1990: 14, 58, 133).

democracy, based in a broad catalogue of programmatic integrative rights. The Weimar Constitution was based in a highly ramified model of state inclusion, in which the principle of citizenship was extended from persons holding formal civil and political rights to persons holding rights of material entitlement, cross-class collaboration and stake holding in industrial production. Indeed, the labour-law sections of the constitution reflected the belief that the integration of citizens as holders of multiple political and economic rights could create a high degree of identity between state and society to support the state's authority and to ensure that the state was consolidated as a powerful and structurally legitimate actor.[28] These material rights in the constitution were grouped together as a corpus of collective objective entitlements, and, in principle at least, the legitimacy of the state was made contingent on the extent to which it could activate and enforce these rights, or to which associated claimants over material/participatory rights in civil society could be satisfied in their demands for the even distribution of material goods and the equitable arbitration of labour disputes. The pattern of material constitutionalism that emerged in the early Weimar years is often construed as a distinctive system of *organized capitalism*, in which trade unions and associations of big business, under the constitutionally defined supervision of the state, acted as democratic partners in economic legislation, whose legislative authority was deduced from, and transmitted through, the inclusive group rights of their memberships.[29] This system of interpenetrated capitalism was originally promoted on the political left: it was an important part of Marxist revisionist orthodoxy throughout and after the First World War.[30] However, it also had advocates on the right (Winkler 1973: 22). By the mid 1920s, in fact, even theorists originally in the liberal camp openly advocated economic organization including the 'institution of compulsory syndicates under state control' as the most effective means of economic control and stabilization (Sombart 1925: 64).

---

[28] Note here the impact of the works of Hugo Sinzheimer (1916). Sinzheimer argued that corporate agreements could form a material constitution on which to found the state and its legitimacy. He represented the SPD in the drafting of the Weimar Constitution.

[29] For discussion see Feldman (1974). For important critical analysis of this system, see Hartwich (1967: 18); Könke (1987: 46).

[30] The origins of this theory can be found in Rudolf Hilferding's revisionist analysis of class struggle as mediated through high-level negotiations between rival mass associations (unions and entrepreneurial bodies) (1947 [1910]: 505).

Third, although the provisions for economic regulation were the most distinctive aspects of the Weimar Constitution, perhaps the most impassioned intention of the constitutional fathers of the Weimar Republic focused, not on questions of material distribution, but on the construction of a fully abstracted and unified state in Germany, and on the elimination of regional privileges and variations retained under the imperial constitution. For this reason, the 1919 Constitution stipulated emphatically that the competences of federal states were subordinate to imperial authority (Art. 13), and it even made provision (fateful, as it transpired) for the imperial executive to use emergency powers in order to break federal resistance to central legislation. The insistent unitary conception of the 1919 Constitution was to no small degree a result of the fact that some framers of the constitution, notably Hugo Preuß and Max Weber, were prominent representatives of the late-imperial German liberal class. As such, they represented a social group whose reformist ambitions (and the ambitions of their parents) had been consistently thwarted by the reactionary force of Prussian conservatism. Because of this, they were strongly driven by the aim to create a strong central state, in which imperial power prevailed over the laws of the constituent states and the particularist pull of Prussian interests on the policies of the empire was terminated. Although closer to organic and decentralized ideals than his fellow constitutionalists of 1919, Preuß, in particular, argued that only a unitary constitution would make it possible, finally, to transform the German state into a generalized and inclusive national-democratic state, in which all Germans were equally assimilated, and he saw the final subordination of Prussia to the Reich as the last building block in the creation of an authentic national state.[31] To Preuß, as to other early-Weimar democrats, a constitution founded in principles of political democracy and democratic welfarism, evenly including all members of German society, appeared as the sole effective device for finally eliminating centrifugal elements from the political arena and for constructing the German state as an institution obtaining a monopoly of national power.[32] Just as German liberals in 1848 had viewed national

---

[31] After 1918, Preuß in fact advocated the dissolution of Prussia into smaller regions (1926: 438–9).

[32] As evidence, note Friedrich Naumann's speech in the National Assembly in February 1919 (1919: 100–5). Naumann, who presided over the drafting of the catalogue of basic rights in the Weimar Constitution, argued that the new constitution afforded an opportunity for 'bourgeois transformation', which was the precondition for the emergence of a people's state (*Volksstaat*).

democracy as a strategy of national state building, therefore, the German liberals and liberal socialists of 1918 saw welfare democracy as a technique for obtaining the same end.[33]

On each of these counts, the Weimar Constitution reflected a most decisive attempt, in distinct dimensions, to consolidate the structural density of the German state. It was designed firmly to ensure that the will of the German people (both in its political and its material dimensions) suffused the institutions of the state, and that all instruments of political authority in German society were concentrated in, and subject to, one integrally formed political order. Both of the two most salient (and closely linked) principles of the Weimar Constitution – its commitment to welfarism and its national unitarism – reflected the fact that the Weimar Constitution was designed to overcome the tradition of weak statehood in Germany, and it was intended to produce a model of state power that was at once politically and materially condensed and inclusive. National corporatism and administrative unitarism were thus perceived as complementary correctives to the tradition of weak statehood in Germany.

It is important to note in this that not all newly democratized states after 1918 opted for an expansive model of statehood, and some in fact strategically aimed to avoid the full material transformation of the political order and its sources of legitimacy. Important in this respect was the case of Austria. Like other European states, Austria had been subject to a regime of authoritarian-corporate control during the war. Moreover, after the war, a democratic constituent assembly was convoked in Vienna which, like its counterpart in Weimar, originally aimed to draft a constitution to sanction redefined rights of ownership, to place property under state jurisdiction and to provide for rights of corporate/economic co-determination at the place of work.[34] However, owing in part to disputes over the legal status of property, the final constitution of the First Republic of Austria (ratified in 1920) did not contain a distinct catalogue of rights, and it referred to the rights established in 1867 as the basis of fundamental law. In fact, the Austrian constitution of 1920, drafted largely by the liberal-socialist lawyer Hans Kelsen, was deeply shaped by the

---

[33] Preuß's intention to revivify the ideas of 1848 is widely recorded (Elben 1965: 68–9). The belief that a national state must be not only a legal state, but also a *social state*, was again expressed most emphatically in the writings of Naumann. He argued that rights must be applied as institutions performing a national-social function of integration (Vestring 1987: 265).

[34] This is documented in Ermacora (1980: 60); Berchtold (1998: 165).

sense that the primary function of the constitution was at once abstractly to preserve and place limits on the power of the state, to locate political authority on consistent legal foundations and to offer mechanisms to avoid the absorptive concentration of all societal contests around the state. At one level, this constitution provided for a very powerful legislature. It rejected both the doctrine of the strict separation of powers and the doctrine of the balanced constitution, and it designated the parliament (Nationalrat), acting jointly with a federal council, as the centre of all legislative authority (Art. 24): it opposed the split executive and the plebiscitary provisions typical of other post-1918 constitutions, and, although it provided for presidential office, the president was elected by parliament and federal council (Art. 38) and had restricted powers to dictate parliamentary procedure (Art. 28). At the same time, however, the 1920 Constitution contained the particular innovation that it established a constitutional court. This court, unlike the Supreme Court in the United States, was separated from the regular judiciary, and it was authorized procedurally to oversee all acts of parliamentary legislation. This institution also strengthened the legislature. It was designed both to ensure that federal law prevailed over the laws of particular states within the Austrian federation (Art. 140), so that the central state retained a full monopoly of political power, and to preserve the state against the use of prerogative measures by powerful social actors both within and outside the executive (Art. 139).[35] More importantly, however, the constitutional court was established as the effective guardian of the constitution, and it was given responsibility for determining the legality of all acts of state (including parliamentary laws, acts of the head of state and acts of other supreme federal and regional organs (Art. 142)) by ensuring that the norms established in the constitution acted as the foundation for all legislation.

Central to Kelsen's plans for the Austrian constitution was his belief that the state and the law both automatically fell under the same 'normative order', that the legal basis of the state could always be isolated against any particular act of state or actor within the state, and that the state was not empowered to act without legal formalization of its power (Kelsen 1922: 87). On this basis Kelsen claimed that the state needed to be regulated by a constitutional court, as an 'organ distinct from the

---

[35] This was of particular significance after the prerogative regime in the war, and it was shaped by anxiety about the potentials implicit in emergency laws for the overthrow of democratic government. For commentary see Adamovich (1923: 20); Merkl (1999 [1921]: 416).

legislator and thus also independent of all state authority'. This meant
that the political force (that is, the sovereignty) of the state could not be
applied outside the apolitical norms of constitutional law, interpreted by
the court: the state, in consequence, was always held to its proper
functions by the court (1929: 53). This argument brought towards conclusion the earlier positivist notion that a constitution conferred legitimacy on a state by at once normatively authorizing and factually
depoliticizing the source and the use of state power.[36] In particular,
Kelsen's plan reflected the belief that the task of a constitution was to
form a state that was fully independent of all particular persons, that
state power ought not to be personalized in any group of objective actors
and that all exchanges between state power and society needed to be
subject to pure legal control. Kelsen's ideal of a constitutional depersonalization of the state, thus, was intended specifically to restrict the
particular, volitional dimension of legislation and to construct the state
as an actor with clearly defined and static functions and sources of
legitimacy, yet also to abstract a clear body of public law to facilitate
the positive use of power.

Despite this exception, however, across different national settings the
process of constitutional formation after 1918 normally involved a
strong impulse towards extreme state enlargement, which intensified
the quasi-corporate experiences of the war. In particular, the classical
restrictive or exclusionary function of constitutions was comprehensively transformed during the transition from the imperial to the mass-
democratic era, and the new constitutions after 1918 at once founded
state legitimacy in a strong material will and defined the state as the
ultimate source of arbitration and regulation for all primary antagonisms
pervading society. In many cases, this placed extraordinary burdens on
emergent states, and states were forced to transform themselves in a
short space of time from very limited constitutional monarchies to
highly materialized constitutional orders which derived their legitimacy
at once from political mass representation, expansive guarantees over
economic security and material legislation, and deeply structured, highly
volatile processes of economic bargaining. The First World War, in fact,
created a situation in which most European states were forced to
undergo a transition towards a system of material mass-democracy at a
point in their construction at which they were not yet reliably formed as

---

[36] For Kelsen's reflections on the constitutional court as a subsidiary source of political
statutes, see Kelsen (1942: 187).

democratic, or even – fully – as constitutional, states. Indeed, it is arguable that most of these states underwent a transition to material mass-democracy at a point in their construction at which they were in fact not yet conclusively formed as states *tout court*. Of the greatest importance in this was the fact that after 1918 many European states obtained semi-corporate constitutions and were compelled to legitimize themselves through the objective inclusion of private/volitional or collective actors before they had adequately developed and tested a fully autonomous public legal order. Many states passed, between 1914 and 1918, from half-dualistic constitutions to neo-privatistic constitutions, and the intermediary condition of relatively balanced and extracted public/legal order was not comprehensively elaborated. Above all, most states consolidated in the First World War were states that assumed fullness of state power at a point where that power was subject to extreme inclusionary expansion, and they were forced to legitimize themselves through sporadic techniques of material inclusion before they had effectively legitimized themselves and abstracted their functions through regular patterns of legal – usually, rights-based – inclusion. The autonomous abstraction of political power, which had integrally marked the entire history of state formation in European societies, began to dissolve at the point of its final realization.

The failure of expansive democracy

The first consequence of this expedited constitutional formation after the First World War was that, owing to their semi-corporate and collective voluntaristic structure, many post-1918 European states began immediately to internalize and directly to *politicize* an extraordinarily high volume of social controversies, for which their inclusionary structures were ill-prepared. This meant that conflicts through society that had conventionally been articulated in functionally or regionally discrete fashion now migrated towards and were conducted through the state. Naturally, this was particularly the case in questions of economic regulation: the inclusion of enforceable programmatic rights in many European constitutions meant that states were forced to bind their legitimacy to uniformly satisfactory standards of material provision and arbitration, and all economic antagonisms assumed an immediate relevance for state power or state legitimacy. In many cases, moreover, problems caused by the escalation of claims addressed to the state were exacerbated by the fact that many European states were demonstrably uncertain in their hold on the monopoly of social violence. In post-1918 Italy, for instance, conflict between economic rivals was only secondarily expressed through state institutions, and industrial conflict was routinely enacted outside the parliamentary arena. Moreover, many military units refused to disband after 1918, and the paramilitary *arditi* and *fasci di combattimento* openly contested the power of the state through the widespread use of concerted private violence and attacks on the institutions of left-leaning political parties. In Germany, likewise, in the first months of its existence the central democratic state was imperilled both by radical leftist forces of the council-communist movement, who sought to create a political order based in local and workers' councils, and semi-demobilized, ultra-reactionary military units (*Freikorps*) (which the government ultimately deployed to suppress the council communists). In many settings, further, the ongoing demand for high levels of material integration and distribution was imposed on states whose fiscal systems were based on antiquated models of limited or loosely unified statehood, and which were already afflicted by highly inflationary public economies. These states were often forced to entertain unmanageable levels of public spending and inflation, and their inclusionary requirements forced them to pursue increasingly desperate measures to stabilize public finances and revenue, which diminished their monopolistic hold on power still further.[37]

As a result of these factors, many new post-1918 constitutional states almost immediately began to suffer a *crisis of inclusion*. That is to say, these states struggled to generate legitimating resources to address and resolve all the societal conflicts that they had internalized, and they were unable to stabilize their unitary functions in the face of highly volatile and multi-causal social conflicts. In the extended wake of the constitutional transition after 1918, therefore, many European states responded to their position at the epicentre of different realms of societal expectation and antagonism by entering a condition of rapid institutional fragmentation. Indeed, many states soon began to respond to their material/democratic and socio-conflictual inclusivity by selectively relieving themselves of the functions imputed to them under their new constitutions, they began to dismantle their constitutionally integrated structure, and, under pressure from potent societal interests, they

---

[37] On Italy see Forsyth (1993: 101). For a brilliant account of Germany's fiscal problems as caused in part by weak unification, see Hefeker (2001: 127). For classical background see Witt (1970).

substantially altered the terms under which diverse private actors were integrated into the functions of the state. In this latter respect, the semi-corporate constitutions constructed after 1918 played an important role in the restructuring of European states through the 1920s and beyond, and their provisions for the equilibrated inclusion of different social groups often, across a number of distinct patterns, led to unforeseen and highly deleterious results.

Italy

Some post-1918 states reacted to their problems of inclusion and legitimization by progressively limiting the integrative power of the parliamentary legislature and by filtering out many interests and prerogatives to which the democratic legislature gave expression. Such states normally resorted to a strategy that curtailed the constitutional integrity between the executive and parliament, which had in most cases been established during the war, and they reverted to a governmental regime marked by a partly suspended executive. The key example of this was the Italian state of the years 1918–22, a period which culminated in Mussolini's assumption of power.

In Italy, it transpired soon after 1918 that the democratic state had incorporated a number of societal constituencies, organized in both political parties and extra-parliamentary associations, which could scarcely be accommodated in the same representative system. Most notably, the democratic polity of post-1918 Italy was critically hamstrung by the fact that elements of the numerically largest party, the PSI, openly discredited the parliamentary system and focused many activities on extra-parliamentary agitation. Further, this polity was undermined by the fact that the two largest parties with some sympathy for parliamentary-democratic order – that is, the PSI and the Roman Catholic Italian People's Party (*Partito Popolare Italiano*) – refused to form joint coalition governments. These two factors made it very difficult for any party or group of parties to establish a majoritarian parliamentary mandate to underpin and sustain the executive. Rapidly, then, the inability of the elected parliament to generate majority support for government became a source of chronic instability in the Italian state, and governmental power was increasingly transacted by non-representative means. Post-1918 Italy, in fact, might be seen as a classic example of a polity that ascribed far-reaching constitutional functions to the organs of parliamentary-democratic government, yet whose democratic institutions, including parties themselves, lacked the cohesive force required for the state to preserve integrity in a highly divided socio-political landscape.

This integrative weakness of Italian democratic institutions had three primary consequences. In the first instance, it created a situation in which smaller parties and more informal groups quickly began to play a crucial role in forming governments, which meant that the executive lost broad public support and minority interests were able effectively to compete for political control. Second, it meant that the groups possessing access to the executive could easily assume a semi-autonomous position in relation to political parties in the legislature, and when parliamentary parties did not produce workable majorities or coalitions, a loose alliance of elites almost of necessity arrogated non-mandated powers of governmental direction. Third, it also meant that, as the executive tended to split away from parliament, power stored in the executive was neither subject to full parliamentary control nor bound by normal principles of accountability, and singular political protagonists could assume powerful functions in the state without full parliamentary authority: privileged societal actors could easily use personal contacts to obtain a share in state power (Catalano 1974: 43). For all these reasons, the democratic state of post-1918 Italy soon began to experience a chronic disintegration in the relation between legislature and executive, and entry to the executive became increasingly reliant on personal associations and semi-clientelistic networks. In fact, barely two years after the end of the war the state began retrogressively to dissolve into its more personalistic pre-1914 structure, and prominent actors in the state began selectively to curtail the process of mass inclusion that had been conducted during and after the war.

This process of state disintegration was reflected, initially, in the fact that by 1920 supreme governmental authority was once again placed in the hands of Giolitti, whose parliamentary mandate, as a liberal, was very limited, and who assumed power, as a minority coalition broker, mainly because of the unwillingness of other parties to form coalitions. Giolitti, in fact, soon reverted to a time-honoured policy of personalistic *trasformismo* as a device for stabilizing government against its unpredictable constituents, and he began to steer the executive away from its obligations to the elected legislature. Indeed, by 1921 Giolitti attempted to shore up liberal support by including Mussolini's fascists on the same electoral list as the liberal parties, and he was willing to co-opt fascists as elements in a liberal/nationalist bloc against the parliamentary left. By

1922, the options for forming integrative coalitions between pro-democratic parties had (it appeared) been exhausted, and the representatives of the old liberal elites in parliament around Giolitti began to toy with alternatives to parliamentary democracy. In particular, a number of prominent liberals favoured a system that limited the sensitivity of the executive to the pluralistic interests of parliament, and promised to preserve political order against social groups and political parties (the PSI and the communists) who threatened the liberal elite monopoly of power. Finally, the office of prime minister in a cross-party, highly conservative coalition was handed to Mussolini. In fact, the dissolution of the constitutional state caused by Mussolini's assumption of power in 1922 was approved by Giolitti and by many other, still more morally pliable, old-style liberals and conservatives, notably by Antonio Salandra, who was happy to describe himself as an 'honorary fascist' (Lyttelton 1973: 113). The termination of Italian democracy, thus, was promoted in part by the old liberal and conservative elites, who, sensing that no acceptable coalition of anti-fascist forces could materialize, sought, in the spirit of *trasformismo*, to *normalize* fascism within a liberal governmental regime,[38] and so to reconstruct the state as governed by a semi-accountable executive, crossing the party lines between fascists, conservatives and conservative liberals.

The second stage in the disintegration of the democratic state in Italy occurred after the fascist leadership had been handed power in late 1922. After this point, the fascist party (Partito Nazionale Fascista, PNF), acting in conjunction with some sectors of the late-liberal elites, at once responded to and profited from the integrative weakness of the state by introducing a raft of legislation, with effective constitutional force, that, first, reinforced the quasi-autonomous status of the executive and, second, assigned far-reaching political functions to persons obtaining influence outside the political arena. On the first point, the main legislative packages introduced by Mussolini after 1922 were designed to raise executive power and to dismantle parliament as an independent source of legislative authority, and to suppress both pluralistic sites and procedures of organized political representation. Notably in 1925, Alfredo Rocco supported these policies by arguing, illustratively, that in modern societies the government (executive) has the authority to exercise powers of legislation usually ascribed to parliament, and he claimed that, in all modern states, many laws need to be introduced

---

[38] See the account of widespread liberal 'philo-fascism' in Vivarelli (1981: 157–8).

simply as 'laws by decree [*decreti-leggi*]' (2005: 218, 222). He concluded
that the classic division of powers could not be applied to modern states,
and he defined the parliamentary legislature as an increasingly internalized component of the executive: he described the modern legislature as
a mere 'chamber for registering laws'.[39] Shortly after assuming power,
thus, Mussolini instituted a fascist Grand Council, which absorbed into
the PNF legislative offices formerly occupied by elected members of
parliament. The transformation of the state to include the Grand
Council, which became an integrated component of the state's constitutional structure in 1928, gave legal form to the domestic hegemony of the
fascist party. The most notable law of the early fascist regime, however,
was the Acerbo Law of 1923, which authorized the most successful party
in national elections to take an overall majority of parliamentary seats,
and, after the sham elections of 1924, it enabled Mussolini to introduce
legislation without opposition. At the end of 1925, accordingly,
Mussolini became head of government, holding power over all ministries. By 1926, legislation was introduced that allowed fascist prefects to
dissolve associations perceived to be contrary to the national order: Italy
became a one-party dictatorial state, whose executive was monopolized
by a small coterie of high-ranking party members. This legislation was
flanked by new laws regarding judicial process: in 1926, notably, the
Laws of Public Security assigned far-reaching judicial powers to state
police to suppress activity hostile to the state and to take all necessary
precautions to uphold public order. In each of these instances,
Mussolini's early decrees were designed to strip away the representative
constitution and the inclusionary apparatus of the state, and to reduce
the state to a free-standing, highly personalistic executive. On the second
point, however, after 1922 the new governing forces also began to co-opt
sources of power outside parliament (i.e. local elites, local party bases,
security forces and semi-public corporations) in order to enforce order
throughout society, and they increasingly allocated functions of the state
to essentially private actors. It is widely documented, in fact, that
Mussolini's regime was supported by an extensive semi-private bureaucratic order, and that the early fascist period was marked by a rapid
growth of public corporations and associations (*enti pubblici*), which

---

[39] Rocco's writings reflected a more general confluence of syndicalism and nationalism in
the early years of the Italian fascist movement. Rocco planned corporate laws as devices
for preserving the 'achievements' of the 'labouring masses' by ensuring that these were
integrated 'in full in the life of the nation and the state' (2005: 308).

were linked to the fascist party and were recruited (in order to reduce levels of state bureaucracy) to administer spheres of intersection between the state and the economy (Mellis 1988: 262–3). Indeed, while limiting the politically formalized connection between the executive and parliament, the PNF also acted to tighten its hold on power by securing support from powerful economic associations, which began to take on responsibilities for economic management and social pacification originally accorded to the democratic state after 1918.[40] By 1926, this process also led to the abolition of organizational structures that contradicted the social and economic interests of powerful elites (i.e. trade unions and left-oriented political parties), and the PNF increasingly utilized its executive power to consolidate the private dominance of select socioeconomic groups that gave it support (Lyttelton 1973: 329, 348).

On this basis, the Italian fascist state emerged from the inclusionary crisis of post-1918 democracy as a hybrid state.[41] At one level, the state that developed under Mussolini, after the material suspension of the parliamentary constitution in the years 1922–5, preserved the elemental structure of a classical state executive, and it retained many administrative units and ministerial offices that characterized the European state of the liberal era. Indeed, it is widely asserted that Mussolini preserved and consolidated his regime by obstructing a complete fusion of the party and the state, and by strategically upholding the residual edifice of the state: this enabled him to impose discipline on the turbulent elements of his own party and to consolidate his own hold on power.[42] In its executive apparatus, therefore, Mussolini's state was consolidated around the bare pillars of the late-liberal Italian state: the monarchy, the army and the governmental ministries, which were partly and irregularly fused with the leadership elite of the PNF. At a different level, however, Mussolini's regime was formed as a state in which many functions of governance and regulation were removed from public office and partly reverted to private actors, semi-public corporations and

---

[40] The vital link between the PNF and the association of big business (Confindustria), formed at approximately the same time as the first emergence of the *fasci di combattimento*, is often noted (Adler 1995: 155). More specifically, private companies also provided extensive support for the regime (see Sapelli 1975: 115). Mellis argues that 'entire branches of production' were removed from the control of the economic ministry and placed under the supervision of private corporations (1996: 367).

[41] See Aquarone for analysis of a regime which was controlled neither just by a party nor just by a state (1965: 164).

[42] For an example of this view see Lyttelton (1973: 269–307).

personal/clientelistic elites. In fact, Mussolini's state supported its functions of regulation and social control by allowing administrative power to be surrendered to diffuse private or semi-private groups in order to compensate for its inclusionary insufficiencies, and the party state was sustained by a balanced aggregate of commissioners, industrial technocrats, local prefects and administrators, and federal secretaries, who expansively dilated the societal presence of the state by devolving power to prominent semi-private and regional organizations (Palla 2001: 8). The corporate-constitutional shift in post-1918 Italy ultimately established a state in which private actors, in semi-patrimonial style, obtained access to public offices, and whose executive structure was sustained by a loose mass of private bargains between associations inside and outside the state.[43] Mussolini's state, in short, was designed as a model of governance marked at once by the consolidation of a powerful independent party executive, making extensive use of prerogative legislation, and by the redistribution of public offices among powerful private actors. In this system, the executive relied on power-sharing arrangements with sympathetic societal groups, and it used prerogative instruments to stabilize these arrangements. As a result, political power was substantially re-particularized, and the state as a whole began to resume features of semi-dualistic constitutionalism. Indeed, vitally, the termination of constitutional democracy in the Italian state after 1922 necessarily meant that it resorted to more erratic patterns of inclusion and it began to lose its positive integrity, consistency and abstraction as a state.

Austria and Portugal

This pattern of democratic collapse through partial suspension of the liberal executive was not exclusive to Italy at this time. A similar phenomenon, albeit arising in a different socio-political setting, was observable in some constitutions of the newly formed states of central Europe. The 1921 constitution of Poland, for example, was in many ways close to earlier liberal models, and it borrowed a powerful bicameral legislative system from the Third Republic in France. However, it also included substantial provisions

---

[43] An important article on this argues that the PNF acted in government as a 'body among bodies', using state power to broker semi-public, semi-private bargains which served the solidification of its own power and the private interests of other associations (Bersani 2002: 186).

for material rights, and it placed the labour process under direct jurisdiction of the state (Art. 102): that is, it guaranteed state protection for those suffering from unemployment, illness or accident. This constitution was supplanted through Pilsudski's coup d'état in 1926. Pilsudski initially projected a model of 'guided democracy', and he advocated executive-led republican rule to supersede the democratic order of 1921. But, in 1935, he secured the adoption of a presidential constitution, which placed both parliament and cabinet under his authority (although he did not live to see it in operation), and accorded to the president substantially augmented powers of emergency legislation.

More significant parallels to Italy can be found in the process of democratic fragmentation in inter-war Austria. However, despite certain parallels to Italy, Austria represented a substantially distinct pattern of democratic crisis, and the state that emerged after the collapse of Austrian democracy represented a different model of constitutional order. In Austria, the democratic constitution of 1920 was initially revised through a far-reaching amendment of 1929. This revision was designed to placate the growing factions of the extreme right, and, although approved by the Social Democrats, it entailed a substantial transfer of power from the parliamentary legislature to the president, and it placed the legitimacy of the presidential executive on a direct plebiscitary foundation. Subsequently, in early 1933, the Austrian parliament was dissolved, the Constitutional Court was suspended, and the federal government began to conduct business by authority of provisions for exceptional governance that had been introduced before 1918. After 1933, in fact, the legal basis of government was secured through reference to prerogatives for military-economic regulation (Kriegswirtschaftliches Ermächtigungsgesetz), which had been implemented in 1917, and which had engendered a system of semi-dictatorial economic management during the First World War. This legislation had not been formally rescinded after 1920, and it was integrated in the constitutional order of the First Republic to legitimize prerogative legal measures in cases where the regular constitution was suspended (Hasiba 1981). Ultimately, in 1934, the prerogative laws supporting the Austrian executive were utilized to introduce a new, highly reactionary constitution, implemented by Dollfuß. This constitution, although purporting to guarantee liberal principles of uniform parity before the law and equal entitlement to basic rights (Art. 16), instituted a model of group-managed federal rule (Art. 2), based on the principle of government by sectoral estates, which substantially weakened political rights. In the 1934 Constitution, legislative competence was in part removed from the elected parliament and divided between diverse corporate organs and professional chambers, which were accorded power to pre-form acts of legislation and to nominate members of the legislature (Bundestag) (Arts. 44, 50). Moreover, this constitution foresaw the creation of a federal economic council (Art. 48), in which representatives of different professions were sent to deliberate and determine economic policy and legislation, and whose members then obtained access to the primary legislature. This constitution was designed to dilute the strict and direct political integrity between the elected legislature and the state executive, and it marked a partial return to earlier dualistic or quasi-privatistic constitutions. Indeed, this constitution created a legal order in which private groups, loosely patterned on corporate estates, obtained direct, varied access to the resources of governmental power. It allocated power to private elites, whose qualifications for governance were determined, not by law, but by party-political conviction, and who were specifically empowered to use prerogative measures for the conduct of government (Merkl 1935: 64, 131).

Closely related to this process of constitutional reconstruction in Austria after 1933 was the suspension of constitutional rule at the end of the First Republic of Portugal. In Portugal the liberal-parliamentary constitution of 1911 was abrogated in 1926 when the military seized control of the state. By 1930, Salazar had become the leading figure in Portuguese government: he was appointed first (in 1926 and again in 1928) as minister of finance, and after 1932 he assumed the office of prime minister, thus becoming effective head of government. Salazar initially used military support to promote a governmental system that abolished opposition parties and transformed parliament into a chamber of appointees, and he used this system to introduce austere fiscal policies to reduce high public debt. Salazar then transformed the state from the military junta established in 1926 to a corporatist constitutional order: the Novo Estado. This was legally instituted in 1933, when he established both a new written constitution and a Code of National Labour, in order to regulate industrial relations and conditions of production. In particular, the 1933 Constitution made provision for a powerful ministerial executive, governed by Salazar himself, which was entitled to pass decree-laws with statutory force (Art. 108(3)) and to oversee the administration of the state. This constitution also provided for a weak legislature (which did not meet until 1935) and for a judiciary that was integrated into the organic structure of the state. The legislature, notably, was split into two bodies: one of these comprised a National Assembly of elected delegates and appointees, and the other was a Corporative

Chamber, consisting of appointed representatives of agriculture, commerce, industry, the army and the church. The Corporative Chamber was required to give its opinions on all draft bills prior to their submission to the National Assembly (Art. 103).

Both the post-1934 Austrian state and the Novo Estado created by Salazar, in sum, developed as state forms that in part reflected the pattern of anti-democratic retrenchment pioneered by Mussolini in Italy. Both reflected a reactionary backlash against parliamentary pluralism, and both at once liberated the executive from elected legislative control and, in instituting corporate chambers, both used coercive techniques to regulate production in the economy and stabilized the power of select socio-economic groups within the apparatus of the state. These states, however, differed from Mussolini's regime in that they did not approach the condition of partial executive autonomy that marked Mussolini's state. Although both states concentrated their economic policies on fiscal austerity, in both instances the state executive remained, at least nominally, more integrally locked into processes of material consultation and corporate economic interpenetration. As in Italy, however, both states reacted to the extreme economic conflicts of the 1920s and early 1930s by strategically diminishing their democratic foundations and, in consequence, by privatistically parcelling state power for powerful groups and re-particularizing many core functions of the democratic apparatus.

Germany

A further analogous, yet also substantially divergent, process of state fragmentation, shaped by similar (although not identical) underlying causes, characterized Germany during the collapse of the Weimar Republic. During the Weimar Republic, Germany also witnessed a process, gathering pace in the currency inflation of 1922–3 and culminating in the three years of presidential government from 1930 until 1933, in which the integral relation between legislative and executive institutions was deeply unsettled, and in which the executive intermittently assumed semi-independent status. In both these periods, actors within the German state executive responded to intense economic pressures and conflicts and lack of parliamentary cohesion by making extended use of emergency powers (codified in Arts. 25 and 48 of the 1919 Constitution) to circumvent normal parliamentary procedures in order to introduce decrees on pressing issues of public security, spending and government finance. In 1923, first, precedents were established for the use of exceptional powers to bypass parliament in order to pass budgetary legislation. At the height of the hyperinflation, notably, President Friedrich Ebert (a Social Democrat) prorogued parliament and used emergency laws to implement fiscal packages to stabilize the currency, and many of the most vital decisions in this critical period of German democracy were made without parliamentary debate: crucial decisions regarding economic stabilization became law through executive fiat. This process necessarily led to a reinforcement of the executive in relation to parliament, it both factually and symbolically eroded the legitimacy of parliament, and – importantly – it offered financial experts and strategists direct personal access to the executive (Feldman 1997: 754–802). Between 1930 and 1933, the economic crisis caused by the Wall Street crash of 1929 provoked a similar response: the normal functions of parliament were again, this time more enduringly, suspended, and the day-to-day responsibilities of government were progressively assumed by appointed members of presidential cabinets, authorized to implement policy under Article 48 by the arch-reactionary President Hindenburg. After the Wall Street crash and the withdrawal of US capital from the German public economy in 1929, most major acts of legislation were introduced, as executive prerogatives, by presidential decree. Most legislation at this time was designed to pursue a radically deflationary austerity course, and emergency laws were used to cut public spending, reduce welfare and insurance provisions, and ultimately also to unstitch the collective wage agreements established through the corporate bargains of 1918.[44] The model of government by presidential cabinets under Article 48, in fact, was specifically devised to replace the parliamentary coalition of 1928–30 led by the Social Democratic Party (SPD) with a simultaneously authoritarian and business-friendly executive.

In both crisis periods of the first German democracy, therefore, the parliamentary constitution of 1919 was dramatically weakened, ministerial offices were either partly or largely disconnected from the Reichstag, and a free-standing executive, supported by a conservative civil service, assumed many functions constitutionally accorded to the legislature. Owing to the semi-independence of the executive after 1930, in particular, cabinet positions were often allocated through personal associations and informal arrangements, and core functions of state were rapidly transformed into personally brokered commissions. Notably,

---

[44] Explaining these policies, see Scheuner (1967: 253); Krohn (1978: 119); Patch (1998: 182).

further, because of the primary fiscal orientation of legislation drafted at this time, the concentration of power in the executive also led to a close convergence between governmental and private/economic elites. It is widely recorded that the late-Weimar political apparatus was intensely vulnerable to the machinations and lobbying activities of private organizations, and the personalistic composition of the state executive meant that a number of socio-economic elites, who possessed limited democratic authority and whose access to power ran through personal channels, were able to assume entrenched positions in the margins of government (Böhret 1966: 104, 125; Winkler 1979: 203; Grübler 1982: 189). In addition, this system also gave a consolidated role to the military, which, to speak euphemistically, was not renowned for its democratic credentials: the last German cabinet before the assumption of power by Hitler's National Socialist Party (NSDAP) was closely linked to the army, and from 1932 onwards it was widely anticipated that the military might act as a bulwark for an executive whose societal legitimacy was becoming more and more fractured and illusory. Throughout the last death throes of the Weimar Republic, therefore, the structure of the state was thinned down to a narrowly founded, semi-accountable and extremely personalized executive. By mid 1932 this was close in composition to the ministerial executive of the imperial period, although its reliance on the military reflected a proximity to Italian fascist principles. This state, of necessity, was extremely porous to private interests, it pursued legislative functions through the concerted decisions of non-elected elites, and it freely co-opted representatives of private bodies in its planning apparatus (Patch 1998: 125–8).

As in Italy in 1922, therefore, the elites that assumed control of the German state executive after 1930 ultimately gave supreme political power to a movement loosely falling into the fascist family of political parties: they installed Hitler as chancellor in a cross-party ultra-rightist cabinet in early 1933. The motives of the German elites, it is legitimate to speculate, were probably rather different from those of the late-liberal and conservative elites in Italy more than ten years previously. Indeed, the German ministerial elites did not collapse in the face of extra-parliamentary intimidation quite as meekly as those in Italy. In Germany, between 1930 and 1933 extensive experiments were conducted, using emergency laws as a legal basis, to devise a non-parliamentary or at least executive-led political apparatus, which could be stabilized against the more radical trade unions and without the electoral support of the Social Democratic Party on one side, but by means of which Hitler could also be excluded from power.[45] It was only when, against a rising tide of street-level political violence, the options for constructing an executive bastion against both the left and the extreme right had been exhausted that the introduction of legislation under emergency clauses was suspended and a deal was struck between the old reactionary elites entrenched in the executive and Hitler's party.[46] Moreover, in their numerical strength the National Socialists were far more powerful in 1933 than was the PNF in Italy in 1922, and they were able both to mobilize a violent cross-class front and to exploit procedures of democracy to destabilize the democratic system, much more potently than had been the case in Italy. In Germany, in consequence, the extreme right around Hitler did not follow the Italo-fascist technique of simply using old elites as accomplices in the dislocation of the state executive from the legislature. On the contrary, the old conservatives in Germany had already effectively created a semi-detached minority executive by 1930, or at the latest by 1932. The National Socialists then came to power by mobilizing resources both of mass democracy and mass-political agitation in order finally to overthrow the remnants of this executive, which had been rendered hollow and precarious through the use of prerogative laws. Once in power, in fact, unlike the PNF, the NSDAP began rapidly to dissolve (and, in some cases, to murder) the old elites installed in the state executive, so that the power of the NSDAP was, ultimately, not checked by the residually pluralistic political arrangements that characterized Mussolini's rule. Overall, the pattern of democratic/constitutional collapse in Germany reflected, not solely a process of executive detachment and elite collusion, but also a process in which the executive was colonized by a populist movement that possessed (in numerical/electoral terms) a much stronger mandate than existing governmental alternatives or possible coalitions.

After a short period of government the National Socialists demonstrated the extent of their annexation of the state executive by

---

[45] Chancellor Brüning obtained the passive support, or the 'objective co-operation', of the SPD. His anti-Nazi stance was affirmed by traditionally conservative groups in the business community.

[46] This is an unfashionable argument. Most interpreters see a direct continuum between Papen, Schleicher and Hitler, and they argue that Hitler came to power under Art. 48. In my view, though, Hitler came to power, not through presidential use of prerogative laws, but because Hindenburg renounced the use of such laws. By late 1932, Art. 48 was primarily designed to keep the NSDAP, the largest party in the Reichstag, out of power, and Hitler was – paradoxically – a more democratic alternative to government under Art. 48. To support this, see the half-forgotten essay by Freund (1962: 117).

conducting a dramatic overhaul of the internal structure of the state. In some cases this reflected the policies practised by Mussolini after 1922. In Germany after 1933, in the first instance, the NSDAP immediately abolished free legislative institutions, and Hitler's introduction of the Enabling Law in March 1933 effectively dissolved all opposition parties and suspended the democratic provisions of the 1919 Constitution. As in Italy, this process of institutional demolition was also flanked by a destruction of the liberal judicial order. The early months of Hitler's regime saw a political cleansing of the judiciary, under laws of April 1933. These months also witnessed the introduction of criminal laws, most importantly the 'Lex van der Lubbe', which imposed new measures against treason and allowed retroactive application of criminal law. As a result of this, the People's Court (Volksgerichtshof) was founded in 1934, and it was designed to try special cases of treason, and in particular to apply new laws against political crimes: as in Italy, the politicization of criminal law was a vital instrument in the suspension of liberal-constitutional rule. Moreover, Hitler's regime also followed the pattern created by Mussolini in that it began a selective re-privatization of political power, and it obtained support for the party executive by entrusting the enforcement of power to a diffuse array of private and social actors. As in Italy, this was most especially the case in economic policies, the implementation of which was coloured by deep interpenetration between public and private initiatives. Reflecting the precedent of the PNF in Italy, in fact, Hitler's regime triumphed in a political landscape in which offices of state had already been subject to a process of partial re-privatization, and in which the functions of state had fused in amorphous fashion with extra-political actors. Ultimately, the NSDAP formed a regime in which, for all its claims to political totalism, many social functions were withdrawn from the state, the state began to coalesce with officers, commissioners and special delegates assuming power outside the state, and state power was sustained through society by its hazy convergence with the clientelistic authority of half-private half-public actors.[47]

Despite these similarities, however, Hitler's regime deviated from the model of Italian fascism in several ways. This was most obviously the case in that it began comprehensively to replace the conventional institutions of the state and the state administration by fusing offices of state with the private offices of the governing party and by at once replicating,

---

[47] For an example see Gotto (2006).

multiplying and conflating the centres of formal and informal power through society.[48] Unlike the fascist regime in Italy, the regime pioneered by the National Socialists was a political order in which a political party began comprehensively to absorb the existing state apparatus, and to dissolve the conventional administrative integrity of the state. In Italy after 1922, as discussed, Mussolini's party had been ultimately (albeit haphazardly) integrated into the pre-existing state, and the Fascist Grand Council had been transformed into an institution not, in its institutional construction, categorically distinct from ministerial organs of late-liberal states. In Germany after 1933, in contrast, the formal structure of the state was far more dramatically dismantled, and power formerly concentrated in ministries of state was transferred into divisions of the NSDAP. Hitler's regime had the crucial distinction from other fascist governments that it used a highly orchestrated mass party to annex the state, it substantially abolished the existing lineaments of statehood, and, to a large degree, it forced departments of the state to interlock with originally independent organs of social mobilization. The state, in sum, lost its abstracted status of consistency and differentiation against private social actors, and it began to fuse haphazardly with an array of private associations and coercive personal networks.[49]

The regimes established by Mussolini, Hitler and other authoritarian rulers of inter-war Europe were thus marked by salient distinctions. However, all were regimes that emerged because democratic states created after 1918 had possessed insufficient integrative power to assume the highly expanded functions, necessitating the integration of irremediably antagonistic social groups, imputed to them. Internally, these states had been unable to integrate potent private elites, they had reserved executive power for privatized interests, and they had struggled to build cohesive institutions to solidify the polarized constituencies from which they now derived legitimacy. Externally, these states had struggled to produce generalized legal responses to meet the societal demands placed on them, they had failed to apply power in relatively equal or inclusive manner across different social groups, and they had been unable to obtain a palpably legitimate monopoly of political

---

[48] For an account of this, which also still recognizes a persistent dualism in the relation between state and party, see Caplan (1988: 138). For still the best account of the governmental 'polycracy' established by Hitler, see again Broszat (1969: 363–402).

[49] This argument is made, in diverse fashion, in some of the classical literature on Hitler's regime (Schmitt 1995 [1938]: 118); Neumann (1944).

violence. All European states experienced a process of dramatic expansion and inclusion in the 1914–18 war and its aftermath, during which time they rapidly incorporated, and were required constitutionally to balance the material interests of, a number of (on occasions) intensely hostile collective actors. Ultimately, however, many states were incapable of maintaining an equilibrium between these groups, and as the economic terrain and balance of influence changed as a result of the economic traumas and conflicts of the 1920s, the integrative functions of states were widely re-privatized in favour of dominant economic interest groups, whose representatives availed themselves of weakly integrated state executives in order either to suspend or (more normally) to realign the corporate agreements which states had entered into during and after the war (Blaich 1979: 64). For each of these reasons, inter-war states commonly reacted to their inner inclusionary crisis by selectively devolving state functions to powerful or privileged private actors and by returning to loosely integrated neo-dualistic constitutions. As discussed, in authoritarian Austria and Portugal this occurred through a process in which representative procedures for legislation were suspended, and statutory force was ascribed to semi-private corporate groups, protected by an authoritarian executive. In fascist Italy, this occurred, paradigmatically, through a process in which the state executive was detached from parliament, and the executive at once relied on semi-integrated actors for maintaining social control and used prerogative powers to sustain and preserve elite economic positions throughout society. In Germany under the NSDAP, this occurred through a process in which the state executive was forced to conjoin with a broad-based totalitarian party. This party distributed coercive power through society by means of diffuse organs of local/private control, and it utilized originally private actors as privileged executors of violent political prerogative. In both major fascist states, however, fascism, beneath its ideological veneer of *totalism*, was formed as a system of *compensatory statehood*. In this system, the structural and inclusionary weaknesses of late-liberal states were counterbalanced through diffuse clientelistic support through society, the techniques of prerogative corporatism pioneered during the war were selectively and more coercively preserved, and a broad set of societal actors were co-opted in the margins of the state to perform quasi-political functions of regulation. In each case, the end of democracy meant that the state deprived itself of its most potent instruments of public inclusion, it began to sustain its power with far more erratic, privatistic and locally applied techniques for organizing support, and it eroded its basic abstractive structures of public statehood.

Rights and the Constitution of Fascism

The constitutional trajectory of many inter-war European states, to summarize, described a transition from expansive statist corporatism, pioneered in the First World War, to semi-privatistic authoritarianism, cemented in the fascist and quasi-fascist regimes of the 1920s and 1930s. Notably, both the corporate system of the war years and the fascist systems of the 1920s and 1930s were established by extensive use of emergency laws: in both cases governments used prerogative powers to bind corporate arrangements together. The use of emergency laws to stabilize the economy and the labour market marked a key thread connecting the wartime political economy of 1914–18 and the post-democratic regimes of fascist Europe. In this respect, fascism evolved as a direct continuation of the authoritarian corporatism pioneered in the First World War, and the wartime political-economic structure was the main antecedent for fascist government. In addition to this, however, the democratic constitutions established after 1918, in themselves, created very propitious circumstances for the later formation of authoritarian regimes, and some features of fascist rule evolved directly from the constitutional models of semi-corporate democracy created after 1918. Indeed, the second precondition of fascism might be identified in the constitutional structures with which post-1918 states sought to manage their newly expanded inclusionary obligations. Naturally, it must be re-emphasized here that not all post-1918 European states adopted fully corporate constitutions. However, as discussed, throughout Europe the ideals of corporatism and the quasi-corporate experience of the war engendered a widespread corporate constitutional orientation: this created a social, legal and political terrain in which the solutions to problems of economic management and societal inclusion offered by fascist parties were able to gain resonance and appear plausible, and, as such, corporate constitutionalism itself vitally prefigured fascist governance.

In general, as discussed, the link between corporate constitutionalism and fascism resulted from the fact that, in tying state legitimacy to very expansive material/volitional inclusion and programmatic provisions, corporate constitutions of necessity at once overburdened the state and obscured the functional boundaries of statehood. This then led to the

co-opting of private actors as supports for the basic functional operations of the state, and it allowed members of private elites to obtain
secure positions in the extended peripheries of the state. Corporate
constitutionalism thus eroded the resources of political abstraction and
proportioned inclusion around which states had historically constructed
their functions. This created a fertile terrain for the half-privatistic
clientelism that marked fascist rule. More specifically, however, the
transformation of the *rights fabric* of classical constitutional law in the
corporate constitutions promulgated after 1918 also played a particularly
significant role in the process of democratic-constitutional collapse in
the 1920s and 1930s. The fact that the post-war constitutional landscape
involved an immediate inclusion of singular and collective social actors
in the periphery of the state as claimants to, and volitional producers of,
material rights did much both to over-expand the functions accorded to
the state and to render state power susceptible to authoritarian re-
particularization. Above all, the fact that these constitutions, within
certain constraints, defined rights as institutions bringing legitimacy to
states as expressions of an overarching societal will, and construed state
legitimacy as obtained through the identity of state and society effected
by collective claims over rights, led to an over-taxing of the inclusionary
capacities of states. In consequence, the widened and pluralistic rights
structure in the constitutions created after 1918 eroded the abstracted
structure of the state, and it weakened the ability of states to construct
their political power in relatively autonomous and internally consistent
political fashion. The corporate/pluralist constitutional models evolving
from the First World War, to be sure, were partially based in the
assumption that, in mass-democratic societies, states required highly
inclusive reserves of legitimacy: this legitimacy could be obtained through
the allocation of different sets of rights, and the exercise of multiple rights,
some of collective character, acted to create a substantial and solidifying will
to legitimize the power of the state in all its dimensions as a potent inclusionary force. These models presupposed that the construction of citizens as
bearers of objective corporate rights would allow the state to incorporate the
plural components of society and consolidate the state *from below* as a
powerful apparatus integrating, representing and sustained by, a strong
social will, structured around powerful organizations of societal and material interest. As the political-economic landscape and balance of societal
influence changed throughout the 1920s, however, the principles of corporate constitutionalism underwent a deep transformation, and corporate
pluralism began to evolve in a categorically authoritarian direction. From

1922 onwards, in fact, corporate ideals became the basis for new constitutions in which the integrative force of collective objective rights was still retained, but in which corporate rights were now applied as instruments of strict and exclusive integration *from above*. Corporate constitutional ideals, in constructing plural private activities as objects of programmatic inclusion in state power, thus obstructed the classical restrictive and politically measured functions of rights, and they helped to generate a constitutional system in which the executive could utilize objective rights as elements in an apparatus of socially coercive and semi-privatistic integration and control.

Italy

In Italy, for example, the pre-eminent project of the early years of the Mussolini regime was the transformation of the late-liberal polity into a state with a corporate constitution, based in objective integrative rights. In addition to its reconstruction of the state around a detached executive, in fact, the Italo-fascist constitutional ideal contained a pronounced corporate dimension, which was centred around a deep revision of classical theories of rights: it was founded on the principle that under fascist governance the regulatory functions of the state extended beyond the limited objectives of liberal states, and the state obtained legitimacy by integrating all elements of society as inner/organic constituents of its *total* constitutional apparatus. Underlying this model was the idea that the fascist constitution suspended classical distinctions between private law and public or constitutional law, and it utilized structured syndicates to integrate all societal exchanges – public, private and personal – to elaborate one total unitary legal order, so obtaining legitimacy from an absorptive allocation of rights to organized social collectives. Fascist constitutionalism had its practical centre in the principle that left-oriented syndicalism had to be recast as a model of state-centred corporatism, in which all syndicates were vertically integrated in, and formally responsible to, the state executive, enabling the state to acquire legitimacy as a totalistic legal organization of all *categories of production* existing in society.[50] For example, Ugo Spirito claimed that the fascist

---

[50] Vincenzo Zangara demanded a type of syndicalism designed to serve the 'fortification of the state' (1931: 125). Dario Guidi advocated a corporate system in which syndicates acted in 'subordination' to the state (1931: 139). Nicola Palopoli stressed the interwoven nature of syndicalism and corporatism, but argued for a corporate system as a state-centred 'system of mediation' between different economic groups (1930–1: II, 55).

state necessarily 'extends, through the life of the syndicates, to all individuals', thus founding a political order based in an inclusive 'identity of state and individual' in all societal functions (1932: 45–6). Giovanni Gentile expressed this in more philosophical terms: he defined the fascist state as a state obtaining legitimacy by reflecting that 'immanence of the state in the individual person' which he construed as 'the proper essence of the state' (1929: 50). The Italian fascists thus rejected the traditional constitutional view that the 'juridical personality' of the state was derived from a statically public legal/normative order, under which particular private agents obtained prior or stable rights outside or prior to the state. Instead, they defined the constitution of the state as a total volitional personality or a 'dynamic reality' of inclusion and active/voluntaristic formation, in which all particular social agents were integrated and harmonized by collective-associative involvement in syndicates and corporations, and in which membership in half-public, half-private groups and associations formed the basis of entitlement to rights guaranteed by the state (Bortolotto 1931: 14, 221).

Reflecting these constitutional ideals, the earlier part of Mussolini's regime in Italy saw the introduction of legislation to provide for a new system of labour regulation, designed to subordinate the labour market and the production process to state control, and to integrate and minimize conflict over issues of production. The early part of the regime, for example, gave rise to an accord, the Pact of Palazzo Chigi, between the confederation of fascists and the largest industrial lobby (Confindustria), in which it was agreed that industrial organization in Italy should reflect an endeavour, under the supervision of the party government, to promote co-operative relations between business and labour and to avoid class conflict for the sake of national development. These corporate ideas were then expressed, in highly authoritarian fashion, in the Rocco Law and other pieces of labour legislation of 1926. These laws organized all deputations of organized labour in one vertical syndicate, they created labour courts to settle industrial disputes, and they subjected trade union activity to strict control and repression. They also instituted a National Council of Corporations (consolidated under legislation of 1930 as an 'organ of state'), possessing powers to represent professional interests and shape economic legislation (Palopoli 1930–1: II, 400–5). The corporate orientation of fascist economic and constitutional policy had its centrepiece in the Labour Charter (Carta del Lavoro) of 1927. The Labour Charter, the focus of Mussolini's ambition for a fully corporatistic system of political-economic direction, granted rights of participation in disputes over industrial conditions both for industrialists and delegations of labour. In so doing, it acknowledged the need for balanced rights between both parties in industrial conflict, and it designated the production process in its entirety as subordinate to the aim of national rejuvenation and expansion. In all these respects, the Charter marked a concluding moment in the elaboration of the corporate constitutional principles that had coloured most post-1918 European polities, and it gave intensified expression to the corporatist presumption that economic agents required inclusion in the state through structured material rights and that a legitimate constitution was one that oversaw the allocation and valorization of varied material rights claims. For its apologists, the Charter and the National Council provided foundations for a 'harmoniously unitary state', based in a 'stable balance between contrasting interests' of social classes (Zangara 1931: 147–50). Mussolini himself described fascist corporatism as a 'new synthesis' of liberal and socialist economic elements (1934: 18).

Beneath this constitutional rhetoric, however, it is notable that many elements of corporate order put in place by Mussolini directly contradicted the founding ideals of corporatist doctrine, and fascist corporatism diverged in its core principles from the original corporate principle that states assume legitimacy through equal organic inclusion of all social groups. First, notably, the National Council of Corporations did not possess factually integrative legislative power, and it remained subordinate to the Ministry of Corporations: it merely served as an organ for 'co-ordination of the forces of labour and production' (Palopoli 1930–1: II, 431). This was made still clearer in the Charter of Labour itself. Notably, the Charter strategically abandoned the principle of factual parity in rights holding between corporate parties, and it was clearly tilted to serve the interests of the entrepreneurial side in the industrial bargaining process. Most importantly, the Charter insisted that powers of veto in industrial settlements should fall to industrialists, and it ensured that directive force in the production process remained with the business class. In this respect, the Charter ultimately acted as a document that lent the coercive power of the state to support the economic decisions of powerful economic elites, and it effectively allowed entrepreneurial rulings to assume force of statute. Indeed, the Charter was only instituted after independent trade unions had been prohibited, and because of this the entire corporate experiment precluded dissent and envisaged unilaterally prescribed solutions for industrial disputes. Even in its basic attempt to stabilize relations between unions and employers, moreover, the

Charter only formed a directive framework document, and it had no de iure force.[51]

In the final analysis, in consequence, the early part of the Mussolini regime saw the introduction of a highly selective pattern of corporatism and collective rights attribution. This system renounced the integration-ist aspects of original corporate ideals, and it began to use adapted corporate techniques as strategies of unilateral economic control, selec-tive steering and repressively instrumental industrial management. In this system, in particular, collective claims over rights in the production process became susceptible to partial arbitration by the state, in which representatives of labour were heavily disadvantaged. Under fascism, therefore, material corporate rights, far from serving volitionally to engender an economically balanced state, acted as institutions that authorized the state to colonize independent spheres of social liberty and to solidify existing conditions of production through prerogative intervention, and that brought selective benefits to materially privileged social groups. Leading legal theorists of Mussolini's regime, notably, expressly expanded on these principles to argue that the corporate state was centred in an increase in *judicial power*, they demanded an inclusion of all economic activities under the judicial functions of the state, and they insisted on the application of corporate rights as instru-ments to draw all spheres of socio-economic exchange under direct state jurisdiction (Panunzio 1933: 31–2). Corporate rights, in other words, were progressively defined as the antithesis of personal/subjective rights and, as such, they were enforced, not to channel the material will of the people into the state, but both to eliminate the freedoms guaranteed under personal/subjective rights and selectively to intensify de facto rights and privileges of certain socio-economic groups.

In the case of Italy, in sum, the corporate transformation of constitu-tional ideals during and in the aftermath of the First World War created a situation in which the constitution of the state renounced its classical functions, and it began to promote intensely authoritarian and socially annexationist patterns of governance. In particular, the corporate con-stitutional system in Italy after 1922 relinquished the conventional exclusionary functions of constitutional law and constitutional rights, and it acted, not to trace the boundaries of political abstraction and to reduce the state's political intensity, but instead to augment the volume of exchanges directed to the state, to harden the state's interpenetration

---

[51] For analysis see Adler (1995: 368); Somma (2005: 90).

with private groups in society and to provide instrumental conventions through which the state could sustain strategic control of private inter-actions. In consequence, this constitution extended material rights to such a degree that the state lost both the ability to extract an autonomous account of its power under public law and the ability to trace its dis-tinction against other parts of society in private law: on both counts, it experienced a rapid loss of autonomy and entered a cycle of deep re-particularization. The classical public-legal and private-legal func-tions of rights in upholding an abstracted and differentiated political system, in short, were eroded through corporate experiments, and the uncontrolled inclusivity of the state sanctioned by corporate rights facilitated a dissolution of the abstracted quality of the state and the differentiated structure of society more widely (Stolzi 2007: 76, 190). This meant that rights, in renouncing their exclusionary status, acted at once to dissolve the specific legal distinction of the state and to open the state to private agents and to provide extensive institutions for egregious private use of the means of public coercion. Both constitutional tenden-cies in Italian fascism – that is, the dislocation of the executive from the legislature and the use of collective material rights – thus culminated in the fact that they allowed dominant economic agents privileged access to the resources of the state (Sarti 1971: 2), and they permitted the reallo-cation of coercive reserves of state authority to powerful local, sectoral and neo-patrimonial groups throughout different social spheres.

Portugal and Spain

Analogies to these processes in Italy were also apparent in the destruc-tion of the parliamentary system in Portugal and the establishment of an authoritarian-corporate constitution under Salazar. As in Italy, the for-mation of the Novo Estado was flanked by a partial move away from the socio-organizational forms typical of liberal capitalism, and, once in power, Salazar's government began to disband organs of class associa-tion and, in particular, to transform trade unions into guilds and state-regulated syndicates. Strongly influenced by clerico-corporate ideology, Salazar instituted a model of political-economic interventionism, for-malized in the constitution of 1933, which accorded substantial legisla-tive powers to the professional bodies and organized syndicates assembled in the Corporative Chamber. In this system the state assumed (notional) responsibility for ensuring conditions of economic stability by guaranteeing material rights for all members of society: that is, by limiting the autonomy of economic actors and by subjecting the economy to constraints via price setting, output management and investment selection. Expressly, the 1933 Constitution imputed to the state the obligation to maintain 'equilibrium' between labour and capital and to prevent exaggerated profits for capital (Art. 31), to promote a 'national corporate economy', to limit unrestricted economic competition (Art. 34) and to police property, capital and labour so that their 'social function' was preserved (Art. 35). Salazar's state was based, in appearance at least, in a highly absorptive constitution, which opposed the political, economic and legitimating conventions of formal liberal statehood by defining citizens as materially formative of state power and as authorized claimants to material rights from the state. Like other constitutional documents of the post-liberal epoch, in particular, this constitution also defined rights of persons as privileges obtained through group membership or affiliation, and it implied that all such rights had to be actively made good through the corporate body of the state (Wiarda 1977: 38, 85–6). On this basis, the constitution imagined the state in its entirety as a highly expansionary body composed through multi-levelled corporate membership, and it viewed corporate associations as inclusionary elements of the state, through which members of society were formally integrated into the margins of public authority. The 1933 Constitution included most classical rights, such as rights to life and personal safety, rights of privacy, rights of fair trial and rights of association (Art. 8). However, its catalogue of formal rights was very weak. These rights were in some cases subject to restriction and special laws, and the primary motive of the constitution was, evidently, not to preserve singular rights but to secure legitimacy by solidifying the state's group constituencies through material allocation.

As in Italy, however, it has been widely argued that, although Salazar's constitution was introduced under the inclusionary banner of national/ economic harmony, a fully corporate system was never comprehensively institutionalized in Portugal, and corporate rights and principles were only applied in highly strategic and selective fashion. Although, for example, Salazar created national unions to regulate and control industrial activity, the corporate oversight of employers' associations was much more fitful (Costa Pinto 1995: 62). Moreover, while endorsing consensual bilateral negotiation and state arbitration in disputes relating to production, the constitution effectively prohibited strikes (Art. 39), and it clearly privileged the entrepreneurial side in labour disputes. As under Mussolini, state co-ordination of the economy was proportioned to potent social interests, corporate status was strategically allocated, and group rights (supposedly formative/integrative dimensions of the state) were used to govern proximity to state power: real power was preserved in a central executive, to which certain elites had obtained privileged rights of access.[52] Indeed, Salazar's constitution was perhaps the closest of all the corporate constitutions to a neo-patrimonial social order, in which the state, although purporting to act as an inclusionary political actor, factually purchased support for its power through society via the pluralistic allocation of structural status and selective privilege to influential social groups – and often to particular prominent families. As in Italy, therefore, constitutional rights were re-converted into private privileges, and they effected a corporate or internally pluralistic parcelling of the reserves of political power contained in the state.

A related set of patterns was observable, during and after the destruction of the Second Republic between 1936 and 1939, in the quasi-constitutional documents promulgated by the Franco regime in fascist Spain. More than a decade before the advent of the fascist regime under Franco, Spain had already experienced various experiments in semi-corporatist constitutionalism. In Spain, which had been non-combatant in the First World War, the 1876 Constitution had initially remained in force after 1918. As in Italy, however, the post-war years had seen a wide push for a reinforcement of the power of the Cortes and an attempt to limit *caciquismo*. After 1918, moreover, Spain also experienced a very high level of union militancy, and at the same time the potency of left-syndicalist models of government increased dramatically.[53] In reaction to this, in 1923 the dictatorship of Primo de Rivera was established, which, in parallel to the rise of Mussolini in Italy, founded a governmental system designed to block the rise in parliamentary power and to suppress (albeit in placatory fashion) the radical labour movement. Under the de Rivera dictatorship a body of social legislation was passed, which contained strong clerico-corporate elements, albeit with lower levels of coercive integration and greater support of the organized labour force than in fully fascist states. In the last years of the regime, an attempt (never fulfilled) was made to place the regime on more regular constitutional foundations, with an electoral system combining representative and corporate elements. Subsequently, after the collapse of the de Rivera dictatorship in 1930 the constitution of the Second Republic (1931)

---

[52] To support this see Wiarda (1977: 140); Machado (1991: 61); Meneses (2002: 162).
[53] For discussion see Meaker (1974: 146–88).

established a democratic polity, supported by left-oriented principles of Weimar-style economic legislation. In particular, the democratic constitution of 1931 mirrored the Weimar Constitution in that, although recognizing rights to private property, it authorized the state to expropriate property for the national economy (Art. 44), and it anticipated social legislation to sanction economic redistribution and to enable the participation of workers in collective bargaining and industrial decision making (Art. 46).[54] A further law of 1932 also made land held by nobility subject to expropriation. Indeed, like the Weimar Constitution the 1931 constitution of Spain made extensive provision for prerogative powers. It established far-reaching presidential authority under Article 81, and it was flanked first by a Law for the Defence of the Republic (1931) and then by a Law of Public Order (1933), which concentrated exceptional powers in the executive. Different degrees of emergency legislation became a general feature of daily governance under the Second Republic, and for almost the entire duration of the republic some constitutional rights (although in principle protected by a supreme court) were subject to different degrees of exemption.

Unlike other fully dictatorial regimes of the 1930s, the political system created by Franco contained a distinct and comprehensive constitutional order, sweeping away the radical-liberal documents of the Second Republic. The first decrees and organic laws of the Franco administration, the laws of 1936, 1938 and 1939, transferred full power to Franco as head of state, they suspended the democratic Cortes, and they created a detached ministerial executive, in which all ministries were subordinate to Franco. By 1942, however, laws came into force that replaced this exceptionalist order with a more fully evolved constitution. These included effective constitutional laws, the Constitutive Law of the Cortes, which re-established some functions of the legislature. Under this arrangement, the objectives of the Cortes were restricted to 'elaborating and approving' acts of law (Art. 1) and membership of the Cortes was reserved for appointees, normally already bearing public office, and for representatives of diverse syndicates and other organic associations. The president of the Cortes was directly accountable to Franco. As in Italy, therefore, the primary impetus behind early fascist legislation in Spain was that it removed the executive from the broad-based legislature,

---

[54] On the influence of German constitutionalism on the constitution of the Spanish Second Republic, see Payne (1993: 60). On disputes in the parliamentary commission regarding the status of property, see de Meer (1978: 109).

it eliminated dissent within the legislative apparatus and it freed both legislature and executive from the constraints imposed upon them by catalogues of rights. In 1945, subsequently, a more elaborate order of rights and duties was introduced, bearing a certain resemblance to conventional catalogues of rights. These laws, the Fuero de los Españoles, made partial provision for a legal regularization of the regime. Notably, they forbade retroactive incrimination (Art. 19) and separated judicial procedures from the military authorities that had dispensed gun-barrel justice in the aftermath of the civil war. Nonetheless, this legislation only sanctioned very partial and circumscribed civil rights, and it insisted both that the exercise of rights was subject to conformity with fundamental principles of state (Arts. 12, 16) and that they could be suspended by decree (Art. 35). It also restricted political rights (Art. 10) to rights of participation in public functions through the corporate institutions endorsed by Franco: that is, corporations representing 'the family, the municipality and the syndicate'. It thus abolished the party-political organs in which political rights might ordinarily be articulated, and it contributed further to the reinforcement of a narrow, detached executive.

The political constitution of the Franco regime was accompanied by a distinctive body of semi-corporate economic and industrial legislation. The fundamental laws introduced in 1945, for example, offered (formal) protection for the right to work, they defined work as an activity subject to principles of human dignity and just remuneration (Arts. 25 and 27), and they stated that representatives of labour and capital were entitled to share the benefits of production (Art. 26). In particular, though, these laws described the right to work as a personal obligation, they articulated this right as a coercive directive principle, and they partly devolved responsibility for material welfare to corporate bodies and the Roman Catholic church (Art. 29). Perhaps the key document in the entire raft of Franco's labour statutes was the Fundamental Labour Law (Fuero del Trabajo) of 1938. This text protected the right to work and set minimal wage levels (III/1), and it made explicit reference to the obligations of the state for the poor, especially in family law. It also foresaw a representation and co-ordination of all productive sectors in organic syndicates, acting as 'corporations under public law' (XIII/3), which were expected to oversee, regulate and improve the conditions of production. In this respect, it imagined that syndical organization of the economy might obviate or at least soften intense class conflicts. At the same time, however, this law also gave express sanction (XI/6) to 'private initiative as a fertile source of the economic life of the nation', it specifically sanctioned the existing system of property relations, and, primarily, it ensured that the owners of industrial units retained authority in setting economic objectives (VIII/3) (Dlugosch 2008: 332–3). Like Mussolini's corporate laws, in short, these laws created a highly selective model of corporate economic design, and they assigned far-reaching directive economic authority to industrial elites.

The Franco regime followed other fascist dictatorships in creating a constitutional system marked at once by a semi-autonomous executive and a strategically structured quasi-corporate economy, in which corporate laws, purporting to secure collective material rights, strongly favoured potent private-interest groups. In this setting, the corporate composition of the Cortes clearly involved a selective re-privatization of the apparatus of government, and it expressly permitted, through corporations, the assignation of public office to actors on the basis of their private/economic status and associational connections. To a greater extent even than in Italy, in fact, the Franquist system of executive dictatorship masked a withdrawal of the state from primary public functions, and the reinforcement of the executive as a largely suspended centre of political agency involved both a corporate privileging of certain social groups and a relinquishment of state power to private actors in society. Most particularly, this system was also based in a reconstruction of corporate ideals, in which collective objective rights were redefined as instruments of state control, economic stabilization and neo-patrimonial privilege. Indeed, the commitment to corporatism in Franco's regime was even more strategically deliberated than in other fascist systems, and it did little but offer an ideological facade for a system of personally directed capitalism.

Germany

The distinctive body of corporate and collective material rights contained in the Weimar Constitution also had two longer-term consequences that contributed to democratic/constitutional collapse in Germany. First, the corporate rights and arrangements in the constitution, originally intended to define different actors in the labour process as sources of material legislative power, were progressively transformed in the early years of the Weimar Republic, and through this transformation the influence of corporate groups representing the management side in production (i.e. industrial lobbies) increased disproportionately. By the late 1920s, in fact, little remained of the cross-class organic consensualism of the post-1918 era, and associations of industrialists widely campaigned for suspension of their corporate commitments: notably, the Grand Coalition (the last democratic government in the Weimar Republic) collapsed in 1929–30 owing to the inability of its business-friendly and Social Democratic components to agree spending and taxation policies. After the Wall Street crash of 1929, the final years of the Weimar Republic were marked, not only by a dramatic reduction in the competences of the elected parliamentary legislature, but also by a rapid expulsion of both the Social Democratic party and the trade unions from positions of high bargaining influence and by a selective dismantling of the arrangements for welfare rights that had originally been established through corporate negotiations. As discussed, this period saw the repeated use of executive fiats to diminish welfare spending, and the limiting of parliamentary power coincided with a deep reduction, initiated under the chancellorship of Heinrich Brüning, in the redistributive dimensions of corporate order. In the course of the 1920s, in short, the corporate rights in the Weimar Constitution gave both unions and management powerful roles in the policy-making process. Ultimately, however, actors representing industrial management were the beneficiaries of this arrangement, and after 1930 they were able to utilize their position close to the state executive to renege on their bilateral corporate commitments (Grübler 1982: 353; Meister 1991: 243; Hartwich 1967: 162). The late-Weimar strategy of deflationary economic governance by fiat cut away the bare political superstructure from the objective/consensual foundations that had supported it through the 1920s, and, as examined above, it transformed the corporate/democratic state into a precariously detached executive, reliant on presidential intrigues, private favour and – potentially – the military for its continued existence.

Second, the initial years of the regime established by the National Socialists brought a partial, albeit highly selective, revival of earlier corporate arrangements. This period was initially marked by wide declarations of enthusiasm for a return to an estate-based system of governance, and some National Socialists proclaimed that the party created an organic state founded in political-economic estates (*Ständestaat*), which resolved the divisions of class society by finally establishing rights of social ownership of property (Bülow 1934: 61). In this period, a number of strategic laws concerning industrial design were introduced. In particular, the first years of Hitler's regime witnessed the introduction of various laws to regulate conditions of production, to maintain stability in the production process and to obviate industrial conflicts. First, notably, in May 1933 the German Labour Front (Deutsche Arbeitsfront, DAF) was formed. The DAF was originally heralded as a corporate forum for syndical organization of the workforce, and in its initial functions it was considered a mechanism for securing material rights at the workplace and ameliorating general conditions of employment. In fact, however, although it remained an intermittent platform for labour dissent, the operations of the DAF were soon re-specified, and it acted mainly as an organ of social indoctrination and pacification.[55] The creation of the DAF was followed in 1933 by a law for the forcible creation of industrial cartels, which was designed to facilitate price setting and general economic co-ordination. Additionally, these institutes were soon accompanied by a further package of labour legislation: notably, the Law for the Organization of Labour (Arbeitsordnungsgesetz) of 1934, which was designed to organize industrial relations in a highly authoritarian corporate structure. Like the corporate laws of other fascist states, this law followed the earlier proscription of trade unions and provided for delegations of labour at the place of work, and it established a formal order of industrial arbitration. However, this law prohibited independent industrial representation and it gave supreme authority for the regulation of labour disputes to factory leaders (Betriebsführer), whose position had normally been established under the laws of the free market before 1933. Moreover, this law stressed that the workforce owed obedience to the factory leader, and it stipulated that conflicts within factories or companies fell under the competence of appointed trustees of labour (Treuhänder), whose duty it was to ensure that conflicts were resolved in accordance with wider macroeconomic prerogatives of the regime. As in Italy, this legislation also foresaw an expansion of the judicial power of the state into industrial activity, and it established tribunals at the place of work to apply political sanction for professional misdemeanours (absenteeism, alcohol abuse, etc.). From the late 1930s onwards, these acts of legislation were followed by further laws to promote labour-market regulation, which strengthened the power of the party to channel investment, to prioritize certain areas of production, to determine prices for commodities and for labour and even to regulate labour flows.

As in Italy, in consequence, the material constitution of Hitler's Germany ultimately formed a highly coercive system of corporate societal management. Moreover, as in Italy, although the party state assumed a degree of co-ordinating authority not widespread in pre-1945 liberal economies, the state's regulatory functions left the basic processes of capitalism (i.e. free investment, free accumulation, free exchange of contracts and free selection of markets) intact: indeed, the

[55] See the account of this in Mason (1966).

interventionist policies of production control and investment steering normally served the advantage of high-level industrial elites.[56] In this system, state intervention in the economy and state control of production were designed to manage the production process in favour of specific social groups, and the industrial apparatus as a whole reflected the aims of a regime generally committed to dismantling the welfare arrangements of the Weimar era and upholding a low-wage, low-cost economy.[57] Although evolving from the principles of corporate rights-holding and cross-class economic co-operation underlying Weimar political economy,[58] the industrial legislation of the National Socialists in fact supported a system of legally privileged economic self-administration, in which heightened coercive powers were given to actors promoting national growth targets.[59] If the original corporate-constitutional design of the early-Weimar era contained an aggregate of objective rights and legal institutions to facilitate a simultaneous political and material-democratic inclusion of society in the state, then the corporate structure arising after 1933, following the transformations in industrial relations experienced in the later 1920s, formed an apparatus of coerced material integration, in which state powers of regulation and distribution formed devices for securing cheap labour supplies and intensifying production. As in Italy, in consequence, the expansion and materialization of rights in the legal order of the post-1918 German state acted to widen the periphery of the state and to incorporate potent social groups in the state's periphery. To a yet greater extent than in Italy, however, this material reconstruction of the state's constitutional rights fabric blurred the state's integrity in relation to other spheres of society and other social actors. In particular, this process forced the state in part to

---

[56] For excellent analysis see Buchheim and Scherner (2006: 394); Kahn (2006: 15).

[57] This view is shared by Witt (1978: 258, 259, 272).

[58] On the ambivalent attitudes of the NSDAP to Weimar property laws see Stolleis (1974: 115). On continuities between ideals of property law among the lawyers of the Weimar era and the NSDAP see Kahn (2006: 8).

[59] Some ideologues of the Nazi *Ständestaat* observed it as a political order supporting independent economic 'self-administration' (Frauendorfer 1935: 21). On the deep conflict between the ideal of the *Ständestaat* and Hitler's economic designs see Freise (1994: 19–20). Ernst Rudolf Huber defined 'German socialism' as an economic system in which 'the total economic state' recognized that the economy possessed its own 'vital principle'. This did not negate the contrast of 'ownership and non-ownership' (1934: 14, 20). Similarly, albeit from a position critical of the NSDAP, Franz Böhm saw a combination of 'competition' and 'order' as the foundation of the National Socialist economy (1937: 108).

converge and share power with non-political organizations, and it made the directive sphere of state power extremely vulnerable to privatistic re-particularization or re-convergence with particular societal interests. Elements of this process were ultimately reflected in the material constitution of the regime instituted by the NSDAP: the corporate legislation introduced after 1933 formed a legal system that committed the state to deep interpenetration with the economy, yet it also tied state policy to macroeconomic goals that demanded the technical suppression of collective interests and the coercive management of industrial bargaining structures.[60]

To conclude, therefore, many constitutional systems in Europe in the 1920s were founded in a pluralistic expansion of the state's inclusionary functions, through which states were expected to legitimize themselves by preserving wartime patterns of societal inclusion, by incorporating and reconciling diverse antagonistic social groups, and by allocating collective material rights in order programmatically to integrate and solidify their societal constituencies. In the case of Germany, most particularly, this was based in the assumption that a material democratic constitution was a precondition for a strong unitary state. However, few inter-war states were strong enough to convert the divergent private elements of this material will into a basis for public order, and the widespread failure of European states to translate the particularistic dimensions of the corporately formed will into public constitutional laws transformed the state into a battleground for particular private prerogatives. Owing to this, inter-war states often progressively relinquished the basic instruments through which they had originally (often incompletely) secured their differentiated and sustainably inclusive stability. Above all, inter-war states eroded the normative functions of constitutional rights, under public law and private law, as institutions that extract an internally constructed formula for the state's societal autonomy and that trace the boundaries of political order and regulate processes of reflexive political in- and exclusion. Instead of this, they began to use rights as devices for maintaining an equilibrium between different groups and for objectively controlling and cementing the private social foundations of their legitimacy. In fact, it might be argued, tentatively in the case of Italy and more decisively in the case of Germany, that the expansion of the state's rights fabric counter-intentionally promoted a re-corporation of society, a haphazard fusion

---

[60] See the account of the success of state-directed industrial enterprise in Tooze (2006: 99–134). On the party links of industrial players, see Ferguson and Voth (2008: 127, 134).

of public and private power and a resultant dualistic re-privatization of the state: that is, collective corporate rights were converted into privileges for select social groups and objective rights were converted into institutions for intensely coercive regulation. Through this, the defining quality of the modern state – that is, its ability to extract a normative projection of itself, under public law, as a centre of positive and relatively autonomous statutory power in a differentiated society – was undermined, and the state began to rely on private actors, often using high levels of unmonitored violence, to sustain its power through society.

The high level of pluralistic social interpenetration and notional identity between state and society produced by post-1918 constitutions and constitutional rights thus led, by a circuitous path, to a disastrous depletion of state autonomy. If the definition of a modern state requires that a state can identify a distinct set of political functions, that it can conduct these functions at a reasonably high level of consistency and territorial generality and provide relatively secure checks on the arrogation of public authority by private actors, the constitution of fascist states, marking the supplanting of formal-constitutional democracy through a model of corporate societal management, reflected and enacted a catastrophic dissolution of statehood. Indeed, fascist states, arguably, experienced a return to the crises of statehood that characterized the transition from feudal to early modern social structure, in which some societies were only able to mobilize public power by relocating power in entrenched private and neo-patrimonial milieux and so by purchasing partial compliance through society by outsourcing powers of state administration. The experiment in the corporate/pluralistic expansion of rights and the attempt to establish material/volitional identity between state and society after 1914, in short, destroyed the basic normative fabric of exclusionary abstraction and autonomy in political power. In fact, in abolishing the strict legal distinction between private and public power, it allowed political power to revert, in part at least, to its original form as a privately applied and arbitrarily coercive resource, whose transmission through society was highly inflexible, dependent on personal support, patronage and particular acts and threats of violence, and liable to encounter and produce innumerable sources of low-level obstruction. The varied change in the rights fabric of states after 1914, in other words, produced a dramatic diminution of the reserves of political power possessed by European societies. As a result, the increasingly pluralistic inner structure of the state led to a depletion in society's capacities for pluralism outside the state.

5

Constitutions and democratic transitions

The first wave of transition: constitutional re-foundation after 1945

The period after 1945 witnessed a wave of constitution drafting in many of the states that either converted to fascism in the 1920s or 1930s or were subject to fascist occupation before or during the Second World War. In many instances this process of constitutional reform reflected the extension of Soviet influence across eastern and central Europe, and it was initiated by the government of the Soviet Union. Key examples of constitutions written at this time were the constitution of Hungary of 1949, the constitution of Czechoslovakia of 1948, the Polish constitution of 1952 and the Bulgarian constitution of 1947.

Constitutions reflecting the political dominance of the Soviet Union contained substantial distinctions, and each of them retained elements of indigenous legal culture. However, these constitutions derived some elements from the 1936 constitution of the Soviet Union, and they had important common features. First, they organized the state as a one-party regime committed to a high degree of economic control. Second, they rejected the separation of powers, which was commonly derided in post-1945 eastern Europe as characteristic of bourgeois constitutionalism: they provided for an integrally unified state structure, founded in the notional principle of full popular sovereignty or 'unitary popular power' (Skilling 1952: 208), in which both legislative and executive authority was concentrated in a unicameral legislature, dominated by a single (non-elected) party – this effectively tied legislative power to the prerogatives of a party executive. Third, they rejected judicial independence and strict judicial review (of these states, in fact, only Czechoslovakia had possessed an independent constitutional court before 1945). Indeed, these constitutions ascribed far-reaching political functions to the judiciary, and they often identified judges as custodians of the political will of the people – that is, as instrumental organs of the executive. For example, the Bulgarian constitution of 1947 (Art. 25) laid down that only the National Assembly could decide on questions of statutory constitutionality and that judges were accountable to the legislature and so, effectively, to the party executive. Similarly, the Hungarian Constitution (Art. 41) stated that judges were required to 'punish the enemies of working people'. In these respects, these constitutions condensed all power in a party-based legislature, they relativized the higher-law principles underpinning many earlier constitutions, and in key matters they made the constitution subordinate to regular legislative functions. Fourth, these constitutions instituted a rights structure that simultaneously stipulated extensive declamatory portfolios of material rights and subordinated civil and political rights to restrictive laws. The Polish constitution exemplified this by establishing a sequence of clauses guaranteeing social and material rights (Arts. 57–65). Yet it also prohibited the exercise of certain political rights (Art. 72). The Czechoslovakian constitution, similarly, placed legal sanction on the exercise of rights likely to cause a 'threat to the independence, integrity and unity of the state' or to undermine 'popular-democratic order' (§ 37). Analogously, the Bulgarian constitution allowed the exercise of political rights only on condition that they did not obstruct the material objectives of the constitution (Art. 87).

In select respects, the constitutions of eastern Europe were proclaimed as legal bulwarks against the constitutional preconditions of fascism, and they employed (in remote and residual fashion) a neo-Jacobin legislative model to impede (or to claim to impede) pluralistic or neo-patrimonial fragmentation of state power. First, for instance, the strongly integrated concept of the state was promoted in these constitutions as a template for preserving a compact polity against semi-independent political forces in society. Second, in the same way that constitutions of pre-fascist states had aimed to co-opt plural economic associations in the state by granting flexibly interpreted corporate rights, the constitutions of the East European states after 1945 gave collective/material rights primacy over singular subjective rights: indeed, like fascist constitutions, they employed material rights as institutes of coercive social integration and planning. However, their essential design differed from fascist constitutions in this respect as they reserved rights of economic co-ordination to a strictly organized political party, which from the outset monopolized the state executive, and, at least in intention, they were constructed to avoid the fragmentation of state power through the uneven concession of rights in the form of corporate group rights. This redefinition of collective rights was intended, in part at least, to solidify the state against the patterns of erratic inclusion and political diffusion that had been characteristic of fascist rule.

The constitution of the Fourth Republic in France, introduced in 1946, possessed, albeit in a democratic setting, partial similarities with the post-1945 constitutions of Eastern Europe, and it was also devised as the foundation for a strongly integrated state, centred on a powerful legislature. A first draft of the constitution, which was rejected by referendum in May 1946, contained a very strong presumption in favour of legislative sovereignty and, echoing Jacobin ideas of 1793, it contained provisions for a unicameral parliament (Shennan 1989: 129–30). This vision was tempered in the final constitution of October 1946, which endorsed a somewhat diluted principle of legislative authority, reinforced presidential powers, instituted a (still weak) second chamber and established an (also weak) Constitutional Committee (Art. 91) to review the constitutionality of statutes. However, this constitution was supplanted through a process of revisions in the 1950s, used to strengthen the government against shifts in parliamentary formation, and it was finally replaced by the 1958 Constitution, which founded the Fifth Republic. The Gaullist constitution of 1958 deviated paradigmatically from earlier French constitutions. It greatly strengthened the power of the cabinet and the president against the legislature, and it established a Constitutional Council (Conseil Constitutionnel) as a horizontal check on legislative power. Not originally conceived as a review court, the Council initially acted to oversee distribution of competences between legislature and executive. By the early 1970s, however, the Council had unsettled the principle of untrammelled legislative sovereignty, and in 1971 the Council was formally recognized as a protector of rights (see Vroom 1988: 266). Although differing from conventional constitutional courts in that it retained a position within the legislative process and it was not open to appeal by citizens or regular courts, it began, acting both within and outside parliamentary procedures for legislation, to assume a priori powers for judicial review of statutes and to promote non-derogable standards of human rights as legislative norms.[1]

Like the constitutions in Eastern Europe, the strategies of post-1945 constitutional transformation in Germany and Italy, pursued under the influence of the US forces, can also be seen as intended correctives to the constitutional crisis induced by fascism and its social preconditions. These constitutions represented alternative patterns of response to the corrosion of statehood and the depletion of political power affecting societies exposed to fascist governance.

---

[1] For samples of the immense literature on this ambiguity see Stone (1992: 4); Bastien (1997: 399); Delcamp (2004: 82).

Italy

In Italy, for example, the process of constitution writing after 1945 proceeded from a position of substantial political heterogeneity, in which a number of parties contributed to preliminary constitutional drafts. For all their differences, however, the main parties in the first stages of constitutional formation in Italy concurred in advocating the retention of some elements of quasi-corporate constitutionalism, and they sought to preserve aspects of pre-war Italian constitutional ideals.[2] In each stage of the drafting process between 1946 and 1948, delegates of the Italian Communist Party, allied with the PSI, urged the inclusion of a substantial body of material rights in the constitution: they projected a constitutional order committing the state to far-reaching policies of redistribution and trade-union involvement in legislation, and they even defined the exercise of political rights as correlated with the material formation and collective enrichment of society. At the same time, the newly founded Christian Democratic Party opposed these designs, and it placed emphasis on singular subjective rights as the 'preconditions' of the state (Gonella 1946: 38). However, in their constitutional stance the Christian Democrats, or some of their more reactionary elements, also retained a corporate stance: some members of the party sought both to preserve the regional structure of the Italian polity and even (in extreme cases) to form a corporativist Senate, elected both by universal suffrage and by regional and professional councils (Einaudi 1948: 662–4).[3] On these counts, therefore, the primary parties in the constituent body in Italy both originally aimed, in diverse fashion, to institute a diffusely broad-based and societally inclusive system of government.

Through the course of the ratification process, however, the inclusionary demands of different parties in Italy were either weakened or eliminated. The more corporate elements of Christian Democratic theory were not reflected in the final constitution of 1948, and the Senate was finally constituted as a body elected by universal direct suffrage (Art. 58). Moreover, although the partial autonomy of the regions obtained definitive recognition through the establishment of a regional council (Arts. 114, 121), regional competences were strictly

---

[2] The origins of the modern Italian constitution can be traced, first, to the decree laws passed by the interim government in summer 1944, Art. I of which provided for a constituent assembly to establish a new constitution for the state, and, second, to legislation of 1946, which set precise procedures for elections to the assembly.

[3] Irene Stolzi advised me on this. See email exchange, 27 October 2010.

circumscribed in the constitution,[4] and objects falling under the exclusive legislative power of the state were clearly determined (Art. 117). In addition, the 1948 Constitution sanctioned a very extensive bill of rights, which reflected some objectives of the Communist Party and the PSI: this comprised roughly one third of the entire document. These rights included the classical rights of personal and domestic liberty, freedom of assembly, expression and conscience, access to impartial legal hearing, and protection from non-legitimate acts of public administration (Art. 113). Moreover, these rights included key distributory rights, such as rights to medical care (Art. 32), the right to a fair wage (Art. 36), rights to welfare support (Art. 38), and limited rights of union action (Art. 40) and collective bargaining (Art. 39). Despite recognizing the freedom of private economic enterprise (Arts. 41–2), the constitution contained prescriptive provisions for the partial regulation of private-sector economic activity and for state control of enterprises (Art. 43), and it stipulated that workers had rights of consultation in industrial enterprise (Art. 46). In fact, the constitution created a national economic council, comprising representatives of 'productive categories', to perform consultative functions regarding draft bills submitted to it by the government (Art. 99). In these respects the 1948 Constitution, reflecting the policies of the Communist Party, manifestly preserved core aspects of material constitutionalism. Despite this, however, the left-corporate principles implied in this catalogue also fell substantially short of the primary ambitions of the Communist Party, and they marked an attempt, influenced by US economic orthodoxy, to restrict the role of the state in the economic arena. The rights enshrined by the constitution specifically avoided the construction of a full corporate constitution: they preserved clear distinctions between actors in the private economy and in the state, they ensured that private conflicts were not immediately internalized in the state (i.e. that collective agreements were not dependent on state intervention in the bargaining process), and they guaranteed that the state was not forced endlessly to assume full regulatory responsibility for economic interactions through price setting and income stabilization. In this respect, the 1948 Constitution was designed, within broad limits, to delineate the boundaries of the state and to ensure the societal primacy of a strong, central, yet also functionally circumscribed, state.

Of crucial importance in the drafting process in Italy was the fact that the constitution placed particular emphasis on preserving the

---

[4] The new state was thus both 'centralized and decentralized' (Tesauro and Capocelli 1954: 48).

independence, impartiality and normative accountability of the judiciary (Arts. 101, 104, 111), and it consolidated constitutional rights as external to the sphere of immediate politicization around the legislature and the executive. In this respect, the constitution broke with stricter Italian traditions of Roman law, based on literal interpretation of written codes, and it provided for the institution of a Constitutional Court (established in 1953 and operative from 1956). In the first instance, it was the Christian Democrat members of the constitutional assembly whose programme advocated the creation of a Constitutional Court. This was because they saw the court as an eventual counterweight to the left-oriented bloc which they (erroneously) viewed as a probable feature of the first legislatures of the new republic (Furlong 1988: 10–11; Volcansek 1994: 494). After its institution, the court was empowered to decide on the constitutionality of laws of state, to resolve conflicts of legislative and judicial competence between central state and regions, to settle jurisdictional disputes between regions, and to act as final court of impeachment for cases brought against the president of the republic (Art. 134).[5] However, although lacking powers of abstract review in respect of rights,[6] the court also acted to determine normative compatibility of laws with the constitution and its provisions for fundamental rights and to conduct concrete review where cases from ordinary courts were referred to the court for query or confirmation.

The Constitutional Court performed important functions for the emergent republican state in Italy, and it served partially to rectify conventional weaknesses of Italian statehood. This became manifest, first, in the fact that it played a key role in countervailing endemic tendencies towards fragmentation and regional centrifugality in Italian politics (Evans 1968: 603). Although clearly defining spheres of separate regional jurisdiction and giving protection to the regional council, the constitution ensured that proper objects for central legislation were determined and preserved as such, and it enabled the government to question and control the legitimacy of laws made in the regions by referring these to the court (Art. 127). In addition, in appointing the court to clarify the relation between different levels of the legislative

---

[5] This was a matter of key importance. See Farrelly and Chan (1957: 316); Luther (1990: 78).

[6] This extent to which judicial review in Italy entails ensuring compatibility of laws with rights is often disputed. For different views see Bonini (1996: 65); Cappelletti and Adams (1966); Pizzorusso, Vigoriti and Certoma (1983: 504–5). The primary role of concrete review appears to mean that in Italy rights play a less significant role than in Germany.

system, the constitution weakened residual corporate counterweights to the state: it acted to ensure that the central state reserved the power to terminate laws, it abrogated laws, especially repressive public-order legislation dating from before 1948 that ran counter to the constitution or dispersed the power of the state, and – by these means – it raised general confidence in the legal order.[7] Indeed, as a normative forum standing apart both from earlier state institutions and the (deeply tainted) regular judiciary, the court generated a significant reservoir of legitimacy for the new state, which enhanced its ability to concentrate the fullness of power in its acts. One key example of this was in the realm of constitutional relations between church and state. In the aftermath of the war, parts of earlier ecclesiastical legislation, derived from Mussolini's Concordat of 1929, had initially been absorbed into the state. This had significant bearing on the state's capacity for legislation over questions of family and matrimonial law. The Constitutional Court ultimately played a significant role in stripping out this legislation, and it intensified the legislative independence of the state in these spheres of regulation. Furthermore, the court permitted the newly founded state to recruit technical assistance in determining proper objects and procedures for legislation, and this made it possible for actors within the state, under the approval of second-order observers, substantially to assert their sole right to perform specifically allotted legislative functions. In stipulating exact principles for the ratification of statutes, therefore, the constitution created guarantees to make sure that all formative legislative power was condensed in the state administration, and that edicts or prerogatives not emanating from the central state (i.e. perhaps from regional parliaments or corporate groups) could not easily assume the technical force of law and could not dissolve the (albeit socially limited) cohesiveness of state power.[8] In particular, the constitution as a whole aimed specifically to restrict the formation of private/public corporations assuming quasi-state functions in the localities (Bartole and Vandelli 1980: 180). The Constitutional Court, thus, acted as an important block in a process of constitutional state building, and it substantially enforced the capacity of the emergent Italian state for the positive and abstracted use of power.

---

[7] This was a very important feature of the Italian court. See Volcansek (1994: 495); Franciscis and Zannini (1992).

[8] Separately from my argument here, the role of judicialization in consolidating states against fragmentation, especially in post-fascist environments in which trust in legislatures and regular courts was low, has been observed in Ferejohn (2002: 55–7).

In conjunction with this, the systemically stabilizing functions of the Constitutional Court in post-1945 Italy were evident in the fact that it formalized procedures for resolving conflicts over the rights expressed in the constitution, and it enabled the state to deflect to the law many factual contests over political legitimacy. Many of the more expansive and politically resonant rights in the constitution, for instance the right to strike and the right of the state to expropriate private enterprises, were clearly phrased in a manner that anticipated the referral of controversial statutes and judicial rulings to the Constitutional Court. Indeed, although the court was not staffed by political radicals, its rulings, even under conservative governments, tended to support the defence of civil liberties and rights of minority groups. In establishing a relatively hardened set of procedures, withdrawn from everyday political activities, to preserve and resolve issues related to constitutional rights, therefore, the Constitutional Court enabled the state to hold contests over distinctively volatile matters outside the centre of the political system. This meant that particular social groups and particular parties were not unreservedly at liberty to employ state power to address specific prerogatives, and that conflict over rights did not automatically consume vital resources of state legitimacy. The Constitutional Court formed an instrument in which the basic elements of societal design contained in the constitution – rights – could be applied through society at a diminished level of intensity, and the court increased the legitimacy of the state by preserving and enforcing principles enunciated as rights without causing a fully inclusionary convergence of society around singular demands or contests.

In each of these respects, the sentences of the Constitutional Court played a decisive role both in establishing the supremacy of democratic law and in producing a progressively (although still incompletely) unified monopolistic state in post-1945 Italy (Rodotà 1999: 17). The Constitutional Court acted as a significant device both in the transitional consolidation of democratic culture and in the consolidation of the Italian state per se. Above all, the functions of normative displacement and statutory control provided by the court acted, as in earlier cases, to rigidify the autonomous structure of the state and to simplify its selectively inclusionary use of power. In a societal setting in which the national polity had at once been afflicted by low levels of regional control and high levels of intersection with private actors, the Constitutional Court emerged as an institution that substantially fortified the state and substantially facilitated its functions as a monopolistic and relatively autonomous actor.

Federal Republic of Germany

In post-1945 West Germany, the process of constitution drafting also moved from a diffuse advocacy of relative political-economic pluralism towards a pattern of restrictive liberal consolidation. Some of the first post-war constitutions in the German regional states (*Länder*) were based on a social/legal democratic model, and they strongly reflected the concepts of material or economic democracy characteristic of German constitutional principles from the Weimar era. The more controversial clauses of these constitutions, however, were suppressed by the occupying armies and they ultimately became redundant.[9] The ultimate character of the Basic Law of 1949, originally only intended to assume force as a provisional constitution until the united German people were able to establish a nationally legitimate constitution, was in fact specifically conceived as a remedy for the problems resulting from the Weimar Constitution. Strongly influenced by US antitrust law, the Basic Law aimed at once to avoid the executive-led presidentialism and the reliance on emergency laws of the inter-war polity and to restrict highly pluralistic convergence between economy and state. In the latter case, it endeavoured to reinforce the non-derogable status of singular basic rights, to limit the inclusionary allocation of material and corporate rights, and – primarily – to ensure that bearers of rights were strictly located outside, and not formative of, the state. Instead of the semi-corporate rights of the Weimar era, it gave primacy to a catalogue of rights that reflected classical ideas of subjective liberties and defined the primary spheres of human liberty as outside state power. Moreover, it categorically recognized political parties as organs for structuring the will of the people (Art. 21), and in so doing it helped to regulate the conditions of access to public institutions and to formalize procedures for the more consistent rotation of government and opposition. One consequence of this was that the emergent West German state of the post-war era was able, gradually, both to tolerate a higher level of pluralistic activity in society in general and to regulate the ways in which political parties used and appropriated power stored in the executive.

Despite this rejection of corporate constitutionalism, the Basic Law contained certain core ambiguities in its catalogue of rights, which, as in

---

[9] The most important example was the 1946 constitution of Hesse, which contained a clause (Art. 41) that provided for the socialization of key enterprises. This was opposed by the US military, and, partly for that reason, never applied. For documentation of this see Berding (1996: 1068).

1919, resulted from the fact that the Parliamentary Council comprised representatives from a number of different political parties. For this reason, in addition to its provisions for rights of free expression, conscience, ownership and protection from the state, the Basic Law contained significant (although limited) provision for welfare rights, and it set an advanced standard for the institution of social-welfare rights as primary elements of constitutional order. Influenced by delegates of the SPD in the Parliamentary Council, Article 20 defined the new state as a 'democratic and social federal state', and it indicated that formal rights under law needed to be flanked by rights of material dignity: it thus expressed (albeit cautiously) the presumption that the state would evolve as a welfare state.[10] This principle was reinforced, although not clarified, under Article 28. In these respects, the constitution clearly construed state legitimacy as arising from a modification of classical concepts of the democratic-legal state to include principles of material equality. In fact, subsequent legislation extended these principles by introducing rights of co-determination at the workplace in some industrial sectors and by establishing extensive mechanisms for collective bargaining. Notwithstanding this tendency, however, the Basic Law clearly configured its catalogue of rights in order to place limits on the political internalization of societal exchanges. Most significantly, it avoided binding the legitimacy of the state to regulation of conflicts over production and salaries, and, although presupposing moderate levels of state intervention in the economy, it largely removed industrial conflict from immediate state jurisdiction (Art. 9). Indeed, the commitment to material reallocation foreseen by the Basic Law presupposed that redistribution through the state was to be conducted, if at all, under fixed and prior legal terms: that is, it defined material distribution, not as an expression of the variable material will of the sovereign body contained within the state, but as an administered element of the more general rule of law dictated by the constitution. The rights structure of the Basic Law was far less inclined to promote a fragmentary re-privatization of state power than the rights catalogue in the constitution of 1919. Indeed, the construction of the welfare state, founded in social rights, emerged at this point as a model of legal statehood that acted to expand guarantees for classical liberal rights, yet also used the legal form of social rights to

---

[10] On the origins of these ideas in the economic-democratic concepts of the Weimar era see Niclauß (1974: 35, 42).

evade the expansive *material republicanism* that had coloured the corporate proto-welfarism of the 1920s.

In addition to this, the West German Basic Law, again responding to Allied pressure, contained potent protection for an independent judiciary, and for a strict separation of powers. Notably, the entire process of constitutional formation, from the first constitutional drafts of 1948 to the final text of the Basic Law, reflected an express presumption in favour of a powerful neo-Kelsenian constitutional court, situated outside the regular judiciary.[11] Once established, the court assumed designated functions in respect of federal questions: it was responsible for resolving conflicts of competence between highest federal organs, for ensuring the compatibility of new laws (either at the level of the *Länder* or at federal level) with constitutional law and especially with the provisions for basic rights that the constitution enshrined, and for deciding over conflicts of competence between state and *Länder* (Art. 93). However, it had wider normative functions, and it was intended to ensure that principles of international law were reflected in legal findings of ordinary courts (Art. 100), to integrate veto players in the political system to check laws against constitutional norms, and – most importantly at first – to protect the rights-based 'free democratic basic order' from any political party or group of actors which might reject or undermine it (Art. 21).[12]

As in Italy, this Federal Constitutional Court, established in 1951, brought several pronounced structural benefits to the emergent state of the Federal Republic. One benefit of the court, first, was that the statutory authority and judicial consistency of the federal state were increased. Indeed, although the Basic Law originally provided (Art. 95) for a further high court to guarantee unity in legal finding through the Federal Republic, this task fell in large part to the Constitutional Court, which acted as a de facto guarantor of federal legal integrity. This was particularly important in view of the inter-war background: the Weimar Constitution, although containing limited facilities for constitutional review, did not effectively provide for regulation of constitutional conflicts at national level, and statutory uniformity had been very difficult to maintain in the 1920s.[13] After 1949, however, the Constitutional

---

[11] In Austria the Constitutional Court was reactivated shortly after the war.

[12] The power to prohibit anti-constitutional parties, on right and left, was assigned a key function in the original design of the court (see Laufer 1968: 48).

[13] In fact, German states had a long history of judicial review. As early as 1815, Hardenberg proposed a court of last resort for the German Confederation (Klüber 1815: 53). Powers of review were also implicit in the Constitution of 1848–9 (§§ 52, 125–128). Review functions

Court succeeded in enforcing the primacy of federal law over state law without provoking the deep conflicts that had marked the Weimar era, and the technical bolt-tightening functions of the court contributed in quiet yet structurally vital manner to the consolidation of a state with unitary statutory and judicial force (Blair 1981: 112). The fact that the state of the Federal Republic was endowed with a formal corpus of basic rights and a constitutional court to apply these rights and to check legislation contributed greatly to the consolidation of a strong central state, and it both supplemented and augmented the provisions made in other articles to cement the primacy of the federal state over regional legislators (Arts. 31, 70–75). The most influential early theoretical account of the functions of the court, in fact, tellingly defined the court as a 'constitutional organ' equal in status to legislature and executive, which played a vital role 'in the process of state integration' (Leibholz 1957: 149–50).

A further benefit of the court, second, was that the activities by rights allocated by the state to social agents were subject to a process of secondary reflection in singular acts of legislation, and access to and contestation over rights were governed and filtered by an institutionally independent judicial body. Externally, this tended to harden the function of rights in stabilizing the boundaries of the state, and it helped to prevent social agents claiming or disputing rights in haphazard or erratically unsettling fashion. Indeed, in conjunction with the fact that the Basic Law only endorsed weak material rights, the functions of the court served to ensure that rights were located outside the state and were not enacted as elements of a societal will expressed through the state. Internally, this acted (albeit counter-intentionally) to strengthen the legislature against the executive and, in ensuring a strict division of competence between legislative and executive operations and strict procedures for statutory ratification, it protected legislative functions from interference by private actors able to gain access to the executive. This also meant that many vital decisions of state could be referred to the

were transferred to the Bundesrath in imperial Germany. But the Weimar Constitution contained multiple provisions for review by a confusing array of courts, which possessed overlapping remits. The powers of the Reichsgericht were primarily determined under Art. 13. Art. 108 provided for a further high court, the Staatsgerichtshof, which had competence both for administrative and for statutory review. The controversy over review (*richterliches Prüfungsrecht*) had defining status among public lawyers in the 1920s. However, the Weimar Constitution did not create a single constitutional court with powers of abstract review. In keeping with the spirit of the period, advocates of strong powers of review often viewed the power of courts as a means for guaranteeing (if necessary against the will of parliament) strong political direction (Triepel 1929: 8).

constitutional court and subject to external review, so that at critical junctures contests over macro-societal direction could be articulated and addressed in relatively formalized procedures. In this respect, the court created a legitimating framework in which the state could withdraw its power from incessant contest and reflect its authority as secured under formally extracted norms. The construction of the Constitutional Court as a custodian of rights, in short, performed the beneficial function that it enabled the state to presuppose the law as a stable normative condition of its legitimacy, so that express legal support could be invoked to implement contested political rulings. The Constitutional Court thus helped to separate the public order of the state from its day-to-day actions, and it provided a body in which the state could articulate and control a legal order to accompany its use of power. This meant in turn that the political system was not obliged endlessly to generate independent foundations for its legitimacy, it internalized an instrument to de-personalize and facilitate the processes of statutory legitimization, and it greatly alleviated the statutory operations of the state. These functions were of particularly vital importance in Germany as they assumed effect in a socio-historical setting traditionally marked by acute lack of parliamentary stability and state integrity and by an acute excess of political privatism and personalism. The fact that the state could explain itself as obtaining a strongly internalized constitutional order standing alongside or above particular persons bearing power enabled the state to avoid personal monopolies in the use of power, and, for the first time in German history, it permitted the state fully to differentiate itself from persons factually exercising governance and to rotate power between different persons, organs and parties. By creating a facility that allowed the state to displace and internally to control its power and to avoid the concentration of full sovereignty in one highly politicized legislative system, the constitutional court substantially reinforced the factual, positive and effective powers of the state, and it practically enhanced the monopoly of political control and reserves of usable power possessed by the state.[14] The normative construction of power within the state, in short, factually multiplied the volume of power which the state contained.

---

[14] The opposite is usually argued (see especially Waldron 2006). However, in my view, the argument that judicial review weakens democracy revolves around the rather absurdly counter-factual assumption that democracy entails one set of sovereign practices, concentrated in a discursive legislature. The normative case against judicial review usually exemplifies *extreme sociological under-reflection*.

In both West Germany and Italy, in consequence, it is arguable that the constitutional design adopted after 1945, although partly imposed by occupying regimes, marked an important leap forward in the inner-societal process of state construction. In each case, the new constitution substantially consolidated the power of traditionally weak states. In the case of Italy, in fact, it is arguable that it was only with the formation of the 1948 Constitution that the state began to assume reliable features of statehood and gradually to exercise a monopoly of national force. To be sure, this process remained tentative: throughout the 1960s the Italian democracy still resorted to personalistic techniques of consensus manufacture that recalled the strategies of *trasformismo* concluded by Giolitti. The use of state power remained precariously balanced in relation both to the social groups that it represented and to the regions over which it applied power, and the Italian political system remained conditioned by endemic lower-level clientelism. In West Germany, the process of state construction, solidified by the constitution, was more rapid. Although it was widely asserted through the 1950s that the state executive remained in thrall to powerful lobbies and that political power retained a partly privatized core,[15] the federal state evolved quickly to a high level of functional abstraction, and it was capable of establishing inclusive and general bases of support. The double-checking of power by a constitutional court was a core innovation in this respect, and it created the basis for a strongly abstracted and internalized body of public law, for an abstract de-personalization of statehood and for a controlled rotation of governmental power which had not been fully established before 1945. In both settings, the constitutional order augmented the generality of state power, and it stabilized the structure of the state as a relatively autonomous actor. Indeed, it was specific to the functions of constitutional courts in these polities that, although designed to resolve problems of federal and regionalized states, they exercised vital functions of abstraction in post-fascist settings. In tracing the limits of statehood against private regional actors and providing constructed de-politicization for traditionally precarious executives, they hardened the public order of the state against the danger of internal collapse and re-privatization.

---

[15] For example, Otto Stammer warned about a 'structural transformation of parliament' resulting from the power of economic associations to influence political parties (1957: 597). Werner Weber defined economic associations as forming a 'para-constitutional system of forces with public claim to validity' (1985 [1957]: 67).

Of the most critical importance in these processes of state reinforcement was the fact that the establishment of strong procedures of judicial review was tied to the increasing recognition of an international rule of rights. This meant that national legislation was progressively determined, not only by national constitutions, but by wider normative standards, which impacted on specific statutes and rulings of specific courts. In particular, the aftermath of the Second World War witnessed the institution of the International Court of Justice (1946) as successor to the Permanent Court of International Justice. It also saw the ratification (1950) and enforcement (1953) of the European Convention on Human Rights, which fostered the presumption that single states were obliged to act in accordance with universal norms in respect of rights, and that legislation should be passed in conformity with international standards. Overall, although in principle placing external checks on the power of single states, these conventions brought deep functional advantages and heightened factual autonomy for post-war democratic states. Specifically, they established a set of norms to which single states could refer in order to accompany and control the different stages of their legislative processes and insulate themselves against destabilizing movements and temporary interests installed within their executives. The emergence of a strong prejudice in favour of international higher-law review that accompanied the democratic transitions of the post-1945 era thus directly reinforced the authority of states, and the emergent multi-levelled, and increasingly trans-societal, normative order of rights provided a complex legal defence through which states could counteract the inner-societal usurpation or fragmentation of their power. Indeed, the broad presumption in favour of rights that accompanied the post-1945 transitions might be seen, like earlier rights revolutions in the eighteenth century, as a societal occurrence that facilitated the abstract inclusive and generalized application of power, and controlled the contingency involved in statutory legislation in uncertain or evolving political environments.

The second wave of transition: constitutional re-foundation in the 1970s

In contrast to these cases, some European societies preserved an under-evolved rights fabric after 1945, and their adaptive political structures and levels of autonomy were strongly and detrimentally marked by this fact. Generally, states that had not followed the pattern of constitutional transition and rights-based political abstraction after 1945 and still retained constitutions integrating a high volume of social functions into the political system struggled to mobilize power effectively across society, and they proved particularly susceptible to crises of legitimacy. These states, consequently, were also ultimately compelled, normally through loss of political autonomy and quasi-revolutionary transitions, to adopt alternative constitutional forms to react to and manage these crises.

Portugal

The first prominent example of this was the authoritarian regime in Portugal under Salazar and, in its last years, Caetano, which collapsed in 1974. In certain respects, the constitutional transition in Portugal commencing in 1974 reflected the wider causal patterns underlying constitutional formation, and it had its preconditions in a societal condition determined by acute levels of political convergence and structural inflexibility. To illustrate this, for instance, it has been widely argued that the Portuguese turn to a closed corporate economy under Salazar in the 1930s was superseded in the later years of the regime through a process of economic restructuring and international opening, and it was replaced by a technocratic style of capitalist growth management.[16] Owing to this change, the 1960s also witnessed a consolidation of liberal economic design in Portugal: specifically, this period saw an increase in labour mobility, emigration and inflows of foreign capital, which altered the configuration of Portuguese society and disrupted existing patterns of industrial control and highly sedimented stratification. It is also widely documented, however, that Salazar's Novo Estado struggled to accommodate these social changes, and in some respects it preserved a political-constitutional structure adapted to a less fluid system of authoritarian corporate capitalism. Indeed, until 1974, many political dimensions of the corporate structure remained in place: in particular, political activity and opposition remained strictly controlled, opposition remained (at best) only semi-legal, and the repressive, vertically ordered executive/judicial apparatus of the Salazar regime was recurrently utilized for political and economic supervision. This simultaneity of progressively liberalized economic policy and persistent neo-corporate political order had a number of implications for the state. It had the consequence, first, that the state apparatus became highly isolated and

---

[16] For analysis see Lewis (1978: 639); Baklanoff (1992: 6–7); Machado (1991: 19); Chilcote (2010: 60).

rigidified, and it was expected to perform regulatory functions to which it was not adapted and which exceeded its rather inflexible steering capacities.[17] It also had the consequence that, owing to the persistently close links between economic and political co-ordination, the state was deeply susceptible to destabilization caused by economic conflict and unrest: economic instabilities were of necessity internalized as political conflicts, and the failure of government to provide for wage increases or satisfactory settlements over changing production conditions necessarily consumed and drained its legitimacy. In response to this, the government was forced further to suppress independent labour activity, to heighten its policies of economic control and generally to place extreme burdens on its legitimacy in questions of economic direction (Wiarda 1979: 111). The Portuguese state in the last years of the corporate era might thus be seen as suffering classically from a lack of political differentiation or excessive structural convergence: this had the result that material conflicts migrated easily into the state, and it meant that the state lacked autonomous capacities for resolving the economic problems that it assimilated and it was routinely forced to over-consume political legitimacy.

In addition, even in its latter years, the Portuguese regime was still characterized by a high degree of internal pluralism. Notably, it remained characterized by deep interpenetration with prominent private/economic groups, it failed fully to integrate actors based in the military, it was compelled to negotiate bargains with the military as a semi-independent body, and it relied on diverse personal arrangements with the church. Indeed, the fact that the state lacked formal mechanisms for the distribution of power and the control of access to the executive meant that it was sustained by half-internal, half-external support from representatives of different social organizations, and it was obliged to pacify groups only loosely assimilated in its institutional apparatus to preserve practical and ideological legitimacy. The dense yet pluralistic intersection between the state executive and these organizations meant that internal or personal conflicts with or between these groups had the potential to acquire extremely destabilizing consequences for the integrity of the state as a whole. Notably, the connection between the executive and the military gradually became the Achilles heel of Salazar's regime: after an attempted coup in 1961, the degree of military representation at ministerial level declined, and the dependence of the regime

---

[17] Excellent here is Schmitter (1975: 14).

on military support became more uncertain. Moreover, although the majority of clergy remained loyal to the Novo Estado, the regime suffered a weakening of its legitimacy when confronted by opposition within the church, and it remained sensitive to alterations in political orthodoxies sanctioned by the Vatican.[18] By 1974, in short, the Portuguese state struggled to use or apply power in inclusive and abstracted form, it solidified its authority through precarious processes of piecemeal personal inclusion and ideological borrowing and it was susceptible to both external and internal delegitimization. The regime collapse of 1974 was thus an event that responded to these weaknesses and drew impetus from the structural and inclusionary deficiencies of the state.

It is evident that the Portuguese constitutional transition of 1974 did not mark an immediate breach with principles of social organization characterizing the Salazar regime, and some structural features of the Novo Estado remained pronounced throughout and after the Portuguese revolution. In the first instance, the revolution was initiated from within the state machinery – that is, by insurgent corps in the army, supported by diverse anti-dictatorial forces inside and outside the state – and, as a result, the interim revolutionary regime preserved some elements of the pluralism and loose institutional integrity of the old order. After its moderate inception, the revolution veered leftward, and the Armed Forces Movement (MFA), centred around a corps of insurrectionist officers, was, despite a counter-coup in 1975, the dominant force in the provisional governments of the period 1974–6. During this time the MFA provided support for the interim state, and the supreme body of the MFA, the Council of the Revolution, functioned as a transitional political vanguard by purging government departments of those sympathetic to Caetano, by controlling the economy through the cleansing of banks and the nationalization of key industries, and by assuming vital judicial functions. Only gradually was the transitional process brought under the regular rule of law: a central element in this consolidation was a law of 1976 that declared void ideologically driven purges of public-sector institutions (Costa Pinto 2006: 192). However, it was not until 1982 that immediate military supervision of judicial, legislative and executive actions was terminated, and that the state executive was fully detached from the army. Until 1982 the Council of the Revolution assumed final powers of veto over legislation (in fact, it acted as a final court of appeal and served as guardian of the quasi-revolutionary

---

[18] On this point, I consulted Cerqueira (1973: 495, 513).

constitution), and it used its powers to support a powerful presidential executive. The Council of the Revolution was replaced in 1982 by a Council of State.[19]

Against this background, the democratic Portuguese constitution adopted in 1976 was also influenced both by the particular social conditions of the transition period and, more arguably, by the residual corporate configuration of Portuguese society under Salazar. At one level, the constitution created preconditions for the stabilization of a parliamentary-democratic state, and it sanctioned conventional rights and freedoms in respect of political activity, expression and movement. It also limited state intervention in private existence by guaranteeing personal security (Arts. 26–7), and it reduced political control of family life, marriage and belief: it crucially restricted the convergence between the state and the church (Art. 41). Most particularly, the constitution authorized free elections and enshrined principles of governmental accountability (Art. 48), and it recognized the existence of a number of political parties (Art. 47), represented in an independent legislature, standing beside and possessing a position inferior to, but not incorporated within, the presidential executive. Simultaneously, however, many classical functions of constitutional rule were not prominent in the 1976 Constitution. Even though the constitution was written after the defeat of the army radicals and the removal of military assemblies from the institutional structure of government, it still authorized powers of legislative and judicial control assumed by the army during the transition. Article 3 of the constitution stated that the Armed Forces Movement was a 'guarantor of the democratic achievements and the revolutionary process': it was, as such, entitled to share in the exercise of sovereign power. The status of the military forces was further cemented under Article 10. In consequence, although the constitution promised universal human rights (Art. 16), pledged itself to rights of free trial (Arts. 31, 32), and established a judiciary that was independent and subject to law (Art. 208), the judicial power of the state remained subject to external restraints, and the executive authority of the (non-civilian) president was intensified. Indeed, although the constitution formally established a supreme tribunal (Arts. 212, 215), separate interpretation of statutes by judges was restricted as long as the Council of the Revolution retained influence. In this respect, the constitutional text preserved a high degree

---

[19] Throughout this paragraph I consulted Gallagher (1975: 203); Maxwell (1995: 159–60); Magalhães, Guarnieri and Kaminis (2006: 160); Costa Pinto (2006: 176; 2008: 272).

of institutional pluralism within the state, the judicial checks for hardening the state against inner pluralism were not firmly embedded and the
state remained founded on a bargained 'diffusion of power', in which a
number of prominent actors in the 1974 revolution claimed and retained
a stake in state authority (Maxwell 1986: 132).

In addition to this, the system of social rights instituted in the 1976
Constitution also strongly reflected the influence of pre-1974 political
structure, and in some respects the constitutional rights of this era looked
back to the patterns of constitutional foundation typical of inter-war
Europe. As in earlier parallel cases, the 1976 Constitution gave direct
expression to the interests of the diverse parties involved in the constituent
body, and on points of economic policy it contained palpably divergent
stipulations. These divergences were particularly accentuated in the catalogues of rights in the constitution. Notwithstanding the fact that it
enshrined the right of private ownership (Art. 62), for example, the constitution defined Portugal as a sovereign republic in transition towards a
'society with no classes' (Art. 1), and it instituted far-reaching provisions
for economic redistribution and control. To reflect this, it pledged the state
to a programme of 'economic and social planning'. It also guaranteed the
right to work (Art. 52), it established an extended system of social security
(Art. 63), and it recognized the right to reasonable habitation (Art. 65).
Further, it guaranteed the rights of workers to labour under conditions
likely to facilitate personal self-realization (Art. 53), to establish extensive
free trade-union associations (Art. 57), to form workplace committees to
defend their interests (Art. 55), to participate in legislation regarding workplace conditions and to negotiate collective bargains (Art. 58). As a result of
these extensive social provisions, the 1976 Constitution preserved aspects
of a quasi-corporate economic system that had prevailed before 1974. To
be sure, the state now clearly abandoned the authoritarian capitalist design
pioneered by Salazar, and it was re-formed as an actor whose regulatory
powers were oriented towards material redistribution. However, the syndical legislation of the constitution built on and maintained informal
continuity with prominent structures of the corporate system of the
Novo Estado.[20]

The period of constitutional reform in Portugal, however, ultimately
approached conclusion in extensive constitutional revisions completed
in 1982, and it was at this time that the state obtained a fully functional
constitution. These reforms, implemented by the incumbent moderate

---

[20] This point is made in Bruneau (1984: 68) and Chilcote (2010: 78–9).

coalition, altered some of the provisions for basic rights in respect of production and distribution, and they loosened the link between executive and judiciary. In this respect, the constitutional revisions of 1982 accorded greater protection to private-economic enterprise (Art. 85), they gave equal status to private, public and corporate sectors of the economy (Art. 80), and they eliminated programmatic statements about the long-term goal of building a socialist economy. One crucial innovation in these revisions was that, in limiting the programmatic functions of the state, it reduced the powers of the president and the military, and it set preconditions for the relatively apolitical rule of law. In particular, these reforms put an end to the use of the judiciary as an instrument of military/political control and planning, and they established a separate Constitutional Court which placed review of statutes under full civilian control.[21] In consequence, although a high level of societal corporatism persisted in Portugal after this time, the end of the protracted constitutional transition in 1982 reduced the inner pluralism and societal density of the state, and it saw the implementation of a rights regime that delineated stricter boundaries of internal and external state competence, placed activities covered by rights outside the state and concentrated the power of the state in internally controlled institutions.

Spain

The Spanish constitutional transition in the 1970s marked a further important example of societally adaptive and politically abstracted constitutional reform. Until the end of the Franco regime, the Spanish state preserved aspects of the corporatist legal order first instituted in the early years of Franco's rule. This constitutional apparatus had a number of highly deleterious consequences for the state, and by the time of Franco's death in 1975 the Spanish state, like the Portuguese state, was characterized by problems of low differentiation and abstraction, and it suffered from many classical structural problems of *weak statehood*. The constitutional reforms during the post-1975 transition acted in part to rectify this weakness and to raise the autonomous capacities of the state.

First, the structural problems of the pre-1975 Spanish state resulted from the fact that it assumed accountability for a large mass of social

---

[21] It was only in the constitutional revisions of 1982 that the functions of de-controversialization attached to constitutional courts became clear. For expert analysis, see Magalhães (2003). Note also Opello (1990).

problems, and the factual legitimacy of the state was undermined through the diffuse politicization of society. To be sure, in its latter years the Franco regime differed from other salient one-party systems in that the economic responsibilities of the state were limited and the Spanish state, although authoritarian, did not aim comprehensively to control economic production and distribution. Up to 1958, notably, the state had assumed accountability for setting wage levels and it intervened in the economy to ensure that economic conditions were favourable for capitalist enterprise: it acted to suppress independent economic activity and economic conflict, and to regulate living standards and income. From the later 1950s onwards, however, Franco reduced his commitment to corporate economic control, and he accepted an increasing degree of private autonomy and private negotiation, including collective bargaining, in the economy. The official syndicalism of the early Franco period was diluted after this time, and prominent policymakers increasingly favoured more standard liberal modes of economic administration. Yet, despite this, the state continued to uphold extensive quasi-syndical arrangements for wage negotiations, it preserved a large number of unproductive subsidized industries, and it was burdened by heavy regulatory policies, a poor taxation system and a small state budget. Additionally, the latter years of the Franco regime witnessed only a selective, supply-side liberalization of social policy: independent economic organization and attendant patterns of trade-union mobilization and industrial conflict were still subject to intense state repression, and restrictive vetoes were placed on political parties and associations representing rival economic prerogatives. In consequence, the state was forced to internalize a high volume of social conflict, it was very heavily dependent on military support, it was vulnerable to the repercussions of economic violence and protest, and it was forced to exhaust its legitimacy in a very large number of societal exchanges.

Second, as it lacked the inner flexibility in policymaking obtained by states recognizing political organization by more than one party or more than one person, Franco's state, like Salazar's regime, had the paradoxical quality that, simultaneously, it concentrated power in the hands of a few particular persons and state ministries and devolved far-reaching political responsibilities to semi-private groups. Indeed, Franco's political system was deficient in several basic characteristics of statehood, and it even lacked the capacity for reliably regimenting administrative power in the offices of a hegemonic political party. Instead of this, political power was exercised by Franco, his ministers and a loose aggregate of associates and ideological supporters, and the regime as a whole relied on highly particularistic 'channels of interest articulation', existing outside the state administration, to connect the state executive with areas of society relevant for specific policies (Gunther 1980: 259). At one level, in consequence, the regime suffered from an intrinsic lack of policy options, as the personal preferences of individual ministers or privileged interest groups determined key aspects of policymaking (Gunther 1996: 167). Additionally, however, the allocation of power to external groups meant that these groups brought their own unsettling legitimating patterns into the state, and they employed state power for objectives not fully internal to the state. A key example of this was the relation between Franco's regime and the church. During the early part of the regime, Franco had repeatedly sought to obtain legitimacy for his government by recruiting support from the Vatican and by associating his policies with the visceral anti-communism of the Roman Catholic church. Indeed, in return for ideological support Franco ensured that members of the episcopate obtained high political standing, and he even ceded powers of state jurisdiction to the church, notably in marital cases and family law. Throughout the 1950s, moreover, the administration of the state became increasingly porous to Roman Catholic pressure groups, particularly representatives of the Opus Dei movement, who advocated policies of technocratic economic liberalization and assumed responsibility for many aspects of public policy. In each of these respects the state constructed preconditions for societal compliance by borrowing legitimacy from the church. In the 1960s, however, Franco's regime suffered critical ideological deflation through the rulings of Vatican Council II, which underlined the increasing support of the Holy See for human rights and constitutional democracy. As a result of this, the ideological assistance that the state had assimilated from the church began to evaporate, and the state struggled internally to manage its reserves of legitimacy. While repressively restricting levels of pluralism throughout society, in consequence, the Franco regime, like that of Salazar, was shaped by a moderately high level of internal or personalistic administrative pluralism (Rodríguez Díaz 1989: 223), and vital decisions were contested by factions within the state and delegated to groups with only tenuous claim to state authority. Owing to its inner personalistic pluralism, in fact, the state lost the ability autonomously to control its motivational basis, and the absence of open and external competition over ideological resources finally led to a depletion and erosion of its authority.

Third, as the state did not possess a fully independent judiciary, questions of legal contravention were absorbed in intense form into the political system, and this overstrained the legal capacities of the state and overtaxed the resources of legitimacy that it possessed.[22] This was particularly the case because the Franco regime subjected political and ideological dissent to high levels of criminalization, and it used the judiciary as a potent repressive tool. After 1945, to be sure, the status and functions of the Spanish judiciary had been gradually formalized. In particular, the jurisdiction of military courts, prominent in the wake of the civil war, was curtailed through the consolidation of the regime in the 1940s, and the law courts, although their power and competence were limited by the executive and the police, acted less frequently as immediate protagonists of political violence and generally obtained a moderate degree of independence. Despite this, however, the moderating shift to legalism and judicial neutrality was never complete. In 1963, for example, a Tribunal de Orden Público was established, which was responsible for the prosecution of political malfeasance. Even with the institution of this body, however, the state was not easily able to prosecute all deemed guilty of political crimes. After 1963, the military continued to exercise some (although limited) judicial functions, and the state was required to create numerous specialized tribunals for dealing with different categories of crime. The state suffered a number of grave functional disadvantages through its persistent politicization of criminal law: it struggled to sustain all its judicial functions, it was required to rely on personal support from the military for the enforcement of law and it was unable to uphold a controlled unitary legal order in all spheres of jurisdiction. The traditional problem of weak judicial unity that defined Spanish statehood in earlier periods of history persisted at this time, and legal rulings were handed down by a bewildering range of official and semi-official tribunals, some linked to the church and the army (Beck 1979: 297). In addition, the state's criminalization of political opposition meant that the law was applied throughout society as a medium of volatile contestation, so that judicial processes and outcomes were endlessly re-internalized in the state, many judicial findings raised far-reaching questions about the overall construction of the political system, and the state was consequently obliged to translate social conflicts into immediately politicized and disruptive exchanges. In particular, owing to its economic directives, the state

---

[22] For an important study that stresses the independent attitudes of judges under Franco, see Toharia (1975b: 476, 482). See also Magalhães, Guarnieri and Kaminis (2006: 144–7).

was required to prosecute a very large number of cases in the sphere of labour law, and it was forced to engender and confront an erratically politicized mass of labour conflicts (Toharia 1975a: 162). Through its close coupling with the judicial apparatus, therefore, the political system lost its ability to limit its political intensity through law, and it dramatically inflated its vulnerability to socio-political conflicts. Indeed, as the state was unable sensibly to regulate its relation to society through singular rights and uniform laws, it was compelled to register a large number of social contests as posing in principle quasi-totalistic questions about the legitimacy, the political form and the direction of society as a whole. For this reason, the Spanish state under Franco had the defining characteristic that it was exposed to extreme and ideologically intensified conflicts over regional autonomy and identity, it was forced to use repressive legislation to preserve territorial control and it was easily destabilized by the separatist ambitions of the regional/national groups that it incorporated.

The inability of Franco's state to abstract itself from, and to accommodate itself to, a pluralistic external social reality, in short, placed the political system in a condition of high personalism and weak adaptivity, in which it was required to generate and consume large quantities of legitimacy, and it was marked by a shortage of political alternatives in its attempts to address emergent social themes. The process of democratic constitutional transition in Spain after Franco's death in 1975, consequently, marked a reaction to these predicaments of structural density, over-inclusion and pluralism in the Spanish state. One of the key outcomes of the transition was that, although both at a socio-economic and at a political/structural level the transition did not end the prevalence of corporate modes of organization in society,[23] it generally alleviated the political apparatus of the expansive burdens of inclusion that had previously characterized it. Like other democratic transitions, the process of political transformation in post-Franco Spain used constitutional devices to locate objects of political inclusion outside the state and to reduce the intensity of society's material and volitional convergence around the state. The process of constitutional reform was initiated by the Law for Political Reform in late 1976, which abolished the corporatist and highly circumscribed form of the Cortes surviving from the Franco regime. This was followed by a raft of reformist legislation, providing, among other

---

[23] During the failed coup of 1981, for example, it was not primarily parliament, but partners in corporate socio-economic concertation, who stood up for the democratic order (Foweraker 1987: 67).

innovations, for the legalization of independent political parties, the establishment of free trade unions and the introduction of an electoral law allowing all parties equal access to governmental power. On this basis, then, a democratic Cortes was assembled in 1977, whose chief duty was to write a new constitution for the transitional state.

The constitution drafted by the Cortes and approved in 1978 was a key example of the structural re-articulation of a political system by constitutional means. In the first instance, the 1978 Constitution sanctioned a number of plural rights, and it extracted the areas of practice covered by these rights from immediate state jurisdiction. Prominent among these rights were rights of ideological and religious liberty (Art. 16) and rights of free expression of political opinion (Art. 20). As corollaries, the constitution also included rights of free political activity, association (Arts. 21–22) and trade-union activity (Art. 28), so entailing a conclusive sanction for the liberty of political parties and free political formation through society. In addition, while enshrining the right to work and to earn a living wage (Art. 35), the constitution restricted the state's internalization of economic conflicts: it endorsed rights of private ownership of property, rights of inheritance (Art. 33) and rights of entrepreneurial activity (Art. 38), and it abandoned the partly syndicalist model of economic organization utilized under Franco. Notably, the constitution specifically recognized the right of both workers and employers to engage in free collective negotiation regarding conditions of labour (Art. 37) and to exercise, within certain limits, policies of collective bargaining. In this respect, the constitution reflected the influence of the socialist and communist parties in Spain, which had been legalized in 1976. However, rather than fully integrating unions into the state, it used recognition of free trade unions as an instrument for ensuring that the state was not defined or forced internally to act as an organ for industrial control or even as a primary regulator of industrial conflict. In each respect, rights acted as institutes of abstraction within the state which separated the state from the pluralistic aggregate of personal arrangements and intersections fundamental to the Franco regime, and they created far sharper lines of public-legal and private-legal articulation and externalization to support the state.

In addition to these rights, further, the transitional reforms in Spain after Franco's death included crucial regulations to reduce the catalogue of political crimes, to control exchanges between the executive and the judiciary and to guarantee equal personal standing before the law and legal ruling by relatively impartial judges. On one hand, the guarantees over rights of expression, conscience and political action diminished the politicization of criminal law, and the constitutional protection of basic rights ensured that the judicial consumption of legitimacy by the state was limited and the ideological burdens placed on the state were curtailed. The relative depoliticization of criminal law was in fact a key element in the reform process. Additionally, however, the constitution established a fully separate judiciary (Arts. 117, 124), it consolidated a unitary basis for the judicial system, it brought military jurisdiction under full control of the state and it prohibited all independent or exceptional tribunals (Art. 117). The traditional judicial weakness of the Spanish state was partly rectified under the terms of the 1978 Constitution, and the heterogeneous sharing of legal authority between the state, the church and the military was terminated. In this legislation again, therefore, the establishment of rights-based legal uniformity played a key role in preserving the monopoly of state power and in allowing the state to obviate the private contestation and borrowing of power through the legal order.

Furthermore, like other transitional democracies at this time, Spain followed the German and Italian precedent in adopting a Constitutional Court (operative from 1980). This court, unlike in Portugal, was founded at a relatively early stage in the transition, and it played a significant role in the process of stabilization. The institution of the court meant, first, that laws passed by the Cortes were subject to both concrete and abstract review, and that laws could be appealed either by judicial organs or by ordinary citizens. As in post-1945 cases of democratic transition, the court enabled the state to establish and entrench the general rule of law across its territories. Indeed, as in Italy after 1956, the court created a legitimating structure in which residues of earlier legislation, if in violation of formally declared constitutional laws, could be swept away and an effective legal *tabula rasa*, promoting increased confidence in the state, could be instituted. Moreover, as in other post-authoritarian states, the establishment of the Constitutional Court meant that cases reflecting fundamental-rights questions could be referred to special procedures and removed from both ordinary courts and the state executive. Through this function the central state was able, once again, to deflect conflictual decisions to a separate judicial body, and the law both provided resources of political de-concentration for the state and impeded the emergence of legal cases in which private actors used the law to unsettle political power. In each respect the court extracted a body of public law above the functional operations of the state: in so doing, it greatly reinforced the inclusive power of the state and it contributed substantially both to the internal structuring of the state and to the consolidation of the state as the primary bearer of political authority. Of particular significance in this was the fact that the court adjudicated in contests over competence between the central government and the regions (Arts. 161–162), and it did much to weaken the traditional potentials for extreme political conflagration that resided in region/centre antagonisms.

Overall, the emergence of a new constitutional reality in Spain after 1975 brought substantial structural advantages for the state order, and, in using a rights apparatus to split many activities from the state, it facilitated a significant simplification and inclusionary intensification of state power. The societalization of the diffuse regulatory functions previously ascribed to the state, for instance, meant that the state, although still bound to certain corporate functions, was less extensively compelled to incorporate the conflictual dimensions of society, and it could relieve itself at once of the programmatic obligations, the ideological requirements and the attendant conflicts involved in extensive societal planning. Primarily, this had the result that the state was not expected to generate absolutely monopolizing ideological patterns to support all its political acts, and the ideological pluralization of the political landscape established through the constitutional transition meant that societal conflicts could be articulated in a number of different procedures and registers, which did not invariably necessitate direct or centric conflict over state power. Furthermore, crucially, the fact that the reforms also severed the direct link between the state executive and criminal law meant that contested legal cases were referred to separate courts, the law was less widely subject to politicization, and the resources of legitimacy possessed by the state were not incessantly implicated in everyday judicial findings. Additionally, the fact that the new constitution sanctioned independent party-political activity and recognized a number of different parties as protected under law had similar consequences. This meant that the state acquired a legal structure that enabled it increasingly to rotate power and to ensure that its power was distinct from the persons and milieux in which it was temporarily invested. In turn, this had the consequence that the state was not required to condense all its legitimacy into solitary manifestos or highly exclusive political programmes, that it obtained flexibility and adaptivity in responding to new contents or themes in society, and that it assumed new capacities for proposing and legitimizing points of policy. The principle of rights-based *societal pluralism* so fundamental to the laws of the post-1975 democratic transition in Spain thus acted, like more formal elements of the new constitutional system, dramatically to intensify the usable power of the state. The acceptance of society as an aggregate of private exchanges, delineated by rights, outside the state effectively decreased the pluralism and the quasi-privatistic use of political resources within the state itself, and it acted as a precondition for the adaptive and effective use, and indeed the heightened positive production, of political power.[24]

The third wave of transition: constitutional transformation in the 1990s

In Russia and other countries in eastern and central Europe in the late 1980s and 1990s a related set of adaptive processes of state building and political abstraction through constitutional formation was observable. In this context, the process of constitutional transition again reflected functional exigencies within different states and it adjusted the political power of states to a new level of articulation. Indeed, although the constitutions of the east European communist states founded in the aftermath of 1945 were in many ways created in antithesis to fascist governance, the fact that they were marked by weak systems of political rotation, by the absence of an independent parliamentary opposition and by a lack of judicial autonomy meant that these one-party states also began to degenerate into a condition of highly interlocked political privatism. As in other settings, they eventually used constitutional remedies to extricate their power from this condition.

Poland

When analysing the constitutional dimensions of the third wave of democratic transition, it is helpful to focus first on Poland, which in many respects both initiated the longer period of reform and established a legal template that legitimized the subsequent reform process in different countries. The Polish state began a long process of reaction against its post-1945 constitutional structure in the second half of the 1970s. The Polish constitution of 1952 (approved personally by Stalin) reflected the Leninist constitutional doctrine that favoured a highly

---

[24] On the commitment to pluralism in Spain during the transition see Cotarelo (1992: 169–70).

integrated executive/legislative structure, and in which the parliament (Sejm), dominated by one party, monopolized all legislative and executive powers and subordinated constitutional laws to statutory legislative acts. In this constitution, as mentioned above, a catalogue of rights, providing for partial political inclusion of economic activity, was appended as a body of normative rules or *programmatic aspirations* to be objectively applied by the state. As in other Soviet-influenced nations, however, these rights were not placed externally to the state, and they were not applied by an independent judiciary: Article 52 of the constitution stated that judges were independent, yet Article 48 maintained that courts were 'custodians of the social and political system' of the People's Republic of Poland. By the later 1970s, however, the high structural density and inclusionary social centricity of the Polish state made it vulnerable to very diverse social protest. Actors in the executive began progressively to respond to increasingly intense sociopolitical unrest and, especially, to independent trade-union activity by implementing constitutional reforms that gradually transformed and disarticulated the more densely integrated elements of the political system. In particular, primary actors in the state reacted to the social pressures of the late 1970s by accepting (tentatively and in limited fashion) principles of judicial independence and so altering the factual constitution of the state both to incorporate an acknowledgement of human rights as institutes external to the legislature and to endorse a partial separation of powers. This was influenced by the (at least notional) acceptance of the Helsinki Accords throughout eastern Europe, and by the resultant recognition of formally normative standards in human-rights legislation (Procházka 2002: 22).

The reform of the Polish constitution began with measures in the 1970s that assigned to the Council of State responsibility to oversee the constitutionality of new laws. This was followed in 1980 by laws establishing a High Administrative Court, which was designed normatively to review administrative regulations. In 1982, the 1952 Constitution was modified to establish a separate Constitutional Tribunal, which was authorized to ensure the constitutional compatibility of statutes and other normative acts issued by parliament and other state organs. This tribunal was not originally conceived as a horizontal check on the legislature. However, after protracted dispute, the position of the tribunal was established under legislation of 1985, and it began to adjudicate cases in 1986. After 1987 it was supplemented by the powers of an Ombudsman for Citizens' Rights, and in 1989 it began to assert itself more fully as a body empowered concretely to review statutes in the light of provisions for rights, and to restrict both legislative and executive powers: it struck down seven statutes in that year, and by then it had struck down almost all substatutory acts that it reviewed.[25] Finally in 1989, the 1952 Constitution was again amended, and the scope of the review powers held by the court was significantly expanded.

In Poland the separation of judicial power from combined legislative and executive power by means of the Constitutional Tribunal was, in its functional dimensions, a reaction to the difficulties encountered by the pre-1989 state in its attempts to police a large mass of social exchanges. It was one aspect of a process in which the state utilized legal-constitutional reform to reduce its conflictual intensity, to increase its options for policymaking and more effectively to control its societal position and its intersection with other social spheres. In the first instance, the tribunal, increasingly patterned on the Austro-German model of the Constitutional Court, acted as a mechanism that allowed the state to deflect and defuse deeply controversial questions. As in similar transitional settings, rights-based judicial review of statutes enabled the state to place objects of legal inclusion outside the state, and to displace and depoliticize many conflicts previously requiring resolution through highly condensed use of state power. Generally, the tribunal began to operate as a filter through which a unified state could transfer highly charged political conflicts into a legal dimension and utilize the law to reduce the controversy attached both to these conflicts and to its own reactions to them. In addition, however, the fact that actors in the state began to explain their actions through reference to stable juridical norms meant that the state could gradually use the law to release itself from its dense administrative integrity with a single political party, and that the law began to articulate normatively constructed boundaries to determine the state's integrity and consistency. In the Polish setting, and in eastern Europe more generally, the emergence of a tribunal with powers of constitutional review brought about a deep functional division within the state, in which the state could gradually account for itself as normatively distinct from single persons or party officials, and in which it could imagine itself, in distinct normative categories of public law, as an independent positive bearer of power. As a result, these changes in the judicial provisions of the Polish constitution ultimately created an

---

[25] For analysis see Brzezinski and Garlicki (1995: 22); Schwartz (1998: 103; 2000: 56). Generally, see Brzezinski (2000).

environment in which, in 1989, a fundamental recasting of the constitution could be undertaken. In mid 1989 the existing electoral system, strongly favouring one party, was abandoned. In 1992 a new provisional constitutional package was established for Poland: this, although lacking a distinctive catalogue of rights,[26] endorsed full provisions for conventional rights and for constitutional review of statutes, and it accepted a fully pluralistic party landscape (Arts. 18, 23). This was ultimately replaced by the full Polish constitution of 1997, which preserved extensive powers of judicial review (Arts. 79, 122).

In the constitutional interim between 1992 and 1997, the Polish Constitutional Tribunal assumed extensive functions in preserving and securing the transitional apparatus of state, and it played a key role in bringing stability to the state despite the incomplete and at times ambiguous fabric of the legal/constitutional order prior to the final constitution and the catalogue of rights introduced in 1997.[27] In this period, the Constitutional Tribunal interpreted the 1989 constitutional amendments and then the 1992 provisional constitution as instituting a factual commitment to the preservation of a legal state (*Rechtsstaat*), and it construed itself as entitled to apply this presumption to check and at times overrule parliamentary statutes. In this respect, the court served during the transition to insulate the legislative process, to generate normatively stabilizing filters to secure the actions of legislators in an uncertain legal terrain, at once to project and to consolidate continuous guidelines for a transitional constitutional order, and to construct a consistent legal identity for the state, which separated it from its particular acts and positively authorized its legislative rulings.[28] Indeed, in a societal environment marked by relatively weak legislative-democratic legitimacy, the Constitutional Tribunal acted as a legitimating pillar for the state, in reference to which the state could, both functionally and symbolically, increase and incubate its autonomy. The institution of a Constitutional Tribunal provided a vital mechanism for initiating and presiding over longer-term processes of reform, and the devolution of key functions of normative control to the Constitutional Tribunal, even before a fully sanctioned constitution was in place, enabled the Polish state to remove existing legislation, to legislate with externally protected

---

[26] Lech Walesa in fact tried to introduce a Bill of Rights in 1992.

[27] On the weak constitutional position of rights during the interim in Poland, see Osiatynski (1994: 121, 114, 150).

[28] For commentary see Procházka (2002: 207, 209–10); Weber (2008: 275).

legitimacy and to increase the probability of acceptance for new legislation. In this process of transition, therefore, the separation of the judicial apparatus from the executive and the creation of a strong Constitutional Tribunal allowed the state flexibly to isolate its power from highly entrenched interests and personal groups, it enabled the state to produce and preserve a sphere of relative autonomy and positive legitimacy to support its everyday decisions, and it distinctively augmented the *effective power* of the state.

The Polish Constitutional Tribunal was not the first constitutional court to be founded in an east European state. Yugoslavia established constitutional courts in 1963. Czechoslovakia also pursued a short-lived experiment with a constitutional court in 1968, although the court never became fully operative.[29] In the 1980s, the move towards judicial review became more widespread. In 1983 a Constitutional Law Council, with rather more limited powers than in Poland, was established in Hungary. However, the Polish tribunal assumed exemplary significance at a crucial transitional juncture, and it impacted substantially on the widening reformist policies of other east European states, which also began to relinquish the highly integrated constitutions obtained under post-1945 communist regimes. By 1989, for instance, in Hungary, the constitution was amended (or effectively refounded) so that it adopted a Constitutional Court with extremely far-reaching powers of review. Soon the powers of the Hungarian Constitutional Court outreached those of other transitional states: the Constitutional Court defined itself specifically as a guardian of the agreements supporting the peaceful transition in Hungary,[30] it committed itself to the powerful enforcement, in concrete individual cases, of principles of legal statehood, and it struck down a substantial number of the laws that came before it. As in Poland, the Hungarian Constitutional Court was able to oversee the process of transition, solidly to entrench normative/democratic principles, to absorb contest over most controversial aspects of new rights-based legislation, and – where required – to suspend existing laws through reference to core invariable rights (Sólyom 1994: 223, 228). In Bulgaria, similarly, the 1991 Constitution established an important Constitutional Court enjoying full judicial independence. The Czechoslovakian Republic established a Constitutional Court in 1992. Even Latvia, which reverted in part to its constitution of 1922, progressively

---

[29] On the failure of the Czechoslovakian court see Cutler and Schwartz (1991: 519–20); Hartwig (1992: 451, 464).

[30] Scheppele has described Hungary in transition as a 'courtocracy' (2003: 222).

amended the original constitution to create provisions for constitutional review. Throughout the east European transition, the institution of a constitutional court thus played a vital normative and functional role in the process of democratic consolidation (Brunner 1993: 883, 865).

Notable in the third wave of constitutional transition, further, was the importance of international human-rights norms in cases brought before the constitutional courts. In this respect, first, the transitions were driven, in part, by an increasing recognition of transnationally binding human-rights agreements, and standards concerning human rights first promoted in the Helsinki Accords formed a repository in which demands for political de-concentration could be expressed and enacted. Indeed, the increasing consolidation after the 1970s of an international legal domain, which placed emphasis both on singular/personal rights and rights of judicial integrity, acted as a normative matrix to which reformists could refer in order to obtain legitimacy for reforms, to separate the interlocked elements of party-led regimes and, above all, to prise apart judicial and executive functions of statehood and generally to separate the apparatus of state power from its intersection with private actors. During the transitions of the 1980s and early 1990s, then, most new states brought their constitutions into line with international treaties in respect of human rights, and they were keen to obtain legitimacy from the growing international legal order by signing the European Convention on Human Rights. None of this, naturally, is to suggest that each of the transitional post-communist regimes spontaneously implemented a full apparatus of guaranteed human rights. In many transitional states, certain basic freedoms, such as freedom of speech, assembly and conscience, were subject to restrictions, and in more nationally conflictual societies, such as Romania and Bulgaria, many particular minority rights were exposed to constraint (Elster 1991: 465–7). Nonetheless, these societies shared a broad tendency to borrow strict norms from international conventions in respect of human rights. Through this, standard provisions over rights acted clearly to simplify processes of political reorientation and to enunciate guidelines and precedents for rescinding old, and implementing new, acts of legislation. This allowed emergent democratic political systems to unburden themselves of much legislative/constitutional controversy, and, in settings where existing statutes were unreliable and legislative-democratic reserves of legitimacy were fragile, to draw legitimacy and heightened autonomy from acceded general norms over rights. International legal standards exercised a potent unifying function in the consolidation of transitional states after 1989,[31] and international provisions over rights, normally internalized and applied by constitutional courts, once again acted to limit the number of social objects that states internalized, to intercept social conflicts before they entered the state apparatus or required legislative resolution, and to augment the reserves of publicly constructed, usable power contained within the state. Indeed, the central position of international catalogues of rights in post-1989 constitutions was vital for their ability to separate many aspects of political exchange from the state, and, as in Spain in the 1970s, the legal salience of rights even allowed a rights-based 'civil society' to emerge, in which political activities, freed from the concentration around the state, could be performed outside the state and at a lower degree of political intensity.[32] The civil-political pluralism arising through the implementation of normative rights structures was thus also one dimension in a process in which state power was concentrated at a manageable and specified level, and it eliminated excessive or internal pluralism in the state itself and was normally correlated with a rise in state autonomy.

In addition to promoting state legitimacy through courts and international legal standards, most post-1989 constitutions in eastern Europe opted to include extensive provisions for positive social and material rights, and they widely dispensed the 'maximum number of constitutional rights' in respect of socio-economic state performance (Sadurski 2002: 233). For example, the amended Hungarian Constitution of 1989–90 carried many material rights from the post-1945 constitution. The amended Czechoslovakian constitution, replaced in 1992, preserved rights of material security fo those unable to work. The Bulgarian Constitution of 1991 enshrined the right to work, the right to welfare and the right to material support (Arts. 48, 51). The Polish constitution of 1997 then placed work under state protection (Art. 24). These rights performed varied legitimating functions for emergent democratic states. In the first instance, they brought symbolic legitimacy as they committed states to recognition of partly embedded societal values and, in transitions marked by extreme economic adversity, they preserved stability by perpetuating definitions of state legitimacy in material categories. However, these rights were not uniformly enforceable and,

---

[31] See for example Cutler and Schwartz (1991: 534, 537); Sólyom (2003: 144).

[32] On this account, civil society is formed as a result of the political system's need for pluralism. Note my simultaneous critique of and agreement with theories that see rights as institutes protecting 'civil society' (Sunstein 1993: 919).

unlike general civil rights, they were not accorded evenly justiciable status. Most constitutions were in fact endowed with restrictive clauses to ensure that material rights could only be claimed subject to exemptions specified by law (Rapaczynski 1991: 610–11; Sadurski 2002: 235). Many such rights were phrased as general directives to governmental institutions, and they were not easily usable as a basis for litigation or action. To be sure, exceptions to this are identifiable, and some courts took pains to apply weaker positive rights, such as environmental rights, and to insist on environmental duties (Halmai 1996: 352). In general, however, even those rights that aimed to secure transitional state legitimacy by preserving a high degree of societal convergence between the state and other spheres of society served to police and limit the inclusivity of the state, and they reinforced the legitimacy of the political system through a restrictive specification of its operations.

Russia

It was in the Soviet Union under Gorbachev that, in the third wave of democratic transition, the functionally adaptive state-building elements of legal/constitutional transition were most comprehensively observable. The era of *perestroika* as a whole was a period in the Soviet Union in which both the constitution and the legal system were reformed, and this acted to reduce, or restrictively to focus, the mass of power that, owing to the one-party political monopoly established under the Soviet constitutions, had accrued around the state. Indeed, one key cause of the reforms was that the executive apparatus around the Communist Party had become overburdened by the extent and dimensions of its power, and the constitutional monopoly of coercive force granted to one set of actors under the Soviet regime conferred an excessively personalistic form on political power: this, at different levels, drained the reserves of legitimacy in the state, and it diminished the volume of *usable power* possessed by the state. The process of legal reform in the Soviet Union was thus conceived as a means for reducing private/personal control of power, for hardening the procedures for the use of state power against 'centrifugal forces' (i.e. actors in administrative bureaucracies and party hierarchies) incorporated within the political system through its dense attachment to one political party (Hausmaninger 1992: 330), and for liberating the state from the 'network of informal alliances' that had attached to it under the Soviet system (Devlin 1995: 38). In the *perestroika* era, in other words, a strategy of reform was pursued to raise the positive autonomy and the general capacity of the state by using the law to separate it from parasitic semi-private centres of power and to clarify its limits and functional objectives.[33] Central to this was the introduction of a more ordered legal system, which was designed to suppress the structurally hypertrophic corruption in the Soviet Union, to create a barrier against the quasi-patrimonial transacting of public offices, and in so doing to heighten the operative power of the state.

The first decisive point in the *perestroika*-era constitutional reforms in the Soviet Union occurred at the end of 1988, when fifty-five of the 174 articles of the Soviet Constitution of 1977 were amended (Smith 1996: 72–3). This act of reform, effectively creating a new constitution, coincided with provisions for an elected multiparty national parliament in the Soviet Union, and it was flanked by legislation that altered the position of the Communist Party under the Soviet constitution and cemented a functional fissure between state and party. It was declared at this juncture that a stricter 'division of labour' between the party and the state was required, and that the party should assume less responsibility for providing direction in political affairs (White 1990: 33). These measures were in fact accompanied by a proposed amendment to Article 6 of the 1977 Constitution – which had defined the Communist Party as the guiding force of society – thus envisaging an end of one-party rule. This was finally enacted in 1990, in legislation that ended the party's monopoly of state power.

Alongside these most prominent events, however, the reforms in Russia were strongly focused on the legal and judicial dimensions of the political system. As early as 1986 the Communist Party of the Soviet Union passed a resolution 'On the Further Strengthening of Socialist Legality and Legal Order', which was designed to restructure the courts and protect rights of citizens. The year 1987 saw the introduction of a Law on Appeals, enabling citizens to appeal against actions of court officials. In 1988, Gorbachev committed himself at the annual party conference to the implementation of a legal revolution of the existing political apparatus, to the building of a socialist state based in the general rule of law and to the consolidation of judicial independence (Kahn 2002: 87). The year 1989 then saw the introduction of laws enabling judicial review of administrative acts, laws designed to ensure the independence of the courts and a Law on the Status of Judges, to increase

---

[33] On the pre-1989 Soviet Union as a weak state with restricted policy-making autonomy, see McFaul (1995: 221, 224); Easter (1996: 576).

the material independence of judges (Quigley 1990: 67). In the same year, a system for trial by jury was created for the most serious criminal cases. Moreover, the legal reform brought a crucial reduction in the scope of criminal law, so that many activities related to economic exchange and production were removed from criminal-law statutes. The political import of criminal law characteristic of totalitarian regimes was substantially reduced at this time, and the number of political or political/economic crimes was diminished.[34] In parallel, these legal changes included provisions both for the curtailment of political encroachment on judicial functions and for the establishment of a Constitutional Supervision Committee (1989–91), which was designed to promote judicial integrity and to perform constitutional review of normative acts. Members of the committee were elected in 1990, and it assumed functions analogous to those of a constitutional court. Throughout, these pieces of legislation were designed to place a legal apparatus above the everyday acts of the state and to guarantee greater accountability of state officials. At the same time, however, these processes were also intended to prise apart the conventional privatistic attachment between singular persons and political and judicial offices, and to distil the power of the Soviet state as distinct from, and positively usable against, those incumbent in office. The formation of a separate parliamentary legislature and the reform of the judiciary and the state administration were thus designed, in conjunction, to raise the autonomy of the state and, above all, to curtail the centrifugal power exercised by actors obtaining public office by private or clientelistic means, mediated through the party (see Solomon 1990: 185). In many respects, in fact, the legal reforms in the Soviet Union under Gorbachev bear comparison with functional dimensions of much earlier processes of reform, and their basic function was to reduce the privatism of the state apparatus by separating structures of office holding from personal control.[35]

Furthermore, the early move towards constitutional rule under Gorbachev involved, centrally, an expansive concession of rights of economic autonomy, and it was driven by far-reaching goals of economic reform. By 1990, a raft of legislation was introduced in respect of

---

[34] On these changes in criminal law see Feldbrugge (1993: 30).

[35] For a good recent study of patrimonialism and weak statehood in the Soviet Union see William Tompson (2002: 936–8). For brilliant analysis, stressing weak central control and neo-patrimonial brokering of public office as features of the Soviet system, see Anderson and Boettke (1997: 38, 43–4).

proprietary rights: this legislation renounced the principle that municipal or state-owned property could be legally differentiated from private property, and it stipulated that neither private property nor private enterprise were bound by the state (van den Berg 1996: 119, 124). These rights were reinforced by the law on the Principles of Civil Legislation of 1991, which afforded protection under civil law to personal rights and other rights vital for independent economic activity. In 1990, anti-monopoly legislation was introduced, which released enterprises from control by the state ministries, and reduced the degree of immediate convergence between the state and independent economic concerns. In 1991, further, wage agreements were removed from state jurisdiction, so that, outside certain general parameters, the state was not required to act as full guarantor for wage levels or industrial settlements. Importantly, at the end of 1991 the old system of taxation, in which revenue had been transferred directly from public enterprises to the state, was replaced by a fiscal apparatus that enabled the state to raise revenue on economic activities outside its immediate control (Feldbrugge 1996: 288). In these respects, the diffuse process of constitutional reform served to detach the state apparatus from its previous economic obligations, and it provided legal means through which the state could begin to stabilize its relation to the economy as a social field external to itself. Placed alongside political rights, the recognition of independent economic rights immediately restricted the social centrality of the state, and, in allowing the state to position itself in more differentiated manner towards other social spheres, rights also began to evolve as institutions that controlled the boundaries of the state and heightened the autonomy and positive flexibility of state power.

In the first instance, in consequence, the concept of government by general constitutional laws, articulated at once under public and private law, served in the Soviet Union *perestroika* era as a multi-faceted normative principle. The insistence on the rule of law as a normative goal of political transformation acted as a lever in the process of severing the political apparatus from its attachment to government by a single party, and it acted to construct the state as personally distinct from the particular mechanics of governance and functionally to liberate actors committed to reform. Tellingly, by the early 1990s legal elites had assumed a distinctively powerful position in the process of transformation (Trochev 2008: 26–7). In fact, as well as acting to isolate the state as a relatively freestanding and autonomous order, the principle of legal rule also formalized the obligations of the central state within the federal system of the Soviet

Union: this meant that the states within the union could (notionally) be regulated by uniform laws and their relations with the central state simplified. The evolution of the constitutional ideal in the Soviet Union, thus, as in other transitions, formed (or was designed to form) a normative response to the undifferentiated and pluralistic density of the state. The construction of a separate constitutional order within the state formed a reaction in the political system to its relative loss of autonomy and excessively personalized social convergence, and the reinforcement of constitutional provisions over rights and legal uniformity was intended as a principle for substantially intensifying state autonomy.

The constitutional situation in the Soviet Union changed dramatically in 1991 when the Soviet Union collapsed and fifteen independent states withdrew from the union. At this point, government was repeatedly conducted by decree, as Boris Yeltsin assumed extensive emergency powers in order both to introduce further economic reforms and to organize the executive. In 1992, however, a new constitution was drafted for the reformed state of Russia. The 1993 Constitution ultimately consolidated a balanced arrangement between executive and legislature, which concentrated extensive powers in the hands of the president, but also accorded important countervailing, albeit subsidiary, powers to the elected Duma. This constitution also sanctioned a very comprehensive catalogue of basic rights: indeed, it accepted that in cases of legal conflict international law was to take precedence over domestic legislation. The rights acknowledged in the constitution included classic rights of personal integrity, especially rights of ownership, expression, privacy and movement. However, as in other transitional states, the catalogue of rights differed substantially from classical liberal constitutions: it guaranteed the right to shelter and social housing (Art. 40), the right to social security in cases of deprivation (Art. 39), and the right to freedom from racial or religious abuse (Art. 29). Vital for the legitimating role of this constitution was that it guaranteed political freedoms and (formally) decriminalized political dissent (Arts. 29–30), and it stipulated rights of protection against the state in cases of unlawful actions committed by state officials (Arts. 52–53).

Of particular importance in this was the fact that the 1993 Constitution contained strong provisions to support a separate and independent judiciary, and it placed under express protection the independence of the courts (Art. 120), the inviolability of judges (Art. 121) and the right to open trials. The constitution also prohibited irregular judicial proceedings: in Article 118, it eliminated the judicial power of the Communist Party.

After 1996, the traditional dependence of courts on political and logistical control through the Ministry of Justice was (in principle) eradicated. Further, as in earlier transitions, the constitution provided for regulation of the functions of the judiciary by a separate Constitutional Court. This court was in fact established in 1991, and it decided its first case in 1992. However, its position was formalized in the 1993 Constitution. Notably, the Constitutional Court had some distinctive features. Although initially endowed with very strong powers, including the power to initiate cases for review, its status was altered in 1994, owing to its involvement in the struggle between parliament and president: this led to its suspension by Boris Yeltsin, after which its powers were substantially constrained and it was less eager to engage in fractious political dispute. Moreover, unlike other post-communist judicial systems patterned on the Austro-German design, in Russia a model of dual judicial control developed, in which the Constitutional Court existed alongside a Supreme Court, which gradually asserted responsibility for judicial decisions and protection of rights in ordinary courts.[36] Nonetheless, the Constitutional Court remained (notionally) authorized to conduct review (although this repeatedly came under siege). It retained strong powers for ensuring constitutional conformity of federal statutes and for resolving disputes over jurisdiction between federal state bodies and between supreme state bodies of subjects of the Russian Federation (Art. 125). In its original conception, in fact, it created the basis for a thorough legal rationalization of the political order, in principle placing powerful rights-based normative constraints on the operations of government, and it reinforced an abstractive structure for the dislocation of the state executive from private actors assuming state power through party-mediated influence (Fogelklou 2003: 186; Thorson 2004: 196).

In this respect it needs to be stated unequivocally that, naturally, the Constitutional Court in Russia was not able to act with even near impunity, and it could not sidestep serious political restriction. Its provisions for a rights-based *Rechtsstaat* were subject to endemic neglect, and minimum thresholds of respect for rights were, throughout the longer reformist period in the 1990s, barely preserved. Moreover, it needs quite expressly to be emphasized that the development of a constitutional order in Russia only selectively restricted private control of public office, and at different points in the longer transition legal/constitutional regulation of access to political and judicial power failed

---

[36] For excellent analysis see Krug (1996).

almost entirely. It has been widely diagnosed that in the earlier 1990s Russia suffered sporadic collapse of state autonomy, and it witnessed such rapid and comprehensive usurpation of state power and administrative resources by private actors and neo-patrimonial oligarchs that it lost the ability to impose reforms: this was also reflected in a consonant decline in legal order (McFaul 1995: 242; Gel'man 2004: 1024). The constitutional preconditions of integral statehood were thus only formally instituted in transitional Russia: the constitution offered only a partial solution to the internal weaknesses of the state, and it was not strong enough to detach the state structure from private control. Indeed, it has also been widely argued that the presidential system remained very susceptible to lobbying and retained a high porosity to informal groups, that the civil service was not formally brought under constitutional rule and both the civil service and the judiciary remained beset by corruption, and that the federal structure often facilitated violations of general legal rules (Fogelklou 2001: 233–4). In each of these respects, the constitutional system that evolved after 1989 provided for only an incompletely regulated pattern of statehood, and it offered only a precarious normative framework of legitimacy for the state. In short, it would be evidently counterfactual to suggest that the Russian constitution consistently performed the functions attached to other constitutions in maximizing state autonomy or abstracted power.

As in earlier transitional settings, however, the judicialization of political procedures in Russia brought longer-term, although distinctively attenuated, functional benefits to the emergent state, and it acted both to simplify the processes through which the state obtained legitimacy and, ultimately, to perform an overall consolidation of state power. First, for instance, the Constitutional Court gradually led to clarification of the relation between executive and legislative powers within the state, it obstructed the endemic arrogation of legislative power by private persons, and it acted rudimentarily to ensure procedural integrity in legislation. In particular, it opposed the practice of passing joint 'executive-legislative decrees' that had typified Soviet-era legislation and had underpinned the control exercised over the state by the party (Trochev 2008: 105). The court also ultimately, albeit in rivalry with the Supreme Court, established the principle that it alone should have powers of 'binding interpretation' of the constitution, and it subordinated ordinary, regional and subsidiary courts to the directives issued by a clear centre of jurisdictional authority (Sadurski 2007: 20–1). In this respect, the court at once enhanced the general application of the law, ensured that state power was not diluted by conflicting patterns of legal interpretation and enforcement, and impeded personal acquisition of power. Moreover, in assuming responsibility for particularly controversial political contests, the court progressively made sure that the state's requirements for factual coercive power were subject to selective limits and that power was only exceptionally used outside a small group of functions. Indeed, in preserving economic and contractual rights, the constitutional court ensured that the state itself was not forced to intervene in disputes between potent economic actors (for example between banks and clients), it reduced the responsibility of the executive for legal planning and implementation, and it meant that the state's need to politicize its economic policies in a newly differentiated and precariously balanced society was limited (Trochev 2008: 167).

In consequence, the transition to a constitutional system in Russia noticeably, over a longer period, strengthened the positive structure of the state apparatus. The existence of a constitutional court, although less politically interventionist than in Poland or Hungary, was an ultimately important innovation in this respect, and it at once cemented the apparatus of the state as distinct from the particular processes in which its power was consumed and ensured that the deepest legitimating resources of the state were extracted above its factual operations and only exceptionally called into question or directly politicized. In Russia, in fact, the constitutional court assumed a distinctive strategic state-building function, and its technical utility in abstracting and cementing the superstructure of the reformed state outweighed its contribution to preserving social pluralism or socio-political freedom. To illustrate this, it has been widely noted that in Russia the acceptance of an international rights regime and the neutral functions of a Constitutional Court sat easily alongside, and in fact commonly reinforced, a tendency towards selectively authoritarian governance (Kahn 2004: 2). The fact that the dynamic of constitutional reform first originated within the state apparatus and reflected strategies of political consolidation meant that, from the outset, the reforms centred on a highly legalistic and semi-prerogative refinement of state power. Indeed, it has been widely noted that during the early period of constitutional reforms in Russia the state acted as both the object and the initiator of liberalization, and the state reformed itself in order, in part, not to generate conditions of effective socio-political or rights-based inclusion, but to obtain a heightened degree of infrastructural power in society (Weigle 2000: 272). Under Vladimir Putin, finally, a very distinctive model of constitutional order began to emerge. Putin repeatedly took notable steps to reform the judiciary: these included measures to increase the financial independence of courts, to introduce new procedural codes, to expand trial by jury and to harmonize laws between federal government and regions. Rather than enhancing the democratic structure of the state, however, these reforms created a political system in which a rationalized judiciary, centred around the Constitutional Court, acted as a semi-authoritarian instrument of state consolidation. Although at crucial junctures in Putin's presidency the Constitutional Court acted to limit the political branch of government, at other times, and in fact more consistently, the court provided a formal framework to consolidate and solidify a powerful executive and to facilitate Putin's policy of government founded in authoritarian executive-led and judicially rationalized legalism (see Fogelklou 2001: 225; Trochev 2008: 185–7). Indeed, if in the earlier periods of transitional reform the consolidation of state autonomy was insecure and the state was fragmented by privatistic usurpation of offices and benefits, Putin pursued legal and judicial reform as a technical policy for rigidifying public authority against private actors and for consolidating central administrative power against personal corruption and fragmentation. The pattern of constitutional reform in Russia, in fact, had its most obvious antecedent in the minimal executive constitutionalism of the softened Bonapartism of many later nineteenth-century societies, and it produced a model of contemporary constitutionalism *sui generis*, in which regular judicial order and legal constraints on private authority acted, not primarily to check, but rather to underpin a semi-detached executive.

Despite this, nonetheless, during the periods of legal reform in Russia under Gorbachev, Yeltsin and Putin techniques of constitutional transformation were employed partly as a normative framework for the construction of a state that at once was differentiated from other functional spheres and possessed internal checks and legal constraints to preserve it against internal/particularistic fragmentation. The rule of law, however imperfectly, acted as an instrument which ultimately strengthened the power of the state, and the principle of the separation of the powers, governed by a Constitutional Court applying general catalogues of rights, provided a mainstay for the relative stabilization of state functions. If the rule of law, constitutional review and the application of rights were only weakly obtained in Russia, Russia remained an example of the classical sociological functions of constitutional reform. The case of Russia, above all, exemplifies the fact that one-party governmental systems have much in common with pre-democratic systems, and they tend to suffer from the same problems of weak abstraction: privatization of public office, clientelism, weak statutory power, low powers of general integration and political inclusion. Indeed, post-communist Russia might be seen as possessing some of the common features of constitutional rule in the imperial era, and the strategic and minimalistic constitutionalism promoted in particular by Putin might be viewed as a distinct expression of the classical sociological functions of constitutions in eradicating the vestiges of feudal order and excessive privatism in the state.

Conclusion

The first conclusion of this book has a functional focus. It claims that constitutions, although often observed as normative arrangements which are deduced and imposed from outside the socio-political structures and institutions of society, are in fact functional articulations of inner-societal processes. In the first instance, constitutions developed as institutions that made it possible for societies, at different stages in their formation, to abstract resources of distinctively political power, to preserve the differentiation of their power from other functions, and to utilize this power, in measured inclusivity, in the context of a differentiated, functionally pluralistic and increasingly positivized societal environment. Constitutions normally play a vital role in enabling societies to construct and address some of their exchanges as distinctively relevant for and included in power: as *political*. Moreover, constitutions bring the crucial benefit to societies that they allow political systems in modern societies positively to produce power and internally to *multiply* the reserves of power that they contain. Constitutions have the indispensable inner-societal function that they allow political actors to extract a supportive internal definition of their power, which means that political actors can refer to stable and withdrawn self-constructions in order positively to reproduce, procedurally to apply, and internally to maximize their power in a number of different spatial and temporal settings. On these grounds, this book concludes that constitutions are functional preconditions for the positive abstraction of political power and, as such, they are also, over longer periods of time, highly probable preconditions of institutions using power: that is, states. It is argued throughout this book that modern societies are defined by the fact that they have successfully developed institutions that are able to construct and gradually to augment stores of power that are in some way and to some (always precarious) degree *public* (that is, internally reproducible, collectively positivized and autonomously abstracted against singular persons): this fact gives a distinctively inclusive and pluralistic form to modern societies. Constitutions play the most central role in ensuring that modern political institutions, and modern society as a whole, do not forfeit this institutional form through an endemic re-patrimonialization of their power and that, in consequence, societies do not relinquish their ability to reproduce their power in reasonably autonomous manner. As discussed, re-patrimonialization of power is a constant danger for modern societies, and where this occurs societies experience a dramatic diminution of their power and, accordingly, a rapid loss of plurality and freedom.

On these grounds, this book also proposes a second, more methodological, conclusion. This claims that the conventional normative strategies for analysing and evaluating constitutions, the provisions normally contained in constitutions (i.e. rights, separation of powers, procedures for pluralistic democratic self-legislation), and the legitimating functions of constitutions and constitutional rights, have fundamentally misconstructed their object. The institutions of constitutional rule, viewed in normative inquiry as external or deductively constructed preconditions of power's legitimacy, are in fact embedded elements of adaptive societal reflexivity, which act within the structure of political power. If we assume that modern differentiated societies demand, and in fact can only effectively utilize, power as an autonomously abstracted and replicably inclusive phenomenon, the institutions of legitimate constitutional rule can be observed as normative principles that the political system of modern society produces or externalizes *for itself* in order to heighten the societal abstraction of its power and to fulfil the complex requirements for positive statutory laws and rulings that characterize modern societies. The primary norms of constitutional order are thus best explicable within an exclusively internalistic and sociological paradigm. As discussed, first, the constitution per se (defined as an extracted and inclusionary public-legal order within the state) initially evolved as an institution that allowed states to underwrite positive statutory functions through reference to an articulated set of norms, to detach their functions from private social milieux, and to imply a consistent personality in order to unify the acts in which power was transmitted and to stabilize the environments in which power was consumed. The rights enshrined within more modern constitutions then evolved, second, as institutions that permitted states at once to police their social inclusion, and to construct and simplify the terrains to which they applied power in relatively controlled and internally consistent manner. The norm of sovereign-democratic inclusion, third, evolved as a principle that allowed states to authorize their power in highly abstracted and inclusive fashion, to separate their power from external interference, and to transmit their power across wide social spaces at a high level of positive reproducibility. The primary norms of constitutional rule, in consequence, can be seen as adaptive dimensions of political power itself. These are institutions generated within power as power became progressively sensitive to highly differentiated societal environments, and as society as a whole, shaped by its functional extension and differentiation, created and encountered a need for more inclusive and autonomous capacities for using power. In a modern society, in short, political power is always likely to be applied through constitutional laws, through rights, and through reference to the inclusionary norm of popular/sovereign authority. Moreover, political power is always likely to be perceived as *legitimate* if applied in this form: constitutional laws, rights and selective popular inclusion create an internal apparatus within political power through which it can reproduce and transmit itself through society at a high level of internal consistency and with a minimum of unpredictable resistance. Societies that do not articulate power in this internal normative form are (over longer periods of time) unlikely to utilize power very effectively, and they are always susceptible to the threat that they might forfeit their inclusive political structure and erode their defining capacities for spatial and temporal extensibility, relatively rapid and reliable decision making and effective inclusion. To this extent, normative or analytical theory intuits a basic truth in its common claim that the legitimacy of political power depends on its exercise through constitutions and distinct legal rights. However, these primary objects of normative constitutional analysis (constitutions, rights and legitimacy) can only be adequately explained by sociological reconstruction.

The third conclusion of this book has a more formally normative quality. It is that in modern societies political power is always likely to assume certain basic normative legal features. Above all, if we assume that modern societies are usually determined by the fact that they require innumerable positive and replicable decisions (statutes) and they necessitate positive procedures for the positive, extensible political inclusion of very diverse actors and exchanges, it is probable that in these societies political power will assume and preserve an internal normative shape that is defined by constitutional laws, uniform subjective rights and some degree of popular/democratic inclusion. These principles or institutions might be seen as the *functional norms* that underpin modern power, and that permit societies recursively to apply and reproduce their power. To this limited degree, in fact, sociological analysis might allow itself to suggest that the norms of constitutional rule are probable preconditions for the political (and perhaps more general) self-reproduction of modern societies, and it might even indicate, prescriptively, that such norms have a *desirable* status. Indeed, it is observable that societies able to multiply their reserves of power through a normative constitutional apparatus are also societies that, in extracting their power from highly singular processes of coercion, usually (albeit with exceptions) engender relatively high levels of political freedom for their members. Societies capable of generating power as a positive autonomous resource are normally societies in which extreme personal violation is rare (although not unknown): societies in which power is abstractly concentrated in states and in which power can be positively replicated through law without singular personal intervention in different settings tend to permit higher degrees of social liberty than societies in which the means of social coercion are endemically privatized and obdurately resistant to positive reproduction. Constitutions play a central role in this regard: in holding political power at a level of positive abstraction, they create conditions in which, over longer periods of time, power is likely to be applied in equal, internally reproducible, routinely inclusive and, therefore, personally indifferent manner. Across different historical periods, it can be observed that societies that struggle to abstract positive facilities to reproduce political power are defined both by weak constitutional structures and by high levels of personalistic violence and duress. To this degree, a sociological approach to constitutions might suggest that constitutions, although primarily acting, in functional manner, to maximize the reserves of usable power in society, have the benefit that, in multiplying power, they also (normally) produce and multiply social freedom. Indeed, this approach might suggest that societies producing high volumes of power tend to produce the highest degree of social liberty. The coincidence of constitutions and social liberty has often led normative theorists to think that constitutions and constitutional rights are created to secure human freedom, or that the extent to which they facilitate human liberty might even be a measure for the validity of constitutions and constitutional rights. Liberty, in fact, is only an incidental outcome of constitutional functions. Yet it surely authorizes normative endorsement of constitutional rule.

The yield of a sociology of constitutions is, therefore, threefold. First, it allows us functionally to explain the widespread reliance of modern societies on constitutional order. Second, it allows us to correct the foundational reductivism of more conventional lines of normative inquiry into constitutions and political legitimacy. Third, it allows us to illuminate the probable normative structure of modern society, and even to indicate that deviation from certain constitutional norms might (for reasons that are not normative but sociological) be undesirable and might jeopardize the basic resources and structural form of society. On this last point, a sociology of constitutions permits us to bring towards conclusion the first objective of the sociological critique of the Enlightenment, and it enables us to offer a sociological (not deductive) model of political legitimacy. Specifically, it allows us to propose a generalized model of political legitimacy, which defines the legitimacy of the modern state as depending, first, on the exercise of power through uniform public laws; second, on the constitutional guarantee of equal subjective rights, usually differentiating clearly between public rights and private rights; and, third, on constitutional provisions for selective popular/sovereign inclusion. Above all, this sociological perspective suggests that societies diverging egregiously from the abstractive and selectively inclusionary functions of constitutional rule are often exposed to the danger that they erode their conserves of political power, they undermine their ability to utilize political power as an autonomous facility, and they relinquish their capacity for the reliable politicization of social exchanges. In this respect, a sociology of constitutions might even play an evidentially sustained role in debate about ideal or undesirable patterns of governance. Yet a sociology of constitutions has the distinction that in isolating a normative political model for society it is not afflicted by the deductive aporia afflicting rival lines of inquiry, and the grounds of the normative model that it proposes are constructed in pure sociological fashion: through internal analysis of the adaptive pressures underlying the political systems of modern societies.

BIBLIOGRAPHY

Adamovich, Ludwig 1923. *Die Prüfung der Gesetze und Verordnungen durch den österreichischen Verfassungsgerichtshof.* Leipzig: Franz Deuticke.

Adams, George Burton 1926. *Council and Courts in Anglo-Norman England.* New Haven: Yale University Press.

Adams, Willi Paul 2001. *First American Constitutions: Republican Ideology and the Making of the State Constitutions in the Revolutionary Era.* Lanham, Md.: Rowman & Littlefield.

Adler, Franklin Hugh 1995. *Italian Industrialists from Liberalism to Fascism: The Political Development of the Industrial Bourgeoisie, 1906–1934.* Cambridge University Press.

Agócs, Sándor 1971. 'Giolitti's Reform Programme: An Exercise in Equilibrium Politics', *Political Science Quarterly* 86(4), pp. 637–53.

Albertin, Lothar 1974. 'Faktoren eines Arrangements zwischen industriellem und politischem System in der Weimarer Republik', in Mommsen, Hans et al. (eds.), *Industrielles System und politische Entwicklung in der Weimarer Republik.* Düsseldorf: Droste, pp. 658–74.

Alexander, Jeffrey C. 2006. *The Civil Sphere.* Oxford University Press.

Altenstein's *Denkschrift* 1931 [1807]. In Winter, Georg (ed.), *Die Reorganisation des Preußischen Staates unter Stein und Hardenberg: Erster Teil: Allgemeine Verwaltungs- und Behördenreform,* vol. I: *Vom Beginn des Kampfes gegen die Kabinettsregierung bis zum Wiedereintritt des Ministers von Stein.* Leipzig: Hirzel, pp. 364–566.

Althusius, Johannes 1614 [1603]. *Politica,* 3rd edn. Herborn.

Anderson, Gary M. and Boettke, Peter J. 1997. 'Soviet Venality: A Rent-seeking Model of the Communist State', *Public Choice* 93, pp. 37–53.

Angermeier, Heinz 1966. *Königtum und Landfriede im deutschen Mittelalter.* Munich: Beck. 1984. *Die Reichsreform 1410–1555: Die Staatsproblematik in Deutschland zwischen Mittelalter und Gegenwart.* Munich: Beck.

Antoine, Michel 2003. *Le Cœur de l'État: Surintendance, contrôle general et intendances des finances 1552–1791.* Paris: Fayard.

Anton, Hans Hubert 1975. *Studien zu den Klosterprivilegien der Päbste im frühen Mittelalter: Unter besonderer Berücksichtigung der Privilegierung von St: Maurice D'Agaune.* Berlin: de Gruyter.

Appleby, Joyce 1984. *Capitalism and a New Social Order: The Republican Vision of the 1790s*. New York University Press.

Aquarone, Alberto 1965. *L'organizzazione dello stato totalitario*. Turin: Einaudi.

Argyriadis, Chara 1987. 'Über den Bildungsprozeß eines peripheren Staates: Griechenland 1821–1827', *Rechtshistorisches Journal* 6, pp. 158–72.

Ascher, Abraham 1988. *The Revolution of 1905: Russia in Disarray*. Stanford University Press.

Asenjo González, María 2006. 'La aristocracización política en Castilla. El proceso de participación urbana (1252–1520)', in Nieto Soria, José Manuel (ed.), *La monarquía como conflicto en la corona castellano-leonesa (c. 1230–1504)*. Madrid: Sílex, pp. 133–96.

Ashley, Maurice 1962. *Financial and Commercial Policy under the Cromwellian Protectorate*. London: Frank Cass.

Atiyah, P. S. 1979. *The Rise and Fall of Freedom of Contract*. Oxford University Press.

Aubert, Félix 1977. *Le Parlement de Paris: De Philippe le Bel à Charles VII (1314–1422): Sa compétence, ses attributions*. Geneva: Slatkine Reprints.

Ault, Warren Ortmann 1923. *Private Jurisdiction in England*. New Haven: Yale University Press.

Azo, Portius 1506. *Summa super codicem et institutis*. Papie.

Bacon, Francis 1639 [1597]. *The Elements of the Common Lawes of England*. London: Printed by the Assignes of John More, Esquire.

Badinter, Robert 1989. 'Introduction. Naissance d'une justice', in Badinter (ed.), *Une autre justice 1789–1799*. Paris: Fayard, pp. 9–25.

Baklanoff, Eric N. 1992. 'The Political Economy of Portugal's Later "Estado Novo"': A Critique of the Stagnation Thesis', *Luso-Brazilian Review* 29(1), pp. 1–17.

Baldus de Ubaldus 1616. *In primam Digesti veteris Partem Commentaria*. Venice.

Baldwin, James Fosdick 1913. *The King's Council in England during the Middle Ages*. Oxford: Clarendon.

Baldwin, John W. 1986. *The Government of Philip Augustus: Foundations of French Royal Power in the Middle Ages*. Berkeley: University of California Press.

Barbero, Abilío and Vigil, Marcelo 1978. *La formación del feudalismo en la península Ibérica*. Barcelona: Editorial Crítica.

Bardoux, Agénor 1877. *Les Légistes: Leur influence sur la société française*. Paris: Germer Baillière.

Baron, Hans 1966. *The Crisis of the Early Italian Renaissance: Civic Humanism and Republican Liberty in an Age of Classicism and Tyranny*. Princeton University Press.

Barral, Pierre (ed.) 1968. *Les Fondateurs de la Troisième République*. Paris: Colin.

Barthélemy, Dominique 1999. *L'an mil et le paix de Dieu: La France chrétienne et féodale 980–1060*. Paris: Fayard.

Bartlett, Robert 2000. *England under the Norman and Angevin Kings 1075–1225*. Oxford: Clarendon.

Bartole, Sergio and Vandelli, Luciano 1980. *Le regioni nella giurisprudenza*. Bologna: Mulino.

Bartolus de Saxoferrato 1555. *Super prima Parte in Digestum Vetus*. Lyon.

Barudio, Günter 1976. *Absolutismus – Zerstörung der libertären Verfassung: Studien zur Karolinischen Eingewalt in Schweden zwischen 1680 und 1693*. Wiesbaden: Steiner.

Bastid, Paul 1945. *Doctrines et institutions politiques de la Seconde République*, 2 vols. Paris: Hachette.

　　1954. *Les Institutions politiques de la monarchie parlementaire française (1814–1848)*. Paris: Sirey.

Bastien, François 1997. 'Le Conseil Constitutionnel et la Cinquième République. Réflexions sur l'émergence et les effets du contrôle de constitutionnalité en France', *Revue Française de science politique* 47, pp. 377–404.

Baumgart, Peter 1969. 'Zur Geschichte der kurmärkischen Stände im 17. und 18. Jahrhundert', in Gerhard, Dietrich (ed.), *Ständische Vertretungen*. Göttingen: Vandenhoeck & Ruprecht, pp. 131–61.

Beck, Raimund 1979. *Das Spanische Regierungssystem unter Franco*. Bochum: Brockmeyer.

Becker, Marvin B. 1960. 'Some Aspects of Oligarchical, Dictatorial and Popular Signorie in Florence, 1282–1382', *Comparative Studies in Society and History* 2(4), pp. 421–39.

　　1966. 'Economic Change and the Emerging Florentine Territorial State', *Studies in the Renaissance* 13, pp. 7–39.

　　1968. *Florence in Transition*, 2 vols., *Volume I: Studies in the Rise of the Territorial State*. Baltimore: Johns Hopkins Press.

Becker, Seymour 1985. *Nobility and Privilege in Late Imperial Russia*. Dekalb, Ill.: Northern Illinois University Press.

Behrens, Betty 1963. 'Nobles, Privileges and Taxes in France at the End of the Ancien Régime', *Economic History Review* 15(3), pp. 451–75.

Beik, William 1985. *Absolutism and Society in Seventeenth-Century France: State Power and Provincial Aristocracy in Languedoc*. Cambridge University Press.

Bell, David A. 1994. *Lawyers and Citizens: The Making of a Political Elite in Old Regime France*. Oxford University Press.

Bellamy, J. G. 1989. *Bastard Feudalism and the Law*. London: Routledge.

Below, Georg von 1885. *Die landständische Verfassung von Jülich und Berg bis zum Jahre 1511: Eine verfassungsgeschichtliche Studie*, 2 parts, Vol. II. Düsseldorf: Voss.

Bentham, Jeremy 2002. 'Nonsense upon Stilts', in Bentham, *Rights, Representation and Reform: Nonsense upon Stilts and other Writings on the French*

Revolution, ed. P. Schofield, C. Pease-Watkin and C. Blamires. Oxford: Clarendon, pp. 317–97.

Berchtold, Klaus 1998. *Verfassungsgeschichte der Republik Österreich*, Vol. I, *1918–1933*. Vienna: Springer.

Berding, Helmut (ed.) 1996. *Die Entstehung der Hessischen Verfassung*. Wiesbaden: Historische Kommission für Nassau.

Berg, Ger van den 1996. 'The Constitution, the Constitutional Court, and the Development of Russian Civil Law in the Transitional Period', in Ginsburg, George, Barry, Donald D. and Simons, William B. (eds.), *The Revival of Private Law in Central and Eastern Europe*. The Hague: Martinus Nijhoff, pp. 117–60.

Berman, Harold J. 1977. 'The Origins of Western Legal Science', *Harvard Law Review* 90(5), pp. 894–943.

1983. *Law and Revolution: The Formation of the Western Legal Tradition*. Cambridge, Mass.: Harvard University Press.

2003. *Law and Revolution*, Vol. II, *The Impact of the Protestant Reformations on the Western Legal Tradition*. Cambridge, Mass.: Harvard University Press.

Bermbach, Udo 1967. *Vorformen parlamentarischer Kabinettsbildung in Deutschland: Der interfraktionelle Ausschuß 1917/18 und die Parlamentarisierung der Reichsregierung*. Cologne: Westdeutscher Verlag.

Bersani, Carlo 2002. 'Gli enti pubblici tra stato e società 1926–1943', in Mazzacone, Aldo (ed.), *Diritto, economia e istituzioni nell'Italia fascista*. Baden-Baden: Nomos, pp. 165–92.

Bertelli, Sergio 1978. *Il potere oligarchico nello stato-città medievale*. Florence: La Nuova Italia Editrice.

Berton, Henry 1900. *L'évolution constitutionelle du Seconde Empire*. Paris: Félix Alcan.

Bèze, Théodore de 1970 [1574]. *Du droit des magistrats*, introduced and ed. R. M. Kingdon. Geneva: Droz.

Biancalana, Joseph 1988. 'For Want of Justice: Legal Reforms of Henry II', *Columbia Law Review* 88(3), pp. 433–536.

Bickart, Roger 1932. *Les Parlements et la notion de la souverainété nationale au XVIIIe siècle*. Paris: Félix Alcan.

Bien, David D. and Godneff, Nina 1988. 'Les offices et le crédit d'état: l'utilisation des privilèges sous l'Ancien Régime', *Annales: Histoire, Sciences Sociales* 43(2), pp. 379–404.

Bigot, Grégoire 1999. *L'autorité judiciaire et le contentieux de l'administration 1800–1872*. Paris: Librairie générale de droit et de jurisprudence.

Birtsch, Günter 1995. 'Die preußische Sozialverfassung im Spiegel des Allgemeinen Landrechts für den preußischen Staat von 1794', in Wolff,

Jörg (ed.), *Das Preußische Allgemeine Landrecht: Politische, rechtliche und soziale Wechsel- und Fortwirkungen*. Heidelberg: Müller, pp. 133–48.

Bisson, Thomas N. 1969. 'Consultative Functions in the King's Parlements (1250–1314)', *Speculum* 44(3), pp. 353–73.

1972. 'The General Assemblies of Philip the Fair: Their Character Reconsidered', *Studia Gratiana* 15, pp. 537–64.

1994. 'The Feudal Revolution', *Past and Present* 142, pp. 6–42.

2009. *The Crisis of the Twelfth Century: Power, Lordship, and the Origins of European Government*. Princeton University Press.

Black, Stephen F. 1976. '*Coram Protectore*: The Judges of Westminster Hall under the Protectorate of Cromwell', *American Journal of Legal History* 32, pp. 32–64.

Blackstone, William 1979 [1765–9]. *Commentaries on the Laws of England*, 4 vols., Vol. I. University of Chicago Press.

Blaich, Fritz 1979. *Staat und Verbände in Deutschland zwischen 1871 und 1945*. Wiesbaden: Franz Steiner.

Blair, Philip M. 1981. *Federalism and Judicial Review in West Germany*. Oxford: Clarendon.

Blancas, Jeronimo de 1641. *Coronaciones de los serenisimos reyes de Aragon*. Zaragoza: Diego Dormer.

Blasius, Dirk 1978. 'Bürgerliches Recht und bürgerliche Identität. Zu einem Problemzusammenhang in der deutschen Geschichte des 19. Jahrhunderts', in Berding, Helmur et al. (eds.), *Vom Staat des Ancien Regime zum modernen Rechtsstaat: Festschrift für Theodor Schieder*. Munich: Oldenbourg, pp. 213–24.

Blickle, Peter 1973. *Landschaften im Alten Reich: Die staatliche Funktion des gemeinen Mannes in Oberdeutschland*. Munich: Beck.

Bloch, Marc 1949. *La société féodale*, vol. II: *Les classes et le gouvernement des hommes*. Paris: Albin Michel.

1964. *La France sous les derniers Capétiens 1223–1328*. Paris: Colin.

Bodin, Jean 1986 [1576]. *Les six livres de la république*, 6 vols., Vol. III. Paris: Fayard.

Bohle, Thomas 1990. *Einheitliches Arbeitsrecht in der Weimarer Republik: Bemühungen um ein deutsches Arbeitsgesetzbuch*. Tübingen: J. C. B. Mohr.

Böhm, Franz 1937. *Die Ordnung der Wirtschaft als geschichtliche Aufgabe und rechtsschöpferische Leistung*. Stuttgart: Kohlhammer.

Böhret, Carl 1966. *Aktionen gegen die kalte Sozialisierung 1926–1930: Ein Beitrag zum Wirken ökonomischer Einflußverbände in der Weimarer Republik*. Berlin: Duncker & Humblot.

Boissy-D'Anglas, François-Antoine 1795. *Discours préliminaire au projet de la constitution pour la République Française*. Paris: Imprimé par ordre de la convention nationale.

Boldt, Hans 1980. 'Der Artikel 48 der Weimarer Reichsverfassung. Sein historischer Hintergrund und seine politische Funktion', in Stürmer, Michael (ed.), *Die Weimarer Republik: Belagerte Civitas*. Königstein: Athenäum, pp. 288–309.

Bolingbroke, Henry 1786 [1733–4]. *A Dissertation upon Parties*. London: Cadell.

Bonaini, Francesco (ed.) 1854. *Statuti inediti della città di Pisa: Dal XII al XIV secolo*, 3 vols. Florence: Vieusseux.

Boncerf, Pierre-François 1776. *Les inconvéniens des droits féodaux*. London: Valade.

Bonini, Francesco 1996. *Storia della corte costituzonale*. Rome: Nuova Italia Scientifica.

Bonney, Richard 1978. *Political Change in France under Richelieu and Mazarin*. Oxford University Press.

Bortolotto, Guido 1931 [1930]. *Lo stato e la dottrina corporativa: Saggio d'una teoria generale*, new edn. Bologna: Zanichelli.

Bosl, Karl 1972. *Die Grundlagen der modernen Gesellschaft im Mittelalter: Eine deutsche Gesellschaftsgeschichte des Mittelalters*. Stuttgart: Anton Hiersemann.

   1974. *Die Geschichte der Repräsentation in Bayern: Landständische Bewegung, Landständische Verfassung, Landesausschuß und altständische Gesellschaft*. Munich: Beck.

Bossenga, Gail 2006. 'A Divided Nobility: Status, Markets and the Patrimonial State in the Old Regime', in Smith, Jay M. (ed.), *The French Nobility in the Eighteenth Century*. Philadelphia: Pennsylvania University Press, pp. 43–75.

Botero, Giovanni 1590 [1589]. *Della ragione di stato*. Ferrara: Vittorio Baldini.

Botzenhart, Manfred 1983. 'Verfassungsproblematik und Ständepolitik in der preußischen Reformzeit', in Baumgart, Peter (ed.), *Ständetum und Staatsbildung in Brandenburg-Preußen*. Berlin: de Gruyter, pp. 431–55.

Bourdon, Jean 1942. *La Constitution de l'an VIII*. Rodez: Carrere.

Bourjon, François 1767 [1747]. *Le droit commun de la France et la coutume de Paris réduit en principes*, 2 vols., Vol. I. Paris: Grangé.

Boutaric, Edgard 1861. *La France sous Philippe le Bel: Étude sur les institutions politiques et administratives du Moyen Age*. Paris: Henri Plon.

Boutaric, François de 1751 [1745]. *Traité des droits seigneuriaux et des matières féodales*. Toulouse: Gaspard Henault et Jean-François Forest.

Boutruche, Robert 1968. *Seigneurie et Féodalité*, 2 vols., Vol. I, *Le premier âge des liens d'homme à homme*, 2nd edn. Paris: Aubier.

Bracton, Henry de 1968 [Written c. 1235]. *On the Laws and Customs of England*, translated by S. E. Thorne, in 2 vols. Cambridge, Mass.: Harvard University Press.

Braddick, Michael J. 2000. *State Formation in Early Modern England c: 1550–1700*. Cambridge University Press.

Broszat, Martin 1969. *Der Staat Hitlers*. Munich: DTV.

Brubaker, Rogers 1992. *Citizenship and Nationhood in France and Germany.* Cambridge, Mass.: Harvard University Press.

Brunkhorst, Hauke 2000. 'Rights and the Sovereignty of the People in the Crisis of the Nation State', *Ratio Juris* 13, pp. 49–62.

2002. *Solidarität: Von der Bürgerfreundschaft zur globalen Rechtsgenossenschaft.* Frankfurt am Main: Suhrkamp.

Brewer, John 1989. *The Sinews of Power: War, Money and the English State 1688–1783.* London: Unwin.

Brown, Howard G. 2006. *Ending the French Revolution: Violence, Justice, and Repression from the Terror to Napoleon.* Charlottesville: University of Virginia Press.

Bruchey, Stuart 1980. 'The Impact of Concern for the Security of Property Rights on the Legal System of the Early American Republic', *Wisconsin Law Review*, pp. 1135–58.

Brundage, James A. 2008. *The Medieval Origins of the Legal Profession: Canonists, Civilians, and Courts.* Chicago University Press.

Bruneau, Thomas C. 1984. *Politics and Nationhood: Post-Revolutionary Portugal.* New York: Praeger.

Brunner, Georg 1993. 'Die neue Verfassungsgerichtsbarkeit in Osteuropa', *Zeitschrift für ausländisches öffentliches Recht und Völkerrecht* 53, pp. 819–70.

Brunner, Otto 1968. *Neue Wege der Verfassung- und Sozialgeschichte.* Göttingen: Vandenhoeck & Ruprecht.

Brusewitz, Axel (ed.) 1916. *Frihetstidens grundlagar och konstitutionella stadgar.* Stockholm: Norstedt.

Brzezinski, Mark 2000. *The Struggle for Constitutionalism in Poland.* Basingstoke: Palgrave.

Brzezinski, Mark F. and Garlicki, Lezek 1995. 'Judicial Review in Post-Communist Poland: The Emergence of a *Rechtsstaat?*', *Stanford Journal of International Law* 31, pp. 13–59.

Buchheim, Christoph and Scherner, Jonas 2006. 'The Role of Private Property in the Nazi Economy: The Case of Industry', *Journal of Economic History* 66(2), pp. 390–416.

Buck, A. R. 1990. 'The Politics of Land Law in Tudor England, 1529–1540', *Journal of Legal History* 11(2), 200–17.

Bülow, Friedrich 1934. *Der deutsche Ständestaat: Nationalsozialistische Gemeinschaftspolitik und Wirtschaftsorganisation.* Leipzig: Alfred Kröner.

Burdeau, François 1994. *Histoire de l'administration française: Du 18 au 20 siècle,* 2nd edn. Paris: Montchrestien.

1995. *Histoire du droit administratif (de la révolution au début des années 1970).* Paris: Presses Universitaires de France.

Burke, Edmund 1775 [1770]. *Thoughts on the Cause of the Present Discontents.* London: Dodsley.

1910 [1790]. *Reflections on the Revolution in France*. London: Dent.

1981 [1775]. 'Speech on Conciliation with America', in *Burke, The Writings and Speeches of Edmund Burke*, ed. Paul Langford, 8 vols., Vol. III. Oxford: Clarendon, pp. 102–71.

Burrage, Michael 2006. *Revolution and the Making of the Contemporary Legal Profession: England, France and the United States*. Oxford University Press.

Büsch, Otto 1962. *Militärsystem und Sozialleben im Alten Preußen: Die Anfänge der sozialen Militarisierung der preußisch-deutschen Gesellschaft*. Berlin: de Gruyter.

Buschmann, Arno 1999. 'Privilegien in der Verfassung des Heiligen Römischen Reiches im Hochmittelalter', in Dölemeyer, Barbara and Mohnhaupt, Heinz (eds.), *Das Privileg im Europäischen Vergleich*, Vol. II. Frankfurt am Main: Klostermann, pp. 17–44.

Butt, Ronald 1989. *A History of Parliament: The Middle Ages*. London: Constable.

Caggese, Romolo (ed.) 1921. *Statuti della repubblica fiorentina*, 2 vols., Vol. II, *Statuti della Podestà*. Florence: Ariani.

Calasso, Francesco 1949. *Gli ordinamenti giuridici del rinascimento medievale*. Milan: Giuffrè.

1954. *Medio Evo del diritto: Le fonti*. Milan: Giuffrè.

1957. *I glossatori e la teoria della sovranità: Studio di diritto comune pubblico*. Milan: Giuffrè.

1971. *La legislazione statutaria dell'Italia meridionale*. Bari: Edizioni centro librario.

Campbell, Peter 1958. *French Electoral Systems and Elections 1789–1957*. London: Faber & Faber.

Cannon, John 1969. *The Fox–North Coalition: Crisis of the Constitution 1782–4*. Cambridge University Press.

Caplan, Jane 1988. *Government without Administration: State and Civil Service in Weimar and Nazi Germany*. Oxford: Clarendon.

Cappelletti, Mauro and Adams, J. C. 1966. 'Judicial Review of Legislation: European Antecedents and Adaptations', *Harvard Law Review* 79(6), pp. 1207–24.

Carpenter, Christine 1983. 'Law, Justice and Landowners in Late Medieval England', *Law and History Review* 1(2), pp. 205–37.

Carré, Henri 1912. *La Fin des Parlements*. Paris: Hachette.

Carretero Zamora, Jan Manuel 1988. *Cortes, monarquía, ciudades: Las Cortes de Castilla a comenzios de la época moderna (1476–1515)*. Madrid: Siglo XXI de España.

Carruthers, Bruce G. 1996. *City of Capital: Politics and Markets in the English Financial Revolution*. Princeton University Press.

Carsten, F. L. 1959. *Princes and Parliaments in Germany: From the Fifteenth to the Eighteenth Century*. Oxford: Clarendon.

Caspar, Erich (ed.) 1967. *Das Register Gregors VII*. Berlin: Weidmann.

Castellano, Juan Luis 1990. *Las Cortes de Castilla y su Diputacion (1621–1789): Entre Pactismo y Absolutismo*. Madrid: Centro de Estudios Constitucionales.

Catalano, Franco 1974. *Potere economico e fascismo*. Milan: Bompiani.

Catalano, Gaetano 1959. *Impero, regni e sacerdozio nel pensiero di Uguccio da Pisa*. Milan: Giuffrè.

Celta, Stephano Iunio Bruto 1580 [1579]. *Vindiciae contra Tyrannos*. Basel?

Cerqueira, Silas 1973. 'L'Église et la dictature portuguaise', *Revue française de science politique* 23(3), pp. 473–513.

Charles I, king of England 1999 [1642]. 'His Majesties Answer to the Nineteen Propositions of Both Houses of Parliament', in Malcolm, Joyce (ed.), *The Struggle for Sovereignty: Seventeenth-Century English Political Tracts*, 2 vols., Vol. I. Indianapolis, In.: Liberty Fund, pp. 154–78.

Chaussinand-Nogaret, Guy 1976. *La Noblesse au XVIII siècle: De la féodalité aux lumières*. Paris: Hachette.

Chénon, Émile 1923. *Les démembrements de la propriété foncière en France avant et après la revolution*, 2nd edn. Paris: Sirey.

1926. *Histoire générale du droit français public et privé: Des origines à 1815*, 2 vols., Vol. I. Paris: Sirey.

Chester, Norman 1981. *The English Administrative System 1780–1870*. Oxford: Clarendon.

Chilcote, Ronald H. 2010. *The Portuguese Revolution: State and Class in the Transition to Democracy*. Lanham, Md.: Rowman & Littlefield.

Chittolini, Giorgio 1991. 'Statuten und städtische Autonomie: Einleitung', in Chittolini, Giorgio and Willoweit, Dietmar (eds.), *Statuten, Städte und Territorien zwischen Mittelalter und Neuzeit in Italien und Deutschland*. Berlin: Duncker & Humblot, pp. 7–37.

Choper, Jesse 1980. *Judicial Review in the National Political Process: A Functional Reconsideration of the Supreme Court*. Chicago University Press.

Chrimes, S. B. 1936. *English Constitutional Ideas in the Fifteenth Century*. Cambridge University Press.

Church, Clive 1981. *Revolution and Red Tape: The French Ministerial Bureaucracy 1770–1850*. Oxford: Clarendon.

Church, William F. 1972. *Richelieu and the Reason of State*. Princeton University Press.

Clanchy, M. T. 1979. *From Memory to Written Record: England 1066–1307*. London: Edward Arnold.

Clarke, M. V. 1936. *Medieval Representation and Consent*. London: Longman.

Classen, Peter 1973. 'Das Wormser Konkordat in der deutschen Verfassungsgeschichte', in Fleckenstein, Josef (ed.), *Investiturstreit und Reichsverfassung*. Sigmaringen: Jan Thorbecke, pp. 411–60.

Cocceji, Samuel 1791–1799 [1713–18]. *Jus civile controversum*, new edn, 2 vols., Vol. I. Leipzig: Weidmann.

Code Louis 1670. 2 vols., Vol. II. Louvain: Claude de Montauban.

Codex Theresianus 1883 [drafted 1766], 5 vols., Vol. I. Vienna: Carl Gerold's Sohn.

Coke, Edward 1797 [1628–44]. *Institutes of the Laws of England*, 4 parts, Vol. IV. London: Brooke.

   2003 [1608]. 'Calvin's Case', in Coke, *Selected Writings*, ed. Steve Sheppard, 3 vols., Vol. I. Indianapolis: Liberty Fund, pp. 166–232.

Collins, Irene 1979. *Napoleon and his Parliaments, 1800–1815*. London: Arnold.

Collins, James B. 1995. *The State in Early Modern France*. Cambridge University Press.

Colmeiro, Manuel 1883. *Las Cortes de los antiguos reinos de León y de Castilla*. Madrid: Sucesores de Rivadenegra.

Colorni, Vittorio 1967. 'Le tre leggi perdute di Roncaglia (1158) ritrovate in un manoscritto parigino', in *Scritti in memoria di Antonio Giuffrè*, Vol. I. Milan: Giuffrè, pp. 113–70.

Conrad, Hermann, Lieck-Buyken, Thea von der and Wagner, Wolfgang (eds.) 1973. *Die Konstitutionen Friedrichs II von Hohenstaufen für sein Königreich Sizilien*. Cologne: Böhlau.

Constant, Benjamin 1991 [1810]. *Fragments d'un ouvrage abandonné sur la possibilité d'une constitution républicaine dans un grand pays*. Paris: Aubier.

   1997 [1819]. 'De la liberté des anciens comparé à celle des modernes', in Constant, *Écrits politiques*. Paris: Gallimard, pp. 589–619.

   1997 [1815]. 'Principes de politique', in Constant, *Écrits politiques*, ed. M. Gauchet. Paris: Gallimard, pp. 303–506.

Constant, Jean-Marie 1996. *La Ligue*. Paris: Fayard.

Corpus Constitutionum Marchicarum 1737–55. Ed. C. O. Mylius, 6 parts, Part 6. Berlin: Buchladen des Waysenhauses.

Corrigan, Philip and Sayer, Derek 1985. *The Great Arch: English State Formation as Cultural Revolution*. Oxford: Blackwell.

Corwin, Edward S. 1925. 'The Progress of Constitutional Theory between the Declaration of Independence and the Meeting of the Philadelphia Convention', *American Historical Review* 30(3), pp. 511–36.

Costa Pinto, António 1995. *Salazar's Dictatorship and European Fascism: Problems of Interpretation*. New York: Columbia University Press.

   2006. 'Authoritarian Legacies, Transitional Justice and State Crisis in Portugal's Democratization', *Democratization* 13(2), pp. 173–204.

   2008. 'The Legacy of the Authoritarian Past in Portugal's Democratization', *Totalitarian Movements and Political Religions* 9(2), pp. 265–91.

Cotarelo, Juan 1992. 'Valores y principios de la Constitución de 1978', in Cotarelo, Ramon (ed.), *Transicion politica y consolidacion democratica: España (1975–1986)*. Madrid: Centro de investigaciones sociológicas, pp. 163–200.

Cowans, Jon 2001. *To Speak for the People: Public Opinion and the Problem of Legitimacy in the French Revolution*. London: Routledge.

Cowling, Maurice 1971. *The Impact of Labour 1920–1924: The Beginnings of Modern British Politics*. Cambridge University Press.

Cromé, François 1977 [1593]. *Dialogue d'entre le maheustre et le manant*, ed. P. M. Ascoli. Geneva: Droz.

Cronin, James E. 1991. *The Politics of State Expansion: War, State and Society in Twentieth-Century Britain*. London: Routledge.

Currie, David P. 1985. *The Constitution in the Supreme Court*, 2 vols. Chicago University Press.

Curthoys, Mark 2004. *Governments, Labour and the Law in Mid-Victorian Britain: The Trade Union Legislation of the 1870s*. Oxford: Clarendon.

Cust, Richard 1987. *The Forced Loan and English Politics, 1626–1628*. Oxford: Clarendon.

Cutler, Lloyd and Schwartz, Hermann 1991. 'Constitutional Reform in Czechoslovakia: *E Duobus Unum?*, *University of Chicago Law Review* 58, pp. 511–53.

Dahlmann, Friedrich Christoph 1924 [1835]. *Die Politik, auf den Grund und das Maß der gegebenen Zustände zurückgeführt*, introduced by O. Westphal. Berlin: Hobbing.

Dakin, Douglas 1973. *The Greek Struggle for Independence 1821–1833*. London: Batsford.

Dareste, Rodolphe 1862. *La justice administrative en France*. France: Auguste Durand.

David, Marcel 1954. *La souveraineté et les limites juridiques du pouvoir monarchique du IX au XV siècle*. Paris: Dalloz.

Davidheiser, Evelyn B. 1992. 'Strong States, Weak States: The Role of the State in Revolution', *Comparative Politics* 24(4), pp. 463–75.

Davies, Godfrey 1937. *The Early Stuarts 1603–1660*. Oxford: Clarendon.

Davis, John A. 2006. *Naples and Napoleon: Southern Italy and the European Revolutions 1780–1860*. Oxford University Press.

Decretum Gratiani 1676 [written *c.* 1140]. Leiden: Hugueton & Barbier.

Delcamp, Alain 2004. 'Le Conseil Constitutionnel et le Parlement', *Revue française de droit constitutionnel* 57, pp. 37–83.

Dembkowski, Harry E. 1982. *The Union of Lublin: Polish Federalism in the Golden Age*. Boulder: distributed by University of Columbia Press.

Denholm-Young, N. 1939. *Seignorial Administration in England*. Oxford University Press.

Deslanges, Maurice 1932. *Histoire constitutionelle de la France*, Vol. II: *De la chute de l'Empire à l'avènement de la Troisième République (1815–1870)*. Paris: Colin.

Devlin, Judith 1995. *The Rise of the Russian Democrats: The Causes and Consequences of the Elite Revolution*. London: Elgar.

Dicey, Albert Venn 1915 [1885]. *Introduction to the Study of the Law of the Constitution*, 8th edn. London: Macmillan.

Dickinson, H. T. 1976. 'The Eighteenth-Century Debate on the Sovereignty of Parliament', *Transactions of the Royal Historical Society* 5th series, 26, pp. 189–210.

Dickson, P. G. M. 1967. *The Financial Revolution in England: A Study in the Development of Public Credit, 1688–1765*. London: Macmillan.

Diestelkamp, Bernhard 1983. 'Zur Krise des Reichsrechts im 16. Jahrhundert', in Angermeier, Heinz (ed.), *Säkulare Aspekte der Reformationszeit*. Munich: Oldenbourg, pp. 49–64.

Dietz, Frederick C. 1964. *English Public Finance, 1558–1641*. London: Frank Cass.

Di Lalla, Manlio 1976. *Storia del liberalismo italiano dal risorgimento al fascismo*. Bologna: Einaudi.

Dilcher, Gerhard 1967. *Die Entstehung der lombardischen Stadtkommune: Eine rechtsgeschichtliche Untersuchung*. Aalen: Scientia Verlag.

  2003. 'La "renovatio" degli Hohenstaufen fra innovazione e tradizione. Concetti giuridici come orizzonte d'azione della politica italiana di Federico Barbarossa', in Constable, Giles and Cracco, Giorgio (eds.), *Il secolo XII: La 'renovatio' dell'Europa Cristiana*. Bologna: Mulino, pp. 253–88.

Dios, Salustiano de 1982. *El Consejo real de Castilla (1385–1522)*. Madrid: Centro de Estudios Constitucionales.

  1985. 'Sobre la génesis y los caracteres del estado absolutista en Castilla', *Studia historica: Historia moderna* 3(5), pp. 11–46.

Dlugosch, Michaela 2008. 'Geordnetes Wirtschaften. Zur sozialen Ökonomie im Franquismus (1939–1959)', in López, Federico Fernández-Crehuet and Hespanha, Antonio Manuel (eds.), *Franquismus und Salazarismus: Legitimation durch Diktatur?* Frankfurt am Main: Klostermann, pp. 317–48.

Doberl, Ludwig 1967. 'Maximilian von Montgelas und sein Prinzip der Staatssouveränität beim Neubau des Reiches Bayern', in Hofmann, Hanns Hubert (ed.), *Die Entstehung des modernen souveränen Staates*. Cologne: Kiepenheuer & Witsch, pp. 273–92.

Doucet, Roger 1948. *Les institutions de la France au XVIe siècle*. Paris: Picard.

Douglass, Elish P. 1989. *Rebels and Democrats: The Struggle for Equal Political Rights and Majority Rule during the American Revolution*. Chapel Hill: University of North Carolina Press.

Doyle, William 1996. *Venality: The Sale of Offices in Eighteenth-Century France*. Oxford: Clarendon.

Dreier, Horst 2002. 'Kanonistik und Konfessionalisierung – Marksteine auf dem Weg zum Staat', *Juristenzeitung* 57, pp. 1–13.

Dreitzel, Horst 1992. *Absolutismus und ständische Verfassung in Deutschland: Ein Beitrag zu Kontinuität und Diskontinuität der politischen Theorie in der frühen Neuzeit*. Mainz: Philipp von Zabern.

Droege, Georg 1969. *Landrecht und Lehnrecht im hohen Mittelalter*. Bonn: Röhrscheid.

Duguit, Léon 1889. 'Le droit constitutionnel et la sociologie', *Revue internationale de l'Enseignement* 18, pp. 484–505.

1921 [1911]. *Traité de droit constitutionnel*, 5 vols., Vol. I. Paris: Fontemoing & Co.

du Haillan, Bernard de Girard 1572 [1570]. *De l'estat et success des affaires de France*, 4 vols., Vol. III. Paris: Pierre l'Huillier.

Dumbauld, Edward 1958. 'State Precedents for the Bill of Rights', *Journal of Public Law* 7, pp. 232–344.

Dunham, William Huse Jr 1964. 'Regal Power and the Rule of Law: A Tudor Paradox', *Journal of British Studies* 3(2), pp. 24–56.

Dupont-Ferrier, Gustave 1930. *Études sur les institutions financières de la France a la fin du Moyen Age*, 2 vols., Vol. I. Paris: Firmia-Didot.

Dupuy, Pierre (ed.) 1963 [1655]. *Histoire du differend d'entre le pape Boniface VIII et Philippe le Bel Roy de France*. Tucson: Audax Press.

Durchhardt, Heinz 1996. 'Das Reichskammergericht', in Diestelkamp, Bernhard (ed.), *Oberste Gerichtsbarkeit und zentrale Gewalt im Europa der frühen Neuzeit*. Cologne: Böhlau, pp. 1–14.

Durkheim, Émile 1950. *Leçons de sociologie: Physique des moeurs et du droit*. Paris: Presses Universitaires de France.

du Tillet, Jean 1579. *De rebus Gallicis*. Frankfurt am Main: Andrea Wechelum.

Duzinkiewicz, Janusz 1993. *Fateful Transformations: The Four Years' Parliament and the Constitution of May 3, 1791*. New York: Columbia University Press.

Dworkin, Ronald 1977. *Taking Rights Seriously*. London: Duckworth.

Easter, Gerald M. 1996. 'Personal Networks and Postrevolutionary State Building: Soviet Russia Reexamined', *World Politics* 48(4), pp. 551–78.

Eberhard, Winfried 1981. *Konfessionsbildung und Stände in Böhmen 1478–1530*. Vienna: Oldenbourg.

Echeverria, Durand 1985. *The Maupeou Revolution: A Study in the History of Libertarianism: France, 1770–1774*. Baton Rouge: Louisiana State University Press.

Edwards, John 2000. *The Spain of the Catholic Monarchs*. Oxford: Blackwell.

Egret, Jean 1962. *La Pré-révolution Francaise (1787–1788)*. Paris: Presses Universitaires de France.

1970. *Louis XV et l'opposition parlementaire, 1715–1774*. Paris: Colin.

Einaudi, Mario 1948. 'The Constitution of the Italian Republic', *American Political Science Review* 42(4), pp. 661–76.

Elazar, Dahlia S. 2001. *The Making of Fascism: Class, State, and Counter-Revolution, Italy 1919–1922*. Westport, Conn.: Praeger.

Elben, Wolfgang 1965. *Das Problem der Kontinuität in der deutschen Revolution: Die Politik der Staatssekretäre und der militärischen Führung von November 1918 bis Februar 1919*. Düsseldorf: Droste.

Elliott, J. H. 1986. *The Count-Duke Olivares: The Statesman in an Age of Decline*. New Haven: Yale University Press.

Elster, Jon 1991. 'Constitutionalism in Eastern Europe', *University of Chicago Law Review* 58, pp. 447–82.

Elton, G. R. 1966. *The Tudor Revolution in Government: Administrative Changes in the Reign of Henry VIII*. Cambridge University Press.

1972. *Policy and Police: The Enforcement of the Reformation in the Age of Thomas Cromwell*. Cambridge University Press.

Emmons, Terence 1968. *The Russian Landed Gentry and the Peasant Emancipation of 1861*. Cambridge University Press.

Englberger, Josef 1995. *Tarifautonomie im Deutschen Reich: Entwicklung des Tarifvertragswesens in Deutschland von 1870/71 bis 1945*. Berlin: Duncker & Humblot.

Erkens, Franz-Reiner 2002. *Kurfürsten und Königswahl: Zu neuen Theorien über den Königswahlparagraphen im Sachsenspiegel und die Entstehung des Kurfürstenkollegiums*. Hannover: Hahn.

Ermacora, Felix 1980. 'Die Grundrechte in der Verfassungsfrage 1919/20', in Neck, Rudolf and Wandruszka, Adam (eds.), *Die österreichische Verfassung von 1918 bis 1938*. Vienna: Verlag für Geschichte und Politik, pp. 53–61.

Erwin, Holger 2009. *Machtsprüche: Das herrscherliche Gestaltungsrecht 'ex plenitudine potestatis' in der Frühen Neuzeit*. Cologne: Böhlau.

Esmein, Adhémar 1928. *Éléments de droit constitionel français et comparé*, 8th edn, 2 vols., Vol. II. Paris: Sirey.

Estepa Díez, Carlos 1988. 'Curia y cortes en el reino de León', in Congreso científico sobre la historia de las cortes de Castilla y León (ed.), *Las Cortes de Castilla y León en la Edad media*, 2 vols., Vol. I. Valladolid: Cortes de Castilla y León, pp. 23–104.

1989. 'Formación y consolidación del feudalismo en Castilla y León', in Perez Ruiz, Alberto (ed.), *En torno al feudalismo hispanico*. Avial: Fundación Sanchez-Albornoz, pp. 157–256.

Evans, Malcolm 1968. 'The Italian Constitutional Court', *International and Comparative Law Quarterly* 17, pp. 602–33.

Faini, Enrico 2004. 'Il gruppo dirigente fiorentino dell'età consolare', *Achivio storico italiano* 162, pp. 199–231.

Fallows, Thomas S. 1985. 'The Russian Fronde and the Zemstvo Movement: Economic Agitation and Gentry Politics in the Mid-1890s', *Russian Review* 44(2), pp. 119–138.

Farrand, Max (ed.) 1911. *The Records of the Federal Convention of 1787*, 3 vols., Vols. I and II. New Haven: Yale University Press.

Farrelly, David G. and Chan, Stanley H. 1957. 'Italy's Constitutional Court: Procedural Aspects', *The American Journal of Comparative Law* 6(2/3), pp. 314–27.

Fasoli, Gina and Sella, Pietro (eds.) 1937. *Statuti di Bologna dell'anno 1288*, 2 vols. Vatican: Biblioteca Apostolica Vaticana.

Feldbrugge, F. J. M. 1993. *Russian Law: The End of the Soviet System and the Role of Law*. Dordrecht: Nijhoff.

Feldman, Gerald D. 1974. 'Der deutsche organisierte Kapitalismus während der Kriegs- und Inflationsjahre 1914–1923', in Winkler, Heinrich August (ed.), *Organisierter Kapitalismus: Voraussetzungen und Anfänge*. Göttingen: Vandenkoeck & Ruprecht, pp. 150–71.

   1997. *The Great Disorder: Politics, Economics and Society in the German Inflation 1914–1924*. New York: Oxford University Press.

Feldman, Gerald D. and Steinisch, Irmgard 1985. *Industrie und Gewerkschaften 1918–1924: Die überforderte Zentralarbeitsgemeinschaft*. Stuttgart: Deutsche Verlags-Anstalt.

Ferejohn, John 2002. 'Judicializing Politics, Politicizing law', *Law and Contemporary Problems* 65(3), pp. 41–68.

Ferguson, E. James 1961. *The Power of the Purse: A History of American Public Finance 1776–1790*. Williamsburg: University of North Carolina Press.

Ferguson, Thomas and Voth, Hans-Joachim 2008. 'Betting on Hitler – The Value of Political Connections in Nazi Germany', *Quarterly Journal of Economics* 123, pp. 101–37.

Field, Daniel 1976. *The End of Serfdom: Nobility and Bureaucracy in Russia, 1855–1861*. Cambridge, Mass.: Harvard University Press.

Firth, C. H. and Rait, R. S. (eds.) 1911. *Acts and Ordinances of the Interregnum, 1642–1660*, 3 vols., Vol. II. London: Stationery Office.

Fischer, Matthias G. 2007. *Reichsreform und Ewiger Landfrieden: Über die Entwicklung des Fehderechts im 15. Jahrhundert bis zum absoluten Fehdeverbot von 1495*. Aalen: Scientia.

Fischer-Lescano, Andreas and Teubner, Gunther 2006. *Regime-Kollisionen: Zur Fragmentierung des globalen Rechts*. Frankfurt am Main: Suhrkamp.

Fitting, Hermann (ed.) 1876. *Juristische Schriften des früheren Mittelalters*. Halle: Verlag der Buchhandlung des Waisenhauses.

Fitzsimmons, Michael P. 1987. 'Privilege and Polity in France, 1786–1791', *American Historical Review* 92(2), pp. 269–95.

Fogelklou, Anders 2001. 'Constitutional Order in Russia: A New Territory for Constitutionalism', *Review of Central and East European Law* 26(3), pp. 231–57.

   2003. 'Constitutionalism and the Presidency in the Russian Federation', *International Sociology* 18(3), pp. 181–98.

Foord, Archibald S. 1964. *His Majesty's Opposition 1714–1830*. Oxford University Press.

Ford, Franklin 1953. *Robe and Sword: The Regrouping of the French Aristocracy After Louis XIV*. Cambridge, Mass.: Harvard University Press.

Forsyth, Douglas J. 1993. *The Crisis of Liberal Italy: Monetary and Financial Policy, 1914–1922.* Cambridge University Press.

Fortescue, John 1942 [written *c.* 1470]. *De Laudibus Legum Anglie,* ed. S. B. Chrimes. Cambridge University Press.

Foster, Elizabeth Read (ed.) 1966. *Proceedings in Parliament 1610,* 2 vols., Vol. I. New Haven: Yale University Press.

Fournier, Paul 1917. 'Un tournant de l'histoire du droit 1060–1140', *Nouvelle révue historique de droit français et étranger* 41, pp. 129–80.

Foweraker, Joe 1987. 'Corporatist Strategies and the Transition to Democracy', *Comparative Politics* 20(1), pp. 57–72.

Franciscis, Maria Elisabetta de and Zannini, Rosella 1992. 'Judicial Policy-making in Italy: The Constitutional Court', *West European Politics* 15(3), pp. 68–79.

Franklin, Otto von 1867. *Das Reichshofgericht im Mittelalter,* 2 vols. Weimar: Böhlau.

Frauendorfer, Max 1935. *Idee und Gestalt der ständischen Neuordnung.* Berlin: Spaeth & Linde.

Freise, Harald 1994. *Wettweberb und Politik in der Rechtsordnung des Nationalsozialismus: Primat der Politik und ständischer Gedanke im Kartell-, Wettbewerbs- und Organisationsrecht.* Baden-Baden: Nomos.

Freund, Michael 1962. 'Demokratie – Wagnis des Vertrauens', in Arndt, Adolf and Freund, Michael (eds.), *Notstandsgesetz – aber wie?* Cologne: Verlag Wissenschaft und Politik, pp. 69–157.

Fried, Charles (2004) *Saying What the Law Is: The Constitution in the Supreme Court.* Cambridge, Mass.: Harvard University Press.

Friedl, Christian 2005. *Studien zur Beamtenschaft Kaiser Friedrichs II im Königreich Sizilien (1220–1250).* Vienna: Verlag der österreichischen Akademie der Wissenschaften.

Friedman, Gerald 1990. 'Capitalism, Republicanism, Socialism and the State: France, 1871–1914', *Social Science History* 14(2), pp. 151–74.

Friedrich II, king of Prussia 1913–14 [1777]. 'Regierungsformen und Herrscherpflichten', in *Werke,* ed. G. B. Volz, 10 vols., Vol. VII. Berlin: Reimar Hobbing, pp. 225–37.

Fritschy, W. 2003. 'A "Financial Revolution" Reconsidered: Public Finance in Holland during the Dutch Revolt', *Economic History Review* 56(1), pp. 57–89.

Fuentes Ganzo, Eduardo 2008. 'Pactismo, cortes y hermandades en Léon y Castilla. Siglos XIII–XVI', in Foronda, François and Carrasco Manchado, Ana Isabel (eds.), *El contrato politico en la corona de Castilla: Cultura y sociedad políticas entre los siglos X a XVI.* Madrid: Dykinson, pp. 415–52.

Fürbringer, Christoph 1985. *Necessitas und Libertas: Staatsbildung und Landstände im 17. Jahrhundert in Brandenburg.* Frankfurt am Main: Lang.

Furlong, Paul 1988. 'The Constitutional Court in Italian Politics', *West European Politics* 11(3), pp. 7–23.

Galai, Schmuel 1973. *The Liberation Movement in Russia 1900–1905*. Cambridge University Press.

Gallagher, Tom 1975. 'Democracy in Portugal since the 1974 Revolution', *Parliamentary Affairs* 38(2), pp. 202–18.

Gallinato, Bernard 1992. *Les corporations à Bordeaux à la fin de l'Ancien Régime: Vie et mort d'un mode d'organisation du travail*. Bordeaux: Presses Universitaires de Bordeaux.

Garaud, Marcel 1958. *Histoire générale du droit privé français (de 1789 à 1804): La révolution et la propriété foncière*. Paris: Sirey.

García de Cortázar, José Ángel 2000. 'Estructuras sociales y relaciones de poder en León y Castilla en los siglos VIII a XII: La formación de una sociedad feudal', *Settimane di studio de Centro Italiano di studi sull'Alto Medioevo* 47: *Il Feudalesimo nell'alto medioevo*, pp. 497–564.

Gardiner, Samuel Rawson (ed.) 1862. *Parliamentary Debates in 1610*. Westminster: John Bowyer Nichols.

Gauchet, Marcel 1995. *La révolution des pouvoirs: La souveraineté, le people et représentation 1789–1799*. Paris: Gallimard.

Gehrke, Roland 2005. 'Zwischen altständischer Ordnung und monarchischem Konstitutionalismus. Begriffserklärungen und Fragestelungen', in Gehrke, Roland (ed.), *Aufbrüche in die Moderne: Frühparlamentarismus zwischen altständischer Ordnung und monarchischem Konstitutionalismus: Schlesien–Deutschland–Mitteleuropa*. Cologne: Böhlau, pp. 1–13.

Gel'man, Vladimir 2004. 'The Unrule of Law in the Making: The Politics of Informal Institution Building in Russia', *Europe-Asia Studies* 56(7), pp. 1021–40.

Gentile, Giovanni 1929. *Origini e dottrina del Fascismo*. Rome: Libreria del Littorio.

Gentillet, Innocent 1609 [1576]. *Discours d'estat sur les moyens de bien gouverner et maintenir en bonne paix un royaume, ou autre principauté*. Leiden.

Gentz, Friedrich von 1979 [1819]. 'Über den Unterschied zwischen den landständischen und Repräsentativ-Verfassungen', in Brandt, Hartwig (ed.), *Restauration und Frühliberalismus*. Darmstadt: Wissenschaftliche Buchgesellschaft, pp. 218–22.

Ghisalberti, Carlo 1972. *Stato e costituzione nel Risorgimento*. Milan: Giuffrè.

  1995. *La codificazione del diritto in Italia 1865–1942*. Bari: Laterza.

  2000. *Storia costituzionale d'Italia 1848–1948*. Rome–Bari: Laterza.

  2008. *Unità nazionale giuridica in Italia: La codificazione del diritto nel Risorgimento*. Rome: Laterza.

Giesey, Ralph E. 1983. 'State-Building in Early Modern France: The Role of Royal Officialdom', *Journal of Modern History* 55(2), pp. 191–207.

Glasson, Ernest-Désiré 1974. *Le parlement de Paris*, 2 vols., Vol. I. Geneva: Slatkine.

Gloria, Andrea (ed.) 1873. *Statuti del Comune di Padova del secolo XII all'anno 1285*. Padua: Sacchetta.

Godechot, Jacques 1951. *Les institutions de la France sous la Révolution et l'Empire*. Paris: Presses Universitaires de France.

1970. 'Sens et importance de la transformation des institutions révolutionnaires à l'époque napoliénne', *Revue d'histoire moderne et contemporaine* 17(3), pp. 795–813.

Goetz, Walter 1944. *Die Entstehung der italienischen Kommunen im frühen Mittelalter*. Munich: Verlag der Bayerischen Akademie der Wissenschaften.

Gonella, Guido 1946. *Il programma della democrazia cristiana per la nuova costituzione*. Rome: SELI.

González Antón Luis 1989. *Las Cortes en la España del Antiguo Regimen*. Madrid: Siglo XXI de España.

Gotto, Bernhard 2006. 'Polykratische Selbststabilisierung. Mittel- und Unterinstanzen in der NS-Diktatur', in Hachtmann, Rüdiger and Süß, Winfried (eds.), *Hitlers Kommissare: Sondergewalten in der national-sozialistischen Diktatur*. Göttingen: Wallstein-Verlag, pp. 28–51.

Gough, J. W. 1955. *Fundamental Law in English Constitutional History*. Oxford: Clarendon.

Greenleaf, W. H. 1983. *The British Political Tradition*, 3 vols., Vol. I, *The Rise of Collectivism*. London and New York: Methuen.

Grey, Thomas C. 1978. 'Origins of the Unwritten Constitution: Fundamental Law in American Political Thought', *Stanford Law Review* 30(5), pp. 843–93.

Grinberg, Martine 1997. 'La rédaction des coutumes et les droits seigneuriaux: Nommer, classer, exclure', *Annales: Histoire, Sciences Sociales* 52(5), pp. 1017–38.

Grosser, Dieter 1970. *Vom monarchischen Konstitutionalismus zur parlamentar-ischen Demokratie: Die Verfassungspolitik der deutschen Parteien im letzten Jahrzehnt des Kaiserreichs*. The Hague: Nijhoff.

Grübler, Michael 1982. *Die Spitzenverbände der Wirtschaft und das erste Kabinett Brüning: Vom Ende der Großen Koalition 1929/30 bis zum Vorabend der Bankenkrise 1931*. Düsseldorf: Droste.

Gruder, Vivian R. 1968. *The Royal Provincial Intendants: A Governing Elite in eighteenth-century France*. Ithaca, N.Y.: Cornell University Press.

2007. *The Notables and the Nation: The Political Schooling of the French, 1787–1788*. Cambridge, Mass.: Harvard University Press.

Grünthal, Günther 1982. *Parlamentarismus in Preußen 1848/49–1857/58: Preußischer Konstitutionalismus – Parlament und Regierung in der Reaktionsära*. Düsseldorf: Droste.

Guidi, Dario 1931. *Principi generali di diritto corporativo*. Rome: Edizioni del Diritto del Lavoro.

Guizot, François 1855. *Histoire des origines du gouvernement représentatif et des institutions politiques de l'Europe*. Paris: Didier.

Gundling, Nicolaus 1743. *Allgemeines geistliches Recht der drey christlichen Haupt-Religionen.* Frankfurt am Main: Spring.

Gunther, Richard 1980. *Public Policy in a No-Party State: Spanish Planning and Budgeting in the Twilight of the Franquist Era.* Berkeley: University of California Press.

1996. 'The Impact of Regime Change on Public Policy: The Case of Spain', *Journal of Public Policy* 16(2), pp. 157–201.

Habermas, Jürgen 1990 [1962]. *Strukturwandel der Öffentlichkeit: Untersuchungen zu einer Kategorie der bürgerlichen Gesellschaft,* new edn. Frankfurt am Main: Suhrkamp.

Haines, Charles Grove 1944. *The Role of the Supreme Court in American Government and Politics 1789–1835.* Berkeley: University of California Press.

Haller, Johannes 1966. *Pabsttum und Kirchenreform: Vier Kapitel zur Geschichte des ausgehenden Mittelalters,* 3rd edn. Berlin: Weidmann, 1966.

Halmai, Gábor 1996. 'Establishing a State Governed by the Rule of Law in Hungary', *Review of Central and East European Law* 4, pp. 347–64.

Halperin, Jean-Louis 1987. *Le tribunal de cassation sous la révolution (1790–1799).* Paris: Pichon et Durand-Auzias.

Harding, Alan 2002. *Medieval Law and the Foundations of the State.* Oxford University Press.

Harrington, James 1887 [1656]. *The Commenwealth of Oceana.* London: Routledge.

Hart, James S. Jr 2003. *The Rule of Law, 1603–1660: Crowns, Courts and Judges.* London: Longman.

Hart, Marjolein C. 't 1993. *The Making of a Bourgeois State: War, Politics and Finance during the Dutch Revolt.* Manchester University Press.

Hartung, Fritz and Mousnier, Roland 1955. 'Problèmes concernant la monarchie absolue', in *Relazioni del X: Congresso Internazionale di Scienze storiche,* 6 vols., Vol. VI. Florence: Sansoni, pp. 3–55.

Hartwich, Hans-Hermann 1967. *Arbeitsmarkt, Verbände und Staat: Die öffentliche Bindung unternehmerischer Funtionen in der Weimarer Republik.* Berlin: de Gruyter.

Hartwig, Matthias 1992. 'The Institutionalization of the Rule of Law: The Establishment of Constitutional Courts in the Eastern European Countries', *American University Journal of International Law and Policy* 7, pp. 449–70.

Hasiba, Gernot 1981. 'Das kriegswirtschaftliche Ermächtigungsgesetz (KWEG) von 1917. Seine Entstehung und seine Anwendung vor 1933', in Rechtswissenschaftliche Fakultät der Universität Salzburg (ed.), *Aus Österreichs Rechtsleben in Geschichte und Gegenwart: Festschrift für Ernst C. Helbling.* Berlin: Duncker & Humblot, pp. 543–65.

Hauriou, Maurice 1929 [1923]. *Précis de droit constitutionnel*. Paris: Sirey.

Hausmaninger, Herbert 1992. 'From the Soviet Committee of Constitutional Supervision to the Russian Constitutional Court', *Cornell International Law Journal* 305, pp. 305–37.

Haverkamp, Alfred 1971. *Herrschaftsformen der Frühstaufer in Reichsitalien*. Stuttgart: Anton Hiersemann.

Hazareesingh, Sudhir 1998. *From Subject to Citizen: The Second Empire and the Emergence of Modern French Democracy*. Princeton University Press.

Heckel, Martin 1956. 'Staat und Kirche nach den Lehren der evangelischen Juristen Deutschlands in der ersten Hälfte des 17. Jahrhunderts', *Zeitschrift für Rechtsgeschichte* 73, pp. 117–247.

Hefeker, Carsten 2001. 'The Agony of Central Power: Fiscal Federalism in the German Reich', *European Review of Economic History* 5, pp. 119–42.

Hegel, Carl 1847. *Geschichte der Städteverfassung von Italien seit der Zeit der römischen Herrschaft bis zum Ausgang des zwölften Jahrhunderts*, 2 vols., Vol. I. Leipzig: Weidmann.

Hegel, G. W. F. 1969 [1821]. *Grundlinien der Philosophie des Rechts*, in Hegel, *Werke*, ed. E. Moldenhauer and K. M. Michel, 20 vols., Vol. VII. Frankfurt am Main: Suhrkamp.

Heinze, R. W. 1976. *The Proclamations of the Tudor Kings*. Cambridge University Press.

Helbig, Herbert 1955. *Der Wettinische Ständestaat: Untersuchungen zur Geschichte des Ständestaats und der landständischen Verfassung in Mitteldeutschland bis 1485*. Münster: Böhlau.

Helmholz, Richard H. (ed.) 1992. *Canon Law in the Protestant Lands*. Berlin: Duncker & Humblot.

1996. *The Spirit of Classical Canon Law*. Athens: University of Georgia Press.

Henshall, Nicholas 1996. 'Early Modern Absolutism 1550–1700: Political Reality or Propaganda?', in Asch, Ronald G. and Durchhardt, Heinz (eds.), *Der Absolutismus – ein Mythos? Strukturwandel monarchischer Herrschaft (ca. 1550–1700)*. Cologne: Böhlau, pp. 25–56.

Hernández Montalabán, Francisco J. 1999. *La abolición de los señoríos en España (1811–1837)*. Madrid: Biblioteca Nueva.

Hickey, Daniel 1986. *The Coming of French Absolutism: The Struggle for Tax Reform in the Province of Dauphiné 1540–1640*. University of Toronto Press.

Hilferding, Rudolf 1947 [1910]. *Das Finanzkapital: Eine Studie über die jüngste Entwicklung des Kapitalismus*. Berlin: Dietz.

Hill, B. W. 1985. *British Parliamentary Parties 1742–1832: From the Fall of Walpole to the First Reform Act*. London: Allen & Unwin.

Hintze, Otto 1962a [1930]. 'Typologie der ständischen Verfassungen des Abendlandes', in Hintze, *Staat und Verfassung: Gesammelte Abhandlungen zur Allgemeinen Verfassungsgeschichte*, 2nd edn. Göttingen: Vandenhoeck & Ruprecht, pp. 120–39.

1962b [1910]. 'Der Commissarius und seine Bedeutung in der allgemeinen Verwaltungsgeschichte', in Hintze, *Staat und Verfassung: Gesammelte Abhandlungen zur Allgemeinen Verfassungsgeschichte*, 2nd edn. Göttingen: Vandenhoeck & Ruprecht, pp. 242–74.

Hobbes, Thomas 1914 [1651]. *Leviathan*. London: Dent.

Hoensch, Jörg K. 1982. 'Königtum und Adelsnation in Polen,' in Kunisch, Johannes (ed.), *Der dynastische Fürstenstaat: Zur Bedeutung von Sukzessionsordnungen für die Entstehung des frühmodernen Staates*. Berlin: Duncker & Humblotz, pp. 315–44.

Hoffmann, Hartmut 1964. *Gottesfriede und Treuga Dei*. Stuttgart: Hiersemann.

Hofmann, Hanns Hubert 1962. *Adelige Herrschaft und souveräner Staat: Studien über Staat und Gesellschaft in Franken und Bayern im 18. und 19. Jahrhundert*. Munich: Kommission für Bayerische Landesgeschichste.

Holbach, Baron Paul Henri Thiry d' 1773. *La politique naturelle ou discours sur les vrais principes du gouvernement*, 2 vols. London: no publisher.

Holt, J. C. 1972. 'Magna Carta and the Origins of Statute Law', *Studia Gratiana* 15, pp. 487–508.

1992. *Magna Carta*. Cambridge University Press.

Hooker, John 1572. *Order and Usage of Keeping of the Parlements in England*. London: Printed by John Allde, and John Charlewood?

Hooker, Richard 1989 [1593–1662]. *Of the Laws of ecclesiastical Polity*. Cambridge University Press.

Hopcroft, Rosemary 1999. 'Maintaining the Balance of Power: Taxation and Democracy in England and France, 1340–1688', *Sociological Perspectives* 42(1), pp. 69–95.

Höpfl, Harro 1986. 'Fundamental Law and the Constitution in Sixteenth-Century France', in Schnur, Roman (ed.), *Die Rolle der Juristen bei der Entstehung des modernen Staates*. Berlin: Dunker & Humblot, pp. 327–56.

Horn, Jeff 2006. *The Path Not Taken: French Industrialization in the Age of Revolution 1750–1830*. Cambridge, Mass.: MIT Press.

Horne, John N. 1991. *Labour at War: France and Britain 1914–1918*. Oxford: Clarendon.

Hoyle, R. W. 1994. 'Parliament and Taxation in Sixteenth-Century England', *English Historical Review* 109, pp. 1174–96.

Hoyt, Robert S. 1950. 'Royal Taxation and the Growth of the Realm in Medieval England', *Speculum* 25(1), pp. 36–48.

Huber, Ernst Rudolf 1934. *Die Gestalt des deutschen Sozialismus*. Hamburg: Deutsche Verlagsanstalt.

1957. *Deutsche Verfassungsgeschichte seit 1789*, 2nd edn, 6 vols., Vol. I. Stuttgart: Kohlhammer.

Hudson, John 1996. *The Formation of the English Common Law: Law and Society in England from the Norman Conquest to Magna Carta*. London: Longman.

Hugo, Gustav 1823 [1792]. *Lehrbuch der juristischen Encyclopädie, in Lehrbuch eines civilistischen Cursus*, 7 vols. Berlin: August Mylius, Vol. I.

Hume, David 1978 [1739–40]. *A Treatise on Human Nature*. Oxford University Press.

Irnerius? 1894. *Summa Codicis*, ed. Hermann Fitting. Berlin: Guttentag.

Jago, Charles 1981. 'Habsburg Absolutism and the Cortes of Castille', *American Historical Review* 86, pp. 307–26.

1985. 'Philip II and the Cortes of Castille: The Case of the Cortes of 1576', *Past and Present* 109, pp. 24–43.

James VI and I, king of Scotland and England 1994 [1616]. 'Speech in Star Chamber', in *Political Writings*, ed. J. P. Sommerville. Cambridge University Press, pp. 204–28.

Jenkins, David 1647. *Lex Terrae*. London: John Gyles.

Jensen, Merrill 1940. *The Articles of Confederation: An Interpretation of the Social-Historical History of the American Revolution 1774–1781*. Madison, Wis.: University of Wisconsin Press.

1950. *The New Nation: A History of the United States during the Confederation 1781–1789*. New York: Knopf.

Jèze, Gaston 1925 [1904]. *Les principes généraux du droit administratif*, Vol. I, *La technique juridique du droit publique français*. Paris: Dalloz.

John, Michael 1989. *Politics and the Law in Late Nineteenth-Century Germany*. Oxford: Clarendon.

John of Paris 1614 [c. 1302]. 'De Potestate Regia et Papali', in Goldast, Melchior (ed.), *Monarchia S: Romani Imperii sive Tractatus*, 3 vols., Vol. II. Frankfurt am Main, pp. 108–47.

Jolliffe, J. E. A 1955. *Angevin Kingship*. London: Black.

1961. *The Constitutional History of Medieval England: From the English Settlement to 1485*. London: Black.

Jones, P. J. 1965. 'Communes and Despots: The City State in Late-Medieval Italy', *Transactions of the Royal Historical Society*, 5th series, 15, pp. 71–96.

Jones, P. M. 1988. *The Peasantry in the French Revolution*. Cambridge University Press.

Jones, W. J. 1971. *Politics and the Bench: The Judges and the Origins of the English Civil War*. London: Allen & Unwin.

Jouanna, Arlette 1989. *Le devoir de révolte: La noblesse française et la gestation de l'état moderne, 1559–1661*. Paris: Fayard.

Juste, Théodore 1850. *Histoire du congrès nationale de Belgique ou de la fondation de la monarchie belge*, 3 vols., Vol. II. Brussels: Muquardt.

Kaeuper, Richard 1988. *War, Justice, and Public Order: England and France in the later Middle Ages*. Oxford: Clarendon.

Kahn, Daniela 2006. *Die Steuerung der Wirtschaft im nationalsozialistischen Deutschland: Das Beispiel der Reichsgruppe Industrie*. Frankfurt am Main: Klostermann.

Kahn, Jeffrey 2002. *Federalism, Democratization and the Rule of Law in Russia*. Oxford University Press.

2004. 'Russia's "Dictatorship of Law" and the European Court of Human Rights', *Review of Central and East European Law* 29(1), pp. 1–14.

Kamen, Henry 1980. *Spain in the Late Seventeenth Century*. London: Longman.

Kannowski, Bernd 2007. 'Der roncalische Regalienbegriff und seine Vorgeschichte', in Dilcher, Gerhard and Quaglione, Diego (eds.), *Gli inizi del diritto pubblico*. Bologna: Mulino, pp. 157–76.

Kant, Immanuel 1976 [1797]. *Metaphysik der Sitten*, in Kant, *Werkausgabe*, ed. W. Weischedel, 12 vols., Vol. VIII. Frankfurt am Main: Suhrkamp, pp. 309–634.

Keeton, George W. 1966. *The Norman Conquest and the Common Law*. London: Ernest Been.

Kejř, Jiří 1992. 'Anfänge der ständischen Verfassung in Böhmen', in Boockmann, Hartmut (ed.), *Die Anfänge der ständischen Vertretungen in Preußen und seinen Nachbarländern*. Munich: Oldenbourg, pp. 177–217.

Keller, Hagen 1979. *Adelsherrschaft und städtische Gesellschaft in Oberitalien: 9. bis 12. Jahrhundert*. Tübingen: Max Niemeyer.

1982. 'Der Übergang zur Kommune: Zur Entwicklung der italienischen Stadtverfassung im 11. Jahrhundert', in Diestelkamp, Bernhard (ed.), *Beiträge zum hochmittelalterlichen Städtewesen*. Cologne: Böhlau, pp. 55–72.

1991. 'Rechtsgewohnheit, Satzungsrecht und Kodifikation in der Kommune Mailand vor der Errichtung der Signorie', in Keller, Hagen and Busch, Jörg W. (eds.), *Statutencodices des 13: Jahrhunderts als Zeugen pragmatischer Schriftlichkeit: Die Handschriften von Como, Lodi, Novara, Pavia und Voghera*. Munich: Fink, pp. 167–89.

Kelsen, Hans 1922. *Der soziologische und der juristische Staatsbegriff: Kritische Untersuchung des Verhältnisses von Staat und Recht*. Tübingen: Mohr.

1929. 'Wesen und Entwicklung der Staatsgerichtsbarkeit', *Veröffentlichungen der Vereinigung der Deutschen Staatsrechtslehrer* 5, pp. 30–88.

1942. 'Judicial Review of Legislation: A Comparative Study of the Austrian and American Constitution', *Journal of Politics* 4(2), pp. 183–200.

Kent, Dale V. 1978. *The Rise of the Medici: Faction in Florence, 1426–1434*. Oxford University Press.

Kenyon, J. P. (ed.) 1966. *The Stuart Constitution 1603–1688: Documents and Commentary*. Cambridge University Press.

Kern, Robert W. 1974. *Liberals, Reformers and Caciques in Restoration Spain 1875–1909*. Albuquerque: University of New Mexico Press.

Kettering, Sharon 1978. *Judicial Politics and Urban Revolt in Seventeenth-Century France: The Parlement of Aix, 1629–1659*. Princeton University Press.

Kienast, Walther 1975. *Deutschland und Frankreich in der Kaiserzeit (900–1270): Weltkaiser und Einzelkönige*. Stuttgart: Anton Hiersemann.

Kirsch, Martin 1999. *Monarch und Parlament im 19: Jahrhundert: Der monarchische Konstitutionalismus als europäischer Verfassungstyp – Frankreich im Vergleich.* Göttingen: Vandenhoeck & Ruprecht.

Kiser, Edgar and Linton, April 2001. 'Determinants of the Growth of the State: War and Taxation in Early Modern France and England', *Social Forces* 80(2), pp. 411–48.

Klebel, Ernst 1960. 'Territorialstaat und Lehen', in Mayer, Theodor (ed.), *Studien zum mittelalterlichen Lehenswesen.* Lindau: Jan Thorbecke, pp. 195–228.

Klein, Ernst 1965. *Von der Reform zur Restauration: Finanzpolitik und Reformgesetzgebung des preußischen Staatskanzlers Karl August von Hardenberg.* Berlin: de Gruyter.

Kleinmeyer, Gerd 1968. *Die Kaiserlichen Wahlkapitulationen: Geschichte, Wesen und Funktion.* Karlsruhe: Müller.

Klüber, Johann Ludwig (ed.) 1815. *Acten des Wiener Congresses,* 4 vols., Vol. I. Osnabrück: Zeller.

Knichen, Andreas 1603 [1600]. *De sublimi et regio territorii iure.* Frankfurt: In officina literaria Paltheniani Collegi.

Kocher, Gernot 1979. *Höchstgerichtsbarkeit und Privatrechtskodifikation: Die oberste Justizstelle und das allgemeine Privatrecht in Österreich von 1749–1811.* Vienna: Böhlau.

Kocka, Jürgen 1973. *Klassengesellschaft im Krieg: Deutsche Sozialgeschichte 1914–1918.* Göttingen: Vandenhoeck & Ruprecht.

Koenigsberger, H. G. 1994. 'Prince and States General: Charles V and the Netherlands (1506–1555)', *Transactions of the Royal Historical Society,* 6th series, 4, pp. 127–51.

     2001. *Monarchies, States Generals and Parliaments: The Netherlands in the Fifteenth and Sixteenth Centuries.* Cambridge University Press.

König, Reinhard 1614. 'Disputatio Politica', in Goldast, Melchior (ed.), *Politica Imperialia.* Frankfurt am Main: Bringer, pp. 645–56.

Könke, Günter 1987. *Organisierter Kapitalismus, Sozialdemokratie und Staat: Eine Studie zur Ideologie der sozialdemokratischen Arbeiterbewegung in der Weimarer Republik (1924–1932).* Stuttgart: Franz Steiner.

Koselleck, Reinhart 1973 [1959]. *Kritik und Krise: Eine Studie zur Pathogenese der bürgerlichen Welt.* Frankfurt am Main: Suhrkamp.

     1977. *Preußen zwischen Reform und Revolution: Allgemeines Landrecht, Verwaltung und soziale Bewegung von 1791 bid 1848,* 2nd edn. Stuttgart: Klett-Cotta.

Krammer, Mario 1913. *Das Kurfürstenkolleg von seinen Anfängen bis zum Zusammenschluß im Renser Kurverein des Jahres 1338.* Weimar: Böhlau.

Krieger, Karl-Friedrich 1979. *Die Lehnshoheit der deutschen Könige im Spätmittelalter (ca: 1200–1437).* Aalen: Scientia Verlag.

Kroell, Maurice 1910. *L'immunité franque*. Paris: Arthur Rousseau.

Krohn, Claus-Dieter 1978. 'Autoritärer Kapitalismus. Wirtschaftskonzeptionen im Übergang von der Weimarer Republik zum Nationalsozialismus', in Stegmann, Dirk, Wendt, Bernd-Jürgen and Witt, Peter-Christian (eds.), *Industrielle Gesellschaft und politisches System*. Bonn: Verlag Neue Gesellschaft, pp. 113–29.

Krug, Peter 1996. 'Departure from the Centralized Model: The Russian Supreme Court and Constitutional Control of Legislation', *Virginia Journal of International Law* 37, pp. 725–88.

Kruman, Marc W. 1997. *Between Authority and Liberty: State Constitution Making in Revolutionary America*. Chapel Hill: University of North Carolina Press.

Krynen, Jacques 1993. *L'empire du roi: Idées et croyances politiques en France XIIIe–XVe siècle*. Paris: Gallimard.

2009. *L'état de justice: France, XIII–XX siècle: L'idéologie de la magistrature ancienne*. Paris: Gallimard.

Küntzel, Georg 1908. 'Über Ständetum und Fürtstentum, vornemhlich Preußens, im 17. Jahrhundert', in Verein für Geschichte der Mark Brandenburg (ed.), *Beiträge zur brandenburgsichen und preußischen Geschichte: Festschrift zu Gustav Schmollers 70: Geburtstag*. Leipzig: Duncker & Humblot, pp. 100–52.

Lacey, Douglas R. 1969. *Dissent and Parliamentary Politics in England, 1661–1689: A Study in the Perpetuation and Tempering of Parliamentarism*. New Brunswick, N.J.: Rutgers University Press.

Ladner, J. R. 1980. *Government and Community: England, 1450–1509*. Cambridge, Mass.: Harvard University Press.

Laferrière, Édouard 1896. *Traité de la juridiction administrative et des recours contentieux*, 2nd edn, 2 vols., Vol. I. Paris: Berger-Levrault.

Lafon, Jacqueline Lucienne 2001. *La révolution française face au système judiciaire d'ancien régime*. Geneva: Droz.

Lanciotti, Maria Elvira 1993. *La riforma impossibile: Idee, discussioni e progetti sulla modifica del senato regio e vitalizio (1848–1922)*. Bologna: Gedit edizioni.

Lanzinner, Maximilian 1980. *Fürst, Räte und Landstände: Die Entstehung der Zentralbehörden in Bayern 1511–1598*. Göttingen: Vandenhoeck & Ruprecht.

Latorre, Gregorio Colás 2003. 'El justicia de Aragón en el señorío', *Revista Pedralabes* 23, pp. 77–94.

Laufer, Heinz 1968. *Verfassungsgerichtsbarkeit und politischer Prozeß: Studien zum Bundesverfassungsgericht der Bundesrepublik Deutschland*. Tübingen: Mohr.

Le Bret, Cardin 1635 [1632]. *De la souveraineté du roy*. Paris: Toussainct du Bray.

Lehmberg, Stanford E. 1970. *The Reformation Parliament 1529–1536*. Cambridge University Press.

Leibholz, Gerhard 1957. 'Einleitung: Der Status des Bundesverfassungsgerichts', *Jahrbuch des öffentlichen Rechts*, Neue Folge 6, pp. 110–221.

Leibniz, Gottfried Wilhelm 1693. *Codex Juris Gentium*. Hannover: S. Ammonus.

Leisching, Pater 2001. 'Quod illi soli licet pro tempori necessitate noves leges condere', in Pennington, Kenneth, Chodorow, Stanley and Kendall, Keith H. (eds.), *Proceedings of the Tenth International Congress of Medieval Canon Law*. Vatican: Biblioteca Apostolica Vaticanum, pp. 195–243.

Lemaire, André 1907. *Les lois fondamentales de la monarchie française après les théoriciens de l'Ancien Régime*. Paris: Thorin.

Lemarignier, Jean-François 1965. *Le gouvernement royal aux premiers temps capétiens (987–1109)*. Paris: Picard.

Lepointe, Gabriel 1953. *Histoire des institutions du droit publique français au XIX siècle 1789–1914*. Paris: Domat Montchrestien.

Le songe du vergier 1982 [*c*. 1378]. Edited by Schnerb-Lièvre, Marion (ed.). Paris: Éditions du CNRS.

'Lettre des Nobles du Royaume de France' 1901 [1302]. In Picot, Georges (ed.), *Documents relatifs aux États Généraux et Assemblés réunis sous Philippe le Bel*. Paris: Imprimérie Nationale, pp. 12–18.

Lewis, P. S. 1962. 'The Failure of the French Medieval Estates', *Past and Present* 23, pp. 3–24.

1968. *Later Medieval France: The Polity*. London: Macmillan.

Lewis, Paul H. 1978. 'Salazar's Ministerial Elite, 1932–1968', *Journal of Politics* 40(3), pp. 622–47.

Le Yoncourt, Tiphaine 2006. 'Les attributions contentieuses des corps administratifs sous la révolution', in Bigot, Grégoire and Bouvet, Marc (eds.), *Regards sur l'histoire de la justice administrative*. Paris: LexisNexis, pp. 31–72.

L'Hospital, Michel 1824 [1560]. 'Harangue aux État-Généraux en 1560', in *Oeuvres complètes*, 3 vols., Vol. I. Paris: Boulland, pp. 375–411.

Lincoln, W. Bruce 1982. *In the Vanguard of Reform: Russia's Enlightened Bureaucrats 1825–1861*. DeKalb: Northern Illinois University Press.

1990. *The Great Reforms: Autocracy, Bureaucracy, and the Politics of Change in Imperial Russia*. DeKalb: Northern Illinois University Press.

Lindegren, Jan 1985. 'The Swedish "military state", 1560–1720', *Scandinavian Journal of History* 10(4), pp. 305–36.

Linehan, Peter 1993. *History and the Historians of Medieval Spain*. Oxford: Clarendon.

Littré, Émile 1879. *Conservation, Revolution et Positivisme*, 2nd edn. Paris: Aux Bureaux de la Philosophie Positive.

Loades, David 1997. *Tudor Government: Structures of Authority in the Sixteenth Century*. Oxford: Blackwell.

Locke, John 1960 [1689]. *Two Treatises of Government*. Cambridge University Press.

Lockhart, Paul Douglas 2004. *Sweden in the Seventeenth Century*. Basingstoke: Palgrave.

2007. *Denmark, 1513-1660: The Rise and Decline of a Renaissance Monarchy*. Oxford University Press.

Lopez, Robert S. 1998. *The Commercial Revolution of the Middle Ages 950-1350*. Cambridge University Press.

Lourie, Elena 1966. 'A Society Organized for War: Medieval Spain', *Past and Present* 35, pp. 54-76.

Lousse, Émile 1943. *La societé d'Ancien Régime: Organisation et représentation corporatives*. Paris: Deselée, de Bouwer & Co.

Loyseau, Charles 1665 [1610]. *Traité des ordres et simples dignitez*, 4th edn. Paris.

Luebbert, Gregory M. 1987. 'Social Foundations of Political Order in Interwar Europe', *World Politics* 39(4), pp. 449-78.

Luhmann, Niklas 1965. *Grundrechte als Institution: Ein Beitrag zur politischen Soziologie*. Berlin: Duncker & Humblot.

1969. 'Klassische Theorie der Macht: Kritik ihrer Prämissen', *Zeitschrift für Politik* 16(2), pp. 149-70.

1973. 'Politische Verfassungen im Kontext des Gesellschaftssystems, I', *Der Staat* 12(2), pp. 1-22.

1981. 'Selbstlegitimation des Staates', *Archiv für Rechts- und Sozialphilosophie*. Beiheft: Legitimation des modernen Staates, pp. 65-83.

1988. *Macht*, 2nd edn. Stuttgart: Enke.

1991. 'Verfassung als evolutionäre Errungenschaft', *Rechtshistorisches Journal* 9, pp. 176-220.

2000. *Politik der Gesellschaft*. Frankfurt am Main: Suhrkamp.

Lukowski, Jerzy 1991. *Liberty's Folly: The Polish Lithuanian Commonwealth in the Eighteenth Century, 1697-1795*. London: Routledge.

Luther, Jörg 1990. *Die italienische Verfassungsgerichtsbarkeit: Geschichte, Prozessrecht, Rechtsprechung*. Baden-Baden: Nomos.

Luther, Martin 1960 [1515-16]. *Vorlesung über den Römerbrief 1515/1516*, Latin-German edn. Weimar: Böhlau.

Lutz, Donald S. 1980. *Popular Consent and Popular Control: Whig Political Theory in the Early State Constitutions*. Baton Rouge: Louisiana University Press.

Lyttelton, Adrian 1973. *The Seizure of Power: Fascism in Italy 1919-1929*. London: Weidenfeld & Nicolson.

Mably, Gabriel Bonnot de 1972 [written 1758]. *Des droits et des devoirs du citoyen*. Paris: Marcel Didier.

McFaul, Michael 1995. 'State Power, Institutional Change, and the Politics of Privatization in Russia', *World Politics* 47(2), pp. 210-43.

Machado, Diamantino P. 1991. *The Structure of Portuguese Society: The Failure of Fascism*. New York: Praeger.

McIlwain, Charles Howard 1947. *Constitutionalism Ancient and Modern*. Ithaca: Cornell University Press.

Mackay, Ruth 1999. *The Limits of Royal Authority in Spain: Resistance and Obedience in Seventeenth-Century Castile*. Cambridge University Press.

Maddicott, J. R. 2010. *The Origins of the English Parliament, 924-1327*. Oxford University Press.

Madison, James, Hamilton, Alexander and Jay, John 1987 [1787-8]. *The Federalist Papers*. London: Penguin.

Magalhães, Pedro 2003. 'The Limits to Judicialization: Legislative Politics and Constitutional Review in the Iberian Democracies', Ph.D. dissertation, Ohio State University, available at http://etd.ohiolink.edu/view.cgi?acc_num=osu1046117531.

Magalhães, Pedro C., Guarnieri, Carlo and Kaminis, Yorgos 2006. 'Democratic Consolidation, Judicial Reform, and the Judicialization of Politics in Southern Europe', in Gunther, Richard, Diamandouros, P. Nikiforos and Sotiropoulos, Dimitri A. (eds.), *Democracy and the State in the New Southern Europe*. Oxford University Press, pp. 138-96.

Major, J. Russell 1960. *Representative Institutions in Renaissance France 1421-1559*. Madison: University of Wisconsin Press.

  1997. *From Renaissance Monarchy to Absolute Monarchy*. Baltimore, Johns Hopkins University Press.

Mann, Michael 1984. 'The Autonomous Power of the State: Its Origins, Mechanisms and Results', *European Archive of Sociology* 25, pp. 185-213.

Manning, Roberta Thompson 1979. 'Zemstvo and Revolution: The Onset of the Gentry Reaction 1905-1907,' in Haimson, Leopold H. (ed.), *The Politics of Rural Russia*. Bloomington: Indiana University Press, pp. 30-67.

  1982a. *The Crisis of the Old Order in Russia: Gentry and Government*. Princeton University Press.

  1982b. 'The Zemstvo and Politics, 1864-1904', in Emmons, Terence and Vocinich, Wayne S (eds.), *The Zemstvo in Russia: An Experiment in Local Self-Government*. Cambridge University Press, pp. 133-76.

Maravall, José Antonio 1972. *Estado moderno y mentalidad social (siglos XV a XVII)*, 2 vols. Madrid: Ediciones Revista de Occidente.

Marchadier, André 1904. *Les états généraux sous Charles VII*. Bordeaux: Cadoret.

Markoff, John 1996. *The Abolition of Feudalism: Peasants, Lords and Legislators in the French Revolution*. University Park, Pa.: Pennsylvania State University Press.

Marongiu, Antonio 1953. 'Un momento tipico de la monarquia medieval: El rey juz', *Annuario de Historia del Derecho Español* 23, pp. 677-715.

Marsilius of Padua 1956 [1324]. *Defensor Pacis*, trans. and introduced by Alan Gewirth. New York: Columbia University Press.

Martin, Benjamin 1990. *The Agony of Modernization: Labor and Industrialization in Spain*. Ithaca, N.Y.: ILR Press.

Martines, Lauro 1968. *Lawyers and Statecraft in Renaissance Florence*. Princeton University Press.

Marx, Karl 1956–68 [1844]. *Zur Judenfrage*, in Marx and Engels, Friedrich, *Werke*, 43 vols., Vol. I. Berlin: Dietz, pp. 347–377.

1956–68 [1852]. *Der achtzehnte Brumaire des Louis Napoleon*, in Marx and Engels, Friedrich, *Werke*, 43 vols., Vol. VIII. Berlin: Dietz, pp. 113–307.

Mason, Alpheus Thomas 1964. *The States Rights Debate: Antifederalism and the Constitution*. Englewood Cliffs: Prentice Hall.

Mason, Tim 1966. 'Labour in the Third Reich, 1933–1939', *Past and Present* 33, pp. 112–41.

Mauer, Wilhelm 1965. 'Reste des kanonischen Rechtes im Frühprotestantismus', *Zeitschrift für Rechtsgeschichte* 82, pp. 190–253.

Maxwell, Kenneth 1986. 'Regime Overthrow and the Prospects for Democratic Transition in Portugal', in O'Donnell, Guillermo, Schmitter, Philippe and Whitehead, Laurence (eds.), *Transitions from Authoritarian Rule: Southern Europe*. Baltimore: Johns Hopkins University Press, pp. 109–37.

1995. *The Making of Portuguese Democracy*. Cambridge University Press, pp. 159–60.

Mayer, Ernst 1909. *Italienische Verfassungsgeschichte von der Gothenzeit bis zur Zunftherrschaft*. Leipzig: Deichert.

Mayer, Theodor 1939. 'Die Ausbildung der Grundlagen des modernen deutschen Staates im hohen Mittelalter', *Historische Zeitschrift* 159, pp. 457–87.

Mayeur, Jean-Marie 1984. *La vie politique sous la Troisième Republique 1870–1940*. Paris: Editions du Seuil.

Meaker, Gerald 1974. *The Revolutionary Left in Spain 1914–1923*. Stanford University Press.

Meer, Fernando de 1978. *La Constitucion de la II Republica: Autonomias, propriedad, iglesia, enseñanza*. Pamplona: Eunsa.

Meister, Rainer 1991. *Die große Depression: Zwangslagen und Handlungsspielräume der Wirtschafts- und Finanzpolitik in Deutschland 1929–1932*. Regensburg: Transfer Verlag.

Melanchthon, Philipp 1836 [1541]. 'Iudicium de Episc. Naumb. 1. Nov. 1541', in Bretschneider, K. (ed.), *Corpus Reformatorum*, 28 vols., Vol. IV. Halle: A. Schwetschke, pp. 683–94.

Mellis, Guido 1988. *Due modelli di amministrazione tra liberalismo e fascismo: Burocrazie tradizionali e nuovi apparati*. Rome: Ministro per i beni culturali.

1996. *Storia dell'amministrazione italiana 1861–1993*. Bologna: Mulino.

Meneses, Filipe Ribeiro de 2002. 'The Origins and Nature of Authoritarian Rule in Portugal, 1919–1945', *Contemporary European History* 11(1), pp. 153–63.

Merkl, Adolf 1935. *Die ständisch-autoritäre Verfassung Österreichs: Ein kritisch-systematischer Grundriß*. Vienna: Springer.

1999 [1921]. 'Die gerichtliche Prüfung von Gesetzen und Verordnungen', in Merkl, *Gesammelte Schriften*, ed. D. Mayer-Maly, H. Schambeck and W.-D. Grussmann, 3 vols. (6 half-vols.), Vol. II/1. Berlin: Duncker & Humblot, pp. 393–438.

Metcalf, Michael F. 1982. 'Challenges to Economic Orthodoxy and Parliamentary Sovereignty in 18th-Century Sweden', *Legislative Studies Quarterly* 7(2), pp. 251–61.

Milsom, S. F. C. 1976. *The Legal Framework of English Feudalism*. Cambridge University Press.

Minninger, Monika 1978. *Von Clermont zum Wormser Konkordat: Die Auseinandersetzungen um den Lehnsnexus zwischen König und Episkopat*. Vienna: Böhlau.

Mommsen, Wolfgang M. 1990. *Der autoritäre Nationalstaat: Verfassung, Gesellschaft und Kultur im deutschen Kaiserreich*. Frankfurt am Main: Fischer.

Moote, A. Lloyd 1972. *The Revolt of the Judges: The Parlement of Paris and the Fronde 1643–1652*. Princeton University Press.

Moran Orti, Manuel 1986. *Poder y goberno en las Cortes de Cadiz (1810–1813)*. Pamplona: Ediciones Universidad de Navarra.

Moraw, Peter 1980. 'Versuch über die Entstehung des Reichstags', in Weber, Hermann (ed.), *Politische Ordnungen und soziale Kräfte im alten Reich*. Wiesbaden: Franz Steiner, pp. 1–36.

Moreno de Vargas, Bernabé 1622. *Discursos de la Nobleza de Espana*. Madrid: Martin.

Morgan, Edmund S. 1988. *Inventing the People: The Rise of Popular Sovereignty in England and America*. New York/London: Norton.

Morgan, Kenneth O. 1979. *Consensus and Disunity: The Lloyd George Coalition Government 1918–1922*. Oxford: Clarendon.

Morris, Colin 1989. *The Papal Monarchy: The Western Church from 1050 to 1250*. Oxford University Press.

Moser, Johann Jakob 1766–82a. *Von denen deutschen Reichs-Tagen*, in Moser, *Neues deutsches Staatsrecht*, 20 vols., Vol. V/1. Stuttgart: Mezler.

1766–82b. *Von der teutschen Reichs-Stände Landen, deren Landschaften, Unterthanen, Landes-Freyheiten, Beschwerden, Schulden und Zusammenkünften*, in Moser, *Neues Deutsches Staatsrecht*, 20 vols., Vol. XIII. Stuttgart: Mezler.

Mosse, George L. 1950. *The Struggle for Sovereignty in England: From the Reign of Queen Elizabeth to the Petition of Right*. East Lansing: Michigan State College.

Mousnier, Roland 1945. *La venalité des offices sous Henri IV et Louis XIII*. Rouen: Maugard.

1974. *Les institutions de la France sous la monarchie absolue 1598–1789*, 2 vols. Paris: Presses Universitaires de France.

Moxó, Salvador de 1965. *La disolución del regimen señorial en España*. Madrid: Consego superior de investigaciones cientficas.

2000. *Feudalismo, Señorío y Nobleza en la Castilla Medieval*. Madrid: Real Academia de la Historia.

Mullett, Charles F. 1966. *Fundamental Law and the American Revolution 1760-1776*. New York: Octagon Books.

Münch, Richard 1984. *Die Struktur der Moderne: Grundmuster und differentielle Gestaltung des institutionellen Aufbaus der modernen Gesellschaften*. Frankfurt am Main: Suhrkamp.

Mussolini, Benito 1934. *Verso il corporativismo integrale*. Siena.

Musson, Anthony 2001. *Medieval Law in Context: The Growth of Legal Consciousness from Magna Carta to the Peasants' Revolt*. Manchester University Press.

Musson, Anthony and Ormrod, W. M. 1998. *The Evolution of English Justice: Law, Politics and Society in the Fourteenth Century*. Basingstoke: Macmillan.

Nader, Helen 1990. *Liberty in Absolutist Spain: The Habsburg Sale of Towns, 1516-1700*. Baltimore: Johns Hopkins University Press.

Näf, Werner 1951a. 'Frühformen des "Modernen Staates" im Spätmittelalter', *Historische Zeitschrift* 171(2), pp. 225–44.

Näf, Werner (ed.) 1951b. *Herrschaftsverträge des Mittlelalters*. Bern: Lange.

Najemy, John 1979. 'Guild Republicanism in Trecento Florence: The Successes and Ultimate Failure of Corporate Politics', *American Historical Review* 84(1), pp. 53–71.

2006. *A History of Florence, 1200-1575*. Malden, Mass./Oxford: Blackwell Publishing.

Naumann, Friedrich 1919. 'Rede', *Die Hilfe* 9 (1919), pp. 100–5.

Nedham, Marchamont 1767 [1651-2/6]. *The Excellence of a free State*. London: Millar & Cadell.

Neugebauer, Wolfgang 1992. *Politischer Wandel im Osten: Ost- und Westpreußen von den alten Ständen zum Konstitutionalismus*. Stuttgart: Franz Steiner.

Neuhaus, Helmut 1982. *Reichsständische Repräsentativformen im 16: Jahrhundert: Reichstag - Reichskreistag - Reichsdeputationstag*. Berlin: Duncker & Humblot.

Neumann, Franz 1944. *Behemoth: The Structure and Practice of National Socialism 1933-1944*. New York: Harper & Row.

Niclauß, Karlheinz 1974. 'Der Parlamentarische Rat und das Sozialstaatspostulat', *Politische Vierteljahresschrift* 15, pp. 33–52.

Nicolet, Claude 1982. *L'idée républicaine en France (1789-1924): Essai d'Histoire critique*. Paris: Gallimard.

Nieto Soria, José Manuel 2002. 'La nobleza y el "poderío real absoluto" en la Castilla del siglo XV', *Cahiers de linguistique et de civilisation hispaniques médiévales* 25, pp. 237–54.

North, David C. and Weingast, Barry 1989. 'Constitutions and Commitment: The Evolution of Institutions Governing Public Choice in Seventeenth-Century England', *Journal of Economic History* 44, pp. 803–32.

Northcott, Clarence 1917. 'The Organization of Labour in War Time in Great Britain', *Political Science Quarterly* 32(2), pp. 209–23.

O'Callaghan, Joseph F. 1975. *A History of Medieval Spain*. Ithaca/London: Cornell University Press.

1989. *The Cortes of Castile Leon 1188–1350*. Philadelphia: University of Pennsylvania Press.

Occhipinti, Elisa 2000. *L'Italia dei comuni*. Rome: Carocci.

Oestreich, Gerhard 1969. *Geist und Gestalt des frühmodernen Staates*. Berlin: Duncker & Humblot.

1977. 'Vom Herrschaftsvertrag zur Verfassungsurkunde. Die "Regierungsform" des 17. Jahrhunderts als konstitutionelle Instrumente', in Vierhaus, Rudolf (ed.), *Herrschaftsverträge, Wahlkapitulationen, Fundamentalgesetze*. Göttingen: Vandenhoeck & Ruprecht, pp. 45–67.

O'Gorman, Frank 1982. *The Emergence of the British Two-Party System 1760–1832*. London: Arnold.

Oldendorp, Johannes 1549. 'De jure naturali gentium et civili', in *Tractatus ex variis juris interpretibus collecti*, 18 vols., Vol. I. Lyon: Compagnie des libraries, fos. 87–105.

Olivier-Martin, François 1984. *Histoire du droit français des origines à la revolution*. Paris: Éditions du CNRS.

Onory, Sergio Mochi 1951. *Fonti canonistiche dell'idea moderna dello stato*. Milan: Società editrice ‹vita e pensiero›.

Opello, Walter C. Jr 1990. 'The Transition to Democracy and the Constitutional Settlement as Causes of Political Instability in Post-Authoritarian Portugal', *Luso-Brazilian Review* 27(2), pp. 77–94.

Ordonnance du Roy Louis XIII sur les plaintes et doleances faittes par les Deputez des Estats der son Royaume convoquez et assemblez en la ville de Paris en l'année 1614. 1630. Paris: Estienne, Mettayer et Prevost.

Osiatynski, Wiktor 1994. 'Rights in New Constitutions of East Central Europe', *Columbia Human Rights Law Review* 26, pp. 112–65.

Pagès, Georges 1946. *La monarchie d'ancien régime en France (De Henri IV à Louis XIV)*. Paris: Armand Colin.

Palla, Marco (ed.) 2001. *Lo Stato Fascista*. Florence: La Nuova Italia.

Palmer, Robert C. 1982. *The County Courts of Medieval England 1150–1350*. Princeton University Press.

Palopoli, Nicola 1930–1. *Legislazione del lavoro*, 2 vols. Milan: CEDAM.

Panunzio, Sergio 1933. *Rivoluzione e costituzione (Problemi costituzionali della rivoluzione)*. Milan: Fratelli Treves, 1933.

Paradisi, Bruno 1987. *Studi sul medioevo giuridico*. Rome: Nella Sede dell' Istituto Palazzo Borromini.

Parker, Geoffrey 1977. *The Dutch Revolt*. London: Allen Lane.

Parker, Henry? 1643. *A political Catechism, or Certain Questions Concerning the Government of this Land*. London: Gellibrand.

Parris, Henry 1969. *Constitutional Bureaucracy: The Development of British Central Administration since the Eighteenth Century*. London: Allen & Unwin.

Parsons, Talcott 1963. 'On the Concept of Political Power', *Proceedings of the American Philosophical Society* 107(3), pp. 232–62.

1969. *Politics and Social Structure*. New York: The Free Press.

Patch, William L. 1998. *Heinrich Brüning and the Dissolution of the Weimar Republic*. Cambridge University Press.

Payne, Stanley G. 1993. *Spain's First Democracy: The Second Republic, 1931–1936*. Madison, Wis.: University of Wisconsin Press.

Pegues, Franklin J. 1962. *The Lawyers of the Last Capetians*. Princeton University Press.

Pennington, Kenneth 1984. *Pope and Bishops: The Papal Monarchy in the Twelfth and Thirteenth Centuries*. Philadelphia: University of Pennsylvania Press.

Pepe, Gabriele 1951. *Lo stato ghibellino di Federico II*. Bari: Gius Laterza.

Perticone, Giacomo 1960. *Il regime parlamentare nella storia dello Statuto Albertino*. Rome: Edizioni dell'Ateneo.

Pertz, Georg Heinrich (ed.) 1837. *Monumenta Germaniae Historiae: Leges*, Vol. II. Hannover: Hahn.

Petit-Renaud, Sophie 2001. *'Faire Loy' au royaume de France: De Philippe VI à Charles V (1328–1380)*. Paris: De Boccard.

Phillips, John A. and Wetherell, Charles 1995. 'The Great Reform Act of 1832 and the Political Modernization of England', *American Historical Review* 100(2), pp. 411–36.

Pickthorn, Kenneth 1934. *Early Tudor Government: Henry VII*. Cambridge University Press.

Pietri, François 1955. *Napoléon et le parlement, ou la dictature enchainée*. Paris: Fayard.

Pincus, Steve 2009. *1688: The First Modern Revolution*. New Haven: Yale University Press.

Pizzorusso, Alessandro, Vigoriti, Vincenzo and Certoma, G. L. 1983. 'The Constitutional Review of Legislation in Italy', *Temple Law Quarterly* 56, pp. 503–38.

Plucknett, T. F. T. 1922. *Statutes and their Interpretation in the first Half of the Fourteenth Century*. Cambridge University Press.

1926. 'Bonham's Case and Judicial Review', *Harvard Law Review* 40, pp. 30–70.

1949. *Legislation of Edward I*. Oxford: Clarendon.

1956. *A Concise History of the Common Law*. London: Butterworth.

Plumb, J. H. 1968. *The Growth of Political Stability in England 1675–1725.* London: History Book Club.

Pole, J. R. 1966. *Political Representation in England and the Origins of the American Republic.* London/New York: Macmillan.

Pollard, A. F. 1920. *The Evolution of Parliament.* London: Longman.

Pollock, Frederick and Maitland, F. W. 1895. *The History of English Law before the Time of Edward I.* Cambridge University Press.

Pothier, Robert-Joseph 1830a. *Traité de personnes,* in Pothier, *Oeuvres complètes,* 2 vols., Vol. I. Paris: Eugène Crochard, pp. 1–25.

1830b. *Traité du droit de domaine de propriété,* in Pothier, *Oeuvres complètes,* 2 vols. Paris: Eugène Crochard, pp. 143–98.

Prestwich, Michael 1972. *War, Politics and Finance under Edward I.* London: Faber & Faber.

Preuß, Hugo 1889. *Gemeinde, Staat, Reich als Gebietskörperschaften: Versuch einer deutschen Staatskonstruktion auf Grundlage der Genossenschaftstheorie.* Berlin: Julius Springer.

1926. *Staat, Recht und Freiheit.* Tübingen: J.C.B. Mohr.

Price, J. L. 1994. *Holland and the Dutch Republic in the Seventeenth Century: The Politics of Particularism.* Oxford: Clarendon.

Price, Roger 2001. *The French Second Empire: An Anatomy of Political Power.* Cambridge University Press.

Procházka, Radoslav 2002. *Mission Accomplished: On Founding Adjudication in Central Europe.* Budapest: Central European University Press.

Procter, Evelyn S. 1980. *Curia and Cortes in León and Castile 1072–1295.* Cambridge University Press.

Prothero, G. W. (ed.) 1913. *Select Statutes and other Constitutional Documents.* Oxford: Clarendon.

Prynne, William 1643. *The Soveraigne Power of Parliaments and Kingdomes,* 4 vols., Vol. I. London: Michael Sparke.

Pufendorf, Samuel 1687. *De habitu religionis christianae ad vitam civilem.* Bremen: Schwerdfeger.

Puhle, Hans-Jürgen 1970. 'Parlament, Parteien und Interessenverbände 1870–1914', in Stürmer, Michael (ed.), *Das Kaiserliche Deutschland: Politik und Gesellschaft 1870–1918.* Düsseldorf: Droste, 1970, pp. 340–77.

Pütter, Johann Stephan 1777. *Beiträge zum teutschen Staats- und Fürsten-Rechte.* Göttingen: Vandenhoeck.

Quazza, Guido 1957. *Le riforme in Piemonte nella prima metà del Settecento,* 2 vols. Modena: Società tipografica editrice Modenese.

Quigley, John 1990. 'Law Reform and the Soviet Courts', *Columbia Journal of Transnational Law* 28, pp. 59–75.

Rachel, Hugo 1905. *Der Große Kurfürst und die ostpreußischen Stände 1640–1688.* Leipzig: Duncker & Humblot.

Radding, C. M. 1988. *The Origins of Medieval Jurisprudence: Pavia and Bologna 850-1150*. New Haven: Yale University Press.

Rakove, Jack N. 1997. 'The Origins of Judicial Review: A Plea for New Contexts', *Stanford Law Review*, 49(5), pp. 1031-64.

Ranum, Orest 1993. *The Fronde: A French Revolution 1648-1652*. New York: Norton.

Rapaczynski, Andrzej 1991. 'Constitutional Politics in Poland: A Report on the Constitutional Committee of the Polish Parliament', *University of Chicago Law Review* 58, pp. 595-631.

Rauer, K. F. (ed.) 1845. *Die ständische Gesetzgebung der Preußischen Staaten, erster Teil*. Berlin: Carl Heymann.

Raumer, Kurt von 1967. 'Absoluter Staat, korporative Libertät, persönliche Freiheit', in Hofmann, Hanns Hubert (ed.), *Die Entstehung des modernen souveränen Staates*. Cologne: Kiepenheuer & Witsch, pp. 173-202.

Rauty, Natale and Savino, Giancarlo (eds.) 1977. *Lo statuto dei consoli del commune di Pistoia: Frammento del secolo XII*. Pistoia: Società pistoiese di storia patria.

Rebuffa, Giorgio 2003. *Lo statuto albertino*. Bologna: Mulino.

Rebuffi, Pierre 1581 [1551-4]. *Commentarii in constitutiones, seu ordinationes regias*. Lyon: Gulielmum Rovillium.

Reden, Armgard von 1974. *Landständische Verfassung und fürstliches Regiment in Sachsen-Lauenburg (1543-1689)*. Göttingen: Vandenhoeck & Ruprecht.

Reformatio Sigismundi 1497 [*c*. 1438]. Augsburg: Lukas Zeissenmaier.

Reid, John Phillip 1976. '"In an Inherited Way": English Constitutional Rights, the Stamp Act Debates, and the Coming of the American Revolution', *Southern California Law Review* 49, pp. 1109-30.

1989. *The Concept of Representation in the Age of the American Revolution*. Chicago University Press.

Reeve, L. J. 1989. *Charles I and the Road to Personal Rule*. Cambridge University Press.

Révész, László 1968. *Die Anfänge des ungarischen Parlamentarismus*. Munich: Oldenbourg.

1978. 'Parteipolitik, Parlamentarismus und Nationalitätenpolitik im liberalen Ungarn: Die Aprilgesetze 1848', *Ungarn-Jahrbuch*, pp. 123-58.

Reynolds, Susan 1981. '*Law and Communities in Western Christendom, c. 900-1140*', *American Journal of Legal History* 25(3), pp. 205-24.

2003. 'The Emergence of Professional Law in the Long Twelfth Century', *Law and History Review* 21(2), pp. 347-66.

Richardson, H. G. and Sayles, G. O. 1963. *The Governance of Medieval England from the Conquest to Magna Carta*. Edinburgh University Press.

'Rigaer Denkschrift' 1931 [1807]. In Georg Winter (ed.), *Die Reorganisation des Preußischen Staates unter Stein und Hardenberg: Erster Teil: Allgemeine Verwaltungs- und Behördenreform*, Vol. I, *Vom Beginn des Kampfes gegen die Kabinettsregierung bis zum Wiedereintritt des Ministers von Stein.* Leipzig: Hirzel, pp. 297–363.

Rigaudière, Albert 1988. 'Législation royale et construction de l'état dans la France du XIIIe siècle', in Gouron, André and Rigaudière, Albert (eds.), *Renaissance du pouvoir législatif et genèse de l'état.* Montpellier: Publications de la Société d'Histoire du Droit et des Institutions des Anciens Pays de Droit Écrit, pp. 203–36.

Rivière, Jean 1926. *Le problème de l'église et de l'état au temps de Philippe le Bel: Étude de théologie positive.* Paris: Honoré Champion.

Roberts, Clayton 1966. *The Growth of Responsible Government in Stuart England.* Cambridge University Press.

Roberts, David D. 1979. *The Syndicalist Tradition and Italian Fascism.* Manchester University Press.

Roberts, Michael 1962. 'Queen Christina and the General Crisis of the Seventeenth Century', *Past and Present* 22, pp. 36–59.

  1968a. *The Early Vasas: A History of Sweden, 1523–1611.* Cambridge University Press.

  1968b. *Sweden as a Great Power 1611–1697: Government: Society: Foreign Policy.* New York: St. Martin's Press.

  1973. *Swedish and English Parliamentarism in the Eighteenth Century.* Belfast: The Queen's University.

  1986. *The Age of Liberty: Sweden 1719–1772.* Cambridge University Press.

  1991. *From Oxenstierna to Charles XII: Four Studies.* Cambridge University Press.

  2003. *The Age of Liberty: Sweden 1719–1772.* Cambridge University Press.

Robespierre, Maximilien 1910 [1793]. 'Rapport sur les principes du gouvernement révolutionnaire', in Robespierre, *Oeuvres complètes*, ed. M. Bouloiseau and A. Soboul, 10 vols., Vol. X. Paris: Leroux, pp. 273–83.

Rocco, Alfredo 2005. *Discorsi parlamentari.* Bologna: Mulino.

Rodell, Fred 1955. *Nine Men: A Political History of the Supreme Court from 1790 to 1955.* New York: Random House.

Rodolico, Niccolò 1898. *Dal comune alla signoria: Saggio sul governo di Taddeo Pepoli in Bologna.* Bologna: Arnaldo Porn.

Rodotà, Carla 1999. *Storia della Corte costituzionale.* Rome: Laterza.

Rodríguez Díaz, Angel 1989. *Transición politica y consolidación constitucional de los partidos politicos.* Madrid: Centro des Estudios Constitucionales.

Rodríguez-Picavea, Enrique 1994. *La formación del feudalismo en la meseta meridional castellano: Los señoríos de la Orden de Calatrava en los siglos XII–XIII.* Madrid: Siglo XXI de España.

Romanelli, Raffaele 1979. *L'Italia liberale.* Bolgna: Mulino.

Rondoni, Giuseppe (ed.) 1882. *I più antichi frammenti del costituto fiorentino.* Florence: Le Monnier.

Rosanvallon, Pierre 1985. *Le Moment Guizot.* Paris: Gallimard.

2000. *La démocratie inachevée: Histoire de la souveraineté du peuple en France.* Paris: Gallimard.

Rose, Craig 1999. *England in the 1690s: Revolution, Religion and War.* Oxford: Blackwell.

Rosenwein, Barbara 1999. *Negotiating Space: Power, Restraint and Privileges of Immunity in Early Medieval Europe.* Manchester University Press.

Rotteck, Karl von 1997 [1819]. 'Ideen über Landstände', in Schöttle, Rainer (ed.), *Über Landstände und Volksvertretungen: Texte zur Verfassungsdiskussion im Vormärz.* Freiburg: Haufe, pp. 15–88.

Rubin, Gerry R. 1987. *War, Law and Labour: The Munitions Act, State Regulation and the Unions, 1915–1921.* Oxford: Clarendon.

Rubinstein, Nicolai 1997. *The Government of Florence under the Medici (1434 to 1494),* 2nd edn. Oxford University Press.

Rudelle, Odile 1982. *La République absolue: Aux origines de l'instabilité constitutionnelle de la France républicaine 1870–1889.* Paris: Publications de la Sorbonne.

Russell, Conrad 1979. *Parliaments and English Politics 1621–1629.* Oxford: Clarendon.

Sadurski, Wojciech 2002. 'Postcommunist Charters of Rights in Europe and the US Bill of Rights', *Law and Contemporary Problems* 65(2), pp. 223–50.

2007. *Rights before Courts: A Study of Constitutional Courts in Postcommunist States of Central and Eastern Europe.* Dordrecht: Springer.

Saguez-Lovisi, Claire 1984. *Les lois fondamentales au XVIIIe siècle: Recherches sur la loi de dévolution de la couronne.* Paris: Presses Universitaires de France.

Salomone, A. William 1960. *Italy in the Giolittian Era: Italian Democracy in the Making, 1900–1914.* Philadelphia: University of Pennsylvania Press.

Sanchez Agesta, Luis 1955. *Historia del constitucionalismo espanol.* Madrid: Instituto de Estudios Politicos.

Sánchez-Albornoz, Claudio 1942. *En torno a los orígenes de feudalismo,* 3 vols., Vol. III. Mendoza: Universidad Nacional de Cuyo.

Sapelli, Giulio 1975. *Fascismo, grande industria e sindicato: Il caso di Torino 1929/ 1935.* Milan: Feltrinelli.

Sarti, Roland 1971. *Fascism and Industrial Leadership in Italy, 1919–1940: A Study in the Expansion of Private Power under Fascism.* Berkeley: University of California Press.

Saunders, David 1997. *Anti-lawyers: Religion and the Critics of Law and State.* London: Routledge.

Savigny, Friedrich Carl von 1837 [1803]. *Das Recht des Besitzes: Eine civilistische Abhandlung,* 6th edn. Giessen: Georg Friedrich Meyer.

1840. *System des heutigen Römischen Rechts,* 9 vols., Vol. I. Berlin: Veit & Comp.

Schama, Simon 1977. *Patriots and Liberators: Revolution in the Netherlands 1780–1813.* London: Collins.

Schelsky, Helmut 1965 [1949]. 'Über die Stabilität von Institutionen, besonders Verfassungen. Kulturanthropologische Gedanken zu einem rechtssoziologischen Thema', in Schelsky, *Auf der Suche nach Wirklichkeit: Gesammelte Aufsätze*. Düsseldorf: Diederich, pp. 33–58.

Scheppele, Kim Lane 2003. 'Constitutional Negotiations. Political Contexts of Judicial Activism in Post-Soviet Europe', *International Sociology* 18(1), pp. 219–38.

Scheuner, Ulrich 1967. 'Die Anwendung des Art. 48 der Weimarer Reichsverfassung unter den Präsidentschaften von Ebert und Hindenburg', in Hermens, Ferdinand A. and Schieder, Theodor (eds.), *Staat, Wirtschaft und Politik in der Weimarer Republik: Festschrift für Heinrich Brüning*. Berlin: Duncker & Humblot, pp. 249–86.

Schieche, Emil 1964. 'Der schwedische Ratskonstitutionalismus im 17. Jahrhundert', in Repgen, Konrad and Skalweit, Stephan (eds.), *Spiegel der Geschichte: Festgabe für Max Braubach*. Münster: Aschendorff, pp. 388–428.

Schilling, Lothar 2005. *Normsetzung in der Krise: Zum Gesetzgebungsverständnis im Frankreich der Religionskriege*. Frankfurt am Main: Klostermann.

Schmale, Franz-Josef (ed.) 1986. *Italische Quellen über die Taten Kaiser Friedrichs I in Italien und der Brief über den Kreuzzug Kaiser Friedrich II*. Darmstadt: Wissenschaftliche Buchgesellschaft.

Schmid, Peter 1989. *Der Gemeine Pfennig von 1495: Vorgeschichte und Entstehung, verfassungsgeschichtliche, politische und finanzielle Bedeutung*. Göttingen: Vandenhoeck & Ruprecht.

Schmidhauser, John (1958). *The Supreme Court as Final Arbiter in Federal–State Relations 1789–1957*. Chapel Hill: University of North Carolina Press.

Schmitt, Carl 1928. *Verfassungslehre*. Berlin: Duncker & Humblot.

    1995 [1938]. *Der Leviathan in der Staatslehre des Thomas Hobbes: Sinn und Fehlschlag eines politischen Symbols*. Stuttgart: Cotta.

Schmitter, Philippe C. 1975. 'Liberation by Golpe: Retrospective Thoughts on the Demise of Authoritarian Rule in Portugal', *Armed Forces and Society* 2(5), pp. 5–33.

Schramm, Gottfried 1965. *Der Polnische Adel und die Reformation 1548–1607*. Wiesbaden: Franz Steiner.

Schück, Herman 1988. 'Early Swedish Representation: Instrument or Opponent of Government?', *Parliaments, Estates and Representation* 8(1), pp. 23–9.

Schulte, Johann Friedrich von 1870. 'Literaturgeschichte der Compilationes antiquae, besonders der drei ersten', *Sitzungsberichte der kaiserlichen Akademie der Wissenschaften, philosophisch-historische Classe* 66, pp. 51–158.

    1891. *Die Summa des Stephanus Tornacensis*. Giessen: Emil Roth.

Schwartz, Bernhard 1977. *The Great Rights of Mankind: A History of the American Bill of Rights*. Oxford University Press.

Schwartz, Hermann 1998. 'Eastern Europe's Constitutional Courts', *Journal of Democracy* 9(4), pp. 100–14.

2000. *The Struggle for Justice in Post-communist Europe.* University of Chicago Press.

Schwennicke, Andreas 1998. 'Der Einfluß der Landstände auf die Regelungen des Preußischen Allgemeinen Landrechts von 1794', in Birtsch, Günter and Willoweit, Dietmar (eds.), *Reformabsolutismus und ständische Gesellschaft: Zweihundert Jahre Preußisches Landrecht.* Berlin: Duncker & Humblot, pp. 113–29.

Sciulli, David 1992. *Theory of Societal Constitutionalism: Foundations of a non-Marxist Critical Theory.* Cambridge University Press.

Scott, John A. 1951. *Republican Ideas and the Liberal Tradition in France 1870–1914.* New York: Columbia University Press.

Scott, Jonathan 2004. *Commonwealth Principles: Republican Writing of the English Revolution.* Cambridge University Press.

Seaward, Paul 1989. *The Cavalier Parliament and the Reconstruction of the Old Regime, 1661–1667.* Cambridge University Press.

Sebastiá Domingo, Enric and Piqueras, José A. 1987. *Pervivencias feudales y revolución democrática.* Valencia: Edicions Alfons el Magnànimo.

Sellin, Volker 2001. *Die geraubte Revolution: Der Sturz Napoleons und die Restauration in Europa.* Göttingen: Vandenhoeck & Ruprecht.

Selsam, J. Paul 1936. *The Pennsylvania Constitution of 1776: A Study in Revolutionary Democracy.* Philadelphia: University of Pennsylvania Press.

Sewell, William H. 1980. *Work and Revolution in France: The Language of Labor from the Old Regime to 1848.* Cambridge University Press.

Seyssel, Claude de 1961 [1519]. *La monarchie de France.* Paris: D'Argences.

Shapiro, Barbara 1974. 'Codification of the Laws in Seventeenth-Century England', *Wisconsin Law Review* 428, pp. 428–65.

Sharpe, Kevin 1992. *The Personal Rule of Charles I.* New Haven: Yale University Press.

Shennan, Andrew 1989. *Rethinking France: Plans for Renewal 1940–1946.* Oxford: Clarendon.

Shennan, J. H. 1998. *The Parlement of Paris.* Stroud: Sutton.

Sheridan, Charles Francis 1778. *A History of the Late Revolution in Sweden.* London: Dilly.

Sicard, Germain 1990. 'Les États Généraux de la France capétienne', in Congreso científico sobre la historia de las cortes de Castilla y León (ed.), *Las Cortés de Castilla y León 1188–1988*, 2 vols., Vol. I. Valladolid: Cortés de Castilla y León, pp. 57–100.

Siebeck, Hans 1914. *Die landständische Verfassung Hessens im sechzehnten Jahrhundert.* Kassel: Schönhoven.

Sieg, Hans Martin 2003. *Staatsdienst, Staatsdenken und Dienstgesinnung in Brandenburg-Preußen im 18: Jahrhundert (1713–1803): Studien zum Verständnis des Absolutismus.* Berlin: de Gruyter.

Siete Partidas 1807. Madrid: Imprenta real.

Sieyès, Emmanuel 1839 [1789]. *Qu'est-ce que le tiers-état?* Paris: Pagnerre.

Simon, Walter M. 1955. *The Failure of the Prussian Reform Movement, 1807–1819*. Ithaca, N.Y.: Cornell University Press.

Sinzheimer, Hugo 1916. *Ein Arbeitstarifgesetz: Die Idee der sozialen Selbstbestimmung im Recht*. Munich: Duncker & Humblot.

Skilling, H. Gordon 1952. 'The Czechoslovak Constitutional System: The Soviet Impact', *Political Science Quarterly* 67(2), pp. 198–224.

Smedley-Weill, Annette 1995. *Les Intendants de Louis XIV*. Paris: Fayard.

Smend, Rudolf 1968 [1928]. 'Verfassung und Verfassungsrecht', in Smend, *Staatsrechtliche Abhandlungen und andere Aufsätze*, 2nd edn. Berlin: Duncker & Humblot, pp. 119–277.

Smith, Adam 1978 [1762–6]. *Lectures on Jurisprudence*, ed. R. L. Meek, D. D. Raphael and P. G. Stein. Oxford University Press.

Smith, David L. 1994. *Constitutional Royalism and the Search for Settlement, c. 1640–1649*. Cambridge University Press.

Smith, Gordon B. 1996. *Reforming the Russian Legal System*. Cambridge University Press.

Smith, Thomas 1621 [1583]. *The Commonwealth of England and the Maner of Governement thereof*. London: Wiliam Stansby.

Snowiss, Sylvia 1990. *Judicial Review and the Law of the Constitution*. New Haven: Yale University Press.

Solomon, Peter H. 1990. 'Gorbachev's Legal Revolution', *Canadian Business Law Journal* 17, pp. 184–94.

Sólyom, László 1994. 'The Hungarian Constitutional Court and Social Change', *Yale Journal of International Law* 19, pp. 223–37.

     2003. 'The Role of Constitutional Courts in the Transition to Democracy: With Special Reference to Hungary', *International Sociology* 18(1), pp. 143–5.

Sombart, Werner 1925. *Die Ordnung des Wirtschaftslebens*. Berlin: Springer.

Somma, Laessandro 2005. *I giuristi e l'asse culturale Roma-Berlino: Economia e politica nel diritto fascista e nazionalsocialista*. Frankfurt am Main: Klostermann.

Sonenscher, Michael 1989. *Work and Wages: Natural Law, Politics and Eighteenth-Century France*. Cambridge University Press.

Spangenberg, Hans 1912. *Vom Lehnstaat zum Ständestaat: Ein Beitrag zur Entstehung der landständischen Verfassung*. Munich: Oldenbourg.

Sparre, Erik 1924 [1585]. *Pro lege, rege et grege*. Stockholm: Norstedt & söner.

Speck, W. A. 1988. *Reluctant Revolutionaries: Englishmen and the Revolution of 1688*. Oxford University Press.

Spirito, Ugo 1932. *I fondamenti della economia corporativa*. Rome: Treves.

     1934. *Capitalismo e corporativismo*. Florence: Sansoni.

Stacey, Robert C. 1987. *Politics, Policy, and Finance under Henry III 1216–1245*. Oxford: Clarendon.

Stammer, Otto 1957. 'Interessenverbände und Parteien', *Kölner Zeitschrift für Soziologie und Sozialpsychologie* 9, pp. 587–605.

St German, Christopher 1613 [Latin 1523]. *The Dialogue in English, betweene a Doctor of Divinitie, and a Student in the Lawes of England*. London: Company of Stationers.

    1532. *A Treatise concernynge the division between the spirytualtie and temporaltie*. London: Robert Redman.

Starr, S. Frederick 1972. *Decentralization and Self-Government in Russia 1830–1870*. Princeton University Press.

Stasavage, David 2003. *Public Debt and the Birth of the Democratic State: France and Great Britain, 1688–1789*. Cambridge University Press.

Stein, Freiherr von 1961. 'Brief von Stein an Sack', in Stein, *Briefe und Amtliche Schriften*, ed. W. Hubatsch, 11 vols., Vol. III. Stuttgart: Kohlhammer, pp. 351–6.

Steinfeld, Robert J. 2001. *Coercion, Contract and Free Labour in the Nineteenth Century*. Cambridge University Press.

Stengel, Edmund E. 1904. 'Grundherrschaft und Immunität', *Zeitschrift für Rechtsgeschichte* 25, pp. 286–323.

    1948. 'Land- und lehnrechtliche Grundlagen des Reichsfürstenstandes', *Zeitschrift für Rechtsgeschichte* 66, pp. 294–342.

Stenton, Doris M. 1965. *English Justice between the Norman Conquest and the Great Charter 1066–1215*. London: Allen & Unwin.

Stephani, Joachim 1612 [1599]. *Institutiones iuris canonici*. Frankfurt am Main: Kopff.

Stephens, J. N. 1983. *The Fall of the Florentine Republic 1512–1530*. Oxford University Press.

Stipta, István 1998. 'Bestrebungen zur Veränderung der ständischen Komitatsverfassung im ungarischen Vormärz', in Peter, Orsolya Márta and Szabó, Béla (eds.), *A bonis bona discere*. Miskolc: Biber Verlag, pp. 473–84.

Stolleis, Michael 1974. *Gemeinwohlformeln im nationalsozialistichen Recht*. Berlin: Schweitzer.

Stolzi, Irene 2007. *L'ordine corporativo: Poteri organizzati e organizzazione del potere nella riflessione giuridica dell'Italia fascista*. Milan: Giuffrè.

Stone, Alec 1992. *The Birth of Judicial Politics in France: The Constitutional Court in Comparative Perspective*. Oxford University Press.

Stone, Bailey 1981. *The Parlement of Paris, 1774–1789*. Chapel Hill: University of North Carolina Press.

    1986. *The French Parlements and the Crisis of the Old Regime*. Chapel Hill: University of North Carolina Press.

Stone, Lawrence 1968. *The Crisis of the Aristocracy, 1558–1641*. Oxford University Press.

Stourzh, Gerald 1977. 'Staatsformenlehre und Fundamentalgesetze in England und Nordamerika im 17. und 18. Jahrhundert. Zur Genese des modernen

Verfassungsbegriffs', in Vierhaus, Rudolf (ed.), *Herrschaftsverträge, Wahlkapitulationen, Fundamentalgesetze*. Göttingen: Vandenhoeck & Ruprecht, pp. 294–327.

Stradling, R. A. 1988. *Philip IV and the Government of Spain 1621–1665*. Cambridge University Press.

Strakosch, Heinrich 1976. *Privatrechtskodifikation und Staatsbildung in Österreich (1753–1811)*. Munich: Oldenbourg.

Strayer, Joseph R. 1980. *The Reign of Philip the Fair*. Princeton University Press.

Stürmer, Michael 1974. *Regierung und Reichstag im Bismarckstaat 1871–1880: Cäsarismus oder Parlamentarismus*. Düsseldorf: Droste.

Suárez Fernández, Luis 2003. *Nobleza y monarquía: Entendimento y rivalidad: El proceso de construcción de la corona española*. Madrid: La esfera.

Sunstein, Cass R. 1993. 'On Property and Constitutionalism', *Cardozo Law Review* 14, pp. 907–35.

Sutherland, Donald 1963. *Quo Warranto Proceedings in the Reign of Edward I 1278–1294*. Oxford: Clarendon.

Sütterlin, Berthold 1929. *Die Politik Kaiser Friedrichs II und die römischen Kardinäle in den Jahren 1239–1250*. Heidelberg: Carl Winter.

Svarez, Carl Gottlieb 2000 [1791/2]. *Die Kronprinzenvorlesungen*, in Svarez, *Gesammelte Schriften*, ed. Peter Krause, 6 vols. Stuttgart: frommann-holzboog, Vol. 4/1.

Tanner, Duncan 1990. *Political Change and the Labour Party 1900–1918*. Cambridge University Press.

Tanner, J. R. (ed.) 1952. *Constitutional Documents of the Reign of James I*. Cambridge University Press.

    1966. *English Constitutional Conflicts of the Seventeenth Century 1603–1689*. Cambridge University Press.

Tarr, G. Alan 1998. *Understanding State Constitutions*. Princeton University Press.

Taylor, George V. 1964. 'Types of Capitalism in Eighteenth-Century France', *English Historical Review* 79, pp 478–97.

Tellenbach, Gerd 1988. *Die westliche Kirche vom 10. bis zum frühen 12. Jahrhundert*. Göttingen: Vandenhoeck & Ruprecht.

Tesauro, Alfonso and Capocelli, Ginevra 1954. 'The Fundamentals of the New Italian Constitution', *Canadian Journal of Economics and Political Science* 20(1), pp. 44–58.

Teubner, Gunther 2006. 'Die anonyme Matrix: Zu Menschenrechtsverletzungen durch "private" transnationale Akteure', *Der Staat: Zeitschrift für Staatslehre und Verfassungsgeschichte, deutsches und europäisches öffentliches Recht* 44, pp. 161–87.

Thiry, Jean 1947. *Le coup d'état du 18 Brumaire*. Paris: Berger-Levrault.

    1949. *Le sénat de Napoléon (1800–1814)*. Paris: Berger-Levrault.

Thompson, I. A. A. 1990. 'Absolutism in Castile', in Miller, John (ed.), *Absolutism in Seventeenth-Century Europe*. Basingstoke: Macmillan, pp. 69–98.

    1994. 'Castile: Absolutism, Constitutionalism and Liberty', in Hofmann, Philip T. and Norberg, Kathryn (eds.), *Fiscal Crises, Liberty, and Representative Government, 1450–1789*. Stanford University Press, pp. 181–225.

Thornhill, Chris 2008. 'Towards a Historical Sociology of Constitutional Legitimacy', *Theory and Society* 37(2), pp. 161–97.

    2010a. 'Niklas Luhmann and the Sociology of the Constitution', *Journal of Classical Sociology* 10(4), pp. 315–37.

    2010b. 'Re-conceiving Rights Revolutions: On the Persistence of a Sociological Deficit in Theories of Rights', *Zeitschrift für Rechtssoziologie* 31, pp. 109–139.

Thorson, Carla 2004. 'Why Politicians Want Constitutional Courts: The Russian Case', *Communist and Post-Communist Studies* 37, pp. 187–211.

Thouret, Jacques-Guillaume 1790. *Discours: En ouvrant la discussion sur la nouvelle organisation du pouvoir judiciaire*. Paris: Imprimerie nationale.

Tierney, Brian 1955. *Foundations of the Conciliar Theory: The Contribution of the Medieval Canonists from Gratian to the Great Schism*. Cambridge University Press.

    1963. '"The Prince is not bound by the Laws": Accursius and the Origins of the Modern State', *Comparative Studies in Society and History* 5(4), pp. 378–400.

Tilly, Charles 1975. 'Reflections on the History of European State-Making', in Tilly (ed.), *The Formation of National States in Western Europe*. Princeton University Press, pp. 3–83.

    1985. 'War Making and State Making as Organized Crime', in Evans, Peter B., Rueschmeyer, Dietrich and Skocpol, Theda (eds.), *Bringing the State Back In*. Cambridge University Press, pp. 169–91.

Toharia, José-Juan 1975a. *El juez español: Un analisis sociologica*. Madrid: Editorial tecnos.

    1975b. 'Judicial Independence in an Authoritarian Regime: The Case of Contemporary Spain', *Law and Society Review* 9, pp. 475–96.

Tomassini, Luigi 1991. 'Industrial Mobilization and the Labour Market in Italy during the First World War', *Social History* 16(1), pp. 59–87.

Tomlinson, Jim 1990. *Public Policy and the Economy since 1900*. Oxford: Clarendon.

Tompson, William 2002. 'Putin's Challenge: The Politics of Structural Reform in Russia', *Europe-Asia Studies* 54(6), pp. 933–57.

Tooze, Adam 2006. *The Wages of Destruction: The Making and Breaking of the Nazi Economy*. New York: Viking.

Torres, David 1989. 'Las Cortes y la créacion de derecho', in Congreso científico sobre la historia de las Cortes de Castilla y León (ed.), *Las Cortes de Castilla y León en la Edad Moderna*. Valladolid: Cortes de Castilla y León, pp. 89–135.

Touching the Fundamentall Lawes, or Politique Constitution of this Kingdome 1643. London: Thomas Underhill.

Tracy, James D. 1990. *Holland under Habsburg Rule 1506–1566: The Formation of a Body Politic*. Berkeley: University of California Press.

2008. *The Founding of the Dutch Republic: War, Finance, and Politics in Holland, 1572–1588*. Oxford University Press.

Treanor, William Michael 1985. 'The Origins and Original Significance of the Just Compensation Clause of the Fifth Amendment', *Yale Law Journal* 94(3), pp. 694–716.

Treharne, R. F. 1932. *The Baronial Plan of Reform, 1258–1263*. Manchester University Press.

Triepel, Heinrich 1929. 'Wesen und Entwicklung der Staatsgerichtsbarkeit', *Veröffentlichung der Vereinigung der deutschen Staatsrechtslehrer* 5, pp. 2–29.

Trochev, Alexei 2008. *Judging Russia: The Role of the Constitutional Court in Russian Politics 1990–2006*. Cambridge University Press.

Troper, Michel 2006. *Terminer la révolution: La constitution de 1795*. Paris: Fayard.

Turgot, Anne-Robert-Jacques 1787 [1775]. 'Mémoire sur les Municipalités', in Turgot, *Oeuvres posthumes*, ed. Pierre Samuel du Pont de Nemours. Lausanne, pp. 1–181.

1844a [1766]. 'Réflexions sur la formation et la distribution des richesses', in Turgot, *Oeuvres*, ed. E. Daire and H. Dussard in 2 vols., Vol. I. Paris: Guillaumin, pp. 7–71.

1844b [1776]. 'Édit du Roi, portant suppression des jurandes', in Turgot, *Oeuvres*, ed. E. Daire and H. Dussard in 2 vols., Vol. II. Paris: Guillaumin, pp. 302–16.

Turner, Michael J. 2000. *The Age of Unease: Government and Reform in Britain, 1782–1832*. Stroud: Sutton.

Turner, Ralph W. 1985. *The English Judiciary in the Age of Glanvill and Bracton c. 1176–1239*. Cambridge University Press.

Tusell, Javier 1976. *Oligarquia y caciquismo en Andalucia (1890–1923)*. Barcelona: Planeta.

Upton, A. F. 1998. *Charles XI and Swedish Absolutism*. Cambridge University Press.

Van Alstyne, William W. 1969. 'A Critical Guide to Marbury v. Madison', *Duke Law Journal* 1, pp. 36–7.

Vandal, Albert 1903. *L'Avènement de Bonaparte: La genèse du consulat brumaire: La constitution de l'an VIII*. Paris: Plon.

Varela Ortega, José 1977. *Los amigos políticos: Partidos, elecciones y caciquismo en la Restauración (1875–1900)*. Madrid: Alianza Editorial.

Veall, Donald 1970. *The Popular Movement for Law Reform 1640–1660*. Oxford: Clarendon.

Vergne, Arnaud 2006. *La notion de constitution d'après les cours et assemblées à la fin de l'ancien régime (1750–1789)*. Paris: De Boccard.

Vergottini, Giovanni di 1952. *Studi sulla legislazione imperiale di Federico II in Italia*. Milan: Giuffrè.

Vestring, Sigrid 1987. *Die Mehrheitsdemokratie und die Entstehung der Reichsverfassung von Weimar 1918/1919*. Münster: Lit.

Vetter, Klaus 1979. *Kurmärkischer Adel und Preußische Reformen*. Weimar: Böhlau.

Vierhaus, Rudolf 1990. *Staaten und Stände: Vom Westfälischen Frieden bis zum Hubertusburger Frieden 1648 bis 1763*. Frankfurt am Main: Ullstein.

Viora, Mario 1928. *Le costituzioni Piemontesi*. Milan: Bocca.

Vivarelli, Roberto 1981. *Il fallimento del liberalismo*. Bologna: Il Mulino.

1991a. *Storia delle origini del fascismo: L'Italia dalla grande guerra alla Marcia su Roma*, Vol. I. Bologna: Il Mulino.

1991b. *Storia delle origini del fascismo: L'Italia dalla grande guerra alla Marcia su Roma*, Vol. II. Bologna: Il Mulino.

Vogel, Barbara 1981. 'Staatsfinanzen und Gesellschaftsreform', in Berding, Helmut (ed.), *Privatkapital, Staatsfinanzen und Reformpolitik in Deutschland der Napoleonischen Zeit*. Ostfildern: Scripta Mercaturae Verlag, pp. 37–57.

Volcansek, Mary C. 1994. 'Political Power and Judicial Review in Italy', *Comparative Political Studies* 26(4), pp. 492–509.

Volpe, Gioacchino 1902. *Studi sulle istituzioni communali a Pisa: Secoli XII–XIII*. Pisa: Nistri.

1976. *Origini e primo svolgimento dei comuni nell'Italia Langobarda*. Rome: Giovanni Volpe.

Voltaire (François-Marie Arouet) 1771. *Les peuples aux parlements*. No publisher.

Vroom, Cynthia 1988. 'Constitutional Protection of Individual Liberties in France: The *Conseil Constitutionnel* since 1971', *Tulane Law Review*, pp. 265–334.

Waite, P. B. 1959. 'The Struggle of Prerogative and Common Law in the Reign of James I', *Canadian Journal of Economics and Political Science* 25(2), pp. 144–52.

Waldron, Jeremy 2006. 'The Core of the Case against Judicial Review', *Yale Law Journal* 115, pp. 1346–1406.

Wcislo, Francis William 1990. *Reforming Rural Russia: State, Local Society and National Politics, 1855–1914*. Princeton University Press.

Weber, Albrecht 2008. 'Rechtsstaatsprinzip als gemeineuropäisches Verfassungsprinzip', *Zeitschrift für öffentliches Recht* 63, pp. 267–92.

Weber, Max 1921. *Wirtschaft und Gesellschaft: Grundriß der verstehenden Soziologie*. Tübingen: Mohr.

1922 [1917]. 'Die Lehren der deutschen Kanzlerkrisis', in Weber, *Gesammelte Politische Schriften*. Tübingen: J.C.B. Mohr, pp. 216–21.

Weber, Werner 1985 [1957]. 'Der Staat und die Verbände', in Steinberg, Rudolf (ed.), *Staat und Verbände: Zur Theorie der Interessenverbände in der*

Industriegesellschaft. Darmstadt: Wissenschaftliche Buchgesellschaft, pp. 64–76.

Wechsler, Herbert 1954. 'The Political Safeguards of Federalism: The Rôle of the States in the Composition and Selection of the National Government', *Columbia Law Review* 54, pp. 543–60.

Wehler, Hans-Ulrich 1987. *Deutsche Gesellschaftsgeschichte,* Vol. I, *Vom Feudalismus des Alten Reiches bis zur Defensiven Modernisierung der Reformära 1700–1815.* Munich: Beck.

Weidenfeld, Katia 2001. *Les origines médiévales du contentieux administrative (XIVe–XVe siècles).* Paris: De Boccard.

Weigand, Rudolf 1967. *Die Naturrechtslehre der Legisten und Dekretisten von Irnerius bis Accursius und von Gratian bis Johannes Teutonicus.* Munich: Max Hueber.

Weigle, Marcia A. 2000. *Russia's Liberal Project: State–Society Relations in the Transition from Communism.* University Park, Pa.: Pennsylvania State University Press.

Weinrich, Lorenz (ed.) 1983. *Quellen zur Verfassungsgeschichte des römisch-deutschen Reiches im Spätmittelalter (1250–1500).* Darmstadt: Wissenschaftliche Buchgesellschaft.

Weise, Georg 1912. *Königtum und Bischofswahl im fränkischen und deutschen Reich vor dem Investiturstreit.* Berlin: Weidmann.

Weitzel, Jürgen 1976. *Der Kampf um die Appellation ans Reichskammergericht: Zur politischen Geschichte der Rechtsmittel in Deutschland.* Cologne: Böhlau.

Weston, Corinne Comstock and Greenberg, Janelle Renfrow 1981. *Subjects and Sovereigns: The Grand Controversy over Legal Sovereignty in Stuart England.* Cambridge University Press.

Wheeler, James Scott 1999. *The Making of a World Power: War and the Military Revolution in Seventeenth Century England.* Stroud: Sutton.

White, Leonard D. 1948. *The Federalists: A Study in Administrative History.* New York: Macmillan.

White, Stephen 1990. *Gorbachev in Power.* Cambridge University Press.

Wiarda, Howard J. 1977. *Corporatism and Development: The Portuguese Experience.* Amherst: University of Massachusetts Press.

1979. 'The Corporatist Tradition and the Corporative System in Portugal: Structured, Evolving, Transcendent, Persistent', in Graham, Lawrence S. and Makler, Harry M. (eds.), *Contemporary Portugal: The Revolution and its Antecedents.* Austin: University of Texas Press, pp. 89–122.

Wickham, Chris 1984. 'The Other Transition: From the Ancient World to Feudalism', *Past and Present* 103, pp. 3–36.

2003. *Courts and Conflict in Twelfth-Century Tuscany.* Oxford University Press.

Wienfort, Monika 2001. *Patrimonialgerichte in Preußen: Ländliche Gesellschaft und bürgerliches Recht 1770–1848/49.* Göttingen: Vandenhoeck & Ruprecht.

Wilkinson, Bertie 1948–58. *Constitutional History of Medieval England, 1216–1399,* 3 vols., Vol. III, *The Development of the Constitution 1216–1399.* London: Longman.

Willard, James Field 1934. *Parliamentary Taxes on Personal Property 1290 to 1334: A Study in Medieval English Financial Administration.* Cambridge, Mass.: Medieval Academy of America.

William of Ockham 1940 [*c.* 1339]. 'An princeps, pro suo succurso, scilicet guerrae posit recipere bona ecclesiarum etiam papa', in William of Ockham, *Opera Politica,* Vol. I, ed. J. Sikes. Manchester University Press, pp. 223–71.

Williams, E. N. (ed.) 1960. *The Eighteenth Century Constitution.* Cambridge University Press.

Williams, Robert F. 1988. '"Experience Must Be Our Only Guide": The State Constitutional Experience of the Framers of the Federal Constitution', *Hastings Constitutional Law Quarterly* 15, pp. 403–27.

1989. 'The State Constitutions of the Founding Decade: Pennsylvania's Radical 1776 Constitution and its Influences on American Constitutionalism', *Temple Law Review* 62, pp. 541–85.

Willoweit, Dietmar 1975. *Rechtsgrundlagen der deutschen Territorialgewalt.* Cologne: Böhlau.

1983. 'Die Entwicklung und Verwaltung der spätmittelalterlichen Landesherrschaft', in Jeserich, Kurt G. A., Pohl, Hans and Unruh, Georg-Christophe von (eds.), *Deutsche Verwaltungsgeschichte,* 6 vols., Vol. I, *Vom Spätmittelalter bis zum Ende des Reiches.* Stuttgart: Deutsche Verlagsanstalt, pp. 66–176.

Winkler, Heinrich August 1972. *Pluralismus oder Protektionismus? Verfassungspolitische Probleme des Verbandswesens im deutschen Kaiserreich.* Wiesbaden: Fr. Steiner.

1973. 'Unternehmerverbände zwischen Ständeideologie und Nationalsozialismus', in Varain, Heinz Josef (ed.), *Interessenverbände in Deutschland.* Cologne: Kiepenheuer & Witsch, pp. 228–58.

1979. *Liberalismus und Antiliberalismus: Studien zur politischen Sozialgeschichte des 19: und 20 Jahrhunderts.* Göttingen: Vandenhoeck & Ruprecht.

Witt, Peter-Christian 1970. *Die Finanzpolitik des deutschen Reiches von 1903 bis 1913. Eine Studie zur Innenpolitik des Wilhelminischen Deutschlands.* Düsseldorf: Droste.

Witt, Thomas E. J. de 1978. 'The Economics and Politics of Welfare in the Third Reich', *Central European History* 11(3), pp. 256–78.

Wittenberger Gutachten 1851 [1538]. In Richter, Ludwig, *Geschichte der evangelischen Kirchenverfassung in Deutschland.* Leipzig: Tauchnitz, pp. 82–96.

Wolfe, Christopher 1986. *The Rise of Modern Judicial Review: From Constitutional Interpretation to Judge-Made Law.* New York: Basic Books.

Wolfe, Martin 1972. *The Fiscal System of Renaissance France*. New Haven: Yale University Press.

Wolffe, B. P. 1970. *The Crown Lands 1461 to 1536: An Aspect of Yorkist and Early Tudor Government*. London: Allen & Unwin.

Woloch, Isser 1994. *The New Regime: Transformations of the French Civic Order, 1789–1820s*. New York: Norton.

   2001. *Napoleon and his Collaborators: The Making of a Dictatorship*. New York: Norton.

Wood, Gordon S. 1969. *The Creation of the American Republic 1776–1787*. New York/London: Norton.

   1992. *The Radicalism of the American Revolution*. New York: Knopf.

Woolrych, Austin 2002. *Britain in Revolution*. Oxford University Press.

Wyluda, Erich 1969. *Lehnrecht und Beamtentum: Studien zur Entstehung des preußischen Beamtentums*. Berlin: Duncker & Humblot.

Yaney, George L. 1973. *The Systematization of Russian Government: Social Evolution in the Domestic Administration of Imperial Russia, 1711–1905*. Urbana: University of Illinois Press.

Zaller, Robert 2007. *The Discourse of Legitimacy in Early Modern England*. Stanford University Press.

Zangara, Vincenzo 1931. *Rivoluzione sindacale: Lo stato corporativo*. Rome: Libreria del littorio.

Zeeden, Ernst Walter 1940. *Hardenberg und der Gedanke einer Volskvertretung in Preußen 1807–1812*. Berlin: Ebering.

Zeller, Gaston 1948. *Les institutions de la France au XVI siècle*. Paris: Presses Universitaires de France.

Zorzi, Andrea 1994. 'La giustizia imperiale nell'Italia comunale', in Toubert, Pierre and Bagliani, Agostino Paravicini (eds.), *Federico II e le città italiane*. Palermo: Sellerio, pp. 85–103.

   2000. 'I rettori di Firenze: Reclutamento, flussi, scambi (1193–1303)', in Vigueur, Jean-Claude Maire (ed.), *I podestà dell'Italia comunale*, 2 vols., Vol. I. Rome: Italian Historical Institute, pp. 453–94.

Zunkel, Friedrich 1974. *Industrie und Staatssozialismus: Der Kampf um die Wirtschaftsordnung in Deutschland 1914–18*. Düsseldorf: Droste.

INDEX

Lightning Source UK Ltd.
Milton Keynes UK
UKOW04f0604021214

242506UK00002B/355/P